TROUT

The Wildlife Series

Trout

Edited by
Judith Stolz and Judith Schnell

STACKPOLE
BOOKS

Published by
STACKPOLE BOOKS
Cameron and Kelker Streets
P.O. Box 1831
Harrisburg, PA 17105

Printed in the United States of America

10 9 8 7 6 5 4 3 2 1

The photo on page 124 was reprinted with permission from *SCIENCE*, Volume 228, 21 June 1985,
Figure 2, page 1398, D.W. Schindler; copyright 1985
by the AAAS.

The map on page 123 was reprinted with permission
from *SCIENCE*, Volume 239, 8 January 1988, Figure
1, page 150, D.W. Schindler; copyright 1988 by the
AAAS.

Prints on pages 218, 219, 226, and 227 are from
British Freshwater Fishes, by Houghton, drawn from
life by A. F. Lydon, published in 1884; courtesy
of the Smithsonian Institution.

The photo on page 292 was reproduced courtesy
of Dr. Peter G. Sly, Canada Centre for Inland Waters,
Burlington, Ontario, Canada.

The photos on page 257 were originally published by
The Wildlife Society in *The Journal of Wildlife Management*, copyright 1941.

Cover photo by William Roston
With special thanks to Jennifer Byrne and Karen
Atwood for their editorial assistance

Library of Congress Cataloging-in-Publication Data

Trout / edited by Judith Stolz and Judith Schnell.
     p.   cm. – (The Wildlife series)
   Includes bibliographical references and index.
   ISBN 0-8117-1652-X
   1. Trout I. Stolz, Judith. II. Schnell, Judith.
III. Series:
  Wildlife series (Harrisburg, Pa.)
  QL638.S2T78 1991   90-19751
  597'.55–dc20   CIP

Contents

WHAT A TROUT IS

LIFE AS A TROUT

THE TROUTS' ENVIRONS

THE SPECIES

THE FUTURE OF TROUT

Contributors

GAYLORD R. ALEXANDER is biologist in charge at the Hunt Creek Fisheries Research Station in Lewiston, Michigan, for the Michigan Department of Natural Resources (DNR).

ROBERT H. ARMSTRONG is a former fisheries biologist for the Alaska Department of Fish and Game and an associate professor of fisheries at the University of Alaska–Fairbanks.

JIM CHACKO ATHAPPILLY, an associate professor of aquaculture at Unity College in Maine, has published and lectured widely on health and disease in fish. He is a certified fish pathologist.

ROBERT A. BACHMAN, chief of freshwater fisheries for the Maryland Department of Natural Resources, is recognized among both fishery managers and anglers alike as an authority on brown trout, both wild and hatchery-reared.

ROGER A. BARNHART, an employee of the U.S. Fish and Wildlife Service, is leader of the California Cooperative Fishery Research Unit at Humboldt State University.

ROBERT J. BEHNKE, "Mr. Trout" to his colleagues, is a professor in the department of fishery and wildlife biology at Colorado State University–Fort Collins. He frequently advises private firms, state and federal agencies, and foreign governments on fishery-related issues.

PETER A. BISSON, an aquatic biologist with the Weyerhaeuser Company, has studied the relationships between salmonid populations and the biological and physical productivity of streams and has written scientific papers on his research.

THEODORE C. BJORNN, an employee of the U.S. Fish and Wildlife Service, is assistant leader of the Idaho Cooperative Fish and Wildlife Research Unit and a professor of fish and wildlife resources at the University of Idaho–Moscow.

ROBERT L. BUTLER, former professor of biology at the Pennsylvania State University–State College, has written and cowritten extensively on trout and other fish. The responses of trout to their environment, especially the responses of trout to artificial cover and how brown trout use space and time, have been special areas of research.

DAVID OWEN EVANS is a fisheries research scientist with the Ontario Ministry of Natural Resources and adjunct professor in the Biology Department, York University–Toronto, Ontario. His research interests are population and community ecology.

KURT D. FAUSCH is associate professor in the department of fishery and wildlife biology at Colorado State University–Fort Collins. His primary interests are the ecology of stream fishes, especially of trout and salmon.

WILLIAM A. FLICK, a former fishery biologist at Cornell University, has studied brook trout almost exclusively for thirty-three years. He was instrumental in bringing the Temiscamie and Assinica strains of brook trout to the United States from Canada and crossing them with domestic brook trout.

DELANO R. GRAFF, as director of the Bureau of Fisheries for the Pennsylvania Fish Commission, is involved in one of the nation's largest trout propagation and stocking programs.

ROBERT L. HERBST is chairman of the Natural Resources Council of America. He also serves on several national conservation boards. He is a former executive director of Trout Unlimited and a former assistant secretary and former acting secretary of Interior, during which tenure he served as chairman of the Great Lakes Fisheries Commission.

FREDERICK GARDNER JOHNSON, senior lecturer in fishery science at the University of Washington–Seattle, specializes in marine biology and environmental impact, especially the effects of pollution.

LIONEL JOHNSON, an independent research scientist formerly with the Canadian Department of Fisheries and Oceans, specializes in work with Arctic char.

DAVID JUDE is a fishery biologist and limnologist with the Center for Great Lakes and Aquatic Sciences at the University of Michigan–Ann Arbor. He has conducted extensive research on the Great Lakes.

CHARLES KRUEGER, an associate professor of fishery sciences, teaches at Cornell University and does research in such areas as the application of population genetics to fisheries management and the ecology of salmonid populations.

ARTHUR L. LAROCHE III, a regional supervisor for the Virginia Department of Game and Inland Fisheries, is responsible for overseeing the work of state fisheries biologists in twenty-two counties in southcentral Virginia.

ROBB F. LEARY received a doctorate of science in zoology with an emphasis on the evolutionary genetics of cutthroat and rainbow trout from the University of Montana and is continuing evolutionary studies of salmonids at the university.

ROBERT MCCAULEY teaches aquatic biology at Wilfrid Laurier University in Waterloo, Ontario, and is particularly interested in the effects of temperature on fish, especially trout.

JAMES M. MCKIM, a research aquatic biologist with the Environmental Protection Agency's research laboratory in Duluth, Minnesota, earned his doctorate in fisheries and environmental health from the University of Michigan–Ann Arbor. Since 1966 he has worked with the Environmental Protection Agency coordinating and managing research projects on fish toxicology and physiology.

JOHN R. MORING is an employee of the U.S. Fish and Wildlife Service, a fisheries biologist, and an associate professor of zoology at the University of Maine.

THOMAS GORDON NORTHCOTE is a fish ecologist, a limnologist, and a professor at the University of British Columbia, Vancouver. He also is director of the Institute of High Andean Waters at the National University of Altiplano in Puno, Peru.

CHARLES HAROLD OLVER is a fisheries biologist with the Ontario Ministry of Natural Resources. He has written more than two dozen scientific papers, mostly on the biology and management of lake trout.

GILBERT B. PAULEY is a U.S. Fish and Wildlife Service employee, serving as assistant unit leader of the Washington Cooperative Fish and Wildlife Research Unit in Seattle. Since 1983 he has served as a technical adviser to the federal district court on issues regarding harvestable anadromous fish in the state of Washington.

PHIL PISTER studied aquatic biology at the University of California–Berkeley and spent nearly his entire career as a biologist managing golden trout in the eastern Sierra Nevada for the California Department of Fish and Game.

JOHN N. RINNE, a fisheries research biologist with a doctorate in zoology, works with the Rocky Mountain Forest and Range Experiment Station in Tempe, Arizona. His research emphases are riparian ecology and endangered species.

ROBERT HENRY SMITH, an avid trout fisherman and preservationist, has caught, photographed, and released thirty-nine of the forty known geographic races of native trout on this continent. He is the author of *Trout of North America*.

PAT TROTTER is biotechnology project leader for the Weyerhaeuser Company, where he has worked in research for twenty-nine years. As an independent scholar, he also has pursued his interest in trout biology for many years. He is the author of *Cutthroat: Native Trout of the West*.

SPENCER E. TURNER is a research biologist for the Missouri Department of Conservation and a certified fisheries biologist. He helps manage the fisheries of Missouri's Lake Taneycomo.

Photographers and artists

Andy Anderson
Robert H. Armstrong
Allen R. Bachman
Robert A. Bachman
Christopher M. Batin
Adela Batin
Roger A. Barnhart
Erwin & Peggy Bauer
Barry & Cathy Beck
Duane Benoit
Greg Betteridge
Peter A. Bisson
Don Blegen
Denver Bryan
Mason D. Bryant
Robert L. Butler
Scott Campbell
Patrice Ceisel
Fred De Cicco
Mary E. Delany
Brian Dempson
Don Douple
David Owen Evans
Kurt D. Fausch
William A. Flick
Jerry Gibbs
Celia Godkin
Richard T. Grost
Eric Gyselman
Vernon M. Hawthorne
Heiner L. Hertling
Philip J. Howell
David L. Hughes
Ken Hunter
John Hyde
David Jude
Bill Kinney
Fred Kircheis
Charles C. Krueger
Arthur L. LaRoche III
Gerard Lemmo

Georges Lenzi
Worth Mathewson
Dick Mermon
John Merwin
James M. McKim
Patrick Michiel
John R. Moring
William H. Mullins
Tony Oswald
Angela Percival
Robert Pollock
Bob Pratt
John N. Rinne
George E. Robbins
Michel Roggo
Stephen Ross
William Roston
Gilbert van Ryckevorsel
David W. Schindler
Jim Schollmeyer
Rob & Melissa Simpson
Peter G. Sly
Osgood R. Smith
Richard P. Smith
Robert Henry Smith
Buzz Soard
Allan Solonsky
Robert Spateholts
Peter Thompson
Joe Tomelleri
James Tucker
Larry Tullis
Paul Turner
Spencer E. Turner
Paul Updike
Peter Vanriel
David Weigand
Jim Yuskavitch
Adam Zetter
Donna Ziegenfuss

Foreword

Much of the literature available to trout enthusiasts who are not scientists by training focuses on the technique, adventure, and spirituality of angling. Those interested in learning about the natural resource aspect of trout have relied on a small but significant smattering of commercially published writings—sections of *The Trout and the Stream* (1974) by Charles E. Brooks, *Trout* (1978) by Ernest Schwiebert, *Native Trout of North America* (1984) by Robert H. Smith, *Reading Trout Streams* (1988) by Tom Rosenbauer, and Robert J. Behnke's thought-provoking articles in *Trout* magazine.

Until publication of the book now in your hands, no single masterwork had presented an integrated view of trout biology, environment, and resource management.

Trout, the second in The Wildlife Series by Stackpole Books, does a great deal more, however, than fill a gap in the literature of trout. The authors broaden and deepen our understanding of a resource for whose future each and every one of us is responsible. Many of them have shaped coldwater fisheries conservation and management policies. We owe them a profound debt of gratitude for the progress that has been made on conservation and management fronts.

As we look to the next century, we must realize that more science and a greater sense of stewardship are critical elements of the informed activism necessary to protect North America's trout resources from the kind of depredation with which we are all too familiar. Although reading this book may not help you catch more fish, reading this book cannot fail to make you a better fisherman. That, by itself, is no small accomplishment.

One message that appears throughout this book is the superior value of wild trout fisheries in relation to those that exist on a put-and-take basis. We who have been fortunate enough to tangle with wild trout already appreciate this message. Any trout is a thing of beauty, but the beauty of a wild trout reaches far beyond the matter of its outward appearance.

By providing us with scientific and economic analyses demonstrating the benefits of wild trout over hatchery-reared fish, *Trout* takes the cause of wild trout beyond the dimension of aesthetic preference. It will help foster conservation and management policies which emphasize the significance of natural habitat, and it will encourage the return of trout propagation from the concrete tanks of hatcheries to its intended place in the sand and gravel spawning beds of streams whose fish and waters run forever wild.

Charles F. Gauvin
Executive Director,
Trout Unlimited

Publisher's note

*F*or all the millions of people who have fished for trout and the thousands of books that have been published on how to catch trout (and what trying to catch them feels like), only a very few volumes over the years have concentrated on trout biology and natural history. Until now no book has undertaken the daunting task of presenting a thorough survey of what we know about what trout are and how they live.

What exactly is a trout? Apparently even the taxonomists are unsure, judging by their recent decision to reclassify the western trouts. Formerly in the genus *Salmo*, these species now fall into the salmon genus, *Oncorhynchus*; other species that we call trout—bull trout, lake trout, and brook trout—actually are classified in the char genus, *Salvelinus*, along with Dolly Varden and Arctic char. The only trout left in the group of thirteen species commonly thought of as trout is the brown, *Salmo trutta*.

This book covers them all. We have omitted the Atlantic salmon, *Salmo salar*, from this study for two reasons: first because its life cycle is so different from that of the other *Salmo*, and second because virtually no one thinks of the Atlantic salmon as a trout, even though—confusingly enough—it is a member of the trout genus.

As for how trout live and behave, there is much about their nature that remains a mystery. Skittish, dazzlingly beautiful, evasive, ungregarious, cannibalistic, trout are as difficult to pin down scientifically as they are to catch. Precisely how many subspecies *are* there? Is a trout a salmon? Why do trout of the same species living in the same stream and exposed to the same food chain have markedly different diets? Is every rise to a specific target? Can trout learn? Do "rogues" roam at night far beyond their daytime range?

So far we can only speculate. There is so much that we do not know about trout—may never know about trout—that the time-passing fun of unresolved debate is a pleasure we may well be able to pass on to future generations. Thus, any comprehensive study of trout has to accept a measure of imprecision at the outset.

With this caveat, we proudly present Volume Two of Stackpole's Wildlife Series, *Trout*, a view of the fish not as sport-object (though the angler will glean much useful how-to-fish information from the pages that follow), nor as poet's conversation piece (though the grace and seductiveness of the fish come through), but simply as natural creature.

Each of the thirteen species commonly thought of as trout—Apache, Arctic char, brook, brown, bull, cutthroat, Dolly Varden, Gila, golden, lake, Mexican, rainbow, and steelhead—is described in detail with species-specific information on classification, coloration, behavior, diet, environment, ecology, and distribution. Other areas of focus include the trout's evolution, the problems and challenges of genetics, anatomy (external and internal), senses and taxes, diseases, predators, a typical population's annual cycle, rogue trout behavior, migration, food and feeding behavior, environmental requirements, habitat, endangered species, and the effects on trout of weather extremes, pollution, and stocking.

In putting *Trout* together we have been most fortunate to benefit from the efforts and expertise of thirty-one dedicated contributors—the very top names in trout biology—who have called on their own research as well as that of respected colleagues and predecessors to build this authoritative reference text for wildlife scientist, nature lover, and angler alike.

Also, importantly, we have provided a wealth of illustration, for the more common species especially. To show one or a couple of full-color illustrations of brown trout—saying, implicitly, that this is what a brown looks like—makes little sense given the near-infinite variety that evolution, environmental differentiation, and interbreeding have produced.

We show you, in color, a brown trout portrait, a brown from a small eastern stream, a brown from a western stream, a brown from a large river, a brown from a deep, clear lake, two different-looking browns from neighboring creeks, old paintings of browns from the Smithsonian Institution, a brown parr, a spawning female, a close-up of a brown's tail side by side with close-ups of a cutthroat's tail and a rainbow's, and so on, with comments from experts on the vagaries and varieties of coloration and anatomy that the reader is seeing.

What we don't know about trout is a source not only of fascination but also of comfort: the physical world retains its mysteries. What we do know about trout is presented, on the pages that follow, in the hope of adding a valuable text to the library of the naturalist, and also—perhaps—of painting a sometimes-entertaining canvas of one small corner of the impossibly complex, ultimately unknowable natural world of which the trout, and we, are part.

Stackpole Books wishes to thank the writers, photographers, illustrators, and others who contributed enthusiastically to this book and who generously provided additional advice and support during its development.

We also want to thank the many individuals who reviewed the manuscripts for accuracy: Robert J. Behnke and Richard L. Knight of Colorado State University; Gilbert B. Pauley, Thomas Quinn, and Christian Grue of the University of Washington; Kathleen Sullivan and Robert Bilby of The Weyerhaueser Company in Washington; Neil H. Ringler of the State University of New York; Peter Vanriel of Terrestrial and Aquatic Environmental Managers, Limited, in Saskatchewan; Thomas Gordon Northcote of The University of British Columbia; Daniel P. Christensen and Darrell M. Wong of the California Department of Fish and Game; William J. Berg of the University of California; Paul Turner of New Mexico State University; Dave Propst of the New Mexico Department of Game and Fish; Jerry Stefferud of the U.S. Forest Service; Bernie May and David Perkins of Cornell University in New York; John W. Nichols of the U.S. Environmental Protection Agency; and Hugh H. DeWitt of the University of Maine.

M. David Detweiler
President, Stackpole Books

HUNTER

What a trout is

The ancestry of trout

*T*he science – or art – of classification (taxonomy) evaluates evolutionary evidence in an attempt to arrange species on a family tree to denote branching points and degrees of evolutionary relationships. Traditionally, we have relied on skeletal features, anatomical characteristics, and the type and arrangement of teeth for evidence. Now, we also use more modern methods: counting chromosomes, studying protein patterns, and analyzing DNA.

We assume that a change in a character, such as presence or absence of teeth on a certain bone or on a particular part of a bone, denotes a branching sequence on the family tree. Branching sequences then can be arranged in a system of classification by descending orders of relatedness. For example, the outer terminal twigs on the tree represent living species, which are traced to a common stem branch that groups closely related species into a genus. Further down the tree, representing more ancient periods on the geological time scale, branches of genera join to form subfamilies. Finally, the base of the trunk represents the family.

LUMPERS AND SPLITTERS

There is general agreement among modern taxonomists that classification should reflect evolutionary relationships. That is, all species in the same genus should be more closely related to each other than to any species in other genera. And when we recognize a genus as a valid genus, we assume or denote that all species in that genus came from one common ancestral species. But we lack unambiguous criteria and all-encompassing definitions of the categories of classification. Thus, a "lumper" may recognize two or three species in a genus. A "splitter," using the same evidence but with different emphasis, might classify these same fish as two or three subspecies of one species.

Controversies and disagreements regarding what classification scheme best reflects evolutionary relationships, or phylogenies, arise from the fact that if the evidence used is inconclusive, it is open to individual interpretation. For example, the significance and magnitude of evolutionary divergence denoted by a change in the size or shape of a bone, a change in chromosome number, or a change in protein patterns might reflect a major branching classified as a genus or a branching of a lesser magnitude denoting a species or even a subspecies.

A primitive condition and an advanced or derived condition must be established for each character. Otherwise the use of any change in that character to denote the sequence of branches is open to interpretation.

THE FAMILY TREE

Uncertainty is prevalent when we try to reconstruct the lineage of the family Salmonidae, because the fossil record is sparse and contains large gaps. We rely on interpretations of the evidence from the characters we use for classification.

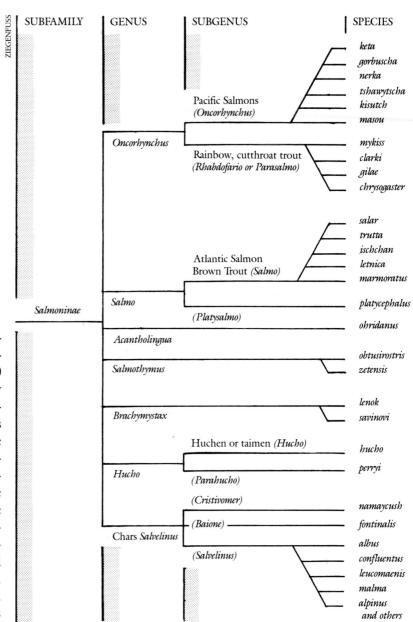

SUBFAMILY	GENUS	SUBGENUS	SPECIES

Pacific Salmons (*Oncorhynchus*)
- *keta*
- *gorbuscha*
- *nerka*
- *tshawytscha*
- *kisutch*
- *masou*

Oncorhynchus

Rainbow, cutthroat trout (*Rhabdofario* or *Parasalmo*)
- *mykiss*
- *clarki*
- *gilae*
- *chrysogaster*

Atlantic Salmon Brown Trout (*Salmo*)
- *salar*
- *trutta*
- *ischchan*
- *letnica*
- *marmoratus*

Salmo

(*Platysalmo*)
- *platycephalus*
- *ohridanus*

Salmoninae

Acantholingua

Salmothymus
- *obtusirostris*
- *zetensis*

Brachymystax
- *lenok*
- *savinovi*

Huchen or taimen (*Hucho*)
- *hucho*

Hucho

(*Parahucho*)
- *perryi*

(*Cristivomer*)
- *namaycush*

(*Baione*)
- *fontinalis*

Chars *Salvelinus*

(*Salvelinus*)
- *albus*
- *confluentus*
- *leucomaenis*
- *malma*
- *alpinus*
  and others

Although the oldest known salmonid fossil, *Eosalmo driftwoodensis* of British Columbia, represents a species living about 45 to 50 million years ago, the origin of the family probably is much older, perhaps on the magnitude of 100 million years. We base this assumption on the primitive nature of the skeletal and anatomical characters of salmonid fishes in relation to other groups of modern bony (teleostean) fishes. What we have learned from *Eosalmo* fossils indicates that the three subfamilies of Salmonidae—Coregoninae (the whitefishes), Thymallinae (graylings), and Salmoninae (trout, salmon, and char)—were already separated from each other 50 million years ago. A gap in the fossil record of about 25 million to 30 million years occurs between the Eocene and Miocene eras. Miocene fossils found in the western United States reveal that several major evolutionary branches of the subfamily Salmoninae were established by this time. These extinct, fossil species represent the same genera in which the living species of trout, salmon, and char are classified. Evidently, the first major branching, or divergence, leading to all living species of trout, salmon, and char, is characterized by a loss of teeth on the shaft of the vomer bone in the roof of the mouth and by a peculiar modification of lateral-line scales. One branch leads to the chars of the genus *Salvelinus* and also includes the lenok of Siberia (genus *Brachymystax*) and Eurasian huchen (the largest living species of Salmonidae, of the genus *Hucho*). The other branch

kingdom	Animalia (animals)
phylum	Chordata (animals with notochords and hollow nerve cords)
subphylum	Vertebrata (animals with backbones)
class	Osteichthes (bony fishes)
order	Salmoniformes (fishes with soft-rayed fins, adipose fins, and abdominal pelvic fins)
family	Salmonidae (trout, salmon, char, whitefish, graylings)
subfamily	Salmoninae (trout, salmon, and char)
genera	*Oncorhynchus* (hooked snout)
	Salmo (salmon)
	Salvelinus (dwelling in springs)
species	*mykiss, trutta, fontinalis,* etc.
subspecies	*lewisi, bouvieri, henshawi,* etc.

Although all subfamily members share certain physical characteristics, they also differ from one another. These differences separate them into distinct genera, subgenera, species, and subspecies. Pacific salmon (genus Oncorhynchus), Atlantic salmon (Salmo) and chars (Salvelinus) are all classified as Salmoninae subfamily members in the family Salmonidae, based on certain physical similarities among them. They are further taxonomically separated into distinct genera, subgenera, species and subspecies, on the basis of the differences among them.

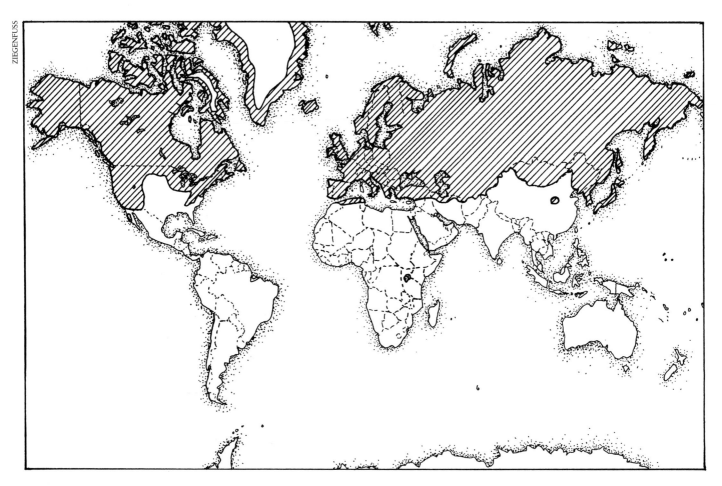

Although originally limited to the northern hemisphere, Salmonids have been successfully introduced into many parts of the southern hemisphere. They inhabit cool and cold waters; the Arctic char, a member of the family, occurs further north than any other freshwater fish.

of this divergence leads to the living species of trout and salmon. By the middle of the Miocene period, the trout and salmon branch forked again, resulting in two major groups. In the North Pacific basin of North America and Asia, one branch subdivided into two main evolutionary lines, one leading to species of Pacific Salmon, the other to rainbow and cutthroat trout—all now classified in the genus *Oncorhynchus*. In the North Atlantic basin of Europe, branchings of the *Salmo* line gave rise to Atlantic salmon and brown trout and related species.

The evolutionary line that developed perhaps 100 million years ago resulting in all of the present species of trout, salmon, char, whitefishes, and graylings probably began when the chromosome number doubled in a common ancestral species. The chromosomes of all species of the family Salmonidae contain about twice the amount of DNA found in related families such as the smelt family, Osmeridae. This indicates that the character change in the chromosomes of a primitive ancestor occurred before the evolutionary separation of the family into three

subfamilies. We do not know whether this most ancient ancestor was a freshwater species or a marine species. All species of Salmonidae must spawn in fresh water, which would indicate a freshwater origin. But most species also have the physiological capability to live in the ocean, which suggests that the ability to excrete salts and retain water, necessary to survival in marine waters, has been inherited from an ancient ancestor.

There are some little-known, troutlike species whose correct positions on the family tree are largely unknown, except that their branches belong in the subfamily Salmoninae part of the tree. A peculiar species (probably two species) classified in the genus *Salmothymus* occurs in a few rivers on the Adriatic coast of Yugoslavia. The generic name implies that this fish originally was thought to be intermediate between trout (genus *Salmo* of subfamily Salmoninae) and grayling (genus *Thymallus* of subfamily Thymallinae). There is no doubt that *Salmothymus* is a trout (subfamily Salmoninae), but where its branching point joins the tree in relation to the *Oncorhynchus* and *Salmo* branches is not clear.

Based on my interpretation of the evidence, *Salmothymus* should be connected to the *Salmo* branch. But others may disagree and place it further down the tree connecting to a common ancestral stem before the separation of this stem into *Salmo* and *Oncorhynchus*.

Another species of dubious relationship occurs only in Lake Ohrid, Yugoslavia, and is classified in the genus *Acantholingua*. This species formerly was classified in the genus *Salmothymus*, but there is little doubt that *Acantholingua* should be recognized as a separate genus. *Acantholingua ohridanus* has a smeltlike appearance and has the most primitive type of skeletal characters and dentition in comparison to all other living species of trout, salmon, and char. *Acantholingua* is an ancient branch in the subfamily, probably connecting to the ancestral trunk well before the separation of *Salmo* and *Oncorhynchus*. All remnants of the *Acantholingua* branch have died out except for the species *ohridanus* in Lake Ohrid.

A species known by only three specimens from a river in Turkey is also of uncertain status. Many years ago I named this species *platycephalus* and created a subgenus *Platysalmo* in the genus *Salmo* for its classification. However, I was not confident about the placement of *platycephalus* on the family tree regarding its precise relationship to *Salmo*.

Now that the branches of the family tree have been classified into genera, we can trace these generic branches to their terminal twigs to assess how many living species of trout, salmon, and char exist in the world. This is not a simple task, and there is disagreement on how many species should be recognized. But we can arrive at a best estimate.

In the genus *Salmo*, I include six species of varying degrees of relatedness. If the Turkish trout *Platysalmo platycephalus* is included as one of the six species, there are three "good" species highly divergent from one another—the Atlantic salmon, *S. salar*; the brown trout, *S. trutta*; and the Turkish trout, *S. (P.) platycephalus*. The other three recognized species are closely related to brown trout. In some rivers tributary to the Adriatic Sea, the marbled trout, *S. marmoratus*, occurs. The marbled trout is a large predaceous fish reaching 23 kilograms (50 pounds) or more. Its coloration and markings differ greatly from those of other species of *Salmo*. It has only light-colored marbled markings (similar to the markings of the char of the genus *Salvelinus*). Genetically, however, *trutta* and *marmoratus* are very closely related and they are known to hybridize where they occur together. The other two species commonly recognized, *S. ischchan* and *S. letnica*, are even more closely related to *S. trutta*. These species probably represent the isolation of *S. trutta* ancestors in single lakes. *S. ischchan* is restricted to Lake Sevan in the Soviet Union and *S. letnica* to Lake Ohrid, Yugoslavia.

The genus *Oncorhynchus* consists of six species of Pacific salmon and four species of western North American trout. Five species of salmon are native to the Pacific drainages of North America: pink, *O. gorbuscha*; chinook, *O. tsawytscha*; coho, *O. kisutch*; sockeye, *O. nerka*; and chum, *O. keta*. In addition, the masu or cherry salmon, *O. masou*, occurs in the Far East. A seventh species, *O. rhodurus*, is often recognized. The *rhodurus* salmon is very closely related to *masou*, and I prefer to classify it as a southern subspecies of

The Atlantic salmon, Salmo salar, *is the closest native relative of the brown trout, which was introduced to this continent from Europe.*

VAN RYCKEVORSEL

masou. Besides rainbow trout, *O. mykiss*, and cutthroat trout, *O. clarki*, I recognize the Mexican golden trout, *O. chrysogaster*; the Gila and Apache trout, in my opinion, are two subspecies of one species: *O. gilae gilae* and *O. gilae apache*. The California golden trout generally is classified as a separate species, *O. aguabonita*. However, my classification, based on the assessment of degrees of relatedness typically used in animal classification, would place it as a subspecies of rainbow trout, making it *O. mykiss aguabonita*.

The Siberian lenok genus *Brachymystax* is generally regarded as a monotypic genus—that is, only one species, *B. lenok*, is recognized in the genus. It has long been known, however, that two distinct forms of lenok occur over a broad geographical area—a "sharp snout" and a "blunt snout" lenok. Because the sharp snout and blunt snout lenok coexist in the Amur River basin, they should be classified as two separate species.

The genus *Hucho*, in my classification, contains two highly divergent species, which I classify in different subgenera. The Danube River basin huchen, *Hucho hucho*, and the Siberian taimen (the world's largest salmonid fish) are very closely related. I classify the huchen and the taimen as two subspecies, *H. hucho hucho* and *H. hucho taimen*, of one species. A very different species of *Hucho* occurs in rivers of Hokkaido and Sakhalin islands in the Far East; it is classified as *H. perryi*. A huchen was described from the upper Yangtze River basin of China as *H. bleekeri*. Virtually nothing is known of the Yangtze huchen. Further study probably will indicate no more than subspecies classification for this fish, but we do not know to which species, *H. hucho* or *H. perryi*, the Yangtze huchen is most closely related.

The char genus, *Salvelinus*, is the most troublesome genus to classify into species. The enormous amount of diversity found throughout the vast distribution of chars in North America, Asia, and Europe creates a classic example for contrasting differences between lumpers and splitters in the emphasis used to define a species. It helps to divide the genus into major evolutionary branches known as subgenera. Two of these branches are represented by single species, the lake trout *S. namaycush* (subgenus *Cristivomer*), and the brook trout, *S. fontinalis* (subgenus *Baione*), of North America. But as for the third major branch (subgenus *Salvelinus*), only best guesses are possible at present to enumerate the "species." This branch appears to include at least two evolutionary clusters of species. One cluster contains the Dolly Varden char, *S. malma*, and Arctic char, *S. alpinus*, but I estimate that about five or six additional species eventually will be recognized for char presently considered as Dolly Varden or Arctic char. The other cluster of char species includes the Far Eastern char, *S. leucomaenis*; the North American bull trout, *S. confluentus*; the Kamchatkan stone char, *S. albus*; and perhaps one or two additional species.

In recent times, two extremely divergent species of char were found in a lake on the Chukokst Peninsula of the USSR (across the Bering Strait from Alaska). This discovery hints at what might be in store for future discoveries of char when the fishes of remote lakes across Siberia are studied. Until then, we may estimate about fifteen species of char in the genus *Salvelinus*, but don't place much confidence in such an estimate—there's much to be learned.

TROUT BY ANY OTHER NAME

Those familiar with the literature of the nineteenth and early twentieth centuries on trout are aware of a confusing proliferation of scientific names used in earlier times. Works

This chinook salmon, Oncorhynchus tsawytscha, (right) has finished spawning and will die soon. Below, a sockeye salmon, O. nerka, shows brilliant red spawning colors. The sockeye is noted for its land-locked varieties.

HOWELL

ROSTON

YUSKAVITCH

referring to the European brown trout, *S. trutta*, might discuss twenty or more species recognized at the time for what we now classify as a single species. In the North American literature, more than thirty species of trout were, at one time or another, recognized for what we now classify as two species—rainbow trout and cutthroat trout. The "lumping" of many species into one species is the result of our changing concept of a species and attempts to make classification more accurately reflect degrees of evolutionary relationships.

One of the basic premises of classification is that all populations of a species can be traced to one common ancestor. That is, all members of a species are more closely related to other members of the same species than to any member of another species.

Another premise is that geographic races (subspecies) of a species would hybridize with others of the same species if they occurred together. If they would not hybridize, they are separate species. The application of the criterion of reproductive isolation resulted in the lumping of many formerly recognized species into a relatively few species at present. In the nineteenth and early twentieth centuries, it was common practice to describe each slight variation found as new species. We now consider many of these older species as geographic variations within one species, although many of the old species names are retained as subspecies.

In earlier times biologists recognized more than twenty different species of what is today classified simply as Salmo trutta, the brown trout.

When what we now recognize as one species has earlier been named as ten or twenty species, which one of the many species names do we keep? The international rules of zoological nomenclature provide the answer. The rule of priority states that when one species has been named two or more times, the valid name for that species must be the first name described and published in the literature; subsequent names for the species then are known as synonyms but can be used for subspecies names.

In 1988 the American Fisheries Society decided to change the genus name for western North American trouts from *Salmo* to *Oncorhynchus* and to change the species name for rainbow trout from *gairdneri* to *mykiss*. The rainbow trout had been named many different species. The oldest name given to any North American rainbow trout was *Salmo gairdneri* in 1836, and *gairdneri* was used to designate rainbow trout for many years. But the same species of rainbow trout also lives on the Kamchatkan Peninsula of the Soviet Far East, and the Kamchatkan rainbow trout was named *mykiss* in 1792. Thus, the name *mykiss* clearly has priority over *gairdneri* as the valid species name for rainbow trout.

The reason rainbow trout, cutthroat trout, and related species were transferred from *Salmo* to *Oncorhynchus* concerns the goal of classification, which is to reflect evolutionary relationships. There is no longer any reasonable doubt that rainbow trout, cutthroat trout, and the western North American trouts are more closely related to the Pacific salmons of the genus *Oncorhynchus* than they are to the Atlantic salmon and brown trout of the genus *Salmo*.

The genus *Oncorhynchus* thus denotes a common ancestor that gave rise to all species of Pacific salmon and also to the western North American trout.

Most people are disturbed over sudden changes in familiar names. It should be remembered, however, that name changes do not affect the fish themselves in any way. A rainbow trout, by any other name, is still the same rainbow trout, just as we have always known it. A rose by any other name still smells as sweet.

—Robert J. Behnke

Judgment calls

*T*here is no single definition or rule that we can apply unambiguously in all instances to decide if a certain fish should be classified as a species or as a subspecies. A standard definition of a subspecies is that it is a geographical race of a species, geographically isolated from other members of its species and recognizably different from other members in one or more characters. This definition assumes that only isolation maintains the subspecies distinctions. If populations of a subspecies were to occur together with other subspecies of the same species, they would hybridize and lose their identity. If two distinct populations occur together without hybridizing, or with very limited hybridization, this is evidence that they should be classified as a separate species rather than subspecies of one species. Thus, in animal classification, the degree of reproductive isolation—the ability to avoid hybridization with nearest relatives—is a major criterion for deciding between species or subspecies classification.

With salmonid fishes, however, many problems arise that require judgment calls regarding correct classification. For example, the California golden trout, the Gila trout of New Mexico, and the Apache trout of Arizona generally are classified as separate species. That is, the American Fisheries Society "officially" recognizes them as three species. The maintenance of their identity, however, depends on geographic isolation. When living with either introduced rainbow trout or cutthroat trout, all of these "species" freely hybridize and lose their identity.

Reproductive isolation between species often is not an all-or-nothing phenomenon, however. The coastal cutthroat trout subspecies coexists with rainbow trout from

northern California to southern Alaska and hybridization is rare—each species maintains its respective integrity over a vast range. Yet when rainbow trout are introduced into interior waters where only the cutthroat species is native, hybridization between rainbow and interior subspecies of cutthroat trout almost always occurs—the two species cannot maintain their integrity in waters where only one species is native and the other is stocked.

The subtle complexities of factors governing reproductive isolation are illustrated also by the interaction of westslope cutthroat trout (subspecies *lewisi*) with rainbow trout. In some parts of the range of *lewisi,* such as the Salmon and Clearwater rivers of Idaho and the John Day River of Oregon, the subspecies evolved with rainbow trout, and hybridization with the native rainbow trout is rare. The two species maintain their integrity. In the Clark Fork River drainage of Montana and the Saint Joe River drainage of Idaho, *lewisi* is native to these waters but the rainbow trout is not; that is, the two species did not evolve together in this geographical area. When rainbow trout were stocked and became established in the Clark Fork and Saint Joe drainages, massive hybridization occurred in most waters where the two species came into contact. In waters where they historically have lived together, ecological and life-history distinctions were evolved that led to reproductive isolation. Where the two species did not coevolve, reproductive isolation is lacking and the species cannot maintain their genetic integrity.

Another extreme of reproductive isolation occurs in rainbow trout. A summer-run steelhead, a winter-run steelhead, and resident rainbow trout all might be found in one river, yet these three distinct groups of rainbow trout maintain reproductive isolation from one another by subtle differences in the times and places of spawning. They behave as if each one is a separate species. The reason we do not classify them as separate species concerns their origins. It is accepted that all members of a species must have a single ancestor—a common origin at the species branch of the system. Considering resident rainbow trout and steelhead, and the different races of steelhead, we are dealing with races of multiple origins. Although all races of resident rainbow trout and all races of steelhead can be traced to a common ancestral rainbow trout (which is why they are all classified as one species), numerous independent evolutionary lines within the species produced a multitude of races.

There is no one common ancestor for all steelhead and no one common ancestor for all resident rainbow trout. One basic life-history form has given rise to the other—that is, the anadromous or the resident has given rise to the resident or the anadromous—independently many times during the past several thousand years. As a result, the races of steelhead and resident rainbow within each major river basin are more closely related to each other within those basins than they are to races of steelhead or resident rainbow in other basins. For example, the resident rainbow of the Colorado River are more closely related to the steelhead of the Colorado River than they are to the resident rainbow of the Sacramento or Fraser river systems. In such a situation, we do not officially recognize anadromous and resident populations as separate species.

—*Robert J. Behnke*

Genes: the code word

*T*he fallen leaves of autumn lie on the banks of a small spring-fed tributary stream. Early November has brought cold nights to the northeastern United States with early morning temperatures in the 20s Fahrenheit. Two days ago a light dusting of snow fell upon the surrounding hills. Now, only the occasional green of a pine breaks the gray and brown monotony of the dormant hardwood trees. In contrast to the winding down of the activities of the landscape, the breeding season of the brook trout is beginning.

A day ago two trout, a male and a female, moved half a mile out of the main river up into a tributary stream and are now resting in a pool under a large fallen spruce log. Just before dusk, the female, drab in color compared with the red-finned, crimson-bellied male, moves out from under the log and drifts downstream out of the pool. Below the pool, partway down the riffle, she senses spring water percolating out of the gravel. Immediately, she turns her head back upstream and holds her position in the current over the spot. The male comes close beside her. The female digs a shallow depression by turning on her side and vigorously thrusting her tail up and down. Soon the redd is completed. The female drops her vent into the depression, the male swiftly comes to her side, and with visible quivering by both, eggs and milt are extruded simultaneously. The female moves a few feet upstream and begins the spawning process again.

What has happened? Just another scene of autumnal reproduction between two trout in a stream? Many would say that the successful spawning of trout is the assurance of future fishing opportunities. Such is true, for the spawning of brook trout this autumn affects the fishing two years hence. For other trouts, such as steelhead (rainbow trout), spawning in the spring affects fishing as much as four to six years into the future. But more is happening here than just the making of new trout.

The combining of an egg, having only one-half of the genes of the mother, with the sperm of the father, which provides the other half, is a precise and complicated process. Most readers will recognize that locked into this process is the code to ensure that brook trout produce more brook trout rather than rainbow trout. Even more interesting, however, is that this code ensures not only a species identity but also a whole suite of traits, such as migration patterns and feeding habits. These traits may be unique to a group or population of trout from a local region and often represent a special adaptation for survival in the streams and lakes where those trout live.

What might the genetic ramifications be if the female trout in our tributary stream represents the original native gene pool and the male trout represents a stocked fish, whose parents in turn represent a domesticated strain held for more than fifty years in a hatchery?

BUILDING BLOCKS OF HEREDITY

Let's briefly consider some key concepts about the genetics of individuals. Genes are the hereditary units that contain the code that affects a trait. The code is contained within the sequence of compounds used to construct a molecule known as dioxyribonucleic acid, or DNA. Genes are located at a specific spot, a locus, on a chromosome. Thus, chromosomes, which are threadlike strands of DNA, carry many genes controlling many traits, which in combination ensure that a functioning organism results. Chromosomes are located in the nucleus of cells and come in pairs. For example, brook trout have eighty-four chromosomes, forty-two pairs. As a result, genes controlling a particular characteristic also come in pairs, one gene copy occurring on each of the paired chromosomes.

The number of chromosomes that contain the genetic code depends on the type of trout species. Lake trout and brook trout have the most chromosomes, eighty-four, in contrast to the Apache trout, which has fifty-six. Trout typically have more chromosomes than other fish. Scientists suspect that, in the distant past, trout chromosome numbers doubled to about ninety-six. As a result of this duplication, trout had four gene copies (tetrasomy), instead of the more normal two (disomy). Since that time, each species is believed to be going through a process of restructuring its genes. Depending on the trout species, some copies of genes appear to have been silenced and some chromosome arms have fused together. As a result, trout have a much greater variation in chromosome numbers among species than are observed in most other fish families.

Hybrids between species may occur but most often they are infertile. For example, the tiger trout is a cross between the native brook trout and the brown trout of European origin, and it has been observed to occur naturally in North American streams. Infertility of the tiger trout may be caused by dissimilarity between the chromosome numbers of the two parent species. Fertile hybrids do occur for species whose chromosome numbers overlap or are the same such as the splake, the hybrid between the lake and brook trout. Stocked rainbow trout in many places in western North America have genetically diluted native cutthroat populations through interbreeding and the forming of fertile hybrids.

For reproductive purposes, trout must develop special cells, eggs and sperm (milt) that contain one representative chromosome from each chromosome pair. Thus, these sex cells have only one-half of the genetic code that normally is contained within other cells. When the egg and sperm unite, each contributes one chromosome to re-form the chromosome pairs characteristic of the species. As a result, the proper number of chromosomes is restored. This describes the genetics of individuals, but what about populations?

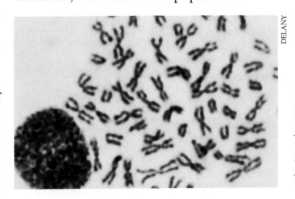

DELANY

Trout chromosomes show tetrasomy—four gene copies—rather than the usual two found in most organisms. Scientists suspect that this extra genetic material may account for the variability found in and among trout species.

REPRODUCTIVE BARRIERS

First, the word *population* should be explained. Biologists, ecologists, and population geneticists use it to mean a group of individuals (trout, in our case) of the same species that live close enough to each other that any member of the population may spawn with any other member, provided, of course, that the two are of opposite sexes. Two populations occur when a barrier exists between them that prevents their members from spawning together.

Separate trout populations often develop as a result of geography. Trout in a remote pond with no inlet or outlet obviously cannot spawn with trout in other ponds. Thus, trout in each isolated pond represent a separate population, according to our definition above. Likewise, trout in one river drainage are unlikely to spawn with trout in other drainages, and, thus, again separate populations result. Sometimes impassable barriers, such as waterfalls on a river, may further subdivide trout into different upstream and downstream populations. In some cases, a trout population may, in theory, have access to other populations through connected waterways, but the actual geographical distance is much greater than what even the most wandering trout might want to travel.

Trout behavior also may help define populations. Trout from many populations may, during some parts of their lives, occupy the same body of water, such as the Great Lakes, Pacific Ocean, or some large reservoir. During the spawning season, these trout aggregate into populations by returning to the individual tributary streams where they were born. Biologists know that at least part of this homing behavior is guided by a memory of the smell of the natal stream.

Waterfalls, though beautiful, are sometimes insurmountable barriers for fish migration. Thus trout populations become isolated and may evolve into distinct geographic races or subspecies.

KRUEGER

DUAL FORCES

The expression of any trait, such as upstream migration of juveniles, is controlled by two forces: genetics and environment. The genetic information coded within an individual provides the innate potential for the expression of a trait. The environment surrounding the individual then controls the expression of the trait within that genetically coded potential. For example, growth is partly controlled by genetics. Some individual trout have the innate capability for rapid growth. However, the ultimate expression of that growth capability is partly regulated by food abundance, a factor in the environment. Without enough food, of course, trout cannot grow.

Just as individuals have traits partly controlled by genetics, so do populations. For example, some wild brook trout populations have the genetic capability to live long lives (eight to ten years) and grow to a large size (2.3 kilograms [5 pounds] or more). This population characteristic is much different from that of many hatchery populations, whose maximum life span may be only four years.

We easily recognize the physical differences among our own family members, yet our family members are more similar and closely related to each other than they are to members of other families. In much the same way, the genetic variation of trout is organized, first, among individuals within populations and, second, among populations. The amount of genetic differences among populations is typically greater than the amount of differences among individuals within a population. The genetic distinctiveness of populations is maintained over time by the reproductive isolating mechanisms that separate populations during the spawning season. Populations may be thought of as the key or fundamental organizational unit of genetic variation, which is why they, rather than a species as a whole, should be the focus of such fishery management actions as stocking and regulations. For example, management of cutthroat trout as a species would be disastrous without recognizing the many distinct populations.

Genetic changes in trout populations may occur as a result of migration and subsequent

mating between populations, adaptation to changing forces of natural selection, or gene mutation. Sometimes they occur just by chance—especially in endangered trout populations that have few individuals. Man often affects these forces of change in an unnatural way, sometimes causing permanent deleterious effects on the genetics of populations. Even well-intended but misguided fishery management efforts can cause permanent genetic damage to trout populations.

GENETIC DIFFERENCES

What are some of the characteristics of populations that have a strong genetic basis? Many examples of genetic differences among trout and salmon populations exist. Most of this information is a direct result of research conducted during the 1970s and 1980s using sophisticated techniques of genetic analysis. Genetic differences have been shown among populations of Atlantic salmon, rainbow trout, brown trout, lake trout, golden trout, cutthroat trout, brook trout, Arctic char, and many species of Pacific salmon. Studies also have been conducted investigating more easily observable traits, such as movement behavior and stress resistance. Though these traits are easier to observe, such studies are more difficult to design and conduct. Nevertheless, whenever populations are compared, they usually demonstrate interesting differences in their genetic adaptations to the environments in which they live.

Cutthroat trout have been studied intensively in the Yellowstone Lake system of Yellowstone National Park in Wyoming. Here cutthroats use the lake for feeding and growth but spawn in streams. During spawning season, the trout migrate out of Yellowstone Lake into stream environments. Note that two different types of stream spawning habitats are used, either inlet streams flowing into the lake or the outlet—the Yellowstone River. But what happens to the fry after they hatch? Are the fry that are hatched in the outlet eventually swept downstream away from the lake, and therefore forever lost to the Yellowstone Lake system? Nature rarely is so wasteful! Or do the fry that hatch in the outlet somehow know to migrate upstream, and do those that hatch in the inlet know to migrate downstream? Indeed after careful

studies, it was discovered that this is the exact situation. Thus, the newly hatched fry are able to find their way to Yellowstone Lake, their nursery lake. This trait for fry migrations is genetically coded. Similar adaptations appear to exist as well among different populations of sockeye salmon and brook trout.

Now contemplate for a moment the potential result of stocking the outlet of Yellowstone Lake with inlet-origin fry in order to increase cutthroat trout numbers in the Yellowstone system. What direction would the fry migrate? Such stocking would be a waste of time and effort! Further consider the genetic damage that could be done if fishery management practices somehow broke down the reproductive isolating mechanisms between the two types of cutthroat populations, or if young cutthroat are propagated from collections of eggs and sperm from both types of populations and then the hybrids are stocked into the system. Remember that fry migration is only one trait that fishery biologists have identified as critical to Yellowstone cutthroat trout. How many other traits are there to be discovered that also are essential to the survival of this population?

APPLIED GENETICS

Studies of lake trout populations have provided us with several examples of important genetic adaptations. For example, as early as the 1800s, different "forms" of lake trout were recognized in the Great Lakes. Sometimes the differences between types of lake trout seemed so great that early biologists such as Louis Agassiz described them as different species. These types include the lean, or shallow-water, form and the siscowet, or deepwater, trout. In the 1960s and 1970s, research by the Ontario Ministry of Natural Resources demonstrated that the ability of a lake char to occupy deep water was an inherited trait. The process controlled by genetics was the ability of a trout to inflate or deflate its swim bladder and thus regulate its position in the water column. Lake trout populations from deep lakes could maintain deeper depth distributions than trout from shallow lakes.

The information about how genetics affects depth distribution of lake trout has been critical in determining what type of lake

Left: *Lake trout in deep lakes evolved a greater ability to regulate their positions in the water column by inflating and deflating their swim bladders, an ability which enables them to maintain deeper depth distributions than trout in shallow lakes. This genetic adaptation caused early observers to describe these two forms of lake trout as two different species—the lean (shallow water) and the siscowet (deepwater) trout.*
Right: *Genetically controlled characteristics have created two recognizably different forms of lake trout, the lean (above) and the siscowet (below).*

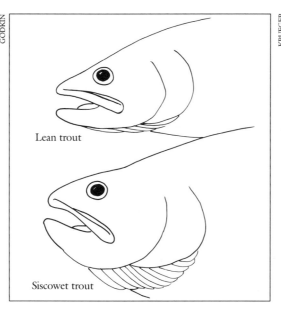

Lean trout

Siscowet trout

trout to stock in the Great Lakes. Here, lake trout are the focus of an international effort to restore this once-native species. In the eastern basin of Lake Ontario, the thermocline, the barrier between the warm upper layer of water and the cool bottom layer, in the summer will sometimes occur as deep as 40 meters (130 feet). However, a lake trout would have to live in deeper water than this to find temperatures cold enough to survive. Clearly, the stocking of deepwater forms of lake trout that are genetically capable of occupying such depths offers the most chance for successful restoration of the species.

Often, fishery biologists know that genetic differences exist among trout populations but cannot explain yet the ecological processes affected. For example, many different strains of lake trout are stocked each year in Lake Ontario as part of the species restoration program. One of them, the Seneca strain, is derived from the population in Seneca Lake, one of the Finger Lakes in New York. This strain represents less than 10 percent of the total stocking of lake trout into Lake Ontario over the past fifteen years. Using genetic techniques, researchers from Cornell University know that at a spawning reef in the eastern basin, the Seneca strain comprises 60 to 80 percent of the naturally produced lake trout fry. The other strains are present at the spawning reef and have viable eggs and milt, so why does the Seneca strain consistently outreproduce them? The trout from Seneca Lake must have a genetic adap-

tation that enhances their reproductive capabilities over those possessed by other, less successful strains.

Rainbow trout from different genetic sources have been evaluated in terms of their movement after being stocked as hatchery yearlings for a put-and-take fishery in Oregon. Researchers found that the Roaring River strain moved downstream much more rapidly than did the Cape Cod strain. For another example, the Skamania and Chambers Creek steelhead stocked in the Great Lakes for put-grow-and-take fisheries have spread rapidly and widely throughout the basin. These trout appear to delay maturity by one to two years longer than the standard domestic strains. In addition, they enter streams in late summer and early fall in preparation for spawning rather than in the spring when the domestic strains enter.

We should always presume that a native population of trout contains specialized genetic adaptations to the home stream or lake that are essential for the survival of the population even if we do not know for sure what they are. Using this presumption, we should be careful not to jeopardize through stocking or other management practices the genetic identities of native populations. Disruption of the genetic combinations essential for survival can cause a long-term problem, and the genetic disruption will be passed from generation to generation until the forces of natural selection can correct it.

—Charles C. Krueger

Changing the code

Specialized genetic technologies are emerging that permit us to radically alter the genetics of fishes in ways other than artificial selection. One technique is the insertion of DNA from one species into the chromosomes of another. For example, the blood antifreeze gene of winter flounder has been reported to be successfully transferred into the chromosomes of the Atlantic salmon, *Salmo salar*. Such technology has the potential of permanently altering the genetics of a species in a most fundamental way–the DNA code. What do you think about having Atlantic salmon with a flounder gene? Society must grapple with the ethical questions of altering the genetics of a species for our benefit at the potential expense of the species' original genetic identity. The book *Population Genetics and Fishery Management*, edited by Ryman and Utter and published by the University of Washington, provides a wealth of information about this subject.

Many other issues arise concerning genetics for which easy answers do not exist. Should we spend tax dollars to save an endangered trout population? Should we restore native trout species to their original habitats? If so, what genetic considerations should be included to speed success? Should we import exotic trout species from Asia? What genetic dangers will exotic trout pose to our wild populations? Should governments promote the DNA manipulation of fish species for aquaculture? If so, what safeguards should be built in to prevent the escape of DNA-altered fish?

When you consider these questions, remember that the fundamental organizational unit of trout genetics is the population. Populations represent special genetic reservoirs that are the products of thousands of years of natural selection. These genetic reservoirs provide trout species with the ability to adapt to changes in their environments. Thus, the conservation of trout populations and their genetic information is vital to ensuring the future of trout species.

–Charles C. Krueger

The beauty of trout

*T*rout can be described as fusiform-shaped, soft-rayed fishes with a terminal mouth, which is to say that they have a body shaped like a dart, fins with flexible spines, and a mouth in which neither the upper nor the lower jaw extends. But the most obvious and the most pleasing feature is their coloration.

The brown trout and the western trouts (cutthroat, rainbow, golden, Mexican golden, Apache, and Gila trout) have a pattern of darker spots against a lighter background. The chars (brook, bull, and lake trout; Arctic and Dolly Varden char) generally have a white leading edge on the anal and pelvic fins and a pattern of lighter-colored spots against a darker background. Beyond basic spotting patterns, various colors may be present. For example, brook trout have spots with blue aureoles; brown trout have faint halos around dark spots.

There may be unique body colorations as well, such as the brown-golden color of brown trout or the reddish lateral stripe of rainbow trout. Or there may be unusual dorsal patterns, such as the wormlike vermiculations on the brook trout. Many species can be truly described as beautiful, but the brightest colors are reserved for those species inhabiting waters at the higher elevations and in the interior regions. The golden trout of the Sierra Nevada of California, for example, has a vivid red to red-orange belly and opercula (gill covers), golden sides, reddish orange lateral bands, and a dark back.

The color patterns are caused by variations in skin pigments. These pigments in the cells reflect light, particularly red, yellow, orange, brown, and black, to produce the trout's external colors. Some of these cells, called chromatophores, contain more than one type of pigment, and some pigments can move in the cytoplasm of the cell to produce changes in colors. The more spectacular colors, blue for example, are produced in special reflecting chromatophores called iridophores. Small, flat structures within the iridophores reflect these unusual colors. These chromatophores and iridophores provide the principal sources of color and occur at many locations in the skin as well as elsewhere in the body, the eyes, for example. When individual fishes undergo color changes, there is a migration of pigment within the chromatophores to create vivid concentrations of color on the fish. The bright red or orange on the undersides of spawning brook trout and Arctic char illustrates this phenomenon.

Young fish in streams, particularly in their first year or two of life, are referred to as parr, and the dark, oblong bars many of them have on their sides are called parr marks. The number and shape of these marks often can be used to distinguish juveniles of many salmonid species at a life stage when other identifying marks may not be so pronounced. In some species, these marks remain through adulthood; in others they disappear as the fish grows and develops distinct species coloration.

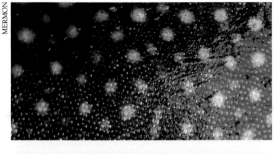

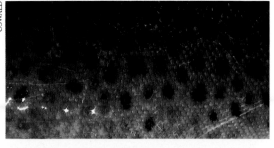

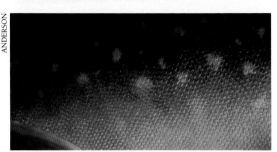

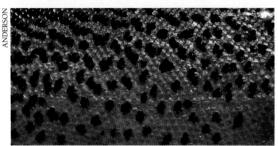

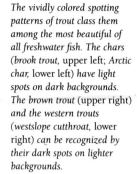

The vividly colored spotting patterns of trout class them among the most beautiful of all freshwater fish. The chars (brook trout, upper left; Arctic char, lower left) have light spots on dark backgrounds. The brown trout (upper right) and the western trouts (westslope cutthroat, lower right) can be recognized by their dark spots on lighter backgrounds.

Anadromous, or sea-run, fish lose their parr marks and develop a silvery coloration as they grow from parr to smolt before migrating to the sea. Sea-run trout generally have a dark dorsal surface and silvery sides while at sea and after returning to fresh water, though trout returning to fresh water for long periods of time may lose this silvery appearance and develop colors similar to those of other freshwater residents. The silvery coloration provides protective countershading at sea, a phenomenon known as Thayer's Principle: Avian predators see only a dark surface, and aquatic predators looking up see only a light pattern against the bright sky.

The basic coloration of trout generally changes only during two stages of life. During development from parr to smolt in anadromous trout, not only do the sides of the body develop a silvery sheen, but also the dorsal, or top, surface usually turns dark and the parr marks fade. The scales during this period are loose, and the fish can be easily stressed and can lose them if it encounters

obstructions to its downstream passage, such as dams.

During spawning as well, trout, particularly the males, often develop different, sometimes quite brilliant, coloration. Males of the Sunapee trout, for example, a subspecies of landlocked Arctic char native to Maine but also transplanted to two lakes in the Sawtooth Mountains of Idaho, develop a bright orange-red underside during fall spawning. Other species, such as sea-run cutthroat trout, darken at the time of spawning.

In addition to color variations caused by these life changes, color patterns can differ between individuals of the same species because of the availability and the type of food, especially the number of red, yellow, and orange carotenoids, or pigments. If trout eat mysid shrimp, for example, they will develop more of a reddish coloration in the flesh, and their external colors often may be more brilliant. So a cutthroat trout in one body of water can look different from one in another locale. For example, cutthroat from the Willamette River in Oregon often are quite pale, but the same subspecies in small tributaries in the Cascade Mountains will have brilliant colors in high contrast.

The color patterns also can be a direct result of such local environmental conditions as lighting, cover, or bottom configuration. Apparently what happens is that the chromatophores in the skin are affected by hormonal and nerve changes in the fish, which are triggered by external stimuli, such as

The oblong bars called parr marks, along with small size, identify juvenile fish, although some species may retain their parr marks into adulthood.

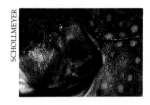

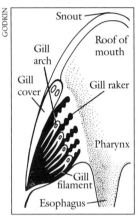

The gills are one of the most critical structures of a fish. The finger-shaped spread of the gill filaments creates a large surface area that maximizes opportunities for oxygen extraction and carbon dioxide removal. Gill filaments are easily damaged by sediments and other water pollutants. Sediments can act like sandpaper on the gill filaments, eroding them away. Other pollutants can cause the filaments to mold together, which reduces their surface area, decreases oxygen extraction potential, and stresses the fish. A stressed fish feeds poorly and is more likely to become disease-stricken.

When an anadromous trout changes from parr to smolt as part of its preparation for migration to the sea, its scales temporarily become loose and are easily dislodged, especially when the fish is handled. Loss of scales makes fish more susceptible to disease and bacterial infection. Trout have scales of the cycloid type.

changes in light, cover, or the color of the substrate. Fish can cause their pigment cells to fade between areas of normal color, bringing on a mottled appearance, or they can cause the cells to darken, creating an appearance that blends well with areas of cover.

Color change in trout often is not as radical as it is in other fishes. Rather, the process is more a change in contrast between color patterns. Nevertheless, experiments by Jenkins in 1969 showed that brook and brown trout could change basic background color, and brown trout could develop mottled bands in response to dark and light colors of the stream bottom.

In 1969 and 1970, Northcote and his associates, studying populations of rainbow trout above and below a waterfall in British Columbia, found that the trout above the falls had a significantly higher number of parr marks than did those below the falls. The difference probably is related to two phenomena: differences in spawning times, so that fish were subjected to different water temperatures, and genetics. Probably a higher number of parr marks led to better survival rates of the trout above the falls, perhaps because the higher numbers of marks made the fish less visible to birds and other predators.

GILLS

Trout, like most fishes, have gills to extract oxygen from the water and to eliminate carbon dioxide as water is passed across a series of gill filaments. Covering the gills on each side are opercula, bony flaps that are open posteriorly, so that water passed along the gill filaments can be extruded. These coverings over the gills are supported by a series of small bones called branchiostegal rays. The gills themselves actually consist of a series of four gill arches, with gill rakers protruding anteriorly and fine gill filaments protruding posteriorly.

The gill filaments are the principal components of gas exchange—extracting oxygen from the water and eliminating carbon dioxide from the trout's system. Tiny protrusions, called lamellae, extend from each filament and thus provide a large surface area in contact with water. Thin epithelial cells compose the outside surface of these lamellae, so

oxygen can easily diffuse across the membrane and enter the blood. When levels of dissolved oxygen are low, trout have the ability to increase the number of lamellae in use so they can extract the greatest amount of oxygen from the water. Booth reported in 1979 that rainbow trout can increase the number of lamellae in use by some 20 percent when placed in conditions with low levels of dissolved oxygen.

LATERAL LINE

Trout also have a lateral line, and only one, unlike some other fish species. The lateral line is a series of sensory pores along the midline of each side of the fish. The external pores actually are mechanoreceptors with which trout detect water movement, avoid objects in their path, and sense certain chemicals in the water, including pheromones from other fish. Scales along the lateral line are unlike scales elsewhere on the body. They have small canals that allow water to flow along the sensory structures of the lateral line.

DELICATE ARMOR

Salmonids have smooth scales called cycloid scales, which are quite thin and are partially embedded in the skin in an overlapping pattern. They are found only on fishes for which speed and reduced friction are essential. Thin scales provide an advantage in regulating buoyancy because they are light, and they do protect the skin, though they

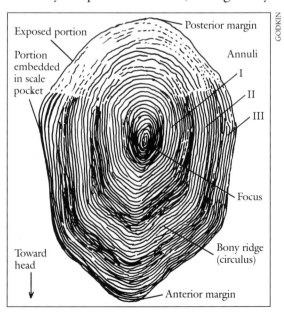

offer little protection from predators. The scales of more primitive fish species often are armorlike and thus provide more protection.

Cycloid scales generally are oval, with rings or ridges similar to those on a cross section of a tree trunk. Unlike tree rings, however, several rings–called circuli–may be deposited each year. Circuli essentially are growth rings. In temperate latitudes, where most trout live, these circuli will appear closer together during winter months when growth slows. The number of these annual clumpings of circuli, called annuli, determine the age of the fish.

In very cold waters, only one circulus or two may be deposited on scales, making the detection of annuli virtually impossible. And, in areas where growth is slow, annuli may not be obvious, in which case we can only speculate upon the age of the fish. Norwegian researchers, working with brown trout, have found that, in very cold waters, scales may not form at all in the first year, so the first annulus may not appear until the trout's second year.

Ocean growth can be distinguished from freshwater growth. The more abundant foods in the ocean produce faster growth, which in turn causes wider spacing between circuli. Thus, an expert can take a scale from a steelhead trout and estimate the number of years the fish spent in fresh water and in salt water and often even the number of spawning runs.

Other hard parts of fishes, such as fin rays, also exhibit circuli and annuli. A cross section of a fin ray, usually from a pectoral or anal fin, clipped at the base, will reveal similar growth lines, though not always in an easily read oval pattern.

The critical function of scales is not entirely understood. Lost scales can be replaced with regenerated scales–indicated by blank areas in the center. However, fish that lose too many can fall victim to stress, disease, and death.

BODY DIMENSIONS

We can describe the typical shape of any fish species as a relationship between normal length and weight. This relationship is defined numerically by the formula for the condition factor: $K = W/L^3$, in which W is the weight of the fish in pounds or grams, and L is the length in inches or millimeters. Fish biologists assign an ideal condition factor value (K) to the species or to a population in a particular area. Then, by comparing the K of an individual fish to the ideal K, they can determine the health of that fish. The K value indicates whether the fish is overweight or undernourished.

The differences in K values of species indicate subtle differences in body shape. A species with a higher condition factor value can be said to be plumper than another species; a species with a lower value can be said to be thinner. For example, the rainbow trout has a higher K than does the westslope cutthroat trout, which in turn has a higher K than does the slimmer lake trout. It should be noted, however, that body dimensions and proportions can differ because of how much the trout eats as well; a trout can grow fat.

A 1989 report by Currens and colleagues of their studies of rainbow trout in Oregon indicated that although the morphometric dimensions of the trunk region can change

BECK

SCHOLLMEYER

GIBBS

Rainbow trout (top) *tend to be plumper than westslope cutthroat* (middle), *which in turn tend to be plumper than the slender lake trout* (bottom). *These differences are reflected in the species' condition factors–numerical values that indicate an ideal relationship between length and weight.*

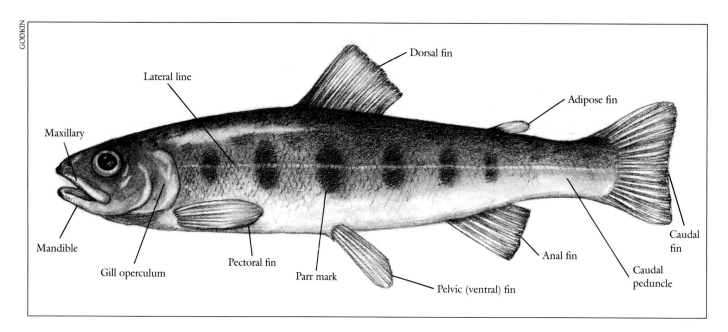

The fusiform or dart-like shape of a trout's body is very aerodynamic and presents a minimum of resistance to water flow. Their terminal mouths, with upper and lower jaws that essentially meet, enable them to feed throughout the water column; they can take a crayfish off the bottom or sip an insect off the surface with equal ease. Cod, in contrast, have an upper jaw that overhangs the lower, facilitating their bottom-feeding behavior. Largemouth bass have a lower jaw that juts out somewhat; they approach their prey from below.

because of the amount of food eaten, the dimensions of the caudal, or tail, region seldom change. It is similar to certain measurements of humans: No matter how fat or thin a person's stomach, the length of the foot or the nose remains about the same.

FINS

Trout have three unpaired, median fins: dorsal, anal, and caudal. The trout use these fins for stabilization and thrust. The caudal fin is homocercal in shape, meaning that both lobes are equal. It is essential for changes in direction and for initial forward movement. The tail may be deeply forked, as in the lake trout, or quite square, as in the brook trout. Most trout species, however, have a tail that is slightly forked.

Like all members of the family Salmonidae, trout possess an adipose fin. This soft, fleshy structure lacks fin rays and is found along the dorsal surface, or upper back, behind the dorsal fin.

Trout also have two sets of paired fins. The pectorals are located on the lower part of each side of the fish, just behind the operculum, or gill covering. They are important for braking. The pelvic, or ventral, fins are located along the ventral surface, about midway along the length of the body in what is called the abdominal position. Trout use these fins for braking, too, as well as for rapid vertical movements. A slight turn of the fins acts against water current to provide lift or descent, much the way adjusting the flaps on a

plane wing does against the air. With such movements, a fish can move up quickly to catch insects drifting in the stream.

Trout maintain their position by a careful balance of swim bladder buoyancy, stabilization by the median fins, and adjustment of the angle of the pelvic fins to compensate for the respiratory currents passing through the gills.

Fins are not simply decorative appendages; they are vital body parts. Although studies have not always been in complete agreement, researchers do concur that partial or complete loss of any fin can have a measurable effect on trout behavior and survival. In studies in California, Nicola and Cordone found that as much as 80 percent of a population of rainbow trout died if they lost their pectoral or dorsal fins.

JAWS

Along the jaw are the lower jaw bone, or mandible, and the upper jaw, or maxillary. In trout, the maxillary is free, or unattached as a flap, at the posterior end of the jaw. Generally, the maxillary extends to a point below the eye. During spawning the males of most species of trout and char, as do male salmon, develop a hooked jaw, called a kype or kuipe. This striking, sexually dimorphic feature helps males as they fight with one another in competition for the females. In extreme cases, male trout are unable to completely close their mouths. After spawning, however, the kype slowly disappears.

IDENTIFYING TROUT

When ichthyologists identify species or subspecies or determine age and other life characteristics, sometimes the best they can do is make an educated guess. This they do based on ranges of measurements of the external characters, because environmental factors such as water temperature and the availability of different foods can affect the identifying features. The ray count of the anal fin of trout in a mountain lake in Idaho, for instance, might differ from that of a member of the same species living in the Willamette River. The study by Northcote and his associates of rainbow trout above and below a waterfall in British Columbia showed that the trout above the falls had significantly higher numbers of lateral-line scales and significantly lower numbers of vertebrae than did those of the same species in the stream below. So a range of counts and factors, such as the number of lateral-line scales, fin rays, gill rakers, and other meristic features, is usually provided in the description of a species.

The presence and location of teeth are used to distinguish species and genera. For example, we can tell brown trout from brook trout by the presence and location of vomerine teeth, those along the roof of the mouth. They are well developed along the length of the mouth in brown trout. In brook trout, though, they are only in a small patch at the front. In addition to these visible characteristics, trout and char lack lower intermuscular bones. In other words, no bones extend

SOLONSKY

deep into the lower part of the body.

The number and type of scale often can be used to determine trout species or subspecies. Salmon and trout, for example, have more and slightly smaller scales—more than 110—along the lateral line than do graylings or whitefishes, which have fewer than 110,

Parr marks provide protective coloration for young fish like this juvenile rainbow.

Meristic counts

*H*istorically, the morphology of fishes has been the primary source of information for taxonomic and evolutionary studies. Characteristic sizes, shapes, pigmentation and spotting patterns, fin placement and the numbers and types of rays within them, and all sorts of other external and internal features have been examined.

Meristic characters are those features that can be counted and once, in evolutionary history, corresponded to the body segmentation. These characters vary within and among species, and are useful in describing or identifying fishes. The problem with meristic characters as indicators of evolutionary relationships is that they can be influenced by environmental factors. Laboratory studies have shown, for example, that temperature during early development can have considerable influence on such characters as scale counts and vertebra numbers. On the other hand, Behnke and his students have tested the amount of nongenetic change due to direct environmental effects by comparing parental populations of many western trouts with their offsprings introduced into different environments. The results, along with the results of meristic counts from thousands of trout specimens collected in the wild, convince Behnke that certain meristic characters are stable; that is, they are largely under genetic, not environmental, influence and can be used to differentiate between species and subspecies of western trouts.

— *Pat Trotter*

although they are all members of the family Salmonidae. A count of lateral-line series scales, that is, the number of vertical rows of scales along the side of the body above the lateral line, is also used. Brook trout typically have 200 to 240 lateral-line series scales, rainbow trout have 140 to 160, golden trout have about 175, and cutthroat trout have 150 to 180.

Recent studies at the University of Rhode Island and elsewhere have shown that even scale shape may be a means of distinguishing between populations or races of individuals. There are indications that the genetics of local populations, which have developed over thousands of years, produce unique variations in scale shape. Thus, the "shape discrimination" can be analyzed by computer, which sometimes can identify the home locale of the fish.

Each scale has a dorsal and a ventral edge, a top and bottom. By measuring the length of a fish at capture and the overall length of the scale, we can estimate the length of the fish at earlier ages by measuring the proportions of the length of the scale at each annulus. This measurement is based on the assumption that scale size increases in proportion to increases in body length. However, Rosa Lee's Phenomenon states that the older the animal is at capture, the less accurate are estimates of its length at specific earlier ages. Thus, back calculations of length can sometimes be slightly in error, because the hard parts of fish, such as bones and scales, do not always grow at a constant rate.

As a rule, trout species that live in the coldest waters live longest, but most age determinations are only estimates. For example, the age of lake trout older than about eight years is difficult to determine from their scales, and maximum age estimates may actually be quite conservative. Instead, a measure of the otolith, a free-floating bone that is the ear of the fish, or fin rays often gives a more reliable estimate.

The most reliable technique for identifying the age of a trout is to retrieve identifiably marked fish. Until recently, scientists, by measuring scales, had estimated the maximum age of sunapee trout at eight years. But similar measurements from scales of an indi-

Common meristic character counts

Certain physical characteristics, when viewed in combination, can be relied upon to distinguish one species from another. Color patterns alone are unreliable for species identification; a trout's colors can vary with water temperature, diet, and other environmental factors. Meristic character counts are recorded in ranges to reflect the differences within a species. Although some of the ranges recorded for specific character counts overlap, no two species share the same combination of traits.

Species	Lateral line series	Anal fin rays	Principal dorsal fin rays	Gill rakers	Vertebral segments
Apache trout	142–170	10–12	11–12	18–22	58–61
Arctic char	about 200	8–11	10–12	19–32	60–71
Brook char	197–240	9–13	10–14	14–22	58–62
Brown trout	116–136	10–12	9–11	14–17	56–61
Bull trout	about 240	9–11	10–12	14–19	62–67
Cutthroat trout	150–180	8–12	8–11	14–28	60–64
Dolly Varden char	186–254	9–11	10–12	11–26	57–70
Gila trout	130–164	9–11	10–12	18–20	59–62
Golden trout	160–210	10–12	10–14	17–21	58–61
Lake trout	185–205	8–10	8–10	16–26	61–69
Mexican golden trout	132–156	8–11	10–12	17–19	56–59
Rainbow trout	140–160	8–12	10–13	16–22	60–66
Steelhead trout	115–177	8–12	10–13	16–22	60–66

vidual previously marked have raised that estimate to nineteen years.

In addition, environmental stresses and injuries can cause the fish to lose scales and grow new ones, which would not accurately reflect the age of the fish. And spawning checks, made at the time of breeding, can provide an indication of spawning history but can also obscure circuli and annuli because such checks scar the scale and can distort various scale features. So it is sometimes difficult to age fish by examining their scales, and even experts will disagree on the age of a given fish.

A count of fin rays, particularly the number of rays in the anal fin, is commonly used to identify trout species. Trout have fewer than thirteen of these soft rays. Lake trout have eight to ten, brown trout ten to twelve. The number of soft rays of the dorsal fin also can be used to identify species, though this meristic count is less common because it is hard to read. Lake trout have eight to ten soft rays; brown trout have nine to eleven.

Other useful meristic measurements include counts of gill rakers, branchiostegal rays, and pectoral and pelvic rays, lengths or heights of fins, and numbers of scale rows above or below the lateral line.

Although differences are often subtle between the trout subspecies and may require genetic examinations, even some subspecies can be distinguished by meristic or color differences. Three subspecies of cutthroat trout demonstrate this. The greenback cut-throat, *Oncorhynchus clarki stomias*, found in Colorado, has the highest number of scales along the lateral line of any western trout. The Lahontan cutthroat, *O. c. henshawi*, confined to the Lahontan Basin of Nevada and California, has the highest number of gill rakers of any western trout. The Paiute trout, *O. c. seleniris*, has meristic characters similar to those of the Lahontan cutthroat but, in many cases, lacks spots, which are typical of other cutthroat.

In addition, measurements of meristic characters, such as length ratios of body segments, numbers of principal and branched fin rays, and number of scales, sometimes can be used to distinguish resident from sea-run varieties of the same species, as McCart and Craig were able to do for Arctic char in Alaska, or between stocks of the same species, as Winter and his associates were able to do for steelhead trout in Oregon.

Biologists often use total length, from snout to tip of caudal fin, or fork length, from snout to fork of tail, if the tail is forked. But ichthyologists typically use standard length, a measurement from the tip of the snout to the most posterior segment of the vertebral column, at the base of the caudal fin. Body proportions are also useful for distinguishing species. For example, the size of the eye in relation to the size of the head may separate two species. In trout, however, other characteristics, such as color and fin ray counts, often are more useful.

—John R. Moring

Inside the trout

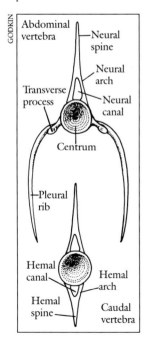

The vertebral framework provides critical support for muscles used in swimming and other activities. Salmonids have no lower inter-muscular bones.

Pleural ribs, which extend around the body cavity, providing form and support for muscles, are attached to the abdominal vertebrae. Caudal vertebrae, located in the tail region, support the caudal musculature; muscles attach to the neural and hemal spines of the vertebrae. The caudal artery and vein are threaded through the hemal arch, present on caudal vertebrae.

GODKIN

Abdominal vertebra — Neural spine

Neural arch

Transverse process — Neural canal

Centrum

Pleural rib

Hemal canal — Hemal arch

Hemal spine — Caudal vertebra

At first glance, the life of a trout seems to be simplicity itself: swim, eat, reproduce. The trout you see rising to the surface to grab an emerging insect is the embodiment of grace and ease. But underlying such simplicity are the complex physiological structures and processes of the trout's body itself that we are still learning about.

SKELETON

The trout skeleton forms a physical support for the body. The backbone is composed of numerous vertebrae, which appear X-shaped in radiographs because of the spines radiating from them into the surrounding muscle tissues. The number of vertebrae varies from fish to fish within a given range for each subspecies. This variation in number is influenced by environmental factors during the early stages of life.

Instead of following the relatively straight line along the length of the fish, the line of the last few vertebrae tends to curve upward in the tail, a condition reminiscent of the ancestral stock. Each vertebra in this section has a dorsal and a ventral spine instead of the somewhat diagonal rays of the vertebrae along the anterior portion of the backbone.

The skull of the trout is complex, consisting of a central piece, the cranium, and many bones that are not tightly connected. So as the trout breathes and eats, the skull bones can move, enlarging the cavity and accommodating the trout's motions.

The appendicular skeleton supports the fins and consists of the pectoral and pelvic girdles underlying the pectoral and pelvic fins, as well as the bony rays of these and the median fins.

MUSCLES

The muscles and the skeleton give the trout its overall shape and provide its means of locomotion. The muscles constitute about 40 percent of the fresh weight. They lie beneath the scales and skin, which make up the integumentary system. The muscles we eat belong to the category of white muscle. The red muscle, with its higher number of mitochondria and rich blood supply, is restricted

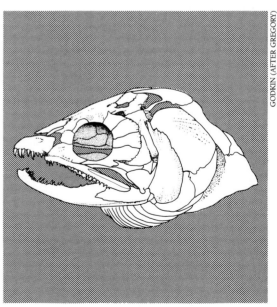

GODKIN (AFTER GREGORY)

to a narrow strip on both sides of the body along the lateral line.

The muscles are in blocks or myotomes, which are arranged in quadrants. A septum, or dividing membrane, separates the myotomes on either side of the body. The blocks of muscle on each side are further separated by a septum into a top one (epaxial muscle) and a bottom one (hypaxial muscle). The muscles, also called myomeres, lie in a zigzag pattern similar to a horizontal "W" that points toward the head. The zigzag muscles are attached to the vertebral column. The trout swims by creating a wave action of the muscles from the head to the tail, as a snake slithers.

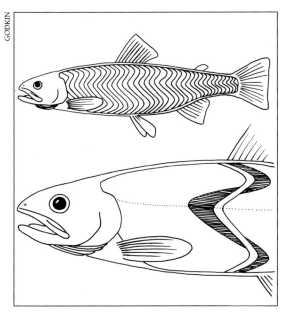

RESPIRATORY SYSTEM

Trout breathe through specialized structures called gills. The gill on either side of the head has four visible gill arches, protected on the outside by a large bony plate called the operculum. Each gill arch has two rows of filaments, and the filaments, in turn, have lamellae, thin flat membranes, which are made up of a respiratory epithelium one layer thick. The epithelial cells are kept in place by pilaster, or pillar, cells.

The trout takes in water through its mouth, maintaining a ventilatory flow by alternately opening and closing its mouth and opercula. As the water passes over the gills, it flows in a direction opposite that of the deoxygenated blood in the gills, which has arrived from the ventral aorta of the heart.

As the deoxygenated blood from the heart is distributed through the fine lamellae, carbon dioxide from the blood exits across the gill membrane and easily dissolves in the water, and the dissolved oxygen from the water diffuses into the red blood cells. The oxygenated blood leaves the gills and is distributed throughout the body. At the same time, the water exits the opercula into the surrounding aquatic environment.

Occasionally, the trout can reverse the flow of the water, to get rid of the accumulated particles from the gill surface. Drummond and his associates suggest that, in brook trout, this reversal of ventilation, or "coughing," indicates copper toxicity.

Salmonids have well-developed muscle systems. Muscular contractions, made possible by vertebral support, make the body bend for swimming and turning, and enable the fish to put on the sporadic bursts of speed often needed to catch its food.

The gill arches are part of the bony operculum (gill cover). Each gill arch has both rakers and filaments. The fine gill filaments are the sites of oxygen and carbon dioxide exchange. The filaments are equipped with thin membranes (lamellae) that allow oxygen from the water to diffuse across them and enter the blood.

Gill arch

Gill rakers

Gill filaments

The amount of oxygen a fish needs for its oxidative metabolic processes in a given period of time is called the oxygen consumption rate. This rate depends on the temperature of the water, the weight of the body of the fish, and the amount of activity. It has been reported that a trout weighing 250 grams (8.8 ounces) will need about 50 milligrams (0.75 grains) of oxygen per hour.

CIRCULATORY SYSTEM

The trout's heart works as a straight pump, sending deoxygenated blood from different parts of the body to the gills for oxygenation. In trout kept at 5°C (41°F), the heart rate slows to 15 beats per minute, and at 15°C (59°F), it can reach 100 beats per minute.

The circulatory system of fish differs from that of birds and mammals. The fish's single pass pump system sends blood from the heart to the gills and then through the whole body, with most of it returning to the heart after passing through the kidney. Birds and mammals have a dual pass heart system that sends blood from the heart to the lungs, back to the heart, and then to the rest of the body, before returning it to the heart.

Fish blood must pass through two to three sets of capillaries before it returns to the heart. Blood pressure drops, due to resistance, with each pass through a capillary set, slowing the flow. Fish generally utilize oxygen at slower rates than birds and mammals.

The heart is enclosed in a two-walled pericardial sac located in front of the abdominal cavity at the base of the throat. A simple organ, it consists of four chambers: the sinus venosus, the atrium, the ventricle, and the bulbus arteriosus. Some authors describe it as two-chambered, but they base their description on the assumption that typically the chambers should have walls composed of cardiac muscles. However, not all chambers of the trout's heart are muscular.

At the top of the heart is the sinus venosus, a thin-walled bag. Blood passes from the sinus venosus through sino-atrial valves into the atrium. From there it enters the thick, cone-shaped ventricle, which does most of the work as the pump. The blood supply to the ventricle to do the pumping work is provided by the coronary artery. The thin-walled atrium is located above the ventricle, and the bulbus arteriosus extends forward from the ventricle as the ventral aorta. This major vessel supplies blood to the gills by paired afferent branchial arteries. The oxygenated blood is collected by smaller vessels that ultimately form efferent branchial arteries in the gills. The branchial arteries in turn merge into the dorsal aorta. Before the blood reaches the dorsal aorta, some is diverted from the first efferent branchial to the brain and eyes. Vessels branch off from the dorsal aorta to the various organs, and from this section on, the dorsal aorta is called the caudal artery.

The deoxygenated blood from the muscles in the tail region is collected by the caudal vein. This vein breaks up into capillaries in the kidney. Venous blood from the kidney is then carried to the sinus venosus. Deoxygenated blood from the stomach, intestine, and other organs is collected in the hepatic portal vein and taken to the liver. From the liver it is

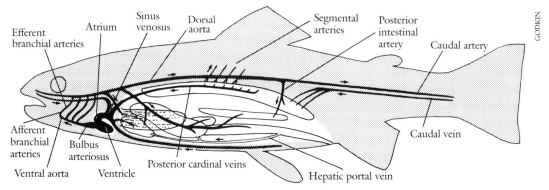

Efferent branchial arteries — Atrium — Sinus venosus — Dorsal aorta — Segmental arteries — Posterior intestinal artery — Caudal artery — Afferent branchial arteries — Bulbus arteriosus — Posterior cardinal veins — Caudal vein — Ventral aorta — Ventricle — Hepatic portal vein

sent to the sinus venosus by way of hepatic veins.

Trout lack bone marrow, which warm-blooded animals have, so the process of hemopoiesis, or blood-cell formation, is carried out mainly in the kidney and the spleen. The blood has both liquid and solid components. Serum, the liquid component, consists of chloride, sodium, magnesium, potassium, calcium, phosphorus, and sulphate. Plasma, the solid part, comprises two kinds of blood corpuscles or cells: the red blood cells, or erythrocytes, and the white blood cells, or leukocytes. Both kinds of cells originate from a common ancestral cell in the blood-forming tissue and later become differentiated and mature in the blood.

SWIM BLADDER

Energy expenditure is kept to a minimum by maintaining neutral buoyancy, which trout do by means of the swim bladder. In an average trout, about 7 percent of the body volume is occupied by the swim bladder, which is a long, thin sac located underneath the kidney and running parallel to it. The swim bladder is physostomous, meaning that the bladder is connected to the esophagus by a duct called the pneumatic duct.

Trout inflate the swim bladder by taking in air through the mouth and forcing it through the pneumatic duct into the bladder. Depending upon the need for buoyancy, air can be sent out from the bladder back into the esophagus and out of the fish.

NERVOUS SYSTEM

The central nervous system of trout consists of the brain and the spinal cord. The peripheral nervous system is composed of nerves running from the central nervous system and terminating in different organs, the same basic kind of system all creatures have.

The brain can be divided into five sections: the telencephalon, the diencephalon, the mesencephalon, the metencephalon, or the cerebellum, and the medulla oblongata.

The telencephalon has centers for smell, vision, and reproduction. The pineal organ is located in the diencephalon. The pineal organ is a photosensitive organ. Secretory function has also been attributed to it. The mesencephalon is the part of the brain con-

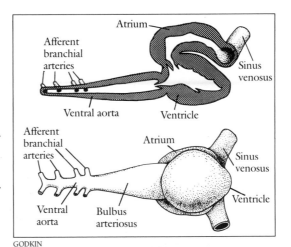

GODKIN

The afferent branchial arteries of the four-chambered heart take unoxygenated blood to the gills for oxygenation.

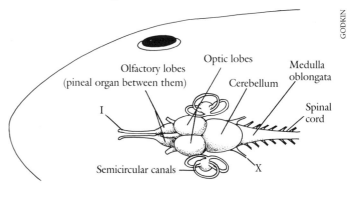

DOUPLE

The trout's heart is near its throat. The large mass to the right of the heart is the liver, where deoxygenated blood from the internal organs is collected. The silvery-gray kidney along the backbone is also visible.

cerned with the reception, integration, and coordination of visual information. The metencephalon, or cerebellum, is involved in the coordination of movement and the integration of balance stimuli. The medulla oblongata acts as the center for the control of chromatophores, or pigment cells, and of the respiratory processes. The spinal cord is a continuation of the medulla oblongata.

The peripheral nervous system consists of nerves originating from the brain and spinal cord. These nerves carry impulses from and to the central nervous system. There are ten cranial nerves arranged in pairs. These nerves have both sensory and motor functions, alerting the trout to stimuli in its environment and enabling it to react to them.

The optic lobes of the fish are relatively large in comparison with the rest of the brain; sight is vital to survival. The large olfactory lobes, which became the cerebrum in higher vertebrates, indicate the importance of scent detection.

SENSE ORGANS

Trout have taste buds, clusters of sensory cells, in the skin of the mouth and the pharynx as well as on the gills. The taste, or gustatory chemoreception, is important to the fish in recognition of food.

Olfactory organs are located in specialized nasal sacs in the snout of the trout. The water is brought into the sacs via nasal openings, or nares. Smell perception occurs when the olfactory epithelium is exposed to different chemicals in the water. The surface of the epithelium is increased by infoldings, or "rosettes," to accommodate more cells. Olfaction is important for migratory species. It has been shown by Hasler and others that migratory fish become imprinted to the smell of the stream where they were born.

The structure of the eye in trout is similar to that of other vertebrates. It consists of a transparent cornea, an internal lens, and a photosensitive retina made up of rods and cones. Trout have no eyelids. The cornea is of uniform thickness. The retina has both rods and cones that convert energy from visible wavelengths of light into nerve impulses. The rods are more sensitive to light than the cones are and allow vision in dim light. The cones operate at higher light intensities and are responsible for color vision. Focusing of the eye for near or far sight is accomplished by moving the spherical lens with muscles attached to the eyeballs. The muscles also allow the turning of the eyes in the necessary direction. The movements of the lens in trout are achieved by the retractor muscle.

Incoming light passes through the lens and reaches the rods and cones of the retina, causing photochemical reactions. The stimuli are conveyed to the brain by optic nerves. Thus does a trout see its surroundings, its enemies, its food.

The lateral-line system is a mechanoreceptor, which enables the trout to detect water movements. It consists of the lateral-line canal, which harbors specialized receptors called neuromasts. Typically, a neuromast will look like a long tube with a swollen base. The base is composed of sensory cells; sensory hairs project into the hollow tube above called the cupula. The base of the sensory cells is highly innervated. Nerve impulses are sent to the brain when the cupula flexes in reaction to changes in pressure caused by movements of the water.

The inner ear, along with the lateral-line system, is sometimes referred to as the acousticolateralis system. Trout do not have a middle ear or an outer ear, which, Behnke points out, are adaptations in vertebrates to compensate for the poor conduction of sound in air. Sound waves propagate five times faster and farther in water than in air.

The inner ear, also called the membranous labyrinth, is an organ of equilibrium and sound perception. It consists of three semicircular canals and three chambers called the utriculus, the sacculus, and the lagena. The whole mechanism is divided into an upper portion consisting of the three canals and a lower portion consisting of the sacculus and the lagena. Two of the canals are in the vertical plane, arranged one behind the other, and the third one is placed horizontally.

Each semicircular canal is a hollow tube. The ends that communicate with the utriculus are swollen to form a structure called the ampulla. Each ampulla encloses a cupula with sensory hairs inside. As the fish moves in the water, the turning of its head will affect the cupula, which in turn will send sensory stimuli through the hairs into the brain, enabling the fish to maintain its equilibrium.

The utriculus, sacculus, and lagena have calcareous concretions inside them called the otoliths. Each otolith is suspended in a fluid inside a chamber. The walls of the chambers are provided with sensory epithelial cells, the cilia of which project into the chamber. The sound vibrations in the water will create movements of otoliths inside the chambers. These movements will cause the mechanical blending of the sensory hairs. Because these hairs are connected to the sensory epithelium, the stimuli thus produced are transmitted to the auditory part of the brain, and the fish hears.

ENDOCRINE SYSTEM

The endocrine system consists of a number of ductless glands or congregations of cells. The principal glands of this system are the pituitary gland, the thyroid gland, the corpuscles of Stannius, the urophysis, and the gonads. Their secretions—hormones—are released into the bloodstream, bringing forth an orchestration of physiological activities.

The pituitary gland, also called the hypophysis or hypothalohypophysial system, is a small pea-shaped gland located under the diencephalon of the brain. It produces several important hormones: prolactin, somatotropin (STH), oxytocin, vasotocin, and melanocyte stimulating hormone (MSH). Prolactin is associated with osmoregulation. STH stimulates growth. Oxytocin and vasotocin have been suggested to have some connection with osmoregulation. MSH helps in the dispersal of melanocytes, the black pigment-bearing cells. This dispersal creates darker coloration. The pituitary gland releases other hormones as well, adrenocorticotropic hormone (ACTH) and thyrotropin, for example, that help in the production of hormones in other glands. ACTH stimulates cortisol production in the interrenal gland; thyrotropin stimulates the production of thyroxin by the thyroid gland.

The thyroid gland in trout is composed of thyroid follicles scattered along the ventral aorta and at the base of the arteries entering the gills. Gorman in 1969 suggested different functions for the hormone thyroxin, produced by the thyroid. Based on the studies in mammals, it is assumed that the thyroid in fish also is associated with metabolism. Migratory behavior also is thought to be controlled by thyroxin.

The adrenal gland has two distinct components, the interrenal bodies and the chromaffin tissue. The interrenal bodies are a group of fluid-containing cells embedded in the anterior part of the kidney. These cells are associated with the production of adrenal cortical steroids. Chromaffin tissues are located inside the kidney. These tissues secrete epinephrin and norepinephrin. It is suggested that epinephrin is involved in regulating the heart rate.

The islets of Langerhans are located within the pancreatic tissue among the pyloric caeca. These cells produce insulin, which is necessary in the conversion of glucose into glycogen.

The ultimobranchial gland is located near the sinus venosus. The hormone produced by this gland is called calcitonin and is thought to have a part in the calcium metabolism.

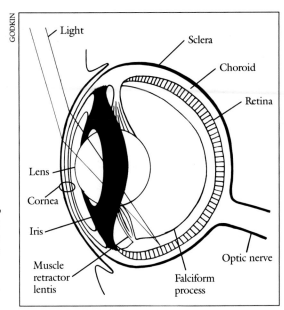

Vision is a vital sense in the fish world. The retractor muscle of the eye moves the lens so the fish can visually track and focus. Photochemical reactions in the retina are stimulated by light; the optic nerve conveys these reactions to the optic lobes of the brain for interpretation.

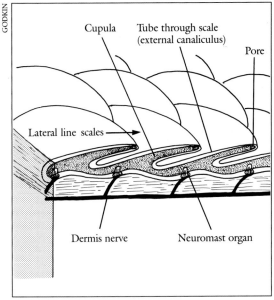

The lateral line system houses a series of pores and sensory structures that pick up wave patterns and changes in water pressure. A large school of fish suddenly changing direction as if it were a single fish is a demonstration of lateral lines in action. The lateral line also enables fish to pick up chemical cues left by other fish—be they potential mates, predators, or prey, and assists migratory fish, in conjunction with the olfactory system, in identifying their natal streams.

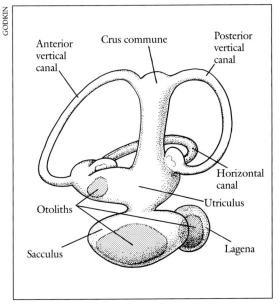

The inner ear enables the trout to keep its balance in the current, and to perceive sound. The otolith is a free-floating, oval-shaped bone often used to accurately age a fish. Growth rings can be clearly distinguished on these bones.

The corpuscles of Stannius are small, compact, dotlike glands, in one to seven pairs located on the ventral surface of the kidney. No established hormone or function has yet been assigned to them.

The urophysis is a gland located toward the end of the spinal cord in the tail region. A series of hormones called urotensins is produced by this gland. Their function is unclear.

The gonads produce hormones called steroids, which trigger reproductive behavior.

REPRODUCTIVE STRUCTURES

Increase in day length and rising water temperature are two important factors that influence the full development of the reproductive structures and the maturation of the sex cells. The time necessary to become sexually mature varies in different trout species. For example, cutthroat become sexually mature in their third or fourth year. Rainbow trout may attain sexual maturity in one year but usually require two or three. Brown trout become sexually mature in the second or third year, brook trout in one or two years. The gonads, or reproductive organs—the testes in the male and the ovaries in the female—can be identified easily in adult trout. Both ovaries and testes are paired structures suspended by a thin membrane from the dorsal part of the body cavity.

The male reproductive glands are off-white in color and smooth in texture, and consist of tubules that contain semen. In the female, the ovaries produce ova, which are extruded through a pore in front of the urinary opening.

The number of eggs each female produces also varies with the species, as well as with the size of the fish. According to Behnke, all species have fecundities averaging about 1,000 eggs (700 to 1,200) per 2.2 kilograms (1 pound) of body weight.

DIGESTION

Trout, which feed on a variety of food organisms, have a simple digestive system, which begins at the mouth, or buccal cavity. The mouth contains short, pointed teeth, which consist of an enamel-like cover, a dentinelike layer, and a pulp cavity. The teeth occur at the head and the shaft of the vomer,

The endocrine system secretes hormones into the bloodstream. Hormones play a major role in a wide range of physiological activities, including the stimulation of growth, osmoregulatory functions, coloration changes, the regulation of metabolism and heart rate, pancreatic functions, and reproductive behavior.

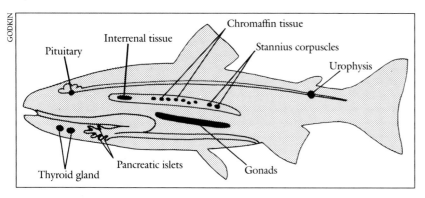

Trout retain a primitive reproductive feature. The open ovary system, like that in humans, results in the eggs being shed directly into the body cavity. Muscular body contractions during spawning force the eggs into the oviduct for conduction to the exterior. In contrast, the large majority of fishes have a closed ovary system in which the ovary and the oviduct are directly connected.

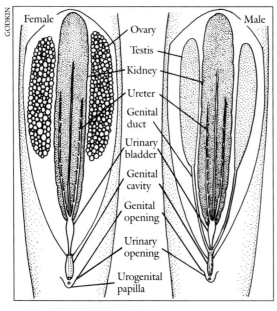

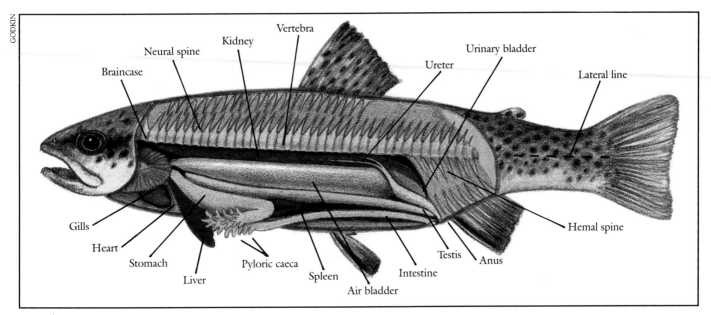

Braincase · Neural spine · Kidney · Vertebra · Urinary bladder · Ureter · Lateral line · Gills · Heart · Stomach · Liver · Pyloric caeca · Spleen · Air bladder · Intestine · Testis · Anus · Hemal spine

Internal organs must be efficiently arranged inside the stream-lined form characteristic of fish that rely upon speed for survival.

the central area in the roof of the mouth. But a trout does not use its teeth to chew. Rather, it uses them to hold large prey.

When a trout catches its prey in its jaws, it maneuvers the mouthful into position for swallowing, and cells in the lining of the buccal cavity secrete mucus that helps the food glide easily into the next region of the digestive system. The food thus passes into the gullet, or esophagus, a short, muscular tube with longitudinal folds that, because of their ability to expand, enable the fish to swallow large prey.

Trout, especially in lakes, also feed on zooplankton as small as 1 millimeter in diameter. Rather than take them in through the mouth, however, trout funnel them through their gill rakers, bony processes on the gill arches, into the esophagus. According to Behnke, the gill rakers of specialized plankton feeders, such as kokanee salmon, are much more developed than those of trout.

From the gullet, the food passes into the stomach, an expandable J-shaped organ, which consists of two regions distinctly different in their tissue structure. The glandular cardiac region, so-called because it is near the heart, at the front of the stomach, releases digestive enzymes. The muscular pyloric region at the back of the stomach, near the entrance to the intestine, grinds and pushes the food into the intestine.

On the outside of the junction of the stomach and the intestine are hollow, fingerlike projections called pyloric caeca, which are similar to the intestine in structure. Digestive enzymes are poured into this junction to break down protein. Because their numbers vary, pyloric caeca have been useful in identifying trout species. For example, brown trout have thirty-six to fifty-seven, according to Burnstick; rainbow trout have fifty-one to eighty-two, according to Mitchum. However, Behnke points out that the great variation by subspecies and even by local populations of a subspecies can make identification difficult.

Two glands—the liver and the pancreas—are associated with the digestive tube and are important in the physiology of digestion. In healthy fish, the liver is a large, dark red or brown organ located in front of the stomach; it does not have distinct lobes as do the livers of mammals. The gallbladder, a small greenish sac, sits atop the liver and stores the bile produced by the hepatocytes, or liver cells. Bile, a green fluid released into the intestine through the bile duct, neutralizes the stomach acids in the digestive process. In an actively feeding trout, the gallbladder empties often. In a starving fish or in a fish that has an obstructed bile passage, no bile is being released, so the gallbladder will be enlarged.

The trout's pancreas is not just one organ. Rather, it consists of diffuse tissues scattered among the pyloric caeca. Poetically called the islets of Langerhans, these groups of specialized cells of pancreatic tissue produce insulin and other pancreatic enzymes that contribute to the metabolic processes.

Steelhead on their long upstream migration require large stores of energy, which they will have exhausted by the end of their run.

gill membrane to the water. The amino acids are absorbed into the bloodstream.

The carbohydrates in the food are broken down into simpler sugars, such as glucose, which then are absorbed into the blood stream and taken into the liver. Some of the glucose is released into the blood to meet the immediate energy requirements. The rest is converted and stored as glycogen. When needed, the stored glycogen is converted back into glucose.

The fats in the food are broken down by the action of the enzyme lipases into fatty acids, glycerol, and glycerides.

Thus, the absorbable portion of the food passes into the blood through the wall of the intestine. The undigested food or roughage passes into the large intestine and is excreted as feces at the anus.

Like humans, trout also need vitamins and minerals to convert the chemical compounds in their food into energy and tissues. These usually occur in sufficient amounts in the trout's natural diet. The deficiency of any of these required elements, called cofactors, will manifest itself in physiological abnormalities, which eventually will lead to disease.

EXCRETORY SYSTEM

The byproducts of metabolic processes as well as the waste products from digestion are removed from the body of trout by the excretory system and the structures of the respiratory system. For example, ammonia is diffused from the gill filaments during respiration.

The kidney is the main excretory organ, although it also serves in the processes of osmoregulation, blood-cell formation, and endocrine secretion. It develops in the trout embryo as a set of paired structures, which unite in the adult trout to become one obvious organ, dark brown to black in color and located beneath the vertebral column in the abdominal cavity.

The kidney is made of numerous structural units called nephrons. A nephron consists of a small double-walled funnel, called the Bowman's capsule, with a long tube, the renal tubule, attached to it and a conglomerate of capillaries—the glomerulus—that fill the mouth of the funnel. Toward the end of the renal tubule are smaller ducts called collect-

Both the stomach and the small intestine have layers of contractile muscles. It is the contraction of the powerful stomach muscles and the acidic action of the digestive enzymes that break down the food, which then passes through the pylorus, a one-way valve to the intestine, which in trout is a short tube. There the food is subjected to further enzymatic action.

The energy sources in the food trout eat are proteins, carbohydrates, and fats. Wild trout obtain most of their protein from aquatic invertebrates. Proteins are broken down into simpler units: amino acids and byproducts of ammonia, carbon dioxide, and water. The circulatory system carries the byproducts to the gills, where they are diffused through the

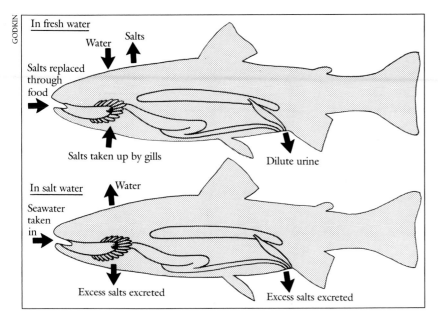

Fish that migrate between freshwater and salt water must change physiologically in order to maintain a certain internal balance of water and salts. This balancing act boils down to a drink-and-desalinate process while in salt water, and a salt-intake-and-water-output process while in freshwater.

ing ducts. These ducts from the multitude of tubules join and form the two ureters, which extend as narrow white tubes along the length of the kidney into the urinary bladder, which is located on the posterior part of the kidney.

Because the trout kidney is primitive on an evolutionary scale, it is incapable of excreting nitrogenous wastes, such as ammonia and trimethylamine oxide. Instead, a part of these nitrogenous compounds is deposited under the skin of the fish in the form of guanine. It is this guanine that reflects light and renders the fish silvery.

OSMOREGULATION AND IONIC BALANCE

A trout living in fresh water is faced with two problems: the continuous entry of water into the body through the gills and skin, and the diffusion of salts from the body by osmosis. The extra water will dilute the blood if not disposed of. The freshwater trout combats this problem by producing large quantities of dilute urine in the kidney. Loss of salt from the body is compensated for by the active uptake of sodium and chloride through the gills and by the absorption from the food through the wall of the gut.

In the sea-going trout the danger of losing water to the saline environment exists. These trout have mechanisms to counteract dehydration and excessive accumulation of salts in the body. The water loss is compensated for by drinking copious amounts, and urine pro-

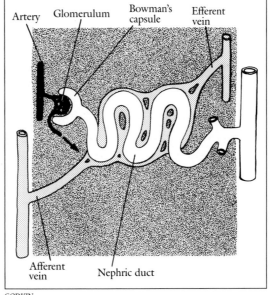

The trout's kidney is an elongate area of specialized tissues in the mid-dorsal wall of the body cavity directly beneath the vertebrae. The kidney assists water balance within the trout's body.

duction is kept to a minimum. But the water also brings in large quantities of salt. The gills in these fish therefore are provided with specialized cells called chloride cells that are capable of excreting sodium salts to help maintain ionic balance.

This brief overview of the physiology of a trout only hints at the complex interweaving of structures and functions underlying the beauty and grace of the fish. Although throughout history the trout has evoked more interest, admiration, and devotion than any other species, there is much we have yet to learn.

—Jim Chacko Athappilly

Senses and taxes

*T*ry to imagine yourself in the watery world of a fish. You suddenly feel water currents along your sides. Slight changes in vibrations carried by the water give you an awareness, even during darkness and without looking, that something is near you. You have to rely less on your vision because the water is ordinarily so murky that visibility is curtailed to short distances. Your sense of smell, however, is extremely acute and provides much more information than is lost by limited visibility. When the water is clear, you may be able to see things approach from above the water surface or from behind you. You feel a sense of direction from Earth's magnetic field, you know what time of day it is, what time of year it is, and you may be able to detect polarized light.

Each factor enhances your ability to navigate or migrate to the right place at the right time. You are like an airline pilot in water, trimming your speed, fins, and trajectory at precisely the right moments, flying on instruments you never look at. You never lie down. You are always naked. The temperature of the water is your body temperature.

RECEPTORS

An animal's senses are the ways that the animal collects information. Most of this information relates to the characteristics of the animal's immediate external environment, but it may also reflect the animal's internal condition. The information-bearing factors that are detected by the senses are called sen-sory stimuli or sensory cues. These cues come in a variety of modes such as light, vibration, pressure, temperature, chemical substances, magnetism, electricity, gravity, and perhaps a few modalities yet to be discovered.

Most sensory functions of a fish are anatomically localized and compartmentalized, usually involving discrete sense organs that are connected with the nervous system. The sense organs are made of specialized cells, some of which are receptors for the specific cue or stimulus type the organ is designed to perceive. Eyes are examples of organs that have localized receptors. Other senses, such as sensitivity to temperature, pressure, and physical contact, rely on diffuse receptors.

Receptors that detect internal stimuli are called proprioceptors and interoceptors; those that detect external stimuli are called exteroceptors. Proprioceptors relay information on such conditions as body position and degree of muscle tension; interoceptors detect gas levels in the blood, for example. Exteroceptors tell a fish where it is and what is going on outside its body. Exteroceptors are sometimes subclassified further into contact receptors and distance receptors. Contact receptors are sensitive to touch, taste, temperature, and pressure; distance receptors are associated with hearing, smell, and vision. The difference between the two categories actually has less to do with the nature of the receptor than the nature of the stimulus. For example, transduction of taste and smell is

A trout's vision must be fairly acute to receive the stimulus of an insect alighting on the surface of the water.

WHAT A TROUT IS

effected by the same mechanism, but taste relies on contact receptors that are physically applied directly to the source, and smell relies on distance receptors that perceive signals propagated through a medium (water for fish, air for people) from a source.

All of these contact receptors, whether used for internal or external monitoring, function as transducers to convert information arriving in many different modes into nerve impulses that can be processed by the animal's nervous system and lead to a favorable response.

TAXES

Taxes are what we might call favorable responses. A taxis is an automatic, genetically programmed response to a given stimulus, such as when an animal that is upside down detects gravity on the wrong side and automatically rights itself. *Taxes* is plural and pronounced as in "taxicab"; the singular form *taxis* rhymes with "axis."

Taxes are relatively simple, genetically inherited behavioral responses to common environmental stimuli. They are often named by the external cue that evokes them. Thus, phototaxis is a reaction to light; geotaxis is a reaction to Earth's gravity; chemotaxis is a reaction to chemicals; and rheotaxis is a reaction to water current. Moreover, some taxes are classified on the basis of whether they involve movement toward or away from the stimulus, so that negative phototaxis means a fish will swim away from light, and positive chemotaxis means it will swim toward a source of chemical stimulus.

Please keep in mind that taxes are very simple behaviors, akin to reflexes, but they may combine with other simple behaviors to form more complicated behaviors. For example, the detection of an attractive chemical substance may cause a positive rheotaxis, which may lead a fish to swim upstream, and a positive chemotaxis, causing the fish to swim toward the source of the chemical attractant. Because taxes are simple and predictable, they are useful for studying fish behavior. So let's look at the senses of trout and char species, representative taxes involving each sense, and then some of the more complicated behaviors that are initiated when the senses receive certain stimuli.

SCHOLLMEYER

BEHAVIORAL COMPLEXITY

A behavioral response may involve a series of many simple events, each of which depends on the sensory stimulus and the animal's response at each step. Often, a series of sensory stimuli will act as releasing factors, each evoking a particular stage of a complicated behavioral sequence. For example, when a fish grabs a mayfly, a number of cues may be involved. The vibration that emanates through the water from the point where the prey strikes the surface may alert the fish, "releasing" a state of alertness. If the water is clear enough, flashing or bright colors may draw the fish toward the prey from a distance, releasing an approach response. After the fish has approached the mayfly, the fish may be further stimulated by visual, chemical, or vibrational cues. These might act either alone or in combination to release a strike from the fish, thereby completing a sequence of steps involved in feeding behavior. If a critical stimulatory releasing factor is lacking, the fish may approach and follow the bait for a time but not strike. Underwater videos of fish behavior taken by White and others prove that this is often the case.

In considering the potential for complexity in fish behavior, we should remember that fish can modify their future behavior on the basis of their past experiences. This results from learning, and there is no question that fish are able to learn from their experiences. If a fish has been attacked by a predator and survives, it can later use the experience to detect the predator's presence more quickly and initiate escape behavior sooner, thereby increasing its chances of surviving and reproducing. Learning also is a factor in the way a fish behaves toward its prey.

Although most research of senses and taxes

has been undertaken on single species of trout or salmon, what is true of one species is generally true of other species within this closely related group, particularly for the senses. Sensory structure and physiology, as well as taxes and more complex behaviors, are usually quite similar in different species within the same genus or family. This similarity reflects the fact that these biological attributes were inherited by this closely related group of species from a common ancestor, and that, for most of these attributes, little divergence has occurred. There are exceptions to this overall pattern of similarity, particularly during spawning periods. In this context, changes in color, body shape, and behavior may enhance mate selection and also may play a role in the evolution of new species.

SENSITIVITY TO LIGHT

We can organize our examination of senses and taxes by sensory mode, beginning with modes familiar to us, such as light and gravity, and proceeding to modes that we are less familiar with, such as water currents and Earth's magnetic field. We will pay special attention to some productive areas of recent research.

Colors. Freshwater teleosts, or bony fishes, such as the trouts and chars, apparently do perceive colors, although it is almost impossible to prove that what another animal sees as a color corresponds with what we see. Through conditioning experiments and other behavioral and physiological research, we have determined that these fishes seem to have sensitivity across a broad range of wavelengths in the visible spectrum, although many other animals do not. Sharks and most mammals, except primates, probably are colorblind. Trouts and other freshwater fishes generally have three cone pigments, as do humans. Each cone pigment absorbs light most effectively at a specific range of light wavelengths out of the total range available in the visual spectrum. Colors refer to specific wavelengths as revealed when light, in which all wavelengths are mixed together, passes through a prism.

The cones of fishes most effectively absorb the light at approximately 455 nanometers (blue light), 530 nanometers (green), and 625 nanometers (red). The peak absorbances of the three cone types in rainbow trout are at 391 to 473 nanometers, 490 to 573 nanometers, and 650 to 669 nanometers, according to Douglas. Brown trout and rainbow trout also have a fourth type of cone that absorbs ultraviolet wavelengths of about 355 nanometers, from which we infer that they can see light wavelengths that are completely invisible to us.

Seeing red. Red is the most interesting portion of what we call the visible spectrum when it comes to fish behavior—fish do not see it, or shun it, or are attracted to it. In deeper marine environments the red wavelengths are filtered out by upper layers of the water column, and most marine fishes have retinal sensitivities that are strong on the blue side of the spectrum but lacking on the red side, which means that they see blue better

SOARD, CONCEPTS WEST

The pupil of the trout's eye has a slightly triangular shape that enhances its forward vision.

The brilliant red of this spawning greenback cutthroat is highly visible to the mate it is trying to attract.

than red. Red coloration among marine fishes is common and allows them to "hide" effectively, because red is a color most predatory fishes see as black, allowing the red fish to match the dark background of deep water, or shallower waters at night. Freshwater fishes often have red coloration for the opposite reason – to act as obvious visual signals for other fish, particularly during spawning periods. Red lures are often very effective for freshwater fishing because they stand out to the fish. Freshwater habitats are more suitable for the detection of red light because red wavelengths are not filtered out completely by the shallower water. The organic substances that leach out of the soil further enrich the proportion of light at the longer wavelengths. These substances absorb and reflect light at the longer visible wavelengths, often giving the water a brownish or reddish appearance. Fishes that live in shallow freshwater habitats generally are able to detect the longer wavelengths of light that are common there. They can better see colors toward the red end of the spectrum than can deepwater marine fishes.

Tinbergen did a great deal of pioneering work in the 1940s in ethology, the study of animal behavior. He studied fighting behavior between small freshwater fish called sticklebacks by placing several males in each of a number of aquaria. At the sight of a patch of red on the underside of a fish, they began behaving aggressively. At times, a red mail truck went by outside the window of his

laboratory, and the male sticklebacks could see it and assumed aggressive postures. More recent research in social interactions of brook trout, brown trout, and rainbow trout reveals that these fishes defend their foraging territories and show agonistic and aggressive behaviors toward other fish in streams. Visual recognition of color patterns, size, and shape seems to be important in mediating these behaviors.

Habitat cues. How visual and nonvisual cues determine what fish do in streams is readily apparent when we study the chronology of early behavior of these fish after they hatch in the gravel redds. Immediately after hatching, and until emergence from the gravel, the alevins obtain energy from their yolk sac and remain in the gravel through a combination of negative phototaxis, positive geotaxis, and positive thigmotaxis. Positive geotaxis prompts them to turn downward until they encounter a solid barrier or poor water quality. If they are too near the top of the gravel, negative phototaxis keeps them moving until they reach a darker area. According to recent research, phototaxis may be more important for finding cover (hiding) and geotaxis more useful for moving up or down. Thigmotaxis (more properly called thigmokinesis) reflects a reaction to touch or physical contact. When in the gravel, physical contact with the gravel is acceptable to the fish.

When it is time to emerge from the gravel, these taxes shift dramatically. The positive

This almost-hatched alevin (left) must remain buried in the gravel for protection. It instinctively turns itself away from light (negative photo-taxis) and toward the pull of gravity (positive geotaxis). Underwater visibility (right) is often limited by the scattering of light in murky water.

thigmotaxis is abandoned, and the negative phototaxis and positive geotaxis are reversed, sending the larvae up and out of the gravel toward the light. Research on the changes in phototaxis and geotaxis of young rainbow trout, brook trout, and lake trout is described in reports by Carey and Noakes in 1981, Carey in 1985, and Nunan and Noakes in 1987 and 1989. After the fry emerge from the gravel, feeding and social behaviors and reactions to current (a positive rheotaxis) begin. The juveniles establish foraging territories, which they defend from other fish, both of the same species and of different species. Within their forage territory, they feed on drifting invertebrates, primarily insects, by visually spotting and approaching the prey as it drifts through their territory.

There are exceptions to the general pattern of visual scan-and-pick drift feeding among salmonids in fresh water. Arctic char, at least, may use nonvisual cues to find prey; they are known to feed along the bottom at night. Dolly Varden char visually scan the bottom for insects, and also may use tactile and perhaps chemosensory (taste or smell) cues to find bottom-dwelling insects. Other lake dwellers typically feed on zooplankton. Many salmonids will visually feed at the surface, or even above the surface, when the opportunity presents itself.

Underwater vision. Besides the visual cues emanating from the prey (including size, shape, movement, and color), the light intensity of the overall environment also affects feeding. Most of the examples I've described deal with diurnal, or daytime, feeding. Often, however, feeding intensity is greatest at the lower light intensities typical of early morning and late afternoon. Many fish species feed most actively during these so-called crepuscular periods. Brown trout are probably the best night feeders and can feed by starlight.

Vision underwater is much more limited by background "noise," or the scattering and dimming of available light, than vision through air. Fish eyes are image-forming "camera" eyes like ours, but the fish eye focuses more like a camera, through lens movement rather than changes in lens curvature. Despite the anatomical ability of fish eyes to produce a focused, visual image complete with colors, shapes, and depth perception (after the visual image is relayed to the optic lobes of the brain by the optic nerves), this visual potential is rarely met, because of ecological limitations. Flowing water in streams (and even static water in lakes and marine habitats) generally has many particles carried in suspension that scatter or absorb light. This creates a "veil" of diffuse light that cannot be focused into an image and that may overwhelm focusable light sources that do not stand out from this bright background. In other words, it can be very difficult for a fish to sort out a meaningful visual image from the excessive background visual stimulation unless the source of the visual image is very close to the fish or the water is very clear.

The circular window to the surface gives the trout a clear picture of the world directly above.

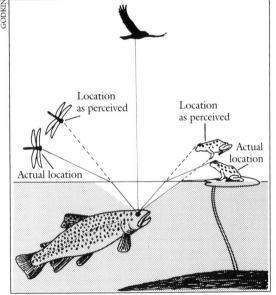

Because of the bending of light rays at the water's surface, fish have a limited field of view as far as perception of the world above the surface goes. Fish perceive an airborne dragonfly as if it were further away from the surface and at a slightly different angle than it actually is, and see a frog that is floating on the surface as if it were actually slightly above the surface. The bird, directly overhead, is perceived in its actual position.

Fish eyes, because they are directed to the sides, are well-situated for wide fields of view underwater. Most fish have a visual field that extends almost all the way back to their tails.

Moreover, if the water surface is rippled by wind or other causes, the surface waves act as lenses to focus sunlight at different depths below the surface. This gives light in shallow water a dancing, flickering effect. Shallow-dwelling fishes seem able to adjust to problems associated with flickering and variable light intensities, however.

The Snell circle. The visual field of a trout is quite a bit wider than ours, because our eyes are directed forward and those of a fish are directed to the sides. Most fishes have a visual field that is nearly hemispherical on each side; it extends almost all the way back to their tails. Their eyes also can be moved within their orbits. Fishes can see through the air above the water surface, but the diffraction of light at the surface causes the visual field above the water to be restricted to a circle or cone extending only 97° rather than 180° (assuming the surface is calm and water is clear). This surface field is called a Snell circle and is only obvious when the surface is flat and smooth. Objects seen near the edge of the circle are near the horizon and are greatly distorted. Outside of the Snell circle field of vision, the surface looks black or silver to the fish, because incident light is reflected away rather than allowed to penetrate the water surface. Within the 97° field, however, a trout can see an avian or human predator's approach.

Salmonids in streams head for cover when approached by a visible human observer. The apparent advantage to this rapid escape response is that it reduces the chances of capture by aerial predators. The disadvantages include the need to be near a source of shaded cover and a loss of foraging time. In a study of this fleeing behavior among brook trout, Grant and Noakes found that the larger fish were more wary of aerial approach. In addition, the closer the fish were to overhead cover, the shorter the escape responses were in duration, which significantly extended the time spent foraging for food. It seems clear that the visual world of a drift-feeding fish is spent striking a balance between the conflicting interests of eating and being eaten.

Despite our initial theme of sensitivity to light, you can see we have wandered among other sensory modes to discuss biologically meaningful reactions to sensory stimulation. This truly represents the real-world situation that a fish faces as it monitors and responds to its environment. The motivations of a fish are continually changing and the sensory cues, which reach the fish collectively rather than one at a time, also may be changing at any given instant.

Polarized light. Some fishes, including brown trout and rainbow trout, may be able to orient themselves by detecting linearly polarized light. That is, they can orient to light that has come directly from the sun, without being confused by light that has been scattered, refracted, or reflected from surfaces. This ability is probably conferred by specialized adaptations of the fish eye, as described by Kuntz and Callaghan in 1989. I noted in the earlier discussion of wavelengths that ultraviolet light may be visible to salmonids; young brown trout have a cone pigment with a peak in light absorption at 355 nanometers. (Many insects also can see ultraviolet light, but humans cannot.) Now we find an even more remarkable possibility for fish vision: directionally enhanced vision. Can nondirectional light be "screened out" by fish as it is by a fisherman wearing polarized sunglasses to see better through the water surface? Ongoing research should greatly add to our understanding of this fascinating field. Whatever the extent of these capabilities, the emerging picture suggests that salmonids have polarotaxes and that underwater light is polarized to a considerable degree; that is, it is more directional than diffuse.

The pineal organ. The second point is that the eyes of a fish are not its only light sensory organs. The pineal organ, located on top of the brain, is also light-sensitive. Having no lens, it cannot form visual images but serves a role in adjusting behavioral activities, hormone levels, and physiological processes that correspond to the day-night cycle and the seasons. Seasonal changes in day length, or photoperiod, are apparently monitored by the pineal organ. In essence, this sensitivity sets the internal time clock of an animal so that it knows the time of day and the time of year, even if other sensory cues are unavailable. Behavioral and physiological activity patterns that are set by this clock are called circadian rhythms. If you take a day-active

Fall colors do not alert trout to the onset of winter, but fish are able to sense the shortening of days.

(diurnal) trout out of its natural environment and place it in a laboratory without natural cues from the sun or daily changes in temperature, it will continue to show a pattern of activity that approximately corresponds to a 24-hour cycle. When placed back into the natural environment, the biological clock will be reset to correspond exactly with the environment, after having drifted slightly from the real 24-hour periodicity.

Experimental manipulation of photoperiod has been shown to affect sexual maturation of rainbow trout and growth rates of Atlantic salmon, as shown by Hoover in 1937 and by Stefanson and colleagues in 1989. Presumably, the biological clock is critical to the timing of migration and spawning runs of anadromous salmonids, and a great number of other precisely timed events as well. Moreover, by knowing the angle of incident sunlight, which may be easier if polarized light is detected, and by knowing the time of day, an animal can navigate by the so-called sun-compass method. In addition, young sockeye salmon apparently were able to navigate by direct sensitivity to Earth's magnetic field, according to a 1980 report by Quinn. A major advantage of geomagnetic orientation over sun-compass orientation is that geomagnetic orientation is possible all the time. Sun-compass orientation is possible only during daylight. Celestial navigation by orientation to the stars also may be a guiding mechanism among migrating salmonids, according to Quinn and Brannon.

MECHANICAL SENSES

Let's go back and bring in a discussion of some other senses. We can use the prespawning behavior of a female salmonid as a case in point. The female first selects a spawning site and then begins to excavate the redd. Many coordinated senses and taxes are employed in this sequence of actions. The fish first makes use of visual cues regarding gravel size as she scans the stream bed for the proper site. Rheotactic cues, which relate to the speed of the current, also are important, because they correspond to how well the incubating eggs will be supplied with oxygen and how well wastes will be carried away. I will discuss the organs involved in rheotaxis shortly.

Next, thigmotactic cues become important as the fish touches and probes a possible nest site, first with her anal and pelvic fins, and finally with her caudal fin as she begins excavation. The touch sensors of a fish are probably like our own. They are scattered, pressure sensitive capsules in the skin that surround nerve endings. During the process of excavating the redd, she lies on her side as her caudal fin and body shake vigorously.

The female trout will select a spawning site and begin to cut her redd only if conditions, such as the size of the gravel and the speed of the current, are right.

Besides the thigmotactic feedback that helps her monitor her position in relation to the stream bed, another organ, the labyrinth, or inner ear, continuously indicates her body position relative to the vertical plane and the force of gravity.

Curiously, the fish organs that detect such widely disparate stimuli as underwater sounds (high-frequency vibrations), gravity, body acceleration, and turning all rely on the same type of sensor unit—the neuromast. Neuromasts sometimes are called hair cells because of the hairlike nerve endings inside the neuromast capsules. They are arranged along the lateral line, externally, and in the labyrinth system in the head, internally. Because the basic sensing units of the labyrinth and lateral-line systems of fishes are equivalent, these two sensory systems often are described as the composite acousticolateralis system. Taxes mediated by this system include geotaxis, which with the muscular system maintains equilibrium, and probably rheotaxis, whereby the fish usually orient themselves or swim up-current. Rheotaxis can also be assisted by vision, through what is

MERMON

known as the optomotor reaction: The fish coordinates its movements by looking at its surroundings or the bottom.

Equilibrium. The ability of a fish to detect the directional force of gravity essentially is the same as ours, based upon the same principles and using the same organs. The sensory mode of transduction involves the resting of dense particles against a field of neuromasts in the labyrinth system. Gravity causes certain heavy particles to bear down on the filaments of specific neuromasts. This in turn causes nerve impulses to be issued from the affected receptors, registering the direction of force when the nerve impulses are integrated by the central nervous system. If the fish tilts its body axis relative to gravity, a new series of neuromasts is stimulated and the shift in body position is indicated. Gravity is a static force that the trout uses to maintain equilibrium.

By similar means, too, the neuromasts register dynamic changes in momentum (speeding up or slowing down) and angular acceleration (turning) because the three semicircular canals of the labyrinth system offer neuromast fields in all three planes of possible motion. Thus, no matter how a fish moves, its movements will be translated into a sloshing of semicircular canal fluid and particles over specific areas of one or more of the semicircular canals. The particles stimulate the neuromast receptors in the sensitive lining of the semicircular canals. These sensitivities that interpret direction and speed provide a feedback system that allows a fish to continuously monitor the outcome of its movements and adjust its actions to produce the desired motion.

Vision also can play a part in maintaining equilibrium. A fish can orient its body relative to sunlight that comes from above. In laboratory experiments in which the labyrinth system was surgically impaired, fish would orient themselves to the direction of incoming light. If the light was placed at the side of the aquarium, the fish lay over on its side rather than remained upright.

Labyrinth system. The labyrinth system also accounts for hearing in fishes. Sounds, which actually are high frequency-compression vibrations or waves that propagate through a medium, carry very well in water over long distances and at great speed. There is a long history of controversy, however, concerning the extent to which fishes make meaningful use of these sounds. On the one hand, many fish produce their own sound signals, and we would think that for those signals to be useful, they would have to be perceived by others. Salmonids apparently are not among the sound-signalling fishes, although they probably hear sounds. On the other hand, the turbulent auditory background of a stream surely must present an overwhelming amount of auditory background noise—perhaps too much to sort through for useful information.

In the late 1800s, an inquisitive researcher found that the trout at a Benedictine monastery, which had been trained to gather at the sound of a bell, would still gather at the sight of a person pretending to ring the bell. This suggested that the sound of the bell was unnecessary for the response, if it was perceived at all.

Sound reception in salmonids involves an association between the otolith organs of the labyrinth system and the three pairs of oto-

The neuromast is a sensor unit responsible for detecting a wide range of stimuli. Nerves connected to the neuromasts conduct incoming stimuli to the brain for interpretation and reaction. These nerves also form part of the inner ear sound perception and balance system. Neuromasts have the same embryonic origin as the inner ear, and migrate onto the head and skin during development.

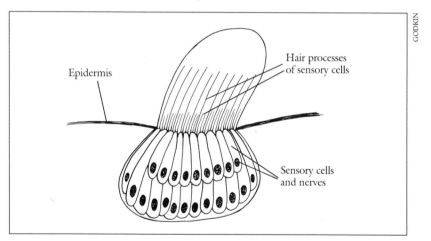

Epidermis

Hair processes of sensory cells

Sensory cells and nerves

GODKIN

The lateral line, a "distant touch" organ, allows a fish to maintain its position in a school.

liths. In some fish species, connections with the swim bladder, which can serve as a resonating chamber, also enter into the sound-detecting association, but salmonids lack the connection of the inner ear with the swim bladder. In comparative terms, carps, catfishes, and sardines have good hearing abilities, cods are intermediate, and flatfishes and salmonids are poor at hearing.

Lateral line. The lateral-line system, also made up of neuromast units, is sensitive to very low frequency vibrations (less than 200 cycles per second) and local water disturbances. The lateral line is sometimes described as an organ that confers a sense of "distant touch." Objects near the fish but not in physical contact cause subtle water disturbances (pressure waves) that indicate a presence to the fish. This system is unique to the fishes and a few amphibians and provides a sense unlike anything we ordinarily experience.

In salmonids, neuromast units are organized within a canal system along the lateral line. In the labyrinth system, neuromasts are clustered. The canals extend along the sides of the fish from head to tail and open at regularly spaced intervals to the water via pores through lateral-line scales. At this point it is hard to say exactly how important the lateral-line system is to rheotactic responses. According to a 1988 report by Denton and Gray, probably the most common stimuli the lateral-line system detects are (1) gradients of local external pressure produced by the fish's swimming movements, (2) mechanical disturbances within the lateral-line canals caused by the bending of the fish's tissues during swimming, and (3) local pressure gradients coming from nearby objects other than the fish itself, including rocks, the bottom, the water surface, and other animals. Fish probably maintain their position in fish schools by detecting the wake waves of the fish around them.

Rheotaxis. Whatever its sensory basis in terms of mechanical transduction, rheotaxis is one of those omnipresent influences on the activities of a stream-dwelling fish. If you walk across a bridge and look down at the silhouettes of fish maintaining their position in the stream bed, you will see that they are all aligned parallel to each other and to the current, with their heads facing upstream. They are usually swimming only enough to maintain their position against the current. If one of the fish displaces itself from this attitude, it quickly realigns itself with the current. From the earlier discussion, you can perhaps imagine how the displacement is registered by the fish using its vision, labyrinth system, and lateral line.

Often a fish will need to change its position by going either upstream or downstream. Migratory behaviors of anadromous salmonids, of course, are well documented, extreme examples of upstream and downstream movement. Even exclusively freshwater salmonid populations are known to make seasonal migrations that relate to changes in food availability between different habitats. For example, Arctic grayling, Arctic char, and brook trout display this behavior in some rivers as they move upstream or downstream to take advantage of seasonal habitat features, according to a 1987 report by Nasland.

The cues fish rely upon to initiate upstream or downstream movements constitute an area of active research, but positive rheotaxis is considered an important element, and negative rheotaxis also may be involved. The rheotactic reactions probably are coupled with responses to temperature and chemical signals associated with ecological productivity. It is even postulated that inexperienced migrants may follow the scent trails of older fish that have learned to migrate to productive feeding areas. In a study reported 1989 by de Leaniz, Atlantic salmon were found to return to an upstream location more readily than a downstream one after being artificially displaced from their habitat, suggesting that positive rheotaxis is one of the strongest influences on the behavior of displaced fish.

In certain freshwater habitats, however, positive rheotaxis can be futile and negative rheotaxis can be lethal. This is the case when there is an impassable waterfall above or below a resident salmonid population. In an interesting study by Northcote reported in 1981, young rainbow trout from a stock above and a stock below waterfalls were reared under hatchery conditions, and tested for their responses to water current. During daylight testing, both groups showed similar rheotactic responses. In tests during darkness, however, offspring from the stock above the waterfalls showed little downstream movement. Offspring from the stock below the waterfalls showed considerable downstream movement. It is clear that these differences in basic behavior are inherited and are significant to the survival and maintenance of the two populations. The results of similar studies, reported in 1981 by Kelso and colleagues and in 1989 by Kaya, on rainbow trout and grayling populations in lakes revealed innate differences in responses to current between offspring of populations that spawn in inlet streams and those that spawn in outlet streams.

As you might expect, there is a strong association between rheotaxis and detection of attractive or repellent chemical cues in stream-dwelling fishes. For example, ripe male rainbow trout initiate a positive rheotaxis and move upstream when they detect the scent of ovarian fluid, a chemical attractant, from spawning females, as noted in a 1979 report by Emanuel and Dodson. Conversely, the scent of a predator may cause a fish to move downstream or hide. Temperature changes, salinity changes, changes in levels of dissolved oxygen, and the scent of food all can be expected to produce rheotactic reactions in appropriate circumstances.

The responses of anadromous salmonids to the water of their home stream have long been known to be important to homing behavior, once the returning adult reaches its natal river system. In fact, Stabell suggested in 1981 that rheotactic behavior can be used in a simple experimental system to screen substances for their attractiveness or repulsiveness to salmonids. Test odors can be added to a flow-through chamber where the responses of fish within the chamber are automatically monitored by photocells. The scientific description for such an assay unit is *positive rheotaxis olfactometer*, and Stabell used one to study the behavior of young Atlantic salmon. The guiding assumption behind Stabell's assay was that the Atlantic salmon remain in a stretch of river by positive rheotaxis to familiar or attractive odors, and leave a section of river by negative rheotaxis in the absence of such odors. Results of the study showed that the fish preferred odors of their own strain to those of another population of the same species. Avoidance of odors from their relatives occurred, however, when the odor source came from fish that were crowded together at high densities.

CHEMORECEPTION

The foregoing comments provide some insight into the importance of rheotaxes in responding to chemical stimuli. The chemical senses, which can be grouped under the general term chemoreception, represent a burgeoning field of inquiry into the biology of fishes. We know our own chemosensory abilities as taste and smell, but as a species we rely far less on these abilities than aquatic animals do. The sense of smell is explicitly called olfaction, and taste is called gustation.

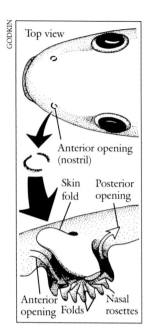

Top view

Anterior opening
(nostril)

Skin
fold

Posterior
opening

Anterior
opening   Folds

Nasal
rosettes

The olfactory system in fish is generally very well-developed. The inner tissues of the nostril—nasal rosettes—are deeply folded, creating a greater surface area for contact with the water around them. Chemical cues gathered through the nostrils alert fish to the presence of other fish, both predator and prey, and assist migratory fish in locating their natal streams.

There is a significant difference between the nature of olfactory stimuli in air and in water. In air, olfactory stimuli must be volatile, or able to evaporate and travel in air. In contrast, an olfactory cue must be soluble to be effective in water. These physical properties are quite distinct. Sugar and salt, for instance, are quite soluble in water but they are not volatile in air. Gustation, even among terrestrial animals, however, takes place in a liquid medium. The differences between olfaction and gustation in aquatic situations are primarily those of quantity and proximity. Olfaction is typically an extremely acute sense. As few as several molecules of an olfactory stimulant reaching the olfactory organs of a fish may be sufficient for the fish to respond to the stimulus. In contrast, gustatory chemoreceptors typically require far higher concentrations of a stimulus to generate a response. As for proximity to the source of the stimulus, olfaction can be described as distance chemoreception; gustation generally amounts to contact chemoreception. The farther the chemical stimulus travels from its source, the more diluted it becomes. Great sensitivity is required to detect extremely diluted individual chemical substances in water among the thousands of other compounds sure to be present. Olfaction is sensitive enough that chemical stimuli can travel great distances and still be perceived; gustatory responses ordinarily result when something is taken into the mouth and sampled by contact with taste buds. Some fishes, including the catfishes, have gustatory chemoreceptors concentrated on their barbels, or "whiskers," and scattered over the skin, and they probably are able to taste over a short distance from a food source.

A chemosensory system works through the binding of chemical stimulus molecules to special protein receptors embedded in the cell membrane of a chemosensitive cell. This binding takes place at a special region of the receptor protein called the active site, where we believe the stimulus molecule fits like a key in a lock if it is the right stimulus for that receptor. Many different receptors may be exposed on the outer surface of a chemosensitive cell. Once the active sites of a sufficient number of receptors are occupied by molecules, a signal is generated and conveyed to

the nervous system. The receptor cells occur in taste buds, and they also are very concentrated in the olfactory rosette, which lies inside the nares, or nostrils, of a fish.

An animal's sense of the strength of a stimulus is dynamic. As a fish swims, water continuously passes across chemosensory cells in the naris on each side of the head. The binding of stimulus molecules to receptor active sites is reversible. It may be that the rates of binding new stimulus molecules and of releasing stimulus molecules from active sites already bound may be able to tell the fish if it is moving toward a higher or lower concentration of stimulus. Moreover, the fish probably can tell which side of its body the higher concentration of stimulus is coming from. Then the fish can turn toward the stimulus and follow the "plume," or scent trail, of the stimulus. You no doubt have heard that sharks can home in on the scent of blood from great distances. The hammerhead shark has widely separated olfactory centers, and thus it can more readily determine differences in scent concentration between the two sides.

Chemotaxis is a behavioral response that brings an animal closer to (positive chemotaxis) or takes it farther from (negative chemotaxis) the source of a chemical stimulus. This behavior is the most primitive and widespread behavior among living things. The sperm of animals and plants and even bacterial cells display chemotactic responses. The cells inside your body depend on chemoreception to coordinate their activities with surrounding cells, respond to hormones, start growing or stop growing, and so forth. Nearly all living cells rely on chemoreception to some degree, so the fact that fishes rely heavily upon this sense for information about their surroundings should not be surprising.

A study by Hara and Zielinsky, reported in 1989, considered the ultrastructure and development of chemosensory cells of rainbow trout. The olfactory cells exhibited various ultrastructural features that presumably increase the surface area available for sampling chemical stimuli, including cilia and microvilli, tiny hairlike extensions of the cell surface. The authors concluded that the olfactory system allows stereochemical sensitivity at an early stage in the fish's life. They also showed that although the olfactory system is well developed by the time of hatching, the gustatory system is not.

In 1980 Rhein and Cagan reported the results of a study of the cilia of rainbow trout olfactory cells in a search for receptors. They isolated fractions from the cilia that were shown to bind with radioactively labeled amino acids. Amino acids are important chemosensory stimuli for rainbow trout and other salmonids. This research yielded direct biochemical evidence of the binding of chemical stimuli to receptors on the cilia. A number of reports have dealt with the neurophysiological (electrical) output of the olfactory system in salmonids, including those by Hara and Brown in 1979 and Døving in 1989. Results of studies of this kind are often quite difficult to interpret because it is so difficult for the researcher to sort the bewildering array of signals into those that are meaningful and those that are just background noise.

Pheromones. A large body of research has been conducted on salmonid pheromones. A pheromone is a chemical signal released into the environment by an individual that can be detected by another individual of the same species. Once detected, it causes a change in either the behavior or the physiology of the recipient. A behavioral response typically might involve search or avoidance behavior; a physiological response could involve something like a release of hormones that cause a more rapid sexual maturation. The research considered earlier that involved detection of ovarian fluid by ripe males indicates a pheromone-mediated response. Among fishes, many other pheromones are associated with glands in the skin or skin mucus.

The range of biological activities mediated by pheromones among freshwater fishes was reviewed by Soloman in 1977 and Liley in 1982. They include homing, shoaling, or aggregating in swarms, communication of alarm or danger, communication of crowding, pair formation, spawning, and other social interactions. There is a large body of recent literature in this area, of which I will consider only a few examples.

Substances released from skin mucus are readily detected by rainbow trout, Arctic char, and other salmonids. An electrophysiological study on rainbow trout by Hara and Macdonald, reported in 1976, showed that the molecules of these substances were small, stable, and nonvolatile. The trout responded to mucus substances from both their own species and other fish species. Similar studies by Døving and colleagues, reported in 1973 and 1974, on Arctic char produced comparable findings. The latter authors speculated that substances in skin mucus might play a part in home-stream recognition, because migratory groups of char responded differently to the odors than did nonmigratory stocks of the same species. It has long been known that salmonid homing within the wa-

Pheromones, chemicals released by one fish that can be detected by another, may be triggers for spawning activity.

DOUPLE

tershed of origin is mediated by olfaction. In early experiments, plugging the nares with wax rendered the fish unable to find their home stream.

The question is, What substances do the fish respond to? Studies reported by Brannon and Quinn in 1989, Quinn and Courtenay in 1989, and Black and Dempson in 1986 dispute the idea that a pheromone is involved, and favor a hypothesis that the homing cues relate to substances associated with the habitat. The skin-mucus cues may have more to do with social behavior than with homing, but this issue remains to be resolved.

Sex pheromones of rainbow trout and Pacific salmon have been investigated in separate studies by Hara, reported in 1989, and Honda, reported in 1980. These substances are released by mature females and elicit responses in males, including enhanced sperm production, sexual arousal, attraction to the spawning area, and persistence of courtship. Females release this sex pheromone from the body via the genital pore.

Amino acids. Day to day, the most important chemosensory cues for a fish undoubtedly relate to the stimulation of feeding behavior. A fish spends more time feeding than doing anything else. Such behaviors as searching, attacking, and biting are initiated at the detection of chemosensory cues. Amino acids and compounds similar in basic structure to amino acids are the primary class of compounds that elicit feeding responses in salmonids, and many other aquatic species as well. Carbohydrates are less potent stimulators for salmonids. For those who have a keen interest in this topic, the following references might be helpful: Adron and Mackie, 1978; Belghaug and Døving 1977; Bres, 1989; Hara, 1973; Hara and colleagues, 1973; McBride and colleagues, 1962; and Satou and Ueda, 1975. Results of these studies indicate that salmonids are extremely sensitive to these stimulants, though not as sensitive as catfishes are. Threshold concentrations necessary for detection of some of the amino acids are quite low. Moreover, feeding stimulants are more effective when mixed together than they are individually. Even some compounds that are individually repulsive can be combined into effective stimulants. Amino acids to which the fishes are relatively sensitive include L-glutamine, L-methionine, L-leucine, L-alanine, and L-asparagine. Actual prey extracts include these and hundreds of other compounds. In most cases, prey extracts are as effective or more effective than amino acids alone in producing feeding responses.

At least one of the amino acids, L-serine, is strongly repellent to salmonids. It causes an alarm reaction, signifying imminent danger nearby or upstream. It is present in water that has been used to rinse human hands, and probably also is released by such fish predators as bears, seals, and sea lions. In 1954, Alderdice and colleagues speculated that skin-rinse substances from seals and sea lions may be effective in repelling migrating salmon at concentrations as dilute as 1 part in 80,000,000,000 parts water! (However, salmon cannot chemically detect predators approaching from downstream.)

Glands that produce alarm substances have been discovered in the skin of minnows and other cyprinid fishes. If a fish is attacked, the special glands in its skin release the alarm pheromones, which alert other fish nearby and give them a better chance to escape. Salmonids do not have these glands in their skin, nor do they respond to the alarm pheromones of minnows, according to a 1983 report by Bernstein and Smith.

Unfortunately, chemosensory activity of fishes can be readily disrupted by pollutants. Acid rain, heavy metals, oil, and other pollutants associated with industrial activity and urbanization are causing subtle changes in the lives of fishes that are hard to assess. Perhaps the more we learn about fish senses and behaviors, the better we will be able to protect fishery resources for future generations of both humans and fish.

– Frederick Gardner Johnson

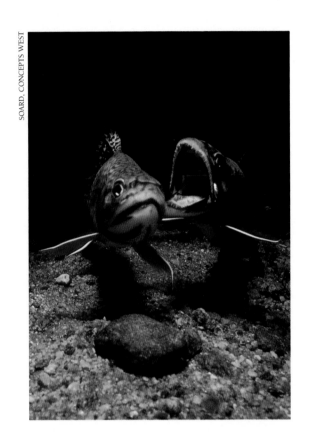

SOARD, CONCEPTS WEST

Life as a trout

View from an observation tank

Similar to plants that flower and form seed in a decreasing length of day and a decreasing mean daily temperature in the fall, the brook trout, under shortening daylight and with decreasing water temperature, experience hormonal changes that bring about the beginning of spawning activity. Such behavior embodies more than those activities that occur at the moment the male and female sex products are discharged. It includes behavior up to that point and others that follow it, which I have witnessed in my studies of wild brook trout from an observation tank in Sagehen Creek in California.

Two to four weeks before spawning, the male brook trout dons more intense colors: a brilliant red on the belly and lower fins, and marked white bands on the fin margins that are emphasized by intense parallel black pigmentation. He also develops strong teeth that are exposed in the newly upturned lower jaw, called a kype. The female, on the other hand, shows little change in color.

The female arrives in the area of spawning

BUTLER

This observation room, located next to Sagehen Creek, California, made possible some pioneering research in fish behavior. The fish, undisturbed in their natural environment, were subjects of intense study.

and begins looking for the correct site supplied with gravel of the appropriate size and an upwelling of water. The female's activity generally is focused on an area just below a pool where intragravel water flow most often can be found. Several cutting acts may occur before intensive action is applied to the substrate in one particular area. From cursory observations, it has been assumed that the male forces or pushes the female to the spawning site. This is not true. He, with his larger size, will often displace the female and therefore appear to be purposefully pushing her. But what looks like a push is nothing more than a courting pass of the male along the side of the female. By the time the male has begun courting the female, she has already selected the site.

The cutting activity of brook trout is much more vigorous than that of other trout species. Perhaps this phenomenon is related to eastern North America, their native home, which is more subject to detritus and organic debris. The western habitats of rainbow and cutthroat generally are of cleaner gravel. The cutting action of the cutthroat and rainbow is perfunctory when compared with that of the brook trout. In fact, the quality of the rainbow's redd reminds me of the lackadaisical construction of the mourning dove's nest.

In the process of cutting the redd, the female places her caudal fin flat against the stream bottom, then begins an intense swimming motion in place. The hydraulics of her activity displace stones and other materials,

The anal fin of a spawning male brook trout shows a vivid contrast of red, black, and white.

and the repeated withdrawal of the caudal fin in a suctionlike action lifts detritus and small stones from the site. In doing so, she cleans from the redd insects, periphyton, which are simple plants attached to the substrate, and organic, oxygen-demanding silt. This effort will provide the eggs with a better chance of survival because she has eliminated materials that compete for the resources that the eggs need.

The first cutting attracts males to the site. They begin courting the female by approaching from downstream and coming alongside her. The male's body vibrates vigorously, close to the female's lateral line. The vibrations are muscular constrictions traveling rapidly from the head to the caudal end, or tail. They can hardly be seen with the unaided eye. The male will make many passes over, under, and beside the female and will try to drive off all other males as they approach and try to court the female. The males then challenge each other in contests of size and dominance—an aggressive process called agonistic behavior. All other conditions being equal, the male with a slightly larger mass has an advantage over his opponent. The lateral line communicates this difference in caudal and frontal displays.

Squaring off

There are four types of display in this contest for the female: frontal display, lateral display, wigwag, and caudal display. Frontal display is an offensive positioning characterized by a stance that is similar to the body position of a trout feeding off the bottom; its head is down and its tail up. The dorsal fin is depressed. The caudal fin is somewhat constricted. This agonistic display may be face to face in a side approach, similar to dancing cheek to cheek. The two swim stiffly in a constrained body motion that is almost stationary. The position is similar to that of courting the female; however, the dorsal fins are depressed, and the opposing pectoral fins are depressed vertically to the substrate, so that the opponents do not touch. The frontal display occurs also in a face-to-flank attack. The frontal display in the rainbow and cutthroat is similar to that of the brook trout.

The lateral display, which is defensive, occurs when the flank is turned toward a frontal-displayed opponent. The head and tail are flexed upward with all fins absolutely erect. The mouth is slightly open and the branchiostegal membranes (just below the gills and neck) are extended. The hyal bones in the middle of the lower jaw, upon being depressed, form what is known as the gular pouch, thus greatly increasing the apparent size of the head. The caudal fin is expanded to full width. Thus, the trout displays itself in its greatest dimensions, much as a young boy threatened by another stands as tall as he can and throws out his chest.

The caudal display and the wigwag display occur when the trout are aligned head to tail. In caudal display the offensive one, with greatly expanded caudal fin, swims in place

BUTLER

A female cuts her redd. Four eggs from a previous spawning are visible in the substrate.

BUTLER

She continues to cut the redd. The large size of the substrate allows water to move through the nest, providing oxygen to the developing eggs.

BUTLER

A male (right) has been attracted by her cutting activity and courts the female over the partially prepared redd.

BUTLER

The mating pair allow their pectoral fins to cross. Their dorsal fins are relaxed.

BUTLER

Another male has moved in to challenge the first. The males depress their dorsal fins and withdraw their pectorals.

with a very vigorous movement that forces water against the head of the opponent—he in effect "slaps the face" of his opponent. The lateral line of the receiver clearly communicates the size of the opponent in this encounter. The wigwag display may be a backward swimming movement into the face of the opponent, or it may be a forward swimming movement as both the aggressor and opponent move upstream. And it may be in a head down or head up movement.

The dominant fish may push, butt, or nip. When all else fails, he may bite his opponent, tearing away some scales and skin. The dominant fish may even hold the subordinate tightly and shake him vigorously. Then, following such a pursuit, the dominant male returns to the female, perhaps to find that another male has taken over the role of courtship. Display, threat, and attack begin again.

Occasionally, the interloper is a very small male, whose sneaky tactic ultimately accomplishes its end: spawning with the large female. When chased away, the little male hides under a nearby rock in a space too small for the attacking aggressor. But the little fellow is always ready to leave his hiding place when the dominant one is absent and court and spawn with the female.

At other times when she is being spawned by the dominant male, others, including the little fellow, get into the act for that short moment. It would be interesting to know whether the behavior of the little interloper is passed on to the offspring through his genes. And what is the nature of his agonistic behavior when he reaches competitive size?

Each behavioral sequence probably does control the potential for survival of the next generation. In other words, the intensity of courting either by the dominant or the sneak and the intensity of the agonistic encounters

BUTLER

The male in the foreground is in frontal display. The male in the background, in lateral display, is trying to make himself look bigger by raising his head and his dorsal fin.

by the dominant provide a higher probability for offspring with that male's genes.

In general, the male has the advantage over the female even when the female is slightly longer. His dominance may arise from body shape rather than length; the male generally has a deeper body and therefore a greater mass. But once the female has begun to cut the redd, she will make a frontal attack against even the dominant male if he should inadvertently approach her face to face. The female's "first claim" to the redd seems to permit her to dominate him here. She also will attack other females that intrude into the area of her redd during her cutting and covering behavior.

THE SPAWNING ACT

Toward the end of the cutting sequence the female begins to test each cut more deliberately with her well-erected anal fin. The erection of the anal fin as it is dragged or probed into the substrate may act as a releasing mechanism to the males. They often rush in as if ready to spawn. But the anal fin must be probed to its full depth before the female is ready. This high intensity of "crouching," as the term is called, happens when the female inserts the anal fin to its full length and depth between the stones of the redd and very tightly arches her back upward from the anal to the caudal portion. She then opens her mouth in a wide gape and simultaneously undulates the dorsal fin intensely.

It is not clear which of these are sign stimuli that release the movement of males to her side. The male, in like manner, opens his mouth very wide. There is an intense tight and fast rippling of the body muscles from head to tail. The head of the male shakes vigorously. Eggs and milt are discharged simultaneously. The redd area clouds with

HAWTHORNE

The dominant fish bites his opponent. Females wait in the background.

BUTLER

Small males use "sneak tactics." While the dominant males engage each other, smaller males attempt to mate with the waiting female.

BUTLER

A female in frontal display attacks a male in lateral display. She will defend her redd against attacks.

BUTLER

The female tests the readiness of her redd by probing it with her anal fin.

The female crouches over her redd to signal to the waiting male that she is ready to spawn.

As the trout spawn, they open their mouths in a wide gape.

A cloud of milt is released by the spawning male.

The female brook trout makes sinuous swimming motions over her redd after spawning.

Once spawning is finished, the female will cover her redd.

milt; the eggs settle to the substrate. The spawning takes place in about three seconds.

Once the spawning is complete, the eggs can be seen in the redd distributed among the crevices and pockets of gravel. The male leaves the area. The female begins a sequence, unique to brook trout, with a long series of slow, undulating swimming movements in place. She drags her anal and caudal fins gently over the area of egg placement. The anal and caudal fins are cupped in a fashion that appears to be purposeful "shoveling." This action washes eggs into the interstices of the gravel and covers them with some of the fines (small gravel of the bottom) that were cleaned in the previous cutting activity. She then begins a series of vigorous cutting actions, called covering, at the edge of the redd that places larger stones over the spawned area.

The brook trout is very thorough, covering the redd from all angles. Again, the rainbow is more perfunctory in her efforts. After a period of from thirty minutes to a full hour, the brook trout completes her task, and the redd appears as a light area of the substrate.

In a day or two she develops another redd as more eggs are released from her ovaries and accumulate in the body cavity. Two or three spawnings are not uncommon. When she has discharged all the eggs, her anal area appears slack and flaccid.

FROM EGG TO FRY

The gravel of the redd must remain permeable throughout the eggs' development. Sedimentation of the redd or formation of anchor ice will kill them. (Anchor ice can form on the bottom of the stream—not the surface of the stream—when the temperature of the water drops to slightly below the freezing point, becoming supercooled.) Among

Before spawning, the anal area of a female before spawning looks full, swollen with eggs. After spawning, the same area appears slack.

brook trout, eggs deposited during October hatch in late February or March.

After incubation, the fry from the hatched eggs move up through the interstices of the gravel and take up a small territory. This is the only time in the life of a trout that a territory as such is well defined. Territoriality implies that the dominant trout defends and keeps out all individuals from its area of use. But this definition does not apply to the trout at any other stage of life. The trout later may have several foraging sites, and at some it may be dominant. But when it is not present, others share the site in an established hierarchy.

The young of the year are visually isolated from other recently emerged trout and protected from strong water currents by the surrounding bottom structures. Those that emerge first have an advantage: They begin to grow first and can defend their small territories. Those that arrive later will have to go elsewhere. The occupied territories generally are in side and riffle areas of the stream, relatively safe areas from predaceous fish, but not necessarily safe from predaceous birds and mammals. Later in their first year, the young trout school with those of the same age and remain in schools in shallow backwaters of the stream.

Those that survive the first year take up foraging sites downstream of a dominant trout or to its side, yet not within the immediate upstream vision of other dominant trout using the same drift corridor. Here the individual can watch the surface drift of insects and anticipate foraging for larger food items. This is a time when the young trout learns to detect acceptable foods. There is a much higher frequency among yearlings of testing and rejecting items as food than can be found among the larger trout. The prey also are smaller than those larger trout usually eat. But the young trout manage to eat plenty. Examination of scales from fish at this age indicates that it generally is a year of rapid growth.

THE PECKING ORDER

This, too, is the year in which the individuals find places in the hierarchy of the species' social group and in the area of stream occupied for the development of the home range. Trout cannot afford to expend energy in continual agonistic "showdowns" throughout the growing season, so they rely on social structure. A short period of testing in the spring determines who is first, second, third, and so on down the pecking order at the various foraging sites, and a social "force field" surrounding each trout indicates its position in the hierarchy. The more dominant the individual, generally the larger its social force field, established from memories of previous agonistic encounters. The contests for hierarchical position occur at the beginning of each year and the resulting social structure remains reasonably stable during the summer. Once it has been established, mere visual recognition maintains it.

Visual acuity, that is, the physical ability to see, generally is not a limiting factor in defining the social structure and the activity centers, those areas used by the fish during the major part of its life. Water velocity, bottom roughness, and opacity of the water provide the greater constraints.

Individuals do not interact with one another during most of the year as intensely as is generally thought. Social structures and activity centers are defined by combinations of size, sex, genetic background, hierarchical position, established residence, stream velocity, opacity of water, visual acuity, and such

MERMON

conditions of food as drift in the stream or locations in the lake environment.

Position in the hierarchy loses its meaning when the trout in a stream section are threatened by an intruder. It has been shown to be greatly disrupted when wild or hatchery trout are introduced into a stabilized population. Small wild resident trout turn into vigorous opponents when larger hatchery trout of the same species are introduced into the area. Bioenergetic costs are high for both the wild residents and the introduced trout. This high cost may largely account for the high number of deaths suffered by hatchery trout compared with those of wild trout.

Hierarchy also falls away when environmental stresses affect the population. I recall an unusually hot spring at Spruce Creek, Pennsylvania, when the water temperatures became too warm for the population of brown trout. The trout abandoned their activity centers and their positions in the social structure and gathered in a current of cold

spring water in the stream without any agonistic behavior. Bioenergetic costs were just those of swimming in the density current of cold water.

As the individuals grow into their third year, they remain in the same general area, moving up in the hierarchy at one or more foraging sites. A trout's energies are directed primarily at growth and reproduction, and since the period of reproduction is relatively short, trout spend most of their time in search of food. There must be a conservation of energy and no net loss if they are to grow. With increases in water velocity, trout tend to swim closer to the substrate, thus reducing the size of their foraging areas. As they come closer to the substrate, bottom roughness further isolates them from the view of others.

The cycle renewed

A change in the length of day and in water temperature initiates hormonal changes in mature fish that accelerate the development of eggs and sperm. Again there is a heightened color change in the male and the primordial eggs present in the female brook trout throughout the summer enlarge. The testes of the male also enlarge.

The female leaves her foraging sites and moves into an area in search of an intragravel flow or upwelling of water where she begins anew the behavioral sequences that lead to the development of another generation of trout.

—Robert L. Butler

Spawning and development

Spawning by most trout and char occurs in the spring or fall. The fish construct redds in areas of streams with suitable-sized gravel substrate, often in riffles. In the northern hemisphere, native cutthroat, rainbow, and steelhead trout spawn in the spring. Brown trout and the chars (lake trout, brook trout, bull trout, Dolly Varden, and Arctic char) spawn in the fall. The lake trout and some Arctic char routinely spawn on the shores of lakes rather than in streams, but other species will attempt to spawn on lake shores if suitable streams are not available. The success of such spawning depends on the substrate and flow of water through the redd. The lake trout, unlike the trouts and other chars, does not construct a redd, but deposits its eggs over the gravel and boulder substrates in the shoals of lakes.

Several factors influence how trout and char select areas in which to build redds: water temperature, flow (depth and velocity of water at the spawning site), substrate in the streambed or lake shore, cover for maturing fish, and size of spawners. In general, large fish, such as steelhead, spawn in larger streams with larger substrates than those selected by small trout.

Temperature. Salmonids have spawned when water temperatures were as low as 1°C (34°F) and as high as 20°C (68°F), but usually the temperatures range from about 6° to 15°C (43° to 59°F) when they spawn. Each native stock of trout and char appears to have a unique time and temperature for spawning that theoretically provides the best chances for survival of offspring. Temperatures before and during spawning must be such that the spawners survive and successfully deposit their eggs, and temperatures during incubation must allow normal development of the embryos and emergence of the young fish from the redd at a time which is favorable for their survival.

In the case of fall spawners, newly spawned embryos must reach a critical stage of development before the water temperatures decline to winter lows, and yet the young fish must not emerge until conditions are suitable during the following spring. Spring spawners likewise do not spawn until after the water has warmed sufficiently to permit normal development of embryos, but as early as possible to allow their offspring to emerge during the summer and grow before the onset of winter.

Location. Trout and char often spawn in the transitional area between pools and riffles where water velocity is accelerating, water is forced through the substrate by the convex slope of the streambed, and the gravel is relatively easy to excavate and free of silt and debris. The amount of space required by trout and char for spawning depends on the size and behavior of the spawners, and the quality of the spawning area. Large fish make large redds, tolerance of nearby fish varies by species, and poor-quality spawning areas may lead to an increased incidence of multiple

Top: *The male, in the background, coaxes the female to begin cutting by swimming alongside her.* Middle: *The female cuts the redd to clear it of fine sediments and debris.* Bottom: *When the redd is complete, she will probe it with her anal fin to signal to the male that she is ready to mate.*

redds per female. Redds range in size from nearly 10 square meters (107 square feet) for large fish to as small as 0.1 square meter (about 1 square foot) for small fish.

Water depth. Water depths measured at redd sites have varied with species and size of fish and ranged from 6 to 300 centimeters (2 inches to about 10 feet). In general, the water was at least deep enough to cover the fish during spawning, large trout requiring 15 to 35 centimeters (6 to 14 inches) and smaller trout 6 to 10 centimeters (2 to 4 inches). Many fish spawned in water deeper than that needed for submergence, but it is not known if the fish preferred the greater depths or were merely using what was available. Velocity of water at the redd sites ranged from 3 to 152 centimeters (1 to 59 inches) per second, but most were in the range of 20 to 100 centimeters (8 to 40 inches) per second.

Cover for salmonids waiting to spawn or in the process of spawning can be provided by overhanging vegetation, undercut banks, submerged vegetation, submerged objects, such as logs and rocks, floating debris, water depth, turbulence, and turbidity. Nearness of cover to spawning areas has been a factor in the selection of spawning sites by some trout.

The suitability of gravel substrate for spawning depends mostly on fish size. Large fish have been observed spawning in substrate with particles up to about 15 centimeters (6 inches) in diameter, and smaller fish in substrates smaller than 5 to 10 centimeters (2 to 4 inches) in diameter. If there are large

TROUT

slightly adhesive, but they soon lose that quality as they absorb water and become more turgid.

At first, salmonid embryos are relatively large single cells, but within hours cleavage occurs and the cell starts to divide into many smaller cells, which develop and differentiate to ultimately become a young fish. Development of the embryo is difficult to discern without a microscope until the eyes become pigmented (the eyed-egg stage). Up until the eyed-egg stage, the embryos are sensitive to movement, but afterward the eggs are quite hardy and can be disturbed or moved with ease until hatching. Hatching occurs about half way through the incubation process. At hatching, the embryo breaks through the chorion and becomes a larval fish, sometimes called an alevin, with limited mobility because of a large attached yolk sac. During the latter half of the incubation period, the alevin stays down in the redd and lives on the remainder of the fats, proteins, and carbohydrates in the yolk sac. When the yolk sac has been absorbed, the young fish emerge from the redd as fully formed miniature trout or char, often called fry.

Temperature. The rate of development and duration of the incubation period depends on the temperature of water flowing through the redd because fish are poikilotherms: Their body temperature changes with water temperature. The length of the incubation period (from fertilization of egg to emergent fry) varies by species and location because each species of trout and char has certain cumulative temperature requirements for development, and temperatures vary from one stream to another. The temperature requirement for development can be expressed as temperature units. One temperature unit is gained per day for each degree of mean daily water temperature above 0°C (32°F).

Development proceeds rapidly at higher temperatures within the suitable range; fry emerge in a month or less. Development from egg to emergent fry can take as long as eight to nine months for salmonids that spawn in the fall, whose offspring incubate during the winter when temperatures are near freezing for many months.

The effect of temperature and season of spawning on the length of the development period can be illustrated by comparing the number of days from fertilization to emergence of steelhead fry in Idaho and large bull trout in Montana, both of whom require about 635 temperature units. The steelhead spawned in the spring when temperatures were increasing. Hatching occurred after about twenty-eight days and the mean date of emergence was fifty-three days after

YUSKAVITCH

YUSKAVITCH

Left: *Incubation involves two distinct stages: the eyed egg (left)* and the alevin (below). *The alevin is nourished in its early weeks by fats stored in the attached yolk sac. When the yolk sac has been absorbed, incubation is complete and the alevins leave the redd.*

This brook trout redd shows the important features of a good incubation ground: large substrate and the absence of fine sediments. The already deposited eggs will receive a steady supply of oxygen from the waters that circulate through the redd.

spawning. Bull trout spawned in the fall. The eggs hatched about 110 days later, and fry emerged about 215 days after spawning.

Trout and char are sensitive to extremes in temperature during the early stages of development, and the optimum temperature is not the same for all species. Mortality or developmental anomalies can result from extremely cold temperatures (less than about 4°C [39°F]) during the early stages of incubation when rapid cell division is occurring. Temperatures that are relatively high (more than 15°C [59°F]) but not out of the suitable range for later life stages can cause losses during the incubation stage for some species.

Varied needs. The requirements of embryos during incubation differ from those of spawning adults, but adults must select sites for spawning that will meet the needs of the embryos or reproduction will not be successful. The incubation of embryos and the emergence of fry depend on many factors within and outside of the redds, including the concentration of dissolved oxygen and the temperature of the water, biochemical oxygen demand of material carried in the water and deposited in the redd, the size of stream substrate in and around the redd (including the amount of fine sediments), channel gradient, channel configuration, water depth (head) above the redd, surface water discharge and velocity, permeability and porosity of gravel in the redd and surrounding streambed, and velocity of water through the redd.

Streambed particles in the redd at the end of spawning, and organic and inorganic particles that settle into the redd and surrounding substrate during incubation, affect the rate of water interchange between the stream and the redd, the amount of oxygen available to the embryos, concentrations of embryo wastes, and the movement of alevins (especially when they are ready to emerge from the redd). During redd construction, fine sediments and organic materials in the stream substrate tend to be washed downstream; consequently the redd environment is as favorable for the embryos immediately after construction as it will ever be. Conditions for embryos within redds may change little or greatly during incubation depending on weather, streamflows, spawning by other fish

in the same area at a later time, and the amount of fine sediments and organic materials transported in the stream.

Disturbance of redds. Redds may be disturbed by later-spawning fish or by floods that displace the streambed containing the redd. Redds that remain intact during incubation may become less suitable for embryos if inorganic fine sediments and organic materials are deposited in the interstitial spaces between the larger particles. The fine particles impede the movement of water and alevins in the redd, and the organic material consumes oxygen during decomposition. Fine sediments transported in a stream, either as bedload or suspended sediments, are likely to be deposited in redds. The amount of deposition and depth of intrusion of the fine sediments depends on the size of substrate in the redd, flow conditions in the stream, and the amount and size of sediment being transported.

During incubation, sufficient water must circulate through the redd as deep as the eggs in the egg pocket (up to 30 centimeters [12 inches] for most trout) to supply the embryos with oxygen and carry away waste products. Circulation of water through redds is a function of the porosity (ratio of pore space to total volume) of the particles in the redd, hydraulic gradient at the redd, and temperature of the water. Porosity is highest in newly constructed redds and declines during the incubation period if the interstitial spaces are filled with fine sediments. The hydraulic gradient through a redd is enhanced by the mounded tailspill created during construction. Survival of embryos will decrease as apparent velocities, an indication of the amount of dissolved oxygen reaching the embryos, decrease. At velocities of less than 10 centimeters (4 inches) per hour, survival was relatively low.

Oxygen levels. Dissolved oxygen that is carried in the water that circulates through the redd must be present in suitable concentrations and saturation levels to provide for respiration and allow normal development of the embryos. Embryos are most sensitive to marginal concentrations of dissolved oxygen during the early stages of development because oxygen uptake by the embryo occurs wholly by diffusion rather than breathing. Once the circulatory system is functional, oxygen transfer to the embryo becomes more efficient.

Survival of salmonid embryos has been positively correlated with the concentration of dissolved oxygen in redds. Phillips and Campbell in 1961 concluded from field studies that intragravel concentrations of dissolved oxygen must average 8 milligrams per liter for high survival rates of embryos and alevins. Although concentrations of dissolved oxygen required for successful incubation depend on the species of fish and developmental stage, concentrations at or near saturation, with temporary reductions no lower than 5 milligrams per liter, will probably allow high survival of salmonids in most cases.

Apparent velocities of water flowing through redds also must be maintained at acceptable rates because high concentrations of dissolved oxygen alone do not guarantee optimum embryo development. Embryos may survive when concentrations of dissolved oxygen are below the saturation level (but above the critical level). But they may be smaller, they may have an increased incidence of anomalies, and their time of hatching may be altered from normal conditions.

Intragravel concentrations of dissolved oxygen are a function of a variety of factors that include water temperature, interchange of water between surface and gravel, apparent velocity of water flow in the redd, permeability of the substrate, and the oxygen demand

of organic material in the redd. The latter factor, organic matter that gets deposited in the redd and decomposes, is probably the most important in causing reduced levels of oxygen. The organic matter can come from logging debris, farming practices, and vegetation in the stream and in the riparian zone along the stream. Relatively small amounts of organic material can cause a reduction in levels of dissolved oxygen if water velocities in the redd are low.

Crowded nests. Egg densities in natural redds are relatively low compared with those in artificial culture facilities, and densities do not become a factor regulating embryo and alevin survival unless the incubation environment is of marginal quality. If a large steelhead deposited 5,000 eggs in a single redd that covered 10 square meters (108 square feet), the density per redd could be calculated as 500 eggs per square meter (10.8 square feet). The density in the egg pockets would be higher, perhaps as high as 2,000 to 5,000 eggs per square meter, if most of the eggs were deposited in one or two pockets. Egg densities of up to 3,000 eggs per square meter have been observed in some streams in Alaska where large numbers of pink salmon spawn, according to a 1969 report by McNeil. In artificial incubators, up to 43,000 chum salmon eggs per square meter have been incubated successfully, according to a 1983 report by Kapuscinski and Lannan.

Emerging alevins. Once incubation is complete and the alevins are ready to emerge from

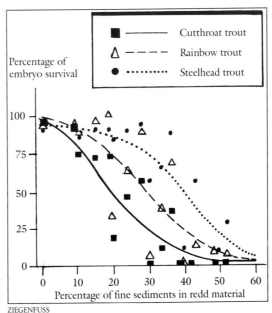

As fine sediments accumulate in the redd material, embryo survival decreases. The fine particles impede water circulation in the redd, reducing the amount of dissolved oxygen delivered to the embryos.

Young trout fry absorb their yolk sacs and emerge from the gravel as fully formed fish.

YUSKAVITCH

the redd and begin life in the stream, they must move from the egg pocket up through interstitial spaces in the gravel of the redd to the surface of the streambed. The upward movement of alevins appears to be a response to gravitational cues rather than to light or intergravel water flow, as noted by Nunan and Noakes in 1985. Emergence of fry from a single redd usually starts with a few fish. The number increases to a peak, then decreases. All fish usually emerge in less than two weeks. Emergence from all the redds in a spawning area may occur over a period of two months or more, depending on the length of the spawning period and temperatures during incubation.

Fry can encounter trouble emerging from a redd if the interstitial spaces between the particles in the redd are not large enough to permit their passage. Although most of the fine sediments in the spawning area are displaced downstream when the redd is constructed, small gravels, sands, and silts carried in the water or moved downstream as bedload after redd construction may settle in the redd. When fine sediments (those less than about 6 millimeters [0.2 inch] in diameter) fill most of the interstitial spaces between larger particles (35 to 45 percent of the volume of a sample from a redd), the alevins have difficulty emerging and survival is reduced.

The incubation stage is an example of the fishes' dependence on a good habitat. The spawning site selected by the adults must be suitable for spawning and suitable for extended periods of incubation by the embryos. During the incubation period, the embryos are immobile and entirely dependent on the quality of the environment in the redd. In the best spawning areas, conditions in the redd change little from the time the eggs are deposited until the fry emerge. In poorer spawning areas, freshets that scour the stream bottom may destroy the redd and dislodge the embryos prematurely. In addition, organic and inorganic sediments may settle in the redd and impede water circulation, reduce the amount of dissolved oxygen delivered to the embryos, and block emergence routes needed by the alevins. Good spawning and incubation areas are usually associated with healthy, well-managed watersheds.

– Theodore C. Bjornn

Trout as predator

On warm summer evenings as the last twilight softens the outlines of streamside objects, trout begin to feed in earnest on emerging insects, dotting the water surface with their rises. Trout feeding at dusk is a scene that repeats itself on lakes and streams throughout the world where trout occur, and it has fascinated humans for centuries. Little else about trout behavior, save perhaps congregations and migrations of spawning fish, seems to excite people as much as watching them feed. Perhaps this is because little else affords the chance to view these fish directly, and to gain a sense of their abundance and size, as does their feeding on prey, especially at the water's surface. It is no wonder then that the earliest writings of naturalists and anglers record relatively detailed observations about what trout eat and when, such as those in Izaak Walton's *The Compleat Angler*, published in 1653.

Fish biologists also have found trout feeding a fascinating subject. These scientists have devoted years of effort to analyzing what trout eat, why they select the prey they do, how and when they feed, and whether they are capable of depleting their invertebrate food supply. One theme common to many of their discoveries is that in both stream and lake environments, the organisms that trout eat have evolved habits that help them avoid being eaten. This places some rather severe constraints on trout feeding, which in turn limits trout growth and survival. The following explores this dynamic interplay among the trout and their prey, and the environments in which both evolved.

What trout eat

There is a consensus among biologists who study fish that trout are generalists and will forage rather opportunistically on the wide range of foods in their environment that fit into their mouths. While this is not to say that trout make no choices about which foods they eat, their behavior contrasts with that of many other fishes that are quite specialized in their diets as a result of having very specialized mouth and jaw shapes. For example, some species of cichlid fishes in large East African lakes have mouths specialized for biting the eyes from other fish.

A rainbow trout rises to the surface to feed.

ZETTER

Order Ephemeroptera
mayflies

Family Ephemerellidae
ephemerella, *4x*

Family Oligonturiidae
isonychia, *2.5x*

Family Ephemerellidae
drunella, *1.725x*

Family Heptageniidae
epeorus, *4x*

Family Ephemerellidae
serratella, *7x*

Trout, on the other hand, are limited in their foraging primarily by mouth size. Large trout, with their larger mouths, can take a much larger range of food sizes than smaller trout can. Although trout often select the largest prey available, certain populations of various trout species have evolved longer or more intricately shaped gill rakers that allow them to trap very small prey, which is a useful adaptation for feeding in lakes.

Food of trout in both streams and lakes consists primarily of three general types: small invertebrates that live in the aquatic environment during some or all of their life stages, terrestrial invertebrates that fall onto the water surface, and larger prey such as large aquatic invertebrates and fish, as well as the odd amphibian, reptile, bird, or mammal.

Food in streams. In streams, the trout diet consists mostly of aquatic invertebrates that drift downstream with the current; these are termed invertebrate drift. Most of these drifting organisms are immature aquatic stages of insects that later metamorphose into winged terrestrial adults, the main groups being mayflies, stoneflies, caddis flies, and midges. For example, immature mayflies, called nymphs, spend from a few months to several years in streams before they metamorphose and emerge as terrestrial adult insects (the sub-imago and imago stages). During a brief few dayq, the imagos mate in swarms near the stream, lay eggs in the water, and die.

Other aquatic invertebrates, such as the freshwater shrimp *Gammarus*, also may make up much of the drift in some streams. Lesser numbers of such invertebrates as aquatic beetles, water mites, and aquatic worms, or oligochaetes, also often appear in the drift—and in trout stomachs.

Although ecologists who study invertebrates still have much to learn about why invertebrates drift, the most important aspect for trout feeding is that most aquatic invertebrates drift primarily at night, reaching their greatest numbers just after dark and just before dawn. This behavior is thought to have evolved partly to avoid predation by fish.

Because trout feed primarily by vision, the greatest numbers of drifting invertebrates are available to trout just before dusk as the drift begins to increase, and again at dawn as it decreases. This is why trout often feed most heavily during these periods, at least in the spring and summer when drifting invertebrates are most abundant. However, some invertebrates drift or emerge during the day, which also can induce trout to feed.

Seasonally, invertebrate drift reaches the greatest abundance during late spring, decreases steadily through the summer and early fall, and is generally lowest during the winter. Overall, although trout put on spectacular feeding displays during relatively brief hatches of emerging adult aquatic insects, such as large mayflies and stoneflies, most of the diet of trout throughout the year is composed of a wide array of smaller organisms captured by more or less continuous feeding from the subsurface drift.

Food in lakes. Many of the small invertebrates on which trout feed in lakes differ from those in streams. In lakes trout eat small, semi-transparent, free-swimming crustaceans called zooplankton, which usually are less than 2 millimeters (0.1 inch) long. They also feed on aquatic insects or other benthic invertebrates that live in the lake-bottom sediment or on aquatic plants. Like invertebrates in streams, zooplankton in lakes have evolved daily schedules to avoid fish predation. They often retreat to deep water just above the lake bed during the day and migrate upward in the water column at night to feed when they are less visible to fish.

Trout in lakes feed primarily by constant roving through the water in search of zooplankton or fish, or by capturing individual benthic prey from aquatic plants or the lake bed. Trout that have lived for tens of thousands of years in lakes where the main food source has been zooplankton, such as the cutthroat trout in Yellowstone Lake, Wyoming, have evolved long, fine gill rakers that increase their efficiency in feeding on these small organisms. After drawing zooplankton and water into their mouths by suction, the trout close their mouths and exhale the water past the gills and gill rakers, which trap the zooplankton. As in streams, trout in lakes tend to time their feeding to coincide with the periods near dawn and dusk when the invertebrates are more active and there is still enough light to allow feeding.

Terrestrial insects and fish. Terrestrial insects that fall on the surface of streams and lakes provide a vital link between the terrestrial and aquatic food webs. In general, terrestrial insects such as ants, bees, wasps, and grasshoppers can form a significant portion of trout diets during late summer when these organisms are abundant. For example, trout caught in high mountain lakes during late summer may have stomachs packed full of flying ants, which often form an important, though transitory, source of food in these unproductive waters.

Trout larger than about 25 centimeters (10 inches) are capable of eating larger prey, such as other fish and crayfish, which can be especially important in producing older and larger trout. Lake trout, which inhabit primarily deep cold lakes in North America, such as the Great Lakes, prey almost exclusively on fish and the freshwater shrimp *Mysis*. Similarly, a recent study by Jude and colleagues indicates that the other trout and salmon introduced into the Great Lakes, including brown and rainbow trout, primarily eat fish, of which about 50 to 75 percent by weight are the exotic alewife, a member of the herring family.

Selecting prey

Anglers who use artificial flies to catch trout frequently report that trout are selective and refuse to strike unless their fly closely matches the color and size of the most abundant prey. Unfortunately, little research has been directed toward determining whether

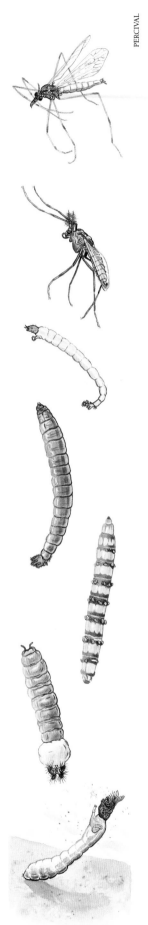

PERCIVAL

Order Diptera
flies

Family Tipulidae
adult, 1.5x

Family Chironomidae
adult, 5x

Family Chironomidae
larva, 3x

Family Tipulidae
larva, .75x

Family Tabanidae
larva, 2x

Family Tipulidae
larva, 2x

Family Simuliidae
larva, 4.25x

trout can discriminate between similar drifting invertebrates. However, several studies have been conducted to learn whether trout select specific prey from the large array of different organisms that drift, swim, or live on the surface or bottom of streams, or whether trout are opportunistic and simply capture prey as the trout encounter them. Because the results of such studies vary widely, I attempt here to organize the information in a useful framework to show what is known about how trout select their prey.

Stomach contents. Fish biologists learn about what trout eat by either removing the stomach or flushing its contents, then identifying the prey, and counting or weighing the various groups of organisms eaten. This analysis usually results in a large table listing the average percentages of the groups of organisms that made up the diet of the sample of trout studied. The organisms eaten then can be compared with the organisms available in the drift if that also is measured and analyzed.

The most striking feature of these results is the vast array of organisms that trout eat. Although at certain times trout may eat primarily one species of prey, especially when a large aquatic insect is emerging so that adults drifting on the water surface are easily captured, most of the time they eat at least some of lots of different organisms and frequently eat about equal proportions of three or four main groups.

These findings have led scientists to believe

Order Trichoptera
caddisflies

Family Phryganeidae
yphria *species, adult, 2x*

Family Limnephilidae
hesperophylax *sp., adult, 2x*
dicosmoecus *sp., 1.25x*
lenarchus *sp., 1.5x*

Family Ryacophilidae
ryacophila *sp., 3x*

Family Hydropsychidae
arctopsyche *sp., 2.5x*

that trout are relatively opportunistic and that they eat primarily those organisms that are most abundant and available. However, experiments designed to test these ideas show that trout do exercise some selection of their prey and indicate that color, size, abundance, and palatability are the most important factors. In addition, trout appear to have some degree of individuality in their feeding habits, which also plays a role in producing the variety of diet usually observed among trout in streams.

Color preferences. Can trout see colors? Do they select prey of some colors over prey of others? Our understanding of color vision in fish comes from two sources. One is microscopic examination of the retina of the eye to determine whether the cone cells and visual pigments required for color vision are present. The other source is experiments with different-colored foods to determine whether fish can discriminate between them and have preferences for certain colors over others. Study of trout retinal cells indicates that trout do have the necessary cone cells and pigments required for color vision, as Behnke recently discussed in a 1987 review of trout vision. However, like humans, fish cannot see colors in low light, because different retinal cells, called rods, are used for vision. Rod cells are much more sensitive to dim light than cones but lack the visual pigments that respond to color.

Although examination of trout retinas revealed that these fish have color vision, it still

did not answer whether fish can distinguish among shades of colors or whether they prefer certain colors of prey. Feeding experiments conducted by Ginetz and Larkin showed that hatchery rainbow trout previously fed only reddish-brown pellets could distinguish among salmon eggs dyed seven different colors, and preferred certain colors over others. Under normal daylight conditions their preference, based on those eggs eaten most, ranked blue, red, black, orange, brown, yellow, and green, when presented against a pale blue-green background.

The researchers also varied background color and light intensity in other experiments and concluded that, although some of the preference could be explained by the contrast between the egg and background colors, especially in dim light, rainbow trout displayed consistent preference for certain colors in relation to others. The best example of this was that the trout selected blue eggs over eggs of other colors under normal light, even when they were presented against a blue background. This finding indicates both that rainbow trout preferred blue among the colors presented and that they could discriminate among shades of blue that were only slightly different.

Other factors influencing selection. Size, abundance, and relative palatability, as well as color, frequently combine to influence which prey trout will select. During the past fifteen years, Ringler has done a series of studies to determine how these factors affect which prey adult brown trout will select. He began his first set of experiments by training brown trout in a laboratory stream to feed on drifting brine shrimp, a small prey 2 to 3 millimeters (0.1 inch) long, during thirty-minute feeding periods each day. When the fish had learned to capture the brine shrimp, Ringler introduced mealworms and crickets of medium and large sizes (6 to 13 millimeters [0.2 to 0.5 inch] long), and increased the proportion of medium-sized prey in different experiments to find out whether the trout chose the most abundant or the largest prey.

The trout almost always selected a larger percentage of the largest prey, regardless of whether they were crickets or mealworms, even when the medium-sized prey were five times more abundant. Moreover, after six days brown trout were able to select a combination of large and medium-sized prey that yielded them nearly the most calories theoretically available within the time allotted for foraging.

Part of the reason that trout fell short of the theoretical optimum was that they continued to eat a few of the small brine shrimp throughout the experiment. Ringler and other scientists suggest that this strategy of periodically "sampling" alternative prey may be important in the long run, because it allows fish to find new prey that yield more energy than the prey they are currently selecting.

Learning and forgetting. In addition to the general finding that brown trout selected the largest prey available, one of the most interesting results of the experiments was how slowly trout learned to capture the mealworms and crickets after these prey were first introduced. Ringler found that trout generally did not respond to the novel larger prey immediately, but required five to twenty-five minutes during which twenty-five to 250 prey drifted by before many were attacked.

Moreover, the percentage of large prey captured continued to increase during the six-day experiment, indicating that the trout were still learning to forage efficiently on these organisms even after 800 to 1,200 prey had been captured. Ringler and others believe that trout learn to search for, recognize, and capture novel prey with increasing efficiency over time. Further experiments indicated that trout retained this learned behavior for at least three weeks but apparently forgot it within three months.

Palatability of prey also affects which ones trout will select. In another set of laboratory-stream experiments, Ringler offered five adult brown trout a choice between drifting mealworms and tent caterpillars, and increased the proportion of tent caterpillars over time. The caterpillars apparently are less palatable to trout either because of their many bristles or chemicals that make them taste bad. All the trout preferred mealworms even when caterpillars were five times more abundant. However, the trout showed wide variation in their preferences, some eating primarily or only mealworms throughout the experiment.

Order Plecoptera
stoneflies

Family Perlodidae
adult, 2x

Family Pteronarcyidae
adult, 2.5x
pteronarcys *sp., 2x*

Family Chloroperlidae
utaperla *sp., 4x*

PERCIVAL

Selectivity in natural streams. Although Ringler's research on prey selection was done in the laboratory, I believe that the results are useful in interpreting whether trout are selective in natural streams. Selectivity can be viewed from two perspectives, however: that of the long-term survival of the trout or that of the angler attempting to catch trout with artificial imitations of aquatic invertebrates. Thus, whereas Ringler's results indicate that fish should be caught relatively easily on any large, palatable prey, the angling literature is full of reports of cases where trout would accept only a certain size and color of artificial fly. Can these seemingly incongruous findings be resolved?

I believe that part of the discrepancy between what scientists find and what anglers observe is due to a difference between the time scale over which anglers perceive trout to be selective and the time scale over which trout change their foraging patterns. Hatches of emerging aquatic insects ebb and flow relatively slowly in rhythms set by the seasons. They require weeks or months to run their courses and provide predictable cues in response to which trout feeding behavior has evolved. Therefore, trout are at no disadvantage if they respond to new prey only after seeing many drift past their feeding positions and if they require several days to become fully efficient at capturing the novel items, because this can be accomplished during the first few days as a new hatch begins. Even rather ephemeral occurrences of terrestrial in-

Family Apidae
bumblebee

Family Flatidae
plant hopper

Family Acrididae
grasshopper

Family Grylladae
field cricket

Family Formicidae
ant

Family Carabidae
ground beetle

sects such as flying ants or grasshoppers are relatively predictable and prolonged.

In contrast, most anglers judge trout to be selective when they refuse a novel fly after drifting it past the fish's position less than a dozen times or so. But because trout have evolved to respond to rhythmic seasonal changes in insect emergence, there is no need for them to respond so quickly in their natural environment.

Selecting large prey. Studies of the sizes of prey that trout eat in natural streams agree with laboratory findings that trout select the largest prey items that they can capture and swallow efficiently. Bannon and Ringler measured the lengths of invertebrates in stomachs of 156 juvenile and adult brown trout that averaged about 15 and 23 centimeters (6 and 9 inches) long, respectively, in a small New York stream on four summer dates. They also measured the lengths of prey in the drift at the same time and found that most were 2 to 3 millimeters (0.1 inch) long and few were longer than 5 millimeters (0.2 inch).

But on every date the trout selected items 1 to 10 millimeters (0.04 to 0.4 inch) longer than the bulk of those found in the drift, including items 8 to 16 millimeters (0.3 to 0.6 inch) long that were so rare that they were not found in the drift at all.

Moreover, laboratory studies indicated that, when the costs of pursuit, capture, and ingestion were balanced against the calories gained, trout of this size could net the most

energy by eating prey 20 to 24 millimeters (0.8 to 0.9 inch) long. Bannon and Ringler hypothesized that the lack of large prey limits growth and survival of trout larger than about 23 to 25 centimeters (9 to 10 inches), which is a view that Behnke, Bachman, and other trout biologists share. The general idea is that unless trout can switch to feeding on large prey, such as freshwater shrimp, crayfish, or fish, when they reach about 25 centimeters (10 inches), they will not grow beyond about 30 centimeters (12 inches) or live much past four years of age. This corresponds well with data from many sources showing that trout begin to feed on larger prey, if available, when the fish reach about 25 centimeters (10 inches) in length.

Cost-effective feeding. But if trout prefer larger prey, why is it that large trout can sometimes be observed foraging mainly on tiny insects? Many anglers are aware of cases when large trout select only very small midges or mayflies (imitated by artificial flies of sizes 18 to 22). Because all trout are limited in their foraging by the energetic costs and benefits, it seems paradoxical that large trout could "make a living" feeding on such small insects that each provide so little energy. The critical question to pose is whether the cost of pursuing such a small insect outweighs its energy content. Observations Ringler made in the laboratory and I made while diving in natural streams may offer a plausible explanation, although this question deserves more scientific study under controlled conditions.

Ringler found that when he drifted small brine shrimp past brown trout at a rate of about one every two seconds, the trout did not always return to their focal point near the streambed between each foray to capture prey but rather swam near the surface and captured many brine shrimp in succession. While diving in the East Branch of the Au Sable River in Michigan, I observed the same behavior by brook trout and brown trout 20 to 30 centimeters (8 to 12 inches) long feeding during mid-morning on emerging *Tricorythodes* mayflies, which are small but emerge in great numbers.

These observations lead me to suspect that larger trout can afford to forage on small prey drifting at some distance from their focal point only when the prey are abundant, so that the energy gained by capturing many items in succession outweighs the cost of swimming to maintain a temporary position in the swifter waters. If this hypothesis is correct, one would also predict that smaller trout would be able to feed profitably on smaller drift items that large trout could not afford to capture, especially at times when emergence is more sporadic so that prey are less abundant, as is the case during most of the daylight hours.

Indeed, in the East Branch Au Sable, I also observed that smaller trout began feeding on small midges that emerged during mid-afternoon in August, whereas the larger trout were enticed to feed only when larger emerging insects became available later in the evening. While some of this response may be due to unwillingness of the larger trout to expose themselves to predation by feeding away from cover during the day, I suspect that much of it relates to their energy balance while foraging.

Individual tastes. Although fish biologists have discovered some of the more important factors that influence which prey trout will select, the reasons that individual trout living together in the same stream section, and exposed to the same drifting organisms, often eat substantially different diets remain largely unsolved. Most of the differences in diet appear to be caused by individual foraging habits and tastes, which surprises scientists because trout display other rather uniform species-specific behaviors—aggressive displays and mating, for example.

Bryan and Larkin reported that the stomach contents flushed from brook trout, rainbow trout, and cutthroat trout that had been captured repeatedly over periods of six to twelve months in a stream in British Columbia were more similar within individuals than between different fish of each species, indicating that at least some trout specialized in their feeding. Another example of diet specialization comes from a recent study by Merna of brook trout and brown trout living in tributary streams of Lake Michigan that salmon use for spawning. He found that only certain trout learned to eat the salmon eggs, either by intercepting those that washed out of the redds or by simply moving in to feed on the eggs during spawning. These fish

Family
daphnia
water flea

Family Mycidae
freshwater shrimp

Family Gammaridae
Gammarus
scud

Family Cottidae
sculpin

Family Cyprinidae
speckled dace

Family Astacidae
crayfish

PERCIVAL

thereby gained a high-calorie food source during the spawning season, whereas other trout did not.

Ringler suggests that such individual variations in diet could be caused by many factors, including differences in abilities to search for and capture prey, hunger levels, activity cycles, experience, and social position. For example, dominant fish occupying more-advantageous positions may have access to the largest prey, which tend to be carried in the swifter currents. These individuals may thereby include more of these larger prey in their diet. Therefore, it is no wonder that the variety in diet among trout is not easily explained by only a few factors.

HOW TROUT FEED

Natural selection dictates that only those trout that maintain a positive balance in the "economics" of feeding can survive to reproduce. Generally food is scarce, even unavailable, in the aquatic environments that trout inhabit. Therefore, if these fish are to grow sufficiently to reproduce, they must minimize the cost of capturing food and at the same time maximize their energy gain from the food available. What feeding strategies have evolved in trout that allow them to stay "in the black" on the energy balance sheet?

This interplay between the benefits and costs of feeding is most easily observed for stream-dwelling trout, because from the stream bank one may often observe an individual fish swimming against the current in a relatively fixed position and watch it make short forays to feed on organisms that drift nearby. Diligently observing the trout in a given pool for many days, one would likely come to the conclusion that the dominant fish appears to hold the "best" position in the pool for feeding, and that a pecking order exists, such that the next most-dominant individual claims rights to the next-best feeding position and so forth.

Foraging-site selection. That adult trout of many species arrange themselves in this sort of linear dominance hierarchy in pools is well known. However, more recently scientists have discovered the strategies that individual trout employ when they choose feeding positions, how this choice affects growth rate, and how it is affected by the dominance hierarchy.

Many fish biologists and anglers have observed that individual trout hold relatively fixed positions in streams, called focal points. These positions usually are in quiet waters downstream from some obstruction that

Foraging sites

*T*here is a difference among the species of trout as they tend to their foraging sites. All species and all sizes of fish come near the surface at the onset of a large hatch of food items. Here they can gain a bioenergetic advantage in a short period of time. Food is abundant, so there is no need to recognize hierarchical position. However, when there is no major hatch but only an occasional food item in the drift, foraging positions are taken that reflect hierarchical status. Brown trout at Sagehen Creek in California orient to the bottom configuration like those trout studied by Bachman at Spruce Creek in Pennsylvania. Large brown trout of Sagehen Creek also use the undercut banks for ambush sites. Here the predator can take advantage of the Tyndall Effect, as the flare of light off the suspended particles in the water partially blinds the prey fish to the predator, the brown trout hidden in the darkness of the undercut bank.

Rainbow and cutthroat, on the other hand, assume foraging sites well above the substrate but do refer to the objects of the substrate to define their foraging sites. Because these species are in faster-flowing water, they must expend much more energy to maintain their position compared with the efforts of brown trout and brook trout.

—Robert L. Butler

offers a refuge from the current but close to swifter currents that sweep large amounts of drift close to the fish's position. The first systematic observations of this phenomenon were published in 1969 by Jenkins, who found that the dominant rainbow and brown trout he observed from towers on the banks of a small stream in the Sierra Nevada of California held fixed positions in pools beneath the principal currents that carried the most surface drift. He was able to map these currents by observing patterns of drifting flotsam on the water surface. Moreover, when he removed the most dominant trout from the pool, the vacant position was filled by the next most dominant individual, whose position was then filled by the third fish in the hierarchy, and so forth. Thus, the entire dominance hierarchy shifted in turn to better positions.

Typically, a "floater" moves into the last position vacated. Floaters, recently described by Puckett and Dill, are subordinate fish in the population that cannot defend positions.

When feeding, a trout seeks to position itself adjacent to swift currents, often taking refuge behind boulders or logs. Such positioning gives it the greatest access to food for the least output of energy. Instead of using its energy to keep from being swept downstream, the trout can put on bursts of speed to snatch its meals from the adjacent conveyor belt of faster currents.

PERCIVAL

Riffles are good feeding sites for trout. They offer protective cover and a good menu.

Nakano at Hokkaido University in northern Japan recently recorded similar position shifts when he removed the dominant individuals from populations of red-spotted Japanese char in stream pools.

Profitable positions. After reading the studies of Jenkins and others as a new graduate student, I became curious about how individual trout select the positions they hold in streams. I realized that the problem could be addressed by measuring the benefits and costs to fish of holding specific stream positions, so I set out to measure the "profitability" of the positions that juvenile trout and salmon selected in a laboratory stream that Ray White and I and others built at Michigan State University. I defined profit as the energy that a fish could gain by feeding on the invertebrates that drifted within its foraging radius, minus the cost of swimming to maintain its position at the focal point, both of which were measured in calories. The objectives were to discover whether trout chose the most profitable positions available to them in the stream, whether those that held the most profitable positions grew the fastest, and whether the more dominant trout

were able to defend the more profitable positions.

The results of these experiments were striking. Indeed, the fish could detect very small changes in water velocity at their focal points and in amounts of invertebrates that drifted adjacent to them, and were thereby able to choose positions that yielded the most net energy or profit. When I compared how fast different trout grew that held positions of different profitability, I found that those holding the most profitable ones grew the fastest, although a threshold was reached above which more energy did not increase the growth rate much.

Because only a limited number of refuges from velocity were available in the laboratory stream, the number of positions that were at least moderately profitable also was limited. Of these, the more upstream refuges nearer the food source were more profitable because the fish there had first chance at the drifting food.

This situation created a hierarchy of positions that ranged from highly profitable to those at which either water was so swift or food was so scarce that a trout holding them could not gain any weight.

Perhaps the most interesting result of my experiments was that the dominance hierarchy observed among the trout matched almost exactly this ranking of position profitability. That is, the most dominant fish held the most profitable position, the next most dominant held the next most profitable, and so on, which indicated that the trout chose positions primarily based on the relative costs and benefits of feeding, within the constraints of the dominance hierarchy. The most subordinate fish, the floaters in the population, held no fixed position but instead moved frequently and fed wherever they could.

Bachman, who in 1984 published the results of an extensive three-year study of the adult brown trout in a large pool of a Pennsylvania spring creek, found that these fish also selected positions that had favorable hydraulic characteristics—and did so with great precision. Not only did the trout spend most of their time feeding from low-velocity focal points adjacent to swift currents, but they also often used the same positions day after day for three summers. In fact, when Bachman compared photographs of one fish taken each of the three years, he found that the position of its eye with respect to the streambed varied only 2 to 4 centimeters (.8 to 1.6 inches) in any direction, and that the position of another fish was nearly identical each year. This precision serves to underscore the importance to trout of the unique flow conditions associated with specific stream positions.

Feeding sequence

It is well known that most fishes and other lower vertebrates display relatively set patterns of behavior. The feeding behavior of trout is no exception, and Ringler has outlined in detail the feeding sequence for adult brown trout he held in a laboratory stream. He fed the fish adult mealworms, crickets, and tent caterpillar larvae drifting on the surface and recorded the following behaviors over many hundreds of feeding sequences. I have supplemented his observations with my own made during many hours of watching trout feed in a laboratory stream and while diving to observe trout in natural streams.

1. Detection. As the prey drifted toward the fish, the trout moved their eyes and elevated their head or trunk from their position near the streambed or moved rapidly from side to side, or did both, all of which indicated that they had detected the prey.

A wild brown trout feeds on a crayfish in Pennsylvania's productive Spring Creek.

2. Approach. The fish then swam relatively rapidly toward the prey by moving upstream and toward the water surface.

3. Fixation. The trout aligned their snouts with the prey, presumably to fix it in the field of binocular vision directly in front of their snouts (30° to 36°, depending on the species), so that they could see it most clearly.

4. Inspection. After fixing the prey in front of the snout, some fish drifted downstream tail first at a fixed distance from the prey and continued to inspect it. When prey were not acceptable, trout aborted the feeding sequence during or after the approach, fixation, or inspection stages.

5. Attack. When attacking prey, a trout swam toward it in a burst. There followed a rapid sequence of movements of its jaws, opercula (gill covers), and branchiostegal membranes, the membranes that enclose the gills on the bottom of the jaw. These actions resulted in rapid suction of the prey into the mouth. A fish typically is able to seal the opercula and branchiostegal membranes shut and at the same time open the mouth and expand the throat region rapidly, which

R.A. Bachman

TROUT

When it sees an insect on the surface, the trout rises and positions itself so that the bug is directly in the trout's line of sight. Floating downstream with its prey, the trout opens its jaws and sips the insect in. The trout then returns to its original position to watch for its next dining opportunity.

the few studies that have been conducted at night and during the winter—most of them recent—have shown some rather surprising results. Can night and winter be important feeding times for trout?

Trout feed primarily by sight, rather than by smell, touch, or taste as do various other fishes, so trout feed most efficiently when there is enough light to allow them to see their prey. However, because many invertebrates avoid fish predation by being most active at night, trout are constrained to feeding on them during brief periods at both dawn and dusk, when light is sufficient for trout vision and invertebrate activity is still high.

creates a strong suction that draws prey into the mouth. The fish then closes the mouth, opens the opercula and branchiostegal membranes, and squeezes the mouth and throat region, thereby forcing water out of the throat and past the gills and gill rakers, structures that prevent the prey from escaping.

6. Manipulation and ingestion. After capturing prey, a trout moved its jaws rapidly and flared its opercula, apparently orienting the prey in its mouth. If prey were large, the trout bit them, spat them out, and then attacked and recaptured them. Once reduced to a sufficiently small size, the prey were swallowed by extreme opening movements of the jaws and opercula, which were followed by normal respiratory movements of the opercula.

7. Rejection. Unpalatable prey were spat out by extreme expansion of the opercula and branchiostegal membranes, followed by quick contraction of these same regions to eject the prey.

8. Return to the focal point. Following each prey encounter the fish generally returned to its focal point to await the next prey. A fish also returned if it failed to capture the prey.

WHEN TROUT FEED

The feeding behavior of trout has been studied most often during daylight of the ice-free months of the year, when the fish are visible and conditions are most conducive to observations by biologists and anglers. Yet

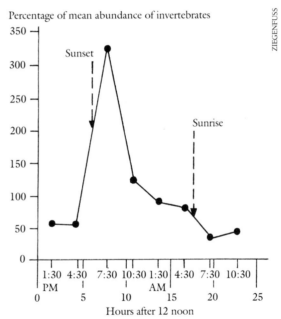

Percentage of mean abundance of invertebrates

ZIEGENFUSS

Invertebrate activity peaks just after sunset, and drops to its lowest point just after sunrise. In spite of the low light conditions, trout successfully feed on invertebrates during these peak activity periods. Perhaps, for individual invertebrates, there is greater safety in drifting along with the night crowd.

Research indicates that moving prey have a much greater chance of being detected and captured by trout than do inactive prey. My observations of young brook trout and brown trout feeding on drifting dead zooplankton in a laboratory stream also indicated that once these prey settled motionless to the streambed the fish had difficulty detecting them, even if the zooplankton fell directly in front of their noses!

Feeding in dim light. One might wonder why some trout have not evolved the capacity for better vision in dim light, if prey are most available then in both streams and lakes. Indeed, this appears to be the case. For example, Henderson and Northcote studied how well coastal cutthroat trout and Dolly

Trout may feed in the evening to take advantage of the peak period of invertebrate activity.

their chins just touching the bottom, apparently detecting benthic invertebrates by touch.

Several investigators have reported that brown trout in streams feed more effectively at night than do certain other trout species. For example, Apache trout, which are native to a small region of Arizona, are observed to feed primarily during the day, whereas brown trout that were introduced into the Apache trout's native watersheds feed at lower light levels. Based on laboratory studies, Robinson and Tash reported that brown trout were able to capture live brine shrimp at light levels in the range provided by starlight, one hundred times dimmer than those required for Apache trout to capture prey, which were in the range of light from a full moon. Thus, it is likely that certain trout species with greater visual acuity feed more effectively than others at lower light levels when more invertebrates are active, though biologists have studied only a few species.

Laboratory studies often tell us what trout are capable of, but the acid test is to measure whether trout actually feed at night in natural streams. Around 1970, Jenkins and colleagues published the results of two studies of night feeding by brown and rainbow trout in the same stream in California mentioned earlier. In one set of experiments Jenkins marked large ants with small dots of paint and introduced twenty to thirty ants per experiment onto the stream surface upstream from groups of five wild brown or rainbow trout holding positions in two different pools. He found that the trout captured up to 20 percent of the ants during experiments under starlight, and up to 40 percent of the ants during various phases of moonlight, but that sometimes they captured no ants. Surprisingly, rainbow trout, which are not known to be adept at night feeding, were about as efficient as brown trout at capturing prey at night, although both species captured higher percentages of ants during twilight and sunlight hours.

Winter feeding. In a second experiment conducted during fall and winter, Jenkins and colleagues introduced single hatchery rainbow trout into three pools and compared their stomach contents with the drift measured during four five-hour periods covering

Varden char, which live together in coastal British Columbia lakes, could find zooplankton prey under light of different intensities. The cutthroat feed on zooplankton and terrestrial insects in well-lit zones near or at the surface and aggressively exclude the char from these zones, so the char are forced to feed on benthic invertebrates and zooplankton at greater depths where little light penetrates.

In the laboratory, the researchers found that Dolly Varden reacted to prey at light levels about ten times lower than those at which cutthroat began to catch prey, and that the distance at which Dolly Varden could detect prey was greatest at light more than one hundred times lower than that at which cutthroat fed best. Moreover, the light intensity at which Dolly Varden could just detect prey was more than one million times less than the light that penetrated the lake surface on a summer day. Henderson and Northcote also observed, using an infrared light and viewer, that at very low light levels below which char could no longer see, the fish detected prey by drifting head down with both day and night. During fall the researchers found that although most aquatic invertebrates drifted at night when trout are less efficient at feeding, trout captured about as many of them at night as during the day when drift rates are low but trout are efficient. In contrast, most terrestrial insects entered the surface drift during the day and were efficiently captured by the trout.

During early winter, aquatic drift was similar during both day and night, but terrestrial drift was low. Despite low drift rates and cold temperatures, fish continued to feed, though they fed primarily during the day. I observed similar daytime winter feeding by trout in a Rocky Mountain stream and suspect that feeding activity is related to water temperature, which often drops below freezing at night in mountain streams during the winter. I noticed that rainbow trout began to feed when temperatures rose above 0°C (32°F) in late morning. It is likely that either trout or their invertebrate prey can be active only above certain temperature thresholds.

Cunjak and Power made the most complete study to date of trout feeding during winter in a southern Ontario stream where water temperatures fall almost to 0°C (32°F). They found that stomachs of brown trout and brook trout were nearly full of invertebrates all winter, which is similar to findings of other winter studies in California mountain streams and in Quebec. However, despite full stomachs and greatly reduced trout activity, which Cunjak observed directly by diving, trout remained thin throughout the winter.

Cunjak and Power suspect that very slow rates of movement of food through the gut at cold temperatures, combined with low rates of digestion, may prevent trout from assimilating much energy from the food they eat during the winter. As a result, they lose weight, especially during the early winter when they must adjust their metabolism to operate at colder temperatures.

CAN TROUT DEPLETE PREY?

Can trout in streams reduce the numbers of their invertebrate prey enough to limit their own growth or survival? Because trout feed primarily on drifting organisms, at least a

A trout eyes its prey before sipping it down.

R.A. BACHMAN

A flash of white gives away the presence of a feeding trout.

portion of which are likely to be surplus individuals emigrating from the population, it seems unlikely that their feeding could markedly affect benthic invertebrate abundance in streams. In contrast, fish predation in lakes on larger and more conspicuous zooplankton and benthic invertebrates is known to produce marked reductions in numbers of prey and shifts toward smaller and less conspicuous species.

One way to test whether trout affect stream invertebrates is to either remove or add fish to stream sections and measure the response. Allan conducted the most complete study of this kind, removing 75 to 90 percent of the brook trout present in a small high-altitude stream in Colorado for four successive years. He found that removing the trout had no measurable effect on the total numbers of invertebrates, nor did it affect the numbers of the four groups of prey that the trout ate most. In a similar study the numbers of coho salmon fry were increased to four times natural levels in enclosures placed in a small stream on Vancouver Island in British Columbia. The results showed that the salmon had little effect on drifting or benthic invertebrates.

Although it may be that the numbers of invertebrates are so variable in streams that the effects of fish predation are not easily detected, a more plausible explanation is that only a small portion of the invertebrate population in streams is being eaten by the fish. This hypothesis becomes even more believable in light of the relatively recent discovery that benthic invertebrates live in the spaces between rocks many meters below the surface of porous streambeds, and so have a very large refuge to which much of the population can escape from fish predation.

Overall, what scientists have discovered about the feeding behavior of trout appears to make good sense, especially when one adopts the perspective of long-term strategies that provide the best chances that individual trout will survive to produce offspring. However, it is clear that we still have much to learn, so the mysteries of why trout eat the prey they do likely will continue to fascinate us for a long time.

—Kurt D. Fausch

Rogue trout

Large trout, especially brown trout, taken by the angler only at night, yet not taken with electrofishing gear by the biologist during the day, often are called "rogue" trout. We have assumed that these few atypical individuals are old enough, large enough, and experienced enough that they are not constrained by the bonds of fish society. In other words, they don't operate by the biological and behavioral rules that affect most members of their species. But I like to be reminded of the caution in thinking given by Epictetus: There may be another explanation. In this case, the explanation may be that rogues live by broader rules.

The large size of the eye and the large optic nerve of the trout indicate the importance of vision, which helps the fish define its home range and its foraging sites. The structure of the eye also indicates that trout see best in high light rather than darkness and close up rather than from a distance. I assume that trout recognize their home range by the familiar sounds of the water as it passes over the substrate and around structures in the stream. They rely on thigmotactic cues (water displacement waves) received through the lateral line, and possibly cues received through the use of olfaction.

Observations of large brown trout from a viewing tank built into Sagehen Creek in the Sierra Nevada in California add credence to the idea that rogue trout differ from other trout commonly seen and caught in daylight. Rogue trout hide in deeply undercut banks or even within the streambed gravel itself. I have often seen huge brown trout burst from the gravel in the evening when light was so dim that I could not film their remarkable behavior. And in the very early morning when light was again too poor for filming, these rogue trout would literally swim into the gravel bottom, head first, and so bury themselves.

Some anglers assume that rogue trout roam beyond their home range at night. Instead, I speculate that rogue trout, after years of experience, are so familiar with their home range that they can move about freely at night because they "remember" the features of their habitat, having thoroughly integrated the information from the senses of sight, sound, olfaction, and function of the lateral line.

Unfortunately, worthwhile data regarding the activity of individual trout at night do not exist. The diurnal and seasonal movements of eight large brown trout in the South Branch of the Au Sable River in Michigan were recorded using radio-tracking. However, this method involves handling the fish to attach or insert the transmitter and thus invokes the Heisenberg Uncertainty Principle—that the observer is part of the observed situation. We cannot be sure that the transmitter and the handling did not affect the behavior of the fish, so we cannot be sure that the resultant information reflects normal activity.

Bachman and I have come up with a possible technique of study drawn from human physiology. Each human has a distinct turbulence of blood flow, which can be measured by the individual's cardiogram. Each is distinct because of the slight differences in structure of the circulatory system, which produce the differences in turbulence. We would expect that similar differences also occur among trout because of their opercular, or gill cover, movements. If proper sonic devices were placed in unobtrusive positions at each of the foraging sites of browns, brooks, or rainbows, records could be made of activities during the daytime and matched with records of activities at night. We could then accept or reject the idea that trout remain in their home ranges at night.

—*Robert L. Butler*

Competition

Fascination with the beauty of trout and their qualities as sport fish has led humans to introduce many species throughout the world to regions where they were not native. In fact, records of fish stocking for any given area often show that most of the eight or so common trout species have been introduced during the last hundred years, although relatively few of the nonnative ones are likely to have been successful. The most successful were the introductions of brown trout into Tasmania, Australia, and New Zealand beginning in the 1860s, into North America in the 1880s, and into Argentina and Chile soon after 1900. Brook trout and rainbow trout were established in many regions of North America outside their native ranges from 1870 to 1890 and soon after were successfully introduced to all continents except Antarctica. Unfortunately, these introductions have often been associated with the demise of native trout. Could introduced trout have been responsible for part of this decline? If so, why?

Native trout and salmon that have lived together for tens or hundreds of thousands of years have evolved so that each uses its environment in subtly different ways and interferes minimally with other species with which it lives. In contrast, species that have not evolved together can be so similar to each other, as are brook trout and brown trout, that when living together they clash as they try to occupy the same preferred space at the same time or eat the same foods. Several examples will illustrate where nonnative species may cause problems for native trout.

Brook trout are distributed throughout the northeastern United States and Canada, but their native range also extends south along the Appalachian Mountains to northern Georgia. Around 1910 rainbow trout were introduced into streams of the Great Smoky Mountains National Park, one of the last strongholds of native Appalachian brook trout located in Tennessee and North Carolina, and became established there. Extensive logging and angling decimated trout populations before 1936 when the park was established. Then, from 1935 to 1975 the length of stream occupied solely by brook trout declined 60 percent in the park. The brook trout retreated into the smaller, steeper streams at higher altitudes each year as rainbow trout invaded upstream, and the cessation of logging and restriction of fishing have not halted the rainbow's advance.

To determine whether rainbow trout are the primary factor causing the demise of brook trout, park fish biologists removed rainbow trout from four streams for six years by electrofishing. They found that the remaining brook trout populations increased after the rainbows were removed, whereas brook trout populations in three other streams that lacked rainbows remained relatively stable during the same period. From this comparison, biologists inferred that the increase in brook trout was most likely due to the removal of the rainbow trout rather than

Rainbow trout eventually replace native brook trout when introduced into brook trout waters.

MERMON

to other factors, such as favorable weather conditions, which also would have affected brook trout in the other three streams.

Other research indicates that brook trout choose positions in slower currents and grow and compete better at colder temperatures than rainbow trout do, which may explain why brook trout appear unable to compete favorably with rainbow trout in these steep, swift Appalachian streams where water temperatures are relatively warm. Based on this evidence, I think it is also possible that any future global warming may contribute indirectly to the decline of Appalachian brook trout populations by warming streams and rendering the brook trout less able to compete with invading rainbow trout.

Similar patterns of distribution of brook trout and rainbow trout have been recorded in streams of the Sierra Nevada in California where they occur together, making interactions between this pair of species the best documented to date. However, competition also is suspected to be important in at least three other cases in North America that have been investigated to varying degrees. Various races of cutthroat trout that inhabit streams of the interior western United States apparently have been excluded from lower-altitude and lower-gradient reaches of streams by brook trout and brown trout, and now maintain populations only in steep headwater reaches or upstream of barriers to fish movement. It is interesting, however, that some cutthroat races are relatively unaffected by brook trout and brown trout, primarily because they are adapted to live in harsh desert streams of the Great Basin in Nevada, Utah, southern Idaho, and eastern Oregon that are unsuitable for the introduced species.

Brook trout are native to the upper Midwest and northeastern United States, but they have declined in abundance and have largely retreated to headwater streams since brown trout were first introduced in 1883. The greater susceptibility of brook trout than brown trout to angling, and their greater sensitivity to stream degradation, thwart efforts to sort out how much of the brook trout's decline is the result of competition by brown trout, a problem common to most studies of trout competition. However, the evidence

suggests that brook trout may be able to withstand competition from brown trout only at colder temperatures, and thereby maintain populations primarily in colder headwater streams throughout the region.

Competition from other nonnative salmonids also can affect resident trout populations. Results of a field and laboratory study I published in 1986 indicate that juveniles of resident brook trout and brown trout in tributaries of Lake Michigan are likely to decline in the face of competition from young coho salmon, a species introduced from the Pacific coast in the mid-1960s. Juvenile coho are always larger than brook trout and brown trout during the first year of life, which they spend in Great Lakes tributaries. Moreover, the coho aggressively exclude the young trout from the most favorable feeding positions in a laboratory stream, even when all are the same size.

We still have much to learn about how nonnative trout eliminate native species from specific environments. However, the body of evidence indicates that introduced salmonids can have far-reaching and unanticipated effects. In our current efforts to preserve the biotic diversity of this planet, we should be ever careful when considering the transplantation of trout to regions where they were not indigenous, lest we cause the decline of yet another race of native salmonid, or for that matter, of any other of Earth's remaining species.

—Kurt D. Fausch

On the eastern slope of the Rocky Mountains, the greenback cutthroat (bottom), a federally threatened species, is being displaced by introduced brook trout (top).

Migration

A reindeer bone dating to about 12,000 B.C. bears a carving of an Atlantic salmon, a species closely related to North American trout. Indians living in the south-central valleys of what is now mainly British Columbia used traps, weirs, and other devices to capture migratory trout hundreds if not thousands of years before the arrival of European man. Yes, humans no doubt have known something of the migratory habits of trout for several thousand years and have used this knowledge to catch them for food.

And today we express wonder, even admiration, at the remarkable distance over which salmonids migrate. Some chinook salmon may swim nearly 4,000 kilometers (2,500 miles) up large river systems on the final leg of their adult spawning migration alone. Anyone who has seen the concentrations of salmon, at times numbering in the millions, that appear each autumn on the spawning grounds of a single river cannot fail to be amazed. Most other members of the salmonid family, particularly trout and char, also migrate, moving long distances and forming large concentrations on their spawning grounds.

But after our initial wonder at the distances and numbers involved and the apparent precision and regularity, as well as the antiquity of trout migrations, interesting and important questions occur to us. What, in fact, is migration? Why do trout migrate? Are there different types and stages of migration? Does

migration involve only long-distance movements in a horizontal plane? What mechanisms do trout use to accomplish these migrations? What are the consequences of migration?

WHAT MIGRATION IS

Obviously migration involves movement by animals from one place to another, though not necessarily movement over long distances or even mainly in a horizontal direction. For example, several species of salmonids, such as young sockeye salmon, migrate daily back and forth between the surface and depths of 9 to 15 meters (30 to 50 feet) or more in lakes. By migrating up to warm and rich feeding areas near the lake surface at dusk and back down to deeper, darker, cooler waters during the day, the young fish may exploit the food resources of the upper waters and avoid much of the risk of heavy predation from larger fish.

The first part of a definition of migration is that it involves a movement between two or more distinct and usually separate habitats: between, say, a feeding habitat, such as a lake or an ocean, and a reproductive or spawning habitat, such as a stream or a river.

Second, to be called migration, the movement must occur regularly. It doesn't just happen at any time but is reasonably predictable, whether it occurs daily, seasonally, annually, or at a specific stage in the life of the fish. Most fishermen (and poachers) know well the regular timing of particular runs of

Spawning migrations are the most common, since all trouts migrate some distance to spawn. The fungi on the fins of these Yellowstone cutthroat are a sign that the rigors of spawning are taking their toll.

salmon, trout, and char into certain streams. For example, the numerical midpoint in the run of salmon spawners migrating into the Fulton River in British Columbia occurred on the same day in five out of six years that it was checked accurately!

In a large river system there often are well-known "early" or "late," "summer" or "winter" spawning runs within a single species of trout or salmon, each appearing at a characteristic and reasonably predictable time every year. Steelhead trout, returning from the ocean a second time to spawn in rivers, apparently time their upstream migration precisely. Nevertheless, environmental conditions can, and often do, cause minor shifts in the timing of migrations. Unfavorable conditions, such as high temperatures or heavy silt loads in streams, can delay the entrance of trout and salmon runs into mouths of rivers or retard their progress upstream once they have entered.

A third point in our characterization of salmonid migration is that a large fraction of any population is involved in the movement at any one time, rather than just a few individuals sporadically. In large populations, of course, this means that many individuals may be migrating together, but the size of the group in itself is not a necessary feature of migration. Small streams may hold only a few trout, so that the total numbers migrating may be small. Nevertheless, migration can be an essential part of the life history of such populations.

A fourth key feature of trout migration is that at some stage it is an active and directed movement by the fish, not merely a passive drifting in the current or a random wandering in open waters. This is not to say that some phase or leg of a migration may not involve such movement. For example, young trout fry may move downstream into a lake largely by drifting at night with the current of an inlet river. But later, the adults migrate up the same river by an active and directed movement against the current.

Taken together, these four features of salmonid migration—movement, periodicity, involvement of most of the population, and directed action—imply a fifth: namely, that the movement phases and patterns eventually complete a cycle, or a return to habitat occupied by an earlier life stage of the fish. Thus the adult spawners usually return to a reproductive habitat from which they themselves started the migratory cycle as young emergent fry, sometimes years earlier.

The migratory cycle may be simple, involving movement between only two habitats, one used for reproduction by adults and the other for feeding by the young to subadult stages. The young of many species of trout move after emergence from their spawning bed in a stream to their first feeding habitat. Later, as juveniles or subadults, they move again to another feeding habitat—sometimes several—before they eventually return as adults to their spawning grounds. In a more complex migratory cycle, the fish could move

The effort of spawning killed this Lahontan cutthroat.

to a wintering habitat from the first feeding area, or the second (or more), and then back and forth seasonally between feeding and wintering habitat until maturity, when they would move to the spawning habitat. Trout do not necessarily die after their first spawning, and the surviving adults may move several times between spawning, feeding, and even wintering habitats, making the migratory cycle still more complex.

WHY TROUT MIGRATE

A large fraction of a population cannot move between habitats without incurring significant effort and loss. The individuals use up energy. Some of them encounter predators. Some of them succumb to diseases and stress. The benefits of migration to the population as a whole must outweigh such costs as these if the process is not to be selectively removed by evolution.

Upstream effort. Although downstream migration of young trout probably does not demand too much energy within stream or river systems with moderate current and few lakes, the return upstream movement of adults undoubtedly does. In rivers with a high gradient or in reaches with steep rapids or falls, upstream movement requires that the fish expend large amounts of energy even though they use pathways where flow is least and jump at locations where they gain hydraulic boosts from the upwelling turbulence. Most salmonid spawners migrating upstream do not feed, so they must rely en-

tirely on their body fat and protein for energy. Over long migratory routes upriver, the spawners on average spend energy from these limited reserves at nearly the maximum rate they can maintain over the course. They have little margin for emergency demands or for delays or stress.

Apart from swimming, other activities, both physical and physiological, use up precious energy. Often there are marked differences in temperature, salinity, and other environmental conditions between habitats, and the fish must develop the physiological abilities and anatomical equipment to adjust to such changes. For example, moving from fresh to salt water, or vice versa, requires major changes in their excretory system. Furthermore, the fish must operate this equipment, so it expends more energy keeping its metabolism in synchrony.

The migrants also expose themselves to a new set of predators and diseases that occur in the different habitats to which the population moves. Juveniles coming from a small stream face a much greater range in number and size of predators when they reach a lake, estuary, or coastal marine habitat than they encountered "back home." And maturing adults from the ocean or from lakes face quite different predators, bears, for example, as well as diseases when they approach upriver spawning grounds, compared with those of the larger bodies of water. Although predators usually do not kill the whole population, diseases such as columnaris can eliminate a large fraction of the adult salmonids before they spawn.

On the other hand, young trout migrating off their spawning grounds in a small river or stream usually reach far richer feeding areas than those they encountered upon emergence from their egg and alevin developmental habitat. Their scales will tell the story, developing more widely spaced growth rings, called circuli, after the stream-reared fry enter more productive lake or estuarine waters and begin to grow faster. The spacing between circuli allows us to distinguish between phases of growth in streams, lakes, and estuaries. By increasing their growth rate, the migratory fish can increase their overall biological fitness—the ability to contribute offspring to the next generation. Larger fish usually survive better when competition or predation is severe. Furthermore, larger females can carry a larger number of eggs at maturity. The stream-resident form in most species of trout is smaller than the form that migrates to lakes; these in turn are smaller than the form that migrates to estuaries or to the open ocean.

Timing. Rich feeding areas may be available or inhabitable only at certain periods in the year, and the fish must enter and leave those areas at appropriate times to gain the benefits without severe costs, including death. For example, after Arctic char migrate to sea, they spend only one to two months there feeding in the productive coastal waters before the sea water becomes too cold and they must return to warmer, spring-fed fresh water to overwinter. But in temperate latitudes, sea-run brook trout may leave the sea in spring to avoid warm summer temperatures. Young brown trout in small coastal streams of Norway migrate to the sea shortly after emergence to avoid low summer flows.

In addition, trout may adjust the time they enter spawning streams and arrive on the spawning grounds so that they usually find conditions that favor successful spawning and development of young. Those migrating to warm streams that are lake outlets spawn much earlier than those in cool streams that are lake inlets, and the young thereby emerge and reach feeding habitats to coincide with the best food production.

In large river systems, migrant trout use

The long migratory journey makes fish vulnerable to predators, which quickly learn where to wait.

ERWIN & PEGGY BAUER

Waterfalls are one of the barriers that migrating fish must negotiate to get to their spawning areas.

completely or become dangerous traps for fish that remain there. Often trout can enter rivers and ascend rapids or falls to upstream spawning areas only when the flow of water is within a particular range of discharge. At levels too high or too low, the rivers may be impassable, so the trout must time their migration closely to use such habitats.

Homing. Trout migrate to the spawning grounds used by their parents—that is, they home—by an instinct that we do not yet thoroughly understand. Biological promptings—hormonal changes—and a series of other cues allow them to gather at the mouth of the river system down which they earlier swam as juveniles. At a signal undetectable to us, they begin their arduous journey to return to their natal stream and often to the exact spawning grounds where they earlier had hatched and emerged from the gravel as fry.

We do not know for sure but we strongly suspect that trout use several senses to remember cues that guide them along the way. Their lateral lines may tell them that these are familiar currents and that the hydraulic conditions are the same ones they drifted through on their downstream journey. Their eyes may tell them that the lay of the riverbed is the same. Most important, their noses tell them that the odors are those of the tributaries that lead to their destination stream, the one to which they are returning to complete the cycle of reproduction.

Sometimes, however, trout misread their homing cues and stray from their intended route. Through such migratory "errors," the species can expand its territory as the trout colonize new areas, especially in northern regions where deglaciation is still occurring. Straying also permits them to recolonize areas where local catastrophic events, such as landslides or temporary blockages, had decimated or eliminated the species.

Migration can provide a sizable transport of nutrients from regions of higher production such as lakes, estuaries, and oceans, to regions of lower production, such as small headwater streams. This increased fertility, in turn, can enhance the growth and survival of the offspring of the migrant adults. The process begins with the spawned-out adults. Many trout—though not necessarily all of

tributaries for spawning, rearing, and feeding in temporal and spatial patterns that seem most conducive to high reproductive success. Where stream spawning grounds are limited and density of the spawning population is high, the young trout migrate downstream to lake rearing habitat directly after emergence from the gravel, thus avoiding severe competition in an environment limited in space and food.

Some areas that are unsuitable as feeding habitats and spawning grounds for months at a time then become available for perhaps only a few weeks. For example, rich feeding areas can develop temporarily in river backwaters or side channels or on seasonally flooded lake shores that later either dry up

TROUT

them—die after spawning, and where the spawning population is large, the gradual decomposition of the bodies can significantly enrich the habitat.

MIGRATION PHASES

Spawning migrations. Usually the most visible, colorful, and dramatic part of the migratory cycle of trout populations is that associated with their movements as maturing adults from a feeding habitat to a spawning habitat. This movement may be one of long distance through many habitats, as when adult steelhead trout move from the open ocean up to the mouth of a major river system, and from there up the river to their spawning grounds in the headwaters of a tributary.

In large river systems there may be genetically different stocks of sea-run trout. Some migrate hundreds of kilometers upriver to their spawning habitat, whereas others spawn in tributaries only a few kilometers from the sea. Different stocks may enter the river at quite different times of the year, summer runs and winter runs of steelhead, for example. Within this same species, some spawning populations may migrate shorter distances yet, as in the forms of lake-dwelling rainbow trout that spawn in streams.

Even more precisely, the lake-dwelling populations may be split into subgroups, some of which migrate upstream to spawn in inlet tributaries and others that migrate downstream at a different time to spawn in an outlet stream. Still in the same species, there may be forms that never leave the lake, spawning in special regions of the lake shoreline after moving only a few hundred meters from their feeding areas within the lake. Some stream-resident forms of rainbow trout move even shorter distances upstream or downstream to spawn. Brown trout, cutthroat trout, and several species of char also show this wide range in migratory behavior.

By using ultrasonic tracking devices implanted in steelhead returning to spawning rivers, we are finding that the adults move erratically on a horizontal plane as they approach a river mouth along the seacoast and also that they make frequent and rapid dives of up to 15 meters (50 feet) to depths where the temperature cools sharply. These movements may help them to locate the smell of water coming from their home stream. Once well within the river, the adults display a much more directional pattern of upstream movement and, even when experimentally displaced, they show a high success in homing ability to their natal spawning site, up to 87 percent in one recent study.

Feeding migrations. Feeding migrations involve movement of trout to habitats where food resources usually are richer than at their spawning areas. In contrast to spawning migrations, feeding migrations commonly occur early in life when the young are small and inconspicuous and usually when streams and rivers are high and turbid.

The numbers of young migrating at this

Large numbers of colorful brook trout making a fall spawning run are a dramatic sight. In selecting spawning grounds they seek upwellings of groundwater. Unlike most other salmonids, brook trout can spawn in lakes and ponds as well as in streams.

TROUT

Left: *Adult anadromous species of trout returning from the sea must battle rapids and other obstacles as they head upstream toward the spawning grounds in which they themselves began life.*

Middle: *Smolts move out from lakes, rivers, and estuaries to the sea. Most species will spend several years there before returning to spawn. The ocean offers them access to greater food supplies, but also increases exposure to predators.*

Right: *As cold weather approaches, some trout migrate from streams into small lakes in search of warmer water temperatures and more reliable food sources.*

time are much greater than those of the adult spawners that produced them, but few people see this stage of migration, despite its great importance to production of the next generation of adult spawners. For example, in the large Fraser River system of British Columbia, people flock to witness the concentration of adult salmonid migrants on their spawning grounds, which in some years exceeds five million adults, but few see or even are aware of the migration of young, which in some years may involve more than 300 million fish!

Similarly, the spectacular upstream spawning run each spring in British Columbia of several hundred large Kootenay Lake rainbow trout, many weighing more than 10 kilograms (22 pounds), attracts many viewers, and rightly so. However, virtually no one would come to watch (even if, indeed, they could) the gradual downstream lakeward migration of the hundreds of thousands of young trout, occurring as it does, mainly at night, when the river is high and dirty with silt.

The feeding migration itself may be divided into two or more stages before the young reach the feeding habitat where they put on the major part of their growth to reach adulthood. For example, young steelhead, after emergence from the spawning beds, first move short distances to feeding habitats within the river, and some remain there for several years before embarking on the next major stage of their feeding migration as smolts down to the ocean. Ocean survival of smolts depends on their size, so the larger the smolt, the more likely it will survive to maturity.

Feeding migrations of young trout from spawning streams to lake rearing habitats include downstream movement from inlet tributaries (largely at night and by fry that have recently emerged), upstream movement from lake outlets (largely during the day and by older fry), and complex patterns of both downstream and upstream movement in tributaries of lake outlet streams. The young of lake-spawning populations of trout, upon emergence from the spawning gravel, move only short distances as they disperse from the parental spawning habitat into their feeding habitat within the lake. Young from stream-dwelling trout populations also may move little after they first disperse from the spawning habitat.

Wintering migrations. Some migrations involve movements not to spawning or feeding habitats but rather to habitats that are refuges from severe environmental conditions common in temperate and arctic regions during winter. Wintering migrations

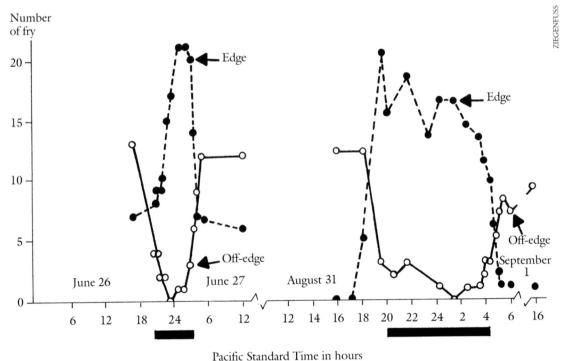

In Loon Creek, British Columbia, the number of rainbow trout fry counted along the creek edges increased significantly during periods of darkness (indicated by solid, black, horizontal bars), and decreased dramatically during daylight hours. Very few fry stay out towards the middle of the creek during the night. The poorer light conditions at night may force them to the edge areas to orient themselves in the current by touch.

have long been known to occur in subadult and adult populations of Arctic char. Each autumn the fish leave coastal marine feeding grounds and migrate into rivers and lakes where they overwinter for several months. Dolly Varden char, brown trout, brook trout, and probably also cutthroat trout make annual wintering migrations of less duration into or within fresh water.

Juvenile trout as well as subadult and adult stages may be involved in wintering migrations. Young cutthroat and steelhead trout migrate into small tributaries of the Clearwater River in Washington during late autumn, apparently to avoid the strong winter freshets in the main river, as do juvenile cutthroat trout in Carnation Creek, British Columbia. Small lakes in a river system also may provide important overwintering habitat for cutthroat trout and Dolly Varden char.

As we gather more detailed information on particular species and stocks, we are finding that wintering migrations are far more common and widespread than we had thought.

Other migrations. Trout, especially young trout in rearing or feeding habitats, may shift their distribution on a regular, predictable basis between day and night. In lakes they often move up and down in the water column, in other cases onshore or offshore, and such movements may be related to feeding opportunities. In streams the trout may move onshore at night, where they remain close to the bottom, and then offshore during the day. Such a shift is well known in young rainbow trout that are temporary stream residents and may be associated with maintaining position in the current by tactile cues during darkness when the visual cues used during the day are lost.

HOW TROUT MIGRATE

The mechanisms trout use to complete their migratory cycles have sparked intense study and research for nearly a century. Whatever guidance cues are involved, the fish depend upon interactions between their sensory capabilities (visual, olfactory, and others), their physiological capabilities (locomotory, osmoregulatory, and others), their recent and present environmental conditions (water temperature, currents, light, and others), their genetically controlled—innate—behavior, and their previous experience and learned behavior. Furthermore, we should not expect to find simple explanations for most migratory stages, nor the same or single explanation for all of the stages.

Let's follow the migration of trout from the spawning bed in a small stream into a river system with a large lake, into a mainstem river to the estuary, into the open ocean, eventually back to the river mouth again, up the main stem to the appropriate tributary, and onto the patch of spawning gravel out of which the adult trout originally emerged as a young fry. Of course any one species or stock would not necessarily use all the mechanisms we will discuss, but we can illustrate the range of potential capabilities in salmonid fishes.

Although salmonid alevins make small vertical and horizontal movements while still in their gravel nests, the first opportunity for much movement comes as they finally emerge from the spawning bed. This event usually occurs at night and places the young, weakly swimming fry in an environment conducive to downstream transport. The timing of their downstream transport is strongly controlled by light both over a 24-hour period and seasonally. Periods of bright moonlight can sharply reduce the numbers of trout migrating down streams at night, whereas dense nocturnal cloud cover can increase such movement. The nightly period of downstream migration is much shorter in June than in September because of seasonal changes in day length.

Physical factors, such as water temperature, and biological factors, such as stock genetics, also influence the timing. Periods of warm water temperature can reduce downstream movement of trout fry in inlet tributaries and promote upstream movement in lake outlets. Particular stocks of trout may be genetically programmed so their young migrate downstream or upstream in certain types of streams.

Although downstream movement of fry may occur largely by passive drift in the water current, this certainly is not the whole explanation. Using an infrared viewing apparatus, I have observed rainbow trout fry actively swimming downstream in their migration at night. Fry from stream-resident populations of trout, and particularly those from lake-outlet spawning populations, greatly restrict early downstream movement and later may begin to move upstream largely during daylight hours.

Water temperature, light intensity, photoperiod, and innate stock differences in behavior seem important in control of such migratory stages. With stream-resident populations, whether temporarily or permanently so, the seasonal wintering migrations to refuge habitat are triggered by decreases in water temperature and day length.

Juvenile trout that undertake long-distance migration toward the sea through large lake and river systems make early physiological adjustments that prepare them for living in sea water. These include external changes, such as a silvery body coloration, which covers the parr marks, and internal changes, such as adjustments in kidney function to cope with the higher salinity. The changes operate under control by both external environmental conditions, day length and temperature, for example, and internal physiological (hormonal) conditions. Furthermore, during this downstream journey, the juveniles apparently learn and remember the sequential and specific differences in water chemistry (organic odors) of tributaries along their route, which play an important role in their return upstream migration as maturing adults.

If trout and char in their open-water migrations through large lakes and in the ocean use similar guidance mechanisms to those of the closely related Pacific salmon, then they probably could navigate by using the sun and other celestial bodies as a compass. It is even possible that they can detect deflections in Earth's magnetic field resulting from large-scale oceanic current patterns, and use these cues in open-sea navigation.

The idea that salmonids use sequential olfactory information gathered on their migration down a river system as juveniles to guide them back up that system as adults to their home stream has had a long history and still seems to be generally supported. Nevertheless, it is by no means the only mechanism used, and alternate theories or modifications have been proposed, especially those first put forward mainly by several Norwegian scien-

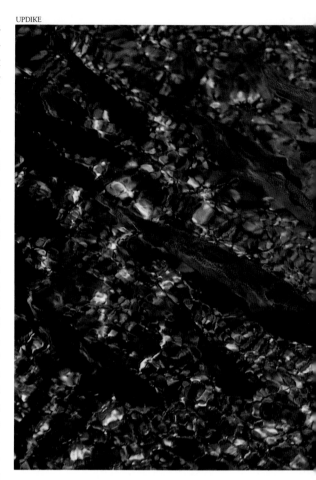

tists. They suggested that nonmigratory fractions of the populations emit specific odor trails, chiefly from their skin mucus, which guide the migratory returning adults upstream. There is no doubt that trout can detect and probably use group-specific odors not only to locate strains within their own population in a spawning stream but also to mark local substrate types that have proven suitable for spawning.

Some of the mechanisms that trout use are more important than others during a particular phase in a migration. At most stages several means of guidance can be used so that if one "fails," as when heavy cloud cover preempts the use of celestial compass mechanisms, others may be brought into play. And, no doubt, as our understanding of their fascinating migrations grows, we will learn other intriguing ways by which trout and char accomplish their incredible and usually precise navigation.

CONSEQUENCES OF MIGRATION

There are several ways by which the migratory behavior of trout enhances their abun-

Timing it right

*T*he migration to spawning areas may begin several months before spawning, as with steelhead, or may precede spawning by only a few days. Summer-run steelhead return to fresh water in summer, migrate most of the way to their spawning areas by late fall, spend the winter in large rivers, and then resume their migration in spring when water temperatures increase. The spawning migrations of bull trout in some large lake drainages of Idaho and Montana are an example of a fall-spawning char that often migrates into the tributaries during spring or early summer during the spring snow-melt runoff, spends the summer in large pools near spawning areas, and spawns in late summer and fall.

The timing of migrations by trout and char to spawning areas is often regulated by water temperatures and flows. Time of entry into tributaries in spring by mature rainbow and cutthroat trout living in lakes can be delayed by cold weather that keeps the water cold. Steelhead do not enter some of the small Pacific coastal streams until fall rains begin and flows increase. Summer-run steelhead migrating to the headwaters of the Columbia River delay entering the Snake River in late summer if water temperatures are too warm, and they overwinter in the large rivers downstream from their spawning streams because water temperatures and ice conditions are unsuitable in their natal streams during the winter.

The differences in timing of maturation and migration to spawning areas observed in trout and char have evolved, in most cases, in response to the specific environment used by each stock of fish. Transplanted stocks of fish can be less successful than native stocks in reproducing themselves if they come from a dissimilar environment and have not had a chance to adapt to conditions in the new environment.

— *Theodore C. Bjornn*

dance and overall fitness. But the advantages gained by the migratory behavior of trout also bring some disadvantages, both for them and for us. The migratory urge builds up dense concentrations of young and adults in locations where they may be heavily exploited by predators, including humans. Furthermore, aside from the problems of predators and disease the trout encounter, the long distances that many migratory populations travel expose them to a range of problems, such as dams and diversions, inflows of toxic chemicals and other pollutants, severe changes in river flow and lake level, dikes and channelizations, disturbances of estuarine marshes, coastal oil spills, and offshore driftnet or longline fisheries.

In addition, migrating trout may transport dangerous chemicals in their flesh far beyond where they were originally dumped, posing a human health hazard.

We can continue to enjoy the many benefits of migratory trout only if we expand our efforts to protect the species and the habitats essential to their survival.

— *Thomas Gordon Northcote*

Anadromous trout

Anadromous trouts and chars are found in the Atlantic, Pacific and Arctic oceans and in the rivers throughout North America that flow into them. In addition, several anadromous salmonids have been transplanted successfully to the Great Lakes. There they continue to behave as anadromous fish, moving between the lakes and tributaries where they spawn.

There are twelve species of salmonids in North America that are in part or entirely anadromous. Included among them are steelhead, sea-run cutthroat trout, brown trout, Arctic char, Dolly Varden char, and eastern brook trout.

The anadromous populations of many of these species often live sympatrically, that is, in the same environment though in different niches, with resident populations of the same species. Anadromous salmonids still occur throughout much of their original range, but their numbers in some of the original locations have been greatly reduced by overfishing, habitat degradation, and natural factors, such as predators and disease. The original ranges of these fish have been extended in some cases and their numbers are continually supplemented by the stocking of hatchery fish.

ANADROMY

Anadromy is a form of diadromy. Both terms refer to the life-history trait of migrating between fresh water and salt water (the Great Lakes species excepted). Anadromy, however, refers more specifically to a stronger preference for salt water during the major feeding and growth phase. After hatching in a freshwater stream and rearing for a period of time, the anadromous species migrate to the marine environment, where they mature. They eventually return as adults to fresh water—usually the natal stream—primarily for spawning.

The trait of anadromy can be obligate, which means that it occurs on a definite natural schedule, or it can be optional, which means that the population merely is capable of it and that there is considerable variation in the schedule. Rounsefell in 1958 indicated that the salmon, trouts, and chars are anadromous to different degrees, from wholly freshwater residents to obligate anadromous fishes. In the family Salmonidae, the bull trout, lake trout, and golden trout are wholly freshwater residents without any anadromous populations. Rounsefell considers the other chars and trouts as well as Atlantic salmon optionally anadromous because all of them exist naturally as distinct races in both the freshwater and anadromous forms. Of these, the Atlantic salmon has the most consistently anadromous life cycle.

The Pacific salmon are the most obligatory anadromous salmonids, although hatchery-stocked chinook, coho, and sockeye salmon all have adapted to wholly freshwater existence and kokanee, a wholly freshwater variation of sockeye, have existed historically in nature without human intervention.

Rounsefell considered chum and pink salmon as obligate anadromous fishes. However, pink salmon have been introduced successfully into the Great Lakes, thereby bypassing the "obligatory" seawater phase of their life cycle.

Rounsefell, in his 1958 review, noted that there appears to be a tendency toward an entirely lacustrine (lake-inhabiting) existence in all anadromous populations and conversely the possibility that exclusively lacustrine salmonids could become anadromous. Non-anadromous members of the Salmonidae family currently are thought to be land-locked relatives of the anadromous species, according to a 1987 report by McDowall. If this is the case, truly non-anadromous species, such as the lake trout, could "revert" to an anadromous phase under the correct environmental circumstances. This hypothesis is supported by the results, reported in 1989, of work by Fraley and Shepard, who observed that non-anadromous bull trout in Flathead Lake, Montana, have migratory tendencies, leaving the lake in the spring and moving into tributary rivers to spawn. Strenberg, in his 1987 review, noted that non-anadromous lake trout, as well as bull trout, occasionally swim from lakes and up rivers to spawn.

EVOLUTION

Anadromy probably developed as described by Gross in 1987, whereby temperate freshwater fishes evolved into anadromous fishes. Freshwater fishes in cold temperate and subpolar regions would more likely cross into marine water as optional wanderers than would freshwater fishes in tropical waters, because in the temperate and subpolar regions, marine productivity often exceeds that of fresh waters, whereas in the tropics, freshwater productivity often exceeds that of marine waters.

An amphidromous habit, a trait that allows growth in both fresh water and salt water with feeding and growth on the return migration before reproduction, could develop in fish that wandered from fresh water into marine water. Subsequently, continued selection could give rise to an anadromous life cycle, in which the anadromous fish would grow most at sea. Finally, natural selection may favor the occurrence of the reproductive phase in the habitat of adult growth, because if the fish becomes wholly marine, the costs of migration back to fresh water have been removed from the biological equation. Therefore, Gross suggested that some marine fishes are of freshwater origin and that anadromy is the next-to-the-last step in the evolutionary development of an exclusively marine existence.

In fact, he said, some populations of pink salmon could be evolving toward an exclusively marine existence. He cited the fact that some of them spawn in saline estuaries rather than in rivers and spend the rest of their lives at sea as evidence to support that statement, and he maintains that such an example supports the hypothesis that anadromy is a step toward total marine existence.

The salmonids are an extremely adaptable group in which anadromy is probably dictated by geography and environment as well as by genetic variation. Differences in life histories as well as physical characteristics, such as growth, among the various anadromous salmonids change with latitude.

For example, northern populations of brook trout are more often anadromous than southern ones. Anadromous brown trout, on the other hand, grow larger in more southern latitudes. In northern latitudes, steelhead spend more time in both fresh water and salt water and grow larger, and sea-run cutthroat trout and Arctic char are wholly anadromous.

Truly anadromous fish migrate to saltwater as juveniles; they must have access to the ocean. Land-locked anadromous fish may display migratory behavior, moving between lakes and the tributaries where they spawn.

Overview of cycle

The life cycles of anadromous trout and char have one characteristic in common: all the anadromous salmonids of North America bury their eggs in redds, or nests, which they construct in gravel. The construction of the redds is similar, although the number of eggs deposited varies among species and according to the size of the female. Within a few weeks the eggs hatch into alevins among the gravel. The time of hatching varies with region, habitat, spawning season, water temperature, dissolved oxygen, and sediment load (fines) in the gravel.

The juvenile fish rear in their natal streams or lakes for a period that extends from fry emergence until their seaward migration. Although this rearing period is usually from one to four years for salmon and trout, actual behavior and rearing time in fresh water varies among species and among races and populations within species, according to a 1987 review by Randall and colleagues. The juvenile rearing period may be less than a year or as long as eight years. Anadromous char have the more extended and irregular period of freshwater rearing, in contrast with salmon and, to some degree, trout. Trout have a more extended and varied freshwater rearing period than do the most obligate anadromous members of the Salmonidae family, the Pacific salmon, but a shorter and more regular rearing period than the char. According to a review made by Pauley and colleagues in 1986, the freshwater rearing period of steelhead can be shortened from the normal two to three years in wild fish to only one year in hatchery fish.

After rearing in fresh water, the juvenile fish undergo a process called smoltification as they ready themselves to migrate into salt water. Few fry survive to reach the open sea because predation, disease, and habitat alterations diminish their populations. Usually less than 1 percent of the fry survive to return as adults to spawn.

At sea

After migrating to the sea as smolts, anadromous salmonids spend a major portion of their lives, usually two to three years, in salt water and attain most of their size, length,

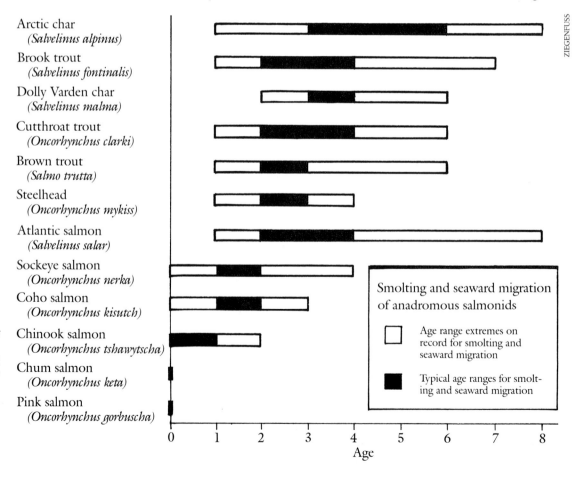

ZIEGENFUSS

Arctic char
(*Salvelinus alpinus*)

Brook trout
(*Salvelinus fontinalis*)

Dolly Varden char
(*Salvelinus malma*)

Cutthroat trout
(*Oncorhynchus clarki*)

Brown trout
(*Salmo trutta*)

Steelhead
(*Oncorhynchus mykiss*)

Atlantic salmon
(*Salvelinus salar*)

Sockeye salmon
(*Oncorhynchus nerka*)

Coho salmon
(*Oncorhynchus kisutch*)

Chinook salmon
(*Oncorhynchus tshawytscha*)

Chum salmon
(*Oncorhynchus keta*)

Pink salmon
(*Oncorhynchus gorbuscha*)

Smolting and seaward migration of anadromous salmonids

☐ Age range extremes on record for smolting and seaward migration

■ Typical age ranges for smolting and seaward migration

0 1 2 3 4 5 6 7 8

Age

Anadromous trout and char species of the Salmoninae subfamily generally spend more of their youth in freshwater than the Pacific salmon species, and journey to salt water at a later age. Sockeye, coho, chinook, chum and pink salmon all smolt and migrate seaward much earlier in life; chum and pink salmon spend almost no time at all in freshwater.

and weight in the marine environment. For example, a 21- to 26-centimeter (8- to 10-inch) steelhead smolt may weigh about .1 kilogram (.25 pound) upon entering salt water; two years later, it returns as an adult that is usually more than 61 centimeters (24 inches) long and weighs 4 to 5 kilograms (8 to 12 pounds). By contrast, a typical stream-dwelling rainbow grows to about 2 kilograms (4.4 pounds) in four years, and a lake-dwelling rainbow may grow to 2 kilograms (4.4 pounds) in four years in a lake with plentiful food.

Average size and the duration of residence in salt water vary among species and also among races and populations within species. (Many of the anadromous salmonids that have successfully adapted to the Great Lakes substitute an extended stay in the large open waters of these lakes for the marine part of their life cycle.) Pauley and colleagues found in a review, that in steelhead, size at first maturity is a function of the number of years spent in salt water. A 1989 study by Trotter indicated the same condition for sea-run cutthroat trout.

Migrations at sea vary from distant, high-seas migrations of brown trout, observed by Solomon in 1982, and steelhead, which Pauley and colleagues reported in 1986, to the short, localized marine excursions of sea-run cutthroat trout near their natal streams. Dempson and Kristofferson in 1987 observed that Arctic char migrate for brief periods and short distances to feed. The tendency to stay close to the natal stream appears to be stronger in anadromous char than in the other anadromous salmonids. This tendency has been noted in the Dolly Varden char by Armstrong and Morrow in 1980; in the Arctic char by Johnson in 1980; and in the brook trout by both Power in 1980 and Naiman and colleagues in 1987.

Return from sea

As mature adults, anadromous salmonids migrate into fresh water to spawn. Homing to the natal stream by the adult fish is quite specific in most, if not all, anadromous salmonids, according to Brannon in his 1982 review of homing mechanisms. This appears to be true for char, such as the Dolly Varden char studied by Armstrong and Morrow in

1980, and trout, such as the sea-run cutthroat studied by Johnston in 1982. However, in certain populations of the Arctic char, adults may stray considerably from their natal streams.

The time between hatching and returning to spawn as adults varies considerably. Among steelhead, it may be as short as two years in some hatchery stocks or as long as seven in some wild stocks. Upon returning to their natal streams where life began when the eggs were laid, the adult fish usually spawn and the life cycle is completed. After spawning, all char and trout, including Atlantic salmon, may live to repeat the cycle a second or third time, whereas all Pacific salmon die after their first spawning. Total life expectancy varies. Pink salmon live only two years, but Arctic char live up to sixteen years, according to Sternberg in his 1987 review of North American game fish. The average life expectancy for most anadromous salmonids is three to seven years. The more obligate anadromous salmonids tend to have shorter life expectancies than the optionally anadromous salmonids.

Pacific salmon species have evolved to be strongly anadromous. Pink salmon tend to maintain anadromous behaviors and life cycles even when isolated from the sea, migrating from lakes into streams to spawn and die. Such obligately anadromous fish tend to have shorter life spans than those Salmoninae subfamily members that can adopt nonanadromous life cycles when landlocked. Under normal conditions, Pacific salmon species migrate seaward at a comparatively early age, and die shortly after they return to freshwater and spawn.

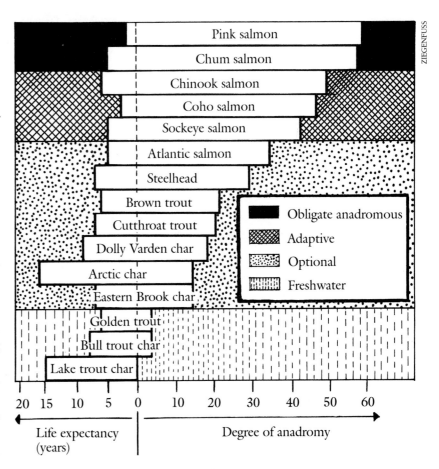

Juvenile rainbows and steelhead are identical until the steelhead (above) undergoes smoltification. The silvery color indicates that this trout is bound for the sea.

PARR TO SMOLT

Young anadromous salmon, trout, and char that migrate to sea change from parr to smolt. The process is a series of changes that transform the characteristically bottom-dwelling young salmonids into pelagic (open-water) smolts fully prepared to enter salt water. According to a 1976 report by Hoar, it's a reversible process, and fish that are prevented access to sea water will reassume the appearance and physiological characteristics of the freshwater parr.

Two morphological changes—in color and shape—are associated with smoltification. The freshwater parr is readily identified by oval-shaped, dark-pigmented melanin bars, called parr marks, on the lateral surface and perpendicular to the lateral line. These marks become obstructed by the accumulation of guanines and purines in the scales and superficial dermal layers, which cause the characteristic silver appearance of the transformed seawater smolt. Changes in body form and condition index (a ratio of length to weight) accompany this color change and result in a slenderer, more streamlined fish.

An increased tolerance for salinity occurs in smolting fish at various minimum sizes, depending upon the species involved. In the more obligate anadromous species of Salmonidae, such as the pink and chum salmon, this size may be only 4 to 5 centimeters (about 2 inches) or even smaller. In the less obligate species, such as the brook trout, the minimum size may be 17 to 20 centimeters (7 to 8 inches). The size of downstream migrant smolts may vary with the age at which they smolt. For example, in sea-run cutthroat trout, according to the 1989 review by Trotter, age-two smolts were 16.5 centimeters (6.5 inches), age-three smolts were 20.3 centimeters (8 inches), and age-four smolts were 21.6 centimeters (8.5 inches).

The development of a preference for salinity is associated with the smoltification process. The ability to osmoregulate, or maintain the balance of fluid in the tissues and control the diffusion of salts across the kidney and gill membranes, at different salinities depends upon the size and age of the individual fish as well as the species. It is not known

whether a gradual increase in salinity enhances the adaptation of the fish to salt water.

Migration to sea water also is associated with smoltification. Before smolting, the parr establish and maintain bottom-feeding territories in specific stream sections through aggressive behavior toward other individuals. At smoltification, the young fish abandon their territories, decrease their aggressive behavior, form loose groups, or aggregations, and move into more open water. The smolts begin to move downstream to reach sea water. Although daylight migrations occur, the downstream migrating smolts prefer to move at night, possibly to protect themselves from predators, because they are in more open water than they occupied as parr.

Numerous biochemical and physiological changes take place during smoltification. In fresh water, anadromous fish are hypertonic. That is, their body fluids have higher ion (salt) concentrations than the surrounding water, so their bodies tend to absorb water. Consequently, they acquire water passively without drinking, primarily through the gill and oral tissues. At the same time, they lose ions across the gill membranes as well as in the feces and urine. To maintain isotonicity, which is the appropriate balance between ions and water, they need to excrete water and conserve the ions. They balance the uptake of water and the loss of ions by producing a relatively salt-free, dilute urine and reabsorbing ions through the kidney tubules.

However, upon entering sea water, trout become hypotonic. That is, the body has fewer ions than the surrounding water, and consequently its fluids tend to be drawn out through the gills and body surfaces, and salts tend to diffuse inward through the gills. So, to maintain isotonicity and prevent dehydration in the ocean, trout drink sea water. To conserve the water they take in, they reduce urine flow and reabsorb water, rather than ions, through the kidney tubules. To rid themselves of the excess ions, they produce urine that is highly saline and feces with large quantities of salt. At the same time, their gill membranes become less permeable to reduce the influx of the ions from the sea water, and they develop more chloride cells to excrete the excess ions from the body.

Several hormones appear to be involved in smoltification and osmoregulation. Endocrine activities occur in the pituitary, thyroid, and interrenal glands, the pancreatic islets, the Stannius corpuscles, and the neurosecretory gland.

McCormick and Saunders in 1987 indicated that the physiological changes associated with the transformation of parr to smolt can occur independently of one another and that the timing of these changes appears in different sequences in the various anadromous salmonids.

Adults

Anatomical, behavioral, and hormonal alterations occur in spawning anadromous salmonids, and they begin in the ocean with

The anadromous Pacific salmon parr wears dark, oval parr marks during its early freshwater days. As the young parr undergoes the physiological changes necessary for successful life in salt water, the parr marks are obscured. The new smolt becomes silvery and streamlined, and migrates to the ocean where it will grow to adulthood. Upon returning to freshwater, the silvery sheen gives way to vivid colors, especially in the males.

Sea-run Arctic char undergo dramatic color changes when they leave the sea to spawn.

the onset of sexual maturity. The degree of change varies among the species of anadromous salmonids, but the changes are most noticeable in the Pacific salmon. Physical changes are more pronounced in the males of the species. Their jaws lengthen, and the lower jaw develops a large upturned hook, or kype. Often the upper jaw also becomes hooked.

The adult fish are still silvery when they enter fresh water. However, they eventually lose this sheen and undergo dramatic changes in color, which usually are more intense and notable in the males. In most cases, the colors are considerably more pronounced. The colors of the char (brook trout, Dolly Varden, and Arctic char) become darker and more brilliant, and their whitish bellies become orange, pinkish, or red. The leading edges of the fins become intensely white. The trout (steelhead, sea-run cutthroat, and brown trout) lose their overall silvery color and become darker. Certain colorings on the trout, such as the red band along the lateral line of the steelhead and the orange fins and reddish slash under the throat of the sea-run cutthroat, may become more intense.

The behavior of the adults changes as spawning time approaches. Both males and females begin a relentless move upstream toward suitable spawning areas. Extremely aggressive behavior occurs among the males. The female picks a nest site and her nest building is accompanied by the male courtship. The mating sequence can go on for many hours. Both spawning partners will aggressively chase away other females and males and jack salmon that intrude.

All of the glands appear to be affected as the anadromous salmonids become sexually mature. However, the pituitary and the adrenal glands are especially important, according to Childerhose and Trim in their 1979 book on salmon biology. In a 1989 study, Dickhoff and colleagues demonstrated that the levels of both thyroxine and insulin increased in Atlantic salmon before the onset of reproductive maturation. The levels of these hormones were higher in male fish than in females during final maturation and entry into fresh water. Thyroid hormone changes during maturation have been observed in several species of anadromous salmonids. The reason for the higher levels of plasma hormones in male fish is not entirely clear. However, Dickhoff and colleagues hypothesize that higher hormone levels in male fish protect against early depletion of energy reserves needed for the lengthier spawning ritual of the males.

COEXISTENCE

Many streams contain several species of both anadromous salmonids and resident trout, with different life histories and preferences for slightly different habitats. The interactions between trout species probably has been most studied between rainbow-steelhead and cutthroat trout. Preferences for different environmental conditions, such as cover, spawning substrate, food organisms, water depth, and water velocity tend to isolate the different species in time and space from one another during their period of freshwater residency. This separation of the species is termed habitat segregation. For example, steelhead use the main streams and their larger tributaries and occupy waters of normal velocities, and the smaller sea-run cutthroat trout move into the headwaters of streams and the smaller tributaries and are found in water of very low velocity in the main streams. Sternberg in 1987 noted that sea-run brook trout will use lake shores with adequate spring upwelling to avoid competing with other spawning trout and char in streams.

The ability of two closely related species, such as cutthroat trout and rainbow trout, to exist sympatrically and yet maintain their species integrity generally has been attributed to the spatial and temporal separation of spawning adults and not to a genetic incompatibility between species. To illustrate this point, it has been noted that steelhead tend to breed and rear in larger, swifter streams than do sea-run cutthroat trout, yet Campton and Utter in 1985 reported evidence of genetic interbreeding between sea-run cutthroat trout and steelhead in some rivers that flow into Puget Sound. Since no two species of trout or char can occupy the same ecological niche at once, differences in habitat preference, morphology, physiology, and behavior have evolved to reduce competitive interactions among the various populations and to provide for the greatest production and survival of each group.

In his 1987 review of salmonid interspecific competition and habitat segregation, Hearn indicated that competition for space replaces the direct competition for food, cover, and other resources. He also noted that even though stream-dwelling salmonids are generalists that usually exhibit considerable dietary overlap, individual fish compete for stream positions based on the value of those positions as food acquisition sites or as cover or access to cover. When competing for preferred stream positions, individuals of different species interact aggressively using similar agonistic displays. In their 1979 book, Childerhose and Trim indicated that if insufficient food is present for the number of fish already present, newly emergent fry will be forced out by aggressive older and larger fry of the same species protecting their own territories. Hearn notes that brook, brown, cutthroat, and rainbow trout all formed localized dominance hierarchies, which confer to dominant individuals greater access to preferred positions in the stream. Thus, streams that have runs of anadromous fish tend to have smaller resident trout than streams without anadromous species. Adult anadromous trout are more robust, as well as larger, than their resident cousins because the anadromous fish have spent time at sea. For example, in Pacific Northwest rivers that con-

The life history traits of anadromous and nondiadromous fish

Anadromous fish generally produce greater numbers of eggs and grow larger than those that do not migrate, perhaps reflecting the greater rigors that migratory fish must withstand.

Species	Age at maturity		Maximum length		Length at maturity		Fecundity		Egg production	
	Anadromous	Nondiadromous	Anadromous	Nondiadromous	Anadromous	Nondiadromous	Anadromous	Nondiadromous	Anadromous	Nondiadromous
Trout										
Cutthroat	4.0 years	3.5 years	99.0 cm	99.1 cm	39.3 cm	20.0 cm	2,323 eggs	1,255 eggs	10,918 grams	5,899 grams
Rainbow	4.0	4.0	122.0	91.5	50.0	42.0	4,483	1,500	17,932	6,000
Brown	4.0	3.5	102.0	82.6	51.5	29.0	1,510	738	6,399	1,390
Brook	4.5	2.5	80.0	86.0	27.0	20.0	2,550	2,550	10,838	9,818
Char										
Arctic	7.0	8.0	96.0	55.0	63.0	27.7	4,582	1,576	19,932	6,777
Dolly Varden	8.0	5.5	127.0	75.0	37.5	15.1	4,250	1,412	19,125	5,013
Salmon										
Atlantic	5.0	5.0	140.0	99.0	67.0	21.5	11,196	2,384	67,176	12,516
Mean	5.2	4.6	109.4	84.0	47.9	25.0	4,413	1,631	21,760	6,773
Standard deviation	1.6	1.8	20.9	15.5	14.3	8.9	3,223	635	20,657	3,552
Sign test	(p = 0.376)		(p = 0.454)		(p = 0.016)*		(p = 0.016)*		(p = 0.016)*	

Two-tailed sign tests are used to test for significant differences between anadromous and nondiadromous means ($p < 0.05$). Adapted from Gross, 1987.

The highly productive waters of the sea allow anadromous trout to grow large. This gives them a spawning advantage over the smaller resident fish in their natal streams.

LENZI

tain resident rainbow trout and anadromous steelhead, the steelhead are considerably larger in all aspects. Coastal cutthroat, which are anadromous (sea-run cutthroat), are considerably larger than the landlocked forms of coastal cutthroat, which usually are found isolated in the headwaters of coastal streams. Likewise, adult anadromous fish of hatchery origin are more robust than their resident hatchery cousins for the same reason.

HUMAN INTERVENTION

Populations of anadromous salmonids may be managed in streams to preserve the species as either native (wild) fish in lightly fished streams or hatchery fish in heavily fished streams. In the most common situation, streams are managed for both types of fish, to prevent overexploitation of the individual stocks of the salmonids. It is often possible to preserve or exploit separately either the hatchery or wild fish components of the run because, although the hatchery and wild stocks overlap as aggregate runs, their peak entries into the river usually are separated by several days or weeks.

Hatcheries provide an equilibrium between production and harvest rates in streams with heavily used anadromous fisheries. Many wild anadromous salmonid runs could not survive without supplemental hatchery stocking programs or protective regulations such as catch and release. In these programs, hatchery fish act as a buffer to protect the wild fish populations from over-exploitation. All of the hatchery fish may be harvested or be used at the hatchery. At the same time, an escapement goal (the number of fish required to perpetuate the run) is established for the native or wild fish.

In his 1976 review of anadromous salmonid management on the Pacific Coast of North America, Narver indicated that the biggest problem facing managers of anadromous salmonids was the reestablishment or maintenance of the proper environment for the adults to spawn and the young fish to rear. With continuous encroachment by man upon the environment, this will continue to be a problem common to all anadromous fish runs. Since rivers of the Pacific Coast contain runs of as many as seven or eight species of anadromous salmonids, and in many instances separate runs of the same species, such as winter- and summer-run steelhead, the integrity of the rivers must be maintained for the benefit of all of the runs.

—Gilbert B. Pauley

Life and death

Most trout become adults by the time they are two to four years old, but the length of time to maturity can vary from one to thirteen years, depending on species and locale. Quite often females mature a year later than do males. In some waters, Arctic char do not mature until age twelve, for instance, and some lake trout not until age thirteen. Some of the classic examples of overexploited fish populations are among species that take longer to mature. For example, the excellent fisheries for Arctic char and lake trout in northern Canada must be closely monitored to prevent overharvest of immature fish. Thus, in the wild, early maturity is an advantage for a fish. The longer a fish takes to mature, the greater the chance that it will die before it reaches adulthood: In other words, the greater the chance that it will succumb to too much stress.

Stress is any stimulus that causes a response, any force or influence exerted on a body: hunger, chill, weight, water pressure, sexual drive. All creatures need some stress to survive, but an excessively stressful stimulus can have debilitating, even fatal, effects. Such a stimulus may be environmental, such as water temperature, or biological, such as a predator. Other factors can cause excessive stress, too: angling, diseases, obstruction by dams, and pollutants.

Trout respond to excessive stress with changes in physiology, such as alterations in osmotic ability; disrupted migration or reproduction; altered behavior; even death.

Studies in Oregon have shown that heavy metals, such as copper, can disrupt downstream migration in many anadromous salmonids. Recent studies of acid rain by the U.S. Fish and Wildlife Service have shown that three subspecies of cutthroat trout are extremely sensitive to acid and aluminum stress. When exposed to these pollutants, their gills erode and respiration and growth are impaired. Other studies have shown that trout panicked by predators change their normal behavior patterns, making themselves visible and thus more vulnerable to predation by birds and other animals.

The connection between too much stress and its effects can be difficult to measure, but scientists usually point to stress when changes occur in levels of blood plasma cortisol or in normal performance or abilities. After extremely stressful situations, normal behavior may return within an hour or two. But in the interim, the behavior patterns of whole communities may change as trout spend more time hiding and less time foraging for food.

Most diseases of trout are related to stress: low levels of dissolved oxygen, extremes in water temperature, and crowding, for example. Under stress, the trout's resistance to disease drops and disease organisms can establish themselves.

Trout can succumb to disease when they are reared in crowded hatchery conditions, an extremely stressful situation. Trout in the wild normally are not so close together, but they, too, are susceptible to disease. In the wild, the number of deaths caused by diseases is not known because dead fish are seldom seen; predators and natural decomposition quickly remove them from view. Some diseases act quickly and trout may die within a matter of days, but many diseases and parasites weaken the fish sufficiently that they die from other causes, such as predation. A weakened fish also is less capable of responding to environmental changes and is less capable of feeding.

Whatever the disease or parasite, there are two means of transmittal: vertical and horizontal. Vertical transmission occurs when a disease is passed from fish to fish through heredity, that is, from parent to offspring.

Horizontal transmission is the passage of disease through water, by nearness to a carrier animal, or by the ingestion of an infected fish, snail, copepod, or other animal. For example, the widely distributed ciliated protozoan, *Ichthyophthirius*, commonly known as ich, travels through the water from the bottom of a pond or stream, and burrows into the skin of trout. Black spot disease is a fluke that passes through fish-eating birds, to snails, and finally to fish. The disease can be quite common in brook trout living in waters infested with the worm.

Bodily invasions. We use several terms to describe the invasion of one organism, in this case a trout, by another. Commensalism means that there is an advantage to the invading organism but no harmful effect on the host organism. Mutualism means that a mutually beneficial symbiosis exists between the organisms. Parasitism occurs when one organism on or in the host uses the host. In large numbers, parasites can damage, weaken, even kill the host animal.

All trout have some degree of natural immunity to diseases and parasites, and the mucous layer and the skin help keep out the bacteria and viruses. But once the skin is broken or abraded, or scales are lost, fish become vulnerable. The severity of their illness then depends on such factors as the age, size, species, and sex, as well as the location of the entry on the body. Once infected, trout can become weak, lose their appetite, change color, develop body lesions or respiratory difficulties, even die. Some diseases, such as the marine bacterium *Vibrio*, can spread rapidly through a population, as cholera can in humans. Other diseases, such as fungal infections, can be much slower to affect the population. In some situations, diseased animals do recover, but often a disease will weaken an animal sufficiently that it dies from other causes.

Death rates. The number of fish in a population that die from a disease and the length of time the disease lingers in the community depend on the infecting organism. A virus will cause a rapid peak in the mortality rate, then a decline; a bacterial infection will cause a slow increase in deaths and an equally slow return to normal survival rates. The number of deaths from parasites rises rapidly, then stays at a constant level, because parasites usually are not expelled from fish. Fish sometimes recover from bacterial or viral infections, but they seldom lose parasites.

Marine infections. Anadromous trout can be affected by diseases in fresh water, then become sick from other diseases in salt water. *Vibrio*, for example, is a particularly devastating bacterium that is transmitted through sea water. It is especially dangerous in warmer water and in the presence of certain nutrients, such as potassium. The combination of diluted sea water and warm water temperatures in a semi-enclosed area, such as a bay or estuary, can result in heavy outbreaks of the disease and many fish deaths.

Sea lice, or "fish lice," are small crustaceans that attach to the sides of anadromous trout. Their presence indicates that the fish recently arrived from the ocean. Steelhead returning to fresh water in Puget Sound, Washington, for example, often can be seen leaping from the water at the Ballard Locks in Seattle, trying to shake off the irritating crustaceans. Surprisingly, sea lice are much less a problem with anadromous char than they are with anadromous brown trout and steelhead, possibly because the char spend less time exposed to sea lice than do the other two species.

The activities of man also can play a role in the susceptibility of fish to disease. Buchanan and other researchers studied steelhead smolts that were delayed at Foster Dam in Oregon for as long as two weeks during downstream migration. By the time the trout reached the lower Willamette and Columbia rivers, water temperatures had increased there, and the young steelhead succumbed in large numbers to the effects of the myxosporidian *Ceratomyxa shasta*.

PARASITES AND DISEASES

Bacteria. Furunculosis (*Aeromonas salmonicida*), named for the furuncle-like lesions found in infected fish, was brought to North America by European brown trout. Furunculosis spread very rapidly across the continent, and it now affects all species of trout in fresh water. Recently, it has been shown that some strains can even attack fishes in salt water. The fish's spleen becomes enlarged and lesions are filled with blood, but the disease can be treated in hatcheries and aquaculture facilities with several drugs, including oxytetracycline (OTC), and vaccines have recently been developed.

Bacterial gill disease (BGD) is caused by a bacterium that attacks the respiratory system of trout and causes the gill lamellae to swell. Fish that have endured stressful conditions, such as crowding, warm water temperatures, and low levels of dissolved oxygen, are probably more susceptible to infection than are other fish. Medical treatments are available for cultured fish, but simply removing or reducing stressful conditions can lead to recovery.

Bacterial kidney disease (BKD), an infection of the kidneys, progresses quite slowly and the bacterium grows within the cells, making treatment difficult. The kidney, spleen, and liver all may have whitish lesions. Although Atlantic and chinook salmon seem to be infected most frequently, BKD readily attacks all species of trout. Injections of erythromycin and the addition of certain compounds in the diet hold promise for cultured fish.

Vibrio (Vibrio anguillarum), a marine disease, is often triggered by elevated water temperatures and other stresses, but it can occur at any time of the year in salt and brackish water. Dozens of strains of the disease exist, each responding to different environmental triggers, particularly temperature. *Vibrio* spreads rapidly and infected fish often have pop eyes, bloody fins, and open lesions. Oxytetracycline has long been added to the diet to treat the disease, although there are several new effective vaccines on the market for cultured fish. The vaccines, however, are not always effective against all strains.

Columnaris (*Chondrococcus columnaris*) generally appears in waters above 13°C (56°F). An infected fish will have lesions and yellow or grayish white areas on its body, gills, and fins. Its skin, muscles, and gills slowly degenerate. The victim eventually suffocates. Stress tends to accelerate the progress of the disease, but columnaris can be treated in hatcheries with some success. Little can be done in the wild, especially if water temperatures are elevated.

Enteric redmouth disease (*Yersinia ruckeri*), or ERM, as it is sometimes known, is related to stress and affects many species of trout, particularly rainbow trout. The trout often bleeds around its mouth, hence the name, and its kidneys can fail. If the disease goes unchecked, mortality can be high.

Fungi. Fungus (*Saprolegnia* spp.), a white mass, is a secondary invader, infecting a fish that has suffered a wound or lesion. Fungus can spread rapidly, causing the fish to become increasingly stressed. There are treatments available for cultured fish, but fungus attaching to wild trout or their eggs will often continue to advance unchecked until the fish dies, particularly if conditions are right for fungal growth.

Viruses. Infectious pancreatic necrosis (IPN) is a highly infectious disease that was first isolated by microbiologists some thirty years ago. It is passed from parent to offspring and has been found in trout in Europe, Japan, and South America, as well as in North America. Some treatments have recently been developed, but IPN is still a rapidly spreading disease that can cause extensive mortalities.

Infectious hematopoietic necrosis (IHN) is another deadly virus that is a particular problem along the Pacific coast. It can be passed from parent to progeny. There are some control methods available for hatcheries, such as isolating parents and young until tests prove negative, but the virus likely will continue to kill unknown numbers of trout in the wild.

Viral hemorrhagic septicemia (VHS) was confined to Europe until recently, when it

Rainbow trout can develop spinal curvature from whirling disease. The disease attacks cartilaginous tissues.

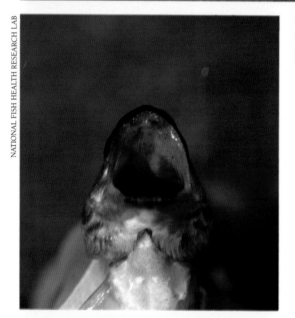

This rainbow trout infected with enteric redmouth disease bears diagnostic hemorrhagic lesions.

Saprolegnia fungus infestations as advanced as this one will almost certainly lead to death.

appeared in the Puget Sound region. It can be particularly devastating to trout in cool waters. Infected fish are listless, dark-colored, and anemic. There is swelling of the belly. The gills, normally red, turn gray-brown. Deaths in the population occur sporadically over an extended period as the disease attacks the kidney, liver, and intestine.

Protozoa. Whirling disease can devastate trout populations, particularly rainbow and brook trout, and there is no known cure. Even freezing fails to destroy the telltale spores containing large polar capsules. The disease attacks the cartilaginous tissues, and infected fish usually show blackened tails and "whirling" swimming movements at the surface of the water. The disease has been known in Europe for more than ninety years and was accidentally introduced to Pennsylvania in the mid-1950s. It is now found in most states that do not have strong fish import laws. Trout become infected when they eat contaminated fish or the intermediate host, tiny worms. In the wild, trout have virtually no protection if they continue to eat infected worms. Brown trout apparently are more resistant to the disease than are brook trout or rainbow trout.

Ceratomyxa shasta attacks virtually all tissues in trout. Lesions can occur almost anywhere, causing the intestinal walls to thicken. These parasitic spores become increasingly numerous with increasing water temperatures, and trout become infected by eating the spores in the water. There is little that can be done to prevent wild trout from becoming infected by this myxosporidian when water temperatures are high.

Ichthyobodo (costia) is produced by a flagellated external protozoan, results in a bluish gray film over the body. Fish become listless and exhibit erratic swimming behavior when this protozoan attaches to the body or gills. It can prevent steelhead smolts from adjusting to seawater, but there is usually little tissue damage. There are some effective treatments available for cultured fish, such as dilute formalin solutions, but the disease is relatively common in the wild.

Ich *(Ichthyophthirius)*, a ciliated protozoan, tends to occur at elevated water temperatures. The immature forms of this protozoan swim through the water and attach themselves under the fish's skin. Ich produces small white spots all over the body. Infected fish sometimes show flashing and other erratic swimming behavior. Some darken in color. In cultured fish, treatments of salt or formalin act to interrupt the life cycle of the organism, but in the wild, trout can be readily attacked, particularly when water temperatures are high.

Parasitic worms. The salmon-poisoning fluke relies on particular species of snail and fish-eating mammals as well as trout in its life cycle. The metacercarial stage, the infective larva, attaches itself to the intestinal walls of the fish. When there are large numbers of encysted metacercaria, fish can become listless or suffer loss of sight. Little can be done to prevent this disease if the snail is present.

Black spot disease attacks many species of trout, particularly brook trout. The characteristic symptom is very obvious black spots. These spots are encysted young flukes that attach to trout after other life stages have passed through birds and snails. When the metacercaria attach to a fish, black-pigmented tissue develops at the cyst. Although this fluke seldom has any long-term consequences to trout, many anglers consider such infected fish to be inedible because of the appearance of the spots.

Crustaceans. Fish lice *(Argulus* spp.), also called sea lice, attach themselves to trout, particularly trout in salt water. Steelhead newly returning to fresh water often carry

Live Argulus, *or sea lice, attach themselves to trout. This parasite can erode the skin.*

NATIONAL FISH HEALTH RESEARCH LAB

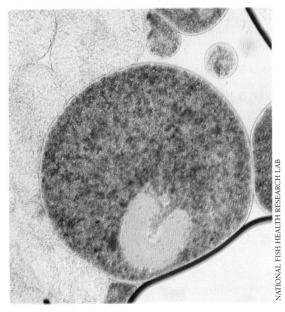

A wet mount of live Ichthyophthirius *shows the characteristic horseshoe-shaped nucleus. Trout infected with Ich may develop impaired swimming ability.*

NATIONAL FISH HEALTH RESEARCH LAB

these crustaceans on their bodies, although the sea lice drop off soon after the fish enter fresh water. In the ocean, however, sea lice can erode the skin. The lice move about on the fish, destroying skin as they go. Large numbers of sea lice can kill steelhead, particularly if they are attached to the head, but there is little a fish can do to prevent such infestation. There are several types of this parasite.

HEALTHY HABITAT

Every species of trout has a range of tolerance for such environmental conditions as temperature. But trout are much less tolerant of extremes of temperature than are sculpins, carp, and catfish. And within the tolerable ranges, much more restrictive ranges of preferred temperatures exist. In general, the salmonids prefer temperatures in the range of 12° to 17°C (54° to 63°F). A trout may be able to survive in temperatures above the preferred range, but it may not grow or behave normally because of the extra stress affecting it. Alcorn found in 1976 that Apache trout ceased feeding at 20°C (68°F), lost equilibrium at 21.2° to 22.3°C (70° to 72°F), and died when temperatures exceeded 23°C (73°F). If slowly acclimated, however, Apache trout can actually survive to 29°C (85°F) before dying.

Though trout in the wild will try to avoid such extremes, the fish can become acclimated to high temperatures within their tolerance ranges if they are subjected gradually to warmer waters. But sudden elevations or drops of temperature can kill them, which is why high death rates among trout are often associated with land disturbances. When forest canopies are removed, solar radiation to streams increases and water temperatures rise. A fifteen-year study of the Alsea Watershed in Oregon documented temperatures reaching 29°C (85°F) after clear-cut logging and slash burning; cutthroat trout population numbers there subsequently dropped sharply. A study in Maine by Garman of the effects of logging reported that water temperatures exceeded 30°C (86°F) after salvage cutting. Brook trout disappeared from the stream studied and were replaced by more temperature-tolerant, nongame species of fish.

At the other extreme, as temperatures fall below preferred levels, trout activity and metabolism decrease. Trout need less food, so growth either slows down or stops altogether. In general, trout do not select water temperatures below the low 50s Fahrenheit. In winter, when the fish are less active, they may have to tolerate lower temperatures or move downstream to warmer waters.

Adequate levels of dissolved oxygen are also critical for fish. Trout do best in well-oxygenated waters. When levels of dissolved oxygen drop below 6 parts per million, because of reduced streamflow, increased water temperature, or rapid respiration of fishes in confined areas, the fish become stressed and their movements slow; below 4 parts per mil-

lion, trout die. Eggs tolerate lower levels of dissolved oxygen better, yet here, too, oxygen is critical. Levels much below 3 parts per million cause eggs to suffocate or, if they live, to develop abnormally.

However, the oxygen demand, stress, and mortality rates in relation to oxygen concentration depend on the temperature, according to Behnke. At temperatures of 14°C (57°F) or lower, there should be no stress at 6 parts per million and no mortality at 4 parts per million. As the temperature nears 0°C (32°F), oxygen concentration must drop to about 1 part per million for trout to die.

HAZARDS

Trout survival also can be affected by several other factors, including pollution, such as acid rain, heavy metals, and pesticides; angling; habitat alterations; and weather. Among the many sources of habitat alterations is grazing. This widespread practice increases siltload to the stream; decreases riparian vegetation, which causes the water temperature to rise; decreases the macroinvertebrate biomass, which reduces the foods for trout; and diminishes water quality. Sedimentation from land disturbances, such as logging, can compact the streambed gravel and reduce oxygen to developing eggs and alevins in the gravel. It also can cause the gills of fish to erode. Many researchers have found an indirect relationship between the percentage of fine sediments in the gravel and the

Grazing cattle can cause significant damage to trout waters by trampling the stream banks, killing streamside vegetation, and otherwise degrading the water quality.

ANDERSON

A healthy trout has low susceptibility to diseases and parasites. It is only when the fish is unnaturally stressed that infections can compromise the trout's ability to survive.

percentage of alevins that survive from hatch to emergence. The more sediment in the gravel, the more compacted the gravel. As a result, many alevins become trapped and never find their way up through it. Reversing the effects of these two sources of habitat destruction—grazing and sedimentation—is considered by many experts to have the greatest potential for increasing production of trout in North America.

Dams can block or delay fish passage, change water temperatures and streamflow patterns, and decrease the downstream flow of natural sediments and insects. In 1985 Buchanan and I documented at Foster Dam on the South Santian River in Oregon that as many as 25 percent of the adult steelhead died as they tried to ascend fish ladders or to return downstream through the deadly blades of turbines.

Logging, in addition to elevating water temperatures, can change the composition of pools and riffles of streams, decrease dissolved oxygen levels, and increase sedimentation and streamflow, or water velocity. Several long-term studies have documented the myriad of direct and indirect effects on trout in streams affected by land disturbances.

Agricultural practices also can divert water and change streamflow, which, in turn, can hurt trout populations by reducing water levels and changing the ratio of pools to riffles. Consider that 46 percent of the water used in the United States is applied to agriculture; in California alone, it accounts for 90 percent of the water used.

Humans cause problems for trout, but nature also can wreak havoc on them. Turner of New Mexico State University found that a population of Gila trout in a New Mexico stream was nearly wiped out after a fire in 1989 swept the area and the associated wave of ash flowed into the stream during subsequent rains. Seegrist and Gard found in 1972 that a rainbow and brook trout community in California changed significantly after natural flooding occurred.

Trout have the ability to respond to natural variations in environmental conditions. Such ability incorporates adaptations bred into them over thousands of years. But radical changes in temperature, dissolved oxygen, and other abiotic factors place trout under unnatural stress. It is these sudden changes that most affect their health and life.

—John R. Moring

Trout as prey

*T*he trout's strategy for existence is to eat, grow, and reproduce before being eaten. Trout predators, like all other animals, follow the same strategy. Thus, in most natural ecosystems, there evolves a balance between predator and prey that normally results in perpetuation of both species.

Research has shown that mortality rates of trout commonly run 50 to 80 percent annually, and of these trout, many are taken by predators. Many species of animals occasionally eat trout or their spawn. However, my research on the North Branch of the Au Sable River in Michigan during the 1960s demonstrated that relatively few predatory species are responsible for most trout mortality.

Trout and salmon that migrate through grizzly bear territory have a significant predator to contend with.

Different arrays of predatory species exist in different parts of the trout's geographic range on Earth. Though this is true, the predator types—predatory birds, mammals, fish, and reptiles—and their effects on trout are similar from one geographic region to another.

Big fish—many times, big trout—are one of the most significant predators. Research on the Au Sable River in Michigan showed that large brown trout eat more trout than does any other predator. Furthermore, they are selective: They eat more brook trout than members of their own kind. Many studies of the diet of salmonids living in lakes have shown that large rainbow trout, cutthroat, lake trout, brown trout, bull trout, and Dolly Varden char and the species of salmon (in addition to the rainbow and cutthroat newly categorized as salmon) eat other salmonids regularly. Yet my Au Sable River research showed that no significant increase in brook trout was found after the removal of predatory brown trout.

Big trout generally prey on trout 5 to 21 centimeters (2 to 8 inches) long. Of course, the larger the trout predator, the larger the prey eaten. Very large lake trout have been known to eat smaller trout weighing 1.4 to 1.8 kilograms (3 to 4 pounds).

In certain trout waters other fish species such as pike, bass, walleye, burbot, lamprey, and eel prey on trout. The exotic sea lamprey that invaded the Great Lakes is a devastating trout predator. Lamprey kill trout by attacking and sucking blood from them.

Pandion haliaetus
osprey

Gavia immer
common loon

Ardea herodias
great blue heron

Megaceryle alcyon
belted kingfisher

Mergus merganser
American merganser

Mergus serrator
redbreasted merganser

H. C. Hertling

Great blue herons are important trout predators in both stream and lake habitats. My studies in Michigan showed that herons ate trout 5 to 33 centimeters (2 to 13 inches) long but preferred fish 15 to 26 centimeters (6 to 10 inches) long. Herons also preyed more heavily on brown trout than on brook trout. In addition, herons kill more trout than they actually eat, sometimes fish as large as 64 centimeters (25 inches) in length, obviously too big for a heron to swallow. Often, a heron will stab or pinch a trout with its beak, trying to capture it, but the trout will escape the attack, only to die later because of the injury.

American mergansers are significant trout predators in many of the larger trout streams of North America. A similar species, the gooseander, or redbreasted merganser, plays a similar role in Europe. Small populations of redbreasted mergansers also live in North America. Mergansers eat trout 5 to 41 centimeters (2 to 16 inches) long, though they prey most heavily on trout 13 to 26 centimeters (5 to 10 inches) long. That a merganser, which weighs about 1.4 kilograms (3 pounds), can swallow a trout that weighs a pound and a half is difficult to believe but true nevertheless. Mergansers eat about one-third their body weight in food a day. Like most predators they eat what's most available; thus mergansers can devastate trout populations in the winter. In the Midwest, for example, the best trout streams have open water free of ice during the winter because of

H.C. Hertling

Esox lucius
northern pike

Micropterus salmoides
largemouth bass

Anguilla rostrata
American eel

Stizostedion vitreum
walleye

Lota lota
burbot

an abundance of spring water inflow. Sometimes wintering flocks of mergansers will congregate on these open waters and, because these waters contain good trout populations, they will eat mostly trout. It was estimated in the studies on the Au Sable River that during winter each resident merganser ate 0.4 kilogram (0.8 pound) of trout per day. Thus, over the winter, a flock of twenty birds ate about 680 kilograms (1,500 pounds) of trout from a 32-kilometer (20-mile) stretch of this stream.

Kingfishers are relatively numerous and common on trout waters. They kill substantial numbers of trout 5 to 13 centimeters (2 to 5 inches) in length. Like many other predators, they also wound fish that escape their attacks to die later from the injuries.

The common loon is a predator of trout on many lakes of North America. Because it is a large bird, weighing about 4 kilograms (9 pounds), it requires about a kilogram (2 to 3 pounds) of food per day. Loons can kill large numbers of trout where trout are the major species in a lake. The largest trout I have taken from a loon's digestive tract was 33 centimeters (13 inches) long, although loons probably swallow much larger fish.

A pair of loons rearing their single young on a small trout lake can kill a significant number of trout. From May to September, the family will consume about 408 kilograms (900 pounds) of food. Even if only half their food is trout, they eat 204 kilograms (450 pounds) of trout. If the trout eaten

Ursus horribilis
grizzly bear

Mustela vison
mink

Procyon lotor
raccoon

Lutra canadensis
river otter

average 23 centimeters (9 inches) and about 0.14 kilogram (0.3 pound), the loons' kill will amount to 1,500 trout for this time period.

Mink are another relatively numerous and common trout predator, but they probably do not hurt trout populations significantly on most waters because they eat a highly varied diet of crayfish, birds, fish, reptiles, and small mammals. However, where trout are concentrated, as in spawning areas or hatcheries, mink can take hundreds, including large trout. They have been known to kill and drag off to their dens trout weighing more than a kilogram (3 pounds). Mink will kill more than they eat and seem to do it just for the joy of killing, when prey are abundant and vulnerable to attack.

River otters also frequent many trout waters and travel great distances to feed. But otters are relatively rare, so they generally are not able to kill many trout overall. However, under certain circumstances, such as when trout are concentrated for spawning, otters, like mink, can have a large effect on the trout population. It has been observed on several occasions that when a family of otters moves in on a beaver pond, it can temporarily wipe out the trout population there.

A study of the diet of several raccoons feeding along trout streams in Michigan showed that raccoons occasionally take trout, but they are not significant trout predators.

The common water snake is a known trout predator and fairly abundant on trout waters

LIFE AS A TROUT

KINNEY

Loons that live on trout lakes can greatly affect trout populations.

Trout mortality

Anglers take twice as many adult brook and brown trout as their closest competitor predators (the brown trout, and the American merganser, respectively). Brown trout, however, out-compete anglers when targeting the yearling class of brook trout: brown trout take nearly half the brook trout that die in their first year of life.

AGE CATEGORIES

Predators of brook and brown trout	Fingerlings taken		Yearlings taken		Adults taken	
	brook	brown	brook	brown	brook	brown
American merganser	0.0%	0.0%	2.6%	6.9%	9.4%	14.6%
Great blue heron	0.1	trace	6.7	6.0	6.8	13.4
Kingfisher	0.8	0.2	4.1	2.6	0.2	0.0
Brown trout	1.8	0.0	45.3	11.2	12.0	4.0
Mink	0.1	0.0	5.4	5.8	5.4	9.4
Otter	trace	0.0	0.7	0.2	1.2	5.8
Angler	0.0	0.0	3.3	3.4	23.6	31.0
Total mortality	2.8%	0.2%	68.1%	36.1%	58.6%	78.2%

of the midwestern United States. These snakes usually eat small fish. However, little is known of their quantitative kill of trout because the number of water snakes along trout waters is difficult to determine.

Sculpins and suckers prey on trout eggs. However, they apparently do not affect trout numbers significantly; in fact, good trout populations coexist with fairly abundant sculpin and sucker populations.

Other trout predators, such as grizzly bears, eat large numbers of spawning adult cutthroat trout in Yellowstone Park, Wyoming, and salmon in both Alaska and British Columbia streams. There are also a few situations where concentrations of pelicans, cormorants, and gulls take large numbers of trout. Eagles and osprey take trout, though the eagles usually eat dead fish. Osprey, however, are very efficient in catching live fish, and when their feeding territory is in trout country, trout will be high on their diet.

Anadromous trout and salmonids that leave freshwater streams and enter the ocean to feed, grow, and return to their natal streams for spawning suffer unquantified losses to predatory marine mammals, birds, and fish. It has been suggested that sea lions, for example, eat large proportions of the adult steelhead that are returning to a stream entering Puget Sound in Washington.

Predators help keep a population fit by culling the sick, weak, malformed, and less alert members. This is not to say that they do not also kill healthy animals. However, the

River otters are efficient trout predators.

process helps the fittest survive. It is natural and essential to maintaining populations that can survive under ever-changing conditions of environment and habitat. Thus, although predation in some circumstances can be a limiting factor, it mainly is a normal factor. If predators are removed, mortality from other factors would increase; the abundance of the target species would not increase.

It appears that predators control prey density. If the density of a trout stock is too high, such as after a new plant of hatchery fish or during a spawning concentration of fish, the predators will zero in. When the prey population drops to normal density, the predators will leave and hunt for better fishing grounds. In fact, where trout occur with other nongame fishes, predators typically select the nongame fish, because they are easier to catch. A study by Colorado State University on otter in a stream with brook trout and suckers found that otters took many more suckers, compared with their ratio, then they did brook trout.

Thus, predators operate under a cost-benefit system. When they are successful in an area they continue fishing until their success rate drops to a point where fishing there is no longer worth their effort. However, once successful in an area, they will keep checking back periodically, because they remember the good fishing.

And, of course, people are important trout predators. Angling is the most significant cause of trout deaths in some waters, especially for older and larger fish.

If people were to control all predators in an attempt to improve their own fishing, trout survival would increase temporarily. However, trout cannot be stockpiled at abnormally high densities for long because some other mortality agent, such as disease, will eventually set in and reduce the population numbers. Thus humans would have to assume the role of the natural predators.

Some fishermen argue for predator control, complaining that predators are taking their fish. However, others argue the reverse, that anglers are taking the predators' food supply.

Ultimately, it is best for all that we share the trout bounty with animal predators.

— *Gaylord R. Alexander*

An osprey with a trout returns to its nest to feed its young.

Pollution's effects

*T*rout and char populations of North America, because of their low temperature requirements, are restricted to the northern half of the continent and to the higher mountain ranges of the West. These less populated areas represent much of North America's last wilderness expanse. Few large industrial or agricultural pollution sources that might directly affect salmonid populations are present there. However, these remote headwater areas contain natural resources such as timber, metals, and fossil fuels, and harvesting of these raw materials has created the major point sources of water pollution. Mining operations, with their accompanying drainage of metals and acids; paper production, with its pulp-mill effluent and wood fibers; oil drilling and coal mining operations, with their drilling fluids and run-off from coal piles; and pesticides sprayed on valuable timber lands all degrade water quality.

Salmonid populations also live in major rivers on the East and West coasts and in the Great Lakes, where industrial discharges that contain both inorganic and organic chemical wastes pollute their water.

TOXIC INORGANIC CHEMICALS

In areas of North America where salmonids live, metallic elements may be present in the environment at concentrations high enough to be detrimental. The metals usually implicated are those mined for industrial uses: aluminum, arsenic, beryllium, cadmium, chromium, copper, iron, nickel, mercury, lead, silver, selenium, tin, and zinc. Metals from specific point sources reach trout and char habitat through direct liquid waste discharge or through leaching from solid waste disposal sites, or both. Metals that reach trout streams are dissolved in the water or are precipitated out, that is, they combine with other chemicals and settle to the bottom as solids.

Lethal effects. Lethal (acute) toxicity of metals to salmonids usually occurs when the dissolved metal or soluble metal complexes act directly on the gills. At high concentrations, these metals damage the delicate respiratory surface, increasing the production of mucous cells, and drawing in white blood cells to battle the inflammation. The in-

POLLOCK

Mining operations can dramatically and severely degrade water quality.

creased thickness of the respiratory surface coupled with the increased production of mucus reduces the ability of oxygen to diffuse from the water across the respiratory surface to the blood, and the fish dies from suffocation. In order of toxicity to fish, mercury ranks highest, then cadmium, copper, nickel, silver, lead, and last, zinc. The concentration of the metals in the water that cause this acute lethal response ranges from 3 to 600 parts per million.

Sublethal effects. Shifting to the more subtle, sublethal effects of metals, an array of responses can occur, from coughing and increased ventilation rates to embryo deaths and deformities. The severity of these effects depends on the metal and the amount of it present in the water. When a fish coughs in response to chemical irritants, a series of violent branchial muscle contractions instantaneously reverses the flow of water across its gills. The severity of the coughing and ventilation rate changes observed correspond directly with the concentration of the metal.

During a three-year study in the mid-1970s of the reproductive life cycle of brook trout in the laboratory, Benoit, working with chromium and cadmium, and McKim, studying copper and mercury, found that these metals increased deaths and deformities among embryos as well as reduced growth of alevins and ninety-day-old juveniles. Holcombe and coworkers in a similar life-cycle exposure described in 1976 the development of severe scoliosis or spinal curvature in ninety-day-old laboratory brook trout populations exposed to low concentrations of lead in water (100 parts per billion). Davies and co-workers in 1973 reported similar symptoms of scoliosis in young laboratory rainbow trout exposed to low lead concentrations. This response to lead seems to be a disruption of nerve impulses to skeletal muscles. In the wild, trout afflicted this way would not be able to find food or escape predators and would rapidly disappear from the population. At the chronic lead concentration of 100 parts per billion, 90 percent of the trout exposed were affected.

Sublethal concentrations of metals weaken the outer protective membrane, or chorion, of trout eggs. The greater the concentration of the metal, the more fragile the shell be-

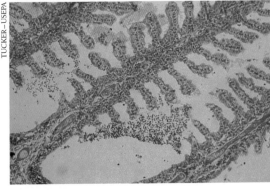

Caustic chemicals do great damage to fish gills. Compare the gills of the control fish (above) with those of a fish exposed to methylmercury (right).

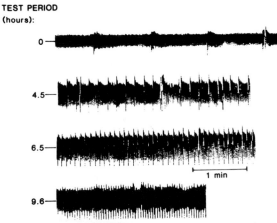

TEST PERIOD
(hours):

0

4.5

6.5

9.6

These respiratory traces show the cough response typical of rainbow trout exposed to caustic skin irritants. Each large spike represents a cough. The coughs become more frequent as the exposure is extended.

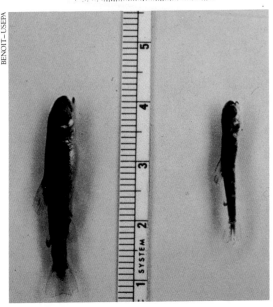

Exposure to sublethal concentrations of metals retards the growth and development of juvenile brook trout.

comes. Holcombe and co-workers, testing the chorion strength of brook trout eggs exposed to different concentrations of zinc, reported in 1979 that at the highest concentration tested—1,360 milligrams per liter—the chorion strength was ten times less than that of untreated eggs. Sublethal exposure to copper and nickel caused a similar reduction in eggshell strength of freshly fertilized brook trout eggs. This response may seem unimportant to the survival of the embryo until one realizes that trout bury their eggs under sometimes as much as 20 to 31 centimeters (8 to 12 inches) of gravel, which could provide the pressure necessary to crush eggs with inferior protective shells.

Because salmonid fishes have a well-developed sense of taste and odor, one might expect that increased pollutant loads in natural waters would be detected rapidly and if possible avoided. According to a 1974 review by Sutterlin, this interaction of the chemical senses with a pollutant can disturb behavioral responses of the fish in several ways: by causing an avoidance reaction, by directly damaging the chemoreceptor of the fish, or by masking or counteracting a meaningful biological odor.

Actually, metals affect trout and salmon in all of these ways. Mercury, copper, and zinc at high environmental concentrations directly damage the highly sensitive, unprotected olfactory bulb of trout and salmon and can block the function of this organ. Sutterlin and Gray, studying adult Atlantic salmon, reported in 1973 that low concentrations of copper render adult salmon less able to follow the odor of their "home-stream water."

At high concentrations of metals, direct damage to the olfactory organ or the masking or counteracting of meaningful biological odors can be highly damaging to established salmon runs. Furthermore, Sprague and co-workers showed the extreme sensitivity of this olfactory sensory system to metal pollution through combined laboratory and field observations in the 1960s. Their laboratory studies show strong avoidance responses to extremely low concentrations (less than $1/50$th the lethal concentration) of copper and zinc separately and in combination.

More importantly, their innovative work was expanded to the field where direct observations on a migrating population of Atlantic salmon were recorded by tagging as the fish migrated through an area of metal mining activities. The number of salmon ascending through a counting gate dropped during periods of elevated copper-zinc discharges from the mine. Some of the salmon fell back and reascended during periods of more favorable water conditions; others that fell back selected a different tributary. The majority of those falling back, however, were not seen again. This left large areas of select spawning gravel unused in the river upstream from the entry point of the mine discharge.

ORGANIC CHEMICALS

Industrial-chemical discharges to major waterways in both rural and urban areas can not only hurt but also kill salmonid populations. Such discharges are considered point-source pollution because they occur at specific sites or by specific processes. Whatever the level of exposure, toxic organic chemicals can enter a fish by two major routes: across the gills or through the digestive tract. During the process of breathing, the most water-soluble industrial organics, such as acetone, toluene, benzene, and phenol, diffuse directly across the semipermeable respiratory membranes of the gills.

The moderately water-soluble organics such as malathion, carbaryl, and industrial organics like trichloroethylene, chlorobenzene, and isopropylbenzene can enter the fish by both routes.

In contrast, the highly water-insoluble chemicals, such as dichloro-diphenyl-trichloro-ethane (DDT), endrin, polychlorinated biphenyls (PCBs), mirex, and dioxin, gain access to the fish primarily through food because they are quickly absorbed by plant and animal plankton (microscopic plants and animals).

The chemicals then move from the plant and animal plankton up through the food chain to larger plankton, aquatic insects, and minnows, to the trout and char, where they accumulate in large quantities in the fatty tissues of these top predators. The accumulation rate of these highly lipophilic, or fat-bonding, chemicals in salmonids is intensified by the fishes' inability to biotransform,

Severe scoliosis results from exposure to malathion, a water-soluble pesticide frequently used by gardeners.

or break down, these persistent chemicals rapidly in the liver to less fat-bonding chemicals that can be excreted.

Trout and char are extremely sensitive to organic pollutants. Mayer and Ellersieck recently analyzed a data set on the acute toxicity of 410 chemicals, most of which were pesticides, to sixty-six species of freshwater animals. Results, reported in 1986, showed that trout and salmon were more sensitive to organic pollutants than any other fish species tested.

Brown trout were most sensitive, followed by rainbow trout, cutthroat, and last, coho salmon. Further studies by Holcombe and his colleagues of the sensitivity of aquatic species to a broad spectrum of industrial organics show that, of those tested, rainbow trout are the most sensitive.

Reactions to organics. As with metals, water-soluble organics can exert acute toxic effects at the respiratory surface of the gills. Generally, however, organics enter the bloodstream and cause diverse systemic effects other than or in addition to gill damage. Over the past few years, Bradbury, McKim, and co-workers have investigated, in the laboratory, the physiological and biochemical responses of rainbow trout exposed to a variety of water-soluble and some insoluble organic chemicals. By evaluating these observations, they identified toxic syndromes for selected groups of chemicals based on each chemical's structure.

Common agricultural and industrial chemical pollutants

Rainbow trout are the "white rats" of the fish scientists' world. Rainbow trout are commonly raised in hatcheries, where laboratory researchers have easy access to them. Scientific research is facilitated by complete and reliable information on age, health, diet, and background.

The extreme sensitivity of rainbow trout to widely differing chemical pollutants including pesticides, metals, industrial solvents, and industrial by-products underscores the importance of good water quality to proper management of the species.

Species	Acrolein	Aniline	Dibutylfumarate	2,4-Dinitrophenol	Guthion®	Nicotine sulfite	Phenol	Rotenone (Rotenoids)	Silver	Systox®	1,2,4-Trichlorobenzene	2,4,6-Trichlorophenol	o-Xylene	Number of chemicals tested with each species	Mean of sensitivity rankings for each species
Fathead Minnow	2	4	3	5	3	5	5	2	3	4	3	4	3	13	3.5
Rainbow Trout	3	2	1	1	1	3	1	1	2	2	2	2	2	13	1.8
Bluegill	4	3	2	2	2	2	4	5	4	1	4	1	3	13	2.8
White Sucker	2	5	–	–	–	–	2	4	–	–	–	–	3	5	3.2
Goldfish	–	6	5	6	4	4	–	–	–	5	–	–	3	7	4.7
Channel Catfish	–	–	4	–	5	–	–	–	–	3	–	–	–	3	4.0
Daphnia	5	1	–	3	–	1	3	3	1	–	6	5	1	10	2.9
Crayfish	–	–	–	7	–	6	–	–	8	–	4	–	–	4	6.3
Leech	–	–	–	–	–	–	–	–	5	–	–	–	–	1	5.0
Midge	6	7	–	7	–	6	6	6	7	–	1	7	–	9	5.9
Xenopus	1	–	–	–	–	–	6	6	–	–	–	3	–	4	4.0
Snail	6	7	–	4	6	6	6	6	6	5	5	6	4	12	5.6

Source: Archives of Environmental Contamination and Toxicology

The work has progressed to the point that six distinct toxic response sets can be identified, based primarily on trout respiratory-cardiovascular responses. The toxic syndromes described to date are (1) respiratory uncoupler syndrome, (2) narcosis syndrome, (3) acetocholinesterase inhibitor syndrome, (4) respiratory irritant syndrome, (5) respiratory blocker syndrome, and (6) convulsant syndrome. Respiratory uncoupler chemicals, such as pentachlorophenol and dinitrophenol, speed up respiration and metabolic rate; narcotic chemicals, such as methane tricane sulfonate and octanol, reduce the respiration and heart rate. Extreme exposures will kill the fish.

Acetocholinesterase inhibitors, such as malathion and carbaryl, both cause dysfunction of the nervous system, reducing oxygen uptake by the gills and slowing the heart rate.

Acrolein and benzaldehyde, typical respiratory irritants, produce irritation of the respiratory surface followed by violent coughing and disruption of the normal breathing pattern necessary to sustain life.

The respiratory blockers cyanide and rotenone cause a loss of the capacity to use oxygen carried by hemoglobin in the blood, effectively reducing swimming ability and eventually killing the fish.

Fenvalerate, a pyrethroid insecticide, is clearly a convulsant-syndrome chemical, which disrupts the normal electrical patterns of the nervous system. Initially it causes slight tremors; periodic seizures lasting up to eight seconds follow. These seizures interrupt normal respiratory-cardiovascular function and eventually become severe enough to kill the fish. Further development of these toxic-response syndromes for specific chemical groups will provide a base from which to predict the effects of environmental chemicals.

LONG-TERM EFFECTS

So far, this discussion has described the responses of salmonids to laboratory exposures of common, moderately water-soluble industrial chemicals and pesticides. Observing these symptoms in wild populations would be possible early in an exposure but not for long, as most of the syndromes described lead to death and the body is quickly dispatched by scavengers or decomposition.

In contrast to the dramatic, lethal results of exposures of short duration and high concentration, the less dramatic, sublethal, long-term exposures to pollutants affect reproduction, growth, development, and survival. Long-term studies of the reproduction of brook trout in the laboratory by Macek, Mayer, and their colleagues indicate that reproduction and early stages of life are the most sensitive to the direct toxicity of organic pollutants. In many respects, the chronic effects of the less water-soluble, more lipid-soluble organic chemicals, or those that accumulate in fat, are the most insidious. They are not initially toxic as their water concentrations are low. Yet they build up over time in fatty tissues to a toxic level. This accumulated dose can cause toxic symptoms in the adult or be passed on in the gametes to the offspring of the next generation.

Effects on eggs and fry. A classic example of genetic damage was described by Burdick and colleagues in 1964 following several years of heavy spraying with DDT in the Lake George watershed area of New York State for gypsy moths, blackflies, and mosquitoes. No direct toxic effects were reported on adult lake trout in this area. However, few of the eggs taken from spawning females by hatchery workers survived.

The loss in egg viability was traced to the amount of DDT passed on in the egg lipids by the parental fish. Experts were able to establish a threshold value of DDT for lake trout egg lipids above which newly hatched fry using these lipids before the fry were free-swimming would not survive. Other persistent organics known to be present in the bodies of animals in our natural waters are thought to act in the same way, but the data base to prove this hypothesis is not now available.

Young brook trout exposed to lead develop skeletal deformities. In the wild, a trout with this affliction would not survive.

TUCKER–USEPA

Skeletal deformities. One of the sublethal effects on growth and development of salmonids is the skeletal deformity scoliosis, described earlier for brook trout exposed to lead. Merle and Mayer have studied the biochemistry of bone formation in young brook trout exposed to toxaphene and have described the cause of this "broken-back" syndrome as a reduction in the collagen matrix, or net, that strengthens and supports the mineral composition of the vertebrae. Reduced collagen in the matrix weakens the bone, which breaks under normal swimming muscle stress. A few fish exhibiting this abnormality have been observed in the wild, but because of its debilitating nature, few would be expected to survive.

Non-point source pollutants

In addition to the problems caused by point sources of toxic chemicals, two major non-point sources of water pollution exist that hurt salmonid populations. Non-point sources are those that are diffuse or unknown. The first is acid rain, caused by the release of anthropogenic (man-made) emissions of nitrogen and sulfur oxides into the atmosphere. These emissions combine with rainwater to form sulfuric and nitric acids.

The second is the atmospheric transport of toxic chemicals generated from fossil fuel combustion, waste incineration, and industrial processes. Contaminants common to this group are pesticides, including DDT, toxaphene, dieldrin, and lindane; industrial chemicals, such as PCBs, dioxin, and hemachlorobenzene; and trace metals, including lead, cadmium, mercury, zinc, and arsenic. These persistent, hazardous chemicals are carried from their origins by the prevailing winds and deposited on the land through local precipitation (toxic rain). Eventually they end up in lakes, streams, and oceans. Because these sources of atmospheric exposure are ubiquitous and favor neither urban nor rural areas, salmonid populations worldwide can be exposed to highly toxic, persistent chemicals.

Acid rain. Acid rain refers to rainwater that has an acid content above that of pure rainwater from uncontaminated areas. Neutral conditions are represented by a pH of 7.0. Values for pH above 7.0 represent more basic conditions; pH values below 7.0 represent more acidic conditions. According to a report in 1985 by Schindler and colleagues, rainwater from pristine uncontaminated areas has a slightly acidic pH of about 5.0, whereas rainwater near urban areas can be as low as pH 2.0. This more acidic rain can lower the pH of nearby surface waters where the buffering capacity of the water is low.

Schindler's review of the extent of acid-sensitive areas in North America identified areas in Minnesota, Wisconsin, upper Michigan, the southeastern United States, the mountainous areas of the West, the northeastern United States, and the very sensitive areas of the six eastern provinces of Canada south of 52° north latitude.

The trout and char populations in the extremely sensitive areas already have been hurt by acid rain and in many cases eliminated. The damage may be due to both direct toxic effects on reproduction and the indirect effects on the food web supporting the trout and char populations. Schindler and co-workers in Canada followed the yearly biological changes that occurred in a small northeastern Canadian acid-sensitive lake as the pH of the lake slowly dropped from 6.8 to 5.1.

The condition of adult lake trout in the lake was excellent at a pH of 5.6, although there were no young trout present, which indicates poor survival conditions for early life stages of lake trout. Over the next three years the forage fish on which adult lake trout

The acid neutralizing capacity of water is determined by its carbonate and organic acids content, which is primarily a measure of the total calcium and magnesium carbonate or alkalinity dissolved in the water. Geographic areas with alkaline soils and adjacent waterways with high alkalinity can successfully neutralize and buffer strong incoming acids. However, this neutralizing capacity can be exhausted by repeated strong acid inputs over long periods of time. Areas in northeastern North America sensitive to acid deposition have average alkalinity-to-calcium and magnesium ratios of less than 0.2. Trout and char populations in such areas can suffer direct physical damage from unbuffered acidity, as well as indirect damage through the loss of food supplies. Areas receiving low levels of acid deposition have average ratios of greater than 0.6, and usually support healthy fish populations.

Average ratios of acid neutralizing capacity to calcium and magnesium.

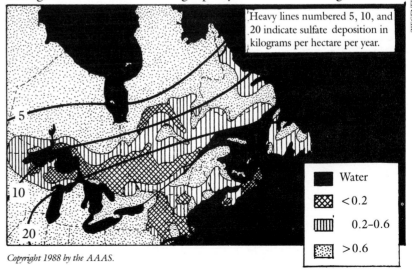

Heavy lines numbered 5, 10, and 20 indicate sulfate deposition in kilograms per hectare per year.

ZIEGENFUSS

	Water
	< 0.2
	0.2–0.6
	> 0.6

Copyright 1988 by the AAAS.

The lake trout from a lake with normal pH (above) appears fat and healthy. The lake trout from an experimentally acidified lake (below) is underweight and in poor condition.

SCHINDLER

ZIEGENFUSS

pH

ACIDIC
0
1
2 — Lemon juice
3 — Vinegar
     Acid rain
4 — Mean pH of
     Adirondack
     Lakes, 1975
5
     "Pure" rain (5.6)
6 — Mean pH of
     Adirondack
     Lakes, 1930s
7 — NEUTRAL
     Distilled H$_2$O
8
     Baking soda
9
10
11
12 — Ammonia
13
14
BASIC

fed, fathead minnows and white suckers, were hit by acid stress and drastically reduced, which starved the adult lake trout.

Bergman and colleagues at the University of Wyoming in 1988 completed a multifaceted five-year project on the effects of acid rain on fisheries. Their work combines laboratory studies on toxicity, physiology, and pathology with field studies on fish populations in areas affected by acid rain. The extensive data produced have provided the base necessary to build models capable of predicting the effect of acid rain on fish populations in acid-sensitive areas.

Wood, McDonald, and co-workers studied the physiological mechanisms in fish of acid and aluminum stress. The results of their work, reported in 1988, demonstrated that acid stress in brook and rainbow trout was characterized by the inability of the gills to control the absorption and excretion of salt. This situation caused fluids to shift within the body, which led to hemoconcentration (the loss of blood fluids and a resultant thickening of the blood) and circulatory collapse. If the animal was to survive, the loss of ions had to be stopped and the balance of water and salts regained.

Depending on the species and the softness of the water (fish in soft water are more sensitive to acid), the threshold for such direct toxic effects on adult salmonids is between a pH of 5.5 and 4.5. In general, the rainbow trout have proven to be the most sensitive to acid stress. Salmon are intermediate in sensitivity, and char are the least sensitive.

Such osmoregulatory (salt balance) problems as were observed in brook and rainbow trout correspond well with the pathological changes in the gill tissue of brook trout described in 1988 by Tiege and his colleagues, who also worked on the Wyoming acid rain project. They described dramatic changes in the cellular structure of the gills of fish that were exposed to acidic water. These cellular changes accounted for the "leakiness" and corresponding loss of plasma sodium and chloride in the exposed animals.

The Bergman acid rain project also included a series of complex laboratory studies of toxicity in brook trout conducted in 1988 by Mount and co-workers. These studies dealt with the effect of acidity, aluminum, and calcium levels representative of acid-sensitive surface waters on the reproductive success of brook trout. They concluded that reproductive failure is not an explanation for lack of young fish in brook trout populations affected by acidification. Rather, their findings led to the conclusion that the loss of the reproductive capabilities of brook trout was caused by the death of fish in the sensitive early life stages.

Toxic rain. In addition to the problem of acid rain, there also is a continuous addition of persistent, highly toxic organic chemicals to North America's lakes and streams from the atmosphere. Swain demonstrated this problem in the early 1980s through the discovery of PCBs and toxaphene in isolated Siskiwit Lake on Michigan's remote Isle Royale in the middle of Lake Superior, a site miles from any production or application of toxic chemicals.

At present, it is well known that concentrations of certain organics like PCB, dieldrin, DDT, chlordane, and dioxin in Great Lakes trout and salmon are above the limits established by the Food and Drug Administration as "safe" for human consumption. The seven Great Lakes states (Michigan, Wisconsin, Minnesota, Illinois, Indiana, Ohio, and New York) have issued public health fish consumption advisories, which state, "Nursing mothers, pregnant women, women who anticipate bearing children, and children age 15 and under should not eat fish listed in any of the categories."

Salmonids listed in these advisories include

Industrial processes that involve coal, such as coke ovens and coal-burning power plants, contribute to acid precipitation. Trout, along with other native flora and fauna, suffer the consequences.

lake, brown, and rainbow trout and coho and chinook salmon. These advisories were based, in part, on the studies reviewed by Swain in 1988 that showed disorders of the nervous system in infants whose mothers consumed more than one fish a week from Lake Michigan. The PCBs causing these disorders passed to the developing fetus through the mother's blood during pregnancy, and from extremely high concentrations of PCBs (twenty-five times higher than the government considers safe for adults) in the mother's breast milk.

Not only are chemical concentrations in fish making them dangerous for consumption by humans and wildlife, but also scientists are concerned about the long-term direct effects of these accumulated, persistent chemicals on the very survival of salmonid populations in the Great Lakes.

In 1982, Hendricks reviewed the use of the rainbow trout as a model animal system for determining the carcinogenicity, or cancer-causing potential, of specific chemicals. He showed that the rainbow is extremely sensitive to known animal carcinogens and that even short exposures to selected chemicals produce a high incidence of tumors. Chemicals causing tumors in laboratory fish are the same as or similar to those chemicals known to accumulate in trout and salmon in the Great Lakes. Although at this time no cancer epidemics are known to have occurred in salmonids, the conditions developing in the Great Lakes combined with the sensitivity of the salmonids could lead to such an occurrence in the future.

Cancer epidemics in other species of wild fish are well documented by Couch and Harshbarger in their 1985 review. However, these occurrences are reported for bottom-feeding nonmigratory species (catfish and suckers) exposed to high concentrations of point-source pollution. Trout and salmon are highly mobile and migratory, and they move rapidly through highly polluted areas, which makes detection of tumors difficult.

Tumorlike growths in the thyroid, although not malignant, reportedly are quite common in Great Lakes salmon populations and are termed goiters by Moccia, Leatherland, and Sonstegard. Their incidence in salmon from the lower Great Lakes exceeds the frequencies noted for these lakes in previous years. The data suggest that environmental pollutants such as PCBs may be involved in causing this thyroid disorder.

The continued deposition of airborne, highly persistent contaminants into the Great Lakes and other surface waters of North America directly threatens not only salmonid populations, but all life that inhabits these waters. Unless we can reduce the rate at which we burn fossil fuels and release industrial chemicals into the atmosphere around the world, we can expect further detrimental effects on these animals, as well as on the humans who depend on them as a food source.

—James M. McKim

The trouts' environs

Aquatic conditions

The ability of a trout to survive, and even thrive, depends on the water in which it lives. Several factors, such as dissolved oxygen content, salinity, temperature, and acidity, affect the quality of a body of water and thus its suitability as trout habitat. When Nature or man alters these factors, the consequences for trout can be devastating.

OXYGEN

Oxygen is essential to the respiration of fish, but the amount dissolved in water is small compared with its concentration in the atmosphere. Even in air-saturated streams, it is less than .01 percent. Moreover, because of the high density and viscosity of water, a substantial fraction of the oxygen consumed is devoted to the metabolic processes of the fish that provide energy to the muscles pumping the gills. The solubility of oxygen decreases with rising temperatures—an unfortunate circumstance because the oxygen requirements of fish increase markedly at elevated temperatures.

Natural bodies of water obtain most of their oxygen from the atmosphere by mixing, by the splashing of running water in streams, or by wave action. The waters of deep lakes in cool, temperate climates are thoroughly aerated during the spring overturn. It is in the spring that the deepest layer of the lake (the hypolimnion), the cool refuge of some species of lake-dwelling trout, receives its oxygen supply for the summer.

The upper story of the lake (the epilimnion), the layer more directly under the influence of the atmosphere, is continually being replenished with oxygen as winds sweep over the water.

Trout, being active fish, inhabit well-aerated waters, and their blood is adapted to extract oxygen from water only near air saturation, that is, at the level at which as much oxygen as possible can be dissolved. Species like carp, in contrast, are able to extract oxygen at low concentrations and survive at high levels of carbon dioxide.

Activity and oxygen. How active fish are and how much oxygen they need are closely related. A trout resting on the bottom of the

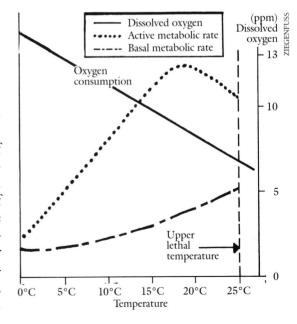

Temperature controls both active and basal metabolic rates in fish. The basal metabolic rate steadily rises with increasing temperatures because chemical reactions and physiological processes are accelerated. At higher temperatures, however, the ability of fish to extract oxygen from the water declines. Decreased oxygen results in less efficient swimming and feeding performance. Performance at a given temperature is proportional to the difference between the active and basal metabolic rates; the temperature at which the difference between these metabolic rates is greatest represents the optimum performance temperature.

quiet area of a stream is consuming oxygen at a rate just over its minimum requirements to maintain vital functions such as pumping water over its gills. The fish is operating close to its basic metabolic rate, comparable to an automobile with an idling motor. At the highest level of activity, when the fish is swimming at the fastest speed possible, its oxygen-consumption rate, that is, its active metabolic rate, can increase markedly, in some species up to five times the basal metabolic rate. Temperature affects both extremes of metabolic rate but not in the same way.

Trout can survive at an oxygen concentration of 2.5 parts per million, but growth would be poor and swimming performance reduced. A rule of thumb for minimum oxygen levels in water is about three quarters of the air saturation value. Ample oxygen is usually present in flowing, unpolluted streams, but during the summer low levels of oxygen can occur in the hypolimnion of deep lakes where there is a high load of organic matter. Trout in deep reservoirs can be squeezed between a cool hypolimnion low in oxygen and an unpleasantly warm epilimnion that is oxygen rich. Then, available habitat is limited.

Embryos and oxygen. Embryos have no functioning respiratory organs, but they obtain oxygen by diffusion from the surrounding water. In perfectly calm water, a shell of hypoxic (oxygen-deficient) water would soon form and suffocate the eggs if the metabolic wastes were not removed. At low concentrations of oxygen, a high proportion of the embryos do not complete development or are born deformed. It is for these reasons that trout deposit their eggs in the gravel of shallow, flowing streams or over submarine springs on the bottom of the lake.

SALINITY

Fish may be classified, on the basis of their salt tolerance, into freshwater and saltwater species. Freshwater fish may be further divided into three categories: primary division, which are highly salt intolerant; secondary, which have some salt tolerance; and peripheral, which can, through physiological adjustment, live in both fresh water and sea water. Oceans are indeed effective barriers to the dispersion of primary division fish, such

Water flowing through riffles absorbs gases from the air, the most important of which is oxygen. Well-aerated water is essential for active trout.

as largemouth bass, which explains the absence of freshwater fish on oceanic islands.

Both marine and freshwater fish have blood and body juices of about the same salt concentration, which in turn are markedly different from that of the surrounding water. Fish in fresh water are in danger of being flooded because of the movement of water molecules from the outside to the inside of the fish down an osmotic gradient. Fortunately, strong kidneys produce a copious supply of dilute urine to bail out the excess water. There also are special cells in the gills for replacing salts that diffuse outward. The marine fish, in contrast, runs the risk of losing its body water to the osmotically stronger sea water. It has developed the physiological "trick" of drinking sea water and secreting the excess salts through special cells in the gills. Urine is produced but only at the minimum required to remove nitrogenous wastes.

Thermal guilds

Fish species are usually confined to particular thermal habitats and, on this basis, are divided into warmwater, coolwater, and coldwater guilds. Largemouth bass and bluegills, for instance, have optimum temperatures around 30°C (86°F) and are representatives of the first guild. Yellow perch and northern pike, favoring temperatures around 20°C (68°F), fall into the second. Salmonids, the family to which trout belong, are classified as coldwater fish and have preferred temperatures in the range of 10° to 16°C (50° to 61°F).

Many people forget that some salmonids also occur in warm, temperate parts of the world—Georgia and Taiwan, for example. Rainbow trout have been even introduced to tropical regions where cooler waters are available only at high altitudes. Thus there is a rainbow trout fishery high in the mountains in Costa Rica—near the heat equator. A trout (*Oncorhynchus apache*) is the state fish of Arizona.

Temperature

Of all the salmonids, the brook trout has perhaps been studied in the most detail, and it can be used to illustrate the role of temperature in the life of salmonids in general.

The temperature zone in which a species can live lies between the species' lower (incipient) and upper (lethal) temperatures. In the laboratory, these boundaries are determined by transferring samples of fish to a series of either warm or cold constant temperature baths and observing how many survive over a suitably long exposure time at each temperature; the temperature at which half a test sample survives is considered the threshold between lethal and nonlethal temperatures. The temperature interval between upper and lower lethal temperatures is known as the zone of tolerance.

Trout can extend this zone of thermal tolerance to a point, given time, by the process of thermal acclimation. Brook trout living in water near the freezing point have an upper

---

Temperature niches

As temperatures approach 21°C (70°F), trout lose out to other species of fish in competition for a common food supply, according to the results of a study by Reeves and colleagues, reported in 1987. In laboratory streams at 12° to 15°C (54° to 59°F), the production of young steelhead did not differ between experiments with and without redside shiners, but at the same temperatures, shiner production with steelhead markedly declined compared with shiners without steelhead. At 19° to 22°C (67° to 72°F), the production of steelhead with shiners declined by 54 percent compared with steelhead without shiners, but the shiner production did not differ with or without steelhead. These results indicate that temperature is a vital factor influencing the niche volume of trout, particularly when trout coexist with other, warmwater species.

—*Robert J. Behnke*

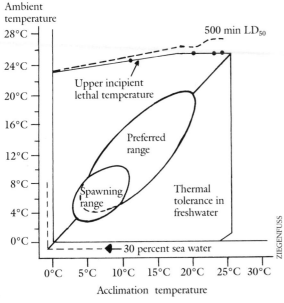

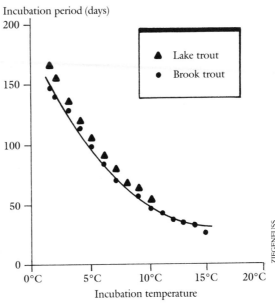

Left: *Lethal temperatures are those at which 50 percent of a fish sample die on exposure for an agreed-upon length of time. Brook trout can tolerate lower temperatures in dilute sea water than in freshwater. The salt content approximates that of fish blood, possibly allowing the fish to conserve some of the energy it would have had to expend in freshwater for osmoregulation.*
Right: *Lake trout require cooler waters than brook trout, and lake trout eggs will not develop and hatch at the higher temperatures tolerated by brook trout eggs.*

"Warmwater" trout

*U*sing the scope for activity, which measures the amount of reserve energy available at a given temperature, Dickson and Kramer in 1971 and Hochachka in 1961 reported that domesticated hatchery rainbow trout have less energy reserves at higher temperatures than do wild rainbow trout. Certain populations of arid-lands redband trout would appear to have a functional temperature tolerance higher than that of other forms of rainbow trout, as indicated by trials at the Bozeman Fish Cultural Development Center in Montana. That is, they can continue to feed and to gain weight at higher temperatures. My experience of catching numerous redband trout in Nevada in water at 28.3°C (83.5°F) and witnessing their excellent fighting ability, which denotes considerable reserve energy, supports an assumption of an unusually high functional temperature.

—*Robert J. Behnke*

lethal temperature of 21°C (70°F), but when acclimated to 20°C (68°F), their lethal temperature increases to 25.4°C (78°F). Upper lethal high temperatures, of course, are rarely encountered by trout in natural waters but serve as an extra safety margin during unusually warm weather.

The highest upper incipient lethal temperature of a species is the ultimate upper lethal temperature—a value that cannot be raised through acclimation. This is the water temperature at which, if it is held constant, the species cannot survive indefinitely. However, according to Behnke, trout could survive daily fluctuations of water temperatures even above the incipient lethal temperature for a few hours if the temperature dropped 6° to 11°C (10° to 20°F) each night.

Lethal water temperatures for trout

Lake trout (*Salvelinus namaycush*)	23.5°C (74.0°F)
Arctic char (*Salvelinus alpinus*)	23.5°C (74.0°F)
Brook trout (*Salvelinus fontinalis*)	25.4°C (78.0°F)
Rainbow trout (*Oncorhynchus mykiss*)	26.0°C (79.0°F)
Brown trout (*Salmo trutta*)	26.4°C (79.5°F)

Brown trout and rainbow trout can tolerate higher water temperatures than other members of the trout family. Lake trout and Arctic char require cooler water temperatures.

At the egg stage. Other temperatures besides lethal temperatures are important. Embryonic stages (eggs) have more narrow requirements and can only develop within the narrow range of 2° to 10°C (36° to 50°F); the rate of development in this range depends upon the temperature. The temperature at which the greatest numbers of eggs hatch is about 8°C (47°F).

Experiments in which the swimming endurance at various water temperatures is determined reveal that 16°C (61°F) is best for sustained swimming. When fish in the laboratory are given the opportunity to select a preferred temperature from a wide range of temperatures, they select those usually well correlated with the best range for such functions as growth and activity. For adult trout this preferred temperature is around l4°C (57°F). There is accumulating evidence that the juvenile forms of most species prefer temperatures several degrees higher, which may explain why young fish are found in warm, shallow waters where protective cover is available.

Although the upper lethal temperature of

MERMON

Fluctuating temperatures, faster growth

*F*luctuating temperatures stimulate trout to eat more and grow more rapidly than does a constant temperature, according to a 1982 report by Spigarelli and colleagues, who compared the feeding and growth rates of three groups of adult brown trout in three temperature regimes during a 57-day period.

One group was reared under a daily cycle of 9° to 18°C (48° to 64.8°F), with a mean temperature of 12.5°C (54.8°F). The second group was reared under a constant temperature of 13°C (55.6°F), and the third group was maintained under an arrhythmic temperature regime of daily fluctuations and gradual increase of daily mean temperatures within a range of 4° to 11°C (39° to 52°F), with a 57-day mean of 7.7°C (46°F). The trout were fed to satiation with alewife twice a day.

At the end of the trials, individuals in the first group had eaten an average of 752 grams (26 ounces) and gained an average of 163 grams (6 ounces). Individuals in the second group had eaten 459 grams (16 ounces) and gained 104 grams (4 ounces) on average. Those in the arrhythmic temperature regime had eaten 476 grams (17 ounces) and gained 94 grams (3 ounces) on average. The low averages of the third group were due not to the arrhythmic temperature regime, which duplicated that of a natural season, but to the extremely low temperatures used in the experiment.

–Robert J. Behnke

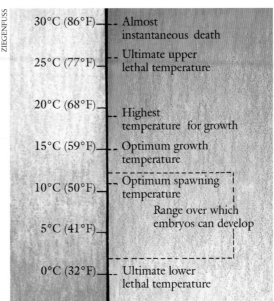

30°C (86°F)	Almost instantaneous death
25°C (77°F)	Ultimate upper lethal temperature
20°C (68°F)	Highest temperature for growth
15°C (59°F)	Optimum growth temperature
10°C (50°F)	Optimum spawning temperature
5°C (41°F)	Range over which embryos can develop
0°C (32°F)	Ultimate lower lethal temperature

Temperature, from the perspective of brook trout, defines life itself. The life cycles of all trout species are critically governed by water temperatures.

brook trout is 25.4°C (78°F), individual fish in streams have been observed in waters several degrees higher. These water temperatures are in the zone of thermal resistance, where fish flirt with thermal death. To survive they must return to waters at nonlethal temperatures. Life expectancy in this zone falls precipitously with increasing temperature. At one degree above the threshold lethal temperature, trout can live for a day, but at several degrees higher, death is instantaneous. Hungry rainbow trout have been induced in the laboratory to invade lethally warm waters temporarily to feed. In general, upper lethal temperatures of salmonids lie in the range of 23° to 26°C (74° to 79°F).

POLLUTION

Before escalating pollution became an important element in our lives, fisheries biologists were concerned with providing the greatest number of fish for an angler's creel by improving habitats and designing effective fishing regulations. Today there are other problems. Deterioration of the water and other parts of the environment now must be reckoned with. Human abuse of natural waters and watersheds has caused the warming of waters, for instance, by the removal of shade from streams. The addition of organic wastes to water depletes the oxygen concentration. Lake trout require deep, cool lakes with high levels of oxygen, but the steady influx of algal nutrients transforms oligotrophic (infertile) lakes into eutrophic

(nutrient-rich) bodies of water, in which the oxygen is depleted by bacteria decomposing the excess organic material.

Degradation of the water through the addition of organic material is usually a slow process that causes the gradual disappearance of fish populations. More dramatic reduction or elimination of the populations can occur through spills of acutely toxic substances or by illegal dumping of industrial waste chemicals. In coal-mining regions, waters flowing over the exposed rocks dissolve sulfur compounds and give rise to sulfuric acid, which renders trout streams uninhabitable by acidification.

ACIDITY

The activity of an acid is measured by the concentration of hydrogen ions in its aqueous solution and is expressed as pH. The higher the concentration of ions, the higher the acidity and, correspondingly, the lower the pH. An increase in acidity in the environment profoundly influences many biochemical reactions of living organisms. It also can affect the water chemistry of lakes, for, at a low pH, toxic metals may form chemical compounds. These compounds, in turn, can be readily taken up by fish.

Acid rain. Many of the waters in which trout are found are threatened not only at ground level but also from the skies in the form of acid rain and snow. We use the atmosphere as a "dump" to dilute the emissions from the burning of fossil fuels and the

Acid mine drainage can weaken and injure individual trout directly—the acidity can alter internal physiological balances critical to survival. Perhaps more important in the long run, though, it can reduce or eliminate populations of invertebrates on which trout feed.

smelting of ores. Impurities such as sulfur and nitrogen react with atmospheric water and oxygen to produce mineral acids. Rain scrubs the air of these acids, but in falling to Earth, they find their way into lakes and streams. In some lakes, those in hard-water regions, the concentration of alkaline compounds in lake water is high enough to neutralize the additional acid, so that the pH remains within a tolerable range. Lakes in regions where the soil is low in calcium carbonate lack this reserve of alkalinity and have become acidulated (slightly acidified) over the recent past. Thousands of such susceptible lakes in the Adirondacks and on the Laurentian shield in eastern Canada and the northeastern United States have already lost their fish populations.

Increased concentration of hydrogen ions has many direct effects on trout and on the animals upon which they feed. At a lowered pH, reproduction and embryonic development are especially vulnerable.

Trout prefer cold, well-aerated waters with a pH between 6 and 9. Brook trout, likely the most acid-tolerant of the salmonids, show signs of stress at pH 5.5 and are believed to perish when the pH falls below 5.0.

At the other extreme of the range of hydrogen-ion tolerance, some populations of trout are threatened when the concentration of hydrogen ions is too low, that is, when the pH is well into the alkaline side of neutrality. Mortality of rainbow trout has been

recorded, for example, in some lakes of the American Southwest when, on occasion, the pH exceeded 9. In these lakes the alkalinity is high, and intense sunlight stimulates the use of dissolved carbon dioxide by green plants, removing this buffering acidic compound.

Acid-resistant trout? Can trout adapt to increasingly acidic waters? Some can in the short term to a limited extent, but long-term adjustment is not so simple. Life on this planet has sometimes—although usually not fast enough—been able to alter its genetic makeup to adapt to changing conditions in the environment. Most species, however, which have appeared on the evolutionary stage during Earth's history are extinct—a sobering thought. Harold Harvey, a Canadian biologist who has spent the last two decades studying the effects of acid precipitation on fish populations, says that the scientific literature contains no records of acid-resistant races of trout. One important reason is the pace with which the pH of lakewater falls after the dissolved alkaline substances have been neutralized. Once the buffering salts are used up during acidification, the pH plummets through the range of 6 to 5 where the harmful effects of low pH first appear, and the fish simply have no time to evolve.

A conclusion can be drawn: It is better to prevent the deterioration of the environment than to rely on the evolutionary ability of trout to cope with these deadly changes.
— *Robert McCauley*

Streams and rivers

*T*rout and char are well adapted for living in flowing water, and they have been very successful in temperate and subarctic streams throughout the northern hemisphere. When introduced into similar environments in the southern hemisphere, they have been equally successful, sometimes spectacularly so.

Trout and char generally are more abundant in cool headwater streams than in warmer rivers, where they face strong competition from fish that are better adapted to higher temperatures, for example sunfish, bass, perch, and carnivorous minnows such as squawfish.

Trout and char are what Webb in 1984 termed locomotor generalists. The salmonid body has large muscle mass in relation to its volume, which gives the fish exceptional endurance, and it has an overall shape and fin structure that permit a wide variety of movements. These characteristics enable the fish to swim long distances at high speeds as well as to dart with quick bursts of energy. Trout need to be able to do both during their life in streams and rivers. In contrast, a pike is a locomotor specialist, whose body is adapted for brief, powerful periods of acceleration but not for sustained cruising.

PRODUCTIVE STREAMS

Productive trout streams are those where trout are naturally abundant and fast growing. The concept of productivity is a bit tricky; it does not indicate the number of trout at any given time. Rather, it refers to the capacity of the stream to produce new trout flesh, a measurement that incorporates both birth and growth rates. The key word is *capacity*. Thus, productive streams that are heavily fished can have relatively few trout, and unproductive streams that are overstocked can have lots of trout.

Biologists measure productivity as the rate at which new trout tissue is produced within a standard unit of stream area, usually over a year's time. It is expressed as the number of grams per square meter per year, or the number of kilograms per hectare per year. With this standardization, biologists can compare the production rates of trout populations in different streams, whether in adjacent drainages or on different continents.

Other ways to express stream productivity, such as the number or weight of fish in an area, are sometimes used, but because their results are subject to interventions–fishing, for example–they are not reliable estimates. This distinction between mere numbers or size and capacity may seem too subtle, but actually it is quite important. The first indicates the present situation, which may be artificially sustained; the second indicates the stream's potential, whether or not it is fulfilled.

Studies of wild trout populations have found that production varies widely from stream to stream and that some streams and

Trout born in steep headwater streams spend their entire lives there.

Why are some streams and rivers more productive than others? To answer this question, we must consider factors that potentially limit salmonid survival and growth at each point in the life cycle.

HOW TROUT USE STREAMS

Some trout that live in steep headwater streams move little during their lives, but many populations migrate long distances, especially in low-gradient rivers where there is access to a lake or the ocean. Although no single location in a stream is likely to satisfy all of the life-cycle requirements of trout, productive river systems contain all the critical elements necessary for high rates of survival and growth, as well as a drainage system that allows access to these elements during the appropriate season.

Even ephemeral streams, those that only flow during the wet season, and intermittent streams, which flow all year but go underground at some points, are important to trout and char, particularly in arid regions. Trout can spawn in them or spend the winter in them if the streams provide the proper combination of low water velocities, abundant cover, and food. Spring-fed ephemeral streams that flow when groundwater levels are high become attractive overwintering sites for many species. Periodically inundated secondary channels, which form when high water braids channels in the flood plain, also provide suitable spawning and rearing habitat when streamflow in the main stem is unfavorable for these activities. Ephemeral streams and flood plain channels are key parts of the river's "highway system" for salmonids.

At any given time, the location of trout in a stream or river is influenced by physical factors, such as substrate or water depth or velocity, and biological factors, such as competition or predation or availability of food. The combined effects of these environmental conditions on trout influence their daily and seasonal movements to feeding, overwintering, and spawning areas. Because the relative importance of these different factors changes constantly, confident predictions about where trout will be at any given time are difficult to make—ask any angler.

Trout movements are influenced to a great

rivers really do seem to be a lot more productive than others. Even where surrogate measures of productivity have been used, such as number or weight, the variation among streams is great, as noted by Platts and McHenry in 1988. Differences between streams may exceed tenfold; that is, they may be greater than an order of magnitude. Likewise, Hall and Knight in 1981, and Platts and Nelson in 1988 reported that the abundance of trout may vary considerably from one year to the next even in the same stream. What is important to remember, however, is that trout and char populations are rarely constant from year to year or from one stream to the next, and that these variations are related to natural differences in productivity.

extent by the flow regime of a stream, that is, the pattern of flow over a year. The flow regime is an outcome of the timing and form of precipitation, including whether the precipitation falls as rain or snow and how often storms occur. Periods of very high streamflow may aid downstream movement of smolts but hinder upstream migration of spawning adults. Extremely low streamflows tend to concentrate fish in deep pools and permit little movement at all. Trout migrations to and from areas for spawning, summer feeding, and overwintering generally coincide with intermediate streamflow. The seasonal timing of these migrations is genetically fixed in trout populations and depends upon the discharge history of the river system in which the population lives.

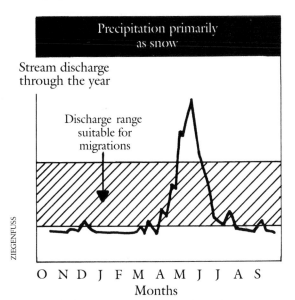

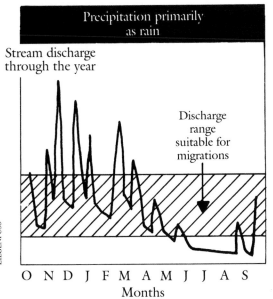

Seasonal movements of trout are timed to take advantage of the flow regime of the river system in which the population lives. Abnormally high or low flow during a critical period may directly affect survival at an especially vulnerable point in the life cycle. Elliott cites evidence, for example, that survival of the early life stages of sea-run brown trout (eggs and alevins in spawning gravel and recently emerged fry) may be critical in determining the overall abundance of a particular year class. Abnormally high or low streamflow at this time, when trout are vulnerable to being stranded or to being swept downstream by high flows, can kill so many fish that even increased survival of later life-history stages may be unable to restore the population to its original numbers.

Spawning. Trout and char prefer to spawn in streams and rivers where gravels will remain clean throughout the time when eggs and alevins are present. Productive streams therefore will be free from heavy sedimentation at least during the spawning season. The size of gravel preferred by different species depends on the size of the adult fish. In general, larger adults use larger gravel. During the process of excavating a redd, a female will remove considerable amounts of sediment and fine organic matter as she digs. Thus redd construction, in addition to providing a pit in the streambed for the eggs, ensures that the eggs will be deposited in clean gravel. Otherwise, fine sediment and decaying organic matter could prevent oxygen from reaching the eggs or could trap fry in the gravel, killing them.

Trout will avoid stream reaches that are prone to large-scale scouring and movement of the bed itself, as these conditions also will kill delicate eggs and alevins.

Thus, productive spawning reaches typi-

Trout streams are usually free of fine materials, especially in spawning areas—the glides and tail-outs of pools.

The regional climate, discharge, and flow patterns of a stream or river strongly influence the timing of trout and char movements.

cally are located on terraces and bars in the stream channel where a low gradient and clean gravel of a relatively uniform size exist. In small streams, trout often select the tail-out of a pool just upstream from a riffle, a location that usually will provide good permeability.

Rearing. Very young trout that have just emerged from spawning gravel cannot easily hold a position against swiftly flowing water because they are so small. Therefore, young-of-the-year trout typically move to the edge of the stream, where they take up feeding stations behind boulders and logs, in undercut banks, and in backwaters. If the stream contains rooted vegetation along the margin, fry will often congregate around the plants for relief from the current as well as for protection from predators and for access to potential prey.

These areas of reduced current velocity along the edges of streams and rivers are critical for trout fry survival, as Moore and Gregory noted in 1988. Efforts to constrain the streambank with riprap or revetments, or to eliminate large structures in the channel that cause streambank erosion, may succeed in deepening the channel; however, they may risk seriously reducing or eliminating important habitat for small fish. The most productive habitat for fry typically contains shallow, complex channel margins with ample cover and will thus be meandering, well-vegetated streams with obstructions that create varying hydraulics. Some of the best locations in the drainage system are in low-gradient areas where vegetated terraces have formed on sediment deposits. The least productive habitat for trout fry is often in streams that cut through steep canyons, with few shallow, calm areas along the edges of the water.

As trout grow, they move into deeper water with swifter current where they are exposed to more drifting invertebrates. They may be at greater risk of being eaten by a predator, but potentially they can find more food. Trout still rely on breaks in the current, which logs, large boulders, and other flow obstructions provide, where they can rest between feeding attempts. Where these flow obstructions are absent, trout can make use of the low-velocity boundary layer of water that exists next to the bottom. The thickness of this low-velocity layer is controlled by the size of the dominant particles that make up the streambed; coarse gravel and boulders have a much thicker boundary layer than does a streambed with fine gravel and sand. Thus streams and rivers with many large boulders and logs, or dense weed beds, provide more usable holding water than streams with a uniform bottom and few large logs or boulders to obstruct the flow.

In the summer, trout use pools and riffles in the main part of the stream. Unless trout are too large to be eaten by other fish or by terrestrial predators, they prefer to remain near such instream cover as undercut banks or crevices created by logs and boulders. Large trout may inhabit large, open pools with little cover; smaller trout prefer small pools where they can hide if threatened. Thus, the most productive stream reaches in summer possess both large and small pools, and contain structures that create cover from predators as well as breaks in the current for feeding. These conditions can exist in nearly all landforms, including canyons.

The least productive locations in summer

Backwater areas serve as nursery waters for growing trout.

GROST

are characterized by uniform, rapidly moving water with few breaks in the current, no hiding places from predators, and low invertebrate production. Such conditions can occur in channelized streams, in streams where the substrate is bedrock, or in streams that are steep, heavily shaded, and very cold.

Extended periods of high streamflow may occur during spring runoff in regions where snow is the main form of precipitation and during winter where rainfall is the main form of precipitation. The risk of predation is reduced during elevated discharge, but the energy required to maintain a feeding station in the main flow becomes too great. Therefore, trout seek refuge in sites away from the main part of the channel in backwater pools, secondary channels, and beaver ponds, and in protected areas under streambanks and behind boulders and logs. In some regions smaller trout burrow into the gravel to escape high flows, but they will do this only where there is little risk of bedload movement, that is, where the water velocity is not great enough to physically dislodge the larger particles in the streambed.

Trout do not seek refuge from high discharge by settling to the bottom of pools. The velocity of water during periods of very high flow actually is greater along the bottom of pools than in riffles. This phenomenon, termed flow reversal by hydrologists, happens where water accelerates as it passes a flow constriction. It is responsible for the scouring action that forms the pool itself. Thus, the presence of pools does not necessarily guarantee suitable refuge from high discharge, even though the same pools may provide excellent rearing conditions at lower flows.

Shallow, protected areas of a stream or river may be good places to escape from rapidly flowing water, but they often are not good places to be during cold winter months when the entire depth of water may freeze. Some of the best overwintering habitat in regions with cold winters includes beaver ponds and other large pools that do not freeze to the bottom. Spring-fed streams, because their temperatures remain above freezing, also provide excellent winter rearing sites.

Trout continue to feed even when stream

Conditions in the summer compel trout to use the entire stream environment. They take advantage of the cover that rocks and logs provide and use breaks in the current for feeding.

Spring snowmelt can dramatically increase the volume of water in a stream. These unfavorable conditions force trout out of their preferred feeding stations.

Springs provide nearly constant flows of nutrient-rich water, creating ideal trout habitat.

Beaver dams and other flow obstructions play an important role in trout waters by slowing the removal of organic matter. Such nutrients are then available to invertebrates, which are important sources of food for trout.

temperatures approach freezing, although their metabolic rate is slowed so much that they are not very hungry. They will seek areas with available food and clear water. Predation, often by birds or mammals, may continue to be an important factor during winter, so instream cover is still critical to winter survival.

Productive winter habitat, therefore, is characterized by the presence of slow-moving water with ample depth and abundant cover. Some of the best sites are located along the edge of a river or on the river's flood plain. Streams that have been channelized or that have been cleared of logs and large boulders through debris torrents (sluice-outs) or channel cleaning tend to have the poorest winter habitat.

FOOD IN THE STREAM

Chapman suggested in 1966 that salmonid populations in streams usually are limited by two critical factors: the amount of available food and the volume of suitable rearing space in the stream channel. He speculated that either determine production and that salmonids would compete for whichever resource was in shorter supply. Subsequent studies have shown that trout populations often are strongly affected by changes in food abundance.

The productivity of aquatic food chains ultimately depends on the energy from sunlight used by aquatic and terrestrial plants to generate new organic matter, which in turn is eaten and recycled by stream-dwelling organisms. Aquatic plants include algae growing on the surface of the streambed and in the water itself, and rooted vascular plants. Terrestrial plants contribute organic matter to streams and rivers in the form of wood debris, leaves, needles, and other plant litter that falls into streams, as well as groundwater containing dissolved organic compounds of terrestrial origin.

Vannote and others have noted that the relative abundance of aquatic and terrestrial plants in aquatic food chains and the way in which plant material is consumed and recycled tend to change in a fairly predictable way from the headwaters of a river system to its mouth. These changes appear as differences in groups of organisms that are adapted to

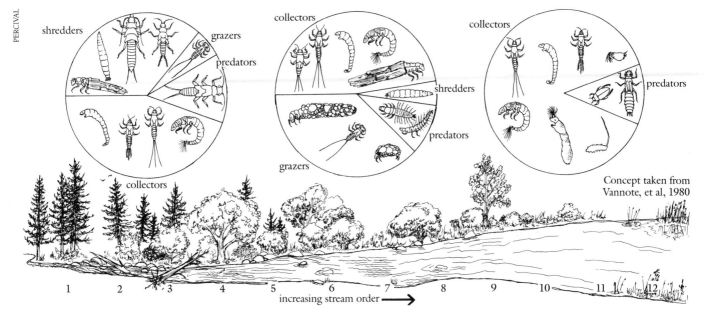

PERCIVAL

shredders

grazers

predators

collectors

collectors

shredders

predators

grazers

collectors

predators

Concept taken from
Vannote, et al, 1980

increasing stream order ➤

1   2   3   4   5   6   7   8   9   10   11   12

certain types of feeding. For example, organic matter of terrestrial origin usually predominates in heavily shaded headwater streams, and many of the invertebrates living there are specialized to feed on this type of plant material, either by shredding large plant fragments or by collecting small plant particles. These invertebrates are called shredders and collectors.

As stream channels become larger and more sunlight reaches the water surface, the contribution of aquatic plants to food chains, relative to terrestrial plants, increases. When algae become more abundant, organisms, called grazers, that feed on algae become more abundant as well. In large rivers most of the organic matter from both terrestrial and aquatic plants has been broken down into minute particles called detritus, and many of the collector invertebrates feed on this fine organic material.

Trout living in headwater streams like to eat relatively large insects such as stoneflies, mayflies, and caddis flies that consume terrestrial organic matter, or that scrape diatoms from the surface of the streambed. Other types of fishes, which are better adapted to feeding on detritus on the bottom, are more successful in larger rivers. In these rivers large insects are relatively rare or are generally inaccessible to trout except when emerging, so the diet of trout often includes small fish.

The role of nutrients. Many of the more productive streams, spring-fed limestone streams, for example, are located in areas with nutrient-rich water. Abundant nutrients typically support abundant plant growth, including diatoms, filamentous algae, and rooted weed species. Many aquatic invertebrates, in turn, feed directly upon the plants themselves or upon microscopic organisms including diatoms, fungi, bacteria, and tiny invertebrates living on plant surfaces.

Plants in streams and rivers make food available to trout in several ways. First, aquatic plants increase the density of potential prey by providing a nutritious and easily digested source of organic matter for invertebrates to eat. Second, by extending into the current, plants place potential prey directly within the path of flowing water, which allows more invertebrates to be carried off in the current. Third, dead aquatic plants contribute an important source of detritus to invertebrates.

The productivity of streams and rivers is strongly influenced by riparian vegetation and by watershed geology. Streams that are open to sunlight and that possess abundant riffles with relatively clean gravel provide an excellent environment for algal growth. In addition to gravel quality, concentrations of nutrients have a marked effect on the rate of plant growth. This situation has been demonstrated by Warren and colleagues in 1964, and Slaney, Perrins, and colleagues in 1986, with fertilization experiments, in which deliberate enrichment of nutrient-poor streams has increased plant growth and stimulated salmonid production.

The mix of invertebrates changes as a stream broadens from its headwaters. Where trees overhang the stream, fallen leaves support lots of shredders. As streams increase in width and more sunlight reaches the water, algae grows, and the number of grazers increases. The smaller organic matter in larger streams supports smaller aquatic invertebrates; trout often feed on small fish, instead.

Floating invertebrates are funneled into plunge pools. The waiting trout are able to feed on them with minimal expense of energy.

Spring-fed streams, especially those in areas where limestone rock predominates, are ideal locations for heavy plant growth. These streams usually have relatively high concentrations of nutrients, low levels of suspended sediment, and moderate temperatures. The highly productive British chalk streams support so much plant production that some are periodically weeded to remove aquatic vegetation, the abundance of which interferes with recreational use.

Although aquatic plants may be a nuisance or may be viewed as evidence of pollution, they are an important source of organic matter for the stream, and they may be the principal food resource for invertebrates that trout eat. In contrast, streams with very low levels of plant growth may be aesthetically pleasing but not biologically productive.

Flow obstructions. Where lack of sunlight, low concentrations of nutrients, and low temperatures limit plant growth, stream invertebrates rely heavily upon the input and retention of terrestrial organic matter for their food supply. This material must be stored in the stream channel without being washed downstream so that aquatic invertebrates have sufficient time to process it. One of the most important functions of logs, large boulders, beaver dams, and backwaters is the retention of organic material and the recycling of dissolved nutrients. Without these structures to hinder the movement of water downstream, organic matter entering a stream from the riparian zone would be rapidly carried out of the system without being consumed and recycled. The result would be a significant reduction in the stream's capacity for production.

If trout are to feed efficiently in flowing water, they must occupy a position in the stream where they are close to a food source but where the energy expended to maintain their position in the current and contend with predators and competitors does not outweigh the benefits provided by the available food. This often means that trout hold in pockets of slow-moving water just downstream from a riffle where food is produced, or near the point where water enters a pool. Logs, large boulders, and other obstacles in streams provide many of the best foraging sites.

The productivity of a stream generally depends upon the availability of food and the quantity and quality of spawning and rearing habitat; the best streams have both abundant food and excellent habitat. Maintaining natural channel complexity, which provides for a variety of food resources as well as essential habitat during different phases of the life cycle of trout and char, is one way to ensure that the productive capacity of a stream or river—and therefore sizable populations of trout and char—will be preserved.

—Peter A. Bisson

Simplified streams

*T*he abundant trout populations native to North America before settlers from the Old World colonized the continent lived in river systems where there was ample interaction between streams and adjacent riparian zones. Where geology and valley topography permitted streams to move laterally, or meander, trees frequently fell into channels, creating a complex flow and increasing the quality of fish habitat. Channel complexity was further enhanced by periodic flooding and other natural events that caused streams to meander. Flood plains were well developed along alluvial valley floors and were used extensively by many fish species.

During the last century, though, social pressure to prevent floods, control river discharge and bank erosion, increase navigational access, and store water for urban and agricultural uses has led to widespread truncation and simplification of most drainage systems, as Sedell and his colleagues noted in 1981. Channelization, diking, the diversion and impoundment of water, bank protection, and the removal of log jams all have had the effect of isolating rivers and their tributaries from riparian zones and flood plains. Consequently few rivers, except those in wilderness areas or national parks, still have the complexity that once characterized their drainage patterns. The effect of simplifying the river's highway system has been the loss of productive capacity for trout and char. They are prevented from moving to seasonally important areas, and material that is es-

sential to trout habitat, fallen trees and plant litter, for example, is prevented from moving from the land into the stream. Sedell and Beschta suggest that attempts to restore habitat quality in trout streams without restoring the natural connections between streams and their riparian zones may be doomed to failure, no matter how carefully and elaborately they are engineered.

— Peter A. Bisson

Streams are often channelized for flood control, but the effect on trout is devastating. The straight, wide, shallow channels provide no usable habitat for trout.

Tailwaters

A tailwater trout fishery, in its broadest sense, is a trout fishery downstream from a dam. It may have been formed on a stream that was a coldwater ecosystem before construction of the dam, or it may have developed on a warmwater stream or lake that was changed to a coldwater ecosystem by discharge from the dam. Some tailwaters are downstream from small, low-head dams, others from massive hydroelectric-power, flood-control, or irrigation-storage structures. They are located all over the country, but the most famous are found in the South and the Southeast, and in the West and the Northwest.

The best known probably is Bull Shoals Dam and the White River tailwater in Arkansas. The White River has produced more world-record trout than any other single aquatic system in the world. Arkansas has three other tailwater trout fisheries of national significance: Norfolk Dam and North Fork of the White River, a 10-kilometer (6-mile) tributary of the White River; the Little Red River downstream from Greers Ferry Dam; and Beaver Dam Tailwater. Missouri also has a major tailwater fishery on the White River system: Lake Taneycomo.

Other significant tailwater trout fisheries include Colorado River and Hoover Dam; Flaming Gorge Reservoir and the Green River in Utah; and Clinch River and Norris Dam and Chilhowee and Dale Hollow reservoirs in Tennessee. Tennessee alone has more than 484 kilometers (300 miles) of tailwaters.

PHYSICAL FEATURES OF TAILWATERS

Trout in tailwaters live in a unique environment. Not only are they influenced by the natural constraints, such as substrate and gradient, as are trout in all streams, but also they are influenced, daily and seasonally, by reservoir operations and upstream water quality. Thus, tailwater trout live within natural laws—physical and biological—as well as under artificial conditions created by the operation of the dams for power, irrigation, or flood control.

Perhaps the most important physical feature of tailwaters is water temperature, which influences the survival, productivity, and growth of the resident trout. Upstream reservoirs, some of them hundreds of feet deep, stratify each year beginning in May and remain stratified until late November. In other words, the water settles into layers with different temperatures—the colder, heavier water on the bottom, the warmer, lighter water at the surface. Hypolimnetic water, or water in the bottom layer, does not mix with the warm surface layer. The temperatures of the hypolimnetic water decrease gradually over the summer, ultimately reaching ambient summer water temperatures in the low 40s Fahrenheit. Water from this cold layer at the bottom is then discharged to the tailwater from the bottom of the reservoir, providing a constant supply of cold water.

The temperatures in tailwaters don't fluctuate as much as they do in natural streams, which can have warm water in the summer and extremely cold water, even solid ice, in the winter. Instead, water temperatures usually range from about 5.5°C (42°F) in the summer to 13.2°C (56°F) in the winter, when the upstream reservoir turns over and mixes. The mixing happens when water temperatures in the surface layer cool in the fall and winter, ultimately allowing the surface to mix with the bottom layer. This warms the bottom layer, providing warmer water to the tailwater during the winter. Such uniformity is important because it provides the best conditions for high productivity and rapid growth year round.

PROBLEMS

This is not to say that tailwaters do not have problems. They do: low levels of dissolved oxygen, even anaerobic conditions, which occur when oxygen is depleted in the upstream reservoir, and extreme variations in water flow. The level of dissolved oxygen in the hypolimnion of the reservoir slowly declines as microscopic plants and animals die in the surface layer, sink to the bottom, and decompose. This natural process gradually uses up available oxygen, which may fall to 1 or 2 parts per million in September, October, and November. (For the best living conditions, trout need 6 parts per million or higher of dissolved oxygen.) When this condition occurs in the reservoir and anaerobic water is discharged, growth of trout and other aquatic organisms in the tailwater slows, and in extreme cases, they die.

The anaerobic conditions created by the depletion of oxygen in the reservoir upstream of the tailwater also may allow heavy metals to be discharged to the tailwater. These pollutants normally are precipitated out of the water to the bottom sediments of the reservoir, but chemical reaction can bring them back into solution. The most serious of these is manganese, which is toxic to aquatic organisms. It occurs naturally in some geographic regions, such as the Ozarks.

The most serious problem facing tailwater organisms is extreme fluctuation in water flow. The dams were built for generation, flood control, and irrigation—not for sustaining trout. Consequently, most operate with little consideration for the aquatic community below the dam. Flows fluctuate from

The tailwaters of hydroelectric dams make productive trout fisheries. The water is usually fast, cold, and well aerated—just what a trout needs.

low or no flow to the equivalent of the Missouri River in some tailwaters, and this situation occurs daily. High flows during peak generation periods act like floods, scouring the bottom of the tailwater, which hurts the aquatic communities and reduces the production of trout and the organisms they feed on. Conversely, reduced flows expose much of the substrate on the stream bottom below the dam, reducing productive habitat for trout and invertebrates on which they feed. Trout and other organisms that moved to areas covered with water, when it was flowing to generate power at the dam, move to isolated pools and shallow riffles when the water is turned off. But trout, as well as algal and benthic, or bottom-dwelling, organisms, need water at least 30 centimeters (1 foot) deep to maintain good levels of growth and productivity.

The constant fluctuation also affects survival of trout in tailwaters. When water is shut down, the isolated pools and shallow riffles make trout in them extremely vulnerable to predators, such as eagles, ospreys, otters, smallmouth bass, and fishermen.

BLESSINGS

But the decomposition process also enriches the hypolimnion with nutrients that encourage the growth of microscopic plants and animals at the bottom of the trout's food chain. This nutrient-enriched water is then discharged to the tailwater, allowing high productivity during most of the year. The

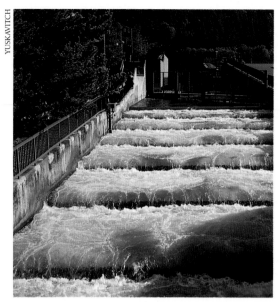

Fish ladders can assist migrating adult trout past otherwise impassable dams during spawning runs. However, the young trout are often injured or killed when passing through the turbines during downstream migration.

low levels of oxygen and anaerobic conditions only occur in the tailwater during a short period of time in the fall; in some years, they do not occur at all.

Tailwaters are clear, thanks to the upstream reservoir, which acts as a silt trap. Sediments that flow into the reservoir sink to the bottom rather than pour into the tailwater with the water that is released into it. This situation and the high levels of nutrients discharged to the tailwater increase algal and insect production, and, ultimately, trout growth. Hoover Dam on the Colorado River cleared one of the most turbid rivers in the country, which allowed a trout fishery to develop.

Most tailwaters have rather simple but highly productive benthic and fish communities. Filter feeders and shredders, such as chironomids, trichopterans, simuliids, oligochaetes, isopods, and amphipods and other microscopic organisms dominate the benthic community. The communities generally have fewer species than do natural trout streams, but their numbers are larger. Fish communities generally consist of a few minnow species, darters, redhorse suckers, sculpins, and trout.

The West and the South

Western tailwaters differ from southern tailwaters. Most western tailwater fisheries contain wild rainbow, brown, cutthroat, and brook trout. But in some tailwaters, reproduction is severely limited for several miles below peak-power dams because of great daily fluctuations in water level. In such tailwaters, on the Colorado River below Lake Powell and the San Juan River below Navajo Reservoir, for example, the fishery must be maintained by stocking, according to Behnke. The populations are maintained by natural reproduction of resident trout. In the West, dams on large rivers, such as the Columbia River and other rivers in the northwestern United States, have severely reduced the numbers of wild juvenile steelhead and other coldwater species leaving the systems each year for the ocean and those returning two to four years later as adults. The dams all have fish ladders, which only partially solve the problem. They concentrate the adults in the tailwaters during the run upstream from the ocean, making them more vulnerable to predators. The stress of passage over the fish ladders and the trip through the many reservoirs also reduces the number of returning adults that survive. However, the greatest mortality happens not to adults but to young trout as they migrate downstream through the dam turbines and as they are exposed to predators below the dams, according to Behnke.

Southern tailwaters, on the other hand, generally are maintained by stocking catchable trout (20.5 to 33 centimeters [8 to 13 inches long]), primarily rainbows. A few brown trout and cutthroats are stocked in select tailwaters. Ten thousand brown trout are stocked each year at Lake Taneycomo in southwestern Missouri, for example, along with more than one million 26-centimeter (10-inch) rainbows.

Dams, especially in the West and the Northwest, have disrupted trout migrations, flooded trout streams, even eliminated trout populations in some areas. However, they also have created trout habitat, especially in the South, and the resulting tailwaters, although artificial environments, provide trout populations that otherwise could not exist in that region.

—Spencer E. Turner

Lakes

*T*rout lakes vary widely in size, origin, geography, and habitat. But despite their diversity, they also have several elements in common that make them suitable for trout. We broadly define trout habitat as those parts of the environment that trout depend on to carry out their life processes. Trout habitat in lakes includes the physical features of the lake—the shorelines and the structure and composition of the lake bottom.

Habitat also includes aquatic vegetation, submerged roots and logs, even the results of such hydrodynamic processes as water currents and vertical and horizontal gradients of temperature. We consider as elements of the habitat dissolved gases, nutrients, and the abundance of prey. Finally, the watershed of the lake, which includes inlet and outlet streams and wetlands, is an important extension of the system. Watershed factors are especially significant as habitat elements when comparisons of trout species compositions and production (reproduction and growth rates minus mortalities) are made between lakes.

When we discuss habitat, we must address two primary attributes: size, which determines how much habitat is available for each life stage, and quality, which determines its suitability for trout. Quality of the habitat comprises two further aspects. The first and more important is water quality, which includes such factors as temperature, dissolved oxygen, pH (acidity), turbidity, ammonia, and a long list of potential trace toxicants

from natural and anthropogenic, or human-caused, sources.

Temperature and dissolved oxygen are the two most dominant water quality features of trout habitat because of their pervasive influence as controlling, directive, limiting, and potentially lethal factors.

Habitat quality also comprises the important structural features, including thermal and dissolved oxygen stratification; cobble gravel or rocky spawning beds; reefs or shoals; submerged trees and roots; and surface or submerged aquatic-plant cover. These features provide nursery habitats for young trout, sources of food, sanctuary from predators, and resting areas.

DIVERSITY

Trout lakes can be small, shallow ponds or huge, deep bodies of water, or any size in between. They are distributed geographically from above the Arctic Circle to as far south as northern Mexico. Johnson noted in 1980 that there is no northern limit to the distribution of Arctic char because they are circumpolar; many landlocked populations exist in small Arctic lakes that became isolated from the sea following the retreat of the glaciers in the last ice age.

Native populations of brook trout are common in small Precambrian shield lakes and also in some very large lakes of eastern Canada. Lake Nipigon in Ontario, for example, which is noted for its brook trout fishery, is 4,480 square kilometers (1,730 square miles) in area.

We can see the diversity of lake types and trout habitats by comparing environs of coastal cutthroat trout with those of lake trout. Cutthroat often inhabit small, shallow lakes and even temporary beaver ponds of the Pacific Northwest. Lake trout prefer large, deep lakes north of 43°00′ north latitude from Alaska to Maine. The deepest trout lake in North America is Great Slave Lake in the Northwest Territories. It is 614 meters (2,014 feet) deep.

Most trout lakes develop as a result of geological processes, and Hutchinson has reviewed them in detail. Glaciation, earthquakes, landslides, volcanic eruptions, and even such uncommon phenomena as meteor collisions have created settings of excellent trout habitat. For example, Ungava Crater Lake in Quebec, 671 meters (2,201 feet) above sea level, is 597 hectares (1,475 acres) in area and 252 meters (827 feet) deep. It has extremely soft water and is one of the world's clearest lakes, with visibility to an exceptional depth of 35 meters (115 feet). Martin reported in 1955 that Ungava Crater Lake is inhabited by a slow-growing population of Arctic char, the only fish species present. In 1952, Meen determined that Ungava Crater Lake was created by a meteor that crashed into Earth sometime before the last continental glaciation.

Artificial introductions have greatly extended the modern distribution of trout in North America. For example, Pennak noted in 1966 that many of the small, high mountain lakes (at elevations greater than 1,700 meters [about 5,600 feet]) of the Rocky Mountain region of the United States were devoid of native fish until about 1880, when extensive trout stocking programs were begun. Similarly, Northcote and Larkin noted the extensive stocking of rainbow trout in the many barren lakes of the southern interior plateau of British Columbia.

Construction of many huge reservoirs in the western United States has also provided extensive new environs for trout. Rainbow trout is the preferred species for stocking in such waters, which include Franklin D. Roosevelt Lake in Washington, Horsetooth Reservoir in Colorado, and Flaming Gorge Reservoir on the border between Utah and Wyoming.

GEOGRAPHIC FACTORS AFFECTING THE DISTRIBUTION

Trout as a group prefer cold to cool water and thus are characterized as coldwater fishes. In fact, this need for cold water explains not only their distribution within lakes but also their geographic distribution in North America and throughout the world. In the northern and northwestern coastal regions of North America, trout occupy a very wide range of lake sizes across their geographic range, but in the southern part of the range, wild, self-sustaining trout populations are found primarily in deep lakes or at high elevations.

Arctic char are adapted to the coldest water, routinely living in waters of 1° to 4°C (34° to 39°F) only north of 45°30′ north latitude, whereas rainbow trout tolerate temperatures between 12° and 20°C (54° and 68°F). Accordingly, rainbow trout have been widely introduced throughout North America where suitable waters exist.

In general, trout have their greatest scope for activity from about 5° to 15°C (41° to 59°F), although this varies widely among species. Scope for activity is the amount of metabolic energy that trout (in this instance) have for such activities as random swimming, capture of prey, escape from predators, courtship, spawning, and growth, after basic physiological functions such as breathing, circulation of the blood, and maintenance of equilibrium, necessary for the integrity of the whole organism, have been taken care of. In the warm temperatures of mid- to late summer, scope for activity is constrained, reducing the potential for physical activity and making trout sluggish.

Trout grow and reproduce best when their scope for activity is near its maximum. This maximum represents the thermal optimum, which occurs near the preferred temperature, for each species. The performance of a species in a given environment, however, is influenced by many other factors, such as the availability of dissolved oxygen and the quality of spawning and nursery habitats.

The most critical period of the year for trout, especially at lower latitudes throughout much of southern Canada and the United States, is summer, when surface

Isolated alpine lakes, when inhabited by trout, naturally preclude migration. The trout that live in them may be genetically distinct from others of the same species as a result of this isolation.

waters reach their highest annual temperature. At this time, trout in the southern range of distribution must have a sanctuary of cool water, which is provided by the large, deep lakes that stratify into well-defined thermal layers and by the cool, high-elevation lakes.

Nevertheless, trout are absent from lakes in some areas of North America, though temperature and habitat factors are ideal, because the geological and glacial histories have simply prevented access to these waters for colonization. Barren lakes that are inaccessible to natural trout colonization are excellent candidates for trout introductions. In such cases, wild, self-sustaining populations can often be established, as lake trout have been in several Ontario lakes, according to a 1986 report by Hitchins and Samis.

TEMPERATURE STRATIFICATION

Lakes in the mid- to southern range of trout in North America stratify during the summer into distinctive layers characterized by their temperatures and the extent of vertical mixing. These lakes vary widely in their patterns of stratification, depending on the latitude, elevation, local climatic conditions, depth, water supplies (surface runoff versus groundwater flows), and flushing rates (the rate at which the total volume of the lake is replaced by inflowing water).

Variation in the circulation patterns of lakes, as described by Mortimer in 1974, has a strong influence on the distribution, feeding, and temperature and oxygen conditions to which juvenile and adult trout are exposed. The relatively common situation of summer stratification reveals some of the major processes and physical habitat features existing in many trout lakes of North America. Two types of lakes stratify: dimictic lakes and monomictic lakes. Dimictic lakes mix from top to bottom twice a year, once in the spring and once in the autumn. Lake Opeongo, Ontario, inhabited by lake trout, and Moosehead Lake, Maine, inhabited by brook trout and lake trout, are examples. Warm monomictic lakes mix only once a year, but continuously over the entire winter period. Cayuga and Seneca lakes in New York, inhabited by lake trout and rainbow trout, and Cowichan Lake, British Columbia, inhabited by cutthroat and rainbow trout, are examples.

Other thermal stratification and mixing patterns also occur in trout lakes. These are amictic (nonmixing) lakes such as Hazen Lake on Ellesmere Island in the Arctic Ocean, inhabited by Arctic char; and cold monomictic lakes, whose surface waters are frozen in the winter but whose waters circulate completely in the summer, such as Ungava Crater Lake in northern Quebec.

After winter ice melts in dimictic lakes, the water column is isothermal, that is, of equal temperature at all depths. Winds readily cause the entire water mass to mix from top to bottom in a process called spring turnover. The entire water column thus becomes recharged with oxygen as the deep waters are brought to the surface by the wind-driven currents. Surface waters of temperate lakes warm rapidly during the spring because of increasing heat energy from solar radiation. The warm surface water, being less dense and therefore lighter, tends to remain at the surface. Wind shear across the surface of these lakes causes mixing of the less dense surface layer, but not the deeper waters.

As warming continues, the surface layer, or epilimnion, becomes thicker, essentially isolating the deeper waters, or hypolimnion, from the atmosphere. The hypolimnion remains isolated until the process reverses itself during autumnal cooling some months later and the lake mixes once again during the fall turnover. The metalimnion, or intermediate thermal stratum, is a zone of rapid temperature change called the thermocline. During the summer, it becomes a blending zone between the warm surface layer and the cold waters of the hypolimnion.

Isolation of the deep waters from contact with the atmosphere during the summer depletes the dissolved oxygen in the hypolimnion as bacteria and other organisms in the water column and associated with the lake bottom break down organic materials. The extent of oxygen depletion depends on the amount of oxygen that is stored relative to the volume of the biologically productive strata above, from which a steady fallout of organic material feeds the oxygen-depleting bacterial processes. In general, the greater the productivity of a thermally stratified lake,

the greater will be the depletion of oxygen in the depths.

Responses to temperature stratification. In the spring, trout frequent the shallow nearshore, or littoral, zone, probably in search of prey, and possibly because of the warmer water that is available there. As the epilimnion temperature exceeds the trouts' preferred range, however, they move deeper in the water column, and they continue to move to deeper water as the thermocline extends to greater depths over the summer.

Baldwin and Martin, in reports in 1948 and 1951 of the response by brook trout and lake trout to temperature, noted that as the summer progressed, the midpoint of the distribution of brook trout descended from a few meters to 8 to 9 meters (26 to 30 feet). Similarly, the mean depth of the distribution of lake trout descended from less than 5 meters (16 feet) to greater than 10 meters (33 feet). Both species inhabited the littoral zone during early spring, when the space available at comfortable temperatures was greatest. Later, as thermal stratification progressed, lake trout usually were found slightly deeper than brook trout. A few lake trout were found in deep water during all seasons, even when most of the population was at shallower depths. This was not the case for brook trout, which consistently inhabited shallower water. Cooper and Fuller found similar patterns of summer depth distribution for these species in Moosehead Lake, Maine, during 1944.

Andrusak and Northcote noted in 1971 that temperature had a strong effect on cutthroat in Placid Lake, British Columbia, which is only 6 meters (20 feet) deep. In the spring, the fish were found in the littoral zone near the surface, but during July and August, they primarily occupied strata below the 15°C (59°F) temperature isotherm, the probable upper limit of their preferred range.

In general, trout respond strongly to thermal gradients in lakes during summer stratification and are found at progressively greater depths as the thickness of the epilimnion increases. Some species—Arctic char and lake trout—will be found below the thermocline. Brook trout, Dolly Varden char, and brown trout will be found inshore, associated with the lake bottom near the base of the thermo-

Brook trout consistently distribute themselves in the water column at shallower, warmer depths than those selected by lake trout. However, both species seek out greater depths as spring changes to summer; the upper levels of a lake are increasingly warmed by sunlight and surface air temperatures, and become less tolerable for trout.

Some lake trout are found in deep water throughout the year. However, the majority move inshore to shallow waters to feed during the spring and to spawn during the fall. (Baldwin, 1948; Martin, 1952; Ontario Ministry of Natural Resources, 1981.)

Depth (m)

| May 7 | May 21 | June 7 | August 12 |

Redrock Lake, Ontario
45°46'N, 78°29'W

Trout species

Brook trout

Lake trout

Lake bottom

ZIEGENFUSS

5°C   10°C   15°C   20°C
Temperature

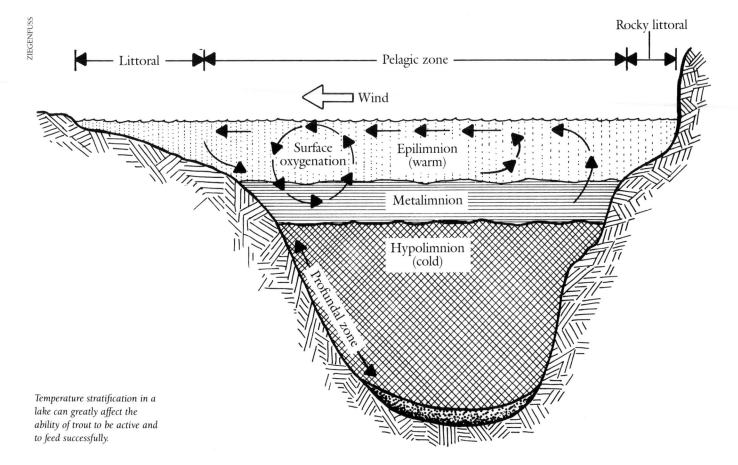

Littoral — Pelagic zone — Rocky littoral

Wind

Surface oxygenation
Epilimnion (warm)
Metalimnion
Hypolimnion (cold)
Profundal zone

Temperature stratification in a lake can greatly affect the ability of trout to be active and to feed successfully.

cline. Rainbow and cutthroat trout select the mid-metalimnion but occupy the midwater and nearshore habitats, respectively. The hydrological and meteorological processes that generate the thermocline, in effect, partition a lake into three distinctive habitats that are in turn partitioned among the trout and other species.

The depth of the thermocline varies among lakes, depending primarily on lake size and the extent of solar warming. Thermocline depth increases directly with increasing fetch or linear distance exposed to the mixing influence of the wind. Trout, therefore, will be found at greater depths during the summer in large lakes.

OXYGEN STRATIFICATION

In deep, oligotrophic (infertile) lakes, thermal stratification presents few problems for trout, but in more productive, mesotrophic or eutrophic (nutrient-enriched) lakes, trout can encounter limiting concentrations of dissolved oxygen in deep water, especially if the hypolimnion is small relative to the volume of the lake. Trout living in the hypolimnia of

these stratified lakes are confined by warm temperature above in the epilimnion and metalimnion and low concentrations of dissolved oxygen in the deep hypolimnion below. In many lakes, a combination of high temperature and low level of dissolved oxygen can limit the production of trout. The rainbow trout, which is relatively tolerant of high temperatures, is not as readily affected by low levels of oxygen in shallow productive lakes, although summer kills in small lakes, even of rainbow trout, are common. In shallow productive lakes, oxygen depletion under the ice also can cause winterkills of trout, as described in Canadian prairie lakes by Ayles and associates in 1976.

Cornett and Rigler reported in 1980 that elevated temperatures increase the metabolism of whole lakes, the total of all the oxygen-consuming, degradative processes in the water column and on the lake bottom.

Trout must have abundant oxygen to survive and reproduce successfully, but they can tolerate reduced concentrations of oxygen. The solubility of oxygen in water is affected by several factors, including the partial pressure of oxygen in the atmosphere above the water, temperature, barometric pressure, and the salinity of the water. Solubility decreases as temperature and salinity increase and as barometric pressure declines at higher elevations. Davis reviewed the effects of low oxygen on fish in 1975 and found, that at a concentration of about 6 milligrams per liter of dissolved oxygen, trout began to show behavioral changes such as decreased swimming. This concentration represents a reduction of about 40 percent from oxygen-saturated water at temperatures in the mid-range frequented by trout. The concentration at which behavior begins to be affected is termed the incipient limiting level. Similarly, the concentration at which the standard metabolic rate begins to be lowered (about 3 milligrams per liter) is termed the incipient lethal level. Finally, the concentration at which death occurs within a predetermined period of time, say twenty-four or ninety-six hours after acute exposure, is the lethal level.

A study, reported in 1977, of Lake Simcoe, Ontario, illustrated the reaction of trout to temperature and dissolved-oxygen stratifications. Lake Simcoe is a mesotrophic lake of 725 square kilometers (280 square miles). It is inhabited by a native stock of lake trout and is located near the southern limit of the species' distribution.

The lake trout followed the isotherms of their preferred temperatures (8° to 10°C [47° to 50°F]) from depths of less than 5 me-

ters (16 feet) in May to greater than 25 meters (82 feet) in July. By mid-July, however, oxygen concentrations in the hypolimnion had reached the incipient limiting level, the concentration at which scope for activity begins to decline. By late August, the incipient lethal oxygen level was reached near the lake bottom, and by mid-September the oxygen-depleted hypolimnion spanned depths from 23 meters (75 feet) to the lake bottom at 32 meters (105 feet). An acutely lethal zone existed for the last two weeks of September at depths greater than 28 meters (92 feet). During most of August and September, therefore, lake trout were expected to move out of their preferred temperature habitat into uncomfortably warm water at 12° to 18°C (54° to 65°F) to avoid areas of low dissolved oxygen. During this period, their ability to be active and to feed successfully was thought to be seriously impaired, although direct observations of their behavior were not made.

During mid-October, adult lake trout return to shallow water to spawn. MacLean and coauthors noted in 1981 that spawning in Lake Simcoe occurs between October 15 and October 30 at depths of less than 5 meters (16 feet) and at temperatures of 9° to 11°C (48° to 52°F). In a recent study, I discovered that lake trout in Lake Simcoe remained near the lake bottom at temperatures of 9° to 11°C (48° to 52°F) during September, even though dissolved oxygen concentrations of 2 to 3 milligrams per liter occurred at that time. Natural recruitment of lake trout in Lake Simcoe has been unsuccessful since the 1950s, and the population is now being maintained by stocking of hatchery-reared yearling trout of Lake Simcoe parental origin each year. Waring and Evans identified loss of summer habitat from reduced dissolved oxygen in the hypolimnion as a possible cause of recruitment failure of lake trout in this lake.

SPAWNING HABITAT

Of all the trout, only the lake trout as a species lives its entire life predominantly in lakes, though Loftus reported in 1957 that there are some populations of lake trout in Lake Superior that leave the lake to spawn in rivers. Some populations of each of the other species spend at least part of their lives in

Lake trout change their locations in Lake Simcoe, Ontario (1977) as water temperatures and levels of dissolved oxygen fluctuate throughout the year. As shallower waters begin to lose oxygen and warm up in the summer months, the lake trout seek deeper, cooler waters within their preferred thermal range, 8° to 10°C (heavy isotherms). During late summer they are displaced from their preferred thermal habitat because of low dissolved oxygen conditions near the lake bottom at depths of 22 to 32 meters. As fall approaches, the upper levels of the lake become cooler, and the adult lake trout move inshore to spawn on shallow, rocky shoals. After spawning they again disperse over a wide range of depths wherever prey is abundant.

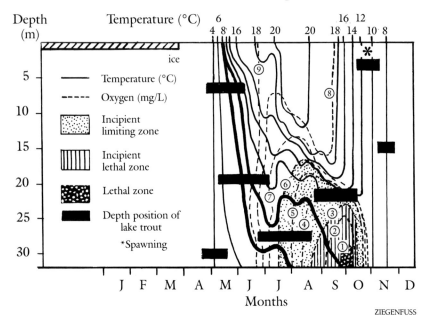

ZIEGENFUSS

lakes and spawn in inlet or outlet streams, which often also serve as extended nursery areas for rearing of the young.

Unlike other species, lake trout do not dig a redd but simply release their eggs a few centimeters above the selected spawning substrate into which the eggs settle. Sly noted that lake trout usually spawn over cobble gravel consisting of stones 5 to 20 centimeters (2 to 8 inches) in diameter with open spaces between them. The spaces must be large enough to entrap the eggs but small enough to exclude egg predators such as crayfish and sculpins.

Sly and Schneider pointed out in 1984 that developing eggs require a stable substrate, so the trout usually do not spawn on beaches where the substrate is moved by strong wave action. However, the trout favor shorelines exposed to autumnal winds because the onshore wave action helps to keep the substrate free of silt and organic material. The eggs generally are deposited below the depth of strong wave action, but above the depth at which suspended sediments settle onto the substrates.

Evans and his associates described four main types of cobble-gravel deposits that lake trout use as spawning habitat: beach deposits; flooded river-channel deposits; scree deposits, which are formed by falling rock at the base of bedrock outcrops; and lag deposits, which are formed of coarse particles that remain after erosion has removed sand, silts, and clays from glacial deposits.

McMurtry reported in 1986 that lake trout in small lakes in Ontario spawn generally at depths of less than 2 meters (7 feet) and have been observed in water as shallow as 15 centimeters (6 inches). Over their entire geographic range, lake trout spawning habitat is found at depths of from less than 1 meter (39 inches) to more than 55 meters (180 feet), and possibly to greater depths in the Great Lakes, according to separate studies by Eschmeyer, DeRoche, Johnson, Goodyear, and Sly and Widmer.

Eastern brook trout usually spawn in streams, but Webster reports that in the Adirondack Mountains of New York, they also spawn in lakes, and Fraser reports seeing them spawn in Dickson Lake, a Precambrian shield Lake in central Ontario. The spawning redds in Dickson Lake were dug in coarse gravel with a diameter of about 1 centimeter (0.4 inch). Nests were in shallow, nearshore areas subject to groundwater upwelling through the gravel. Brook trout also have been observed by Webster and Fraser to occasionally spawn on atypical substrates of tree bark, wood fragments, and other plant debris where groundwater upwelling is present.

HABITAT FOR YOUNG OF THE YEAR AND JUVENILES

Habitats of young-of-the-year trout in lakes are not well known. Except for populations of lake trout and some populations of Arctic char, trout usually spawn in tributary streams, where their young generally remain

These two areas are used by lakeshore brook trout for spawning. Left: The preferred spawning ground has clean areas of substrate that have been created by the upwelling of groundwater through the gravel. Right: This atypical spawning site is littered with organic debris, but upwelling may keep the area clear.

for days or weeks and often up to several years before moving to the parent lake, as Northcote reported in 1969 for rainbow trout. Stream nursery areas have been well documented, but lake nursery areas have not.

In general, young trout in lakes that have cool littoral zones will remain in these nearshore areas where adequate cover exists in the form of boulders, aquatic vegetation, fallen trees, and sunken logs, which provide sanctuary from predation by birds and larger fish. In some cases, nearshore submerged springs provide coldwater sanctuaries for fingerlings, even when the surrounding littoral area exceeds the preferred temperature range, as Carl observed in 1953 in Cowichan Lake, British Columbia. Yearling and two-year-old brown trout were reported in 1983 by Haraldstad and Jonsson to inhabit the littoral areas of a Norwegian lake year round, whereas adult brown trout were found in pelagic (midwater) and benthic areas in all parts of the lake down to but not exceeding 38 meters (125 feet).

In contrast, Benson, reporting in 1961, found that two-year-old juvenile cutthroat trout in Yellowstone Lake, Wyoming, were distributed over the same depths as the adults and that the two-year-olds were more frequently captured below 20 meters (66 feet) than the adults. Arctic char and lake trout young of the year appear to abandon the littoral zone in favor of deep water once temperatures in the nearshore area reach 10°C (50°F). In small lakes in Algonquin Park, Ontario, brook trout fry are readily observed along shorelines in only a few centimeters of water during May and early June. As the water warms, they move offshore, but the exact location has not been observed. Specific information on seasonal distribution of young-of-the-year and juvenile trout in lakes is rare, but it is likely that even the species more tolerant of warm temperatures would move to deeper areas of the littoral or sublittoral zone once surface temperatures reach 18° to 20°C (65° to 68°F).

Latitude affects the choice of habitat by young lake trout because of the associated effects of climate on the aquatic temperature regime. In a 1948 report, Miller and Kennedy noted seeing lake trout from the fry stage

through three years old along a boulder shoreline in Great Bear Lake in the Northwest Territories. Johnson also found juvenile lake trout inhabiting shallow littoral areas or inlet streams during the summer in cold Arctic lakes. However, DeRoche in 1969 reported another observation. He noted that in deep, stratified lakes in the southern part of the range of lake trout, young of the year inhabited the rocky littoral zone adjacent to spawning areas only until early May while temperatures were lower than 10°C (50°F). Near the end of May, young of the year were captured in small trawl nets at depths of 18 to 30 meters (59 to 98 feet), which suggests that the young trout descend to deep water in temperate lakes as the littoral zone warms in early spring. Evans et al. concluded that juveniles move to deep water to avoid being eaten by adult lake trout, which are known for their cannibalistic behavior.

Young Arctic char were reported by Hindar and Jonsson in 1982 to inhabit deep benthic areas in Vangsvatnet Lake, Norway, while the adults were found at shallower depths. Johnson, in his 1980 review, noted several cases of cannibalism among Arctic char, and Martin reported that Arctic char preyed on their own young in Ungava Crater Lake, but cannibalism was not observed in Vangsvatnet Lake.

ADULT HABITAT

The stratification of temperature and oxygen during the summer strongly limits the distribution of adult trout in lakes. During other seasons, and in unstratified and weakly stratified lakes, trout tend to be more widely dispersed, and their choices of habitat will reflect availability of prey. The distribution of their prey is influenced by stream inlets, water currents in the lake, and the structure of shorelines and contours of the lake bottom. Availability of resting habitats, including the presence of cover structures, also can influence the distribution of adult trout.

But during spawning seasons—autumn for Arctic char, lake trout, brook trout, Dolly Varden char, and brown trout, spring for rainbow trout and cutthroat trout—migration to spawning areas and breeding behavior dominate all activities. Trout tend to return to their natal sites, as reported by Jahn in

1969 and LaBar in 1971 for cutthroat trout in Yellowstone Lake tributaries, and by Northcote in 1969 for rainbow trout in various lakes in British Columbia. Brook trout and lake trout also apparently return to traditional spawning sites, although MacLean and coauthors reported in 1981 that Lake Opeongo lake trout, especially females, moved extensively during the spawning period between sites that were 1 to 3 kilometers (0.62 to 1.86 miles) apart. Cutthroat trout in Yellowstone Lake also were frequently found in non-natal streams during the spawning period, according to Jahn and LaBar. This suggests some degree of interbreeding among the subpopulations.

The presence of other trout species can also influence how coexisting trout species use their habitat. A study by Andrusak and Northcote, reported in 1971, of sympatric coastal cutthroat trout and Dolly Varden char in a small coastal lake in British Columbia revealed horizontal, as well as vertical, partitioning of the available habitat. In the nearshore zone, cutthroat trout were found closer to the surface and Dolly Varden char were nearer the bottom. Further offshore, cutthroat also were near the surface but much less abundant. Dolly Varden were found throughout the water column but were more likely to be feeding on the bottom. Cutthroat fed on terrestrial insects and small zooplankton; Dolly Varden fed on benthic insect larvae, small clams, and large zooplankton. In the absence of Dolly Varden, cutthroat trout occupied and fed in the mid-zone of the water.

Similarly, Nilsson and Northcote noted in 1981 that cutthroat abandon the midwater zone to the rainbow trout when they occur together, but in this case, cutthroat feed on both surface and bottom organisms. Similar changes were noted by Johnson and Hammar in 1981 for Arctic char and brown trout in isolation and when together. Both species, when occurring alone, will feed on benthos, but when together, the char switches to a midwater life pattern and feeds more on plankton.

The brown trout is less flexible, occupying the littoral areas and feeding on bottom organisms and terrestrial insects. The abundance of brown trout apparently always declines in the presence of the Arctic char, possibly due to a competitive disadvantage of the trout. Some trout prefer the lake bottom, including lake trout, brook trout, and Dolly Varden. These species, therefore, are often found near physical structures on the lake bottom, a ledge, for example, especially if prey species are nearby. But lake trout also will take to the bottom over featureless deep-water substrates, especially during the summer. Cooper and Fuller, reporting in 1945, clearly showed that lake trout and brook trout in Moosehead Lake, Maine, were located close to the lake bottom, while co-inhabiting landlocked Atlantic salmon preferred the middle stratum of the water. Similarly, more midwater species, such as rainbow trout and Arctic char, especially when the char are coinhabitants with brown trout, would not seek out structural features in the habitat as frequently as would the more benthic or littoral species.

Littoral species, such as cutthroat and brown trout, tend to prefer nearshore structural habitat that provides not only sources of food but also secure resting and hiding places. For example, Shepherd in 1974 reported observing cutthroat trout apparently seeking shelter under floating mats of sphagnum, which extended 10 meters (33 feet) from shore. Cutthroats also can often be observed cruising under log booms near shore in coastal British Columbia lakes, perhaps seeking cover as well as feeding on terrestrial insects that fall from the logs.

PRODUCTIVITY

The productivity of whole lakes depends on many factors, including the availability of minerals and nutrients, such as nitrogen and phosphorus, that phytoplankton at the base of the aquatic food web need; climatic factors associated with both latitude and regional geographic features, such as elevation and nearness to ocean coastlines; and local factors, including lake area and depth, geology, and materials that are imported by streams from the surrounding watershed. The productivity of fish also is determined by these factors, as shown by the work of Lawson, Northcote and Larkin, Ryder, and others. For example, production of Arctic char is extremely low in the crystal-clear waters of

Cold, deep lakes with adequate spawning areas offer excellent trout habitat.

Ungava Crater Lake. Production is higher, but still relatively low, for lake trout and brook trout (about 0.5 kilogram per hectare [0.45 pound per acre]) in lakes on the granitic, infertile soils of the Precambrian shield in Ontario, and reaches a maximum for rainbow trout in United States reservoirs. Jenkins in 1982 reported average annual yields of 11 kilograms per hectare (10 pounds per acre) for eighty-six such lakes.

When trout have the highest amount of surplus energy for such activities as capturing prey, avoiding predators, growing, producing eggs, migrating, and spawning, we would expect to find viable, productive populations. Habitats, therefore, that provide adequate quantities of space and food under the most suitable conditions of temperature, dissolved oxygen, and pH, for example, will be the most productive for self-sustaining wild trout populations.

The availability of adequate quantities of habitat resources, such as spawning habitat, nursery or juvenile rearing habitat, and adult habitat, also will influence the level of trout production. Fraser concluded, for example, that limited shoreline spawning habitat was probably limiting the production of brook trout in Dickson Lake, Ontario. Christie and Regier reported in 1988 that sustained yields of lake trout in twenty-one large North American lakes are well predicted by the volume of habitat within the lake trout's range of preferred temperatures. My colleagues and I found that as the amount of deepwater nursery habitat for lake trout increased in small inland lakes in Ontario, the angling yields for that species also increased.

Yields of lake trout in these waters also significantly declined as total dissolved solids (TDS) in the water increased, suggesting that the quality of lake trout habitat declined as nutrient levels and general lake productivity increased. Lake trout production declines as TDS increases, and therefore as primary production increases, because of the sensitivity of this species to loss of dissolved oxygen in the deepwater habitat and degradation of the littoral spawning habitat, both of which can occur as a result of decomposition of excessive organic material.

Healthy, self-sustaining populations of wild trout thrive in relatively undisturbed temperate watersheds, and lakes that have well-oxygenated waters at all depths. The sensitivity of trout habitat to general environmental degradation has special significance to us, because the quality of habitats for trout is one reflection of the general state of well-being of the human environment. Because of their responsiveness to environmental change, trout populations and their habitats can, in effect, serve as sensitive barometers of the health of the human life-support system. The tranquility and natural beauty of the wild places inhabited by trout go beyond the habitat needs of trout. We need to protect these places in their natural state not only for the trout, but also for ourselves.

—*David Owen Evans*

156 TROUT

The Great Lakes

The Great Lakes were formed 10,000 to 12,000 years ago by the retreating glaciers and now are centrally located between a watershed draining south to the Gulf of Mexico and one draining north to Hudson Bay.

The five Laurentian Great Lakes constitute the largest freshwater system in the world. They extend over an area greater than 243,000 square kilometers (94,000 square miles) and hold enough water to cover the entire contiguous United States to a depth of more than 3 meters (10 feet). Consolidated, this water nevertheless covers a vast area of different substrates and provides habitat for many species of fish.

Six species of salmonines have attained prominence in the Great Lakes: brook trout, lake trout, brown trout, rainbow trout, and coho and chinook salmon. A seventh, the Atlantic salmon, can occasionally be found in Lakes Michigan, Huron, and Superior, and more frequently in Ontario, where the many efforts in recent years to reintroduce it to where it once was native have met with partial success.

The lake trout has been extirpated in all the lakes but Superior. Brook trout, called coasters, brown trout, and various strains of rainbow trout were stocked to fill niches left vacant by the demise of the lake trout. Brook trout are native to inland streams and to Lake Superior and its tributaries. Brown trout were introduced from Europe, rainbow trout from the Pacific coast.

Native fish communities

Fish faunas in all the Great Lakes have changed dramatically since the 1800s, when conditions were pristine: They bear little resemblance to what they were then. At one time, Great Lakes fish communities comprised only native species that had evolved together and thus were in harmony within their ecosystems. The stocks were diverse, and individuals were larger on average than they are today. The ecosystem also was inherently more stable and resilient than it is now.

Historically, lake trout and burbot topped the aquatic food chain and fed on ciscoes, whitefishes, and other subspecies of *Coregonus*. Lake trout stocks were diverse, occupying every available habitat in the Great Lakes and even in some rivers, as Brown and his colleagues have noted. The lake trout was the dominant and most abundant terminal predator in Lakes Superior, Michigan, and Huron. According to a 1985 report by Ryder and Edwards, it became dominant in Lake Ontario after the Atlantic salmon population declined and became extinct in that lake during the last half of the 1800s. The lake trout also may have been the dominant predator of the limnetic zone (open water) of eastern Lake Erie, at least until about 1890.

Intruders

Habitat modification, eutrophication, (nutrient enrichment), pollution, overfishing, and invasions by nonindigenous species, all human-induced changes to habitat and fish communities, have caused changes more far-reaching in the Great Lakes than in any other large freshwater lakes in the world. The completion of the Welland Canal around Niagara Falls in 1910, for instance, which connected Erie, Michigan, Huron, and Superior to the Atlantic Ocean, inadvertently created a conduit for species alien to Great Lakes ecosystems. These species invaded the disrupted fish communities and flourished. They had no predators to consume them and no competitors to modulate population increases, since they had evolved in a different environment.

The sea lamprey was the most devastating intruder, preying on the largest fish in the lakes, generally top predators. Sea lampreys coexisted with large lake trout in Lake Ontario after the lamprey gained entry in the 1800s. As a result of years of overfishing, lake trout mean size declined. They were then too small to overcome attacks by this parasite, which attaches itself to the fish, rasps a hole in its victim's side, and removes blood using anticoagulants—a piscine Dracula.

Sea lampreys have weakened populations of top predators, such as lake trout, in the Great Lakes.

JUDE

Deforestation caused increased accumulations of organic matter and higher water temperatures in potential spawning streams, making them more favorable for sea lamprey and allowing successful reproduction of this alien in those Great Lakes with suitable streams: Michigan, Ontario, Huron, and Superior. Ironically, recent improvements in water quality of some of these tributary streams have increased the amount of habitat suitable for sea lamprey spawning.

Loss of top predators because of sea lamprey predation destabilized fish communities. This major disruption allowed another nonindigenous species, the marine alewife, a member of the herring family, to thrive in three of the Great Lakes that had become

devoid of top predators and had suffered major changes to their formerly well integrated fish communities. Alewife populations exploded in Lakes Ontario, Michigan, and Huron (Lake Erie gets too cold in winter and Lake Superior is too cold most of the time).

Subsequent plantings of many species of salmonines have reestablished a predator-prey system in the lakes based totally on exotic prey fish and mostly on hatchery-reared salmonines. (Some natural reproduction by stocked salmonines has occurred in all the Great Lakes.) This fish community is dominated by alewife because of their abundance, their central role as prey for salmonines, and their depressing effect on such prey species as yellow perch, bloater, deepwater sculpin, and emerald shiner. Alewife compete with prey species by feeding on their required food, zooplankton, and by preying on their young, thus reducing their numbers both indirectly and directly.

INTRODUCED SPECIES

There have been many purposeful introductions of predatory fish into the Great Lakes. Rainbow trout were introduced widely at the end of the 1800s, and naturally reproducing populations now provide a substantial sport fishery, according to a 1971 report by Hansen and Stauffer. There also is the possibility, according to a 1972 report by MacCrimmon and Gots, of early hybridization of rainbow trout with cutthroat trout, which were introduced into Michigan streams as early as 1895. The current populations are now a mixture of wild and domestic strains, and many more new "strains" are being added to enhance various fisheries.

The rainbow trout, unlike its fellow salmonine predators, exhibits considerable variation in its life history. Spawning runs occur typically in spring, though some stocks spawn in fall. Rainbow trout now occur in all the Great Lakes, and substantial natural spawning runs occur in those lakes with adjacent large, clean rivers and streams—Michigan, Huron, Superior, and, to some extent, Ontario. Pollution, the sea lamprey in the late 1940s, and dams have limited growth and reproduction of this species. Current management efforts are aimed at removing

dams, installing fish ladders, stocking fish above and below dams, and introducing new strains that spawn at different times.

Data on movement of rainbow trout are scarce, but Betteridge reported in 1985 that, in an Ontario inland lake, rainbows moved in response to movements of prey, rather than with waters of their preferred temperatures. They ranged widely throughout the lake, which is characteristic of rainbow trout in the Great Lakes as well. (One rainbow trout, which was marked near Zion, Illinois, was collected on the other side of Lake Michigan near St. Joseph.) Rainbows have often been found in warmer, nearshore waters, preferring and growing best at temperatures between 17° and 20°C (51° and 68°F), accord-

ing to a 1971 report by McCauley and Pond.

We know little about brook trout movements in the Great Lakes, but a 1969 report by Alexander and Shetter of brook and rainbow trout stocked in inland lakes suggests that brook trout stayed near shore and sought areas where springs and inlets occur, whereas rainbows generally stayed in water deeper than 3 meters (10 feet).

Brown trout in Lake Superior reproduce naturally, spawning in the fall in tributary streams. They are bottom oriented, and most are confined to the margins of the lakes, unlike salmon, which range widely in the thermocline area through the lakes. They prefer temperatures between 12.4° and 17.6°C (54.6° and 64.0°F).

Lake Superior, one of the largest bodies of fresh water in the world, is home to several species of salmonid fish.

More than 100 million lake trout were stocked in the Great Lakes between 1965 and 1984. Yet as of 1989, only Lake Superior has regained a substantial population of self-sustaining native lake trout. In all the other Great Lakes, massive stocking efforts have replaced the native lake trout and their many component "stocks" with hatchery-reared lake trout, which lack genetic diversity. Little natural reproduction has occurred, and managers have been reluctant to tackle this problem on an experimental basis, such as stocking all the lake trout into one lake in one year.

Eshenroder and colleagues in a 1984 report suggested several causes for the lack of reproduction: inadequate numbers of spawners, reduction of egg viability, predation, inappropriate fish stocking methods, maladaptation for reproduction in the selected habitat, reduction in the genetic diversity of hatchery fish, contaminants, and eutrophication of spawning habitat.

Attempts to restore lake trout populations by stocking have included introducing one hybrid strain, splake (brook trout × lake trout). This hybrid grows faster and is more prolific than lake trout of similar size. Splake were stocked in the hope that they would reproduce before sea lamprey or commercial fishermen exterminated them. They have enjoyed limited success.

There exists a great range of habitats for lake trout across the Great Lakes. Reproductive success has been the greatest in the most oligotrophic Lake Superior, though maximum growth would be expected in Lake Erie. With general degradation of habitat, especially increased levels of nutrients brought on by civilization and development in the nearshore zones, spawning habitat may have been degraded. Additional nutrients encourage more plant growth. When the plant materials decompose, they generate toxic substances and reduce dissolved oxygen concentrations in the incubation environment, thus decreasing egg-hatching success. Resolution of this problem in the Great Lakes will focus greater emphasis on viewing the Great Lakes as a total ecosystem. Such resolution dictates that we concentrate on restoring native fish natural reproduction whenever possible and retreat from the temporary fixes of artificial stocking.

The restoration of top predators (salmonines) has created a sportfishing mecca, whose cornucopia is not without its drawbacks. On one hand are a Great Lakes sport fishery valued at more than $4 billion per year and high expectations of numerous catches of large fish. On the other hand are nagging concerns about increasing attacks by sea lamprey on northern Lake Huron predators, a declining catch rate (and size, in some areas) of salmon, shifts in fishing emphasis to lake trout, which we are trying to rehabilitate, unexplained large die-offs of chinook salmon in Lake Michigan, a declining forage base of alewife, loss of genetic diversity in hatchery fish, and diseases of hatchery fish, which have wiped out whole stocks in recent years.

LAKE STRUCTURE

Lake morphology (structure) profoundly influences the quality and quantity of important fish habitat and in turn fish communities. The most important habitat is often near shore and thus subject to human disruption. We can divide the overall structure of each of the Great Lakes into two zones: offshore, or pelagic, and nearshore. The pelagic zone is generally uniform, and sediments below it are soft and organic. It also tends to be oligotrophic and thus generally cannot support a highly productive fish community. The nearshore zone is a highly energetic zone because of wave activity and is the receptacle for nutrients as well as contaminants and sediments from the surrounding watershed. It has a diversity of sediments, dominated by sand and rocks, and a variety of habitats, including important spawning and nursery areas.

Basin morphometry is an important confining factor, for it sets limits within which fish reproduce, feed, and compete. For example, Lake Erie, which is shallow and receives high levels of nutrients from the watershed, accounts for only 2 percent of the total volume of water in the Great Lakes, yet it produces about the same biomass of fish in the commercial catch as do the other four deeper and more oligotrophic lakes combined.

The oligotrophic nature of the Great Lakes, excluding Lake Erie, is exacerbated by the relatively low input of annual energy from the sun, which in turn contributes to inordinately low mean water temperatures, relatively slow growth rates in fishes, and low fish biomass turnover rates (low harvest each year). Rawson in 1955 expressed the relationship this way: The standing crop of fish per unit area in large lakes decreased as the mean depth increased.

The morphology of the Great Lakes also affects the concentration of such toxic substances as PCBs (polychlorinated biphenyls). Lake Superior, because of its enormous surface area, takes in more atmospheric toxic substances, but has a low sedimentation rate, a large volume, and lower temperatures, which retard biological uptake compared with the other lakes. Contamination of fish there is low compared with Lake Michigan, where more tributary inputs, moderate productivity, and contaminated sediments result in higher concentrations of contaminants in fish. Lake Erie receives large tributary inputs of toxic substances but has a high sedimentation rate, which tends to tie up and remove toxic substances from the water column.

Contaminants generally occur in low concentrations in the water of the Great Lakes. In these ecosystems, detrimental chemicals move up through the food chain and accumulate in top predators. Experiments conducted by Willford and colleagues and reported in 1981 demonstrated that water from Lake Michigan was of such poor quality that it impeded the survival of newly hatched lake trout carrying maternally inherited residues.

Substrate

Habitat diversity begets fish diversity. Generally, the diversity of the substrate is highest near shore because of the influences of rivers, bays, and strong currents, which shape the kinds and amounts of substrate in this zone. Thus, many more species are found near shore.

Progressing offshore, there is a gradient of sediment types and decreasing sizes to the deepest basins and areas of deposition where fine organic material accumulates. Sediment type determines the amount of benthic (bottom fauna) production, which is important for fish production. In many areas of the Great Lakes, the offshore abyss, where habitat varies least, is characterized by only a few common species, most notably the deep-water sculpin in the upper Great Lakes.

Water chemistry

Beeton in 1969 compiled the chemical data for the Great Lakes, which showed that concentrations of major ions have remained virtually unchanged in Lake Superior. However, increases began to occur about 1910 in the lower lakes, especially of nitrates in Lake Ontario. Chapra in 1977 noted two major periods of change in water quality: the late nineteenth century, when large areas of forest were cleared and agricultural practices were developed, and after World War II, when the population increased and detergents were introduced.

The general response to cultural eutrophication (man's addition of too many nutrients to the aquatic environment) has varied from lake to lake. The morphology of the Great Lakes has strongly influenced the magnitude of effects. In the upper Great Lakes, the effects of accelerated additions of nutrients were confined to the nearshore zones and shallow bays and diluted because of the immense volume and depth in the main lake basins. But in the lower lakes, Ontario and especially shallow Erie, the effects were dramatic. Nutrients caused massive growths of algae, which died, decomposed, and consumed dissolved oxygen in the deeper parts of Lake Erie. The oxygen depletion prevented fish habitation in these waters and caused the demise of most of the large may-

Lake trout probably spawned on Charlevoix Reef before they were extirpated from Lake Michigan.

JUDE

Dead carp and algal mats are a sure sign that nutrient enrichment is a problem in Lake Huron.

flies, *Hexagenia*, critically important food organisms that live in bottom sediments. Consequently, for part of each summer, fish production ceases in the entire hypolimnion, or bottom layer of water, of the western basin of Lake Erie.

There were changes in abundance of various fish species, and these changes followed predictable patterns in each of the Great Lakes as these stocks underwent human-induced stresses. The ultimate biological extinction of lake trout populations in Lake Erie probably was related to environmental stresses, particularly to depletion of dissolved oxygen in the central basin hypolimnion, according to a 1973 report by Hartman. It appears that excessive phosphorus loading, mainly from domestic wastes indirectly caused extinction or a reduction in size of lake trout stocks by decreasing the amount of habitable water, according to Ryder and Edwards. A major secondary effect of nutrient loadings, increased rates of organic sedimentation, may have adversely affected the quality of spawning grounds for walleye and lake trout and, in Lake Erie, the habitat of the burrowing mayfly, according to a study by Regier and colleagues in 1969.

To assure survival of lake trout in the summer hypolimnion of the Great Lakes, levels of dissolved oxygen must be at least 5.5 parts per million, according to Ryder and Edwards. Relatively high nutrient levels occur in Lakes Michigan and Huron, which are mesotrophic rather than oligotrophic, as is Lake Superior. Such levels allow good growth rates but may limit or eliminate successful reproduction as the accumulation of organic matter on spawning grounds causes ammonia production and depletes the dissolved oxygen supply.

TEMPERATURE

All fish have thermal preferences, temperatures at which they grow and perform other life functions best, and the interplay between the physical characteristics of the water and the changes in distribution of prey constrain fish into certain strata or areas within a lake. Prey fish, such as alewife, rainbow smelt, gizzard shad, and sculpin, prefer different habitats, temperatures, and depth strata, a situation that complicates immensely the predictability of finding salmonines in the Great Lakes.

Christie and Regier give an example of the way in which temperature configures a lake and its trout populations. Much of Lake Ontario is very cold from May to September. Less than 20 percent of the available habitat is warmer than 8 C° (46°F). Because lake trout prefer temperatures ranging from 8° to 12°C (46° to 54°F), only a small proportion of the lake is in their preferred thermal zone. A similar situation exists in all the other Great Lakes. In fact, even less preferred habitat would be available for lake trout in Lake Superior (based on the total volume available) because so much of it is below the minimum preferred temperature. On the other hand, lake trout cannot inhabit much of the available habitat in shallow Lake Erie because, except for the eastern basin, it becomes too warm.

Christie and Regier further state that the availability during the summer of water in a temperature range that is physiologically optimal for a species contributes strongly to the productive capacity of that species. It also affects the number of species. Lake Erie, the warmest, has the highest number: around 100. Lake Superior, the deepest and coldest, has the lowest: forty-four.

Another strong force that controls fish in the Great Lakes is the stratification pattern that develops seasonally. Water is densest at 4°C (39°F) rather than at 0°C (32°F). This unique property combined with the thermal energy from sunlight and mixing from the wind creates typical sequences of temperature patterns over the year. As you might expect, these patterns again are strongest in shallow Lake Erie and weakest in cold, deep Lake Superior.

Spring. Bear in mind the relationship of depth to temperature. At some point in spring, the surface waters of a lake warm. When they reach 4°C (39°F), they sink until the lake becomes isothermal. That is, it has the same temperature from surface to bottom and is subject to wind-induced mixing. This makes spring a time of replenishment of the entire water mass as dissolved substances (nutrients, for example) derived from the decomposition of organic sediments on the bottom are mixed throughout the water column, fueling algae that grow in upper layers. Dissolved oxygen from upper layers and chemical substances that may have built up in bottom waters because of the decomposition of bottom sediments are evenly mixed throughout the body of water. This condition is especially true in Lake Erie where water near the bottom loses some of its dissolved oxygen over the winter due to bacterial decomposition of accumulated bottom sediments. However, because cold temperatures retard bacterial metabolism, depletion of dissolved oxygen is considerably less than that observed during the summer anoxic period.

Spring is also the time when a phenomenon called the thermal bar develops. It occurs when the lake begins to warm in spring, first in shallow, nearshore water. (A similar phenomenon occurs in reverse in fall.) Remember that in spring the main mass of water is at 4°C (39°F) and thus at maximum density. So when water in the nearshore zone warms, a vertical thermal gradient or front forms with warm water on one side and cold water on the other. This front continues to move lakeward as air temperatures rise and warm runoff from tributaries accumulates in the nearshore zone. Nutrients and toxic substances are thus temporarily confined there. In addition, many fish species, which prefer temperatures higher than 4°C (39°F), seek this warmer water, and prey fish can accumulate in exceedingly large numbers in this very narrow bar along the lake shore. In turn,

ZIEGENFUSS

Warm   Warm

< 4°C

Thermal bar

In the spring, as the surface waters warm, wind-induced mixing adds oxygen to the bottom waters and resuspends nutrients in the surface waters. The thermal bar is a temperature zone that forms when colder offshore waters of less than 4°C (39°F) and warmer near-shore waters of greater than 4°C encounter each other in a lake. This mixing zone between the two temporarily prevents warmer waters from moving out away from the shoreline, and keeps cooler waters offshore, affecting the distribution of predator and prey species within the lake.

predators seek these warmer waters and the large populations of prey fish that inhabit them.

Summer. In summer, vertical thermal stratification is at a maximum, and depending on the lake, three layers form in various thicknesses. The top layer, or epilimnion, is the warmest layer with uniformly high temperatures in general, usually greater than 15°C (59°F). The thermocline, the middle layer, is a transition zone where the thermal gradient is at a maximum, generally ranging from 13°C (55°F) to 8°C (46°F) within the layer. The bottom layer, or hypolimnion, is often only 4°C (39°F).

This stratification pattern is slight in Lake Superior because it is deep, large, and far north. Maximum stratification occurs in Lake Erie, because it is shallow and the farthest south. In Lake Erie, summer stratification, along with the high input of nutrients, creates a high accumulation rate of sediments (dead algae, plants, and animals, and eroded soil). This sedimentation caused the depletion of dissolved oxygen from the hypolimnion in the 1960s, and it was this loss of oxygen from bottom waters that precipitated the extinction and suppression of several species of fish and bottom-dwelling organisms.

The area where the thermocline stratum intersects the slanting lake bottom is also an area of concentrated and intense fish activity. Prey fish apparently find preferred temperatures and abundant food at this intersection, and they in turn attract trout, which also often find preferred temperatures here. Demersal, or bottom-dwelling, fish such as the lake trout also do not have to suspend above the bottom to find optimal temperatures, which sometimes are available at the intersection of the thermocline and the lake bottom.

The summer stratification period also gives rise to two phenomena that can cause changes in fish distribution. Seiches are oscillations of the lake surface, caused by wind or an atmospheric pressure differential between two widely separated points on a body of water. This fluctuation causes the lake to slosh. Changes up to 3 meters (10 feet) have been recorded in Lake Erie. There are two types of seiches, surface and internal. The internal seiche has the most substantial impact on the physical environment, and hence on fish distribution. Changes in depth and receding water from nearshore habitat can kill small fishes and benthos populations when this area is dewatered.

The second phenomenon is upwelling, in which cold, hypolimnetic waters from the lake bottom rise near shore to replace warmer water that has been pushed toward the other end of the lake by offshore winds. This is another major disrupter of fish distributions, because predatory fish move in with the cold water to nearshore areas to feed on prey fish, which are separated from these predators by their preference for warm water. In addition, there is undoubtedly considerable movement of prey fish living near shore or in or near the thermocline where it intersects the lake bottom. Movement of the water mass allows trout access to these fish, which may well be stressed by the incoming cold water to which they have not had time to acclimate.

Fall and winter. In fall, the process is reversed as the lakes cool down to 4°C (39°F)

and fall overturn occurs, again making the entire lake similar in physical and chemical characteristics. As the process moves into winter, the period of winter stratification begins. Temperature again most affects Lake Erie. The 4°C (39°F) water sinks to the bottom (because it is densest, remember), the upper layer cools further but floats, because the water colder or warmer than 4°C (39°F) is less dense. Surface temperature rapidly reaches 0°C (32°F), and water freezes.

This process depends, of course, on winter severity and wind intensity, which can prevent freezing and, instead, supercool the water. In fact, the Great Lakes, except for Lake Erie, seldom or never freeze over entirely. Lake Erie is the shallowest of the lakes and has the smallest volume. Thus, it stores less heat per unit surface area in warm months, so it cools faster than do the other lakes. Their volumes of water are so large and wave activity so high that winters usually are not severe enough to cool the water mass above 4°C (39°F) to freezing temperatures.

Winter can be severe for fish in Lake Erie. During extremely cold winters with a lot of wind, a large part of the surface water can become cooled to 0°C (32°F) or below, which can stress, even kill, some fish. Gizzard shad, an immigrant to Lake Erie and an important forage fish, is susceptible to winterkill because of this phenomenon. In addition, the poor success of alewife in Lake Erie sometimes is attributed to the lack of suitable deepwater habitat of warmer water, which generally does exist in Lakes Huron, Michigan, and Ontario. Still, cold winters in these lakes can kill large numbers of alewife, according to a 1985 report by Eck and Brown. All fish activity during this time of the year is low, but several species, including deepwater sculpin, important prey fish such as the bloater, and the predatory burbot spawn during the winter period.

The thermal cycle is completed the following spring when warming once again occurs, heating upper waters until the entire water column is once again 4°C (39°F) and the lake undergoes spring mixing.

Langmuir circulation lines. You often see foam lines on lakes, and they indicate some interesting activity. These wind-parallel streaks, called Langmuir circulation lines, occur on windswept lakes and coincide with downward motion of the water, according to a 1974 report by Mortimer. Between the streaks are zones of upwelling. Thus, the energy of the wind, transferred to the waves, is one of the vehicles, perhaps a principal vehicle, for the downward flux of turbulence and for the formation of the upper mixed layer. In addition to indicating this transfer of energy from wind to water, the Langmuir circulation lines also accumulate terrestrial insects that trout often prey on.

Weather conditions. Climate, especially in years of unusually warm or cold temperatures, can enhance or retard the reproduction of fishes and can cause the thermocline to move far offshore, meaning that preferred trout habitat also moves far offshore. A study, reported in 1982, by Heufelder and colleagues on Lake Michigan documented that cold summers and frequent offshore winds produced unusually large numbers of upwellings. These upwellings in turn inhibited alewife reproduction, which in Lake Michigan occurs in warmed nearshore waters. More alewife than average die in cold years, according to Eck and Brown, and cold years also can reduce the growth of fish. Lake Michigan almost froze over in 1977, which reduced the wind-caused resuspension of phosphorus from sediments, which in turn reduced phytoplankton production, the basis of the aquatic food chain, the following year, according to a 1986 report by Scavia and colleagues. Years of drought or high water levels, alternately decrease or enhance production of fish that use nearshore areas for spawning and as a nursery.

GLOBAL WARMING

Lake trout are stenothermal. They maintain themselves within a narrow temperature range, with specific temperature requirements for survival, growth, and successful reproduction, according to a 1980 report by Martin and Olver. These thermal specifications are currently manifested in two examples: optimal reproduction but poor growth in cold Lake Superior, and dismal to no reproduction but good growth in warm, productive Lake Erie.

So, depending on the lake, the effect on lake trout of increases in mean temperature of the Great Lakes may lead first to reproductive and recruitment failure, increased growth, and eventually, if the temperature trend persists, to subsequent reductions in growth rates, even death if the trend is prolonged. In mesotrophic Lakes Michigan and Huron, thermal habitat for lake trout may be expanded because of global warming, which presumably would cause increased growth and production.

LIGHT

Light controls fish by influencing their daily behavior patterns, especially those of distribution and feeding. Annually, light initiates the reproductive cycle, and temperature regulates the timing. But light is modified by turbidity and currents, wind-induced changes to the water body, cloud cover, and plankton blooms. Thus, these conditions set the boundaries of habitat conditions for fish and provide spatial and temporal structure to the environment. Light can be one of the major factors that effect final species dominance in an aquatic system.

Part of the reason gizzard shad do well in highly turbid lakes, such as Lake Erie, is that they must feed on zooplankton; alewife do not do as well. However, the water is much clearer in Lakes Michigan, Huron, and Ontario, and alewife, which feed on individual particles of food as well as passively filter water for zooplankton, dominate these systems.

TROPHIC INTERACTIONS

Habitat characteristics and biotic interactions can be changed in startling ways from the bottom up, by changes in nutrient supply coming into the system, or from the top down, by top predators preying on dominant planktivores in a system. Banning phosphorus in detergents and curbing sewage input in the Detroit River, and hence into Lake Erie, resurrected that lake. Productivity, which is determined by the level of nutrients in the lake, dropped as nutrient inputs slowed. As a consequence of this bottom-up force, algal blooms decreased, prey fish production decreased, and water clarity increased. These changes have allowed fish managers to restore the lake's walleye population as habitat conditions for this species improved and controls on the commercial fishery were instituted.

Changes to the overall function of the ecosystem can also be wrought from the top of the food chain. Since the late 1970s, the alewife has declined in Lake Michigan because of cold winters and predation by salmonines, according to studies done separately by Eck and Brown, Stewart and colleagues, and Tesar and Jude. Changes triggered by this decline have cascaded through the ecosystem. As the major zooplankton predator, the alewife, declined, its main prey, the larger zooplankton and *Daphnia pulicaria*, increased. Because these larger zooplankton are more efficient at removing particles, including algae, from the water column than were the former smaller zooplankton populations, dramatic increases in water clarity were observed in the early 1980s, recorded by Scavia and colleagues.

Other changes can occur when the largest lake trout are harvested or otherwise eliminated from the system. Prey fish can grow too large for smaller lake trout, so large proportions of the prey-fish community become immune to predation. This situation in turn leads to an inefficient transfer of energy (fewer trout to harvest) from prey to predator populations and is one reason why fish managers try to maintain the appropriate sizes and abundances of prey for the top predators in the Great Lakes.

PREDATOR AND PREY

Changes in habitat affect the distribution of prey fish and sometimes the predators that feed on them. To understand the effects, let's look at some general distribution patterns for fish in Lake Michigan. These generalities apply to lakes Ontario and Huron, but to a lesser extent in lakes Erie and Superior, where conditions are extreme and where either the array of fish species is different or a different species dominates the food chain (for example, gizzard shad in Lake Erie).

Prey become vulnerable to coevolved predators when the prey change behavior, perhaps because of disease, spawning, lack of escape cover, starvation, or upwelling, or when their habitat overlaps that of many predators. However, in the case of predator-prey dynamics in the Great Lakes, the generalities are clouded, because in some cases the predator and prey had not shared the ecosystem before the development of the current potpourri of fish that now inhabit the Great Lakes. Nevertheless, some patterns emerge.

Alewife is an exotic marine fish. It reaches lengths up to 20 centimeters (8 inches) in the Great Lakes. This species entered the Great Lakes above Lake Ontario through the Welland Canal in the 1950s and exploded in numbers and biomass in lakes devoid of predators and competitors. Alewife attained highest abundance in Lake Michigan in 1966, when they experienced a catastrophic die-off and littered the beaches by the tons. They have formed a large part of the diet of salmonines since then.

Alewife are pelagic (midwater), schooling fish whose age groups occupy different parts of the lake during the four periods of the thermal cycle: spring overturn, summer stratification, fall overturn, and winter stratification. In Lake Michigan, alewife replaced the now extinct seven-species complex of deepwater ciscoes, which occupied the entire lake more completely and, hence, used food and habitat more efficiently than do the current dominant exotic species complex of alewife and rainbow smelt.

Because alewife are pelagic, salmon were stocked to feed on them. Salmon, continuous-swimming pelagic predators, key in on these fish, whose schools present large and silvery targets. As a result, salmon eat more alewife than trout, which tend to feed slightly more on demersal species and therefore eat a greater diversity of food items.

Some observations of Great Lakes piscine predators in studies at the Shedd Aquarium in Chicago support these statements, according to a 1989 report by Savitz and Bardygula. Salmon were very fast and could catch any prey they decided to eat, but they had difficulty seeing rainbow smelt in the water column, because of the transparency of these prey, and seldom went after demersal species such as the yellow perch, which were not in the midwater cruising territory of the salmon. On the other hand, rainbow trout would chase yellow perch all around the aquarium but had difficulty catching them.

Adult alewife come inshore in the spring first to inhabit the warmest water, then later to spawn in June through August, after which they return to deeper water. Some juvenile alewife also are attracted to this warmer area in the spring. Young of the year inhabit nearshore water less than 6 meters (20 feet) deep until it begins to cool during fall turnover. Yearlings inhabit the thermocline areas of the lake. A combination of reproduction and preferred temperatures determines where in the available thermal habitat this particular fish lives. Jude and colleagues found that lake trout, brown trout, and, to a lesser extent, rainbow trout feed on adult alewife in the spring when the preferred temperatures of the predator and prey, and consequently the habitats, overlap.

In summer, lake trout feed on much larger alewife than do any of the other predators, because adult alewife stay low in the hypolimnion, where lake trout generally reside. Salmon feed on smaller fish, including yearling alewife, which are present in the thermocline area, the preferred-temperature habitat for salmon. Young of the year escape extensive predation by salmonines during summer by staying inshore, where temperature generally is too warm for the trout and salmon. However, some rainbow trout and small brown trout commonly are found in this zone feeding on young alewife.

When young-of-the-year alewife migrate offshore in the fall as waters cool, they face extensive predation, because they move into colder water preferred by salmonine predators. A similar scenario exists for yellow perch, which stay even more closely associated with the shallow, nearshore zone. They are fed on during spring and fall overturns, when prey fish move into preferred thermal habitat of salmonines, and during upwellings, when salmonines move into nearshore zones occupied by both forage fish.

Upwellings must be a dynamic phenomenon for fish in the Great Lakes, as large, warm, nearshore masses of water are blown offshore by strong, offshore breezes. The size of the nearshore water mass depends on the spatial extent of the wind and its force but can extend for 80 kilometers (50 miles). This water mass then is replaced with cold hypolimnetic water with its complement of coldwater fish, including trout predators. Up-

wellings must cause prey fish to move either horizontally or vertically, as fish may experience a decline in temperature of up to 15°C (27°F) from ambient conditions before the upwelling. Such thermal changes in Lake Ontario stressed and killed fish, according to a 1970 report by Emery. Thus, it appears that predators take advantage of this disruption and feed on prey that are thermally stressed and seldom available to them otherwise. The spottail shiner is one of the species that are abundant nearshore yet seldom eaten by predators. They are confined to the warmed nearshore zone above the thermocline and, therefore, are usually out of the preferred thermal habitat of their piscine predators.

Rainbow smelt were fed on extensively during their spring spawning migrations to the tributaries and the nearshore zone, and slimy sculpins, which prefer cold water, did not appear to be susceptible to predation, except during spawning activities in spring. Slimy sculpins are nocturnal crevice-seeking animals that prefer to live close to the bottom, in or under rocks or other kinds of shelter during the day. They nest on the underside of the substrate and males guard the nests. Apparently these behaviors during the spring spawning season result in high mortality caused by trout predators, especially brown trout. Eck and Wells found in 1986 that age-1 and age-2 lake trout ate young-of-the-year alewife in December after offshore dispersal due to nearshore cooling. They ate slimy sculpin in March when predator and prey distributions forged by environmental factors caused populations to overlap.

The deepwater sculpin is demersal, abundant, and wholly distributed in the deepwater abyss of the upper Great Lakes, generally in water deeper than 50 meters (164 feet). This species lives in water of about

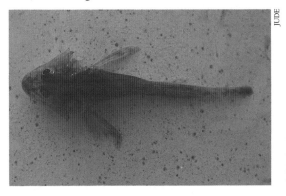

The deepwater sculpin is a regular food item of lake trout, but other salmonids do not venture that deep to feed.

Of the five Great Lakes, Lake Superior has been the least affected by human activity and thus sustains the largest populations of trout.

4° to 8°C (39° to 47°F) and, as a consequence, generally is out of the range of the current suite of predators in most of the Great Lakes, except for Lake Superior, where increasing native lake trout populations are distributed throughout the lake. Here, lake trout eat deepwater sculpin regularly.

However, predators in Lakes Michigan and Huron, except some recent stockings of lake trout on offshore reefs, do not venture into the offshore abyss because the fish are of hatchery origin; we no longer have the strains of fish that once inhabited these offshore areas.

In this discussion, we have seen how latitude, lake shape, and the effects of man, especially the addition of nutrients, modification of habitat, and overfishing, have dramatically altered the fish species complexes and the places where fish live, eat, and reproduce in the Great Lakes. Lake Superior, the largest,

remains least affected by the human and fish aliens that have assailed its terrestrial and aquatic environments. Lake Erie, the shallowest and most productive, has experienced the most dramatic swings, from "dead sea" in the 1960s to walleye mecca in the 1990s. In the three other lakes, many species have been extinguished, native fish communities have changed, edible fish have become contaminated with toxic substances, and, more recently, resurgences have occurred in both native stock and the salmonine fisheries that now enjoy world-class status.

We enjoy the scenery, eat the fish, drink the water, and create many of the problems for the Great Lakes. If we are to leave a Great Lakes legacy to following generations, we must reduce resource consumption, restore clean air, and lower our impact on the ecosystem.

—*David Jude*

Oceans and estuaries

With the exception of some strictly interior species, such as the golden trout and the Apache trout, most salmonid species in North America have some anadromous component within their range. The more common examples include steelhead and sea-run Dolly Varden and cutthroat trout along the Pacific Coast, and sea-run Arctic char and brown trout along the Atlantic Coast. But there are unusual examples of anadromy as well. The lake trout, for example, is known primarily as a fish of cool, deep lakes. But even this species enters coastal waters along Labrador and other parts of northern Canada. Although lake trout are the least tolerant of salt water, Boulva and Simard found in the 1960s that this species can be found in brackish waters with salinity of up to 13 parts per thousand. Brook trout are most commonly a freshwater-only species, but there are sea-run populations in Maine, Massachusetts, and the Maritime Provinces.

Sea-run brown trout are common throughout the British Isles and northern Europe. Non-anadromous brown trout were introduced to North America in 1883, and some of these fish have developed anadromous tendencies, moving into the estuary and coastal areas along the northeastern coast of the United States and Canada. True sea-run brown trout, however, are rarely found in North America, though eggs from sea-run populations have been imported from Europe.

ESTUARIES AND COASTAL WATERS

The steelhead is one of the few species of trout that undertake distant migrations. Steelhead from North American waters have been encountered as far north as the Gulf of Alaska and as far west as 185° west longitude, at the tip of the Aleutian Island chain.

Most anadromous trout, however, only move into the estuaries or coastal waters. Sea-run brown trout in Europe are known to migrate relatively great distances along the coast, sometimes hundreds of miles, but never far out to sea. Brown trout in North America are thought to behave the same way, though there have been a few tag recoveries at sea. Non-anadromous brown trout grow rapidly in estuaries of southern Maine, but they are almost never encountered along the coast. Sea-run brook trout and cutthroat trout, as well as Arctic char and Dolly Varden char, do venture into coastal waters but almost never far from their natal streams. There are, of course, exceptions. One tagged Arctic char was recaptured 129 kilometers (80 miles) from its home stream. But such examples are rare for trout.

As a consequence of these limited movements, estuarine and coastal areas are extremely important to anadromous trout. The Fraser River estuary in British Columbia, through which pass steelhead and sea-run cutthroat trout and some of the largest Pacific salmon runs in the world, is surrounded by the port facilities of Vancouver and some 1.3 million people. Because the Fraser estu-

Steelhead and sea-run cutthroats pass through this estuary in Puget Sound.

and salt water. Anadromous trout move to these areas because estuaries and coastal areas are extremely productive; under normal conditions, trout attain their highest growth rates in these waters.

Fish production can be more than 600 times higher on the continental shelf and more than 70,000 times higher in upwelling areas along the coast than in open ocean waters. Upwelling is common along many coastal regions where bottom waters move inshore, replacing surface waters that are pushed offshore by winds. The result is a mixed, nutrient-rich environment.

Carlander made an exhaustive study of available information on brown trout in 1969, and concluded: "Growth, in general, is faster in lakes than in streams . . . and is fastest in the ocean." The abundant food supplies result in larger trout in the sea than in fresh water for fish of the same age. The largest trout have spent the least time in fresh water.

Because estuaries are relatively shallow, light can penetrate and phytoplankton multiply. This in turn promotes zooplankton populations and abundant food for fish. Salinities and temperatures can fluctuate greatly, especially with the ebb and flow of the tides. But these fluctuations cause rapid turnover of the ecosystem and high productivity. The diluted salinity results in especially rich and diverse animal life.

The two most important characteristics dictating the appearance and distribution of trout in estuaries and ocean waters are water temperature and food. If temperatures are suitable and food supplies are abundant, trout will remain in salt water. When temperatures rise or fall beyond preferred ranges, or food supplies become limited, trout will return to fresh water or will move to other oceanic areas.

Temperature dictates the appearance or disappearance of anadromous trout in estuaries and at sea. Arctic char, for example, move downstream to estuaries soon after ice-out. A decline in water temperatures in the fall often influences sea-run Arctic char and Dolly Varden to return to fresh water.

Temperatures at sea are particularly important for steelhead because they influence distribution of the fish in the open ocean. These trout follow isotherms—invisible lines of

ary and other such areas can be influenced by man, habitat destruction and pollution are always concerns. When such pollution and habitat destruction occurs, the estuary or river mouth can actually act as a barrier to returning fish. And, because most anadromous trout rely on the estuary and do not travel far to sea, whole populations can be adversely affected.

It is difficult to describe trout habitat in estuaries and coastal areas in the same way as streams and lakes. The depth of the water and the large area make measurements of bottom configuration, cover, shading, and other habitat inventory terms meaningless. But, to a large degree, habitat selection in these areas is dictated by environmental conditions and the availability of food. When these are limiting, fish will move on.

As a consequence, any time estuarine habitat is adversely affected by pollutants or manmade structures, such as breakwaters or jetties, the attractive features of estuaries and coastal areas for trout are reduced, and fish will migrate in search of preferred water temperatures, prey, and other attributes.

Estuaries are semi-enclosed bodies of water forming the interface between fresh water

PRATT

temperature in the sea—in much the same way as do albacore, though tuna are more temperature-specific. Fish that follow specific isotherms at sea have a restricted range of preferred water temperatures. Thus, they move within those narrow temperature bands at sea. As the locations of isotherms change, so too do the fish. Steelhead are usually distributed in the North Pacific between the 5°C (41°F) isotherm to the north and the 14.8°C (59°F) isotherm to the south.

Food influences the distribution of trout and the time spent in any location. The rapid growth rate of anadromous trout is primarily due to the consumption of abundant marine fishes and invertebrates. Steelhead feed on amphipods, squid, herring, and other fishes

in salt water; sea-run Dolly Varden concentrate on capelin and sand lance, supplemented by young salmon, greenling, sculpins, euphausids, and polychaetes. Similarly, Arctic char have a broad diet of amphipods, mysids, sculpins, lumpfish, seasnails, sand lance, capelin, and young cod and char while in coastal waters.

In general, anadromous trout are opportunistic feeders, adjusting their food habits to the availability of prey. But the diversity and abundance of food items is greater in estuaries and coastal areas than in fresh water. Because trout are opportunistic, their movement patterns often are related to the presence of prey. Trout often will follow schools of small fish for miles along a coastline, be-

In estuaries the abundance of crustaceans, killifish, small herring, and other organisms means rapid growth rates for trout. Risks accompany the rewards, however; predators such as the great blue heron and the osprey supplement their diets with young fish.

Estuaries, like this one at the mouth of the Harris River in Alaska, are invaluable trout habitat. Where fresh water meets salt water, the richness and diversity of species provide trout with plenty of food.

cause of the concentration of food. Smaller trout often will remain for months in estuaries because zooplankton blooms are dense. When food supplies dwindle or pollutants reduce species richness and diversity, anadromous trout will move along the coast in search of better conditions.

Several species of anadromous trout are active predators on young salmonids. One advantage of estuarine residence for any predator species is that large numbers of salmon migrate downstream in the spring, and must pass through estuaries. Sea-run cutthroat trout, for example, may actually move from estuaries into river mouths during that time of year to take advantage of salmon prey. A large number of smolts are moving down the river. Once they reach the estuary, they spread out into the larger area and opportunities for predators to eat them are less than in the river. So some cutthroat will move into the river where the density of the prey is greater. When smolts are available in the spring, the cutthroat will try to position themselves so they can eat as many as possible. After the peak migration, however, most cutthroat trout return to the estuaries to forage because saltwater areas provide a broader menu of fish and invertebrate prey during most of the year.

RETURN TO FRESH WATER

The length of estuarine or oceanic residence depends on species, and even varies within a species. Steelhead, for example, may remain at sea for two to three years, and occasionally longer; Dolly Varden and Arctic char remain in salt water only two to five months.

The return to fresh water is often related to spawning, but the patterns can be quite unusual. Sea-run brook trout in Massachusetts migrate to the sea in late October to early December following spawning, and most spend the winter months in salt water becauqe of more favorable water temperatures there. But Arctic char return from estuaries in late summer or autumn and spend the winter months in protected areas in fresh water. The timing of these returns is largely a function of local conditions, particularly water temperature and streamflow.

Trout entering estuarine and coastal areas can encounter problems different from those of fish remaining exclusively in fresh water. Not only must they have suitable spawning and nursery habitat in fresh water, but they also must have suitable conditions in the estuaries and at sea.

Trout entering areas of lower rivers and coastal zones encounter many predators not found in freshwater zones, such as seals, sharks, and marine fishes. Several types of aquatic birds, cormorants, mergansers, terns, loons, even white pelicans, also are known to feed on anadromous trout, particularly smolts, in the lower rivers. Moving into salt water, trout can also become susceptible to marine diseases and parasites.

—John R. Moring

Weather extremes

*T*rout species can tolerate a tremendous range of habitats. Consider the variety of situations encountered by an anadromous population as it migrates from the natal stream to the ocean. All along the route, the trout must adapt to new, sometimes harsh, conditions: changing oxygen levels and temperatures, different salinities and chemical mixes, and varying flows, for example.

The seasons of the year change the environment, too, and trout, like all creatures, must alter their behavior and metabolism to accommodate those changes. If the process is gradual and within the trout's range of tolerance, they can adjust without much difficulty. They can tolerate the stress. But unusual or extreme weather conditions can inflict devastating damage that can, in the worst situations, wipe out the population.

FLOODS

Floods wreak havoc in many ways. They tear away valuable cover that protects trout. They scour gravel beds that trout use for spawning and, if they occur during the time the eggs are incubating, they destroy the eggs and thus the next generation of fish.

Floods also reduce the overall productivity of the stream by damaging the habitat of all species in the food chain on which the trout depend, and they reduce the carrying capacity of the stream, the number and weight of trout that the stream can support.

They can kill the trout themselves, which not only reduces the current population but also suppresses the numbers of future generations because there are fewer adults to reproduce.

As waters recede from flooded areas, trout that have moved into these backwaters can become stranded and die.

Flooding on abused land magnifies these problems by increasing the erosion-caused sediment in streams. Studies by Bjornn and his associates, and by Hausle and Coble showed that increased sedimentation can reduce food production, lower the oxygen-enriched, intergravel flow necessary for the development of eggs and larvae, and damage spawning habitat. In turn, these factors cause poor year-class strength, that is, a reduction

Catastrophic floods, if they occur while trout eggs are still incubating, may wipe out an entire generation.

YUSKAVITCH

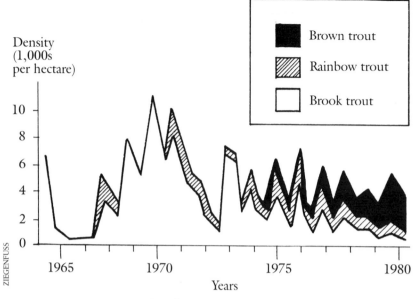

Density
(1,000s
per hectare)

ZIEGENFUSS

Brown trout

Rainbow trout

Brook trout

Years

In Valley Creek (Minnesota) repeated episodes of flooding changed the creek environment extensively, resulting in changes in the fish populations residing there. The native brook trout populations were drastically diminished by the effects of flooding, gradually opening the door for the expansion of rainbow and brown trout populations.

in the numbers of fish at a given age. In addition, Waters found that floods on Valley Creek in Minnesota reduced the number of brook trout, and allowed rainbow and brown trout to expand their population ranges, thus changing the trout species mix.

Waters found that mean annual precipitation, fluctuation in annual precipitation, the number of notable single-day rains, and the number of floods all increased in a fifteen-year span compared to the previous ten years. These weather extremes and the resulting increase in erosion and siltation appeared to be the causes of observed weak year-classes of trout, decreases in invertebrate food production, and loss of cover for small trout. A shift in the trout community occurred, from 100 percent brook trout in 1965 to 70 percent brown trout, 15 percent brook trout, and 15 percent rainbow trout in 1980.

DROUGHTS

The effects of drought and low flows can be just as devastating to salmonid populations. Many biologists, Lennon, Latta, McNeil, and I, for example, have documented direct correlations between population size and surface-water and groundwater flow. While studying the trout populations of the Tye River system in Virginia, I found that native brook trout density decreased by about 85 percent after the region suffered two consecutive years of severe summer drought and one severe winter. Reduced streamflow caused fish to crowd together, which in-

During drought conditions trout may crowd together in a deep pool.

creased their competition for food, feeding stations, spawning sites, and shelter.

Corning found that larger trout suffered more during droughts than did smaller trout, which can feed in shallow riffle areas. Larger trout generally must feed in pools, which are less productive. In addition to finding less to eat, trout restricted to pools become more vulnerable to predation by raccoons, otters, birds, and other animals. Streamflows lowered by drought also have been found to restrict spawning migration of adults and subsequent egg deposition.

In many areas, lower water levels mean higher stream temperatures. If the temperatures remain above the species' thermal tolerance level for even a couple of hours, they can kill the trout. In addition, elevated temperatures also can increase susceptibility to disease and can cause fish to react abnormally in the presence of predators. For example, they may become lethargic and may not flee predators, or they may exhibit irregular body movements, such as flashing, which attracts predators. Finally, low flows, dwindling food supplies, and elevated stream temperatures can reduce feeding efficiency and may cause the loss of gamete production as trout reabsorb their eggs or milt to conserve energy.

During droughts, the flow of water may actually dry up or run subterranean. In extreme cases, extended droughts may result in a loss of riparian vegetation, increased sedimentation, increased water temperatures, and loss of trout habitat.

DOUPLE

TROUT

The South Fork of the Tye River subjects its resident trout populations to both drought and severe winter conditions.

ICE AND SNOW

Winter extremes such as cold temperatures and ice and snow also can hurt salmonid populations. Ice or snow shelves may collapse and suffocate trout or crush them against the bottom of the stream. Ice dams, which have backed up water, can fail, draining flooded side channels and stranding trout. Sometimes when ice dams break, downstream flooding occurs as well. In turn, as in other floods, the water there recedes and strands fish that wandered from the streambed. As the broken ice dams move downstream, they can scour gravel areas, thus reducing food production and egg survival. In a study of Michigan streams, Benson found that trout fry in the egg-sac stage are vulnerable to ice formations if formation coincides with emergence. The swim-up fry could be entrapped because of their inability to escape quickly. However, losses appeared to be greater among adults and juveniles.

Extended ice and snow cover also can reduce light penetration to stream bottoms during winter months and reduce the development of algae and other food organisms.

In straightened or channelized streams, ice damage may be greater because of increased velocities as the ice and water travel downstream. Many abused streams carry less water or are shallower; thus, ice formation can be more extreme and cause greater damage.

DAMAGE CONTROL

The extremes of weather often are worse on

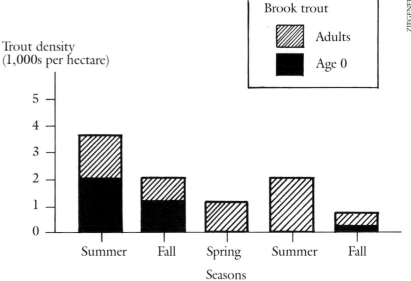

land or in waterways that we have misused. Clear-cut areas are more prone to floods, for example. Streams stripped of their riparian habitat suffer more from the extremes of temperature than do streams where overhanging trees and brush shade the water.

Trout population managers and the public should be aware that different strategies may be needed to correct the ravages of the weather. For example, habitat may need to be replaced so that population densities can return to previous levels. And, unfortunately, decreases in population densities also may dictate the need for an emergency reduction of creel and size limits to prevent the overharvest of the remaining population.

–Arthur L. LaRoche III

Drought, low flow conditions, and winter ice and snow severely affected the native populations of brook trout in the Tye River system (Virginia). The density of adults per hectare was greatly decreased, and an entire year class of fish was essentially eliminated.

Anchor ice

On clear, cold winter nights when the air is still and the temperature is 10 to 20 degrees below zero Fahrenheit, most of us are safe in the warmth of our homes. But in those trout streams without an abundant supply of spring water and a good cover of snow on the watershed, a devastating phenomenon takes place: The streams become "supercooled." That is, the temperature of the water drops below freezing without causing any surface ice to form. Instead, ice forms in the water, on condensation nuclei, or sediment. The result is what is called frazil ice. The development of this frazil ice creates a veritable snowstorm in the water, a whiteout. As with humans and land animals in a blizzard, the fish lose their orientation to all stream structures and to other fish, and they swim aimlessly through the mixture of ice and water.

Anchor ice may be beautiful to see, shown here from the observation station at Sagehen Creek, but its disorienting effect on trout can be lethal.

The frazil ice floats downstream and becomes attached to solid bottom structures, forming what is known as anchor ice. This anchor ice builds up from the bottom until it impounds the stream in many sections. Water backs up and overflows the streambanks. At this point, the disoriented fish may leave the streambed and swim out into the flooding water.

In the morning, with the first warming of the sun, the anchor ice is released and all is chaos. Some of the bottom gravel, and along with it bottom-dwelling insects torn loose from their refuges, is carried downstream, often away from the stream channel. Thin ice that formed late on the impounded areas behind the dams of anchor ice is also carried down. The full water flow returns to the stream channel, but the collapse of mushy ice and thin surface ice formed on the streambanks traps fish and aquatic insects caught out of the streambed in the flooded areas.

Although there are no quantitative studies of mortality caused by anchor ice, it is known from population studies that winter and early spring are periods of high mortality. I assume anchor ice is one of the major factors of winter mortality of trout and insects as well as of trout eggs laid in the fall.

At Sagehen Creek in the Sierra Nevada of California, where snow falls at the rate of more than 205 centimeters (80 inches) per month during January and February, there was no snow on the watershed in the early winter of 1963. Clear, calm, and very cold nights brought on a succession of anchor ice conditions. Hawthorne and I photographed many of the conditions and in a short time recovered trout, sculpin, and aquatic insects.

The phenomenon of anchor ice is not restricted to high mountain streams; I have seen it frequently on the streams of Pennsylvania as well.

—Robert L. Butler

ANDERSON

The species

Apache trout

Oncorhynchus apache

The Apache trout of the Southwest, a small, rare jewel of a fish, lives a precarious existence. By the time it was officially described in 1972, it had been forced or fished out of its range so that today it occupies less than 5 percent of its original 965 kilometers (599 miles) of stream habitat. It has recovered somewhat from its *endangered* status, so designated by the U.S. Department of the Interior in 1967 and the International Union for the Conservation of Nature in 1969. Today it is *threatened*.

CLASSIFICATION

In the late 1800s scientific explorers encountered native trout in the headwaters of the Gila River in Arizona and New Mexico. They called them speckled or yellowbelly trout to distinguish them from the rainbow trout, *Oncorhynchus mykiss*; brown trout, *Salmo trutta*; and brook trout, *Salvelinus fontinalis*, that were being rapidly and widely introduced for sport fishing in the region. Based on three specimens collected in 1873 from the White River in Arizona, these yellowbellied-speckled trout were reported first in 1875 as a variety of the cutthroat trout named *Salmo pleuriticus*.

Three-quarters of a century later, Miller analyzed and described the Gila trout, *S. gilae*, from Main Diamond Creek, New Mexico. At that time, all native trout in the White Mountains of East-Central Arizona were provisionally included under this name. Another twenty-five years passed before Miller described the native trout from the East Fork of the White River as *S. apache*. However, the type series, or specimen used in the description of this species, did not include the full range of morphometric and meristic variation, the possible variations of characteristics used to classify a species that we know today.

Based on osteological studies in 1988, this species of Pacific trout is now in the same genus as the salmons, *Oncorhynchus*, and the official scientific designation for the native trout in the White Mountains is *Oncorhynchus apache*.

DESCRIPTION

The Apache trout is golden olive-yellow with spotted fins and a yellow "cutthroat" mark under the lower jaw. Purple and pink tints often occur as well, though not in the colorful lateral band that is characteristic of rainbow trout. The uniformly spaced, pronounced spots are medium-sized and slightly smaller than those on interior species of cutthroat trout.

Both spotting and coloration vary among Apache trout, partly because of natural occurrence and partly because of the influence of rainbow and perhaps cutthroat trout genes. A population of Apache trout from Soldier Creek, on the boundary of the reservation and the national forest, was found on examination in 1989 to have atypical bright orange-red fins, similar in color to those of cutthroat.

The large dorsal fin and the pelvic and anal

TOMELLERI

fins each have a conspicuous cream-colored or yellowish tip. The body is deeper than that of a typical rainbow trout; it also is compressed laterally, that is, thin.

DISTRIBUTION

We do know that Apache trout originally occupied the headwaters of the Little Colorado, Salt, and San Francisco rivers in Arizona. In the late 1800s fishermen caught them easily, at the rate of one hundred per hour. They were salted in barrels, to be used as food during the winter.

But the decline in range and numbers has made it difficult to determine the former distribution of Apache trout relative to that of the closely related Gila trout. Specimens collected at the geographic limits of the historic salmonid range in Arizona have exhibited characteristics of both species. Specimens from KP Creek in the San Francisco Creek drainage display spotting patterns characteristic of Apache trout but also have the red

RINNE

band characteristic of Gila trout. On the extreme western limits of the range, trout collected a century ago from Oak Creek in Arizona morphologically are Apache trout but contain the spotting patterns of Gila trout. Ambiguity in both cases could reflect either historic hybridization of the two natives with rainbow trout or close similarity of genetic makeup of the two species.

Geographic patterns of the purity of Apache trout populations closely parallel relative stocking histories of rainbow trout on the two major land-management areas in the White Mountain region, the Fort Apache Indian Reservation and the Apache-Sitgreaves National Forest. These two areas are the only places where Apache trout can be found now. Purity of wild stocks is greater on the reservation where fewer rainbow trout have been stocked and where the streams have been closed to angling. Conversely, extensive stocking of rainbow trout in streams on the national forest has resulted in fewer pure stocks in this area.

Pure populations of Apache trout have been reported to occur either naturally or by introduction in twenty streams, and nearly pure populations in another twenty streams. About half of the pure populations of this rare trout live in streams on the Fort Apache Indian Reservation.

Since about 1950, only catchable rainbow trout larger than 20 centimeters (8 inches) have been stocked in the streams of Fort Apache Indian Reservation and the Apache-

A conspicuous cream-colored dorsal fin is one of the identifying characteristics of the Apache trout.

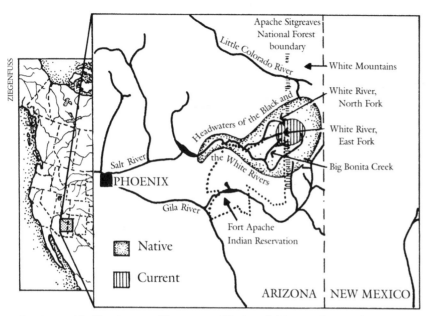

Native

Current

ARIZONA | NEW MEXICO

Apache Sitgreaves National Forest boundary

Little Colorado River

White Mountains

White River, North Fork

White River, East Fork

Big Bonita Creek

Headwaters of the Black and the White Rivers

Salt River

PHOENIX

Gila River

Fort Apache Indian Reservation

Logging, road-building, live-stock grazing, dams, and water diversion projects have contributed to the degradation and loss of habitat that has forced the Apache trout onto the list of threatened species. Hybridization and competition with introduced species has also taken its toll. Apache trout now occupy less than 5 percent of their original nearly 600 miles of stream habitat; their current range is restricted to the headwaters of the Black and the White Rivers, east of Phoenix, Arizona.

This headwater stream on the Fort Apache Indian Reservation is one of the few places where Apache trout can be found.

Sitgreaves National Forest for angling. This practice explains why any existing hybridized populations have not originated in the past thirty-five years. First, hatchery-reared trout may be of inferior reproductive capability because they have been genetically selected for domestication and rapid growth. Second, many hatchery-reared rainbow trout either are caught by anglers within the first year after stocking or move downstream to larger waters. Such fates have largely precluded extensive interbreeding with native trout in headwater areas. Finally, artificial hatchery crossing of rainbow and Apache trout does not always result in an equal mix of characteristics. Innate genetic barriers to successful hybridization may be present; in other words the species may be genetically incompatible.

In the mid-1960s to mid-1980s, pure-strain Apache trout from Ord Creek were introduced into man-made lakes in the Arizona rim country and the White Mountains. On national forest lands, Bear Canyon and Lee Valley in the White Mountains and Riggs Flat Lake in Coronado National Forest in the Graham Mountains were stocked with Apache trout. On the Fort Apache Indian Reservation, Christmas Tree Lake was first stocked in 1965 with subsequent stockings through 1973. Hurricane Lake was stocked in 1970 and again in the mid-1980s. These typically are small, shallow, high-elevation reservoirs of less than 4 hectares (10 acres) that stratify thermally in summer and become icebound in winter.

HABITAT

Both hybridization, which creates a fish that is less than pure strain, and the loss of habitat have left pure-strain Apache trout only in the extreme headwaters of drainages. These streams are subject to highly variable, extreme conditions: flooding, drought, anchor ice, wildfire. Nevertheless, the species exists in comparatively high densities and biomass in these unsparing habitats.

The salt or dissolved-solid content of these waters, which drain high-montane (higher than 2,100 meters [6,900 feet]) conifer forest and alpine meadows, is extremely low, approaching that of distilled water in some of the streams. In general, conductivity is low, too, pH is near neutral, and dissolved oxygen is variable but, at more than 8 parts per million, adequate for survival. During drought, large numbers of Apache trout can survive in pools with elevated water temperature (18°C [64.8°F] or greater) and low levels of dissolved oxygen (less than 6 parts per million).

Lakes with Apache trout generally are small (less than 10 hectares [25 acres] in area) and shallow (less than 15 meters [50 feet] in depth) and stratify thermally in winter. Summer surface water temperatures may reach 20°C (68.4°F). Large aquatic plants may produce elevated levels of alkalinity (above pH 8.0) and fish kills.

Life history

When increased recovery efforts began for the Apache trout in the mid-1970s, information on its basic biology and ecology was lacking. Its scarcity and protected status made obtaining valid biological information about the species difficult. The size of sample groups had to be minimized and study areas carefully selected and limited in number and size to prevent adverse effects on this already-rare native trout. Most of the available information on the biology, ecology, and habitat requirements was collected, analyzed, and published by the U.S. Forest Service, the U.S. Fish and Wildlife Service, and the White Mountain Apache tribe between 1975 and 1986.

In 1979 Ken Harper, Apache tribal biologist, provided the results of detailed research he conducted on the biology of the Apache trout in Big Bonita Creek in Arizona. Examination of otoliths, or bony growths of the inner ear, of sample fish showed that Apache trout grow slowly. Total length increased an average of only 50 millimeters (2 inches) between the formations of scale annuli, or scale growth rings. Mean population biomass (13 grams per square meter) of Apache trout, that is, the average amount of trout "flesh" per square meter, was very similar to that estimated for Gila trout (15 grams per square meter).

Female Apache trout mature at three years of age or a petite 13 centimeters (5 inches) in length. They produce about 3,000 eggs per kilogram (about 1,400 eggs per pound) of body weight, which they deposit in several redds they build on gravel-pebble substrate of 0.8 to 3.2 centimeters in diameter (0.3 to 1.2 inches). Spawning occurs during receding water flows, and activity begins at midday when water temperatures reach 8°C (46.6°F), and recedes in late afternoon, about 6 P.M.

The eggs hatch in thirty days. The fry emerge from the gravel in sixty days and move downstream to locate and occupy new territories in which to grow and reproduce. Migration occurs only at night; during the day, fry burrow into gravel interstices.

The temperature of the water is a vital factor for Apache trout. They spawn at a brisk 8°C (46.6°F), for example. Relatively high temperatures affect them adversely. Fingerlings cease feeding at 20°C (68°F). They lose their equilibrium at 21° to 22°C (70° to 72°F), and they die at 23°C (73.9°F). Adults succumb at higher temperatures of 28° to 29°C (82° to 84°F).

In lakes Apache trout can grow to lengths of more than 50 centimeters (20 inches). The world record Apache trout was caught in Bear Canyon Lake, Arizona. It was 56 centimeters (22 inches) long and weighed 1.6 kilograms (3.6 pounds). However, in the restricted headwater environments they inhabit, they are generally less than 25 centimeters (10 inches) long.

Apache trout are opportunistic feeders and prey mostly on mayflies. Thirty percent of their diet is terrestrial insects. Laboratory feeding experiments suggest that Apache trout do not feed at the same time as the brown trout that inhabit their waters, so feeding does not appear to be a critical factor of competition between these two species. Instead, competition by brown trout and brook trout for living space and cover, and direct predation by both species on Apache trout probably hurt the native trout more.

The introduced rainbow trout, a spring spawner, readily hybridizes with the native Apache trout, so until the mid-1980s the genetic purity of Apache trout populations

The Apache trout lives a precarious existence in waters subject to flooding, drought, anchor ice, and wildfire.

ROSTON

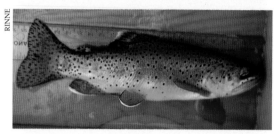

Even though native Apache trout from Big Bonita Creek (top) and Ord Creek (second from top) show differences in coloring, they are both likely to be pure Apache stock. The Apache-rainbow hybrid (second from bottom) shows the influence of rainbow (bottom) genes.

Physical characteristics of Apache and rainbow trout

The threatened, native wild Apache trout generally has larger fins in proportion to body size than its hatchery-bred, introduced competitor, the rainbow trout. In addition, although both species have about the same number of vertebral segments, the Apache trout has more scales above the lateral line—Apache scales are smaller in size than those of the rainbow. The ratios of snout and fin sizes to total body length, and counts of scales, vertebrae, and fingerlike projections in the intestines provide a composite picture that allows observers to determine whether it is a pure, native Apache trout or a hybrid resulting from Apache-rainbow cross-breeding.

Morphometric character	Apache trout		Rainbow trout	
	Range of means	Total range	Range of means	Total range
Snout length	71–76	68–89	56–70	49–77
Dorsal fin base	153–187	144–200	124–159	106–162
Dorsal fin, depressed length	265–267	245–299	218–255	195–270
Adipose fin, depressed length	113–117	106–128	65–95	60–100
Anal fin base	122–124	117–136	104–118	92–128
Anal fin, depressed length	181–183	170–198	149–172	148–187
Meristic character				
Scales above lateral line	34–36	32–40	22–29	25–30
Vertebral segments	59–60	58–61	59–62	56–65
Pyloric caeca	26–33	22–40	55–62	35–70

was undefined. Hybridization thus precluded accurate estimates of total numbers in the wild.

However, between 1976 and 1985 Rinne conducted a comprehensive study of trout from Ord Creek, East Fork of the White River, and of trout populations in more than forty streams in the White Mountains of Arizona. The results suggested that some populations formerly considered to be genetically impure because of hybridization with the introduced rainbow trout actually consist of pure-strain Apache trout. Subsequent genetic analyses of selected trout populations from the White Mountains corroborated those conclusions. Current research on mitochondrial DNA (mtDNA) has substantiated the influence of extensive introduction of nonnative rainbow and cutthroat trouts and hybridization in the White Mountain trout populations. So far, though, the specifics of the mechanisms of genetic interactions of those species with Apache trout have not been fully analyzed.

Hybridization with rainbow trout, competition with brown trout and brook trout, and habitat degradation and loss have contributed most to the decline of the native Apache trout in the Southwest. Land-management activities, logging, livestock grazing, road building, damming, and water diversion, for example, have altered pristine habitats once occupied by the Apache trout. In some situations they have caused the total loss of populations.

HUMAN INTERVENTION

Efforts to conserve the Apache trout began even before it was officially described in 1972. In the late 1940s and early 1950s, the White Mountain Apache tribe, recognizing that the only remaining pure populations of Apache trout might be on their lands, closed all

streams in the Mount Baldy Wilderness Area to sport fishing. Subsequently, all additional streams that contained Apache trout were closed and remain so today. However, Christmas Tree Lake provides a quality sport fishery, open for an abbreviated season of less than a month.

In the 1960s the U.S. Fish and Wildlife Service and the Arizona Department of Game and Fish conducted population surveys, and the department, in cooperation with the tribe, began a hatchery propagation program, in which eighty-two Apache trout initially were collected from Ord Creek and transferred to the department's Sterling Springs Hatchery. Between 1964 and 1973 almost 87,000 Apache trout were reared at this facility and stocked in lakes and streams throughout Arizona's highlands.

The tribe adopted a plan in 1964 that included renovation of streams and construction of fish barriers to limit potential upstream movement of rainbow trout. But despite a 2-meter (6-foot) barrier, brown trout and brook trout gained access to Ord Creek and eventually reduced the native Apache trout to a remnant population. Chemical treatment of this stream with fish toxicant was conducted in 1980, but the nonnative salmonids were not successfully removed because numerous springheads and cienegas (wet meadows) diluted and oxidized the fish toxicant. Recent genetic analyses also indicate that the population stocked from nearby Paradise Creek is hybridized.

An official plan to recover the Apache trout was completed in 1980 with a primary objective of restoring the Apache trout to nonthreatened status. A major criterion is to establish thirty pure, self-sustaining populations of Apache trout.

Up to now, Apache trout have simply been transplanted from a stream with pure stock to the reestablishment stream, saving time and avoiding the cost of hatchery rearing as well as the potential development of undesirable hatchery traits. Currently the U.S. Fish and Wildlife Service is rearing Apache trout from the type locality, or the habitat from which the species was first described, the East Fork of the White River. However, this population contains the least genetic variability of the Apache trout populations and, therefore, perhaps the least adaptability. That is, the population's genetics have adapted it well to a very specific environment, and to introduce it in a different environment, however slight the difference, could result ultimately in failure.

Therefore, any hatchery program must consider the genetic diversity of species. Hatcheries may be vital as "halfway houses" in case of future endangerment of a species or for holding during stream renovation. Further, hatchery facilities provide for development of the sport-fish potential of this species in numerous lakes throughout its historic habitat, which in turn encourages interest and support from the public.

—John N. Rinne

Preservation of the Apache trout's genetic variability will ensure the survival of this beautiful southwestern jewel.

THE SPECIES

Arctic char

Salvelinus alpinus

---

*T*he Arctic char, also sometimes called Arctic trout, thrives in the icy waters near the shores of the Arctic Ocean. There it reaches its largest size, greatest abundance, and most brilliant color. In the northernmost part of its range, where fresh waters connect directly to the sea, the Arctic char, like salmon, is anadromous, spawning in fresh water but going to the sea to feed and grow. However, it occurs also as a lacustrine, or lake-dwelling, form, both in waters containing the anadromous stocks and in landlocked lakes where the connection to the sea no longer exists.

CLASSIFICATION

The word *char*, also spelled *charr*, is believed to be derived from the Celtic word *ceara*, meaning red or blood-colored. It was first applied to a troutlike fish occurring in the Lake District of England. This species was later discovered to be widespread throughout northern Europe and in isolated locations farther south and was referred to by many common, local names.

Originally given the scientific name *Salmo alpinus* by Linnaeus, the great Swedish taxonomist of the eighteenth century, it was thereby placed in the same genus as Atlantic salmon, *Salmo salar*, and brown trout, *Salmo trutta*, in the family Salmonidae. *Salmo alpinus* implied "salmon of the (Lapland) mountains," rather than "salmon of the (European) Alps," where it is also found. The variability of European chars suggested their subdivision into many species and subspecies of *Salmo*. According to Behnke, in 1832 Nilsson first published the name *Salvelini* to group chars but did not propose it as a genus name. In 1836 Richardson used the name *Salvelinus* as a genus.

The same species is found in North America, but in addition, there are several closely related species not found in Europe: Dolly Varden char, *Salvelinus malma*; brook trout, *S. fontinalis*; and lake trout, *S. namaycush*. Several species of Arctic char were initially identified in eastern North America: the blueback trout of Maine, *S. oquassa*; the Sunapee trout, *S. aureolus*, from Sunapee Lake in New Hampshire, which is also considered to be a form of *S. oquassa*; and the Quebec red trout, *S. marstoni*. Today all are grouped together under the general term *Salvelinus alpinus* complex.

DESCRIPTION

The chars, *Salvelinus* spp., are most readily distinguished from the trouts by their smaller scales, their pink-to-red spots along the back and sides, and the brilliant white leading edge on their paired fins, dorsal fin, and tail, or caudal fin. These characteristics are true of Arctic char, brook trout, and Dolly Varden, but lake trout, which some authorities classify in a different genus, *Cristivomer*, has less colorful markings. With the exception of lake trout, chars at spawning time are brightly colored; the males in particular turn brilliant red. Simultaneously, males frequently form a

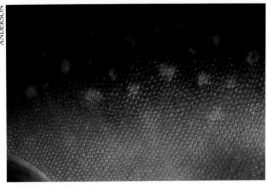

strong kype, a pronounced hook to the lower jaw that is characteristic of most male salmonids. Color at other times of the year varies and is not a reliable distinguishing characteristic, particularly in the juvenile stages. Anadromous char returning from the sea often have a dark green or brown back and a brilliant white belly. Lake-dwelling forms vary from brown to green even within one lake, but they frequently retain a permanent orange tinge to the fins and ventral regions. The skeleton of the Arctic char is soft and cartilaginous compared to that of lake trout and other salmonids, in which the bones are ossified and hard.

The relationship between Arctic char and Dolly Varden in Alaska, the Yukon, and British Columbia is still under consideration, frequently even in dispute. Dolly Varden, *Salvelinus malma*, are distinguished externally from Arctic char mainly by their blunter snout and by the smaller spots on their body, and internally by their smaller numbers of gill rakers and pyloric caeca, or outgrowths of the intestinal wall. Despite the relatively small differences, the distinction is clearly maintained in several bodies of water, such as Karluk Lake in Alaska, where the two forms occur sympatrically, that is, together, within the same lake system, without evident interbreeding.

DISTRIBUTION AND HABITAT

The Arctic char is circumpolar in its distribution, existing between 47° north latitude and 82° north latitude. It occurs in northern Russia, Norway, Iceland, Greenland, Canada, and Alaska, as well as the isolated islands of Jan Mayn and Spitzbergen. In the far North, in the islands of the Queen Elizabeth Archipelago, Arctic char is the only freshwater fish encountered.

North of the southern limit of anadromy, which, in the east, is on the northern peninsula of Newfoundland (51° north latitude), both anadromous and lacustrine forms may occur together in the same waters, but in lakes where postglacial uplift of the land has created impassable falls, only the landlocked form occurs. South of the limit of anadromy in Russia, Finland, Sweden, the British Isles, France, Germany, Austria, Switzerland, and the continental United States and Canada, char do not go to sea even when the opportunity exists.

In North America, lake-dwelling populations exist in isolated locations in Quebec along the north shore of the Gulf of Saint Lawrence. According to Behnke, Sunapee

Vivid pink-to-red spots cover the sides and back of spawning Arctic char.

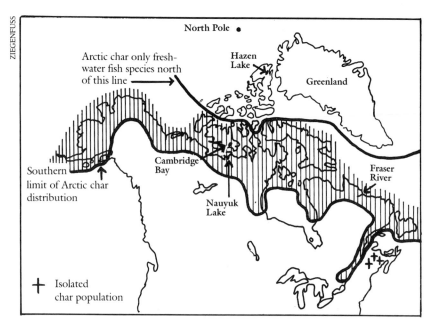

North Pole •

Arctic char only fresh-
water fish species north
of this line →

Hazen
Lake

Greenland

Southern
limit of Arctic char
distribution

Cambridge
Bay

Fraser
River

Nauyuk
Lake

✝ Isolated
  char population

The Arctic char is essentially a coastal species, and is the only species of fish found in the northernmost latitudes. Isolated Arctic char populations have been found in Maine and New Brunswick.

trout originally were known from Averill Lake in Vermont, Sunapee Lake and Don Hole Pond in New Hampshire, and Flood's Pond in Maine. Today, only Flood's Pond has the native population. The original populations in Vermont and New Hampshire no longer exist in native waters. In the West, populations occur throughout the coastal regions of Alaska and British Columbia. The southern limit of distribution is Lake Baikal in Russia and the alpine lakes in Europe. In the European Alps, populations exist in lakes at elevations of up to 2,591 meters (8,500 feet).

The geographical distribution of Arctic char is closely bound up with events of the Pleistocene glaciations. Populations that

existed in the northern regions before the glacial period retreated south in the face of advancing ice, which thereby eliminated all populations from the Arctic Ocean. Thus the original stock was separated into Atlantic and Pacific forms, which, over many thousands of years, evolved independently. With the melting of the ice, the char repopulated their original domain. Over the course of the four glaciations, whole ecosystems tracked these ice movements. The most recent retreat of the ice allowed mingling of the formerly separate stocks, giving rise to the present systematic confusion. In Europe, during the most recent glaciation, ice dammed north-flowing rivers such as the Rhine, converting them into immense lakes, which provided char access to higher elevations. Above a certain altitude these regions, too, were covered by ice, but when the ice melted, the present region of alpine lakes was exposed. The cold, deep water of these lakes allowed char to survive the warmer conditions of the postglacial period. In addition they survived the immigration into the habitat of many other fish species, which occupied the warmer, more productive, upper levels of these lakes.

In North America similar conditions prevailed, but distribution of Arctic char on this continent was restricted by the presence of lake char. These species can coexist, particularly in the Arctic, but it is evident that, in southerly regions, only those lakes that are devoid of lake char can support populations of Arctic char. No Arctic char have been

Nauyuk Lake in Canada's Northwest Territories supports a large population of Arctic char. As many as 12,000 may spend the winter here.

186

found in the Great Lakes, or the large lakes of central and northern Canada, where lake char predominate, although Arctic char may be presumed to have had access to many of these lakes during the retreat of the ice.

Life history

Migration patterns. The migration pattern of anadromous Arctic char is extremely complex and differs in the spawning and non-spawning segments of the population. In contrast to salmon and trout, Arctic char migrate to the sea each year, specifically for feeding; spawning frequently involves upstream migration. L. Johnson worked out the migration pattern of char in considerable detail from research at Nauyuk Lake on the Kent Peninsula in the Central Canadian Arctic. This is a general system, with which the unique characteristics of individual systems may be compared.

Feeding migration. In spring, at Nauyuk Lake, as soon as water begins to flow in the river, which is sometime between the fifth and the twentieth of June, char begin to migrate downstream. The largest char (65 to 95 centimeters [25 to 37 inches] in length) migrate first, followed by the mass of medium-sized fish (55 to 65 centimeters [22 to 25 inches] long). This outward migration takes nearly a month, and mean daily size of the fish gradually declines over this period. When the main group of adult char has passed, there is a waiting period of a few days before the first-time sea-migrants, or smolts, begin to descend. These smolts have spent the first four to eight years of their lives in fresh water. They move to the sea for the first time at a mean length of about 22 centimeters (9 inches). The first fish to descend spend up to fifty-six days at sea; those that migrate later spend only about thirty-five days.

During the early part of the migration the sea is still frozen to a depth of 1 to 2 meters (39 to 79 inches), but the char make the passage to neighboring river systems underneath the sea ice. Most of them remain in the relatively warm estuarine waters until the ice melts, making short excursions to the sea to feed. Most of the population remains within 25 to 30 kilometers (16 to 19 miles) of the stream they descended in spring, feeding

These spawning Arctic char (right, male; below, female) sport brilliant white leading edges on their paired fins.

These sea-run Arctic char are from the Fraser River in Labrador.

The Sunapee char, here from an isolated population in Flood's Pond, Maine, was once recognized as an independent species (S. oquassa), but now is considered a form of the Arctic char.

Arctic char pass along the Nauyuk River in the spring on their way to the sea to feed, and again in the fall as they return to Nauyuk Lake for the winter.

voraciously on the short burst of marine production, which occurs mainly in June and July. However, some char from Nauyuk Lake, marked with individually identifiable tags, have been recaught up to 550 kilometers (341 miles) away.

The char begin to return to fresh water in early August. The migration reaches a peak about ten days later and is complete by early September. As with the descent, the upstream run is characterized by size precedence among the adults; returning smolts again are the last to arrive. Tag returns indicate that many fish migrate into systems other than the one occupied the previous winter, and it also has been shown that the first char to descend in spring, and therefore generally the largest, are the most likely to wander from their former home. Anadromous char may penetrate inland up to 150 kilometers (93 miles). They are extremely powerful swimmers and can force their way upstream against strong currents. However, they are less powerful jumpers than most salmon and trout and therefore less able to negotiate waterfalls.

Char spend the winter under the ice in fresh water at temperatures between 0° and 2°C (32° and 35.6°F). They do not feed for the ten months following their return from the sea. Large Nauyuk Lake char (greater than 40 centimeters [16 inches] long) lose about 14 percent of their body weight over the winter, and smaller fish may lose more. Char also are relatively quiescent during this

period. Welch, during dives under the ice to study arctic lake ecology in Char Lake on Cornwallis Island, observed char resting on the bottom for much of the year, becoming active only during the summer feeding period.

Glova and McCart, in their 1974 report, describe how large adults in the Firth River in the Yukon occupy the central regions of the stream, whereas juveniles occupy the stream margins close to where ice and substratum meet and the water flows less rapidly. This separation of juveniles occupying the rocky shorelines and adults in the more open waters is also evident in lakes.

Spawning. Char spawn in fresh water either in lakes or in rivers that flow continuously throughout the year. River spawning is confined to the eastern and western Arctic; the rivers in the central region freeze solid. In lakes, char prefer to spawn on gravel beds at variable depths of from 3 or 4 meters to 80 meters (10 feet to 262 feet) where currents sweep the gravel free of silt.

Anadromous stocks spawn in the fall, although spring-spawning stocks are known to exist in some lakes, and both fall-spawning and spring-spawning stocks exist in Lake Windermere in England's Lake District. Spawning first occurs when the fish reaches the modal, or most numerous, size of the population; in many anadromous stocks this is a length of 60 to 65 centimeters (23 to 25 inches) at about ten years of age. However, the limitations of environment and life history ensure that the actual egg production per female Arctic char is well below that of most salmonids.

The char of Nauyuk Lake return from the sea in the fall to overwinter there; none of these fish has been known to spawn the year they return from the sea. Prespawners overwinter in Nauyuk Lake before moving up a small stream, Willow Creek, to Willow Lake in the spring. Dutil showed that these char are in better condition than those returning to the sea at this time. The mean size of females in this prespawning run is a length of about 67 centimeters (26 inches) and a weight of about 3 kilograms (7 pounds); the males are somewhat larger, averaging 75 centimeters (29 inches) in length and about 4.2 kilograms (9.3 pounds) in weight. Females

The spawning Arctic char male (left) *and female* (below) *develop their eye-catching colors during the summer, in preparation for the fall spawning.*

considerably outnumber males; the ratio varies between 3:1 and 10:1 from year to year.

Prespawners pass the summer in Willow Lake, while their gonads gradually mature and their vivid spawning colors develop, preparatory to spawning in mid- to late September, about the time the first ice begins to form. Fabricius in his studies in 1953 and 1954 found that the males are the first to arrive at the spawning grounds on gravel beds in water 3 to 4 meters (10 to 13 feet) deep. They divide the suitable substratum into specific territories through aggressive display. The females approach the males' territories one by one, then begin to dig in the redd by lying sideways and rapidly moving their tails. After a prolonged courting sequence, the females deposit their eggs and the males fertilize them. They spawn several times in the same nest before the female covers the eggs with gravel, a process different from that of other salmonids. In other species, the female moves upstream to the next site after each spawning act. The digging of the next nest covers the fertilized eggs.

Spawning continues over two to three weeks, after which the postspawners over-

winter in Willow Lake. With the melting of the ice in spring, the postspawners pass down Willow Creek at the same time the next crop of prespawners move up. Many postspawning fish die during this time. After spending twenty-one months in fresh water virtually without feeding, they have lost up to 35 percent of their original body weight and are in extremely poor condition. In fact, many are so weakened that they have difficulty negotiating the passage down Willow Creek. They become stranded among the sedges bordering the stream, and here, in this exhausted state, they fall ready prey to the waiting gulls, who peck out their eyes before they have even ceased to struggle. Those char that reach Nauyuk Lake join the main body of the

This lacustrine Arctic char is in the poor condition typical of postspawners after their many months without feeding.

population in its migration to the sea. In a good year, they recover rapidly in the sea and can almost double their weight during the short summer season.

This sequence of events in Nauyuk Lake imposes on individual spawners a minimum interval of two years between spawnings, but this frequency can be attained only when the fish grow very well in the sea in the intervening year. More usual is a three- or four-year interval between spawnings, which allows two or three summers in the sea to attain the condition necessary to trigger spawning. Given such constraints, individual char probably spawn only two to four times over their average lifespan of about fifteen years. This means that only a small proportion – 5 to 10 percent – of the population spawn in any one year.

As in most salmonids there is a homing instinct in Arctic char. It has not been definitely established that char home to the river system in which they themselves hatched, but it has been shown by McCleave and colleagues that char in Flood's Pond in Maine experimentally displaced during the spawning season return quite quickly to their original spawning site. Comparably, the tagging data from Willow Creek indicate that many fish repeat the spawning process on the same ground during consecutive spawnings, even though these consecutive spawnings are separated by intervals of two or more years. A number of char, recognized by their individual tags, are known to have spawned twice, and some even three times, in Willow Lake. It also has been observed that some of the females in the category of smallest spawners (55 to 60 centimeters [21 to 23 inches]) moving into Willow Lake do not actually spawn. Their relatively good condition on the return down Willow Creek identifies them as maidens.

Feeding. The outstanding characteristic of Arctic char is their capacity to live in a lean environment. They are supreme generalists, feeding on whatever may be available. Lean environments are created by cold temperatures, relatively few hours of sunlight during the year, and barren lands surrounding the lakes. The most extreme example of this situation is Hazen Lake at 82° north latitude. It is located at the northern end of Ellesmere

Although they prefer deep water, Arctic char move toward shore and compete with brown trout for freshwater shrimp when the shrimp are plentiful.

Island, the land nearest the North Pole, where the ice only clears completely in relatively warm years.

Char, although generalists, do not appear to feed at random. I characterize their behavior as following the principle of the smorgasbord: If the crowd is large and the table long, one moves to the position where maximum consumption with least interference can be effected; but if few others are present, one can pick and choose with greater discrimination.

In the sea, where char experience little competition, they feed on a variety of organisms: *Mysis* spp., a small shrimplike creature, a variety of amphipods (freshwater shrimp), and small fish such as Arctic cod, Greenland cod, capelin, sand lance, and small sculpins. There is considerable variation in feeding and growth in the sea from year to year. Much seems to depend on the time of ice breakup; in years when breakup is early the movement is more concentrated and the fish return in very good condition, whereas when breakup is toward the end of June many char seem undecided as to whether or not to go, spend-

ing much time around the source of the river and growing very little. For a char of about 60 centimeters (23 inches) in length, summer weight gain in a good year may be up to 1 kilogram (2.2 pounds); in poor years the gain is negligible.

Landlocked char feed on a wider variety of organisms, depending on what is available. Their diet can include small freshwater clams, amphipods, and an interesting group of organisms found in northern waters collectively known as marine-glacial relicts: an amphipod, *Gammaracanthus*; an isopod, *Mesidotea*; a copepod, *Limnocalanus*; and a small fish, the deepwater sculpin. All of these species, originally marine in origin, frequently occur together in many waters both in Scandinavia and in Arctic Canada. In fresh water Arctic char rarely feed on fish, and when they do, they frequently prey on other Arctic char.

Generalized feeding and flexibility of life pattern appear to be associated with lack of an ability to compete effectively against more specialized species. Nilsson studied the interaction of Arctic char and brown trout over a year's time. The results of this classic study in Sweden, which were published in 1963 and 1965, showed that brown trout occupied the more productive littoral, or shore, region of the lake for most of the year. But in spring, when production was at its peak, char joined them to feed mainly on the abundant amphipod, *Gammarus lacustris*. When the peak declined, the trout remained, but the char moved off into the pelagic, or open, regions to feed on plankton.

Char, when feeding at the surface, may select several items in succession. Brown trout, in contrast, take one item at a time, then return to their territory.

Growth. Undisturbed char populations tend to be old compared to most freshwater fish populations. The mean age of many anadromous stocks is between fifteen and sixteen years, though individuals can be more than twenty-five years old. The mean length of such stocks is between 60 and 70 centimeters (23 to 27 inches), the mean weight between 2 and 4 kilograms (4 and 9 pounds). Age is determined, not by growth rings on the scales, which are usually too distorted to read satisfactorily, but by rings on the otolith, a small concretion, or bony growth, that is part of the balance mechanism in the inner ear. The oldest fish found so far was estimated to be more than thirty-two years old. The world record char, caught in the Tree River northwest of Hudson Bay, weighed 14.5 kilograms (32 pounds).

Growth in char varies greatly between lakes, and even within one lake, fish of the same size may vary greatly in age. In fact, relatively uniform length with great variation in age is characteristic of most populations examined. Detailed age and length distributions were compiled from Nauyuk Lake in

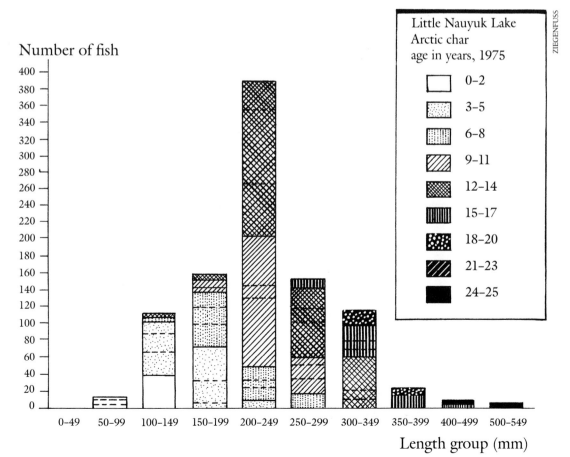

Little Nauyuk Lake
Arctic char
age in years, 1975

☐	0–2
	3–5
	6–8
	9–11
	12–14
	15–17
	18–20
	21–23
■	24–25

ZIEGENFUSS

Number of fish

Length group (mm)

Most of the Arctic char in Little Nauyuk Lake (in the Central Canadian Arctic) in 1975 were 200 to 249 millimeters (8 to 10 inches) long, and ranged in age from 5 to 14 years. Life in lean arctic environments tends to produce small fish with relatively long life spans.

1974, when the population appeared relatively unexploited. The main body of the population is relatively homogeneous in length but diverse in age. The modal length class, or length group into which most of the population falls (60 to 65 centimeters [23 to 25 inches]), has a wide range of ages: from eight to fourteen years. There also is a smaller mode, composed of juveniles 18 to 22 centimeters (7 to 9 inches) in length that range from five to seven years of age.

After one or two years in the seas, when a length of 28 to 30 centimeters (about 11 inches) has been attained, growth rate increases rapidly for two to three years, then gradually declines as the length of the larger modal size is approached at a mean age of about ten years.

Comparable age and length distributions also are found in freshwater lakes. In Little Nauyuk Lake, a previously undisturbed, completely landlocked lake, most of the fish were 20 to 25 centimeters (8 to 10 inches) long and ranged in age from five to fourteen years.

The landlocked trout (char) from Sunapee Lake were reported by Kircheis to have reached a weight of 5 kilograms (11 pounds) in earlier times. The largest fish he actually observed was a female that weighed 2.2 kilograms (4.9 pounds) and was 60 centimeters (23 inches) long. Blueback trout (char) generally are much smaller: about 20 to 25 centimeters (8 to 10 inches) long and between 125 and 250 grams (4 and 9 ounces) in weight. However, when stocked in new lakes in Maine with good food sources, bluebacks have reached 2.3 kilograms (5.1 pounds).

In some northern lakes extreme dwarfism occurs; the modal size of the population is only 10 to 12 centimeters (about 4 inches), and reproduction occurs in fish of that size.

These dwarf Arctic char were found in a small lake; they did not migrate to sea.

In one small lake at the head of Borup Fjord in Ellesmere Island, investigated by Parker, the modal size was 10 centimeters (about 4 inches) and the largest fish nearly 12 centimeters (about 5 inches); the oldest fish was ten years old. In a nearby but somewhat larger lake there were two population modes. The size of the larger and more numerous mode was 41 centimeters (16 inches), comprising fish between thirteen and twenty-one years of age. The oldest fish was twenty-six years old and 53 centimeters (21 inches) long. The smaller modal size was about 16 centimeters (6 inches), comprising fish four to eleven years old. Both modes contained fish in a reproductive state.

Predators. Large anadromous Arctic char face few predators, and it may be supposed that many live out their physiological lifespan. Marine mammals, seals, walrus, and beluga (white whales) might be expected to be more important predators on char, but although there are isolated reports of Arctic char in stomachs of ringed seals in Cumberland Sound at Baffin Island and of beluga in the White Sea, there is little further evidence to indicate that these or other marine mammals are significant predators. There are also reports of wolves, polar bears, and otters feeding on char in the northern Yukon and Alaska.

In the early stages of their life history, small Arctic char are preyed upon by loons, terns, and gulls, and also by lake trout, but once they reach a length of about 25 centimeters (10 inches), they appear to be unaffected.

Parasites. Many lacustrine char populations frequently are infested with parasites, but the intensity of infestation varies greatly even between neighboring lakes. Anadromous char, on the other hand, are relatively free of parasites. The most frequent external parasites, usually found attached to the gills and the walls of the gill cavity, are of the species *Salmincola*, a parasitic copepod.

In the body cavity, most immediately evident on the wall of the intestine, are cysts of the tapeworm *Diphyllobothrium* spp. In fact, in older fish these cysts frequently are so abundant that they appear to fuse the internal organs to the body wall. This tapeworm occurs in char only in the encysted stage; the final reproductive stage occurs in the gut of

Arctic char can tolerate colder, deeper water than lake trout. In North America they are found north of the northern-most edge of the lake trout range.

birds, particularly loons and gulls. When the eggs are returned to the lake in the birds' feces, they hatch as free-living (unattached) coracidia, the larval stage of the tapeworm. Copepods eat the coracidia, which then develop into infective larvae. When char eat the copepods, the coracidia burrow through the stomach wall of the fish and encyst as worm-like plerocercoid larvae. The life cycle is finally closed when the char are consumed by fishing birds. The incidence of this tapeworm appears to decline westward from Baffin Island, and it is absent from Alaska. Often found in the gut of the char itself are acantho-cephalan parasites (named for their thorny head) of the genus *Metechinorhynchus* and cestodes, or tapeworms, of the genus *Eubothrium.*

The roundworm *Cystidicola* is another evident parasite. Two species of this nematode, indistinguishable to the naked eye, occur in the swim bladder of the char. Heavy infestations appear as a mass of very fine vermicelli once the swim bladder has ruptured. The intermediate hosts of these parasites are *Mysis relicta*, and the amphipods *Gammarus* and *Hyalella*.

Dick has listed sixty-six species of parasites of Arctic char in North America, but apart from those mentioned above, most appear to have little general significance. The high level of infection in many otherwise apparently healthy individuals indicates that they kill relatively few fish.

Physiology. One of the most remarkable characteristics of the salmons, trouts, and chars is their capacity for anadromy: the ability to move from fresh water to salt water and to return to fresh water. Of the salmonids, chars of the genus *Salvelinus* are the least adapted to marine life; they have difficulty remaining in salt water for extended periods. They have never been known to overwinter in the sea, even where water temperatures do not fall below 0°C (32°F), and they have been found difficult to rear in salt water continuously, that is, from the time they reach a size of 15 to 20 centimeters (6 to 8 inches), when they can first tolerate sea water, until they reach "market size," say 35 centimeters (about 14 inches).

According to Hoar, Arctic char lack all the adaptations to life in salt water that are found in Pacific salmon. These adaptations largely are physiological. In addition, they do not show the characteristic smoltification, the change to a slender body form and silvery coloration at the time of first seaward migration, to anywhere near the same extent as, for example, Atlantic salmon. Arctic char and Dolly Varden generally make a concerted movement to the sea following ice breakup and again on their return in the fall. They thus exhibit anadromy to a greater extent than do brook trout, which seem casual about movement to and from the sea, coming and going over the summer without any apparent schedule. Lake trout, on the other hand, are unable to tolerate any significant degree of salinity.

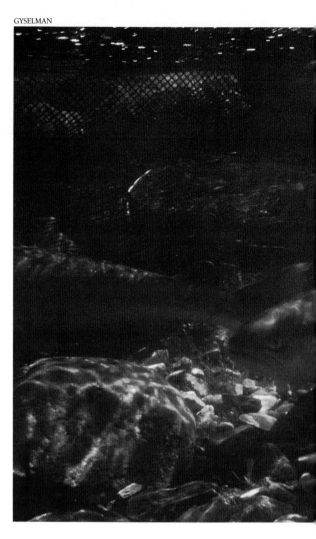

Most salmon and trout migrate to the sea at a variety of ages and sizes, depending on the species. They remain in the sea for two years or more before they return to fresh water to spawn and, frequently, to die. Arctic char, on the other hand, may make the transition twice each year for up to a dozen years. Arctic char and Dolly Varden make the transition more frequently than do any other salmonid species.

The move into fresh water in winter allows the char to escape the subzero temperatures in the Arctic Ocean that can reach $-1.7°C$ (29°F). A char probably could not withstand these temperatures if it remained in the sea. It lacks the antifreeze glycoproteins found in truly arctic marine fishes and would therefore be in constant danger of becoming supercooled and instantly freezing solid. Nevertheless, char are known to travel up to 15 kilometers (9 miles) from their overwintering stream under the sea ice when the water is still well below freezing. A thin layer of relatively warm water, that is, above freezing, does appear to form just under the ice a considerable time before actual breakup. I believe the char may use this layer. However, no Arctic char have been captured in the sea in winter, even in northern Norway where winter sea temperatures are mild relative to the Canadian Arctic. The explanation is that Arctic char probably have difficulty remaining in salt water for prolonged periods during the winter. Researchers have found it difficult to rear them in cages in salt water over the winter, even at moderate temperatures.

Several interesting studies have been conducted on the olfactory ability of char to discover the extent to which smell contributes to their food-finding ability, homing to the lake in which they previously spawned, and returning to the same lake after a summer in the ocean. Olsen showed that Arctic char are attracted to water in which other char have been present and that juveniles could distinguish between their own and other stocks. He found also that a mixture of amino acids at low concentrations stimulated food-searching behavior.

HUMAN INTERVENTION

The study of Arctic char raises questions of great interest and importance in the field of general biology. What is a species? Are arctic ecosystems different from those at lower latitudes?

The first question arises from the existence of several forms, or morphs, in the same lake, a characteristic that is virtually exclusive to arctic species. In some lakes in Sweden and to a lesser extent in Norway and North America, up to five different forms may occur. The scientific consensus is that new species arise only when small groups of individuals are isolated from the parental stock. But this theory generates another question: Have these different morphs of Arctic char originated in the lake in which they now exist, or have they migrated there from their area of origin?

One possibility is that these morphs arise within the lake in different habitats to which specific groups respond in the best way their genetic endowment allows. Char, being the only species able to survive in the lake (or the only species to have arrived there), fill these

niches in the same way that a range of fish species would fill them in a lake with more diverse fauna.

The Arctic provides some of the few ecosystems left on Earth that are largely undisturbed by human activities. Small arctic lakes with their universal populations of Arctic char are not only undisturbed, but they also are largely autonomous and relatively simple. In their autonomy, they form a microcosm of the whole living world, and their simplicity makes it possible to determine the most important factors contributing to ecosystem structure. Such ecosystems thus provide a vital reference against which other systems more complex, more open, and more disturbed may be compared and contrasted, in the hope that the forces creating structured ecosystems may be better understood.

Conservation. In Europe, in the region of the great alpine lakes and in the English Lake District, well-established Arctic char fisheries have existed for centuries. In the Arctic itself, since time immemorial, char has been a staple food among the Lapps in Scandinavia, the Inuit (Eskimo) in Greenland and North America, and their relatives in northern Siberia. Traditionally, much of the summer catch of the Inuit, taken either by spearing or in stone weirs during the seasonal migration, was dried and used in early spring as food for both humans and dogs during the main traveling season on the sea ice. In winter, char are caught by jigging through holes cut in the lake ice. Commercial fisheries, which supply limited quantities of fresh and frozen Arctic char to southern markets, have been established in Labrador, on Baffin Island, and on Victoria Island in the vicinity of Cambridge Bay.

In the alpine-lake region of Central Europe and England's Lake District, where Arctic char are an item of considerable gastronomic as well as economic importance, and in other parts of its southern range, cultural eutrophication—the stimulation of algal growth by the addition of nutrients—is causing deterioration of spawning beds and inducing low oxygen levels in the deeper waters during summer. To maintain present populations in some lakes, new gravel is being deposited regularly to rejuvenate spawning beds, hatchery-raised stock is being planted, and water quality is being upgraded by improving sewage treatment.

In the North, the anadromous habit allows Arctic char to be readily captured, particularly with the introduction of modern fishing methods. In many areas, it has therefore suffered over-exploitation, giving rise to the need to impose management restrictions. Armstrong called Dolly Varden a manager's nightmare; he just as easily could have the said the same thing about Arctic char because they have the same behavior patterns. The tendency to move from stream to stream in search of overwintering habitat and the seasonal variability in spawning and feeding, combined with slow growth and a tendency for fish populations to retain a uniform size distribution in the face of declining stock abundance, all make successful management difficult. But Arctic char have the capacity to recover if left completely alone for several years.

—Lionel Johnson

Brook trout

Salvelinus fontinalis

---

*I*nterest in the brook trout of North America developed as the colonists discovered this game fish, plentiful in the early days of our history, in the streams and lakes of the Northeast. Such renowned figures as Daniel Webster, Cotton Mather, and Henry Ward Beecher took to the waters of Long Island in quest of its beauty, its grace—and its high quality as table fare. Adaptable though it is to conditions that other fish species cannot tolerate—water that is extremely acidic, for example—its numbers have dropped since then. Nevertheless, it can be found in the widest diversity of habitats, providing water temperatures are favorable and competition is not excessive.

CLASSIFICATION

The North American brook trout, *Salvelinus fontinalis*, actually is a char, the common English name given to all members of the genus *Salvelinus*. The early English and European immigrants considered the brook trout similar to the European brown trout. It was first described taxonomically by Samuel Latham Mitchell in 1814 from specimens collected near New York City.

It has since been extensively studied, yet its taxonomic structure is only vaguely defined. Its wide distribution, from large lakes and rivers of the North to small headwater streams in the South, has encouraged differences in growth, body conformation, longevity, and coloration, particularly concerning the size and number of spots. Even brook trout from adjacent but isolated watersheds may be quite different in markings. Thus, the question about whether there should be several subspecies is not an unexpected one. Behnke, the leading authority on this subject, recognizes only two subspecies. One, the aurora trout, *S. timagiensis*, is found in three lakes in the headwaters of the Montreal River in Ontario, Canada. At one time this fish was considered related to the Arctic char, because of its lack of vermiculation, but subsequent studies show it derived from the brook trout.

Another interesting variety of char, the silver trout, was discovered in Monadnock Lake near Dublin, New Hampshire. In the early 1800s it was thought to be a form of lake trout, for it would move into the shallow waters of the lake to spawn in October. In 1885 it was described as a new species, *Salvelinus agassizi*. However, in 1967 Behnke found, on examining preserved specimens, that it actually had evolved from the brook trout. Unfortunately, the silver trout now may be extinct.

DESCRIPTION

In most instances the coloration and markings of the brook trout are sufficient to distinguish it from other members of the genus *Salvelinus*, all of which are characterized by the lack of black spots and the absence of teeth on the shaft of the vomerine bone in the roof of the mouth. The brook trout is the most colorful member of the group, with

TOMELLERI

scales that are exceedingly small. In fact, many early anglers did not believe brook trout had scales. The wormlike vermiculations on the back, dorsal fin, and tail stand out clearly, and its ruby red spots with their bluish halos are truly spectacular. It has a chalky white edging and black stripe on the foreparts of the pectoral, ventral, and anal fins. This white-and-black edging also may occur on the lower edge of the tail.

Season and environment can greatly influence the coloration. Sea-run brook trout or those from clear, deep lakes may be very light or even silvery; those from small spring-fed streams or waters stained with tannic acid in watersheds of spruce and tamarack will be darker and more colorful. Examining the vivid and varied coloration of brook trout closely, it is easy to see why many consider them the most beautiful freshwater fish in the world.

DISTRIBUTION

The brook trout is truly a North American species. In 1969 MacCrimmon described its historical range in the United States with southern limits in the Chattahoochee and Catawba rivers in Georgia north through the headwater streams in the Appalachian Mountains in the Carolinas on through the Coastal States. Its western boundary was the northwestern counties of Maryland, northeastern Ohio, Iowa, and eastern Minnesota. In Canada the brook trout was found on the east coast north to the George River in

the Ungava region of Quebec, throughout the James Bay region and the tributaries of the Great Lakes but absent from southwest Ontario. In northwestern Ontario, Ryder in 1964 collected brook trout from the Patricia district and in the Severn and Fawn rivers but did not find them in the Nelson River or Lake of the Woods. The western limit of brook trout in Canada was in Manitoba where they were found in the Kettle Rapids, Wier, Limestone, Seal, North Knife, and Churchill rivers, south of Island Lake, and Red Sucker, Stull, and Echoing rivers.

The popularity of the brook trout as a sport fish has encouraged the introduction of the species into an additional fourteen states and four provinces in North America and into

Brook trout were native to nearly all North American waters where temperatures were favorable and competition from warmwater species was absent; brook trout prefer temperatures of between 13° and 18°C (55° and 65°F). Logging and dam construction, however, raised water temperatures and prevented spawning runs, and introduced species increased the competition for food and habitat. Brook trout are now extinct in some parts of their native range, but have been successfully introduced into other areas.

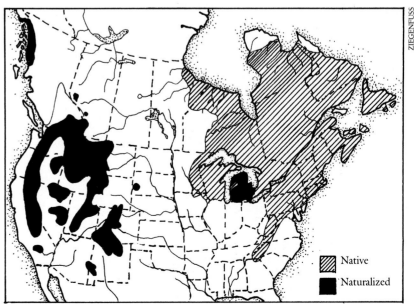

Native

Naturalized

ZIEGENFUSS

Assinica (above) and Temiscamie (below) brook trout exhibit rather striking color differences even when reared in the same Adirondack ponds.

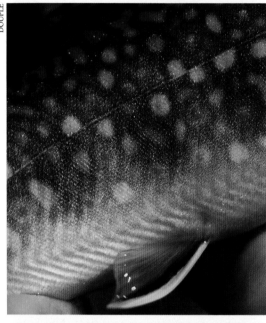

The colors of a brook trout are stunning. Red spots surrounded by blue halos and light vermiculations on a dark background are trademarks of the beautiful Salvelinus fontinalis.

Waters stained with tannic acid from spruce and tamarack contain darker, more colorful brook trout (left). Sea-run and lacustrine brook trout are silvery and less colorful (below).

nineteen countries in Eurasia, Central and South America, Africa, and New Zealand. In some areas brook trout have adapted extremely well, and in many western states they now dominate the fish populations in cold waters at high altitudes. But water temperature is the major limitation in the distribution of the species, so its range probably will not expand much beyond its present limits.

HABITAT

Of all the members of the char family, brook trout adapt most easily to their environment and will tolerate the widest range of conditions, including extremes in temperature and pH level.

Brook trout, which like other char and trout are a coldwater species, can survive a wide range of temperatures, from near 0°C (32°F) to around 22°C (72°F). However, they have been known to tolerate temperatures above 25.6°C (78°F) for up to a few hours. They grow and survive best in temperatures between 13° and 18°C (55° and 65°F). In streams or high mountain lakes where temperatures remain below 10°C (50°F), brook trout may be abundant, but they will grow slowly and probably will not exceed 15 to 20 centimeters (about 6 to 8 inches) in length.

Brook trout tolerate acidic conditions particularly well, compared with other species. They have been known to survive at pH 3.5 (7.0 is neutral), though only in unusual circumstances. Realistically, the lower limits are around pH 4.8. The presence of aluminum ions or other heavy metals may raise the lowest pH level at which brook trout can survive. Where pH levels are low, brook trout may be the only game fish that can survive. But even this species has suffered because of acid rain, particularly in the northeastern United States and southeastern Canada.

High alkalinity, the other extreme of the pH condition, is not a critical factor under natural conditions. In fact, survival has been recorded at pH levels of 9.8.

Stream habitat. Brook trout can be found in even the smallest spring-fed streams, especially where cover is available. Fingerlings prefer shallow water about 41 centimeters (16 inches) deep, and adults do not need much more than that. In northern latitudes where water temperatures are cool throughout the summer, brook trout are abundant in the larger rivers as well.

In streams, they prefer areas where the substrate consists of gravel or cobble with diameters of between 2 and 25 centimeters (0.8 to 10 inches). The movement of water in streams is important because it brings food that drifts with the current. However, chars prefer lower water velocities than do other salmonids. Brook trout fry use stream velocities of about 16 centimeters (0.5 feet) per second. Fingerlings are found in flows of 15 to 55 centimeters (0.5 to 1.8 feet) per second. Griffith found in his studies in Idaho that adult brook trout prefer slightly lower velocities in the range of 8 to 10 centimeters (0.25 to 0.33 feet) per second.

Stream fish have small home territories, or stations, and may remain by a given rock or log throughout the season, provided it is close to cover. If at all possible, dominant trout will seek out feeding stations that include overhead cover. Subdominant adults and juveniles often settle for less protected stations. Trout establish hierarchies and exhibit agonistic behavior at feeding stations, but they often will share escape cover. They will use deep water more often only as escape cover than as a preferred feeding area. As stream temperature drops in the fall and winter to the low 40s Fahrenheit, brook trout feed less and move closer to cover.

Lake habitat. Many people mistakenly consider deep, coldwater lakes the ideal habitat for brook trout. However, brook trout are not a deep-water species. They can tolerate that environment, but seldom will they use depths greater than 4.6 to 6 meters (15 to 20 feet) unless temperatures in shallower water are too high and no other coldwater refuge areas exist. In fact, when water temperatures are high, brook trout are more likely to concentrate where a spring seeps, in cold water that may be only a foot deep, than to venture into deeper water of favorable temperature. Such behaviors contrast with those of most other chars, particularly lake trout.

Studies by Cornell University have shown that maximum growth and standing crops of brook trout occur in shallow ponds and lakes that contain no competing species. But in contrast to brook trout in streams and rivers, those in ponds and lakes do not have feeding stations. Instead they cruise in search of food or move to areas with favorable temperatures. Cover in such environments is of minor importance.

LIFE HISTORY

Feeding. Brook trout are opportunistic feeders: Though primarily insectivorous, they eat whatever food is available and easy to get. They eat other fish only when those prey are particularly vulnerable. The importance of vulnerability was noted in Cornell University studies in which the stomachs of brook trout were examined. In a lake where alewife were abundant, few were eaten during the summer months, but in the winter when they were inactive because of low water temperatures, they became an important source of food. A similar situation has been noted in lakes with rainbow smelt. This species is taken readily by brook trout during the period when smelt are spawning, and thus more vulnerable, but they are of minor importance to brook trout the rest of the year.

The brook trout, like other salmonids, is an opportunist and feeds on whatever it can find.

HUGHES

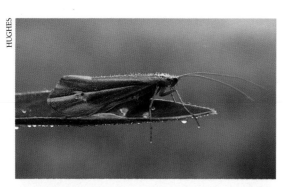

Right: Caddis flies are abundant and are found in the slower waters inhabited by brook trout, making them a staple food item in the brook trout's diet. Below: A brook trout strikes at the water's surface.

MERMON

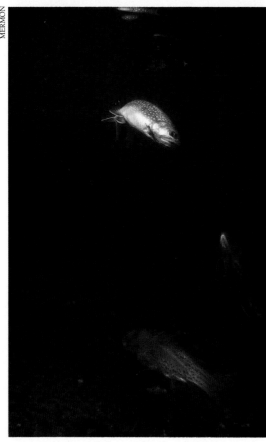

In a study of stomachs of large brook trout (1 to 2 kilograms [2 to 5 pounds]) from Mistassini Lake and Lake Albanel in Quebec, I found that the diet was nearly 100 percent insects. This finding was a surprise; these large fish were assumed to be primarily piscivorous. It should be noted, however, that stomachs were obtained during the summer months. Food habits may be different in other seasons. Over about thirty years, I have examined the stomachs of several thousand brook trout from ponds and lakes. Few have contained fish remains. Those with fish remains indicated that the brook trout had fed predominantly on spawning minnows or smelt or on alewife during the winter months.

In studies of stream environments in Idaho, Griffith found that brook trout fed extensively on caddis fly nymphs and adults, and cutthroat fed more extensively on midges. This again probably represents the opportunistic nature of brook trout. Cutthroat inhabited the faster water where there were more midges, and the brook trout stayed in slower water and nearer the bottom where there were more caddis flies. Caddis fly and midge larvae and adults are abundant in most environments and are usually at the top of the list when stomachs are examined for content. However, the opportunistic feeding behavior of brook trout makes listing preferred foods impossible. Depending on the season and the particular environment, terrestrial insects, mayflies, snails, leeches, and dragonfly and damselfly nymphs also may be important foods.

Growth. The generalized feeding habits of brook trout encourage fast growth when food is abundant and water temperatures are favorable. In much of the brook trout range, particularly in the Northeast, waters are basically unproductive, but even here trout may reach 1.4 to 1.8 kilograms (3 to 4 pounds) by age three. Brook trout from Assinica Lake in the province of Quebec weigh 3 to 5 kilograms (6 to 10 pounds) at ages seven to eight. The record brook trout was taken from the Nipigon region in Ontario in 1916 and weighed 6.6 kilograms (14.5 pounds). Fish nearly this size have been taken from various waters throughout Canada and Argentina. However, brook trout of 2 kilograms (4.4 pounds) or larger are considered trophies, and most are taken from lakes. Those taken from streams generally have migrated from lakes.

In contrast to the relatively fast growth that can occur in lakes, brook trout grow slowly in most infertile, cold mountain streams or high-altitude lakes. In some instances brook trout from such environments become sexually mature at 10 to 13 centimeters (4 to 5 inches) in length, and an 18-centimeter (7-inch) fish is a trophy. There has been speculation that the slow growth of many populations is genetic rather than environmental. But, although there are exceptions, studies by Cornell University have shown that when the progeny of slow-growing populations are stocked in productive environments, growth has been similar to that of resident fish.

Even in a rich aquatic environment, however, brook trout do not always reach a large size. If spawning conditions are favorable, this species often overpopulates its habitat and stunting occurs, which is why brook trout are not regarded highly in some western states. Thus, one cannot generalize about growth rates. Interspecific and intraspecific competition, water temperature, and the productivity of the environment all affect the species, more than such factors affect most other salmonids.

Brook trout reach sexual maturity early. Most males mature at age 1 + (at the end of the second summer of growth). Some females also will mature at this age, depending on their size and the environment. Except for a few isolated strains, or those in northern latitudes or high, cold mountain lakes, all brook trout have matured by age 2 +.

Genetic makeup is the major factor that influences the age at which brook trout mature; extremes in environment, such as high-altitude, infertile lakes, also affect it. Hatcheries have been selecting for early maturity, along with other traits, for about a hundred years, and most hatchery-strain brook trout are mature at age 1 +. Some males mature at the end of the first summer of growth, even though they may only be 13 to 15 centimeters (5 to 6 inches) long. The stocking of these early maturing fish in waters with self-sustaining populations of wild brook trout may be altering the genetic makeup of the wild trout.

In contrast to the early maturity of hatchery strains, studies by Cornell University have found later maturity in the strain of large brook trout from Assinica Lake and the

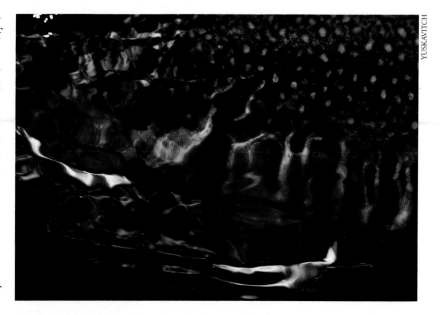

Broadback River in Quebec, as well as from some other waters in northern latitudes. In Assinica Lake, brook trout do not reach maturity until age 3 + to 4 +, even though some weigh 1.4 to 1.8 kilograms (3 to 4 pounds). This trait generally has held even when these strains have been transplanted to waters in more southern latitudes.

Spawning. Brook trout spawn in the fall, and as spawning time approaches, males put on their grandest garb. Their sides turn shades of red and the colors often are intense. The white edging on the fins becomes more pronounced and the red spots with their blue halos become more striking. Even the females develop more coloration, though not to the degree that the males do. Males also develop a kype, or hooked lower jaw, but it is not as pronounced as in other salmonids.

Brook trout prefer to select their spawning sites at places where groundwater wells up, a condition that is more important to them than the size of the substrate. This preference makes them highly successful spawners and enables them to spawn in ponds and lakes as well as in streams; most other salmonids spawn only in streams. Brook trout have an amazing ability to detect even minute amounts of groundwater seepage even when water temperatures in the stream or lake are similar to the upwelling water. If no upwelling groundwater is available, brook trout will use the tails of pools or riffles for spawning where the gravel is about 0.34 to 5.05 centimeters (0.13 to 2 inches) in diameter and

The spawning colors of the brook trout cannot be matched for brilliance or elegance.

The male brook trout's kype is not as pronounced as that of other salmonid species.

Above: The much larger male swims alongside the female at the onset of spawning. Above right: The spawning site abuts a rock, which makes it easier for the male to defend his place next to the female.

water velocity is 1 centimeter (0.39 inches) per second, according to a 1973 report by Smith, to 92 centimeters (36 inches) per second, according to Thompson in 1972 and Hooper in 1973. Water temperatures at the time of spawning are usually 4° to 13°C (40° to 55°F). The spawning act is similar to that of other salmonids except lake trout.

Development and survival. Egg development in the redd is similar to that of other salmonids. It depends on the temperature of the water and ranges from forty-seven days at 10°C (50°F) to 165 days at 3°C (37°F). More than 80 percent of the eggs hatch unless siltation smothers them. Usually, though, the upwelling groundwater continuously clears the redd of sediment.

After absorbing the yolk sac, the fry are about 2 centimeters (0.8 inches) long. At this point, they emerge from the gravel to start feeding on plankton and other minute food items. During this early stage they quickly disperse from the redd site and seek out water only a few inches deep.

The survival of brook trout varies greatly with environmental factors, including com-

petition from other species and water temperature. Brash showed that only 1 to 2 percent of the fry in streams survived to become nine-month-old fingerlings. But with an increase in size and age, it is common for the survival rate to improve. Brash found that 39 percent of the fingerlings lived to ages 1 to 2, and 73 percent of those lived to ages 2 to 3. In many populations, however, brook trout are short-lived, and Brash noted a decrease in survival to 39 percent at ages 3 to 4.

Here is an example. Of a thousand eggs that hatch, at most only about twenty will live to nine months of age. Because the survival rate usually increases with size, about eight of those will live to ages 1 to 2. As growth continues, the survival rate continues to climb, so of those, perhaps six will live to ages 2 to 3. However, of these short-lived trout, only two will survive to ages 3 to 4.

Because the environment of ponds and lakes is less hostile, survival is much higher there than it is in streams. In a study by Cornell University, 78 percent of 4.6-centimeter (1.8-inch) fingerlings in a sample pond survived the first year after stocking. This is

An alevin (left) doesn't stand much chance of reaching fingerling size (below).

an exception, however; survival rates of 40 to 65 percent in the year that follows stocking at fingerling size are more common. In the absence of fishing pressure the survival may be higher than 60 percent once brook trout have grown to a length of 15 to 18 centimeters (6 to 7 inches).

It should be noted, however, that brook trout are highly vulnerable to angling. In fact under heavy fishing pressure, catch rates can approach 100 percent of the population. Thus loss of brook trout populations of yearling size and larger may not always be due to high natural mortality.

Migration. Most brook trout that live in streams do not travel far, except in search of spawning areas or water with more favorable temperatures. In some coastal areas, however, there are anadromous populations that move to salt water. No set pattern exists for such movements, in contrast to salmon, and only a portion of the population may migrate. White determined in 1940 that 79 percent of the brook trout going to sea were age 2, the others age 3. In 1958 Smith and Saunders reported brook trout going to sea

every month, although fewer migrated in midsummer or midwinter. The length of time in salt water also varies. Smith and Saunders reported that, at Prince Edward Island, half the population returned to fresh water within a month. As stream temperatures decline fewer brook trout move back to fresh water, and instead overwinter in the estuary. Movement also varies between watersheds. Populations from some of the larger rivers in New Brunswick spend longer periods in the estuaries or at sea.

Parasites and diseases. Mullen reported in 1958 that brook trout can be affected by about twenty-five organisms: five trematoda, four cestoda, four nematoda, two acanthocephala, one copepoda, five protozoa, two bacteria, and two fungi. However, populations of brook trout in the wild normally do not have severe loss of epidemic proportions unless a pathogen is introduced from a fish hatchery and the fish are under stress from high water temperature, low levels of dissolved oxygen, or pollution. Under any of these conditions, epidemics of the bacterial disease *Furunculosis* are the most common. Even an infestation of this bacterium normally will not continue in epidemic proportions once the stress is reduced.

In natural environments the copepod *Salmoncola edwardsii* may be a serious problem when trout populations in ponds or lakes are high. This copepod is specific to brook trout. Only the female is parasitic; the male swims freely. The females attach themselves to the gills or, sometimes, to the fins, and are commonly called gill lice. In streams infestation is usually light and unimportant; trout seldom have more than one to three of the parasites

Wavy, wormlike vermiculations are the brook trout's trademark.

attached. This parasite can, however, be a major concern if an infestation completely covers the gills and impedes the animal's respiration. Larger trout usually have the heaviest infestation and may become emaciated and die.

After the young of the copepod hatch from the two elongated egg pouches, the female offspring must attach to a brook trout within twenty-four to forty-eight hours or they will expire.

This life-history trait can be exploited to ultimately eliminate the infestation of gill lice. Fish toxicants such as rotenone are applied to the water to kill the brook trout hosts, after which the lake or pond can be restocked with fish free of copepods. This program has successfully restored brook trout to numerous waters.

Gill lice can become a serious problem. A heavy infestation may interfere with the trout's respiration.

HUMAN INTERVENTION

Settlers of eastern North America found brook trout in nearly all waters where temperatures were favorable and competition from warmwater species was absent. The clearing of forests and the construction of dams, however, raised the water temperatures in many streams and prevented spawning migrations, thus eliminating viable populations of brook trout in many areas. In the early 1900s it also was a common practice to introduce other fish species, many of which—pike, bass, and yellow perch, for example—were serious competitors to brook trout. This situation further added to the decline of brook trout, as it is rare for a pond or lake with yellow perch to have a viable brook trout population.

With the advent of successful fish culture operations for trout in the late 1880s, stocking was considered the remedy for the decline of brook trout, and fish hatcheries became an important tool in fish management. However, except where natural reproduction was a limiting factor, stocking rarely provided more than a short-term increase in catch rates. But fisheries managers continued to stock, adding other trout species in the hopes of increasing fishing potential.

In most streams brook trout could not compete successfully with brown and rainbow trout except in headwaters where cold temperatures limited species other than brook trout. Not until the early 1950s were detailed, scientifically valid studies initiated

This healthy brook trout has a full, well-formed body.

to evaluate trout stocking and survival in various habitats.

The inability of brook trout to compete with warmwater species, particularly yellow perch, led to early measures of population control. Initially dams were built to regulate water levels so that yellow perch could be destroyed at spawning, and nets were used to physically remove warmwater species and suckers, and thus reduce competition with brook trout. But such measures were not successful, and it was not until the early 1950s that the use of fish toxicants, such as rotenone, became important in management of brook-trout waters.

From detailed studies of seven lakes in the Adirondack Mountains in New York, I reported in 1987 that the standing crop of non-trout species in these relatively unproductive waters was nearly 46 kilograms (100 pounds) per acre and that brook trout amounted to less than half a kilogram (one pound) per acre. These waters were then reclaimed with rotenone and restocked with brook trout. In the absence of competing species, natural reproduction was excellent and only one, which lacked favorable spawning areas, needed more than an introductory planting. Within two years the standing crop of brook trout ranged from 3 to 7 kilograms (6 to 16 pounds) where previously populations were too low to provide good fishing.

In fact, brook trout populations responded so well that, to prevent stunting, three waters

Wild brook trout (left) try to avoid the researcher's hand. The hatchery trout (below) show little fear.

The native brook trout (left) is not only more colorful than the stocked fish (below), but also more likely to survive and adapt to life in the wild.

had to have trout removed by netting, in addition to angling. The total annual harvest from one lake of 59 hectares (146 acres) was 6 kilograms (13.2 pounds) per acre; previously this water did not have a viable trout population.

For nearly a hundred years hatchery stocks of brook trout were selected for early maturity, fast growth, heavy body conformation, and ease of handling. Field investigations by fishery biologists indicated, however, that even high-quality waters stocked with these fish yielded few trout that were large or more than two or three years of age.

In 1957 Cornell University biologists studied the growth and survival rates of hatchery-strain brook trout as well as wild strains reared under identical conditions. Differences in behavior were noted immediately. Fingerlings of hatchery strains showed little fear of human activity. They took readily to hatchery diets, grew more rapidly in the hatchery, and used the upper portion of the water column where they received the most food when fed. In contrast, the wild strains were very nervous and frightened by any movement near their trough, remained near the bottom of the water column to take advantage of any shade or cover, took artificial food poorly and thus grew slowly, and in general were more difficult to rear.

But the hatchery strain, when stocked in a wild environment, had lower survival rates, matured earlier in life, and seldom lived to more than two or three years. The wild strains survived better than did their hatchery-strain counterparts. Although smaller when stocked, they soon caught up with or passed the hatchery strains in size. Some wild strains lived two to six years longer than did the hatchery strains, thus allowing greater potential for maximum size.

Further studies by Cornell showed that crosses between strains of brook trout from the James Bay area of Quebec and hatchery-strain brook trout exhibited hybrid vigor, growing faster than either parent, with survival and longevity characteristics of the wild parent. It was thus apparent that the genetic makeup that governs various traits is complex. Selection of characteristics desirable in the hatchery may be successful, but others important for survival in the wild may be

lost. Thus, the intention to improve populations of brook trout through stocking has backfired to a degree and has had to be re-evaluated. Stocking still is an important management tool, but it is more complex than originally realized.

Degradation of many streams through human activities has reduced stream cover and pools, lowering the carrying capacity of these waters. Increasing cover and pools through stream improvement activities has thus become another important management tool. Studies on Lawrence Creek in Wisconsin by Hunt showed the beneficial effect of intensive stream management. Following stream improvement work on a one-mile section of stream, the brook trout population increased from 1,747 to 4,306 trout. The total biomass (weight of brook trout) also increased nearly threefold, from 59 to 175 kilograms (130 to 385 pounds). The stream environment itself improved most dramatically: Stream cover increased 416 percent and the number of pools increased 289 percent. This program was an intensive stream-improvement effort, but it demonstrates the relationship between stream cover and pools and the size of trout populations.

We will never see brook trout of the size and numbers that historically occurred in eastern North America, but with our knowledge of its biology and life history, we can make sure that it continues to exist.

—William A. Flick

THE SPECIES

Brown trout

Salmo trutta

"*T*here is a river called Astraeus, flowing midway between Berea and Thessalonica, in which are produced certain spotted fish . . . whose food consists of insects which fly about the water. The natives call this insect *hippurus*. As the flies float on the top of the water in pursuit of their food they attract the notice of the fish, which swim upon them. When a fish spies one of these insects on the top of the water, it swims quietly underneath it, taking care not to agitate the surface, lest it should scare away the prey; so approaching it, as it were, under its shadow, it opens its mouth and gulps it down, just as a wolf seizes a sheep from the flock, or an eagle a goose from the yard; and having done this it swims away beneath the ripple." (Claudius Aelianus, *Natura Animalium*, A.D. 230.)

The "certain spotted fish" in Aelianus' description is *the* trout: the brown trout, the essence and definition of "troutness." From the brown trout, Western civilization derives the very idea of what a trout is.

The word *trout* stems from the Middle English *troute* and *trute*, Old English and Anglo-Saxon *truht*, and the Late Latin *tructa*. The latter undoubtedly is derived from the Greek word τρώκτης (trouk-tas), meaning *gnawer*, *nibbler*, or *greedy creature*, and according to Maxwell, this same word seems originally to have been used by ancient peoples to refer to fish in general. If so, the brown trout might not only claim precedence as *the* trout, but possibly also *the fish*.

All of these ancient words are cognates of the French *truite*, and all refer to the various forms and varieties of trout that now are collectively called brown trout. The brown trout was the trout described by Piscator in Izaak Walton's *The Compleat Angler*: "his name is of a German offspring . . . he may justly contend with all freshwater fish . . . for precedency and daintiness of taste." It was the trout of fifteenth-century Dame Juliana Berners of the Abbey of Saint Albans and the trout of the sixteenth- and seventeenth-century outdoor writers Leonard Mascall, John Dennys, Gervase Markham, William Lawson, and Thomas Barker.

It was the only trout known to these early European writers. The North American brook trout, *Salvelinus fontinalis*, and the rainbow trout, *Salmo gairdneri* (recently renamed *Oncorhynchus mykiss*), had not yet been introduced into Europe, and the various forms of Arctic char are sufficiently different in appearance as to be easily distinguished from the brown trout. From Claudius Aelianus through Juliana Berner, Izaak Walton, F. M. Halford, Theodore Gordon, and Vince Marinaro, the brown trout began and sustains our long love affair with trout.

EVOLUTION

The trout and salmon of the Atlantic (*Salmo*) diverged from the trout and salmon of the Pacific (*Oncorhynchus*) some 20 million years ago. Just when and under what condi-

tions the divergence between the Atlantic salmon, *Salmo salar*, and brown trout, *Salmo trutta*, occurred is unknown, but there is more than circumstantial evidence that the various forms of brown trout all stem from one or more anadromous forms of brown trout, which in turn either stem from the Atlantic salmon or have a common ancestor with the Atlantic salmon.

Chromosome differences between the Atlantic salmon and the brown trout (fifty-six to fifty-eight for *S. salar* and eighty for *S. trutta*) clearly separate the salmon and brown, but the similarity of markings for the juveniles or parr of both species (black and red spots on a dark background, and well-developed double row of teeth on the vomer in the roof of the mouth) are strong evidence of a relatively recent common heritage. The observation that the vomerine teeth of the adult Atlantic salmon are restricted to the anterior portion of the vomer, that adult freshwater forms of brown trout have vomerine teeth extending along the entire length of the vomer, and that certain sea trout have vomerine teeth intermediate between the Atlantic salmon and the freshwater resident trout, would suggest that the Atlantic salmon is the ancestral form, and that the brown trout might have evolved by a process known as neoteny, in which immature characters are retained in adulthood. Further, the greater number of chromosomes in the brown trout also suggests that the brown trout may have resulted from the duplication

of some of the chromosomes of the Atlantic salmon.

This rather convincing scenario, however, appears not to be what happened. According to Behnke, more recent studies show that both *trutta* and *salar* have the same amount of DNA. If *trutta* evolved by partial chromosome doubling, it should have approximately 40 percent more DNA than *salar*. Because the amount of DNA is approximately the same for both species, it seems that, instead, the brown trout is the ancestral form and the Atlantic salmon is derived from it by fusion of some of the chromosomes. *S. salar* has many very long one-arm chromosomes, apparently a fusion of two-arm *trutta* chromosomes.

Svardson notes that there have been eight glacial and interglacial periods within the past 700,000 years, and at least seventeen in the period since the split between *Salmo* and *Oncorhynchus*. Along with whitefish, *Coregonus*, and char, *Salvelinus*, the origins of the Atlantic salmon and the various races or subspecies of brown trout undoubtedly are associated with the events of the Pleistocene glaciations. During these periods, most of the British Isles and Northern Europe was covered with ice, and freshwater fishes would have been eliminated in the regions of glaciation. However, the migratory salmonids undoubtedly retreated southward, permitting these forms to invade the Mediterranean, Black, and Caspian seas. The glaciations were not continuous, however, and alternate advances and

THE SPECIES

retreats of ice in separate geographical areas most likely resulted in long periods of genetic isolation (as indeed is still the case where introduction by humans has not occurred), allowing genetic differentiation to take place.

Payne and others have postulated, for example, that two races of salmon, *Salmo salar* L., in the British Isles—a northern "boreal" race and a southwestern "Celtic" race—evolved in isolated refugia during the final phase of the last glaciation. They suggest that when the ice covered the northern part of the British Isles, the boreal race was isolated in the present North Sea area and that when the ice retreated, the rivers in the northern parts of the British Isles were recolonized by this race. The Celtic race is assumed to have remained in the ice-free southwest area throughout this time.

Similar mechanisms are postulated for the origins of the many forms of brown trout. There is no reason to believe that the glacial advances and retreats followed the same routes each time. Consequently, different patterns of isolation and subsequent interbreeding seem to explain, if not confirm, the variations in form and distribution of "native" brown trout.

CLASSIFICATION

At one time or another, as many as fifty separate "species" of brown trout have been identified and described. However, after many years of tortuous categorizing, comparing, synonymizing, lumping, and splitting, the International Commission on Zoological Nomenclature now recognizes the forms, varieties, strains, subspecies, or ecotypes of trout as belonging to one highly variable species, *Salmo trutta* Linnaeus.

The classification of the brown trout is complicated not only by the incredible number of kinds of brown trout that have been lumped into one species, but also by the wealth of information that is available about the trout as a popular game fish. Because so many highly respected taxonomists, working independently and relying on different classification schemes, arrived at workable but conflicting and overlapping results, the grouping of many forms under one name, *Salmo trutta* L., appears to have been more of an attempt to sweep the problem under the

rug than to deal with it. But there is evidence that some original populations have remained reproductively isolated for hundreds of thousands of years—some in Europe within the same lakes and streams. What is perhaps even more interesting is that the generic brown trout, which has been produced by intermingling various forms and strains of trout in fish hatcheries and which has been distributed all over the globe, may over time and generations be reverting to the original "name brands."

In classifying and cataloging the fishes of the British Museum, Albert C. L. G. Günther commented on the genus *Salmo*: "We know of no other group of fishes which offers so many difficulties to ichthyologists with regard to the distinction of the species." In his 1847 book *Angler Companion*, referring to the brown trout of the British Isles, Stoddart wrote, "unquestionably there exists no species of fish which, judging of it by the external marks, holds claim to so many varieties as the common freshwater trout. In Scotland almost every lake, river, and streamlet possesses a breed peculiar in outward appearance to itself." Heacox, in *The Compleat Brown Trout*, borrows from Winston Churchill to describe the brown trout as "a riddle wrapped in mystery inside an enigma." And as to scientific names, Trewas exclaimed simply, "The trouble is that the Linnaean system of binomial nomenclature is simple and the trout situation is complex." Exemplifying the difficulty of classifying brown trout was a proposal by Lunel to combine all of the four so-called species residing in Lake Constance under a single name, *Salmo variabilis*.

Carlolus Linnaeus, in his historical work *Systema Naturae*, published in 1758, named three types of trout in Sweden by the binomial nomenclature now universally used: *S. trutta*, the trout of large rivers; *S. fario*, the trout of small brooks; and *S. eriox*, the migratory sea trout.

Before the work of Linnaeus, the various forms of brown trout went under a multitude of common and Latin names, some of which referred collectively to both the brown trout and its close relative, the Atlantic salmon. In 1686, for example, Willoughby described the salmon and several kinds of trout: the salmon; the gray trout; the scurf, or bull trout, *Trutta salmonata*; the stream or river trout, *T. fluviatilis*; and *Salmulus*, a term used for the parr of both salmon and trout. In 1713, Ray gave the salmon the Latin name *Salmo*, the young salmon and trout (samlet) the name *Salmulus*, the gray trout the name *Salmo griseus seu cinereus*, the salmon trout *Trutta salmonata*, and the common trout of streams *T. fluviatilis*. The mixture of common and Latin terms used by these two naturalists reflects the lack of any formal terminology or classification system at the time.

Common terms in use in the British Isles to describe the various life stages and races of sea trout included: samlet, skegger, sewen, white salmon, whitling, salmon-peal or simply peal, Galway trout, Orkney trout, Fordidge, or Fordwich, trout of Kent, phinnock or finnock, herling, truff, and eight kinds of "bull trout." These, along with local names for strictly freshwater trout of rivers, streams, and lakes—gillaroo, sonaghen, ferox, buddagh, great lake trout, black-finned trout, Loch Leven trout, Lough Neagh trout, to name but a few—were an open invitation and challenge for naturalists of the eighteenth and nineteenth centuries. Swept by an almost fanatical desire to describe and catalog, and the excitement of Darwin's concepts of evolution and natural selection, British taxonomists and naturalists generated a prodigious list of species of brown trout. And by no means was this cataloging and naming restricted to the British Isles!

Within this plethora of terms, however, lay four distinct forms that early naturalists and taxonomists used for grouping, comparison, and further study: the immature forms of salmon and trout, or parr; the resident brown trout of freshwater lakes and streams; the sea-run trout, or salmon trout; and the true salmon. Because all these forms readily hybridize, or exhibit coloring, marking, anatomical, and physiological characteristics that intergrade, but breed true for successive generations (exhibit inherited characteristics), the process of classifying and naming has been complex and, for many, a frustrating experience.

Disparate classification schemes by systematists and naturalists working sometimes independently and sometimes in outright dis-

Brown trout have pronounced dark spots on a lighter background.

agreement resulted in an interesting and informative, if somewhat confusing, array of species lists. The following lists of European trout and salmon, while by no means exhaustive, are illustrative of differing viewpoints, and provide a useful reference to the many different common and Latin names by which the brown trout *Salmo trutta* L. was and sometimes still is known.

Of the eighty-three species of *Salmo* described by Günther alone, approximately thirty today are considered forms of brown trout. In his 1866 herculean work, *Catalog of Fishes in the British Museum*, Günther described ten species of brown trout from the British Isles that deserve special attention because of recent phylogenetic and taxonomic studies. These are: the river trout or "common trout," *S. fario*; the sea trout or salmon-trout, *S. trutta*; the great lake trout, *S. ferox*; the Loch Leven trout, *S. levenensis*; the Welsh black-finned trout, *S. nigripinnis*; the Irish gilaroo, *S. stomachicus*; the sewin, or western sea trout, *S. cambricus*; the phinnox, or eastern sea trout, *S. brachypoma*; the Galway sea trout, *S. gallivensis*; and the Orkney sea trout, *S. orcadensis*.

In 1863, Widegren had suggested that anadromous sea trout and nonmigratory freshwater forms of British and Irish trout were simply varieties of one common species, the differences being merely the consequence of local environments. Günther vigorously objected to such crass lumping, declaring that these views were the outcome of the "incapacity or ignorance of the observers." As we shall see later, Günther seems to have been at least partly vindicated in this somewhat arrogant viewpoint.

In 1884, Francis Day, who rarely agreed with Günther on the matter of fishes, gave detailed descriptions of the numerous forms of brown trout and sea trout of Ireland and Britain. But following the line of thought of Widegren, Malmgren of Finland, Collett of Norway, and Fedderson of Denmark, he concluded that all were, in actuality, one species.

Regan concurred with Day that the various forms all correctly belonged to one species. But loath to dispense with the commonality of certain species and differences between others, in 1911 he organized the eighteen different so-called species into six groups of British Isles and Continental strains of brown trout.

David Starr Jordan, Carl Hubbs, and others later argued that the separate species should all be accorded one name, and by 1930, the name *Salmo trutta* L. had been accepted by virtually all taxonomists as the proper name for the various forms and descriptions of brown trout.

This was not to be the end of the matter, however. In 1932, L. S. Berg, a highly respected Russian authority of fishes of Eurasia, agreed that all forms of brown trout deserved to be recognized as belonging to only one species, but saw enough differences in geographical subdivisions to recognize six subspecies stemming from geographic separation: *Salmo trutta trutta*, northern and western Europe; *S. t. labrax*, Black Sea and tributaries; *S. t. caspius*, Caspian Sea and tributaries; *S. t. macrostigma*, Mediterranean region; *S. t. carpio*, Lake Garda, Italy; and *S. t. aralensis*, Sea of Aral and Amu Dar'ya River.

Berg regarded *S. t. trutta* as one subspecies, which, throughout its range, was present in three forms: a migratory (stem) form, a lake trout of more restricted migrations, and a relatively stationary brook, or stream, form. However, he argued that these forms, or 'morpha' as he called them, were unstable and that a change in the environment caused the form to revert to its first state. That is, it had no tendency to transmit its characters by means of heredity except when the environment remained constant. Gunnar Alm and others were later to disprove this assertion.

DESCRIPTION

The almost limitless variations of color, shape, spot patterns, fin markings, number of vertebrae, fin rays, lateral-line scales, caecal appendages, food preferences, growth rates, spawning habitats, age at maturation, and behavior of the brown trout have been the source of frustration, confusion, acrimonious debate, and resignation for more than a hundred years. Not only is the issue far from being settled, but also recent advances in genetic fingerprinting have brought the arguments virtually full circle.

The brown trout is best described as being olive green to brown on top, shading to yel-

low or white on the lower sides and belly, and having many pronounced black spots, most numerous on the upper portions of the body, each usually surrounded by a conspicuous light halo. In addition to these dark brown or black spots, brown trout usually also sport haloed reddish spots ranging from light orange to brilliant crimson. The tail, or caudal fin, is rarely spotted, but when it is, the spots are few in number, irregular in pattern, and restricted to the upper margin of the fin. The leading edge of the dorsal, anal, and pelvic fins often is fringed with white and black. The pectoral fins are more uniformly yellow, amber, or dusky gray in color.

The adipose fin of the brown trout is spotted, and highly colored specimens sport an adipose fin margined with orange or crimson spots. The brown trout is the only salmonid that has red on the adipose fin, and although not always present (hatchery-reared trout rarely exhibit this coloration; neither do trout in lakes), a red adipose fin, if present, of and by itself positively identifies the brown trout.

Variations. The above description applies best to juvenile brown trout and brown trout that are permanent residents of streams and rivers. Although all forms and races of brown trout exhibit some or all of the above characteristics in the juvenile, or parr stages, much of this coloration disappears or is masked by a silvery coloration when the trout lives in deep, clear lakes or when it smoltifies, that is, when it undergoes physio-

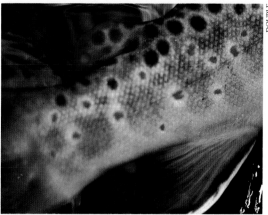

The dark spots with light halos (above) and the red spot on the adipose fin (left) are characteristic of many brown trout.

The brown trout's pectoral fins are unspotted and may be yellow, amber, or gray.

Markings and color are not always good identifiers. This trout has irregularly shaped spots, and the colors are masked by the silvery guanophores.

Fish have jaw, palatine and vomerine teeth. Trout teeth are structurally similar to human teeth, although all conical in shape. Fish teeth are composed of a soft pulp cavity containing blood vessels and nerves, an inner dentine portion and a harder, external enamel cover. The teeth are continuously replaced when lost.

Brown trout have two rows of teeth on the vomer bone in the center of the roof of the mouth; brook trout only have one row. Vomerine teeth probably assist in gripping and holding prey.

logical changes in preparation for life in salt water. Further, the black and red spots on some forms are more irregularly shaped than on other forms, and when the coloration is masked by a proliferation of guanophores (cells that contain the pale iridescent crystals of guanine that account for the silvery appearance of salmon and trout in lakes and in the sea), markings and coloration are poor, if not useless, means of identification.

One should always be mindful of the ichthyologist's warning, *Nimium ne crede colori* (place little credence in color). Because of similarities in coloration, the brown trout has often been confused with its closest relative, the Atlantic salmon, and not until techniques for counting chromosomes were perfected was it possible to distinguish adult brown trout from adult Atlantic salmon in every instance.

Forms. By habitat and behavior, the brown trout now is distinguished in at least four different forms: trout that reside permanently in small streams and brooks—the "brook" trout (not to be confused with the North American brook trout, *Salvelinus fontinalis*); trout that live in freshwater lakes and migrate into rivers and streams to spawn—lacustrine trout; trout that spend most of their time in large rivers and estuaries—river or estuarine trout; and trout that spend most of their adult lives in the sea—salmon trout or sea trout.

Sexual dimorphism. For those who wish to go beyond merely identifying a fish as a brown trout, there is a simple means of determining the gender by means of a pronounced sexual dimorphism among sexually mature, adult brown trout. As in most salmonids, the male has a somewhat flattened head, larger than the female's. In addition, large old males often develop a kype on the lower jaw. The

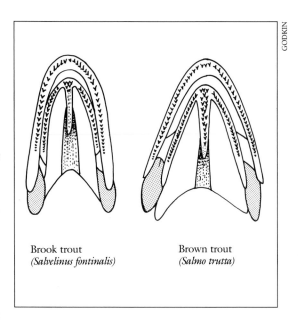

Brook trout
(*Salvelinus fontinalis*)

Brown trout
(*Salmo trutta*)

difference in the shape of the head, including the development of the kype, however, is not always pronounced in smaller adult brown trout, and without two fish for comparison, it may be difficult to discern.

Gruchy and Vladikov, however, have described an additional method for sexing adult brown trout by examination of the anal fin. Upon becoming sexually mature, male brown trout develop a convex anal fin, whereas female brown trout retain the concave or falcate anal fin typical of immature brown trout. If the trout is large enough to be assumed mature, then lack of the convex anal fin is evidence that it is a female.

Comparison with other North American salmonids. Because the brown trout is so variable in color, shape, and morphology, no single character or set of characters can be used to identify a brown trout with certainty. Nevertheless, certain characters, when present, can be used to readily distinguish the brown trout from other species of trout. In addition to the adipose fin, scaled body, scaleless head, and pseudobranchs (small partial gill beneath each operculum) of all salmonids, all brown trout have pronounced dark spots on a lighter background.

Brown trout can be distinguished most readily from other trout by the degree and location of dark spots on the tail or caudal fin. If present at all on the tail, the dark spots are restricted to the dorsal portion. This characteristic readily distinguishes it from the rainbow trout and cutthroat trout, both of

The kype is a sure indicator of a sexually mature male fish.

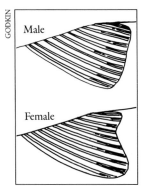

Male

Female

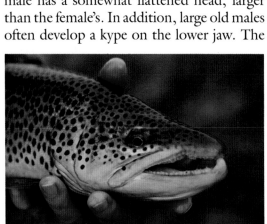

MERWIN

which have profuse spotting on the tail. An additional character, but one that is not always present, that distinguishes a brown trout from all other salmonids except juvenile Atlantic salmon is the presence of orange or red spots on a light background. Although some North American char—brook trout, bull trout, and Dolly Varden—also have orange or red spots, the char are characterized by a dark background surrounding such spots.

Even more distinctive, if present, are red or orange spots on the margin of the adipose fin. No other salmonid has this distinguishing character. The red or orange spots on the adipose fin are also a strong, if not definitive, distinction between hatchery-reared and wild brown trout. Unless the hatchery trout are fed a special diet, or unless they survive long enough and eat enough natural food to color up, brown trout of hatchery origin rarely, if ever, have red markings on the adipose fin.

In addition to these red or orange markings, the brown trout can be distinguished from the Atlantic salmon, its closest relative, by the shape of the tail and the length of the upper jaw. The brown trout generally has a square or even slightly rounded tail, whereas the Atlantic salmon usually has a forked tail. The maxilla or upper jaw of the brown trout extends well behind the eye, whereas that of the Atlantic salmon terminates below the center of the eye.

One final distinguishing feature, of which

Brown trout can usually be easily distinguished from other trout by examination of the tail. The tail of a brown trout (right) has few or no spots. Cutthroat (below) and rainbow tails are heavily spotted.

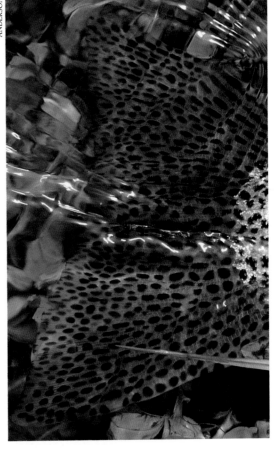

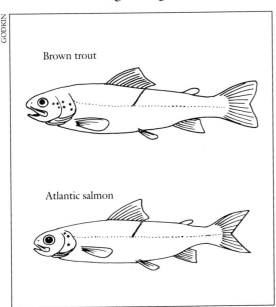

Brown trout

Atlantic salmon

Brown trout and Atlantic salmon can be differentiated by their tails and upper jaws. Scales for assessing ages are usually taken from the back edge of the dorsal fin in a diagonal line down to the lateral line; these scales are the least apt to be misshapen.

THE SPECIES

SCHOLLMEYER

much has been made by various taxonomists and naturalists, is the presence of two zigzag rows of well-developed teeth on the brown trout's vomer, the raised shaft of bone in the center of the roof of the mouth. The presence of these vomerine teeth on the shaft and body of the vomer is a relatively sure distinguishing character of the brown trout.

DISTRIBUTION

The historical account of efforts to define and name the various kinds of brown trout gives us a basis for describing the so-called original distribution of the brown trout. Before humans effected a mass translocation throughout the globe, the brown trout lived in its many freshwater and sea-run forms from Iceland, the British Isles, and the northern coast of Europe as far east as the White Sea drainage of the USSR, southward to the watersheds of the European Mediterranean Sea, the Atlas mountains of North Africa in Algiers and Morocco, and Corsica and Sardinia. Marshal and others report evidence that brown trout inhabited tributaries of the Adriatic and Aegean seas in Yugoslavia, Albania, and Greece, the Oronte River in Lebanon, and the headwaters of the Tigris and Euphrates rivers. The original range of the brown trout extended eastward as far as the Amu Dar'ya River of the Aral Sea, the Timanskiy and Ural mountain ranges of the USSR, and the Black and Caspian seas and their tributaries. Behnke also reports a previously undescribed subspecies of brown

trout having many small black and red spots from one small stream in the Rezaiyeh Basin of Iran.

Transplantation. The first attempt to transplant brown trout outside their native range seems to have occurred in 1852 with an unsuccessful attempt to establish brown trout in Chudskoe Lake in the Baltic region of the USSR. The earliest successful introduction of brown trout beyond its native range was a planting of fry in Tasmania in 1864, hatched from ova from the Wey and Itchen rivers of England. Progeny of these and a subsequent shipment of eggs the following year were eventually successfully introduced into other waters of Tasmania, mainland Australia, and New Zealand.

The distribution of brown trout throughout the world appears to have been so extensive that within the past 125 years, most areas of the world capable of supporting brown trout have received introductions at one time or another. Naturalized populations of brown trout have been confirmed in India, West Pakistan, Japan, South Africa, Kenya, Rhodesia, Uganda, Madagascar, the Kerguelen Islands, Bolivia, Argentina, Chile, Peru, and the Falkland Islands, and attempts are still being made in other countries.

Profound differences in morphology, behavior, food preferences, growth rates, longevity, and age at sexual maturity persist in various brown trout populations. However, because of widespread introductions throughout the world, the contamination of gene pools by undocumented introductions, and the intentional mixing and backcrossing of stocks in hatcheries, it is virtually impossible to track lineages and thus difficult, perhaps impossible, to retain or determine either species or subspecies distinctions. The introductions into North America illustrate this point.

The first brown trout in North America. There are reports that a Mr. Gilbert may have imported brown trout for the Old Colony Trout Hatchery in Massachusetts in 1882, and references of importation of trout, salmon, char, and huchen ("salmon of the Danube") for a private club on Long Island appear in the New York Tribune as early as 1865. However, the New York fish culturist, Fred Mather, generally is credited for bring-

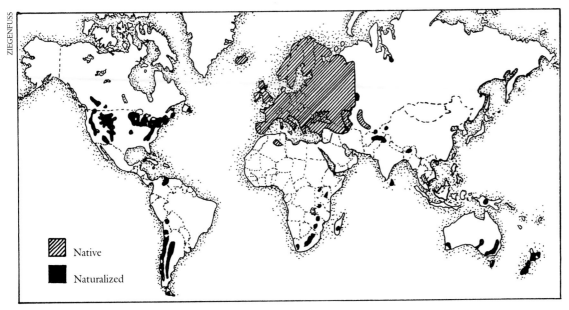

Native

Naturalized

Brown trout were not native to North America. They were introduced here in the late 1800s and are now widespread throughout the world. Brown trout tend to live longer, grow bigger, produce more eggs, and spawn more frequently than our native brook trout—all of which may explain the brown trout's ability to out-compete many other species. Brown trout also seem better able to cope with degraded habitats.

ing brown trout to North America.

In 1880, while visiting the International Fisheries Exposition in Berlin as a representative of the United States Fish Commission, Mather met Baron von Behr, president of the German Fishery Association. It was during this visit that Mather caught his first brown trout in the Black Forest. He was so taken with the trout that he became determined to introduce the species into America. After a long bureaucratic hassle, Mather received a shipment of 80,000 brown trout eggs (60,000 from a strain resident in a large lake, and 20,000 from a strain living in a small mountain stream) at New York's Cold Spring Harbor hatchery on Long Island on February 28, 1883—a gift from Baron von Behr. The brown trout eggs were in poor condition by the time they reached Cold Spring Harbor. Because of limited space, interagency politics, and conditions of agreements made at the Berlin Exposition, a portion of the eggs was sent to New York's sister hatchery at Caldonia, New York, and another lot to the U.S. Fish Commission hatchery at Northville, Michigan. Of this first batch of eggs from von Behr, fewer than fifty trout were still alive at Cold Spring Harbor by September 1883, and only 1,330 at Northville, Michigan.

By Seth Green's accounts, the von Behr trout fared better at the Caldonia hatchery than at Cold Spring Harbor and Northville. There are no records of what Green did with the original von Behr fry that hatched at

Caldonia, but because it was his practice to use new fish for brood stock, it is unlikely that many of his original "German trout," as he called them, were stocked. Green did report, however, that the first take of brown trout spawn occurred at the Caldonia hatchery in November 1885, so it is clear that at least some trout of the first shipment survived to spawning age.

The fish that survived at Cold Spring Harbor and Northville also were held for exposition and for brood stock. There is no record that any of these trout were ever stocked either. The record is not entirely clear, but it seems that few if any of the first batch of trout from von Behr were ever intentionally stocked. One incident confounds the story, however. A 1.4-kilogram (3-pound) brown trout reportedly was caught in Allen's Creek, a tributary of the Genesee River in New York, in July 1886. This fish was estimated to be three years old, which would mean that it would have to have come from one of the first lots of eggs received in America. Whether this trout was one of a batch that was stocked or whether it escaped from the Caldonia hatchery is not known.

A second shipment of eggs from von Behr arrived at Cold Spring Harbor in February 1884. As in the previous year, this shipment was split between New York and the U.S. Fish Commission, some going to Northville, Michigan, and the rest to Wytheville, Virginia. Although many of the eggs at Wytheville hatched, all died in the sac-fry

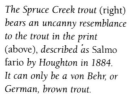

The Spruce Creek trout (right) bears an uncanny resemblance to the trout in the print (above), described as Salmo fario *by Houghton in 1884. It can only be a von Behr, or German, brown trout.*

stage. The fry at Northville fared better, and on April 11, 1884, J. F. Ellis stocked 4,900 brown trout fry from the second batch of von Behr eggs into Michigan's Pere Marquette River. This, then, is the first documented introduction of brown trout into American waters.

After this initial introduction in 1884, distribution of brown trout was swift and wide. Fry from the 1884 hatch at Cold Springs Harbor were distributed to at least six places on Long Island, and the following year a third shipment of eggs from von Behr was distributed even more widely.

The first North American introduction of Loch Leven trout, *Salmo trutta levenensis* (a lake form), appears to have been made in Long Pond near Saint John's, Newfoundland, in 1884. The following year Sir James Gibson Maitland of the Howieton fishery, Stirlingshire, Scotland, sent 100,000 Loch Leven eggs to Cold Spring Harbor. These eggs were immediately distributed to hatcheries in Maine, New Hampshire, Iowa, Minnesota, and Michigan, and to the Bisby Club of Herkimer County, New York. Another shipment of Loch Leven eggs arrived at Cold Spring Harbor in 1887.

Brown trout arrived in Pennsylvania in 1886, and by the end of the following year, Colorado, Illinois, Massachusetts, New Hampshire, North Carolina, and Wisconsin all had received at least one shipment of brown trout. Minnesota received browns in 1888, Montana and Nebraska in 1889. By

1900, brown trout had been stocked in thirty-eight states. Naturalized populations of brown trout have now been documented in at least thirty-four states.

After the first North American introduction of the Loch Leven trout occurred in Newfoundland in 1884, brown trout were introduced into nine of the ten Canadian provinces, but naturalized populations are much less widely distributed in Canada than in the United States. Although the brown trout was introduced into every province of Canada except Prince Edward Island (none was ever introduced into the Yukon or the Northwest Territories), significant wild brown trout fisheries currently exist only in Newfoundland (especially the Avalon Peninsula), Nova Scotia, southern Ontario, and Alberta.

Incredibly, there was little or no attempt to keep the Loch Leven and the von Behr strains isolated or distinct. For a time, state and federal fish distribution records listed both Loch Leven and von Behr trout, but widespread shipment from one hatchery to another and introduction of both strains into the same waters apparently resulted in the disappearance or merging of the original distinguishing characteristics.

At this point it may be useful to recall the differences between the von Behr, or German, brown trout and the Loch Leven trout, because it is from these two stocks that most North American brown trout undoubtedly are descended. As was mentioned earlier,

The Loch Leven trout, in contrast with the German brown, has few or no red spots and is much more heavily spotted.

some of the von Behr trout, *S. fario*, lived in small streams, were brightly colored, and rarely exceeded a length of 31 centimeters (12 inches). In contrast, the Loch Leven trout, *S. levenensis*, was a lake-dwelling form, which at one time reportedly reached a size of about 8 kilograms (18 pounds). The Loch Leven was described by Francis Day as being a silvery gray with black spots but no red ones up to the fourth or fifth year of life. He further noted that the "undergrown ones take on the color of the brown trout (common English brook trout), *S. fario*." Although Loch Leven continues to be one of the most productive large lakes in Great Britain, the trout now rarely exceed a weight of about 1 kilogram (2.2 pounds).

According to Maitland, there was free access to the sea from Loch Leven until the beginning of the nineteenth century, and until then the Loch Leven trout was thoroughly migratory. Maitland contended that *S. levenensis* still retained many of the characteristics of a sea-going salmonid, but loss of access to the sea may have accounted for the decrease in size of the Loch Leven trout.

If, as reported, the von Behr and Loch Leven strains have been widely interbred and broadly distributed, and if the brown trout has as plastic a genetic variability as hypothesized, we should not be surprised to find here in North America brown trout that are, in appearance and life history, similar to practically every form originally described in Europe.

Wiggins, in his 1950 review of the ecology of brown trout and their introduction to North America, continued to use the trinomial subspecies convention to refer to the forms from which North American brown trout are descendant. Grouping them in an ecological context, he listed: *Salmo trutta fario*, the European trout which are permanent freshwater inhabitants, especially those that spend most or all of their time as residents of small streams; *S. t. levenensis*, the trout of Loch Leven and other Scottish and north England waters; and *S. t. trutta*, the sea-run forms of European trout.

Certainly the two former subspecies have progeny that are naturalized Americans. Whether the latter migratory genetic structure was ever introduced, either in its pure form, through hatchery contamination in Europe, or latent in the Loch Leven form, is impossible to discern. All three forms exhibit downstream migratory behavior to some extent, and sea-run strains are currently known to exist in Nova Scotia and Massachusetts.

The introduced European trout took to America much the same as did their earlier human predecessors: They thrived under adverse conditions and in many places displaced the resident natives. Their ability to survive in habitat degraded by their human predecessors was initially greeted with delight, but once anglers discovered that the new trout were difficult to catch (part of the reason for the species' success), their popularity faded. They were regarded as cannibals, a

The brown trout spawns in early winter, usually November. The female will go to great lengths to find the right sort of gravel before she begins to cut her redd.

poor investment in terms of returns to the fisherman and not good to eat. As early as 1897, just thirteen years after their first introduction into Michigan waters, the Michigan Conservation Commission, spurred by irate fishermen, stated: "A few years of experiment and experience have convinced us that the brown trout is inferior in every respect to the brook or rainbow." The Montana fisheries people were a bit more appreciative of the brown trout's qualities, and more to the point: "The brown trout is a good fish, but the average angler is not skilled enough to catch it."

Because the brown trout was more difficult to catch than the native brook trout, and because it was able to survive in slightly warmer water, naturalized populations of brown trout survived in North America despite episodes of unpopularity. Its propensity to feed on emerging aquatic insects was a major force in the origin and evolution of dry-fly fishing in America, and before long the brown trout regained and exceeded its original preeminence as a noble game fish. Its ability to survive in the face of intense angling pressure, its wariness, longevity, and readiness to feed on surface insects have made it one of the most popular and economically important North American game fishes.

LIFE HISTORY

Spawning. November is the most common time for spawning, but it occurs from late October, and in some regions, as late as December or early January. Both photoperiod and water temperature play a role in sexual maturation. Responding to hormonal changes, the trout gradually move from their summer feeding sites, begin false cutting, and start moving to the spawning areas. The spawning gravel may be many miles upstream from the summer feeding area or just a few yards, depending upon the origin of the individual fish itself. It is not unlikely that some trout may return to the same gravel bar or stream reach where they hatched, but no definitive studies have been done to document this.

Trout that spend their adult lives in the sea, lakes, and large rivers tend to congregate at the mouths of streams in the fall to await a rise in water after a rain. Fall drought conditions can have a profound influence in the time and success of spawning. If the spawning tributary remains low until late in the spawning season, the trout all may move up into the tributary within a day or two after a heavy rain, and the spawning activity all takes place within just a few days. Otherwise, spawning may extend over a period of several weeks.

Trout resident in streams mature at an early age (two to three years), but in streams where food is scarce females may spawn only every other year. Some strains of lake-dwelling brown trout and some sea trout may not attain sexual maturity until the fourth or fifth year, and consequently spawn at a much larger size. Large trout, because of their size, are able to obtain the best spawning sites and produce more and larger eggs. Larger eggs produce larger fry, which have been shown to have higher survival rates. Consequently there is a selection pressure for rapid growth and large size in environments that can produce large trout.

The spawning behavior of brown trout is in many ways similar to that of most other salmonids. Stream-resident males usually become sexually mature by the end of their second or third summer, and females typically mature a year later. The female selects the spawning site in gravelly areas of a stream, most frequently at the tail end of a pool where water is flowing down into the gravel as a result of the pressure differential between the pool level and the water level in the downstream riffle. The female uses her tail to clear an oval-shaped redd. She does this by turning on her side, and with vigorous vibrations of her body and caudal fin, dislodges silt, sand, and fine gravel.

The preparation of the redd, known as redd cutting, may last several days. This behavior attracts males, and the latter stages of the cutting are accompanied with the male's courting behavior and aggressiveness as he drives off all other fish, especially other male trout.

The male's courting seems to stimulate the female to cut more intensely. During the redd cutting and courting, the female may stop to rest periodically. During this rest period she may move upstream a short distance into quiet water, and the male may guard the partially prepared redd.

As the female enlarges the redd, she periodically probes the cleared gravel with her anal fin. By this process, the female apparently can assess the readiness of the redd to accept eggs. As probing increases in frequency, the courting of the male intensifies. In courting, the male lies parallel to the female, periodically nudges the side of her body, and vigorously drives off other males. Occasionally two males may court a female at the same time, one on each side.

During the actual spawning event, the female arches her body, pressing her anal fin deeply into the gravel. The male lies close alongside, and both fish vibrate their bodies vigorously, open their mouths widely in an exaggerated gape, and simultaneously release eggs and milt. During the spawning event, it is not unusual for a smaller male that has been driven off repeatedly during the redd cutting and spawning activity to dash in and participate in the spawning act by simultaneously releasing milt on the other side of the female. By this means some precocious small males, despite their obvious inferior hierarchical status, get some of their genes into the next generation.

Age and growth. If not caught by anglers, brown trout usually reach an age of five or six years, although ages of eight and nine are not uncommon. Lake-dwelling trout mature later and live longer.

The official world record for a hook-and-line-caught brown trout recognized by the International Game Fish Association is a 16.3-kilogram (35-pound 15-ounce) trout caught in Argentina in 1951. A 17.9-kilogram (39.5-pound) brown trout caught in Loch Awe, Scotland, in 1866 was ruled invalid, but a 17.5-kilogram (38-pound 9-ounce) brown caught in the White River, Arkansas, in 1988 may qualify as a new world's record.

Both longevity and food availability are important in determining the size a brown trout may attain. Genetic factors also may play a role. A genetic marker, known as the

The female flexes and arches her tail energetically. She is preparing the gravel for egg deposition by clearing it of fine debris.

The juvenile brown trout, like other trout, has prominent parr marks that will disappear with maturity.

LDH-5 allele, has been shown to be associated with the large brown trout known as ferox in certain lakes of Britain and Ireland, and with long-lived sea trout. Although this allele itself has not been shown to have a functional significance, the common possession of this genetic marker by both ferox and long-lived sea trout suggests there might be a genetic factor responsible for longevity and large size. As with other factors—migratory behavior, food preference, coloration, and age at sexual maturity—both nature and nurture play an interdependent role in the growth of brown trout.

Many of the earlier estimates of age came from analysis of scales, but recent studies have cast some doubt on the reliability of scales in determining the age of slow-growing trout in small streams. One male brown trout observed regularly over a period of five years in a Pennsylvania stream was assessed to be three years old by scale analysis. But examination of its otoliths, which are small bones in the inner ear, confirmed that this 34.6-centimeter (13.5-inch) trout was at least nine years old. Other trout in the same stream that had grown more rapidly were correctly aged at five and six years and had attained a length of 41 to 46 centimeters (16 to 18 inches). Comparisons of age by means of scales and otoliths have shown a tendency to overestimate the age of young trout and underestimate the age of older fish. These results have, in turn, cast some doubt on the growth studies that used scale analysis for growth rates.

It has long been known that brown trout grow to different sizes in different waters, and there has been much speculation concerning the factors determining these differences. Dahl suggested that the food supply and the degree of crowding were important and that small, slowly growing trout were derived from smaller ova than were those growing more rapidly. Southern demonstrated that in Ireland the more rapidly growing fish are found in hard or alkaline waters. Those growing slowly live in soft, acid waters. This correlation also was upheld in Great Britain. Therefore the size attained by trout in different waters may vary depending on their rate of growth during the first year of life, the age at which they begin to spawn, and their

Larger fish eat larger prey. As they grow, trout switch from a diet composed primarily of insects to one of fish and crayfish.

average length of life. In soft waters, brown trout grow slowly during the first year, begin to spawn when three or four years old, and seldom live more than five years. In hard waters, they generally have a higher specific growth rate during the first year, begin to spawn at an older age, and may live for twelve years or more.

Food. The food of brown trout ranges widely as a function of the size and age of the trout and the kind of food available. Newly emergent swim-up fry feed on zooplankton and other small invertebrates. As the young trout become stronger and able to maintain position in faster current, they gradually move into deeper, faster water and begin to feed more and more on terrestrial and aquatic insects.

In especially productive streams, the diet of resident brown trout may consist almost entirely of aquatic insects. Direct observation of a population of resident trout in Spruce Creek, Pennsylvania, revealed that trout of all ages, ranging in length from 10 to 41 centimeters (4 to 16 inches), obtained most of their food from insects drifting by feeding sites. Trout ranging from one to nine years of age took less than 12 percent of their food items directly off the bottom; for the remainder, they foraged about equally at the surface and somewhere between the bottom and the surface. Next in order of importance were crayfish, followed by small fish species such as sculpins and dace.

Elsewhere, as trout grow, other food items play a greater importance in their diet. In streams that support luxuriant growths of aquatic vegetation, crustaceans such as iso-

The most important criterion that must be met by trout prey is availability.

pods and amphipods (often called freshwater shrimp) may equal or exceed aquatic insects in importance, and in still other waters snails and other mollusks form a large part of the diet of brown trout. In larger streams and rivers, and especially in lakes, fish are a very important component of the brown trout's diet. As a general rule, brown trout switch from a diet of insects to one of fish and crayfish when they reach a length of about 31 centimeters (12 inches), and in most cases very large trout feed almost exclusively on fish. However, especially productive rivers and lakes that support dense populations of aquatic insects may produce brown trout of up to about 4 kilograms (8 pounds) on a diet consisting almost entirely of aquatic insects and other aquatic invertebrates.

In most cases the food of brown trout in lakes appears to consist primarily of fish, although notable exceptions are reported. The large lake trout of Europe, once regarded as a separate species, *Salmo ferox* (ferocious) feeds almost entirely on fish, and attains enormous size. Likewise brown trout in the Great Lakes, exposed to abundant forage fish, such as alewife, attain weights averaging 4 to 7 kilograms (8 to 15 pounds), some even larger. These exceptionally large fish are silvery in appearance, lack the brilliant red spots and yellow bellies of the smaller resident stream forms, and often have numerous X-shaped black spots rather than the haloed round black spots of the trout resident in streams and rivers.

Brown trout that have a high proportion of crustaceans in their diet invariably are highly colored and have an intense red flesh color. This red color is derived from the fat-soluble carotene found in crustaceans, and this same nutrient is partially responsible for the delicate flavor of these highly colored fish. An example is the gillaroo, or "red fellow," of Irish lakes, a brown trout that is specially adapted to feed on crustaceans and mollusks. It has a thickened stomach wall.

Whether the brown trout is a specialist or a generalist in its food habits and preferences is a function both of genetic makeup and environmental factors. Where abundant, frogs, salamanders, rodents, and leeches all may constitute an important part of the trout's diet. For example, in 1988 brown trout gorged themselves on the seventeen-year cicada in many parts of the eastern United States. Occurrences such as this reveal yet another facet of the amazing plasticity and adaptability of the brown trout.

Feeding behavior. The feeding behavior of brown trout, especially of those living in streams, may be part of the reason for their longevity and their ability to successfully compete with other trout. Their wariness and conservative behavior make them harder

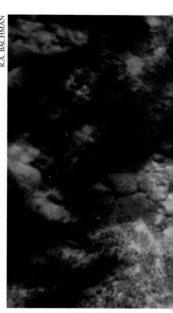

Brown trout occupy feeding stations from which they watch and wait for their prey. They seek positions that offer them protection from the current while affording easy access to drifting invertebrates.

to catch than most other trout, and where fishing pressure is intense, brown trout are more likely to persist. Direct observation of wild brown trout feeding in streams has shown that the trout feed from a more-or-less-stationary feeding station, the fish's "lie." This feeding site typically is located in front of or behind an object, usually a rock, that affords some protection from the current, but from which the trout can dart to capture food items drifting by in the current. Measurements of water velocity in and around feeding sites have revealed that the water velocity in the location where the trout "sits and waits" is about 0.2 meter (0.5 foot) per second, and that water velocity just inches or less from the position of the head of the trout is about 0.6 meter (2 feet) per second. In addition, the trout position themselves in such a way that they are protected from the current but have a clear view of objects drifting toward them from upstream.

Because insects drifting helplessly on the surface provide much of the brown trout's diet, the trout frequently selects feeding sites in fairly shallow water ranging in depth from 15 to 62 centimeters (6 to 24 inches). Such feeding sites permit the trout to capture food items on the surface with the least effort.

Competition with other species. Although much more study needs to be done, all other things being equal, brown trout seem to select feeding sites in shallower water than do brook trout and in water of slower velocity than do rainbow trout. Observations of brook, brown, and rainbow trout in an aquarium reveal that brown trout are more wary than either brook or rainbow trout, stay closer to the bottom, feed less frequently than do either the rainbow trout or brook trout, and over the short run do not fare as well as the other two species. Brook trout tend to swim about slowly near the surface but are aggressive and dominant. The rainbow trout generally are more active, moving about in all levels of the aquarium, and are quicker to capture food introduced into the aquarium. Such marked differences in behavior undoubtedly account, in part, for the differences in "catchability."

Brown trout are now commonly found in waters that historically contained brook trout. Brook trout need clean, cold water and a relatively stable environment in order to flourish. Siltation, increased runoff after storms, and elevated temperature, all consequences of human activity, decrease the stability of the environment and the likelihood of successful reproduction. Because brook trout mature earlier than brown trout and rarely live longer than three or four years, they must spawn successfully every year, or at least not miss more than one year, if the population is to be maintained. But because brown trout typically live longer than brook trout, attain a larger size, produce more eggs, and spawn more often than brook trout, brown trout populations are not as sensitive to spawning failure as are those of brook trout. Conditions that are unfavorable for

successful reproduction in two successive years are devastating to a brook trout population but may confer an advantage to brown trout where both species could otherwise thrive. If one then adds the higher vulnerability of brook trout to angling, it is no wonder that the brown trout has survived so well in heavily populated areas.

Temperature and pH tolerance. The assumption that the brown trout can tolerate warmer temperatures than most other salmonids can is not entirely accurate. Although brown trout are capable of surviving in water temperatures of 26.4°C (80°F) for short periods of time, they are most active and grow best when water temperatures range between 12.6° and 15.4°C (55° and 60°F). In contrast, brook trout do not tolerate temperatures much above 20.9°C (70°F). Experimental data from domesticated strains of brown trout and rainbow trout suggest that brown trout have more reserve energy or greater scope for activity as the temperatures approach upper lethal limits than do rainbow trout, but some wild strains of rainbows may actually be able to survive and grow in warmer water than brown trout. As with temperature, brown trout are able to tolerate a fairly wide pH range, thriving in waters ranging from a pH of 4.95 to 8.0 or higher.

VARIATION AND GENETIC PLASTICITY

When one considers the gene pool from which North American brown trout have descended, and the genetic plasticity of brown

trout, it is not surprising that brown trout come in many different sizes, shapes, and colors. The differences among these various forms are just beginning to be fully appreciated. It is generally agreed that the many naturalized populations, some of which may now have existed for thirty or more generations, derive from the small, early maturing, highly colored, von Behr "brook" form, and the larger, later-maturing, silvery Loch Leven "lake" form. For the most part, wild brown trout that live in small to moderate-sized streams have yellow bellies, bright red spots (particularly on the lateral line), pronounced dark brown or black spots on the opercula and sides, black and white margins on the anal and dorsal fins, and look remarkably like the original von Behr brown trout (*Salmo fario*). Brown trout found in the lower reaches of large rivers (sometimes termed *transition zones*) typically have more and larger irregular black spots and few or no red spots. These trout are strikingly similar in appearance to the Loch Leven (*S. levenensis* or

This wild brown trout looks remarkably like the original von Behr brown trout.

Many of the various forms of trout known today as brown trout were once thought to be separate species. Salmo ferox (right) and Salmo nigripinnis (far right), painted from life in 1884, are both actually Salmo trutta.

This transition-zone fish, found in larger bodies of water, is heavily spotted and has no red spots. It looks much like the ferox.

S. ferox) brown trout. Brown trout caught in deep, clear lakes are usually silvery in color, have conspicuous X-shaped black spots, and few or no red spots, and resemble the sea or salmon-trout of English and Scottish lochs. Occasionally a reddish-hued, heavily spotted trout with many large red spots is taken from streams and rivers that have an abundance of crustaceans. These vividly colored trout bear a striking resemblance to the Irish gillaroo, S. stomachicus. Sometimes all three forms are found within the same river or stream.

Whether the differences in these trout, so varied in appearance, are genetic or just random selections in behavior and feeding habit, or whether the habitat and food supply is primarily responsible for these differences, has not yet been fully investigated. Wright and his colleagues at The Pennsylvania State University have shown that brown trout can be selected for heavy spottedness and light spottedness. He and his co-workers have shown not only that

brown trout (and other salmonids) are tetraploids, that is, they have four sets of chromosomes rather than the two sets of most other fish, called diploids, but also that salmonids appear to be in the evolutionary process of going from tetraploidy to diploidy. The studies of Wright, May, and Johnson have revealed that the chromosomes are able to combine in an amazing variety of ways and that the genetic plasticity is higher in males than in females. This special trait seems to account for the remarkable genetic plasticity of brown trout and their ability to adapt within just a few generations to a wide range of habitats and food sources. These discoveries shed important light on the amazing variance in physiologic and morphologic characters among the native European strains of brown trout, and the difficulties early naturalists and taxonomists had in describing and naming the various forms of brown trout.

It is speculated that the various forms and strains of brown trout that were thoroughly mixed in North American hatcheries produced a polytypic gene pool from which, over many generations, the environment is gradually selecting the forms that are best suited for that particular stream, river, or lake, or microhabitat of specific river systems. For this reason, fisheries managers are now more cautious about introducing new strains of brown trout into waters that have long-standing naturalized populations.

HUMAN INTERVENTION: BACK TO THE SPLITTERS?

Despite the taxonomical lumping that has taken place over the past sixty to seventy years, the pendulum may be starting to swing toward splitting again. New methods of as-

Other forms of brown trout were once described as Salmo cambricus (far left) *and* Salmo stomachicus (left).

sessing the genetic makeup of organisms, such as electrophoresis, which provides a means of identifying structural proteins called isozymes, are beginning to shed new light on the perplexing taxonomic issue of whether the brown trout is one species or many subspecies—or even many species!

In 1981, Ferguson and Mason demonstrated that four distinct forms of brown trout exist in Lough Melvin in Ireland: the gilaroo, ferox, sonaghen, and "common brown trout." The gilaroo is a highly colorful, yellowish trout with large red spots and thickened stomach wall. It feeds predominantly on crustaceans and mollusks. As we saw earlier, it once was regarded as a distinct species, *Salmo stomachicus.* The ferox is a large, less colorful, late-maturing trout, with little or no spotting. It has a disproportionately long head and many large teeth, and it feeds predominantly on fish. It is the great lake trout, *S. ferox*, described by Günther and Regan. The sonaghen is characterized as having elongated black fins, many large black spots, and few red spots. If present, the red spots are restricted to the posterior half of the body. It feeds predominantly on plankton and aquatic insects. This form, of course, is similar to the species previously described as the Welsh black-finned *S. nigripinnis*. All other brown trout that did not fit these three descriptions and were more similar to the *S. fario* were referred to by Ferguson and Mason as the common brown trout. On the basis of enzyme analysis, Ferguson and Mason concluded that the ferox and gilaroo in Lough Melvin represented genetically distinct and reproductively isolated populations. There was less genetic distinction between the sonaghen and common brown trout, and these forms were not considered

The stomachicus, or Irish gillaroo trout is reddish and has large red spots.

to be completely reproductively isolated. Both of these forms ascend one of the main inflowing streams at the same time of year, which probably accounts for the more similar genetic structure found in these two types of trout.

Little is known about the spawning behavior of the gilaroo in Lough Melvin, or that of the ferox, but the gilaroo in other lakes is said to spawn in the shallower parts of the lake. It does not ascend streams to spawn. Campbell reports that in Scotland a ferox type of brown trout spawns in the same rivers as ordinary brown trout but, because of its large size, selects deeper water and larger gravel in the lower reaches of the river.

Allendorf and others also have reported reproductive isolation of two forms of brown trout in Lake Bunnersjoarna in northern Sweden, and other investigators have reported two genetically distinct populations in a Norwegian stream, even though the home ranges of these trout overlap to a certain extent. These new discoveries have led Allendorf, Ryman, Stennek, and Stahl to conclude that the pattern of genetic diversity present in these populations is too great to classify them all simply as *Salmo trutta*.

Nei's method for estimating the time of divergence of populations gives a time of 230,000 to 265,000 years ago for the Lough Melvin ferox and 40,000 to 65,000 for the gillaroo and sonaghen–compatible with an early stage of the last glaciation. It should be noted, however, that some evolutionary taxonomists consider this method imprecise, and these dates highly speculative. Regardless of the time of divergence, the inherent tendency of brown trout to spawn in their natal areas makes it very likely that reproductive isolation, once achieved, will be maintained. The discovery that the ferox, sonaghen, and gillaroo are indeed genetically different and reproductively isolated in Lough Melvin (and presumably elsewhere) prompted Alastair Stephen, fisheries officer of the West Galloway Fisheries Trust in England, to write, "The Victorian system may well be shown to be a model for the future rather than a relic of the past."

If it is generally true, as several of the earlier-mentioned authors have asserted, that the brown trout, unlike the leopard, does change its spots, how and under what conditions? Do environmental factors such as water clarity, color of the substrate, and diet alter the appearance of brown trout, or do these factors rapidly select from the enormous genetic range of forms present, the genetic formula best suited for that environment? Are brown trout more genetically plastic than other trout, or is the genetic variance simply more noticeable in this widely distributed, adaptable fish? Probably neither.

According to Behnke, genetic variation among cutthroat trout is considerably higher than in brown trout, and future studies will undoubtedly reveal similar confounding results with other salmonids. But one thing is certain. The designation *Salmo trutta* does not adequately reflect the genetic variability of this remarkable fish. As Behnke says, "We must learn to live with [the binomial system]. . . . Salmonids are not unique." Perhaps so, but some system of identifying and cataloging the ecological significance of the various forms of brown trout is undoubtedly necessary.

Whether one species or many, the brown trout comes in many liveries, is one of the most widely distributed and widely studied of all salmonids, and is a highly variable and adaptable fish. The ability to survive under the adverse conditions of elevated water temperatures, intermittent losses of successive year classes, and perhaps most important of all, intense angling pressure, accounts for the still-expanding distribution of brown trout in North America. The ability to adapt has made the brown trout one of the most popular and successful of North American salmonids.

–Robert A. Bachman

Bull trout

Salvelinus confluentus

---

*T*he bull trout acquired its name because of its notable characteristics: a broad head, a large mouth, prominent jaws, and a predilection for fish in its diet. Despite the image of strength and aggression its name conveys, however, the bull trout often succumbs in competition with other, introduced species, such as brook trout.

CLASSIFICATION

Bull trout actually are char, classified in the genus *Salvelinus* with brook trout, *S. fontinalis*; lake trout, *S. namaycush*; Dolly Varden trout, *S. malma*; and Arctic char, *S. alpinus*. At one time, most populations now called bull trout, *S. confluentus*, were thought to be Dolly Varden, but in 1978 taxonomists formally recognized them as a distinct species based on the work of Cavender.

DESCRIPTION

The bull trout is shaped like a trout, but, as with the other chars, its coloration–light spots on a dark background–differentiates it from the trouts, which have black spots on a light background. A white margin on the leading edges of the ventral fins is often apparent on bull trout, as on other chars, and they have teeth only at the head of the vomer. The trouts have teeth on the head and shaft of the vomer.

As for distinguishing bull trout from the other chars–sometimes it's easy, sometimes not. If you lay a bull trout next to a lake trout, for example, you'll see that the bull

The bull trout, like other chars, displays light spots on a dark background. It lacks the deeply forked tail of a lake trout and the vermiculations of a brook trout, but is not so easily distinguished from Dolly Varden and Arctic char.

trout's tail is less deeply forked than the lake trout's and that the spots on the bull trout are colored rather than whitish. If you lay it next to a brook trout, you'll notice that it lacks the brook trout's vermiculations on the back and the dorsal fin.

But correctly identifying a bull trout laid beside a Dolly Varden and an Arctic char is trickier, and taxonomists use several less obvious characteristics, including the shape and size of the head and lower jaw; the number and arrangement of basibranchial teeth, which are on the roof of the mouth; the morphology of the gill rakers; the number of pores on the mandibles; the number of branchiostegal rays, located on the throat; and the configuration of bones in the cranium.

DISTRIBUTION

The bull trout is one of four species of char native to western North America; the other three are the Dolly Varden, the Arctic char, *S. alpinus*, and the lake trout, *S. namaycush*. In particular, bull trout are native to most of

MULLINS

the interior and some coastal drainages of the Northwest, from northern California to Alaska. They have been found with cutthroat trout, *Oncorhynchus clarki*, and mountain whitefish, *Prosopium williamsoni*, in many inland drainages both upstream and downstream from natural barriers, which means that they were early colonizers of those waters. In drainages colonized later by anadromous salmon and steelhead, the bull trout have coexisted successfully by occupying a different niche.

Specimens of fish now classified as bull trout have been collected from headwaters of the Sacramento River drainage on the southern end of its range in California, from the headwaters of the Yukon River in Alaska and Canada at the northern end of its range, from Pacific coastal rivers, and as far east as tributaries of the Saskatchewan, Peace, and Liard rivers in Canada.

The bull trout has been lost or virtually eliminated from many streams in its original range, but relatively viable populations still exist in portions of the Columbia and Fraser river drainages, some coastal rivers, and some streams on the east slope of the Continental Divide in Montana.

HABITAT

Bull trout live in a variety of habitats: small headwater streams, large rivers, even lakes and reservoirs if such environments are accessible to them. They appear to do best in relatively cool drainages.

They can complete their life cycle in small headwater streams, but more often they move from their natal streams to larger rivers or lakes when they are two to three years old. There they grow at faster rates than they would in small streams. In lakes and reservoirs, bull trout are usually found near shore or the bottom at depths with temperatures lower than about 10° to 12°C (50° to 53.8°F). In streams, bull trout prefer to live in pools and stay close to the bottom, except to feed.

LIFE HISTORY

Bull trout usually mature at four to ten years of age, and range in length from less than 200 millimeters (8 inches) to more than

Good habitat in the small tributary streams where they tend to feed and spawn is important to the bull trout, a char native to western North America.

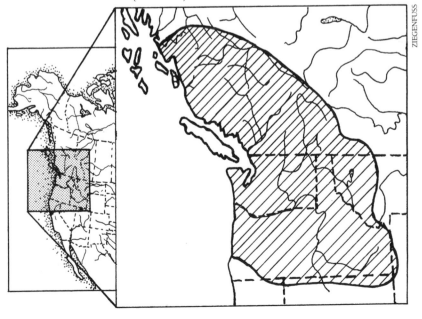

700 millimeters (28 inches), depending on the environment. The adults spawn in the fall, from late August through early October, when stream temperatures have dropped below 10°C (50°F). Fish that have spent part of their lives in lakes or large rivers migrate back to their natal streams during the spring or summer preceding spawning. It is not uncommon for large adult bull trout to spend one to two months waiting in the natal stream before spawning, and they have little inclination to feed during this period.

Spawning. The female bull trout digs the redd in a gravel riffle in which she deposits the eggs. The male bull trout may spawn with more than one female, though investigators found some evidence of pairing during the upstream migration in the Flathead River in Montana.

The fecundity of the female bull trout depends on her size. Small adults from cold tributaries have only 100 to 200 eggs; larger adults have thousands of eggs. Fraley and Shepard reported that 32 adults from the Flathead River system with a mean length of 645 millimeters (nearly 26 inches) averaged 5,482 eggs per female. One fish weighing 6.8 kilograms (15 pounds) had 12,000 eggs.

After the eggs have been deposited and the redd completed, the adult bull trout leave the spawning site and move downstream to the large river or lake if that is where they grew to maturity. Some of the bull trout may die from the rigors of spawning. Others live to spawn a second, even a third time, though usually not in successive years.

Development. As with the onset of spawning, the rate of development of the bull trout embryos in the redds depends on temperature. In most environments, the embryos develop rapidly at first in the relatively warm temperatures (4° to 10°C [39° to 50°F]) of autumn. The pace slows as temperatures drop during the winter to near freezing, then quickens again as temperatures increase in the spring just before the young fish emerge from the redds. In the Flathead drainage of Montana and British Columbia, the eggs hatch in midwinter, about 100 to 120 days after spawning, and the fry emerge from the redd in April, about 200 to 230 days after spawning. They need an accumulation of about 635 temperature units: one unit for

Both the female (above right) and the male (right) bull trout can attain large sizes. Young bull trout (below) grow rapidly, especially if they move to lakes where food is more abundant than in their natal streams.

Bull trout are easily caught by anglers and thus susceptible to overfishing.

each degree that the water is above 0°C each day.

Soon after emergence, the small bull trout (23 to 28 millimeters [about an inch] long) disperse both upstream and downstream to find suitable rearing areas for the summer. During their first summer they usually stay close to the bottom in side channels, backwaters, and stream margins with slow water velocity. They feed on aquatic invertebrates, often dipterans and ephemeropterans, and add 20 to 60 millimeters (.8 to nearly 2.5 inches) to their length during their first growing season.

In some streams throughout their range, bull trout may spend their entire life in their home stream. In others the fish spend the first one to four years in their natal stream and then migrate down to a larger stream or lake during the spring or summer. There they spend another two to four years before maturing and returning to their natal stream to spawn. They do not return to their natal stream until they spawn, and if they do not spawn in successive years, they do not return to the natal stream each year.

Growth. Usually those that move to larger rivers or lakes grow faster. While in the small natal tributaries, the young bull trout probably face less risk of predation, but growth is constrained by lower temperatures and less food. After the fish are two to three years old,

larger, and better able to avoid predators, they can take advantage of the warmer temperatures and more diverse food supply in the larger rivers and lakes. In Flathead Lake, Montana, and Priest Lake, Idaho, bull trout growth has been recorded at 75 to 100 millimeters (3 to 4 inches) per year, a result of the forage fish diet that is available in those lakes. Fish up to 14.5 kilograms (32 pounds) have been produced in lakes with abundant forage fish, such as kokanee, *Oncorhynchus nerka*, a landlocked variety of the sockeye salmon.

Abundance. The abundance of bull trout in some drainages may be limited by the number of spawners available there. Bull trout are easily caught by anglers and they have not been universally protected from overexploitation to insure an adequate number of spawners. In addition, other fish species introduced into a drainage may compete with bull trout or prey on them, reducing the number that reach maturity. Exactly such a scenario has occurred in Priest Lake, where brook trout compete with young bull trout in tributary streams, and lake trout prey on them as the bull trout enter the lake.

In areas where there are adequate numbers of spawners, the number of bull trout produced is probably limited by the carrying capacity of streams where the young fish spend their first two to three years. The number of larger adult fish is limited by the

Bull trout are more piscivorous than other salmonids. The Rocky Mountain whitefish makes up a significant portion of the bull trout's diet in some areas.

number of fish that can be produced in the small streams used for spawning and initial rearing, regardless of the food resources available in downstream rivers and lakes where bull trout may spend a portion of their lives. Productive rearing areas in rivers and lakes result in larger adults with more eggs that can help assure full seeding of the tributary rearing areas, but they do not change the carrying capacity of the tributaries.

Feeding. Although bull trout have evolved with other salmonids in the streams of western North America, the behavior of the bull trout differs. The young of all salmonids stay close to the stream substrate immediately after emergence from redds, but many of the trouts and salmons soon move up into the water column to feed on invertebrates drifting in the water column and on the water surface. The bull trout, on the other hand, remain close to the bottom, feeding on invertebrates there.

All of the species of trout, char, and salmon are opportunistic feeders and will feed on fish, given the opportunity, but bull trout, as they grow larger, tend to be more piscivorous than do the other species of trout and salmon. Following predation studies at the University of Idaho, Horner reported in 1978 that bull trout 150 to 200 millimeters (6 to 8 inches) long were more active predators than were brook, cutthroat, or steelhead trout of similar size. When forage fish are available, bull trout longer than 200 to 300 millimeters (8 to 12 inches) will switch to a diet of fish almost exclusively, whereas cutthroats living in the same stream or lake may rarely eat fish.

During the summer, bull trout, like other salmonids, are primarily interested in feeding, and they select areas of the habitat where they have the best chance of obtaining food. But as temperatures drop in the fall, the behavior of juvenile bull trout in streams changes. The smaller fish often hide in the interstitial spaces of the stream substrate, and the larger fish may move downstream to larger streams and congregate in large pools with little or no current. Investigators noted that larger juvenile bull trout in the Middle Fork of the Salmon River in Idaho moved as much as 100 kilometers (62 miles) downstream to larger rivers in the fall, then migrated back upstream in the spring as water temperatures increased.

HUMAN INTERVENTION

Some populations of bull trout have been lost or seriously reduced through overexploitation, loss or deterioration of habitat, and introductions of exotic species. Now that the effects of overexploitation have been recognized, fisheries managers have taken steps to reduce fishing mortality in many areas. Habitat losses and deterioration, however, are chronic problems, and survival of the bull trout depends on good-quality habi-

tat in small tributary streams.

The introduction of exotic species has hurt the population of bull trout in some drainages and lakes. For example, the introduction of opossum shrimp, *Mysis relicta*, into Idaho's Priest Lake increased the productivity of the lake trout, which was introduced many years before. The larger numbers of lake trout resulted in intense fishing that bull trout could not sustain. In other words, more anglers now fish here, catching bull trout as well as lake trout. Kamloops rainbow trout, *Oncorhynchus gairdneri*, introduced into lakes and drainages formerly occupied only by bull trout and cutthroat, have increased the competition of the native species for food and space both in the lakes and in the streams used by juveniles. Brook trout have been introduced in many streams of the Northwest and have become a serious competitor and predator for the native bull trout and cutthroat trout.

In many of the large lake systems that produced large bull trout, Priest Lake and Pend Oreille in Idaho and Flathead Lake in Montana, for example, it's too late, and the damage is done; the introduction of the exotic species cannot be reversed. But the recent development of efforts to culture bull trout in hatcheries may help to maintain populations in those areas.

In others, though, primarily river systems without lakes, the introduced species could be removed from tributary streams and the bull trout protected from overexploitation if enough interest existed in reserving the drainages for the native fish species.

— *Theodore C. Bjornn*

THE SPECIES

Cutthroat trout

Oncorhynchus clarki

---

*T*he name *cutthroat* was coined by Charles Hallock in an article in *The American Angler* dated October 4, 1884. He was describing the trout his party encountered in Montana's Rosebud Creek:

"It resembles the iridea of Colorado in respect to the metallic black markings scattered like lustrous grains of coarse black powder over its shoulders and body; but it lacked the rainbow lateral stripe. Its distinctive feature, however, was a slash of intense carmine across each gill cover, as large as my little finger. It was most striking. For lack of a better description we called them cut-throat trout."

However, the cutthroat trout was known long before Hallock coined the name. Coronado's army noted it in a small creek near the Pueblo Indian town of Cicuye in 1541, thereby becoming the first European men to record trout in the New World. The Franciscan friars Escalante and Dominguez found the trout in Utah Lake and the Provo River during their explorations in Colorado and Utah in 1776.

Lewis and Clark's men encountered the cutthroat trout at the Great Falls of the Missouri River in 1805. Meriwether Lewis even described teeth on the pallet of the fish, one of the cutthroat's characteristic features, as well as the two dashes of red at the throat that later prompted the name.

Journals of the fur trappers and explorers who followed Lewis and Clark into the Rocky Mountains and the Great Basin contain references to many other encounters with cutthroat trout. They called it by many names, salmon-trout being a common one because of the migratory habit of the fish at spawning time.

An employee of a fur-trapping enterprise was responsible for the first collection of the species for science. Meredith Gairdner was a physician employed by the Hudson Bay Company at their Columbia River outpost, Fort Vancouver. A naturalist at heart, he either himself collected or arranged for the collection by others of many specimens of northwest trout and salmon, which he shipped to Sir John Richardson at the University of Edinborough in Scotland. Richardson examined the specimens carefully and recorded the descriptions in his book, *Fauna Boreali-Americana*, published in 1836. To one of Gairdner's specimens Richardson assigned the scientific name *Salmo clarkii*, (later changed to *Salmo clarki* and more recently to *Oncorhynchus clarki*).

CLASSIFICATION

Genetic analysis confirms that the cutthroat trout is a polytypic species; that is, it can be subdivided into several more or less distinct subspecies. Behnke recognizes fourteen of them. Four he categorizes as major subspecies, which through evolution have developed distinct characteristics. The other ten he calls minor subspecies, as they developed from two of the major ones in more recent evolutionary time.

Three of the major subspecies diverged

roughly one to five million years ago: the coastal cutthroat, *O. c. clarki*; the westslope cutthroat, *O. c. lewisi*; and an interior form, *O. c. bouvieri*. The fourth divergence occurred later, when the *O. c. bouvieri* subspecies split into two groups. *O. c. henshawi* occupied the Lahontan drainage on the west side of the Great Basin. The other lineage, retaining the name *O. c. bouvieri*, occupied the Bonneville drainage on the east side of the Great Basin as well as the upper Snake and Yellowstone river basins of Idaho, Montana, and Wyoming; the upper Green and Colorado river drainages of Wyoming, Utah, and Colorado; and the drainages of the upper Rio Grande and the Pecos River in Colorado, Arizona, and New Mexico.

Although taxonomic and genetic evidence supports the differentiation of cutthroat trout into these four major subspecies, further subdivision is subject to how one interprets the evidence. Behnke interprets it to indicate that the early divergences of cutthroat trout were associated with the Columbia River basin in the western United States and British Columbia. The first two major divergences, which occurred roughly one to five million years ago, led to three characteristic karyotypes, or chromosome counts: 2N = 68 for the coastal cutthroat trout; 2N = 66 for the westslope cutthroat trout, which colonized the upper reaches of the Columbia River proper; and 2N = 64 for a *bouvieri* ancestor that colonized the Snake River drainage. An early member of the 64-chromosome group then gained access to the Lahontan Basin to give rise to the fourth major subspecies group, *henshawi*.

The coastal and westslope cutthroat trouts gave rise to no other surviving subspecies. The Lahontan Basin cutthroat trout gave rise to four additional subspecies: the Paiute cutthroat trout, *O. c. seleniris*, isolated in Silver King Creek, California; an unnamed fluviatile, or stream-dwelling, subspecies indigenous to the Humboldt River drainage in Nevada on the east side of the basin; and two additional unnamed subspecies established by transfer into the Alvord and the Whitehorse and Willow creek basins in Nevada and Oregon, which are contiguous with the Lahontan Basin on its north rim. The *henshawi* subspecies is found on the west side of the basin. Behnke speculates that the Humboldt cutthroat trout, the Alvord cutthroat trout, and the Willow-Whitehorse cutthroat trout probably arose during the early to middle part of the last glacial epoch, perhaps 40,000 to 70,000 years ago. The Paiute cutthroat trout probably did not arise until postglacial time.

The ancestral *bouvieri* also gave rise to new subspecies, six in all, most likely in the latter part of the last glacial period. One of these, an unnamed fine-spotted subspecies, is indigenous to the upper Snake River from Jackson Lake downstream to the Wyoming-Idaho border. Headwater transfers allowed cutthroat trout from the Snake River to colonize the Bonneville Basin, the upper

Colorado and Green river basins, the upper South Platte and Arkansas river drainages in Colorado, and the upper Rio Grande and Pecos River drainages, where there evolved the Bonneville cutthroat, *O. c. utah*; the Colorado River cutthroat, *O. c. pleuriticus*; the greenback cutthroat, *O. c. stomias*; and the Rio Grande cutthroat, *O. c. virginalis*. An extinct subspecies, the yellowfin cutthroat of Twin Lakes, Colorado, *O. c. macdonaldi*, also may have arisen from this lineage.

There is an alternative interpretation of the evidence for dispersal of the several cutthroat subspecies into the interior West. Loudenslager, who has studied these trouts quite extensively, believes that the 66-chromosome westslope cutthroat did indeed result from one colonization that involved the Snake River in a more roundabout way. Loudenslager points out that geological evidence, as well as evidence based on other faunal relationships, connects the upper Snake River with the Klamath or the Sacramento river systems in Oregon and California, perhaps both, at the time of the colonizations in question rather than with the Columbia River. He also indicates that faunal evidence connects the Lahontan and Bonneville basins with that ancient drainage. He notes also that cutthroat trout from the western and southern parts of the Bonneville Basin are genetically more similar to Colorado River cutthroat trout than they are to Bonneville cutthroat trout from the Bear River drainage in Utah in the northeast corner of the basin, and the Bear River cutthroat trout are indistinguishable from Snake River *O. c. bouvieri*. One could thus envision the radiation of the 64-chromosome cutthroat trouts happening almost in reverse of what Behnke suggests, that is, from the Lahontan Basin to the Bonneville Basin and from there into both the Rocky Mountain drainages and the upper Snake River.

Logical arguments undoubtedly could be made for several other scenarios to explain these observations. Perhaps it is best, as Loudenslager observed in a recent letter, to acknowledge the range of possibilities and recognize our limitations in distinguishing them.

DESCRIPTION

The name cutthroat derives from the red or sometimes orange slash marks found on each side of the lower jaw. This field mark must be used with caution, however, because the Apache trout, *O. apache*; the Gila trout, *O. gilae*; and the redband trout, *O. m. gairdneri*, often have yellowish or orange slash marks as well, and some true cutthroat trout, such as sea-run coastal cutthroat trout, may lose the cutthroat marks in salt water.

Fish identification keys often list the presence of basibranchial teeth, located on the basibranchial plate behind the tongue, to separate cutthroat trout from rainbow trout, *O. mykiss*. Basibranchial teeth do occur in more than 90 percent of the specimens in pure cutthroat trout populations, and the

Four major subspecies of cutthroat trout are differentiated, and then further separated according to chromosome counts. There is some disagreement among the experts about further separation of these four major subspecies into minor subspecies of cutthroat, although many minor subspecies are generally recognized.

ZIEGENFUSS

Cutthroat trout

Coastal rainforest belt evolution — Coastal cutthroat trout *O. clarki clarki*

Upper Columbia river evolution — Westslope cutthroat trout *O.c. lewisi*

Lahontan Basin evolution — *O.c. henshawi* / *seleniris* / Humboldt / Alvord / Willow and Whitehorse

Snake River evolution — *O.c. bouvieri* / *utah* / *pleuriticus* / *stomias,* / *virginalis* / *macdonaldi* (extinct) / fine-spotted Snake River form loss of basibranchial teeth, one of the influences of hybridization with rainbow trout, is detectable much earlier than changes in color or spotting pattern become discernible. Again, however, some redband trout, Apache trout, and Gila trout have vestigial basibranchial teeth, although this characteristic usually does not occur in more than 10 percent of a population.

Another field mark that is sometimes listed is the length of the upper jaw. Cutthroat trout are long-jawed, the upper jaw length being typically more than half the length of the head. This positions the eye well forward of the back of the maxilla, or upper jaw. In rainbow trout, the upper jaw is half or less the length of the head, and except in very large specimens, the eye often is in line with the back of the maxilla.

Cutthroat trout typically have nine rays in their pelvic fins, whereas coastal rainbow trout typically have ten. But this is not an absolute field guide either, because interior rainbow trout can have either nine or ten pelvic fin rays.

Coastal cutthroat (O. c. clarki). The coastal cutthroat trout is a profusely spotted fish, with small to medium, irregularly shaped, dense and closely packed spots distributed more or less evenly over the sides of the body, on the head, and often on the ventral surface, or belly, and anal fin as well. It is not noted for developing brilliant colors, however. Coloration of sea-run individuals is silvery with a faint yellowish or brassy wash (the silvery de-

posits often mask the body spots), and the cutthroat markings are sometimes faded. Freshwater fish are darker and brassier or more coppery in sheen. Pale yellow colors may appear on the body, and the lower fins may be yellow to red-orange. Rosy-colored tints may appear on the gill plates, sides, and ventral regions as spawning time draws near, and male fish will become more intensely colored than females. Sea-run fish darken and take on these colors after a period in fresh water.

Meristic characters of coastal cutthroat trout with direct access to the sea are quite similar throughout the subspecies range. (Meristic characters are particular body parts counted or measured to identify species and subspecies.) The lack of clinal variation, or distinction attributable to latitude, suggests that sea-run cutthroat trout wander and thus gene flow occurs among populations. Analysis of genetic proteins indicates that this is not so, however. Campton examined sea-run cutthroat trout populations from northern Puget Sound in Washington and from the

SCHOLLMEYER

The coastal cutthroat is profusely spotted and shows the silvery coloration of sea-run fish.

GROST

northern and southern ends of Hood Canal, also in Washington. These populations were found to constitute three genetically divergent stocks, with little if any straying and gene flow between them. If this, rather than meristics, portrays the true picture of the population structure of coastal cutthroat trout, then there could be dozens or hundreds of genetically distinct stocks spread throughout the range of the subspecies. Studies of additional populations are needed to clarify this picture.

Westslope cutthroat (O. c. lewisi). The spots on the westslope cutthroat are small and irregular in shape like those on the coastal cutthroat trout, but the pattern is quite different and distinctive. In westslope cutthroat trout,

the body usually is free of spots within an arc drawn from the front of the anal fin up and above the lateral line, then back down to the pectoral fin. The colors generally are brighter too. Westslope cutthroat trout develop bright yellow, orange, and red colors, especially with the onset of spawning, and particularly in male fish. The entire ventral region of some male fish becomes bright red.

Many westslope cutthroat populations exhibit differences in meristic characters which may reflect long isolation of those populations. For example, populations from the Salmon and Clearwater drainages in Idaho typically have more lateral-series scales than other populations, and specimens of the so-called mountain cutthroat, described in the

Meristic character counts of cutthroat trout subspecies

Combinations of certain physical characteristics can be relied upon to distinguish among cutthroat subspecies. Trout color patterns can vary with water temperature, diet, and other environmental factors, but when observed in conjunction with other traits, color can help identify a subspecies.

Meristic character counts are recorded in ranges because differences within a species may result from environmental and other factors. Two ranges exist for the number of scales in lateral series found on coastal cutthroats: some coarse-scaled resident coastal cutthroats typically have fewer. Although some of the ranges for specific character counts overlap, no two subspecies share the same combination of traits.

Species	Lateral line series scales	Scales above lateral line	Pyloric caeca	Gill rakers	Vertebral segments
Coastal (*Onchorhynchus clarki clarki*)	140–180 (120–140)	30–40	25–55	15–21	59–64
Westslope (*O. c. lewisi*)	150–200+	30–40	25–50	17–21	59–63
Lahontan (*O. c. henshawi*)	150–180	30–40	40–75	21–28	60–63
Humboldt (*O. c.* unnamed)	125–150	26–40	40–70	19–23	–
Paiute (*O. c. seleniris*)	150–180	–	50–70	21–27	–
Alvord basin (*O. c.* unnamed)	122–152	33–37	34–39	20–26	59–63
Willow or Whitehorse (*O. c.* unnamed)	140–155	34–45	40–58	19–23	59–64
Yellowstone (*O. c. bouvieri*)	165–180	–	25–50	17–23	60–63
Fine-spotted Snake River (*O. c.* unnamed)	153–176	–	32–51	17–23	–
Bonneville (*O. c. utah*)	135–190	33–46	25–60	16–24	60–62
Colorado River (*O. c. pleuriticus*)	170–205	38–48	25–45	17–21	60–63
Greenback (*O. c. stomias*)	189–217	44–57	25–45	18–21	60–63
Rio Grande (*O. c. virginalis*)	150–180	35–45	30–50	–	61–62
Yellowfin (*O. c. macdonaldi*), extinct	159–185	42	–	20–22	–

1930s from the upper Columbia and Fraser river basins, British Columbia, have the most lateral-series scales of all. Upper Missouri Basin specimens typically have fewer pyloric caeca (small fingerlike pouches on the intestine) than do specimens from elsewhere in the subspecies range.

Population distinctions also are reflected in genetic analyses of this subspecies. Allendorf, Leary, and their colleagues have examined many westslope cutthroat populations and have found that each local population bears a unique share of the genetic diversity of the subspecies. Preserving the genetic diversity thus entails the preservation of as many local populations as possible.

Lahontan cutthroat (O. c. henshawi). Cutthroat trout of the Great Basin are dull in color. Lahontan cutthroat run generally to yellowish brown, brassy, or golden olive. Sometimes there are rosy tints on the sides and cheeks, and they become more intense as spawning time approaches. The spots are medium to large, rounded, and more or less evenly distributed over the sides of the body, the top of the head, and often on the abdomen. In lake-dwelling fish, which are often silvery, the silvery deposits can obscure the spots and make them appear smaller and star-shaped.

The evenly distributed large round spots combined with the highest number of gill

ANDERSON

MULLINS

Above: *The Westslope cutthroat has profuse small spots, but few or no spots in an arc from the pectoral fin to the anal fin.* Left: *This Westslope displays the prominent red cut mark for which the species is known.*

ROSTON

HYDE

The Lahontan cutthroat has medium to large spots evenly distributed over a dull background. The difference between spots and parr marks can be seen in the juvenile (right), which has both.

rakers (comblike projections on the gill arches) of any trout, plus generally a higher number of pyloric caeca than any other cutthroat trout has, are trademark characters of cutthroat trout native to the west side of the Lahontan Basin. Behnke believes these characters to be lacustrine, or lake-related, specialized features that reflect long isolation and evolution in ancient Lake Lahontan, and he believes them to be distinctive enough to set west-side *henshawi* apart from cutthroat trout native to the east side of the Lahontan Basin as a separate subspecies. Behnke points out that cutthroat trout from the east side of the Lahontan Basin, which encompasses the Humboldt River and its tributary drainages, have developed more fluviatile characters.

Protein electrophoresis presents a different picture of this subdivision, however. This evidence suggests that there is only a single Lahontan Basin subspecies, *O. c. henshawi*, but one with electrophoretically distinct races or stocks existing in the Carson River, Summit Lake, Walker River, Humboldt River, and Reece River drainages (the Reece River is a Humboldt tributary) in Nevada.

In all probability, the trout of the Lake Tahoe-Truckee River-Pyramid Lake system in

California and Nevada also were a distinct race. This race, before it became extinct in Pyramid Lake, produced the greatest size of any western North American trout. The world hook-and-line record cutthroat trout is a fish of 18.6 kilograms (41 pounds), taken from Pyramid Lake in 1925, and larger ones were taken in commercial nets. Lake Tahoe produced the California hook-and-line record, a fish of 14.3 kilograms (31.5 pounds), taken in 1911.

Paiute cutthroat (O. c. seleniris). Paiute cutthroat trout evolved from Lahontan cutthroat, *O. c. henshawi*, in relatively recent geological time after isolation in Silver King Creek. The only feature that distinguishes the two is the absence of spots on the body of *seleniris*. Meristic characters are identical, and likewise there is electrophoretic identity in the products of several gene loci between *seleniris* of Silver King Creek and *henshawi* from the drainage of the East Fork Carson River.

Even the absence of spotting is not an absolute characteristic. Up to nine spots were found when the type specimens used to name *seleniris* were reexamined, and Behnke, writing in his 1979 monograph, told of ob-

BARNHART

The Paiute cutthroat is identical in every way to the Lahontan, except that it lacks spots.

serving specimens of a remnant *henshawi* population high in the headwaters of the East Fork of the Carson River with so few spots on their bodies that he would have called them *seleniris* had he found them in Silver King Creek.

Cutthroat of the Humboldt River drainage (unnamed). The Humboldt cutthroat has never been formally described as a subspecies, although Behnke considers it one, differentiated from *O. c. henshawi* based on meristic characters. He and his students have distinguished Humboldt drainage specimens (including those from Reece River tributaries) from west-side specimens 100 percent of the time using computer analysis of these characters. Humboldt drainage trout have typically fewer scales in the lateral series, fewer scales above the lateral line, and fewer gill rakers than *henshawi*, all reflective of the fluviatile adaptation mentioned earlier. Other meristic characters are similar to *henshawi*.

Loudenslager and his colleagues argue against subspecies status for the Humboldt cutthroat trout, citing insufficient differentiation in electrophoretically detectable gene loci. On the other hand, analysis of mtDNA does reveal a unique haplotype in specimens from the Humboldt River drainage.

There is little difference in the appearance of the trout from either side of the Lahontan Basin. Both are dull-colored, with perhaps a tendency for the east-side fish, especially the larger specimens, to be more ruddy-colored.

Spotting varies, but experts who have examined many, many specimens say there typically are fewer spots on trout in the Humboldt drainage than on west-side *henshawi*, and those spots tend to be concentrated on the posterior of the body.

Cutthroat of Alvord Basin (unnamed). Cutthroat trout were first collected from streams flowing into the Alvord Basin of northwestern Nevada and southeastern Oregon by Hubbs and his family in 1934, but hybridization and replacement by introduced rainbow trout were already under way. This form was believed to be extinct until 1984, when a few specimens were discovered in a remote corner of the drainage.

Observations of those 1984 specimens and others collected in 1985 and 1986 led to the following description. Alvord Basin cutthroat trout are bronze-olive on the back, shading to lighter colors on the sides and belly, much like Lahontan Basin cutthroat trout. Large specimens have pinkish rose hues on the head and sides, and large spawning males develop broad bands of rose or brick red along the sides from gill covers to tail. The spots on these fish, and also on the museum specimens collected by Hubbs, are

Although the unnamed Alvord Basin cutthroats are much like the Lahontan cutthroats, their spots are more concentrated toward the tail.

THE SPECIES

243

large, round, and sparsely distributed, more concentrated on the posterior and only rarely present below the lateral line.

The number of gill rakers in Alvord Basin trout is high, possibly indicative of lacustrine adaptation by way of a Lahontan ancestor or because of residence in the large lake that is known to have existed in the Alvord Basin at the time of the last ice age. The sparse spotting, lower scale counts, and poor development of basibranchial teeth suggest long separation from Lahontan stocks, although the latter two characters also could suggest hybridization with rainbow trout. About 30 percent of the museum specimens had eight rather than nine pelvic fin rays.

Electrophoretic examination of the fish collected in 1985 and 1986 revealed alleles associated with Lahontan cutthroat trout, but also one unique allele that investigators at first thought would serve to distinguish Alvord Basin cutthroat trout. But that allele was subsequently found also in Lahontan cutthroat trout from the Quinn River drainage, and so is probably not diagnostic. Unfortunately, rainbow trout alleles also were found in high frequency in the Alvord Basin collections, indicating extensive hybridization. This again casts doubt on the existence of a pure Alvord Basin subspecies.

Cutthroat of Whitehorse Basin (unnamed). The cutthroat of Willow and Whitehorse creeks, too, exhibit the same dull colors one sees in Lahontan Basin cutthroat trout. The spotting pattern is more like Alvord Basin trout, that is, large spots sparsely distributed and tending to concentrate posteriorly. Few spots are found below the lateral line on the fore part of the body. Willow Creek specimens average about ten more lateral-series scales than Whitehorse Creek specimens.

Willow Creek and Whitehorse Creek specimens are indistinguishable from Lahontan cutthroat trout by protein electrophoresis. Analysis of mtDNA likewise reveals only one haplotype in Willow Creek specimens, that being the common western Great Basin haplotype found in the Lahontan cutthroat trout. But Whitehorse Creek specimens exhibit two haplotypes in about equal frequency. One is the common Lahontan haplotype, but the other is unique and represents a unique genetic lineage.

The cutthroats of the White-horse Basin are an unnamed species, nearly indistinguishable from the Lahontan cutthroats.

MATHEWSON

Yellowstone cutthroats have large, pronounced round spots. The rosy tints (right) indicate mature fish.

ROSTON

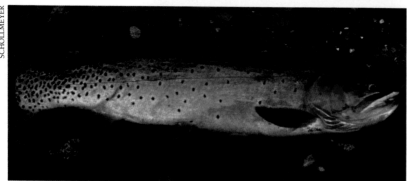

SCHOLLMEYER

ROSTON

The fine-spotted cutthroat of the Snake River has not yet been named, but its unique "ground-pepper" spotting pattern sets it apart from its near relatives.

TULLIS

Yellowstone cutthroat (O. c. bouvieri). The Yellowstone cutthroat is another dull-colored cutthroat. It typically is yellowish brown, brassy, or golden olive, although rosy tints may sometimes develop on mature fish. The spots are medium to large, round, quite pronounced, and concentrated on the caudal peduncle, which is just ahead of the caudal fin, or tail, except in the Yellowstone Lake population, which has spots more evenly distributed over the body. Yellowstone Lake fish typically have higher counts of gill rakers than do stream-dwelling fish.

Fine-spotted cutthroat in Snake River (unnamed). The unnamed fine-spotted cutthroat in the Snake River, whose range lies totally within that of *O. c. bouvieri*, cannot be distinguished from *bouvieri* either by meristic character analysis or by protein electrophoresis. Even in coloration the two fishes are alike, although experts say there is a tendency for the fine-spotted Snake River cutthroat trout to develop more dull silver or dull yellow colors than *bouvieri*, and for the fins to become more orange or red.

What does set the fine-spotted form apart

from *bouvieri* and from other members of its subspecies complex is its unique spotting pattern. It has the smallest spots of any trout native to western North America. The spots are profuse and have been described as a heavy sprinkling of ground pepper on the sides of the fish. They are most heavily concentrated on the caudal peduncle area, and on the fore part of the body there are more spots above the lateral line than below it.

Bonneville cutthroat (O. c. utah). The Bonneville cutthroat is yet another generally dull-colored trout. Stream-dwelling populations are similar in appearance and in most meristic characters to *O. c. bouvieri*, but they differ from *bouvieri* in that they typically have larger, more evenly distributed spots. Snake Valley trout have more and smaller spots than fish from elsewhere in the basin.

Populations of Bonneville cutthroat dwelling in large lakes are quite different in appearance from stream-dwelling fish. Historically the Bonneville Basin had at least two lake populations, and it was one of these, in Utah

The Bonneville cutthroat is generally indistinguishable from the Yellowstone, except that its spots may be somewhat larger and more evenly distributed.

ROSTON

The trout of the Colorado River drainage are much more brightly colored than any other cutthroats. The Colorado River cutthroats (above) show brilliant reds, oranges, and yellows when mature. The most striking characteristic of the greenback cutthroat (above right) is its spots, which are the largest in any of the cutthroat species.

Lake, to which George Suckley, in the mid-1800s, conferred the name *Salmo utah* to distinguish it from trout found in nearby mountain streams, which were called *Salmo virginalis* at the time. Suckley and other early collecters described Utah Lake fish as being silvery with small, speckle-like spots. Bear Lake cutthroat trout are similar in spotting to those early descriptions, but Bear Lake fish often take on a distinctive robin's-egg blue cast, a trait that has earned them the nickname "bluenose." Males develop a rosy orange hue at spawning time.

Meristic character analysis suggests that there are three slightly differentiated groups of trout native to the Bonneville Basin: one group associated with the basin itself—the Jordan, Provo, Weber, and Sevier river drainages; another group associated with the Bear River drainage in the northeast corner of the basin; and the third group associated with the Snake Mountain Range and Snake Valley along the western edge of the basin. Small but interesting differences in population structure also show up in protein electrophoresis. Loudenslager has reported that *O. c. utah* from the Bear River drainage are indistinguishable from Snake River *O. c. bouvieri*, and both groups of fish exhibit fixed allelic differences from *O. c. pleuriticus* (described next) at two gene loci. But trout from the Sevier River drainage and trout from the Snake Valley streams are more similar to *O. c. pleuriticus* than they are to Bear River populations.

Colorado River cutthroat (*O. c. pleuriticus*). It would be possible to know when one has crossed from either the Bonneville Basin or the upper Snake-upper Yellowstone drainage into the Green River-Colorado River drainage, even though headwater tributaries are less than a mile apart in many places, simply by looking at the native trout. A striking change in coloration occurs. The dull, somber hues of *O. c. utah* and *O. c. bouvieri* give way to the brilliant colors of *O. c. pleuriticus*, the Colorado River cutthroat.

The Colorado River cutthroat trout, along with the greenback cutthroat, develops the most brilliant red, orange, and yellow colors of all of the cutthroat trout subspecies. Mature male fish in lakes show off these colors best. The area along the lateral line turns red, the ventral region a bright orange or crimson, and golden yellow colors spread over the rest of the lower body.

The spotting pattern of *pleuriticus* varies. On trout in the tributaries of the upper Green River, Wyoming, the spots are as small as or smaller than the pupil of the eye and are distributed mainly on the caudal peduncle and above the lateral line in front of the dorsal fin. Elsewhere in the native range, the spots are larger. On all specimens, they are pronounced and round.

The Colorado River cutthroat trout, as well as the greenback cutthroat, consistently exhibits the highest scale counts of any of the cutthroat subspecies. Pure *pleuriticus* populations average more than 180 scales in the

RINNE

The Rio Grande cutthroat, related to the Colorado River and greenback cutthroats, has clublike spots clustered near the tail.

lateral series and more than forty-three scales above the lateral line.

Distinctions between the genetic proteins of *pleuriticus* and *bouvieri* have been reported by Loudenslager. Allendorf, Leary, and their colleagues also have examined these fish but find little genetic divergence between them.

Greenback cutthroat (O. c. stomias). Based purely on taxonomics, the greenback cutthroat and the Colorado River cutthroat might be considered together as a single subspecies. There is a broad overlap of characters between them. Many specimens known to have come from a greenback drainage have been misclassified as Colorado River cutthroat and vice versa when meristic characters were processed in a discriminate function computer analysis, which tests for statistically significant differences between groups of data. In addition, little genetic divergence can be found electrophoretically. Both trouts also develop similar brilliant colors.

On the other hand, experts who have handled many specimens say that the greenback has the largest spots and the most scales of any cutthroat subspecies. And Behnke points out that the name *pleuriticus* has long been recognized to designate the cutthroats native to the upper Colorado River basin and the name *stomias* to designate those native to the South Platte and Arkansas river drainages.

Rio Grande cutthroat (O. c. virginalis). The coloration of the Rio Grande cutthroat trout is similar to that of the Colorado River and greenback cutthroats, but it is not quite so intensely expressed. Spotting is distinctive: On the Rio Grande cutthroat, virtually all spots are clustered on the caudal peduncle in a close-set patch, and they are more clublike, not round. Trout of the Pecos River drainage have larger spots than trout associated with the Rio Grande itself. Pecos River trout also have more lateral-series scales than do Rio Grande trout. Basibranchial teeth typically are feebly developed in both populations.

Yellowfin cutthroat (O. c. macdonaldi)—extinct. The yellowfin cutthroat, now extinct, is known only from Twin Lakes, Colorado, in the Arkansas River drainage, which is the native range of the greenback cutthroat trout. A greenback population also lived in the lakes. The yellowfin cutthroat grew much larger than the greenback trout did, but it was something of a mystery fish. Twin Lakes was popular with anglers, but yellowfin cutthroat trout were never reported in the catch before 1885, nor after 1903.

David Starr Jordan collected specimens of yellowfin cutthroat trout in 1889 and named the fish *Salmo mykiss macdonaldi*. He described it as silvery olive in color with a broad band of lemon yellow along the sides, lower fins of bright golden yellow, and no red anywhere except the deep red dash on each side of the throat. The rear of the body and the dorsal and caudal fins were profusely speckled with small, pepperlike spots which extended forward to the head on some speci-

This rainbow fine-spotted cut-throat hybrid most likely resulted from the introduction of rainbows to waters where they were not native. Such introductions are almost always to the detriment of local populations of native species.

mens, but spotting was usually sparse on the front half of the body.

Behnke examined Jordan's old museum specimens and reported that the small star-shaped spots and silvery coloration clearly stood out from the dark coloration and large, round, pronounced spots of greenback trout specimens taken at the same time from Twin Lakes. Behnke reported 159 to 185 scales in the lateral series of the yellowfin trout; the greenback specimens he examined had 170 to 208 scales. The yellowfins had twenty to twenty-two gill rakers, the greenbacks eighteen to twenty-one. He concluded that two distinct and reproductively isolated forms of cutthroat trout did exist in Twin Lakes in 1889.

Hybrids and hybridization

Where two species of trout are native to the same waters, that is, where they have evolved in sympatry, the mixing of their gene pools normally is prevented by some slight difference in behavior that results in reproductive isolation. Thus, along the Pacific coast, both rainbow trout and coastal cutthroat trout are native and share many of the same waters without hybridizing. Likewise, in Idaho's Salmon and Clearwater rivers, native rainbow trout coexist with native westslope cutthroat trout without hybridizing. But in waters inhabited naturally by just one species, hybridization will nearly always result when a closely related nonnative species is introduced.

The degree of hybridization will depend upon the magnitude of the introduction and the type of habitat. Sometimes there is only a small infusion of one gene pool into the other; that is, only a few nonnative fish mate with the native species. Other times the infusion is sufficient to completely obscure the genotype of the native trout. Hybridization shows up in the meristic characters; for example, rainbow x cutthroat hybrids may have reduced numbers of basibranchial teeth or lack them altogether. They also may exhibit low scale counts, higher numbers of pyloric caeca and vertebrae, and erratic spotting. Crosses between Yellowstone cutthroat trout and westslope cutthroat trout exhibit higher scale counts as well as higher counts of gill rakers and basibranchial teeth. They also have larger, rounder spots than typical westslope populations.

In the Colorado River and Green River drainages where the Colorado River cutthroat is the native trout, hybridization had become so extensive that by the early 1970s, pure populations were rare indeed. The introduction of nonnative trout had resulted in all degrees of hybridization.

Distribution

Historically, *Oncorhynchus clarki* was distributed more broadly in North America than were any other species of trout. It is the only trout native to Colorado, Wyoming, Utah, and Alberta, and was more widely distributed in Nevada, Idaho, Montana, and perhaps also New Mexico than were other trout native to those waters. In addition, its historic range included parts of California, Oregon, Washington, British Columbia, Alaska, and, in Alberta, the headwaters of the South Saskatchewan River. But as the American frontier moved westward, the fish was exploited for food and commerce, its habitat was conscripted for other uses, and nonnative salmonids were introduced into its waters. In less than one hundred years after the first settlements were established, the native cutthroat trout had vanished from most of its vast range.

Coastal cutthroat. Of the individual subspecies of cutthroat trout, the coastal cutthroat has the broadest distribution: from the Humboldt Bay area of California northward to Gore Point on the Kenai Peninsula, Alaska, a distance of about 3,025 kilometers (1,876 miles). Its distribution extends inland to the crest of the Cascade Mountains in Oregon and Washington and to the coast range crest in British Columbia, an average distance of about 160 kilometers (99 miles). (In British Columbia, the coast range includes the northern ranges of the Rocky Mountains, which converge with the Cascades.) This distribution closely overlaps the Pacific coast rain forest belt.

Although coastal cutthroats have been affected by man's activities less than interior subspecies and are still widely distributed throughout their native range, anadromous populations have declined sharply in recent years; many are now listed as at risk. Environmental alteration, mainly logging, and conscription of habitat for urbanization and for the rearing of millions of stocked salmon and steelhead in places that historically did not support them, and over-exploitation by anglers continue to contribute to coastal cutthroat trout declines.

Westslope cutthroat. The westslope cutthroat trout also embraced an extensive historic range. *O. c. lewisi* territory includes the upper Columbia River basin in Idaho, Montana, and southeastern British Columbia (that is, the west slope of the northern Rocky Mountains, hence the name), then straddles the Continental Divide to include the upper Missouri and South Saskatchewan river basins. On the east side of the divide, the historic range extends down the Missouri River to below Great Falls, Montana, and includes the headwaters of the Judith, Musselshell, Milk, and Marias rivers. The historic range also includes the Madison and Gallatin rivers to their headwaters in Yellowstone National Park. In the South Saskatchewan system, the range includes all headwater tributaries in Montana and Alberta from the Bow River southward.

The westernmost extent of the range is not so certain. It may have extended as far as the crest of the Cascade Mountains in Washington, based on historical accounts of "mountain trout" and "speckled trout" from locations across northeastern Washington and the presence of a native stock of westslope cutthroat in the Lake Chelan drainage. There

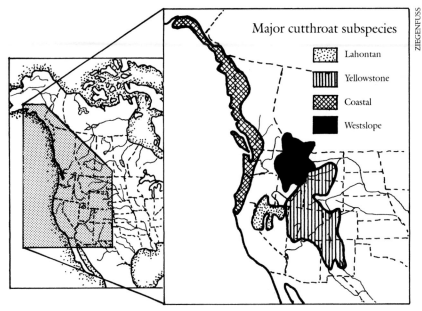

Major cutthroat subspecies

Lahontan
Yellowstone
Coastal
Westslope

ZIEGENFUSS

The four major subspecies divisions of cutthroat trout are based on significant genetic differences. They are the coastal cutthroat (Oncorhynchus clarki clarki), the westslope cutthroat (Oncorhynchus clarki lewisi), the Yellowstone cutthroat (Oncorhynchus clarki bouvieri), and the Lahontan (Oncorhynchus clarki henshawi) cutthroat trout.

also is a population of apparently native westslope cutthroat trout in the upper John Day River drainage in northeastern Oregon. In addition, a westward and northward extension of the range may be represented by isolated pockets of cutthroat trout that occur in the upper Fraser River drainage in British Columbia. In 1931, Dymond described these as a new subspecies with the name *Salmo clarki alpestris*, the mountain cutthroat trout. The current view is that the mountain cutthroat trout is another isolated form of *lewisi*.

Based on the glacial history and geology of the area, the movement of the westslope cutthroat trout across the Continental Divide to occupy the upper Missouri and South Saskatchewan river drainages must have been a postglacial occurrence. An apparent anomaly in the distribution of *lewisi*, its occurrence as the native species of trout in the Clearwater and Salmon river drainages of Idaho, both tributaries of the Snake River, also may be explained by the Ice Age history of the area. Ancient Lake Missoula, which covered the Clark Fork and Bitterroot valleys of western Montana, may have provided a refugium for westslope cutthroat trout, and, by way of headwater stream transfers, avenues for dispersal of these fish into the Salmon and Clearwater drainages.

But few wild, genetically pure populations of westslope cutthroat remain. Montana and Glacier National Park found that only seventy-two pure stream populations in nine

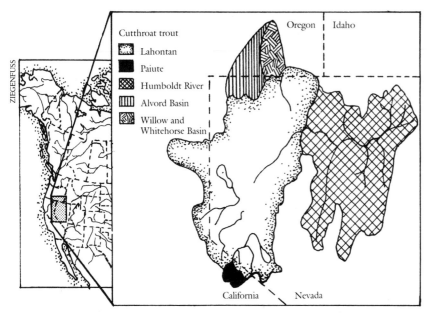

The Western Great Basin genetic group of cutthroat trout currently includes one major and 4 minor subspecies groups, two of which are recognized as separate subspecies – the Lahontan cutthroat (Oncorhynchus clarki henshawi) and the Paiute cutthroat (Oncorhynchus clarki seleniris). The major subspecies group, the Lahontan cutthroats, and the three minor subspecies which have not been recognized as genetically distinct and therefore remain officially unnamed – the Humboldt River cutthroat, the Alvord Basin cutthroat, and the Whitehorse and Willow Creek Basin subspecies – are also currently included in this group.

river drainages remain, a mere 2.5 percent of Montana's historic stream range. Many other stream populations of cutthroat trout are present, but they are hybridized. Only twenty-two pure lake populations were found, and nineteen of those are in the Flathead River drainage of Glacier National Park. Hybrid westslope cutthroats were found in another 243 lakes in Montana.

Surveys of cutthroat populations have not been done in Idaho or Canada, but Idaho is known to have several genetically pure westslope cutthroat trout populations in the Middle Fork Salmon, North Fork Clearwater, Lochsa, Selway, St. Joe, and Coeur d'Alene rivers.

Western Great Basin genetic group. The native historic range of the western Great Basin genetic group is the ancient Lake Lahontan drainage plus two much smaller basins contiguous with the Lahontan Basin on its north rim: the Alvord Lake Basin and the Whitehorse Basin. This region is home to two recognized subspecies, the Lahontan cutthroat, *O. c. henshawi*, and the Paiute cutthroat, *O. c. seleniris*, as well as the three subspecies, whose status is still being debated, from the Humboldt River, Alvord Lake, and Whitehorse-Willow creek drainages. Today, fewer than one hundred locations, representing only 7 percent of the stream habitat once occupied in the Lahontan Basin, are now known to contain genetically pure, self-sustaining populations of cutthroat trout.

Historically, Lahontan cutthroat occurred in almost all of the cooler perennial streams of the Truckee, Walker, and Carson river drainages, plus streams in the Honey Lake, Smoke Creek Desert, and Black Rock Desert subbasins in California and Nevada, some 2,600 kilometers (1,612 miles) of stream in all on the west side of the basin. In addition, *henshawi* was known to occur in Tahoe, Cascade, Fallen Leaf, Independence, Donner, Pyramid, Winnemucca, Walker, Upper Twin, Lower Twin, and Summit lakes in California and Nevada, a combined surface area of 135,000 hectares (333,450 acres). Today remnant populations of *henshawi* can be found in small, isolated headwater tributaries of the Truckee, Carson, and Walker river drainages on the west side of the basin, and genetically pure, self-sustaining lake populations of *henshawi* are down to only two: Summit Lake in Nevada and Independence Lake in California. In Independence Lake, there have been fewer than one hundred *henshawi* spawners annually since 1960.

The Humboldt cutthroat trout historically occupied about 3,500 kilometers (2,170 miles) of stream in the Humboldt River drainage in Nevada, which included the watersheds of Rock Creek, Maggie Creek, North Fork Humboldt, Little Humboldt, and Reese rivers, and the main Humboldt River itself to below the town of Carlin, Nevada. Remnant Humboldt cutthroat trout still hold out in small headwater tributaries in the Humboldt River drainage on the east side of the basin. It is not known to have occurred historically in lakes.

Probably no one today would know the Paiute cutthroat trout but for a "coffee can transplant" made by a sheepherder in the early twentieth century. The historic range is a section of Silver King Creek, East Fork Carson River drainage, Alpine County, California, from Llewellyn Falls downstream about 6 kilometers (4 miles) to the site of another impassible falls. That lower falls had been formed in the stream channel, stranding a population of Lahontan cutthroat trout, by some flood event that occurred long before recorded time. It was in this reach that the Paiute cutthroat trout evolved from its Lahontan cutthroat ancestor. Above Llewellyn Falls, the water was barren of fish.

Then the herder, tending his sheep in the valleys of upper Silver King Creek, moved fish into the barren waters above Llewellyn Falls in 1912. A few years later, the lower falls washed out. Trout remaining in the original reach were exposed to new infusions of trout from below. In addition, rainbow trout were introduced into the East Fork Carson River and lower Silver King Creek. By 1933, when Snyder published the first scientific description of Paiute cutthroat trout and named the fish *Salmo seleniris*, the trout in the original range were thoroughly hybridized. Snyder's type specimens, collected above Llewellyn Falls, were descendants of that "coffee can transplant." Silver King Creek above Llewellyn Falls and two or three small tributaries in the same drainage make up the present range of this rare subspecies, which numbers only about five hundred fish.

The historic range of the Alvord Basin cutthroat trout is not really known. The Alvord Basin is desert country now with few perennial streams, but at the time of the last ice age, a lake about 47 kilometers (29 miles) long and maybe 3 to 6 kilometers (2 to 4 miles) wide existed there, fed by streams running off the ranges that form the rim of the basin. No doubt most of these streams and the lake itself were once inhabited by cutthroat trout, but specimens were not collected from Alvord Basin streams until 1934, by which time rainbow trout had already been introduced. Hubbs and his family obtained cutthroat trout specimens from two

sites: Virgin Creek, which flows out of the Pine Forest Range on the south rim of the basin, and Trout Creek, which flows out of the Trout Creek Mountains along the eastern rim. The Trout Creek specimens showed evidence of hybridization.

In 1984, after a fifty-year period in which the Alvord Basin cutthroat trout was thought to be extinct, a crew from the Nevada Department of Wildlife collected specimens from an isolated reach that were similar in appearance to the type specimens collected by the Hubbs family in 1934. Behnke examined specimens collected in 1985 and reported their meristic characters to be identical with the Hubbs specimens; however other specimens collected in 1985 were shown by electrophoresis to be hybridized with rainbow trout. Nevertheless, in 1986 an effort was mounted to recover and protect genetically pure individuals if they could be found or, if not, individuals selected to be phenotypically good examples of the Alvord Basin trout. No genetically pure fish were discovered in this effort; all showed a history of hybridization with rainbow trout. But twenty-five fish were selected based on appearance, and these were successfully transplanted into a nearby creek that was barren of fish. This hybrid population, plus the trout remaining in the reach where they were discovered, is all that remains of the Alvord Basin cutthroat trout. It is probably extinct in genetically pure form for all practical purposes, unless—and this seems unlikely—an-

The Alvord Basin is desert country with only a few perennial streams, some of which are home to the Alvord Basin cutthroat.

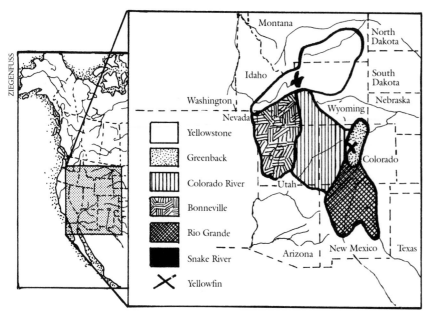

The cutthroat species native to the Bonneville Basin, like most other interior cutthroat subspecies, occupy very little of their native range because of habitat degradation and loss, and hybridization with introduced species. Most of the native Bonneville Basin cutthroat population is now restricted to the Bear River drainage in Wyoming.

other population remains undiscovered in some other remote corner of the Alvord Basin.

The range of the cutthroat trout of Willow and Whitehorse creeks has been these creeks, which feed into the Whitehorse Basin, Harney County, Oregon, just east of the Alvord Basin. Willow Creek and Whitehorse Creek are presently isolated from one another, but they probably were connected during wetter climes. No Ice Age lake is listed for this basin, but such a lake may have existed. There is a playa, or shallow desert depression, called Coyote Lake out on the basin floor. No other species of fish is found in Willow Creek or Whitehorse Creek, and both of these waters appear to have escaped the introduction of nonnative trouts.

The Willow-Whitehorse Creek cutthroat trout exists under marginal conditions at best. Comparisons of population estimates made by the Bureau of Land Management (BLM) in 1980 with estimates made in 1970 seem to show that the fish are holding their own, but their numbers are not large.

Yellowstone and Bonneville cutthroats and other subspecies. The historic range of the fourth major genetic group comprises the Bonneville Basin and the interior Rocky Mountain region, including the drainages of the upper Snake and Yellowstone rivers, the upper Colorado and Green rivers, the upper South Platte and Arkansas rivers, and the upper Rio Grande and the Pecos River. This area is home to five existing, named sub-

species: Yellowstone, *O. c. bouvieri*; Bonneville, *O. c. utah*; Colorado River, *O. c. pleuriticus*; greenback, *O. c. stomias*; and Rio Grande, *O. c. virginalis*. It also is home to one unclassified subspecies, the fine-spotted cutthroat. A seventh subspecies, the yellowfin cutthroat, which formerly occupied this area, is extinct.

The western extent of the historical range of the Yellowstone cutthroat trout is not known for certain. The type locality for fishes with the name *bouvieri* is Waha Lake, Idaho, an isolated lake in the lower Snake River system near the Washington border. A cutthroat trout reported in 1909 from Crab Creek, an isolated stream in the channeled scablands of eastern Washington, was also apparently identical with *bouvieri*. (The scablands were carved when the floodwaters of ancient Lake Missoula washed across eastern Washington after the ice dam that backed up the lake gave way.) Above Shoshone Falls on the Snake River, the Yellowstone cutthroat trout is native to the entire Snake River system except for that section of the main Snake River (known to locals as the South Fork) between Palisades Reservoir and Jackson Lake, where the fine-spotted Snake River cutthroat trout occurs. All of the Snake River tributaries between Palisades Reservoir and Shoshone Falls have native *bouvieri*. Likewise, in Pacific Creek, Buffalo Fork, and Spread Creek, the first three Snake River tributaries below Jackson Lake, *bouvieri* is the native species. In the Gros Ventre River, *bouvieri* occupy the upper tributaries and fine-spotted cutthroat occur in the lower reaches.

We do not know how far downstream in the Snake River the range of the fine-spotted Snake River cutthroat trout extended before the dam that created Palisades Reservoir was built. I have no quantitative information about the present distribution of the fine-spotted Snake River cutthroat, but Behnke, writing in 1979, stated that it is the only subspecies of *O. clarki* that is more abundant now than it was historically.

We also do not know which fish—the Yellowstone or the fine-spotted Snake River cutthroat—was native to Jackson Lake before the dam was built, backing up the water. There was no barrier to free movement between the river and the lake before then.

On the Yellowstone River side of the Continental Divide, *bouvieri* spread downstream in all tributaries as far as the Tongue River. The Powder River drainage, which is the next one downstream, never had a native trout. The Yellowstone cutthroat trout undoubtedly crossed the Continental Divide by way of Two Ocean Pass from Pacific Creek in the Snake River drainage to Atlantic Creek in the Yellowstone River drainage. This must have been a postglacial occurrence based on the glacial history and geology of the area.

The Yellowstone cutthroat is still found in genetically pure form in about 85 percent of its original lake habitat but in only 10 percent of its historic stream range. Within Yellowstone National Park, *bouvieri* populations are healthy and doing well. Outside the park in Montana and Idaho, *bouvieri* is of special concern because of its low numbers. In the Snake River drainage of Idaho, major indigenous populations still exist in the Blackfoot and Teton rivers and Willow Creek, as well as in the Snake River itself, but recent surveys document high angling mortality and declining numbers in several of these populations.

The Bonneville cutthroat trout, *O. c. utah*, is endemic to the Bonneville Basin, which contained the largest of the ancient Great Basin lakes. At its largest, Lake Bonneville rivaled present-day Lake Michigan. The Great Salt Lake and Utah Lake are remnants of this vast Ice Age lake.

The Bonneville cutthroat trout was distributed in all of the suitable waters of the basin, including Bear and Utah lakes, the Bear, Logan, Weber, Provo, Jordan, and Sevier river drainages, and most all of the cooler perennial streams that flowed down off the ranges around the perimeter of the basin.

Only forty-one genetically pure populations of Bonneville cutthroat trout remain. Thirty-nine of these are in headwater streams and two are in lakes: Bear Lake and Lake Alice, Wyoming. Idaho has three stream populations, Nevada five, Wyoming ten, and Utah twenty-one. These are all small, isolated, widely distributed populations, but each of the slightly differentiated forms previously discussed is represented.

The Colorado River cutthroat trout is native to the upper Colorado River basin above the Grand Canyon, except that historically the Colorado River itself below the town of Rifle, Colorado, and the Green River below the town of Green River, Wyoming, were too warm and silt-laden to be trout habitat. Therefore, the range of *pleuriticus* was a discontinuous one and included the waters of the mountain and foothill zones on either side of the river valleys, extending downstream to encompass the Dirty Devil River drainage of Utah on the west and the San Juan River drainage of Colorado on the east. The line of demarcation between Colorado River cutthroat and the greenback and Rio Grande cutthroat is the Continental Divide.

Since 1977, fishery managers in Colorado and Wyoming have used the relative-purity rating system developed by Binns to gauge the purity of *pleuriticus* populations as they strove to recover this rare and troubled subspecies. In 1985, Colorado believed it had at least twenty stable pure populations within the historic range. However, research reported by Martinez in 1988 cast doubt upon this number and suggested that *pleuriticus* may yet be in jeopardy in Colorado.

The native historic range of the greenback cutthroat trout is the mountains and foothills of the South Platte and Arkansas river drainages on the east side of the Continental Divide. The greenback cutthroat is the only trout native to these drainages, except for the now extinct yellowfin cutthroat trout that was found in Twin Lakes, Colorado, in the Arkansas River drainage. The North Platte River drainage never had a native trout.

This desert basin once held Lake Bonneville, the largest of the ancient Great Basin lakes.

The greenback cutthroat represents another case of historical abundance and precipitous decline after settlers occupied its range. But eventually, five populations were discovered that were judged to be pure using the Binns system. These five remnant populations occupy four streams totalling about 13 stream kilometers (8 miles), and one population is in a 5-hectare (12-acre) lake. These waters are closed to angling and are managed as refugia, or areas that are existing undisturbed. As of 1988, reintroductions had been made into twelve streams totalling 64 kilometers (40 miles) and five lakes totalling 20 hectares (49 acres), and seven of those reintroduced populations had stabilized, meaning that they are reproducing naturally and have developed multiple age classes. Thus, the number of pure greenback cutthroat trout populations presently stands at twelve.

The Rio Grande cutthroat trout is native to the upper Rio Grande Basin in Colorado and New Mexico, and to the upper Pecos River drainage in New Mexico. The only unknown concerning its historic range is the southernmost extension. There are nineteenth-century reports of cutthroat trout from Mexico, and anecdotes from the same period about "speckled trout" in streams in the Rio Grande and Pecos River drainages in Texas. The known southern limit of the range of *virginalis* is Sierra Blanca Peak, New Mexico, which still makes this form the most southerly distributed of the cutthroat trout subspecies.

Like the other interior subspecies, the Rio Grande cutthroat trout has been extirpated from nearly all of its historic range in the past one hundred years. New Mexico and the U.S. Forest Service have been able to identify just thirty-nine genetically pure populations of Rio Grande cutthroat trout in New Mexico streams, and Colorado has at least ten stable self-reproducing populations in streams on public lands.

LIFE HISTORY

In addition to being a polytypic species, the cutthroat trout also exhibits considerable diversity in its life history and ecology. There are five general life-history forms: anadromous, fluvial-adfluvial, lacustrine-fluvial, allacustrine, and fluvial.

Anadromous populations migrate between marine waters and small freshwater tributary streams to spawn. The coastal cutthroat trout, being the only subspecies whose populations have access to salt water, is the only cutthroat that exhibits this particular life history.

All cutthroat trout, regardless of life history, are considered spring spawners. Actual spawning time depends on latitude, altitude, water temperature, and runoff conditions. The peak period for anadromous coastal cutthroat trout in Washington, Oregon, and southern British Columbia is February; in Alaska, the fish spawn as a rule in April and May. Spawning commences when the water temperature reaches about 5°C (41°F).

Anadromous coastal cutthroat trout predominate in streams with very small watersheds (total area less than 13 square kilometers [5 square miles]) and in streams with moderate-sized watersheds (up to about 120 square kilometers [46 square miles]) where the gradient is low throughout or where the lower reaches flow through extensive sloughs or meadowlands. Moderate-sized streams with higher gradients, and also large streams may be used as well, but in these, steelhead usually predominate. It has been suggested that anadromous cutthroat trout select small streams for spawning so that the nursery areas will be isolated, and interactions with other salmonids will be at a minimum. In streams shared with coho salmon, which show a preference for the same kinds of watersheds and natal tributaries despite their larger size, sea-run cutthroat trout spawning and nursery areas are usually found immediately above the reaches used by coho.

Adult sea-run cutthroat trout select the upper reaches of small, low-gradient tributaries for spawning, and there is evidence from population genetics studies that homing to these tributaries is precise. The volume of water in natal streams seldom exceeds 0.28 cubic meters (less than 1 cubic foot) per second during summer low flows and most of them average about half of that. These streams are sometimes found in the headwaters of the drainage, but not always.

Few female sea-run cutthroat trout spawn before age 4. Data correlating age to length, compiled from many agency reports, indicate that the fish average 330 to 355 millimeters (13 to 14 inches) total length at that age, and may carry 1,000 to 1,200 eggs. Spawning takes place in riffles ranging in depth from 150 to 450 millimeters (6 to 18 inches), in clean, pea-sized gravel. Preferred spawning sites are not far from deep pools, often right in the tail-outs, perhaps so the pools can be used as escape cover.

Spawning is rigorous, yet sea-run cutthroat trout withstand the stress well, and repeat spawning is common. In a study carried out in Oregon a few years ago, 39 percent of the run were second-time spawners, 17 percent were third-time spawners, and 12 percent were returning for their fourth spawning effort.

Spawned-out fish recover their condition rapidly and return to salt water around late March or early April in Washington and Oregon and toward the end of April in Alaska. The timing is about one month before the peak downstream movement of sea-run cutthroat smolts in those areas. The spawned-out fish also precede the seaward migration of pink and chum salmon smolts in rivers with those species.

Sea-run cutthroat trout eggs require about 300 temperature units for incubation. Another 150 to 200 temperature units must pass before the newly hatched fry are mature enough to emerge from the gravel. Peak emergence of fry occurs from March through June, depending on the locale and the timing of actual spawning.

Newly emerged fry are only about 25 millimeters (1 inch) long. They move quickly into low-velocity margins, backwaters, and side channels, where they remain throughout the summer, gradually moving into pools if competing species are absent in them. However, coho salmon often spawn in the immediate vicinity, and coho fry emerge earlier and at a somewhat larger size than cutthroat fry. Coho fry exert social dominance in sympatric situations, driving the little cutthroat trout into riffles, where they will remain until decreasing water temperatures at the onset of fall and winter reduce the assertiveness of the cohos.

Yearling sea-run cutthroat trout range more widely in the stream than do young-of-the-year fish. As water temperatures start to warm, the yearling fish begin to move downstream out of the nursery tributaries and disperse throughout the main stem. The onset of winter freshets triggers an upstream movement that often takes the juvenile trout back into the tributaries.

Age one is the earliest recorded age at which an anadromous cutthroat trout has smolted, or become physiologically able to tolerate salt water, and migrated to sea, and the oldest recorded is age six. The majority smolt at age two, three, or four, depending on the locality. In some streams the smolts begin migrating seaward as early as March. In Washington and Oregon the peak of the migration is mid-May. In one Washington stream, also populated by steelhead, cut-

The tiny, newly emerged cutthroat fry are vulnerable and must move quickly into safe, low-velocity areas to feed and grow.

GROST

throat smolts followed the peak steelhead smolt migration by about two weeks.

There appears to be a relationship between age and size at smolting, and the type of saltwater environment the smolts will enter. In sheltered saltwater reaches where there is little pounding surf, smolts are predominately age two with an average fork length, the measurement from snout to fork of the tail, of about 160 millimeters (6.4 inches). Smolts that migrate to places where they must cope with heavy, inhospitable surf are predominately age three or four with an average fork length of about 210 millimeters (8 inches).

Once in the marine environment, sea-run cutthroat trout remain fairly close inshore.

This young coastal cutthroat is beginning to lose its parr marks.

HOWELL

They do not migrate far out into the open seas as other anadromous salmonids do, and they are reluctant to cross even narrow stretches of deep open water. Their migrations in the marine environment seldom take them more than 50 to 70 kilometers (31 to 43 miles) from their home streams. They forage about in little schools along the gravel beaches, off the mouths of tiny creeks and beach trickles, around oyster beds, and in the patches of eel grass where they feed opportunistically on amphipods, isopods, shrimp, stickleback, sand lance, and other small fishes, including the occasional juvenile salmonid. They are in turn preyed upon by adult salmon as well as steelhead and Dolly Varden char, by hake and dogfish, by harbor seals, and by seabirds. Sea-run cutthroat trout grow about 25 millimeters (1 inch) per month while they are in salt water.

A very few scale samples taken from sea-run cutthroat by the Washington Department of Wildlife indicate that some fish did not return to fresh water at regular times, which leads to speculation that in rare instances, some sea-run cutthroat may overwinter in salt water. However, nearly all return to fresh water the same year that they migrate to sea. For many of the returning fish, this first freshwater reentry will not be for spawning but simply for overwintering. These fish will not become sexually mature until after they return a second time after another season at sea.

Two distinct freshwater reentry times have been noted for sea-run cutthroat trout. The runs occur typically from July through November, reaching a peak in September and October in most parts of the range. However, stocks in the sheltered waters of Puget Sound in Washington, Hood Canal in Oregon and Washington, and the waters of southern British Columbia between the mainland and Vancouver Island enter small streams that flow directly into salt water, and they migrate much later, from December through March, with the peak in January. That is, they migrate just before the onset of spawning. In Alaska, small numbers of mature cutthroat trout enter some streams in May. Some of Hood Canal's moderate-sized streams receive both early-entry and late-entry fish.

How returning sea-run cutthroat trout spend the overwintering period is not documented. One can speculate that their instream behavior and movements would not be unlike those of older premigrant juveniles, that is, dispersing throughout the upper reaches in pools and other sheltered habitat where they can remain until spawning or returning to salt water in the spring.

Fluvial-adfluvial populations migrate from larger rivers to smaller tributaries to spawn. These tributaries may be upstream or downstream of areas frequented by the trout during their growing and feeding period within the main stream. All subspecies, except perhaps the now-extinct *macdonaldi* and the unnamed Alvord Basin and Willow-Whitehorse forms, either do exhibit this life history, or did as a matter of historical record.

In simplest terms, one could say that cutthroat trout exhibiting this life history use mainstem rivers for feeding and growth, much as anadromous coastal cutthroat trout use salt water. Aside from details of timing and the like that are associated with specific locales and environments, life history characteristics are otherwise quite similar.

But there is one major difference: the timing of migration into spawning tributaries. Anadromous cutthroats move into spawning tributaries in the fall or winter. But fluvial-adfluvial cutthroats move into them in the spring. Fluvial-adfluvial populations of westslope cutthroat trout in Montana spawn between March and July; fluvial-adfluvial Yellowstone cutthroat trout in Idaho spawn

These photos, first published in 1941, show a pair of Lahontan cutthroats spawning. Right: The female, her tail flat against the gravel, begins to dig the redd. A male hovers nearby. Below right: At the moment of spawning a cloud of milt appears below the fish. Bottom right: Immediately after spawning, the pair separate.

from May through early July; river-dwelling Lahontan cutthroat trout in California and Nevada spawn from April through July. Spawning fish choose the same kinds of low-gradient reaches in small tributaries that sea-run cutthroat trout do, and spawning commences when water temperatures reach about 5°C (41°F).

In 1941, Smith published a description and a set of photos of the spawning ritual of Lahontan cutthroat trout. The female fish builds the redd while the male fish hovers nearby. She turns on her side and flips her tail vigorously against the gravel half a dozen times, and a small cloud of silt and pebbles swirls away. After a brief rest, she repeats the process. This continues for two or three hours until she has fashioned a pocket some 10 to 15 centimeters (4 to 6 inches) deep and just a little shorter than her length. From time to time toward the end of the digging, she settles into the pocket as though to test the fit. She settles in again, but this time some indefinable signal draws the male fish to her side. He bumps her gently, persistently, as she presses her anal fin into the gravel. Then both fish quiver, their mouths gape, and eggs and milt are extruded together into the pocket.

The female trout now moves upstream a bit and begins to sweep out a new depression, simultaneously covering the first one with the displaced gravel. Occasionally, rather than spawning again in this new pocket, she may select another spot entirely

THE SPECIES

257

and start digging anew. And once in a while, one fish or the other will abandon its mate and continue spawning with a new partner. In any event, the process continues for two to three days until all of the female's eggs are safely covered with mounds of gravel.

After spawning, the trout usually remain in the tributaries for another two to four weeks before dropping back to the main rivers. Adult westslope cutthroat trout will sometimes take up residence in the tributaries for the entire summer, not returning to the main rivers until fall or early winter.

Like anadromous cutthroat trout, fluvial-adfluvial females attain sexual maturity most commonly at age four although occasionally, fish are reported mature at age three and undoubtedly some individuals mature later. Size at maturity varies widely. Some westslope cutthroat trout in drainages where growth rates are slow are as small as 150 millimeters (6 inches) in total length; elsewhere they are as long as 350 millimeters (14 inches). Fluvial-adfluvial Yellowstone cutthroat trout are generally larger and may average between 300 and 500 millimeters (12 to 20 inches) in total length at first spawning. Fluvial-adfluvial Lahontan cutthroat trout average about the same. In most cutthroat, fecundity is about 340 to 550 eggs per kilogram (750 to 1,200 eggs per pound) of body weight.

The percentage of repeat spawners in runs of fluvial-adfluvial cutthroat trout is somewhat lower than what is reported for anadromous cutthroat trout. Fifteen percent is close to the norm, although 20 to 24 percent has been reported in some westslope cutthroat trout populations. This may not all be because of high death rates of first-time spawners, since it appears to be common for fluvial-adfluvial fish to skip a year before spawning a second time. It is reported that females outnumber males in many spawning migrations by anywhere from 3:1 to 6:1.

Like sea-run cutthroat trout, juvenile fluvial-adfluvial trout normally spend two to three years in their natal tributaries, but there are some exceptions. Fry of Yellowstone cutthroat trout that spawn in small intermittent streams in the upper Snake River drainage move out of the tributaries immediately. In contrast, there are seasonally intermittent streams in the Humboldt River drainage where the young-of-the-year fish stay in the tributary reaches, sheltered in tiny pools with no apparent surface flow. Downstream migration of juveniles is bimodal in many places; that is, there are two peaks, one in the spring, coinciding with springtime high flows, and the other in the fall or early winter when water temperatures decrease.

Fluvial-adfluvial cutthroat trout form dominance hierarchies in pools and runs. Juveniles distribute themselves evenly along the margins and larger, older trout choose the better positions in pools. They all are opportunistic feeders, usually taking insects that come to them in the drift. Some subspecies, notably the Yellowstone, fine-spotted Snake River, and Lahontan subspecies, become more piscivorous when they reach about 305 millimeters (12 inches) in length. Westslope cutthroat trout do not show this piscivorous shift. This subspecies coevolved with bull trout and northern squawfish, which occupy the piscivory niche. In sympatry with bull trout, westslope cutthroat trout hierarchies align vertically in the water column and use the midwater feeding zones, leaving the bottom zone to the bull trout. Cutthroat trout need more energy to maintain midwater positions, but if being there puts them in better position to intercept more drifting food, it may be worth the trade-off.

Coastal cutthroat trout, and the westslope cutthroat trout in some parts of its range, coevolved with steelhead and resident rainbow trout. These forms have survived in sympatry by partitioning the habitat. Rainbow trout and steelhead are found in riffles and higher-gradient reaches while the cutthroat trout frequent pools and generally slower, quieter reaches. Rainbow trout and steelhead usually also predominate in the lower reaches of jointly occupied watersheds; cutthroat trout will be found in the upper reaches. The other interior subspecies of cutthroat trout evolved in the absence of other trouts and do not coexist well with them. When other trouts are introduced, the native cutthroat trout populations seldom last more than a decade.

Fluvial-adfluvial cutthroat trout can live to nine years of age, and some subspecies have the potential to reach large sizes. River-dwelling Yellowstone and fine-spotted Snake River cutthroat trout commonly attain lengths exceeding 500 millimeters (20 inches) and weights of 2 to 3 kilograms (4 to 7 pounds). Occasionally they reach 600 millimeters (24 inches) and more than 4 kilograms (9 pounds). Lahontan cutthroat trout also can grow quite large in rivers, and the historical record indicates that river-dwelling Colorado River cutthroat trout also were capable of great size. (There are reports in old angling literature of trout weighing up to 9 kilograms [20 pounds]). However, westslope cutthroat trout seldom exceed 500 millimeters (20 inches) in length, and the historical record tells us that river-dwelling greenback cutthroat trout also were small fish.

Lacustrine-adfluvial populations live in lakes and ascend inlet tributaries to spawn. This also is a common life-history form. Even subspecies not known to have expressed this life history in their native condition, the Humboldt cutthroat trout, for example, have adapted such behavior when stocked in lakes. Populations with the fluvial-adfluvial life history have adapted lacustrine-adfluvial behavior (or the allacustrine life history described next) when isolated above empoundments formed on rivers in which they live.

Allacustrine populations reside in lakes but migrate downstream through lake outlets to spawn. This may not be as common as lacustrine-adfluvial behavior, but it is nevertheless well represented. Along with several different inlet-spawning populations, Yellowstone Lake has a population of *bouvieri* that spawns in the Yellowstone River below the lake. The Heart Lake population of *bouvieri*, also in Yellowstone National Park, is another outlet-spawning population. The coastal cutthroat trout of Crescent Lake, Washington, is an outlet-spawning population, as is Washington's Twin Lakes strain of westslope cutthroat trout.

Spawning migrations for lacustrine cutthroat trout begin in the spring when threshold water temperatures reach 5°C (41°F). This could happen anytime from May through July for interior locations, but it occurs in late winter in many coastal locations. At Yellowstone Lake, older and larger fish migrate first; the age, length, weight, and condition factor of migrating individuals de-

ANDERSON

Westslope cutthroat that evolved for life in lakes do not shift to feeding on fish as they get larger; they remain in midwater feeding zones. Bull trout and northern squawfish, also lake residents, fill the fish-eating niche in lacustrine environments; they inhabit the deeper waters with their prey.

cline as the run progresses. There is also evidence that the older, larger Yellowstone trout travel the greatest distance upstream. At Walker Lake, Nevada, some Lahontan cutthroat traveled as far as 200 kilometers (124 miles) before spawning. At Yellowstone Lake, males migrate earlier than females and remain longer in the spawning streams.

In the absence of fishing pressure, about 26 percent of the spawning fish in Yellowstone Lake populations survive to spawn again. Repeat spawning in alternate years is more prevalent than consecutive-year spawning at Yellowstone Lake, but Pierce found in 1984 that the coastal cutthroat trout of Lake Crescent, Washington, spawn every year with few exceptions.

Lacustrine trout select spawning streams and sites similar to those of sea-run and fluvial trout: small, low-gradient tributaries with shallow riffles over pea-sized gravel. They prefer streams that flow year round, although some populations do spawn in intermittent streams. When they do, young-of-the-year fry usually leave the stream just before it goes dry in late summer.

Spawning populations in Yellowstone Lake comprise individuals age three and older, primarily age four through seven. This span of years seems to be the norm for lacustrine cutthroat trout throughout the range, except for the Bear Lake form of Bonneville cutthroat trout, which matures later. More than 92 percent of the fish in the 1987 Bear Lake spawning run were age six or older, and repeat spawners made up only 4 percent of that particular run. Length at first spawning for Yellowstone Lake females usually averages about 350 millimeters (14 inches). As you would expect, Bear Lake females are larger at first spawning, and might reach 560 millimeters (22 inches) in length.

A typical Yellowstone Lake female trout of 39 centimeters (15 inches) in length will deposit 1,300 eggs, which could be considered the fecundity norm for lacustrine cutthroat trout populations. Lahontan cutthroat females exceed this norm; a lake-dwelling Lahontan 39 centimeters (15 inches) long might carry as many as 2,000 eggs, even more than a stream-dwelling counterpart. In alpine lakes where growth is slower, the trout at maturity is smaller and less fecund.

Eggs incubate for about 330 temperature units to time of hatching, and the fry emerge from the gravel after another 150 to 200 temperature units. As do the fry of other life-history forms of cutthroat, they congregate in the shallow, slower places along the stream margins. At Yellowstone Lake most of the fry exit the natal tributaries for the lake before their first summer is over. The same is true of the fry of lake-dwelling Lahontan cutthroat trout. This behavior contrasts with that of fluvial-adfluvial fry, as well as with the behavior of fry of lake-dwelling coastal cutthroat trout, which spend one, two, or sometimes three years in natal tributaries if the streams flow year round.

Nilsson and Northcote reported in 1981 that coastal cutthroat trout living as the sole salmonid in several British Columbia lakes make broad use of the habitat, foraging in all areas from shallow to open water, and at all levels from bottom to surface, feeding mostly on crustacean plankton and insects, and eating fish only occasionally. On the other hand Pierce, in 1984, found that coastal cutthroat trout in Lake Crescent, Washington, become highly piscivorous when they reached a length of about 305 millimeters (12 inches), feeding mainly on the lake's abundant supply of kokanee salmon. The Bear Lake form of Bonneville cutthroat trout also is highly piscivorous, as was the Pyramid Lake strain of Lahontan cutthroat trout, which now exists only as an introduced population in Utah, according to Behnke.

When cutthroat trout share a lake with other salmonids, they partition the habitat and resources. Coastal cutthroat trout share many lakes with rainbow trout and Dolly Varden char. In such lakes, the cutthroat trout congregate inshore and the rainbow trout (or Dolly Varden) congregate offshore. In sympatry with rainbow trout, the cutthroat trout also relinquish the midwater feeding zone almost completely and rely more on surface prey. They also become more piscivorous when in sympatry with rainbow trout. In sympatry with Dolly Varden char, coastal cutthroat trout feed mostly near the surface in littoral areas. At Yellowstone Lake, another interesting form of habitat partitioning occurs between juvenile and older cutthroat trout. Juvenile fish move offshore and tend to stay there, whereas older, larger trout remain in the littoral zone the year around.

In aquarium experiments comparing the feeding behavior and social interactions of cutthroat and rainbow trout, cutthroat are found to be cautious, deliberate feeders, whereas rainbow attack food items. Cutthroat trout also are the less aggressive fish in agonistic encounters, and generally are dominated by rainbow trout of equal size.

Growth rates of lacustrine cutthroat trout are highly variable, depending on the particular stock and environmental conditions, but some can attain great size. I have already mentioned the enormous size of the Pyramid Lake strain of Lahontan cutthroat trout. The Bear Lake strain of Bonneville cutthroat trout is another one capable of large size, and even coastal cutthroat trout can reach impressive sizes in some lakes. The trout of Lake Crescent, for example, commonly reach a weight of 3.6 kilograms (7.9 pounds), and the Washington state hook-and-line record is a Lake Crescent fish of 5.5 kilograms (12.1 pounds). Some subspecies, on the other hand, do not seem to be noted for large size, even in lakes. The westslope cutthroat trout, for example, seldom exceeds 500 millimeters (20 inches) in length, and the historical record for the greenback cutthroat trout is devoid of fish weighing more than about 2 kilograms (4.4 pounds). The maximum age for most subspecies seems to be about six or seven, but Yellowstone cutthroat trout of age eleven have been recorded.

Fluvial populations do not migrate. They do disperse locally to spawn near their home territories within streams, but this is not migration in the general sense. The term fluvial is most often used to describe populations dwelling in small headwater streams, but there is a population of Yellowstone cutthroat trout that both resides and spawns in the Yellowstone River in the area between the Yellowstone Lake outlet and Upper Falls.

Nonmigratory stream populations do not move far within their streams. Fry, upon emergence, take up positions in stream margins, side channels, and backwaters near their redds. As they grow over the summer, they may move short distances and gradually take up foraging stations in pools. In winter they also may move upstream or downstream to more secure habitat. But these seasonal movements are not extensive; most fluvial cutthroat trout spend their entire lives within about 200 meters (219 yards) of the places where they were born. Adults move to spawning gravels in spring when water temperatures increase to 5°C (41°F) or higher.

Some stream-resident forms can grow quite large; examples are the Humboldt cutthroat trout of the Mary's River, Nevada, which often reach a length of 380 millimeters (15 inches), and the Alvord Basin trout, of which an individual, age seven, measuring 508 millimeters (20 inches) in length was recorded. However, most are considerably smaller, and few exceed 150 to 250 millimeters (6 to 10 inches) in length. This is because typical stream homes of fluvial cutthroat trout are cold, nutrient-poor headwaters where conditions for growth are less than optimal.

Nor do these fish generally live to a very old age. Most small-stream cutthroat trout mature early, age two or three, and seldom do they live beyond age four or five. The fluvial Alvord Basin trout, which can live to age seven or beyond, is an exception.

HUMAN INTERVENTION

From the beginning, native cutthroat trout were a source of food for the trappers, miners, settlers, and railroad builders. The Utah Lake population of Bonneville cutthroat trout was so important in maintaining the early settlers of the Salt Lake Valley that one Mormon legislator proposed that it be put in the historical record on a par with the gull. Gulls saved the Mormons' crops during an infestation of locusts by eating up the insects. Extensive commercial fisheries developed on Utah and Bear lakes, on Pyramid and Walker lakes, and on Lake Tahoe. Market fishermen also worked the Humboldt River and its tributaries, the upper Colorado and Arkansas drainages, and Henry's Lake, among others, to supply trout to the mining camps, hotels, and "sporting houses" that sprang up around new mineral strikes and settlements. Overfishing led in large part to the demise of the Utah Lake and Lake Tahoe populations (although in the latter case the introduction of nonnative salmonids certainly contributed), and to the near-collapse of the Bear Lake and Walker Lake populations.

It was not overfishing that did in the Lahontan cutthroat trout of Pyramid Lake, however; it was a 1906 water-diversion project. The construction of Derby Dam, the keystone of the brand-new federal Bureau of Reclamation's Newlands Project, cut off miles of spawning habitat on the Truckee River, and the diversion of water left habitat in the river below the dam desiccated during the key spawning and rearing periods. Lake Winnemucca, a large, shallow companion of Pyramid Lake, dried up completely, and a sand bar developed across the mouth of the Truckee River.

Less noticeable, but even more insidious because of its wider effect, was the diversion of water from spawning tributaries by individual agricultural and ranching users. This is one of the key reasons for the decline of the greenback cutthroat trout in Colorado, Lahontan cutthroat trout in California, and Yellowstone cutthroat trout in Montana and parts of Idaho. It also was another major contributor to the decline of the Bear Lake cutthroat trout in Utah and Idaho. All over the interior West, where water was so necessary for all forms of enterprise, diversions to supply that water hurt native cutthroat trout populations. In 1889, David Starr Jordan

The diversion of water for agricultural purposes can be devastating to trout populations. In dry years, irrigation demands can reduce flow to the extent that spawning isn't possible.

surveyed and reported on the streams of Colorado and Utah:

"In the progress of settlement of the valleys of Colorado the streams have become more and more largely used for irrigation. Below the mouths of the canyons dam after dam and ditch after ditch turn off the water. In summer the beds of even large rivers (as the Rio Grande) are left wholly dry, all the water being turned into these ditches."

In years of little precipitation, when land users divert water, fish either do not spawn, or they interrupt spawning and leave the stream as flows become inadequate. Or, even if the fish do spawn successfully, flows drop so much that the redds are desiccated and the eggs die. In Jordan's day, adult trout trying to find spawning habitat would themselves become diverted:

"Great numbers of trout, in many cases thousands of them, pass into these irrigation ditches and are left to perish in the fields. The destruction of trout by this agency is far greater than that due to all others combined, and it is going on in almost every irrigating ditch in Colorado."

Habitat degradation and destruction began with the mining booms. Jordan reported on this problem as well, saying that placer mining and stamp mills had rendered the waters of otherwise clear streams yellow or red with clay and had made the streams uninhabitable for trout. Many parts of the Grand (upper Colorado) and Arkansas rivers had been ruined as trout streams by mining operations

by the time Jordan saw them in 1889. In addition, every cycle of mining, and railroad building, too, required that the watersheds be logged to supply timbers for the mines, fuel for the ore-extraction mills, ties for the railroads, and lumber for the homes and towns that sprang up in their wake.

Much of the interior West is cattle country. Cattle like to come down to the water and stay, grazing the streamside vegetation until it is gone and trampling the banks, showing no inclination to leave until something or someone disturbs them and pushes them along. They are the major cause of streambank erosion and deterioration in areas where grazing is a principal land use. In the course of western settlement, much native cutthroat trout habitat was lost for this reason. It still is a major problem today.

Coastal cutthroat trout have been affected far less than the interior subspecies. Sea-run cutthroat are still widely distributed throughout their native range, although they too have declined in abundance in many areas. Anadromous populations probably have suffered from overexploitation by anglers. And environmental alteration and conscription of habitat for urbanization continue to contribute to coastal cutthroat trout declines. Logging and forest road-building in watersheds that support both anadromous and resident forms of coastal cutthroat trout have been intense in recent years. The Pacific Northwest also is experiencing an unprecedented explosion of new growth. Sea-run cutthroat trout favor low-lying, low-gradient reaches that, unfortunately, lie right in the path of this development.

Detrimental introductions. But as detrimental as these factors have been, the most devastating has been the widespread and indiscriminate introduction of nonnative trouts. Within about a decade after rainbow trout were introduced into Colorado, they had replaced native Colorado River cutthroat trout populations in all of the mainstem rivers and had hybridized many populations of native cutthroat trout in upper reaches. Rainbow trout were introduced into streams in the Bonneville Basin, the Humboldt River drainage, the Lahontan Basin, the Alvord Basin, and the historic ranges of the greenback and Rio Grande cutthroat trouts, whether or not there were native cutthroat trout already present in the receiving streams. The result was the same: The native cutthroat trout either died out or were hybridized. Brown trout and eastern brook trout, too, were introduced into many waters. Those introductions also caused the loss of native cutthroat trout in all but the most remote or marginal habitats.

Even when the introduced fish were cutthroat trout, no regard was given to the native forms already present. The attitude of the times was, "a cutthroat is a cutthroat."

Also contributing to declines in numbers of both sea-run and resident forms of coastal cutthroat trout are the efforts of management agencies to boost production of salmon and steelhead. One way they attempt to increase the numbers of these more popular species is to plant millions of steelhead and salmon fry in habitats formerly occupied only by coastal cutthroat trout or where coastal cutthroat trout were historically predominant. In doing so, they disrupt the niche separation so vital to coastal cutthroat trout survival.

To my knowledge, there have been no introductions of coastal cutthroat trout outside its historic range. However, locally adapted stocks have been transported to other places within the subspecies range. For example, a coastal Oregon stock was introduced into southwest Washington streams. That particular introduction was not successful.

The westslope cutthroat trout is another subspecies that has not been introduced outside its native range except in Washington, which has two westslope cutthroat broodstocks: the King's Lake stock and the Twin Lakes stock. Self-reproducing populations of these introduced fish have become established in several lakes. Those on the west side of the Cascade Range are in coastal cutthroat trout territory.

Several Lahontan cutthroat trout populations have become established outside the historic range. Between 1883 and 1938, millions of fry were obtained from eggs of adults trapped in Lake Tahoe spawning tributaries and were planted in lakes and streams throughout California. Most of these populations were themselves displaced by subsequent introductions of other trout species, but seven of them still exist in California streams outside the Lahontan Basin. Records from Nevada also allude to the large numbers of cutthroat trout that were hatched from Pyramid Lake stock, reared, and sent throughout Nevada and even Utah until the diminishing population in Pyramid Lake ended that activity. However, one of those old introductions, into Donner Creek, Utah, outside the Lahontan Basin, may have preserved the original Pyramid Lake gene pool.

In recent years, fishery managers have exploited the Lahontan cutthroat trout's ability to adapt to highly alkaline waters, and introduced this fish into other waters outside the native range. Many of these populations are maintained by stocking, but some have developed spawning migrations into tributary streams.

Because the native range of the Paiute cutthroat trout has always been small, and there now are so few viable fish within the native range, it wouldn't take much to extinguish this rare form. Neither would it take much in the way of introduction into new waters to increase the Paiute cutthroat's abundance—at least, that was the reasoning in the past. In 1946, Paiute trout collected from Corral Valley and Coyote Valley creeks in the Silver King watershed were stocked into Cottonwood Creek, Mono County, California. From there, and from the Silver King drainage, subsequent transplants were made into several southern California streams and lakes. Most of these populations were either displaced or hybridized, but two of the transplanted populations have apparently survived in pure form in the North Fork of Cottonwood Creek, Mono County, and Stairway Creek, Madera County, California.

It is difficult to define the extent to which the Yellowstone cutthroat trout exists outside its historic range. In the period between 1899 and 1957, more than 800 million eggs and fry were shipped from Yellowstone National Park. In addition, several egg-taking and shipping stations operated outside the park. Yellowstone cutthroats went to more than half of the fifty United States, to most of the Canadian provinces, and to several foreign countries.

Most of these Yellowstone cutthroat introductions were failures. The vast majority of the introduced fish were from the highly specialized lacustrine Yellowstone Lake stock, which proved to have an intrinsic lack of adaptability in new habitats. Transplants that did "take" occurred when the trout were stocked into small lakes that were formerly fishless. But enough successes did occur throughout the western states to have a profound adverse effect on local subspecies of cutthroat trout that existed in waters receiving transplants of the alien subspecies. Hybridization with Yellowstone cutthroat trout has been blamed for the demise of many westslope cutthroat trout populations, and for the loss of genetic integrity of other rarer subspecies. Populations of Yellowstone cutthroat trout have been established, outside the native range, in Montana, Wyoming, Idaho, Nevada, Utah, Oregon, Colorado, Arkansas, and perhaps some other states as well, and also in British Columbia, Alberta, and Quebec.

Unlike the highly lake-specialized Yellowstone Lake *bouvieri*, the evolutionary programming of the fine-spotted Snake River cutthroat trout is influenced by its historical coexistence with a variety of fishes in a big river environment. The result is a trout with a wide range of adaptive responses that allows for successful introduction into just about all environments except small streams. Consequently, this trout too has been propagated in hatcheries and widely distributed outside its original range.

Three genetically pure populations of Bonneville cutthroat trout occur just outside the Bonneville Basin in Nevada, in tiny, intermittent headwater streams on the backside of the range that forms the western rim of the basin. Some of the stocking that led to these populations were coffee-can transplants and took place many years ago. Other transplants were for the purpose of preserving remnant populations of this rare subspecies.

Amended ways. The cumulative effect of these factors—overfishing, habitat degradation, indiscriminate stocking—reduced the interior forms of cutthroat trout from a condition of abundance to virtual extinction in little more than one hundred years. Behnke once estimated that at least 99 percent of the original populations of the interior subspecies of cutthroat trout have been lost since the wagon trains rolled west. The greenback and Bonneville cutthroat trouts actually were believed to be extinct until the small, remnant populations were discovered in isolated drainages in remote parts of their range. Numbers were so low that when the U.S. Endangered Species Act of 1973 was passed, ten of the interior cutthroat trout subspecies were proposed for listing. Only three of them actually were listed: Lahontan—listed as endangered, reduced to threatened in 1975; Paiute—listed as endangered, reduced to threatened in 1975; and greenback—listed as endangered, reduced to threatened in 1978.

Several of the western states passed endangered species legislation of their own and have listed six additional cutthroat subspecies as threatened or as species of special concern because of low numbers: westslope cutthroat—species of special concern in Montana and Idaho; Yellowstone cutthroat—species of special concern in Montana and Idaho; fine-spotted Snake River cutthroat—species of special concern in Idaho; Bonneville cutthroat—threatened in Utah, species of special concern in Idaho, Nevada, and Wyoming; Colorado River cutthroat—threatened in Utah, species of special concern in Colorado and Wyoming; and Rio Grande cutthroat—species of special concern in Colorado and New Mexico.

Plans for recovery. After years of relative indifference, management agencies have at last begun to show new interest in the preservation, protection, and perpetuation of wild native trouts. At the federal level, listing as an endangered or threatened species requires that the U.S. Fish and Wildlife Service prepare a comprehensive recovery plan. But beyond that, federal land management agencies have mandates to protect and preserve unique forms in areas under their jurisdiction. The native cutthroat trout has been made an indicator species for the health of aquatic habitat in several national forests, notably the Carson and Santa Fe national forests in New Mexico and the Humboldt National Forest in Nevada. In addition, the Forest Service, the BLM, and now the Bureau of Reclamation have signed agreements with Trout Unlimited, a nationwide organization of trout anglers and conservationists, to provide for habitat improvements that should benefit wild native cutthroat trouts.

At the state level, several western states (Washington, Oregon, California, Utah, Nevada, Idaho, and Montana are examples) have adopted wild fish management policies which give special consideration to native forms. In addition, states having their own endangered species legislation have written management plans directed toward recovery of cutthroat trout subspecies recognized as threatened or as species of special concern in those states.

Because much cutthroat habitat has been irretrievably lost, and because so many quality populations of introduced trouts have been established, it seems to me unlikely that wild cutthroat trout abundance can ever approach historic levels. However, if the plans for preserving, protecting, and perpetuating the native cutthroat trout subspecies can be brought to fruition, these fishes should remain a permanent part of our heritage.

– Pat Trotter

Dolly Varden char

Salvelinus malma

Dolly Varden char, *Salvelinus malma*, also sometimes called Dolly Varden trout, live in some of the most beautiful waters in the world. Imagine a long, winding fjord bordered by snowcapped mountains and cliffs. Waterfalls cascade to the edge of the salt water. A stream teeming with Pacific salmon snakes its way from the head of the fjord up the valley through ancient forests of Sitka spruce and western hemlock. These are environs typical of the Dolly Varden char.

As one walks along these streams, schools of Dolly Varden seem to slowly materialize, for they are well camouflaged and almost motionless. Occasionally the observer may see an individual fish dart out of the school to grab something. Each sizable pool has a school of about fifty to a hundred char, most of which seem to be waiting patiently for something to happen. Some wait for Nature to signal the onset of spawning, which begins one to three months after they enter the stream. Others, for no apparent reason, leave that stream for the ocean; a few miles down the coast, they enter another stream. In the riffles between the pools, salmon already are spawning, and each pair seems to have a few Dolly Varden in close attendance. These char wait for the numerous salmon eggs that are knocked out of the gravel during the salmons' nest-building activities and gorge themselves on the nutritious delicacies.

In the side channels, beneath undercut banks, quiet shallow areas, and side tributaries of the stream small Dolly Varden, up to three years old, ranging in length to 13 centimeters (from only a little over an inch to almost 5 inches), are visible, the progeny of Dolly Varden that have previously spawned in the stream. Most of these fry and fingerlings occupy territories and some, the despots, viciously defend their territories from other Dolly Varden and from other species such as coho salmon.

Dolly Varden char occupy most of the available habitats. Such a variety exists in size and behavior that the complexity of their natural history becomes more apparent. Few other species of fish have been more maligned and misunderstood. People once killed them by the millions, considering them serious predators of salmon eggs and young. The results of numerous scientific studies finally exonerated them, but not until the 1970s did we begin to uncover a natural history of the species that has proven not only fascinating but also unique in the world of trout and char.

CLASSIFICATION

The classification of the Dolly Varden char has been a continuing source of disagreement among ichthyologists. It did not start off well. In 1792 Johann Walbaum described the Dolly Varden and named it *Salmo malma*. However, according to Behnke, his description was not original nor was it based on the examination of specimens. Rather, Walbaum seems to have based his description on the

work of George Wilhelm Steller, who wrote two large volumes on the fishes of Kamchatka, USSR.

Today one has to use special care when looking in the literature for information on Dolly Varden. Confusion in the references has been created by the classification of a new species, bull trout, *Salvelinus confluentus*, by Cavender in 1978 and a reworking by Morrow in 1980 of the classification of Dolly Varden in Alaska that provided a more clear separation from Arctic char, *Salvelinus alpinus*. Thus, much of the literature that discusses the Dolly Varden in British Columbia, Washington, Idaho, Oregon, and California actually may refer to the bull trout, especially when the material concerns the large char that live in lakes within British Columbia and the continental United States. And much of the literature that discusses Arctic char in Alaska actually may refer to the Dolly Varden, especially when the char being discussed are anadromous, or sea-run. Based on present nomenclature, no anadromous Arctic char exist in Alaska.

Field identification of Arctic char and Dolly Varden is difficult for most people because the characteristics used to identify them are internal and include the number of gill rakers, vertebrae, and pyloric caeca. Thus the Alaska Department of Fish and Game refers to the fish as Arctic char/Dolly Varden when it issues catch information. Some ichthyologists still believe that Dolly Varden and Arctic char should be one species, although the evidence does seem to support the separation. The classification of Dolly Varden will probably never be universally accepted.

The origin of the common name, Dolly Varden, however, is without controversy. The fish was named by a landlady at the Upper Soda Springs Hotel on the McCloud River in California. Upon seeing the fish, she said it looked like a regular Dolly Varden, referring to the character of the same name, who wore a pink spotted dress and hat in the Charles Dickens novel *Barnaby Rudge*. The scientist who received the specimen reportedly said, "That's a good name; call it Dolly Varden." That the fish named actually was a bull trout, according to Behnke, illustrates the confusion in differentiating these very similar species.

DESCRIPTION

The appearance of the beautiful Dolly Varden depends on maturity and on the water in which they live. Young freshwater residents have about eight to twelve wide, dark oval blotches, or parr marks, on each side, which contrast with the mottled olive-brown color of their bodies. Their sides and backs are sprinkled with small, red spots, their fins are dusky, and their bellies white. As they become older, these freshwater residents often darken.

The young of sea-run Dolly Varden, before they go to sea, resemble the freshwater residents except that they look more streamlined. Those that live in glacial rivers may be

silvery with only a hint of parr marks. During their first migration to sea and thereafter until maturity, they look silvery overall with olive-green to brown on the dorsal surface and numerous red to orange spots on their sides. These spots may be faint until maturity when they become quite vivid.

At maturity the lower body of the males turns brilliant red, and their lower fins become reddish black with white along the leading edges. Males exhibit more brilliant and more intense breeding colors than do females. Males develop a kype, which hooks upward and fits into a groove that develops in the upper jaw. Females also develop a kype, but it is considerably less pronounced.

DISTRIBUTION

The Dolly Varden char is widely distributed in western North America and is particularly abundant in Alaska. Its range extends from the Arctic coast of Alaska and western Canada south into Washington. Some of the eastern records probably refer to the bull trout; hence the eastern extent of its range is vague.

According to Behnke, as presently understood its range consists of two well-marked geographical groups. In North America, the southern Dolly Varden is known from Puget Sound drainages along the Pacific coast to the Alaskan Peninsula. The northern subspecies extends from the Alaskan Peninsula to the Mackenzie River.

In the Far East, the same northern form occurs from Kamchatka to the Chukokst Peninsula. The southern form occurs south of the Amur River on the mainland to Korea and on Sakhalin and Hokkaido islands.

Most Dolly Varden are native throughout their range. Apparently no hatchery fish have been stocked, and only occasionally have Dolly Varden been transplanted from one freshwater system to another. Usually transplants have been on a small scale: a handful of fish moved by local residents to a barren lake. The Alaska Department of Fish and Game recently tried to rear the young of sea-run Dolly Varden on an experimental basis. Their efforts were only partially successful, however, probably because of the difficulty of working with the species and the lack of strong commitment from the agency.

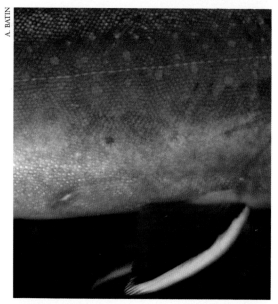

A spawning Dolly Varden has a green back with bright red spots and a reddish belly. The edges of the fins are a brilliant white; the balance is rusty red.

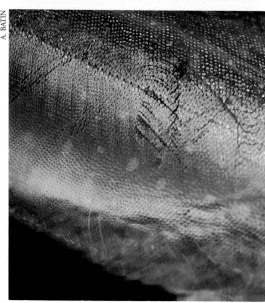

The spots on a sea-run fish are so faint that they can easily be overlooked.

Habitat

Dolly Varden have adapted to a variety of habitats: lakes of all sizes with and without access to the sea, tiny, isolated ponds, large rivers, streams, sections of water both above and below barriers to anadromous fish, even intermittent rivulets. Glacial rivers and lakes in Alaska harbor Dolly Varden from September to May. In salt water some are present nearly all year round, though populations are highest during late spring and early summer before they begin to enter streams. They inhabit both offshore and inshore saltwater areas but prefer the latter.

Life history

Most Dolly Varden that live their entire lives in streams, and small lakes and ponds, are small and seldom grow longer than 26 centimeters (10 inches). Those that inhabit the larger lakes often grow to a foot or more but still do not reach a size that can be discussed in pounds, with one exception: the few lakes in southeast Alaska that contain kokanee (small landlocked sockeye salmon) may produce Dolly Varden that weigh up to 4 kilograms (9 pounds). These occasional lunkers probably are feeding on the kokanee. Also, they seem to live longer, up to nineteen years, whereas most other Dolly Varden do not live longer than eight to ten years.

Most sea-run Dolly Varden grow no larger than 38 to 56 centimeters (15 to 22 inches) in length and 0.5 to 1.4 kilograms (1 to 3 pounds) in weight. Occasional large fish weighing more than 5 kilograms (10 pounds) are hauled from the large mainland rivers of Alaska, such as the Taku River near Juneau and the Wulik River near the Eskimo village of Kivulina in northwestern Alaska. The largest Dolly Varden char on record in Alaska was caught in the Wulik River. It weighed 7.9 kilograms (17.5 pounds).

We know more about the anadromous Dolly Varden char than about those fish that spend their entire lives in lakes, ponds, rivers, and streams. Only a few studies have ever been made of freshwater-resident Dolly Varden, and none of them examined the complete natural history. The sea-run fish, on the other hand, have received a considerable amount of attention over the years, especially in Alaska, because they are more sought after

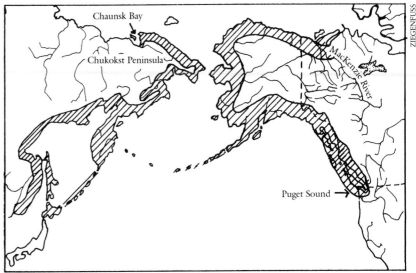

by sport fishermen. The results of these studies have revealed one of the most unusual patterns of life history for any sea-going fish.

In most southern coastal areas of Alaska, thousands of Dolly Varden migrate from the sea into lakes to spend the winter. Most of these fish come from the numerous streams of small to medium size that intersect Alaska's shoreline. They are the offspring of fish that previously spawned in these streams. After living for three to four years in the stream in which they were hatched, they make their first trip to the sea. They migrate along the shoreline during this first summer at sea, entering several streams until they find one with a lake. Although they migrate to sea each spring from their chosen lake, they will

Most Dolly Varden char are native throughout the range they now occupy. Overharvesting has caused severe declines in Dolly Varden populations in some areas, and environmental degradation has also taken its toll. These fish congregate for overwintering, and frequently move from one freshwater system to another; they may appear more abundant than they actually are.

Eva Lake on Baranof Island is prime wintering habitat for Dolly Varden.

C. BATIN

GROST

Anadromous Dolly Varden grow large at sea before returning to their natal streams to spawn.

not return to their natal stream until they reach maturity, up to three years later.

Up to 70 percent of the Dolly Varden entering each lake consist of these small fish (18 to 23 centimeters [7 to 9 inches]) coming from other streams. The rest of the run are fish that originated from that lake system, immature fish on their second or third annual trip from the sea, and fish that spawned in other streams along the coast. In fact, these lakes attract Dolly Varden that originated from streams as far as 161 kilometers (100 miles) away.

Most southern coastal streams in Alaska serve as spawning grounds for adults and as early rearing habitat for their young. Lakes and some large rivers in southern Alaska pro-

vide overwintering areas for Dolly Varden after migration, but most rivers and streams without access to lakes are not used as overwintering habitat, for reasons we do not know yet.

Dolly Varden benefit greatly by overwintering in lakes. Because of ice cover there are few, if any, predators. Fresh water in southern Alaska may be several degrees cooler than the sea in winter, so fish need fewer calories and less food. And they may live longer because they do not need to burn energy to avoid predators, search for food, or swim to maintain themselves in currents as they do in streams or in the ocean. One study I did in 1965 at Eva Lake on Baranof Island in southeastern Alaska showed that about 93 percent of the nearly 100,000 Dolly Varden that entered this lake left the following spring, a figure that indicates an amazing rate of overwinter survival.

At maturity the Dolly Varden leave lakes in the spring. They migrate to sea, then swim to their home streams to spawn in late fall without entering other streams as younger Dolly Varden do. After spawning they return to sea and migrate to a lake for the winter. Our studies also showed that mature Dolly Varden have strong homing tendencies, returning each year to spawn in the system from which they originated.

The sea-run Dolly Varden that live in the most northerly Arctic areas of Alaska and western Canada must cope with special conditions. Most parts of Arctic rivers freeze solid in the winter and inhabitable lakes with access to the sea are few, so sites for spawning and overwintering are, probably without exception, associated with major springs in the larger rivers. Spawning, rearing, and overwintering sites are the same for Dolly Varden in the northern Arctic, so these char do not need to move from one freshwater system to another. Nevertheless some tagged non-spawning char in the Arctic have been found to migrate into other systems, though in nowhere near the numbers that move about in the other coastal areas of Alaska.

The blood of Dolly Varden in the Arctic areas of Alaska would probably freeze if the fish remained at sea during the winter because seawater temperatures fall below the freezing point of their blood. Most marine fish living in the Arctic are thought to have antifreeze compounds in their blood. However, Dolly Varden probably do not, so to survive they must either enter fresh water for the winter or, like the progeny from Pacific salmon that spawn in Arctic rivers, migrate hundreds of miles to warmer ocean areas. Dolly Varden choose the shorter route and return to freshwater rivers where they seek out the warmer, ice-free spring areas.

According to DeCicco, the movements of Dolly Varden in northwestern Alaska also are complex. Two spawning groups—summer and fall—exist. They differ in timing and location of spawning and in the selection of areas they use for overwintering. In general, Dolly Varden appear to home for their natal

streams to spawn. In rivers where the species overwinters, different stocks coexist.

In southern Alaska, Dolly Varden spawn every year until they die. However, in the Arctic, they seem to spawn only every other year, because they need more than one season to recover. This is probably an adaptation to the colder temperatures and lower food supplies. In addition, many Arctic Dolly Varden, especially spawners, do not migrate to sea every year.

In the southern coastal areas of Alaska and in British Columbia, Dolly Varden often inhabit lakes that also contain cutthroat trout, but the two species live in different parts of the lake and feed on different foods. Andrusak and Northcote reported in 1971 that the cutthroat trout occupied, and fed near, the lake surface along the shorelines, whereas the Dolly Varden occupied the deeper areas near the bottom of the lake and fed mostly on benthic, or bottom-dwelling, organisms. In these multi-species lakes, such segregation seems to allow an underharvest of Dolly Varden by anglers, who often fish closer to the surface by spin casting or trolling. Sea-run Dolly Varden overwintering in lakes usually bunch in only one or two select areas.

HUMAN INTERVENTION

Between 1921 and 1940, the U.S. Bureau of Fisheries administered a bounty program on Alaskan Dolly Varden because they were thought to be serious predators on salmon eggs and young. From 2½ to 5 cents was paid

Most mature Dolly Varden spawn every year. Those in the Arctic spawn every other year.

ANDERSON

for each tail, and the records indicated that more than six million Dolly Varden were killed.

However, in 1939, almost twenty years after the bounty program was initiated, biologists were called in to investigate its effectiveness. What they found showed it to be one of the greatest boondoggles in the history of Alaska fisheries. They discovered that many—and in some instances most—of the tails being turned in for bounty were from rainbow trout and salmon, the very species the Bureau of Fisheries was trying to save. For instance, in the office of the U.S. Bureau of Fisheries in Yakutat, Alaska, biologists examined 20,000 tails, all of which were supposedly Dolly Varden. The examination showed that only 2,040 of these tails were from Dolly Varden; 3,760 were from rainbows, 14,200 from coho salmon. In Bristol Bay even the magnificent trophy rainbows of the Newhalen and Naknek rivers were being killed and discarded after their tails were cut off for a bounty of 2½ cents each.

Numerous studies have been done since the early 1940s to determine whether or not Dolly Varden are serious predators of salmon eggs and young. These studies have shown not only that they were not harming salmon populations but also that in fact Dolly Varden may actually benefit salmon, because the char eat drifting salmon eggs that would not have survived. These eggs, were they not eliminated, would eventually die and become hosts for fungi, which could infect the live eggs and alevins in the gravel. Another possible benefit is that Dolly Varden in lakes feed heavily on freshwater snails, which are intermediate hosts of a parasite that infects the eyes of coho and sockeye salmon young and eventually causes blindness. Hence the chars' feeding on these snails may help reduce this parasite. Even the competition for space that seems to occur with Dolly Varden and more serious predators of salmon young, such as cutthroat trout, may play a role in reducing overall predation of salmon young by all species of fish.

Although its effects have not been well studied, environmental degradation no doubt has reduced the numbers of Dolly Varden. Clear-cut logging, stream channelization, urban development, and placer min-

ing, in which the gravel is dredged from an open pit and washed to settle out the minerals, all have caused obvious damage to streams where Dolly Varden live.

Overharvest by sport fishermen has caused severe declines of Dolly Varden in some areas of Alaska. In the Juneau area, for example, over a period of only eight years, the catch rate dropped from more than 4 char per angler hour to less than 0.2 char per angler hour. This situation prompted the Alaskan Board of Fisheries to close several waters around Juneau to sport fishing for Dolly Varden and, where open, to reduce the daily bag limit to two fish.

A few subsistence fisheries of Dolly Varden exist in Alaska. The estimated subsistence catches by Eskimos from the village of Kivalina have numbered from 7,000 to 49,000 Dolly Varden char annually from the Wulik River in western Alaska, for instance, and some biologists are concerned about the ability of Dolly Varden to withstand this level of harvest.

Dolly Varden are also taken incidentally in commercial fisheries for other fish. Documentation exists suggesting that in one year, for example, more than 3,000 mature Dolly Varden were taken in the commercial salmon fishery near Kotzebue in western Alaska. The effects of such fisheries on Dolly Varden populations have not been studied, and usually the numbers taken are not reported.

Dolly Varden are not nearly as abundant as most people believe. Their behavior of moving from one freshwater system to another and concentrating in lakes and rivers for the winter makes them appear much more numerous than they really are. Thus they can be easily overharvested. In addition, populations in a vast area could be decimated by harming one key wintering lake or river.

In summary, certain types of habitat alteration and harvest may be extremely detrimental to the sea-run Dolly Varden populations. It is especially important that we protect the small tributary streams that juvenile char use before they leave streams and lakes as smolt; spring-fed areas in the Arctic rivers that juveniles and overwintering adults use; and the lakes and rivers that different populations use as overwintering areas.

—*Robert H. Armstrong*

Gathering data

The Alaska Department of Fish and Game began studying the natural history of Dolly Varden char in 1963. In early March of that year, two of my colleagues and I, with a huge amount of lumber and provisions, were dropped off by boat during a snowstorm in a remote bay on Baranof Island in southeastern Alaska. We built a fish weir, a research station, and living quarters there and in the wilds of Admiralty Island. Those two locations became our homes and bases of operations for the next ten years.

For many, many nonstop days and nights, we dip-netted thousands of Dolly Varden from weir traps to try to determine the characteristics of the population we were studying. We anesthetized them and measured their length to determine migration differences by size. We clipped their fins and tagged them to identify them in future sightings. We took a representative sample of them each day and examined their stomach contents to determine what they had eaten. We measured their ovaries and their testes to determine the degree of maturity and removed their otoliths for age analysis.

We also sampled the Dolly Varden at sea and in the lake to determine their feeding habits and distribution. Numerous surveys and samples were taken of young fish to determine the rearing habitat for each age class. We walked streams every day, usually past several brown bear, to observe the behavior of spawning Dolly Varden.

When a logging camp 30 miles from our first research system reported that most of the Dolly Varden in their local streams were missing a fin or had a yellow tag, we realized that "our" Dolly Varden were migrating significant distances between freshwater systems. So over the next several years we put weirs and temporary research stations on four other streams.

Throughout our ten-year study, we fin-clipped and measured more than 300,000 adult and subadult char, tagged about 50,000 of them, and sampled 7,000 for age, maturity, and stomach content before we were able to piece together the hows and whys of their strange migrations among so many different streams.

Our emotions throughout this study ranged to the extremes. We were euphoric when our research plans worked and when we discovered something that had not been known before. We were horrified when a co-worker was mauled by a brown bear, and devastated when two colleagues, working on Dolly Varden in the Arctic, disappeared without a trace.

Typical of many research projects, this one involved myriad details, mind-dulling routine, physical discomfort, even tragedy. Ultimately, when we were called upon to present our results at the first international symposium on char, it also brought the satisfaction of a job well done.

—Robert H. Armstrong

Gila trout

Oncorhynchus gilae

Nature adorned the tiny Gila trout of the Southwest with an extravagant iridescence that contrasts mightily with the severity of its environment. Surviving in headwaters sometimes only a few inches deep, it fell in 1967 among the endangered species listed by the U.S. Department of the Interior. Recovery to *threatened* status seemed imminent until the summer of 1989 when a drought and wildfire nearly dashed hopes of recovery and reminded governmental planning teams that even our best efforts cannot control natural events.

CLASSIFICATION

In 1950 Miller first analyzed and identified the Gila trout, *Salmo gilae*, taken from Main Diamond Creek in the Gila National Forest of New Mexico. Subsequently, Gila trout were discovered in South Diamond, McKenna, Iron, and Spruce creeks in the Gila National Forest. Each of these populations is distinct because of physical isolation by barrier falls and dry streambeds, yet the populations of Main Diamond, McKenna, and Iron creeks do resemble one another. The Gila trout of South Diamond Creek, though, has significantly more spotting on its body, and the Spruce Creek population is not yet clearly defined taxonomically; that is, it resembles Apache trout in some characteristics.

In his description of Gila trout, Miller noted that it had characteristics of two of the major evolutionary lines of western trouts: cutthroat, *Oncorhynchus clarki*, and rainbow, *O. mykiss*. He ultimately suggested that the Gila trout derived from the rainbow rather than the cutthroat. Ongoing research at Arizona State University and analyses in the mid-1980s to determine genetic relationships substantiate that the Gila trout is of rainbow trout ancestry.

Based on osteological studies in 1988, this species of Pacific trout is now in the same genus as the salmons, *Oncorhynchus*, and its official scientific designation is *Oncorhynchus gilae*.

The Gila trout and the Apache trout, *O. apache*, are more closely related to each other than to other *Oncorhynchus* species in western North America. Genetic differences between these two native southwestern trouts are even less than differences between some subspecies of cutthroat trout of the western United States. This similarity has led Behnke to suggest they eventually may be demonstrated to be subspecies of Gila trout, *O. gilae gilae* and *O. gilae apache*, rather than full species.

DESCRIPTION

Compared with the Apache trout, the Gila trout typically is more iridescent gold. This color blends laterally to dark shades of copper on the opercula, or gill covers. Spots, though larger and more numerous than on the Apache trout, are small and diffuse. They reach their extreme in the South Diamond Creek population. They generally are confined to the areas above the lateral line

Joseph R. Tomelleri
© '87

along the sides and increase in size from the lateral line up across the back. On the sides they are irregularly shaped.

Scattered spotting dots the fins, but the adipose fin is typically well spotted with larger spots. Dorsal, pelvic, and anal fins have a white to yellowish tip. Adults have a faint, salmon-pink lateral band often with yellow and orange streaks.

The Gila trout has the characteristic golden or yellowish "cutthroat" mark on the lower jaw. Parr marks are obvious on small adults, but on larger fish they may be faint or may disappear entirely. Turner reported rearing specimens in the laboratory to 44 centimeters (17 inches) before parr marks disappeared completely.

DISTRIBUTION

Gila trout were collected in 1888 and 1889 from Oak Creek, Arizona, a tributary of the Verde River. Research by Regan indicates that in 1896 Gila trout also had extended from extremely cold headwater habitats downstream to the town of Cliff, New Mexico, and had been so abundant that fishermen could catch one a minute almost effortlessly in Willow and Gilita creeks, tributaries of the Gila River.

Miller included native trout populations of the White Mountains in Arizona. Based on interviews with people who had lived in the area for years, he concluded that Gila trout inhabited all tributaries of the Gila River in New Mexico from the extreme headwaters

downstream to the mouth of the box canyon near Cliff, New Mexico.

Gila trout in the San Francisco River in New Mexico purportedly were introduced by miners in 1905. But the presence and uniqueness of the Spruce Creek population suggest that instead it may be indigenous to this drainage. The presence of Gila trout in Eagle Creek in Arizona, the next major drainage west of the San Francisco, is further evidence for the natural occurrence of the species in the San Francisco drainage.

However, Chitty Creek, a tributary of Eagle Creek, supports a remnant population of trout that, based on the most recent genetic analyses, are rainbow trout. The population of trout in Sycamore Creek, a tributary

Gila trout are now extinct over much of their native range. Populations are currently limited to the upper portions of the Gila River headwaters in New Mexico.

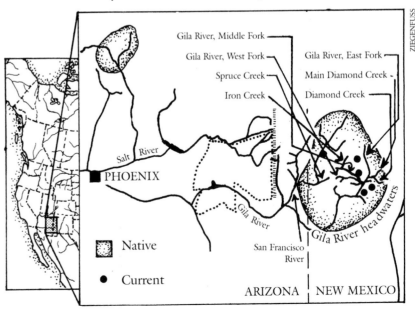

of the Agua Fria River in the Prescott National Forest of Arizona, is either a Gila-rainbow hybrid or an isolated population of rainbows. These two situations are evidence of stocking programs and inadvertent transplant of fish by well-meaning individuals.

But despite these notations, the original distribution of the Gila trout is not well defined because of the lack of collections before 1950. Further complicating the delineation is the species' close relationship to the Apache trout.

Gila trout have been introduced into McKnight Creek, Sheep Corral Creek, the East Fork of Mogollon Creek, and Little Dry and Big Dry creeks in New Mexico, and in Gap Creek, Arizona.

In the late 1960s almost 60 percent of the total population of Gila trout lived in Main Diamond Creek, the type locality. By the mid-1980s, an introduced population in McKnight Creek in the headwaters of the Mimbres River was the second largest, consisting of about 3,000 fish. At the other extreme, introduced populations in Gap Creek, Arizona, and Sheep Corral Canyon, New Mexico, contain fewer than one hundred adults.

HABITAT

Waterfalls or dry streambeds, both natural barriers, now restrict the Gila trout to five extreme headwater streams. Although isolation has prevented hybridization with rainbow trout in these five streams, it has caused marked changes in the characteristics of the respective populations. The most divergent group, in both genetic makeup and appearance, are the Gila trout in Spruce Creek. Indeed, this population even shares character traits with the Apache trout.

Drought and flooding control the abundance and age structure of the precarious Gila trout populations, but wildfire on the watersheds of their streams has always been a special concern. A "hot" wildfire can immediately raise the temperature of the water, causing thermal stress and killing the trout. In the long term, increased flooding can cause extensive stream morphological changes and increased turbidity of the water. In the summer of 1989, such a fire occurred

The Gila trout (right) is typically more golden than the Apache trout (below right). Its spots are small and numerous. The Gila-rainbow hybrid (bottom right) is less colorful and more heavily spotted than the pure Gila.

Physical characteristics of Apache, Gila, and rainbow trout

The Gila trout *(top photo)* is typically more gold in color than the Apache trout *(middle)*. The Gila x rainbow hybrid *(bottom)* is less colorful and more heavily spotted than the pure Gila. Although these color patterns are helpful clues, other physical traits provide the definitive information necessary to distinguish pure forms from hybrids, and from other species. These physical traits include ratios of snout and fin sizes to total body length, and counts of scales, vertebral segments, and the pyloric caeca of the intestines.

The Gila and the Apache generally have larger fins in proportion to body size than their introduced competitor, the rainbow trout. Hybrid forms have morphometric and meristic profiles that differ from the range of means typical for pure forms.

Morphometric character	Gila trout Range of means	Rainbow trout Range of means	Apache trout Range of means
Snout length	71–72	56–70	71–76
Dorsal fin, base length	139–142	124–159	153–187
Dorsal fin, depressed length	235–243	218–255	265–267
Adipose fin, depressed length	110–122	65–95	113–117
Anal fin, base length	112–113	104–118	122–124
Anal fin, depressed length	164–180	149–172	181–183
Meristic character			
Scales above lateral line	31–34	22–29	34–36
Vertebral segments	59–62	59–62	59–60
Pyloric caeca	31–36	55–62	26–33

over 10,000 acres in the Main and South Diamond Creek watersheds. Because of concern for the immediate effects of the fire, 566 Gila trout were removed and later reintroduced. Then rains and subsequent flooding almost decimated the population because there was little vegetation on the watershed to hold back the water. Comparing the situation on the Diamond Creek watershed with the long-term, continuing effects of a similar fire on the headwaters of McKnight Creek in 1950, we can expect the Gila trout in Main Diamond Creek to remain in jeopardy for several decades until the vegetation grows back. The effects of increased frequency and duration of floods will prevent populations from returning to prefire levels.

Water depth correlates with the size of the fish and, to a lesser extent, to their numbers and biomass, which suggests that large Gila trout prefer pools, if the pools have satisfactory cover and water quality. One study showed that pools deeper than 50 centimeters (20 inches) support fish 20 centimeters (8 inches) or more in size 60 percent of the time. The Gila trout requires compara-

tively less space than do introduced salmonids, such as rainbow and brown trout, and it appears to be an effective steward of space in its small headwater environments. Recent analyses and comparisons by Platts suggest that the Gila trout averages a higher biomass than do other western trout species.

Studies that included marking and recapturing Gila trout show that the fish moved, on the average, less than 100 meters (328 feet) over a period of eight months. Compared with other trout, they are homebodies. When Gila trout move, they usually go downstream. They are not the jumpers that many anadromous trout are, so that few of those that move upstream can surmount log stream-improvement structures more than half a meter tall. In South Diamond Creek, Gila trout oriented toward a central, permanent-water reach, staying in it or living nearby so they could move there during a drought. During the drought in the summer of 1989, all of South Diamond Creek below Burnt Canyon dried up, and many of the trout died.

Hanson reported that Main Diamond

Hybridization with other species, both native and introduced, and harsh environmental conditions leave the future of the Gila trout in doubt.

ROSTON

Creek became intermittent several times in the 1960s and again in 1971. In 1969 and 1970, streamflow in Main Diamond Creek in November dropped to one-fourth the volume that occurred in May. The trout survived in pools, many of these created by artificial log structures.

LIFE HISTORY

Regan was the first to evaluate the ecology of the Gila trout in Main Diamond Creek, where the fish was originally described. In 1963, the population in this creek had been estimated at 4,300 fish. A decade later, estimates of 3,000 to 4,000 were reported. Specimens were ages one to six, and no fish collected were longer than 22 centimeters (9 inches).

Regan found that fecundity is extremely low in the adults found in small headwater streams, compared with that of rainbow and cutthroat. Adult females, typically 12.5 to 22.5 centimeters (4.9 to 8.8 inches) long, produce only about 70 to 300 eggs each.

The interaction of receding water flow and rising water temperature induces spawning, though the temperature determines more when spawning will occur. Both Regan and Hanson reported that Gila trout in Main Diamond Creek spawn from April through June. In 1982 Rinne recorded spawning habitat and behavior in Main and South Diamond creeks and McKnight Creek.

Fish begin building their redds in 6 to 15 centimeters (a mere 2 to 6 inches) of water when the temperature reaches 8°C (46.6°F) (April). They generally construct them near the bank and within 5 meters (16.4 feet) of instream or streambank cover. Gravel 0.2 to 3.8 centimeters (0.8 to 1.5 inches) in diameter makes up the spawning substrate. Spawning begins earlier in the season in McKnight Creek, which is at an elevation of about 2,100 meters (6,900 feet), and later in Main and South Diamond creeks, which are at elevations of about 2,300 to 2,400 meters (7,500 to 7,900 feet).

In line with this seasonal sequence to higher altitudes, spawning commences at the downstream end of McKnight, where waters warm earlier to the required 8°C (46.6°F), and progresses upstream with time. Redds range in size from 0.3 to 2 square meters (3 to 18 square feet). Females produce about 1,300 eggs per kilogram (about 590 per pound) of body weight.

Spawning behavior is similar to that of other salmonids. A female and an attendant male hover over a redd while one male or more flank downstream. The female's digging attracts males from as far as 4.6 to 6 meters (15 to 20 feet) downstream. Most spawning activity occurs between 1 and 4 P.M. and almost never before 11 A.M.

The condition of Gila trout in Main Diamond Creek drops after spawning and during summer low-flow periods, but it usually improves by autumn following an increased summer food base of aquatic macroinvertebrates. In autumn fish congregate in pools, and competition for space and food limits the size of the population. Fish in the poorest condition die because of direct abuse by larger Gila trout and probably because they can't compete for the available food.

Fry emerge from the gravel in eight to ten weeks. (Although no research has been done on the length of time the eggs need to develop, it probably is similar to that of Apache trout: about thirty days.) Gila trout fry inhabit the riffles and apparently avoid the pools because of competition from and potential cannibalism by larger Gila trout. A pecking order from large to small fish has been observed during feeding and may explain the higher KTL of the larger fish. (KTL, also called condition factor, is a measure of weight per length and indicates the health of the fish.)

Laboratory experiments and field observations have demonstrated that Gila trout can tolerate waters up to 27°C (81°F) for about two hours. During droughts, they congregate at the heads of intermittent pools where cooler intragravel flow apparently sustains them through peak afternoon temperatures.

Analysis of internal parasites indicates a distinct, unique helminth (flatworm) fauna in this rare southwestern trout, which it tolerates well. Mammals and birds, such as the great blue heron, prey on Gila trout, and in many areas, it must compete for habitat with rainbow trout.

HUMAN INTERVENTION

Hybridization with rainbow trout, inter-

Flooding in Main Diamond Creek on the heels of a devastating wildfire severely cut the creek's trout population.

specific competition, and habitat degradation and loss have been major factors in the decline of the Gila trout in the Southwest, as they have for the Apache trout. Conservation agencies have adopted strict guidelines for stocking programs to reduce the likelihood of losing populations through hybridization and interspecific competition with nonnative trouts.

In 1970 the native suckers in McKnight Creek were killed out with fish toxicant and 307 Gila trout were transplanted from Main Diamond Creek. A severe drought in 1971 markedly reduced the population, so in 1972, 110 more fish were transplanted. The population grew, stabilizing in the 1980s at about 3,000 fish. But periodic, intense flooding has limited the number of Gila trout. In the most recent flood of 1988, more than 90 percent of the fish either died or were swept downstream by strong currents. Gila trout also were transplanted into Sheep Corral Creek in 1972 and into Gap Creek in 1974.

In the mid-1960s, the Gila National Forest and the New Mexico Game and Fish Department repaired more than one hundred log stream-improvement structures in Main Diamond Creek to enhance stream habitat. These structures generally do improve habitat for fish and aquatic macroinvertebrates. However, they may impede the movements of trouts in small, restricted headwater habitats. Such restriction could hurt the population if a flood were to occur, followed by a drought. The fish would move downstream with the higher water, then be unable to move back upstream as the stream dried.

Initial efforts to conserve the Gila trout were initiated by the New Mexico Department of Game and Fish, which in 1923 built a hatchery at a place called Jenks Cabin in the Gila Wilderness Area. Its sole purpose was to propagate this native trout. However, poor access and limited production of fish here as well as limited success in subsequent attempts by the Arizona Game and Fish Department indicated this species was not easily cultured. The New Mexico Department of Game and Fish closed Main Diamond Creek to fishing in 1958, and streams that support native Gila trout were not stocked.

A plan to save the Gila trout was developed in the mid-1970s, the main objective of which is to secure viable populations of all five genotypes in the wild. Studying the fish, keeping the numbers up, and increasing extant, pure populations have been the most important steps. The goal was reached in 1988, but the Main Diamond Creek loss in summer 1989 and the fact that the Iron Creek population has not been duplicated have caused the recovery team to recommend waiting at least one year before considering downlisting the species.

Another important goal of the recovery plan is to develop this rare trout to the extent that perhaps some day it can support a sport fishery, which will generate more interest and support for safeguarding the fish as well as provide more research potential. This step will be possible, however, only when the Gila trout has been dropped from *endangered* status and additional populations have been established.

—John N. Rinne

Golden trout

Oncorhynchus aguabonita

———————

*I*t seems appropriate that California's state fish should have descended from such royalty as the steelhead rainbow. From time immemorial, steelhead on their spawning journey have entered the Golden Gate from the Pacific Ocean and ascended the tributaries of the Sacramento and San Joaquin rivers that, before man's indiscretions, flowed unimpaired to the sea. It was many thousands of years ago, likely about the boundary of the Pleistocene and Holocene epochs, that the southernmost of these migrant populations, because of geologic changes, became isolated within the drainages of the Little Kern River, Golden Trout Creek, and the South Fork of the Kern River. Thus permanently separated from their parental stock, the two groups began their slow evolutionary journey to become the golden trout that we know today, their brilliant coloration reflecting warm hues of the decomposed granite and volcanic rock that predominate in the substrate of these stream systems.

CLASSIFICATION

The Civil War was still fresh in the memory of Colonel Sherman Stevens when he moved west and in 1873 built a sawmill in the upper reaches of Cottonwood Creek, California. It perplexed him, at the end of a hard day of hauling and milling the foxtail and lodgepole pine logs that supplied the lifeblood of the mines at Cerro Gordo, that the beautiful stream powering his mill could not also provide him and his crews with an occasional platter of trout. The usual austere fare had to be transported by pack train for more than 12 kilometers (20 miles), and up 1,500 meters (5,000 feet), from Lone Pine in the southern Owens Valley.

His quest for saw logs had taken him southwest over the low divide separating Cottonwood Creek from the small tributaries feeding the South Fork of the Kern River, where he marveled at the small, brilliantly colored trout that abounded there. It then became only a matter of time until, in the company of A. C. Stevens and Thomas George, Colonel Stevens journeyed to Mulkey Creek, where the Hockett Trail enters Mulkey Meadow, and caught thirteen trout with hook and line. This was in July 1876.

Mulkey Creek appears to have been effectively separated from the South Fork of the Kern River by major rock slides that preceded invasion of the area by fishes. Although these slides allow the passage of water through and beneath them, they serve as effective barriers to upstream migration by trout. Early records reveal that Mulkey Creek was planted with Volcano Creek fish at an unknown date before 1876. Similar transplants of other native Kern River trout species were taking place in other waters within and adjacent to the Kern River drainage at about this same time.

After a short journey (about 2.5 kilometers [4 miles]) over the Hockett Trail in a coffee pot, twelve of the fish caught in Mulkey

Creek (one died in transit) were planted about a mile above the sawmill. The fish found an abundance of food and an ideal habitat in barren Cottonwood Creek, and they thrived there. In 1879 Colonel Stevens and Judge A. C. Harvey of Lone Pine reported catching a string of 21-centimeter (8-inch) golden trout from Cottonwood Creek, one of the first of countless catches taken since the initial introduction.

In 1891 a small branch of Cottonwood Creek was diverted from its channel, and about a hundred fish were collected and taken upstream past barrier waterfalls about 4 kilometers (3 miles) to the Cottonwood Lakes. Only about fifty survived the journey, but they adapted quickly to their new home, and 5-pounders were soon reported.

The following year, ichthyologist and Stanford University president David Starr Jordan received from George T. Mills, fish commissioner of Nevada, three specimens of golden trout collected from the Cottonwood Creek Basin, probably from Cottonwood Creek below the lakes. Jordan described these fish under the appellation *aguabonita*, which means "pretty water." Largely because of the golden trout's brilliant coloration, Jordan initially thought that they may have been related to the Colorado River cutthroat trout. However, in 1894 he corrected his assessment and recognized *aguabonita* as a close relative of the rainbow trout. An appropriate common name for this fish is Volcano Creek golden trout, which refers to its site of origin.

Novelist Stewart Edward White was impressed by the vulnerability of the golden trout and, with perception unusual for the times, registered deep concern that they be adequately protected from extinction. "Well-meaning people used to laugh at the idea that the buffalo and wild pigeons would ever disappear. They are gone," White wrote in 1904 in *The Mountains*.

He told of two individuals who were known to have taken 600 golden trout in a day's angling. It may have been this same incident that prompted Jordan to comment in 1907 on trout hogs, ". . . the most vulgar of all beasts of prey . . . who caught six hundred in one afternoon, leaving four hundred and fifty lying on the bank. Two other idiots at the same time caught two hundred in an afternoon." Such indignance is refreshing, especially from an individual whose deeply ingrained background as an academic ichthyologist and conservationist obviously overcame the cautious reserve normally associated with university presidents!

White reported his findings to President Theodore Roosevelt, emphasizing his concern over the apparent ease with which the species could be rendered extinct. The president delegated the matter to the commissioner of fisheries, who directed that a study be undertaken to cover virtually all phases of golden trout life history and management. A key part of the investigation was to be devoted to a determination of measures necessary to assure preservation of the species. Bar-

THE SPECIES

ton Warren Evermann, assistant in charge of scientific inquiry for the U.S. Bureau of Fisheries, was appointed to conduct the study during the summer of 1904.

Evermann's survey party accumulated a vast fund of information on the fishery resources of the upper Kern River drainage, with major emphasis devoted to the golden trout. The proposed protection plan was based upon enlarging the boundaries of the Mount Whitney Military Reservation to include all major golden trout waters, including the headwaters of Cottonwood Creek, and closing this entire area to angling for a period of three years. It would then be opened to angling under a set of restrictive regulations including a size and number limit and a closure during the spawning season.

This report also recommended implementation of a fish cultural program as a means of stocking barren waters in the Kern River region and throughout the southern High Sierra. Many facets of Evermann's general plan were adopted and provided a sound basis for successful management of the golden trout for over half a century.

Evermann gave full species status to the Kern River rainbow trout described as a subspecies by Jordan in 1894, and discovered a new form of golden trout in the upper Kaweah River, transplanted there from Soda Spring Creek, a tributary of Little Kern River. Evermann honored Stewart Edward White in 1906 by naming the Little Kern golden trout *Salmo whitei*.

These beautiful paintings of the Volcano Creek golden trout (Oncorhynchus aguabonita aguabonita, top) and the Little Kern golden trout (O. a. whitei, right) show the vivid colors for which this species is known.

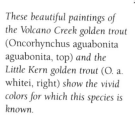

The Volcano Creek golden trout and Little Kern River golden trout are acknowledged to be closely related. Many fishery biologists consider them to be only subspecifically distinct. Furthermore, recent advances in systematic methodology have resolved that the Pacific salmon and trout are much more closely related to each other than either is to the Atlantic salmon, *Salmo salar*, and the brown trout, *Salmo trutta*. Morphologic, behavioral, genetic, and biogeographic data argue that native trout of western North America should be considered in the same genus as the Pacific salmon. Hence, the complete specific designations are *Oncorhynchus aguabonita aguabonita* for the Volcano Creek golden trout, originally described by Jordan in 1892, and *Oncorhynchus aguabonita whitei* for the Little Kern golden trout, based on Evermann's description in 1906.

DESCRIPTION

In 1903 White visited the Kern Plateau and in glowing terms wrote of the golden trout: "I can liken it to nothing more accurately than the twenty-dollar gold-piece, the same satin finish, the same pale yellow. The fish was fairly molten. It did not glitter in gaudy burnishment, as does our aquarium goldfish, for example, but gleamed and melted and glowed as though fresh from the mold. . . . Furthermore, along either side of the belly ran two broad longitudinal stripes of exactly the color and burnish of the copper paint used on racing yachts. I thought then, and have ever since, that the Golden Trout, fresh from the water, is one of the most beautiful fish that swims."

DISTRIBUTION

During the late nineteenth century and the early part of the twentieth, people began moving native trout northward from the trout's home waters in the Kern River watershed to other waters in the Sierra Nevada, the great majority of which were barren of fish. Pleistocene ice, which carved many high lake basins during the four major glacial stages, left no fish life outside of the Kern River drainage. This portion of the Sierra Nevada was largely excluded from glacial action by its southerly location.

Trout are not native to east slope drainages of the southern Sierra, and major barriers prevented the invasion of fishes into the extreme upper reaches of Pacific slope drainages. The California Fish and Game Commission, assisted by sportsmen's groups, maintained an active transplanting program at the turn of the century, sometimes using twenty-mule pack trains to move trout from native waters to new locations.

LIFE HISTORY

Spawning. The life history and biology of the golden trout are not greatly different from those of other spring-spawning trouts, such as the rainbow and cutthroat. Egg development in the female golden trout for the following year begins early in their short

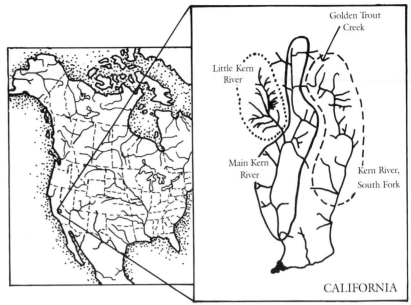

growing season (even before the current year's eggs are released), achieving near ripeness when decreasing temperatures arrest development at the beginning of winter. They are thus ready to spawn at the earliest opportunity the following spring. In their high mountain environments spring comes late. Snow melt and thawing of streams stimulate the spawning process, which can begin any time from March through July, depending upon elevation, severity of winter, and onset of warmer weather. Spawning activity, egg development (incubation), hatching, and early growth stages are essentially the same as for other spring spawners. In high lakes the spawning urge appears to be triggered by longer days and increasing water tempera-

California golden trout (Oncorhynchus aguabonita aguabonita) are found in the upper South Fork of the Kern River, and in Golden Trout Creek. They have been widely stocked in mountain lakes in the western United States, particularly in California, Wyoming and Montana. Little Kern golden trout (whitei) inhabit the waters of the Little Kern River drainage. Kern River rainbow trout (gilberti) are originally native to the Main Kern River; they occur there now in hybrid populations.

This trout, with its few, large spots, is probably a Volcano Creek golden.

THE SPECIES   **283**

ture, which is often highest in the outlet stream. This causes golden trout to enter the outlet stream to spawn, and they often become stranded below waterfalls. Sometimes it becomes necessary to build outlet screens with spawning gravel on the upstream side to encourage spawners to remain in the lake.

Coloration. In their native habitats, and in most streams where they have been introduced, golden trout retain the brilliant coloration for which they have become famous. In some locations (particularly in lower, warmer habitats and in many lakes), their colors often fade to dull grays and reds. It is for this reason that wild Cottonwood Lakes populations, rather than hatchery broodstocks, are used for rearing purposes. Color development and retention within golden trout from the Cottonwood Lakes are comparable to that of trout within their native habitats.

Other factors affecting golden trout coloration include plant pigments in the available food, the effect of cold incubation temperatures on metabolism, and degree of sexual maturity. Sexually mature golden trout attain their most vivid coloration during the spawning season. Curtis found in 1935 that Cottonwood Lakes fish may not mature until the end of their fourth year, at which time they may exceed 26 centimeters (10 inches) in length. For this reason anglers may suspect that their favorite golden trout lake was mistakenly planted with the much paler and more silvery rainbow trout. Either their fish are just not old enough to attain the most intense color, or color-producing food materials are insufficient in their diet. Trout with red and oily flesh usually are found in lakes with heavy populations of red plankton organisms.

Size. Golden trout are better known for their beauty than for their size. In streams a 20-centimeter (8-inch) fish is a large one, and it is interesting to note that workers studying golden trout at the turn of the twentieth century reported the same size. The large lake goldens reported during the first half of the century usually resulted from fish planted in a previously barren lake with a yet unexploited insect population. Then, as numbers of trout increased through natural reproduction, they encountered a diminishing food supply, and growth rates declined. It is now rare to take a golden larger than a pound from a Sierra Nevada lake, and experienced anglers are pleased to catch a few goldens up to a foot long (about half a pound).

High Sierra lakes generally are unproductive. There is inadequate nutrient material in the water to support a significant food chain. Consequently, resident trout must compete vigorously for available food. As a general rule, if a lake has a large population of trout, the trout will be small; if there are just a few fish, they are more likely to be "lunkers." Trying to raise an abundance of large trout in nearly any High Sierra lake is akin to trying to raise alfalfa on a tennis court.

The world-record golden trout (5 kilograms [11 pounds]) was taken in 1948 from a lake in the Wind River Mountains of Wyoming. The California record (4.5 kilograms [9 pounds 14 ounces]) was taken in 1952 from Virginia Lake, adjacent to the John Muir Trail in Fresno County. Golden trout of this size now exist only in photographs and memories. They will never occur again.

Although golden trout are normally associated with cold, clear streams and lakes—and indeed that is where most goldens are found—they evolved under very different circumstances. Late-summer water temperatures in their native streams in the Kern River drainage often reach well into the 70s Fahrenheit. They are found in coldwater habitats only because they were planted there.

HUMAN INTERVENTION

In 1918 hatchery crews began to use the Cottonwood Lakes as a brood source for golden trout. The egg-taking program at Cottonwood Lakes continues today almost exactly as before, but more advanced rearing methods are now used once the eggs reach the hatchery. Whereas before World War II all planting of golden trout was done with pack animals, planting of backcountry lakes is now accomplished with fixed-wing aircraft. Equipped with carefully prepared schedules, maps, and aerial photographs, pilots for the California Department of Fish and Game now plant as many fish in a few hours as pack strings could in an entire summer.

The golden trout planting program has continued virtually uninterrupted since

1918, with the exception of World War II and rare years when egg taking is precluded by abnormal weather and runoff conditions. Only the Volcano Creek golden trout has been used in the planting program. In recent years the Kern River Hatchery near Kernville has developed broodstocks of Little Kern golden trout, not for general stocking, but as part of a plan to remove the fish from its status as a threatened species under the federal Endangered Species Act.

Efforts of the California Department of Fish and Game have resulted in establishment of golden trout in about 300 lakes and 1,129 kilometers (700 miles) of streams within thirteen counties in California, primarily in the Sierra Nevada. Between 1928 and 1937 golden trout were sent to Wyoming, Colorado, Utah, Washington, Montana, and New York, as well as to England. For reasons not entirely clear, the California Legislature in 1939 prohibited exportation of golden trout eggs or fry.

The brink of extinction. During the past twenty-five years, both the Little Kern and Volcano Creek golden trout have hovered on the brink of extinction, and for essentially the same reasons: stream habitats and watersheds severely degraded by livestock, competition and predation from introduced nonnative species, and hybridization with introduced hatchery rainbow trout. Recovery programs for the two golden trout therefore have been similar, beginning in the 1960s. Major chemical treatment projects have been conducted along hundreds of miles of stream to remove nonnative species (brown and rainbow trouts in the drainage of the Kern River's South Fork, and eastern brook trout and rainbow trout in the Little Kern drainage) and hybrid forms. Major migration barriers preventing reinvasion of nonnative species and erosion control devices have been constructed in both drainages, and key areas are being fenced along the South Fork of the Kern in an effort to reestablish riparian vegetation.

Following chemical treatment, restocking projects have been conducted using stocks known to be genetically pure (transplanted or salvaged natives and artificially propagated golden trout from broodstock of wild origin).

Efforts to recreate the natural circumstances that molded the trout through the evolutionary process have required the removal of beavers from the South Fork of the Kern River. Beavers are not native to the area and in the long run are highly detrimental to trout populations. Also required was the reestablishment of native Sacramento suckers in the drainages of the Little Kern River and the South Fork of the Kern River following chemical treatment. Although stocking suckers may seem inconsistent with a conservation project, the interaction between suckers and golden trout over thousands of years may have been significant in the evolution of the golden trout. A golden trout wilderness without pure golden trout obviously is unacceptable.

—Phil Pister

Lake trout

Salvelinus namaycush

In North America, the native lake trout has long been prized for its beauty, its size, its sporting characteristics, and its quality as table fare, from the time of the early explorers, who reported seeing lake trout nearly five feet long, to the present day, when catching a lake trout larger than 4.5 kilograms (10 pounds) is the exception in most places.

However, lake trout require pristine conditions to survive, and individual populations of the species are subject to extinction because of acidification and other forms of pollution of their waters. In addition, because of its popularity and rigorous habitat requirements, the species as a whole is susceptible to overexploitation.

CLASSIFICATION

The common name *lake trout* has been somewhat controversial. The term *lake* is not totally appropriate, as many populations in the Arctic live in rivers the year around, and the word *trout* originally referred to the brown trout, *Salmo trutta*, in Europe. Many scientists favor the name *lake char*, because the fish is a char, not a trout. Yet even that term is not completely satisfactory, because *char* comes from a Gaelic word that means red, which the lake trout is not. To add to the confusion, some authorities prefer the spelling *charr*. Confusion notwithstanding, the accepted name remains lake trout.

Descriptions of the lake trout occur in many of the notes and journals of explorers, missionaries, and fur traders in central and northern Canada. In late July of 1615, while travelling on Georgian Bay of Lake Huron, the French explorer Samuel de Champlain recorded in his journal a description of enormous trout two and a half feet to four and a half feet long. Their size is probably an exaggeration, but the fish likely were lake trout, because at that time the lake trout was the only salmonid of that size in the area. Other historical figures commented on the lake trout, including Father Hennepin in 1698 and Charlevoix in 1761, both of whom referred to the Indian fishery of "salmon trout" in the Straits of Mackinac between Lakes Huron and Michigan. Samuel Hearne, the great Arctic barren-grounds explorer, made frequent mention of the trout in his journals in the period from 1770 to 1772.

However, credit for the description that eventually was used to name the species belongs to a Hudson Bay employee named Alexander Graham, even though his account confuses the lake trout with the Arctic char, *S. alpinus*. Thomas Pennant, in volume one of his famous *Arctic Zoology*, published in 1784, used the work of Thomas Hutchins for a description of the fishes of the Hudson Bay area. Hutchins was a contemporary and associate of Graham on Hudson Bay who, like Graham, was interested in natural history. But Hutchins' account, including that of the lake trout, was a direct plagiarism of Graham's journals, which had been published a dozen or so years earlier.

Joseph R. Tomelleri
© '88

In 1792, J. Walbaum, a German doctor and naturalist, applied the scientific name *Salmo namaycush* to the lake trout. The generic name of most other trouts at that time also was *Salmo*. He based his classification on Graham's description, which he incorrectly credited to Pennant. In 1878, Gill and Jordan proposed *Cristivomer* as the generic name, separating the lake trout from the other chars because of minor morphological differences, mainly in the structure and shape of the vomerine bone. This name persisted only until 1882 when Jordan and Gilbert placed the lake trout in the genus *Salvelinus*, along with the other chars, determining that the morphological differences were not sufficient to warrant a separate genus. In the intervening years, the generic name of the lake trout changed back and forth between *Cristivomer* and *Salvelinus*, but since 1960, the American Fisheries Society has recognized *Salvelinus* as the valid generic name of the lake trout. The specific name, *namaycush*, from Graham's original description, is but one of many attempts by Europeans at pronouncing and spelling the various North American Indian names for lake trout. Namaycush purportedly means "dweller of the deep."

Subpopulations. The siscowet, a deepwater form of the lake trout, found in Lake Superior, has at times been considered a subspecies, and was classified by Agassiz as *S. namaycush siscowet*. Several varieties or subpopulations of lake trout exist in Lake Superior, including the siscowet, and they are physically distinguishable from one another.

According to Goodier, commercial fishermen on Lake Superior have given them such colorful names as leans (the common form of lake trout elsewhere); half-breeds; humpers, also known as paperbellies or bankers; and siscowets or fats. Various forms or "breeds" of lean trout have been identified on the basis of differences in their behavior, particularly during the spawning season, habitat preferences, and physical appearance. Among the names commercial fisherman call these variants of lake trout are blacks, redfins, yellowfins, and sand trout, to name just a few.

The lake trout is not known to mate with any other species, at least in part because no other closely related fish, except perhaps Arctic char, spawns at the same time and place as the lake trout. However, successful artificial hybridization has been carried out between the lake trout and species of salmon, trout, and other char. The best known example is the cross between a female lake trout and a male brook trout, the progeny being known as the splake, *S. namaycush* x *S. fontinalis*. Splake have been crossed with female lake trout to produce a fish called the lake trout backcross.

DESCRIPTION

Scott and Crossman, and Martin and Olver have described lake trout in detail. Members of the species have large mouths with prominent teeth along the jaws and on the tongue. Like other char, they also have teeth at the

SIMPSON

The lake trout's large jaw permits it to take large food items into its mouth.

GIBBS

A deeply forked tail is the lake trout's most distinguishing characteristic.

COURTESY OF ALGONQUIN FISHERIES ASSESSMENT UNIT

Right: *Lake trout are not very colorful fish, but the rusty orange on their paired fins is striking.* Below: *These full-bodied lake trout have probably stuffed themselves on smelt.*

head of the vomer bone on the roof of the mouth. This is one feature that distinguishes them from trout, which have teeth on both the head and the shaft of the vomer.

The most apparent features of the lake trout, which readily separate it from the other chars, are a deeply forked caudal fin and the absence of red spots on the sides of the fish. Internally, the lake trout has more pyloric caeca (81 to 210) than other members of the genus, which each have less than 75. The number of small embedded cycloid scales along the lateral line on the sides of the fish varies between 116 and 138. Scales do not occur on the head.

The long, slender form typical of salmonids often is more pronounced in the lake trout. Large fish, however, may be quite full-bodied. The greatest body depth occurs below or in front of the dorsal fin. The head is large, roughly equal in size to body depth, and is about one quarter of the body length. The eyes are near the top of the head, a position typical of a visual predator.

Generally, lake trout are lighter in color overall than are other salmonids and may range from silver to gray to green to almost black, although the most common color is a greenish gray. Water color and local environmental conditions seem to affect external color variations, whereas diet influences flesh color. Piscivorous lake trout generally have pale or white flesh, and carotenoids in the diet of planktivorous lake trout cause a deep red or, more usually, a bright orange flesh.

The darkest colors are on the top, or dorsal side, of the fish and the top of the head. The back may be quite vermiculated, although these markings are not as prominent as in a common species associate, the brook trout, *S. fontinalis*. The sides of the fish are paler than the top, and the belly tends to white, although it may sometimes have a bronze hue. The body, except for the throat, belly, and paired fins, is covered with large, pale roundish spots, which have been described as white, silvery, gray, yellow, or golden. Lake trout do not have red spots, though other salmonids, such as the brook trout, do. The dorsal and caudal fins may have dark wavy lines. Bright color on the lake trout is usually restricted to the anal and paired fins, which may have a distinct light yellow or orange cast. The leading edges of these fins are white, but here too they are not as prominent as those of the brook trout. The roof of the mouth and the tips of the jaws are white.

There are some differences in physical appearance between males and females, but they are not as prominent as in most other salmonids. Dark bands may be noticeable on the sides of spawning male lake trout, but they are not present in all populations. Otherwise, the sexes cannot be distinguished on the basis of color. Pearl organs, which add a rough texture to the scales, have been noted on both sexes during the breeding season in some lakes; in other bodies of water, they occur only on the males. These organs, which may appear on the head in other fishes such as minnows, are also called nuptial tubercles. They are hormonal growths that occur during the reproductive part of the life cycle.

DISTRIBUTION

The lake trout is native only to North America and is found mainly in glaciated areas in Alaska; northern British Columbia; the Yukon Territory; the Northwest Territories, including some offshore Arctic islands; the prairie provinces of Alberta, Saskatchewan, and Manitoba; Ontario; Quebec; the Labrador portion of Newfoundland (but not the island itself); and the maritime provinces of New Brunswick and Nova Scotia. In the continental United States, native stocks occur in Maine, Vermont, New Hampshire, New York, Pennsylvania, Michigan, Wisconsin, Minnesota, and Montana. The species also occurred in the Great Lakes waters of Illinois, Indiana, and Ohio before the native stocks were extirpated in Lakes Michigan and Erie.

The lake trout has been widely introduced outside its native range. In the United States, successful introductions have occurred in California, Nevada, Washington, Oregon, Idaho, Utah, Colorado, Massachusetts, and Connecticut. Lake trout have also been introduced into Argentina, Peru, Bolivia, Finland, France, Sweden, Switzerland, and New Zealand.

In large part, glacial activity accounts for the present distribution of native lake trout. During the Pleistocene glaciation, some

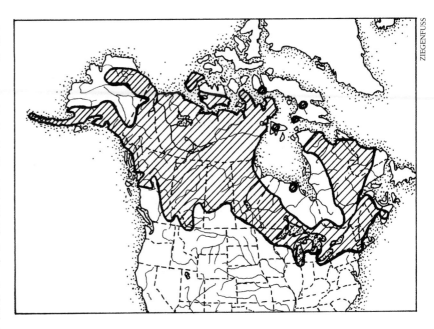

15,000 years ago, lake trout moved to several areas to escape the ice sheet. These areas, known as glacial refugia, were outside the species' present range. During the final stages of Pleistocene glaciation some 8,000 to 10,000 years ago, the Wisconsin ice sheet retreated north. In the moderating climate, meltwaters created many dispersal routes, and glacial scouring produced habitat for the lake trout. Consequently, the species was able to recolonize much of its previous range. Today, at least 90 percent of all native lake-trout stocks are found on the Canadian (Precambrian) Shield in lakes created during the demise of the last ice age.

Although lake trout are found primarily in fresh water, they can tolerate waters of low salinity, which is probably why they were able to colonize several Canadian Arctic islands. Lake trout probably were not able to establish native stocks in areas close to their existing range, such as Siberia and Newfoundland, because of the higher salinities in the Bering Sea and the Atlantic Ocean.

It is estimated that 8,000 to 10,000 lakes around the world contain lake trout. Probably about 75 percent of all lake trout lakes occur in Ontario, Quebec, and the Northwest Territories.

HABITAT

Lake trout typically inhabit deep, clear, cold, well-oxygenated, rocky, infertile freshwater lakes that offer clean rubble for spawn-

Lake trout prefer deep, cold, well-oxygenated but nutrient-poor waters. Members of this species grow slowly, mature late, and produce small numbers of eggs. All of these factors cause the lake trout to be very susceptible to harm from environmental degradation and change.

Lake trout are found most often in nutrient-poor northern lakes with rugged, rocky shorelines.

ing. They also inhabit shallow lakes and rivers in the northern part of their range and subalpine lakes. In fact, many arctic populations live in rivers the year around. Lake trout also can tolerate low salinities and are sometimes found in brackish waters.

Temperature and oxygen conditions are the primary factors governing their presence and distribution in those systems. Their upper lethal temperature of 23.5°C (74.3°F) is one of the lowest for freshwater fish. In the wild, they prefer water that is about 10°C (50°F); thus, the annual temperature fluctuations strongly influence their seasonal movements. During the spring, fall, and winter when water temperatures are close to homothermous, or nearly the same from surface to bottom, the lake trout may be found at all depths. They begin to move to deeper water in the spring as surface water temperatures approach 12° to 15°C (54° to 59°F). In thermally stratified lakes, waters from 6° to 13°C (43° to 56°F) constitute their summer habitat, though the temperature range will vary slightly from lake to lake. Occasionally lake trout may move into much warmer water above the thermocline, the layer of water that separates the warm upper layer from the cold bottom layer. These movements likely are short excursions in search of food.

Lake trout can tolerate oxygen levels of less than 4 parts per million, but they will move up in the water column if higher amounts are available there. They seem to prefer oxygen levels between 6 and 12 parts per million. Such conditions are present in most, but certainly not all, lakes that contain lake trout.

The lake trout is a bottom-oriented species regardless of depth. Juvenile fish are generally found in deeper water than are adults. This segregation may have considerable survival value for the younger fish, as adult lake trout are cannibalistic.

Lake trout normally occur in lakes from as small as 4 hectares (about 10 acres) to as large as several thousand square kilometers in size, such as the Great Lakes. Martin reported finding them in the Ungava region of northern Quebec in small tundra ponds of less than 0.5 hectares (just over an acre) in size, but this situation is unusual.

In temperate areas, lake trout seldom occur

in lakes less than about 15 meters (49 feet) deep. However, depth is not a critical factor at high latitudes and altitudes because of the colder annual water temperatures. Lake trout also occur in very deep lakes and they have been captured at depths of more than 400 meters (1,312 feet) in Great Bear Lake in the Northwest Territories, and Lake Tahoe on the border between California and Nevada.

LIFE HISTORY

Spawning. Lake trout are fall spawners. In a large part of their natural range, they reproduce primarily in September and October. However, siscowets in Lake Superior have been known to breed as early as June, and lake trout in Lake Tahoe have reportedly spawned as late as January. Lake trout at high latitudes and in subalpine lakes spawn earlier than those in more southerly regions.

Lake trout of different populations reach maturity at different ages, ranging from four to fifteen years. In southerly lakes, they usually are mature by ages six to eight. Many factors affect maturation: the sex of the fish, the growth rate, the location, even the diet. Males generally mature one year earlier than females. Fish in northern waters mature at older ages than do their southern counterparts. Planktivorous fish, which grow slowly and live only a few years, usually mature at a smaller size and at a younger age than do piscivorous lake trout, which grow faster and live longer.

Length and weight upon maturity vary considerably, too, ranging from 28 to 65 centimeters (11 to 25 inches) and from 0.5 to 2.5 kilograms (1 to 5.5 pounds).

Lake trout may not spawn every year, and there is an inverse relationship between frequency of spawning and latitude. The more northerly stocks tend to have fewer spawning fish in any one year. The different photoperiods in northerly lakes, together with shorter growing seasons, less abundant food supplies, and the very unproductive nature of the lakes themselves, all likely cause intermittent spawning and even affect egg development.

Temperature, light, and wind contribute to the onset and duration of spawning activities. Spawning begins when water temperatures fall toward about 10°C (50°F) and con-tinues as they drop further. It may coincide with the fall overturn of the lake water, or it may occur well afterward. Lake trout are negatively phototropic; that is, they avoid light. Thus, the shortening daylight hours of fall, as well as the fading light at the end of each day, also induce them to begin spawning behavior. In continuous, strong onshore winds, spawning may be completed in only a few nights.

Prolonged calm periods, especially with bright, warm, sunny days, may extend spawning over several weeks because the temperature, wind, and light "cues" are absent. Following a prolonged period of calm weather, it may be completed in a few nights during or after a strong wind.

Lake trout spawn primarily in lakes; on occasion they spawn in rivers. Spawning typically occurs on offshore shoals, near shorelines off points, and near islands exposed to the prevailing winds—usually northerly or westerly. The spawning substrate is usually a combination of broken rubble and sharp-edged rocks, 3 to 15 centimeters (about 1 to 6 inches) in diameter, perhaps with large boulders scattered about. In the Great Lakes, before the collapse of the lake trout populations, they were known to spawn on honeycombed limestone. The effects of wave action and ice movement keep the spawning beds clear of vegetation and fine material such as sand and silt.

In small inland bodies of water, lake trout usually spawn in less than 6 meters (about

These lake trout eggs have been exposed by a receding waterline.

Three large male lake trout pursue a female on spawning substrate in Lake Opeongo, Ontario. An instant after this photo was taken, the males overshot the female, causing her to roll over.

20 feet) of water, in fact often in water less than 1 meter (about 39 inches) deep. Such populations are particularly vulnerable to fluctuations in water level. The depth of the spawning beds increases with the size of the lake. In the Great Lakes, siscowets have been known to spawn at depths greater than 90 meters (295 feet), although the leans spawn in much shallower water.

The lake trout is one of the few salmonids, if not the only one, that spawns just at night—from dusk to late evening. Males usually arrive at the spawning sites a few days before females and remain longer. Females leave immediately after spawning. Males usually outnumber females on these shoals by a margin of 2:1 or 3:1, although balanced sex ratios are normal at other times of the year. The younger and smaller mature trout of both sexes tend to spawn earlier than do the older and larger fish. Lake trout also may spawn earlier in shallower and smaller lakes, where water temperatures drop more rapidly.

Researchers think that lake trout home—that is, that they return to their natal shoal each year they spawn. There is some question

about how specific this activity is, however. Lake trout, more particularly, female lake trout, are known to visit different spawning beds, but it is unclear whether they are searching for their natal shoal or selecting males with which to spawn, and whether they actually are depositing eggs on more than one shoal.

Unlike most other salmonids, the lake trout does not construct a redd, and lake trout do not form single pairs for spawning. The spawning act itself may involve one or more males and one to several females. The eggs are broadcast over the spawning bed where they settle into crevices in the rocks to depths of 10 to 50 centimeters (4 to 20 inches). The fish do not cover the eggs, though the crevices afford protection from most predators, nor is there any parental care of the eggs.

The lake trout is not a very fecund fish. Egg counts in most populations vary between 800 and 1,800 eggs per kilogram (about 360 to 800 per pound) of body weight. The maximum numbers of eggs per female vary between a low of about 500 and a high of about 20,000. Hence, the lake trout, like other chars and trouts, is considered to have a low reproductive potential, compared with carp, walleye, and burbot, for example.

Development. The eggs incubate and hatch, the fry emerging from their egg shells within the spawning beds, over the winter and usually under ice cover. The length of the incubation period depends on temperature and oxygen levels; generally it requires about four to five months. The eggs usually hatch between mid-February and late March or early April in temperate zone lakes. The fry spend about a month within the rubble on these sites while they slowly absorb the yolk sac.

The lake trout, like most soft-rayed fishes, is physostomous. That is, the swim bladder and the esophagus are connected, as they are in many fishes, including other salmonids. It therefore must fill its swim bladder with air to regulate buoyancy. This it normally does at the time of the final absorption of the yolk sac, usually in May.

The swim-up fry migrate to the surface to fill their swim bladders. Though most spawning sites are in shallow water, the fry can swim long vertical distances if necessary. They also can swim for long periods without filling their swim bladder if ice covers the surface of the water. Usually, though, extensive air pockets exist under the ice, especially near shore, where the process can be completed.

Afterward, the young free-swimming fish, known as alevins, move to deep water, at least in northern temperate lakes. For most of the next two to three years of their lives, these young juvenile lake trout remain in deep water.

Movements. Generally, lake trout move in response to changes in environmental conditions, in search of food, or at the onset of spawning. In large bodies of water, such as the Great Lakes, lake trout may migrate up to 300 kilometers (186 miles) to their spawning grounds. In fact, large fish may be rather nomadic. Some specimens have been recaptured more than 600 kilometers (372 miles) from where they were tagged by researchers. In small bodies of water, lake trout are more likely to respond to seasonal adjustments in temperature, oxygen, and light. In thermally stratified lakes, the trout generally stay in the deeper parts of the lake below the thermocline, except for brief feeding forays into warmer water.

Adult lake trout are generally solitary creatures. Although young fish are often found with others of the same size and age, the lake trout, as a species, does not school.

In the spring, the younger fish tend to move to deeper water later than do the larger trout. This may be a survival mechanism, as older and larger lake trout prey on smaller lake trout.

Food and feeding. The lake trout is an opportunistic and omnivorous feeder, essentially eating whatever is available. Although mollusks, small mammals, and even birds occasionally have been reported in the diet of lake trout, the fish usually eat zooplankton, crustaceans, insects, and other fish. Large

The alewife, an introduced species in the Great Lakes, is commonly found in the lake trout's diet.

lakes generally have more fish species than do smaller ones, and in these habitats the lake trout generally is piscivorous. Smaller lakes usually have fewer forage species and lake trout may be mainly planktivorous for all or a large part of the year.

Small planktonic crustaceans, such as cladocerans and copepods, and several immature stages of aquatic insects, such as chironomids, blackflies, dragonflies, damselflies, and mayflies, are the major food items in the diet of young-of-the-year and juvenile lake trout. Large crustaceans, such as the opossum shrimp, *Mysis relicta*, and the amphipod *Pontoporeia affinis*, may replace the smaller prey as lake trout increase in size. Even larger lake trout, which are capable of feeding on fish, may continue to eat crustaceans. In some lakes, *Mysis* remains an important food item in the diet of lake trout throughout the life of the fish.

With increasing size and age, lake trout usually turn to fish as the staple in their diet. Coregonids, such as the lake herring and the lake whitefish, are two of the most important forage species. They occur throughout most of the natural range of the lake trout and occupy similar habitats. Both alewives and rainbow smelt have become major food items in the diet of the lake trout in areas where invasions or introductions of these species have been successful, as in the Great Lakes and in some inland lakes in the Great Lakes watershed. Such other fish as yellow perch, various species of suckers, primarily *Catostomus*, and minnows may be of local or seasonal importance in the diet of lake trout. In general, the larger the predator, the larger the prey. However, large lake trout also may eat several species of the relatively small sculpins and during the spring will feed at the surface on terrestrial insects in shallow areas.

Seasonal changes in the diet of lake trout are related mainly to changing water temperatures, which affect the distribution of the lake trout as well as their prey. In the Arctic, where annual changes in the water temperature are quite small, the diet of the lake trout may be similar throughout the year. In the spring, the adults and some of the larger juveniles may feed on and near the surface, at which time they may gorge themselves on terrestrial insects and minnows. As the surface waters warm in temperate lakes and the lake trout move to deeper water, they generally eat more fish. However, if the lake trout are spatially separated from their normal fish forage by thermal barriers, or if few deepwater forage species occur in a lake, the lake trout become planktivorous. As lake trout move into shallower water again in the fall, prey unavailable during the summer may reappear in their diet. Mature fish in most populations do not feed as consistently as juveniles throughout the summer. Lake trout may not feed as actively in the winter as they do at other times of the year, because some food items are less abundant, and in addition, their metabolic requirements are lower.

Growth. The growth rate and longevity of lake trout depend on temperature, which affects the length of the growing season, and lake productivity, which affects the abundance of the food supply. Lake trout in northern lakes grow more slowly but live longer than more southerly but faster-growing fish because the water is less fertile and because the colder water in northern lakes shortens the length of the growing season.

Assessing the age of lake trout has proven difficult. At one time, researchers, reading the scales of the fish, estimated the maximum age at about twenty-five years. We now know that ages of more than about eight years determined by measuring scales are unreliable, because the annuli on the scales cannot be distinguished. Instead, age can be determined much more accurately by reading the otoliths, which are calcified tissues used for equilibrium, balance, and hearing. Using this method, researchers aged a lake trout from a lake in the Northwest Territories at sixty-two years, the oldest determined so far.

Lake trout that feed on fish grow faster and larger and live longer than those that feed primarily on plankton. A fish weighing 1 kilogram (about 2 pounds) would be large in a planktivorous population, small to average in a piscivorous one. Fish-eating lake

CEISEL, VISUALS UNLIMITED

This small lake trout could grow to weigh as much as 20 to 25 kilograms.

trout can exceed 25 kilograms (55 pounds) in weight.

The growth rate in lake trout increases when the fish are able to switch from a diet primarily of plankton to one of fish. In lakes where both foods are available, this generally occurs when the lake trout are about 35 to 40 centimeters (14 to 16 inches) long.

Genetics and environmental conditions both play a role in the growth rate, although it does not appear to be genetically fixed. Each unique genetic stock has its own inherent growth rate, but growth can be altered by environmental conditions. In addition, different genetic stocks put into the same environment likely would have different growth rates. For example, introductions of forage species such as lake herring, rainbow smelt, and *Mysis* into lake trout lakes, or conversely the introduction of lake trout into lakes containing these forage species, can result in a marked increase in the growth rate of the lake trout. The growth rate of the sexes is similar, although in some stocks, female lake trout may grow slightly faster, and the largest fish in most lakes usually are females.

Growth generally is more rapid in immature fish and also just after a switch to piscivory. The onset of sexual maturity may signal a decline of growth in length, although growth in weight may continue markedly. The largest lake trout on record is one that weighed 46.3 kilograms (102 pounds), taken in the commercial fishery in Lake Athabaska, Saskatchewan, in 1961. The angling record is a fish weighing 29 kilograms (65 pounds), caught in Great Bear Lake, Northwest Territories, in 1970. Today, few lake trout exceed 20 kilograms (44 pounds). In fact, most caught by anglers weigh 1 to 5 kilograms (2 to 11 pounds) and are four to ten years old. In many planktivorous stocks, fish weighing 0.25 to 0.5 kilogram (0.5 to 1.1 pounds) are common in the creel.

Parasites and diseases. Lake trout have a normal complement of diseases and parasites. Parasite loads in wild populations generally have no major effects on the well-being of the fish. However, cysts of the cestode tapeworm *Triaenophorous crassus* may, on occasion, be heavy enough to affect the marketability of commercially caught lake trout. The fungus *Saprolegnia* can cause major mor-

Growth rates in lake trout

The slowest growth rate recorded to date for lake trout (based on otoliths) was from a population in a subalpine lake in Jasper National Park, Alberta, Canada (Donald and Alger, 1986). Subalpine lakes are harsh, nutrient-poor environments.

Age	Range in fork length
2 years	18–28 cm
4	23–44
6	22–59
8	28–79
10	33–83
12	39–90

Lake trout are opportunistic feeders. The abundance and nature of available food supplies shape the growth rates of local populations, resulting in tremendous variability within the species (from Martin and Olver, 1980).

talities of the eggs of wild lake trout.

Diseases can present very serious problems in fish hatcheries. Infections can spread rapidly due to the high densities at which fish are often held. Outbreaks of such diseases as infectious pancreatic necrosis (IPN), enteric redmouth, and bacterial gill disease (BKD) can kill many lake trout. In extreme cases, outbreaks of the bacterial disease furunculosis and, more recently, the virus epizootic epitheliotropic disease (EED) have killed large numbers of hatchery fish. The remaining lake trout then had to be destroyed and the hatcheries closed and disinfected.

Predation. The lake trout is the terminal predator in most water bodies, and adults are seldom eaten by other fish species. The exception is the decimation of lake trout stocks by the parasitic sea lamprey in the Great Lakes following the opening of the Welland Canal between Lake Ontario and Lake Erie in 1829. However, predation on lake trout eggs by several species of fish, including the lake trout itself, is common. It is likely that any fish species found on the lake trout's spawning ground during the spawning season of the species are trying to prey on lake trout eggs. The mud puppy is a serious predator on lake trout eggs in some lakes. In recent years, crayfish, such as *Orconectes propinquus* and especially *O. rusticus,* have invaded several lakes in the Great Lakes basin that have lake trout. Their effect as predators on lake trout eggs is unclear. In most situations, egg mortality likely does not have a serious effect on the production of lake trout,

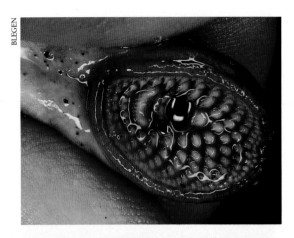

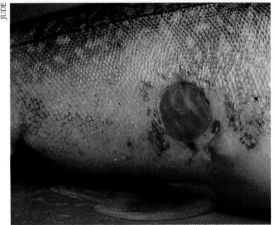

Although the lake trout is the top predator throughout most of its habitat, the sea lamprey decimated lake trout populations in the Great Lakes after the opening of the Welland Canal.

may compete with lake trout for many of the same food resources. The biomass or standing stock of lake trout might be higher if some of these species were absent, but many of them also are part of the diet of lake trout. The lake trout is a keystone predator; it helps to maintain the stability of the fish community by controlling the predator-prey balance. With its ability to occupy all depths and make extensive horizontal and vertical movements, the lake trout is an important energy vector and transfer agent in the recycling of nutrients between the shallow, inshore areas and the deep, offshore waters.

Lake trout may compete with other salmonids where they occur together, although each species may occupy slightly different habitats and supplement their diets with a wide variety of prey. Brook trout commonly occur with lake trout in eastern Canada, and lake trout and Arctic char may be found together in arctic and subarctic lakes. Burbot, ciscoes, lake whitefish, and some sculpin species are common deepwater associates of lake trout. Walleye and northern pike often occur with lake trout in lakes that have diverse habitat conditions. Yellow perch, rock bass, and smallmouth bass, which are often introduced into lake trout habitats, are common in lakes near the southern extent of the lake trout's range.

Species diversity is related to a variety of factors including: glacial history, lake area, latitude, water temperature, and activities of humans. The most diverse fish communities with lake trout occur near the southerly limits of its natural range and close to population centers—particularly in the Great Lakes, which contain several introduced species, including brown trout, *Salmo trutta*; rainbow trout, *Oncorhynchus mykiss*; chinook salmon, *O. tshawytscha*; coho salmon, *O. kisutch*; pink salmon, *O. gorbuscha*; and alewife and rainbow smelt.

HUMAN INTERVENTIONS

The rigorous life-history requirements of the lake trout (slow growth, late maturity, low reproductive potential, and slow turnover rate), coupled with the low nutrient-low energy ecosystems that the lake trout inhabits, make the species particularly intolerant of, and acutely vulnerable to, degrada-

except perhaps where they are forced to spawn on substrate that is less than favorable so that many eggs remain on the surface of a shoal, rather than fall into the crevices of the rocks. However, such exposed eggs likely would die anyway.

Cannibalism occurs frequently in arctic and subarctic lakes where food supplies may be severely limited. Recent evidence suggests that it may be important in many other lakes, as well, particularly those with degraded water quality, because juvenile lake trout may be forced to abandon their deepwater nursery habitat and enter that occupied by the adults.

In such situations, cannibalism by large lake trout could control the number of juveniles that survive to become adults, thus limiting the size of the population.

Community ecology. The lake trout is the terminal predator in most lakes, so competition with other species for food generally is limited and not a serious problem for the lake trout. Seasonally and throughout its life history, the lake trout interacts with several species, each of which, at similar life stages,

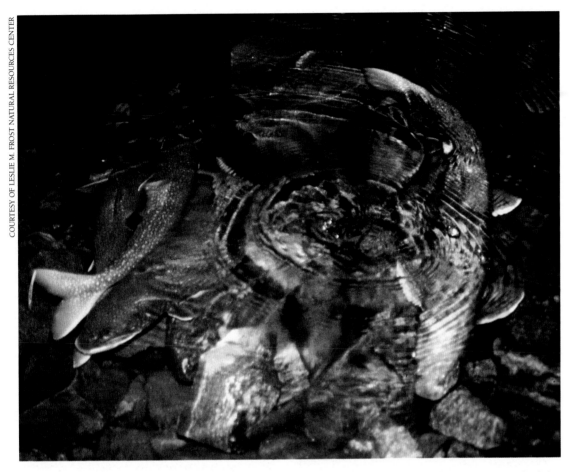

In small inland lakes, lake trout may spawn in shallow water, often with their bodies exposed. Lake trout do not make redds, but simply scatter their eggs in the crevices of large substrate.

tion of its habitat.

Introductions, whether deliberate or inadvertent, or invasions of species can severely damage the populations of the lake trout. Predation by the sea lamprey, for example, caused the collapse and extinction of many stocks in the Great Lakes in the 1940s and 1950s. Most scientists believe that even without the arrival of the sea lamprey, most lake trout stocks eventually would have collapsed from overfishing. Native lake trout stocks disappeared from lakes Ontario and Michigan, and only two small remnant stocks survive in Lake Huron. The loss of lake trout in Lake Erie probably came about because of intense exploitation and habitat degradation rather than predation by the sea lamprey.

Massive restocking programs for lake trout began in the 1960s and 1970s. Since then, about 120 million lake trout, most of them yearlings, have been planted in the Great Lakes. This has certainly produced an abundance of lake trout, but the results have been questioned. Eshenroder and colleagues have noted that most of the fish caught still are hatchery fish; there has been little evidence of

natural reproduction by the planted fish. However, rehabilitation of lake trout stocks has been encouraging in Lake Superior, where many native stocks, particularly those offshore, were not decimated or eradicated by the sea lamprey.

There is serious concern that stocked fish may reduce the overall genetic fitness of wild stocks and cause their eventual demise. This could occur through the combined efforts of introgression (the mixing of the genes of the less fit hatchery fish with those of the wild fish), and increased exploitation on stocked lakes. In heavily fished lakes, the native fish are overexploited and not enough are left to replenish the population. As hatchery fish are stocked to replenish the declining numbers, the populations change from native to hatchery-reared fish. Eventually, the populations consist mainly of stocked fish, which must be artificially replenished continually, both because many of them are harvested before they have the chance to reproduce and because the hatchery fish are less efficient spawners than the native fish.

The poor reproductive success of stocked

lake trout is partly the result of the loss of genetic diversity caused by the extinction of many native, locally adapted stocks, so that managers now have fewer options to match hatchery fish to their intended environment. In replenishing a population, the first choice is to rehabilitate it with fish hatched from native stocks from the same area. The second is to use native fish from another area in the same lake as brood stocks. The third choice is to use native fish from another lake as brood stocks.

The lack of reproductive success also may be related to the age at which most lake trout have been planted. The imprinting of wild fish to their natal shoals during their early life history seems to be a critical process in the return of the fish to these shoals as adult spawners. This process, of course, does not occur in the hatchery where the fish are raised from eggs to yearling size. Experiments with eggs are being conducted in an effort to learn if this lack of imprinting can be overcome by planting eggs instead of yearlings.

The behavior of hatchery fish released into the wild often is quite different from that of native stocks. Hatchery fish tend to remain closer to shore, near areas where they are (usually) planted. They often occur in areas not frequented by native fish, and they may try to spawn at nontraditional sites and on less than favorable substrates. Hatchery-reared fish also are less efficient spawners than are wild fish. The inshore distribution and movements of hatchery fish may be reinforced by reliance on exotics in their diet—rainbow smelt and alewife. The forage fish themselves tend to be found closer to shore than does the complex of coregonid species that were staples in the diet of native stocks in the Great Lakes before the arrival of these exotics.

Stocking has been important in replenishing depleted stocks in numerous lakes besides the Great Lakes—or in appearing to do so. The harvest of planted fish often leads to unrealistically high expectations by anglers about the productivity of such lakes. However, the number of fish stocked is usually far above the carrying capacity of the lakes in which they are stocked. Because hatchery-reared fish are not an intrinsic product of these systems, stocking may engender a false

sense of well-being about the health of these aquatic ecosystems, camouflaging environmental problems by deflecting attention from them.

The degradation and loss of habitat have seriously depleted lake trout stocks because the species is so sensitive to changes in water quality. Thus cultural eutrophication, or human-related enrichment of the habitat with nutrients, particularly phosphorous, may cause a depletion of oxygen in the hypolimnion, or bottom layer of water, and reduce or even eliminate deepwater habitat. Profuse growths of such algae as *Cladophora* and increased sedimentation and siltation on the spawning beds may render them unsuitable for egg incubation. Urban areas within a watershed may increase to the extent that the ability of these oligotrophic systems to absorb an influx of nutrients may be overwhelmed.

There are many other ways in which the habitat of lake trout is affected. Lakes that support lake trout are poorly buffered and thus vulnerable to acidification, particularly in eastern Canada and the northeastern United States. For example, in one Canadian study, Beggs and colleagues estimated acidic precipitation has eliminated lake trout populations in 3 percent of the 2,200 lakes containing lake trout in the province of Ontario and that a further 16 percent of these lakes are presently either acidified (3.5 percent) or extremely sensitive to acidification (12.5 percent). Other contaminants, such as myrex, PCBs, and dioxin, are a serious problem too, particularly in the Great Lakes basin, and have rendered the lake trout in many places unsafe to eat.

Fertilizers, pesticides, insecticides, and herbicides, toxic mine effluents, physical destruction of habitat, and airborne contamination with heavy metals have diminished both the quality and quantity of lake trout habitat. Hydroelectric developments, such as dams; water-level manipulations; dredging and filling activities; and shoreline development, such as the building of cottages and marinas, also have damaged lake trout habitat.

The lake trout is easily caught and with its innate biological characteristics and its preference for cold, nutrient-poor waters, it is quite susceptible to overexploitation. Sustainable harvests are extremely low (about 0.25 to 0.75 kilogram per hectare [about 0.25 to 0.7 pound per acre]). A phenomenal growth in sport fishing followed the Second World War because improvements in access (modern highways, forest access roads), improvement in methods of access (airplanes, snow machines, all-terrain vehicles), and the development of sophisticated fishing gear (depth sounders, downriggers) provided humans with the ability to overexploit virtually any lake trout population, in any lake, anywhere. In fact, many lakes have been overfished, and even a small amount of continued fishing likely will prevent the complete recovery of the lake trout stocks in them.

Species such as the lake trout, which are sensitive to changing environmental conditions and have only a limited ability to adapt, require austere and pristine conditions to thrive. As we approach the twenty-first century, the outlook for the lake trout is not bright—given our shameful environmental record of the last fifty years. If the well-being of the lake trout—like that of other species—is to be assured, an environmental conscience or ethic must emerge in which protection and resource maintenance are the first priorities.

—Charles Harold Olver

Mexican golden trout

Oncorhynchus chrysogaster

Until recently, at least by taxonomic standards, the Mexican golden trout was known only to villagers who lived near the mountain streams it inhabited and to those few anglers who ventured there. Given the remoteness of the area, the fact that we know little about the trout is no surprise. However, inaccessibility also causes us some concern, for we have been unable to determine the abundance of this remarkable fish at the same time that we are aware of two factors that threaten it as well as many other species: pollution and hybridization.

CLASSIFICATION

It has long been known that trout occur in high elevation streams draining the Sierra Madre Occidental range to the Gulf of California on the mainland of Mexico. But how many kinds of trout occur in Mexico and how they should be classified remain largely unknown. The only trout of mainland Mexico that has been officially classified is the Mexican golden trout, named *Salmo* (now *Oncorhynchus*) *chrysogaster* in 1964. To place the Mexican golden trout in its proper perspective in relation to the evolution and classification of western North American trout, the other Mexican trout also must be considered.

The Gulf of California (also known as the Sea of Cortez) appears to have been an important center in the evolution of western trouts. At least four ancestral evolutionary lines gave rise to their present diversity. These four (or more) ancestral groups migrated south from the Gulf of California into mainland rivers during glacial periods when marine waters were much colder. There were four major glacial epochs during the last two million years of the Pleistocene era. These four glacial epochs neatly correlate with the four evolutionary lines, but this circumstance may be coincidental. For example, two or more ancestral evolutionary lines may have been displaced from the north into the Gulf of California during a single glacial period. The four lines probably evolved outside the gulf at various periods; each line moved south into the gulf at some unknown time.

From the fossil record, we know that other, more ancient evolutionary lines of trout also dispersed from waters that are tributaries to the Gulf of California. The extinct *Salmo* (now *Oncorhynchus*) *australis* occurred in the Lake Chapala basin, about 155 kilometers (250 miles) south of the present distribution of native trout in Mexico.

Proceeding from north to south, the first apparent evolutionary line associated with dispersal from the Gulf of California is represented by the Gila and Apache trout of New Mexico and Arizona—assuming that their common ancestor moved up the lower Colorado River and dispersed in the Gila River system. The chromosomes of Gila and Apache trout have a common ancestral trait: Both species have fifty-six chromosomes with 106 chromosomal arms. In comparison, various forms of rainbow and cutthroat trout

have fifty-eight to sixty-eight chromosomes with 104 arms.

The next evolutionary line is represented by the trout native to the Rio Yaqui and the Rio Mayo, tributaries to the Gulf of California. The Yaqui and Mayo trout have never been classified. Their coloration and spotting pattern is somewhat similar to Gila trout, but the Rio Mayo trout was found to have sixty-four chromosomes. The Yaqui and Mayo trout may represent a primitive line in the evolution of rainbow trout, which would indicate their classification as a subspecies of *Oncorhynchus mykiss*.

The three river systems south of the Rio Mayo from north to south–Rio Fuerte, Rio Sinaloa, and Rio Culiacan–contain the Mexican golden trout, *O. chrysogaster*, the third distinct evolutionary line associated with the Gulf of California. The precise position of *chrysogaster* in the evolution of western trouts is uncertain, but they probably represent an early branch closer to rainbow trout than to cutthroat trout.

The fourth and apparently most recently established form of Mexican trout is found in headwaters of the Rio del Presidio. At about 24° north latitude, near the Tropic of Cancer, the Rio del Presidio trout represents the southernmost natural distribution of any living salmonid fish in the world. The Rio del Presidio trout has not been formally classified, but it is more similar to common rainbow trout than are the other evolutionary lines. The Rio del Presidio trout probably represents the most recent invasion from the Gulf of California, perhaps occurring during the last glacial epoch.

The Rio San Lorenzo drains to the Gulf between the Rio Culiacan to the north and the Rio del Presidio to the south. A peculiar trout has been recorded from one tributary of the Rio San Lorenzo, the Rio Truchas (Trout River). The Rio Truchas trout may represent a fifth distinct evolutionary line or it may have resulted from hybridization between Mexican golden trout and the form of rainbow trout found in the Rio del Presidio drainage. In most of its characters, the Rio Truchas trout is intermediate between the Mexican golden trout and the Rio del Presidio rainbow trout. It has not been classified.

DESCRIPTION

The Mexican golden trout is characterized by rose coloration along the midline of the body, light yellowish colors on the lower sides with more intense orange coloration on the abdomen and lower fins. A light yellow-orange "cutthroat" mark is present beneath the lower jaws. The black spots are relatively small and sparsely scattered along the greenish dorsal part of the body. The general appearance has similarities to that of Gila trout and to those of certain inland forms of more primitive rainbow trout, often called redband trout. These similarities of coloration, spotting, and configuration of parr marks on the body probably reflect the traits of a primi-

The Gila trout (right) *and the Rio Yaqui trout* (below) *represent two of the four ancestral evolutionary lines that gave rise to trout native to the extreme Southwest.*

The limited range of the Mexican golden trout makes it vulnerable to overfishing, pollution and hybridization. Reservoirs, which often serve as introduction points for nonnative species, have been built in the three river drainages where the Mexican golden is found.

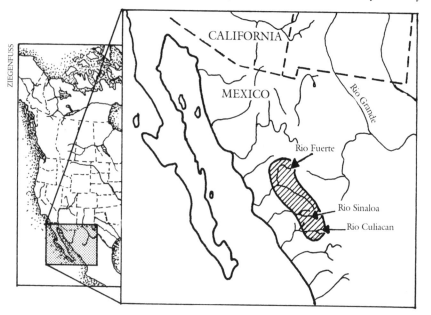

tive common ancestor at an evolutionary stage soon after a major divergence separated a common ancestor into two radiations, one leading to cutthroat trout, the other to rainbow trout. That Mexican golden trout have sixty chromosomes indicates a closer relationship to the rainbow trout line rather than to cutthroat trout. Among all western North American trout (rainbow, cutthroat, Gila, Apache, California, golden), the Mexican golden trout typically has the lowest number of vertebrae (fifty-five to fifty-nine) and the lowest number of pyloric caeca, which are appendages on the intestine, averaging twenty to twenty-three in different populations. Other western trout typically have sixty to sixty-five vertebrae and thirty to sixty

pyloric caeca. The numbers of vertebrae and pyloric caeca of the Mexican golden trout are most similar to those found in Gila, Apache, and California golden trout.

DISTRIBUTION

The range of Mexican golden trout is restricted to higher-elevation, cold-headwater tributaries of only three river systems—Rio Fuerte, Rio Sinaloa, and Rio Culiacan. These rivers drain the west slope of the Sierra Madre Occidental range to the Gulf of California in the Mexican states of Sinaloa, Chihuahua, and Durango. Most of the trout habitat in these drainages occurs at elevations of between 1,800 and 2,400 meters (6,000 and 8,000 feet).

LIFE HISTORY

No studies have been made on the life history of this trout. Information on its ecology and habitat consists only of casual observations of a very few people who have fished for and written about Mexican golden trout. We can assume, however, that *chrysogaster* has no major traits of life history or behavior that would differ from those of other species of trout. In their small-stream habitat, Mexican golden trout probably prefer essentially the same depths, current velocities, substrates, and types of cover that would be used by brook, brown, rainbow, or cutthroat trout if any of these species lived in these Mexican streams. They probably feed opportunistically on the same organisms that other

The Mexican golden trout is the only trout of mainland Mexico that has been officially classified.

species of trout would feed on under similar conditions, that is, on insects of the same species as those that occur in the Pacific streams of the United States.

Similar to Apache and Gila trout living in small-stream habitat, the Mexican golden trout does not grow very big. About 25 centimeters (10 inches or so) would be a large fish in most of the populations. If Mexican golden trout were stocked in a pond or lake with an abundance of food, they could be expected to grow to several pounds in weight, similar to what has been demonstrated with Gila and Apache trout.

Although detailed documentation is lacking, it appears that under the prevailing climatic regime of the area, Mexican golden trout spawn in the winter, from January to March.

HUMAN INTERVENTION

No inventory of abundance has been made and a detailed account of the distribution of Mexican golden trout within the three river drainages is unknown, but some general observations can be noted on the species' status and prospects for survival. Where roads and villages occur near streams, the Mexican golden trout is rare because fishing is not controlled. In addition, these streams historically have been used for refuse and effluent disposal. Thus pollution is a problem.

The greatest danger to the survival of this trout, however, is the introduction of nonnative trout. Reservoirs are a prime target for the introduction of hatchery rainbow trout and other nonnative species, and some reservoirs have been constructed in the drainages. If rainbow trout become established in these drainages, we can predict, based on what has happened to interior subspecies of California trout after rainbow trout were stocked, that hybridization between Mexican golden trout and rainbow trout will occur and the Mexican golden trout will lose their identity as a separate species.

We need a conservation program for Mexican golden trout so that we can gather data on distribution and abundance and document all potential threats to the continued existence of this species. The introduction of nonnative fishes, especially rainbow trout, should be prohibited and key areas of critical habitat should be identified for environmental protection. The conservation program should include setting aside sections of "ideal" trout streams and ponds and lakes where Mexican golden trout populations can be enhanced for catch-and-release or special regulation fisheries attractive to tourist anglers. If a rare and beautiful trout can be used to stimulate the local tourist industry, the economic benefits of a conservation program will become apparent and the survival of the species should be assured.

—Robert J. Behnke

Rainbow trout

Oncorhynchus mykiss

The rainbow trout, formerly *Salmo gairdneri*, now classified as *Oncorhynchus mykiss*, is an extremely wide-ranging and diverse salmonid. Under this broad umbrella are included all of the rainbowlike trout of the Pacific slope from the Tropic of Cancer in Mexico to the Arctic Circle in Alaska and the enclosed drainage basins of the high desert in eastern Oregon. Across the Bering Sea in Asia they occur on the Kamchatka Peninsula, in drainages to the Okhotsk Sea basin, and in the Commander Islands. In addition to these native populations, rainbows of hatchery origin have been introduced worldwide.

CLASSIFICATION

The scientific classification of rainbow trout has had a long and turbulent history. From the latter half of the last century to the present, there has been much uncertainty and some controversy regarding the designation and validity of species and geographical races or subspecies. The number of recognized species has ranged from one to more than fifteen; now we are back to one.

Johann Walbaum, a Swede, while cataloging the fishes George Wilhelm Steller recorded in the Arctic, was the first to describe rainbow trout in 1792, naming it *Salmo mykiss*. *Salmo* means "to leap"; *mykiss* is the native name for the fish. This was an Asian fish from Kamchatka and was largely unknown or ignored in North America. More than forty years later, Meredith Gairdner, a naturalist in the employ of the Hudson Bay Company, collected a rainbow specimen in the lower Columbia River and sent it to the renowned British naturalist, Sir John Richardson, in London, who in 1836 named the fish *Salmo gairdneri* after its donor. This specimen is now thought to have been a redband steelhead because this race of anadromous rainbows dominated the steelhead runs of the Columbia River before it was dammed. For more than two decades, *S. gairdneri* was the generally accepted scientific name for all known North American rainbows.

Then in the latter half of the nineteenth century came a spate of western explorations and natural history surveys in which a host of new species of both plants and animals were described and named. David Starr Jordan, the eminent ichthyologist of that period and the early twentieth century, and his colleagues were the leaders in describing and naming new species and races of fishes, including more than fifteen rainbow trout as full species and one redband rainbow, which they described with the cutthroat species. Most of the species named during this period have since proved to be invalid, synonymous with others, or merely subspecies, but they were generally accepted then and were published in the Report of the U.S. Commissioner of Fisheries for the fiscal year 1928. *S. gairdneri* generally referred to anadromous rainbows and *S. irideus* to resident rainbows.

In those early, less critical days, a description of a species was based largely on how it

differed from others by outward appearance: phenotypic characters and linear measurements. If it looked different or had different body proportions, it was named a separate species. Now, relying on more stringent criteria, improved techniques, and a large base of information from many studies, taxonomists evaluate the meristic characters, biochemical genetic data, and chromosomal numbers as well as phenotypic, linear, and zoogeographic information. They have shown that all of the western North American native trout formerly in the genus *Salmo* and Pacific salmon of the genus *Oncorhynchus* evolved from one common ancestral line and are more closely related to each other than any of them are to the Atlantic salmon and the brown trout of the genus *Salmo*. Hence rainbows are now classified in the genus *Oncorhynchus*. It also has been shown that the Kamchatkan trout, described in 1792, is conspecific, or identical, to the coastal rainbows in general. Therefore, to conform with the international rules of nomenclature, which state that the first name used has priority, the specific name *gairdneri* has been changed to *mykiss*, the name bestowed by Walbaum on the Kamchatkan trout almost 200 years ago. So we now have *Oncorhynchus mykiss* as the approved scientific name for all rainbows, which were first listed as such in the 1990 checklist of the American Fisheries Society.

Fine-scaled and coarse-scaled rainbows.
Under the broad but specific umbrella of *O. mykiss*, as all rainbows are now classified,

are two greatly differentiated groups, the fine-scaled, highly colorful redbands and the coarse-scaled, much less colorful coastal rainbows. It is the redband group, particularly, that has caused the confusion and controversy among taxonomists from the time of its first description in 1858. Redbands have been variously described as cutthroats, subspecies of rainbow, a link between cutthroats and rainbows, and new species altogether. In an attempt to resolve this dilemma, Behnke in 1979 tentatively proposed placing the redbands in a separate species, *S. newberrii*, named after the first one described from Oregon's Upper Klamath Lake in 1858. Meristically, phenotypically, and in chromosomal values, this proposal has biological reality and would simplify the subspeciation of the group into logical divisions. However, electrophoretic studies, charting biochemical genetic data, have failed to find any clear-cut difference between the two groups at any gene locus so far examined and therein lies the basis of the controversy.

The sequence of events leading to the differentiation between coastal rainbows and redbands began millions of years ago. According to the model accepted by most ichthyologists, the rainbow tribe diverged from the ancestral line leading to the cutthroats possibly as early as the Pliocene epoch. Later, this rainbow branch diverged again, leading to the ancestral stocks of coastal rainbows and redbands essentially as we know them today. The cutthroats came first in the colo-

THE SPECIES

nization of Pacific watersheds by western trout from the sea, penetrating the intermountain region to the Continental Divide and even beyond. The redbands came next but were stopped by barriers in the upper Columbia River system that were absent when the cutthroats went through. However, below the barriers they replaced the cutthroats almost entirely. In fact the only waters where the two are known to have coexisted without massive hybridization are headwater tributaries of the John Day River in Oregon, as Smith noted in 1984. Behnke has recently reported a similar situation in headwater tributaries of the Methow and Wenatchee rivers in Washington's Cascade Mountains, and the Salmon and Clearwater river drainages of Idaho.

The last to invade the Pacific watersheds were the coastal rainbows, and they in turn replaced the redbands eastward to the Cascade Range. The coastal rainbows did not penetrate as far inland as the redbands were able to do, however, so redbands still exist in the closed drainage basins of eastern Oregon, the mid-Columbia basin below the barriers, the Frazer River system above Hells Gate, the upper Klamath tributaries, and the upper Sacramento River system. It is noteworthy that these four rivers are the only ones in the region that have cut through the Cascade Mountain barrier and that all known populations of redbands lie east of the Cascades.

Where the ranges of the two groups overlapped there was undoubtedly some introgression, and to compound the problem we have a hundred-year history of massive introductions of hatchery fish whose origins are mostly in coastal rainbows. Consequently there are some "grey areas" where it is difficult to identify the subspecies. Fortunately many of the domesticated strains of hatchery fish could not survive the rigors of a stream environment and failed to completely contaminate the native stock.

Now only four subspecies of rainbows have some degree of acceptance–and not all ichthyologists are in accord on this. These subspecies are classified as the Kamchatkan rainbow, *O. m. mykiss*, the nominative subspecies from the type locality of the species in Kamchatka, where it was first identified; the coastal rainbow, *O. m. irideus*; the red-band, or interior rainbow, *O. m. gairdneri*; and the Eagle Lake rainbow, *O. m. aquilarum*. It should be noted, however, that the redbands are not one homogeneous group and cannot all be lumped under the subspecies *gairdneri*. According to Behnke, *gairdneri* refers only to those redbands of the Columbia and Frazer river basins east of the Cascades, and all other redbands of the upper Sacramento and upper Klamath rivers and the Oregon desert basins remain unclassified.

DESCRIPTION

Because of the great diversity within the resident or non-migratory rainbow group, only a few generalized descriptive characters can be listed that apply to the species as a whole. All are soft-rayed, short-headed, streamlined fishes with caudal fins that are noticeably forked in juveniles and almost truncate in large adults. All show the red or pink rainbow stripe at least when in spawning condition. Lake-dwelling fish are less colorful, more silvery than riverine populations.

Redbands. In general two broad categories of coloration and spotting patterns exist in the redband group and coastal rainbows. The redbands, excepting the lake-dwelling populations, are the most flamboyant of the rainbows. Some of the most colorful races could be compared to golden trout. They show varying intensities of yellow and orange on the lower sides, have eight to thirteen large, dark elliptical parr marks in a horizontal row,

The beautiful redband rainbow trout retain their parr marks into adulthood.

which are bisected by the lateral line, and sport a brick-red to purplish "rainbow stripe," which ends usually just above the anal fin. Above, below, and sometimes slightly between the elliptical parr marks are smaller, round, supplementary parr marks. Except in lake fish, the parr marks are retained into adulthood.

The back, as in most other species of trout, varies from olive green to grey or tannish, and the belly varies from white to yellowish. The cheeks are rose to carmine with a dark spot or blotch behind the eye similar to those found on cutthroats.

The lower fins usually are dusky or may show an orange tint. The pelvic and anal fins are tipped with white, the dorsal fin with white or yellow. The adipose fin usually is bordered with black or may have a few small black spots. The dorsal and caudal fins, however, are profusely spotted. Slash marks similar to those of the cutthroat appear under the lower jaw. They may be faint or prominent, and brassy to yellow, but they are usually present.

The spotting pattern on the body may vary in different populations. In some, the spots are confined to the area above the lateral line and on the caudal peduncle; others also are spotted on the lower sides and belly. The spots are generally small to medium-sized. In different populations they may vary in shape from round to irregular.

Other characteristics of the redband group are not readily apparent in a casual examina-tion but they are important to ichthyologists and taxonomists: vestigial basibranchial teeth, fifty-eight chromosomes (coastal rainbow have fifty-eight to sixty-four); finer scales, fewer pyloric caeca, and fewer gill rakers than in coastal rainbows.

Many of these attributes of the redbands are considered primitive traits and are shared with the Apache and Gila trouts, the Mexican golden trout, and the golden trout of the High Sierras.

Coastal rainbows. Compared with the colorful redbands, coastal rainbows are drab. They do not show the yellow and orange

The profusely spotted dorsal fin with the white tip (above) and the rose-to-carmine cheeks (left) are characteristic of the redband group of rainbows.

In contrast with the brightly colored redbands, coastal rainbows are rather drab. They lack the white tip on the dorsal fin and the rosy cheek blotch (lower right). Lake-dwelling fish (lower left) lose almost all markings beneath the guanine deposits.

body shades; their rainbow stripe and cheeks are much paler, more pink than red; their parr marks are not as dark and are round rather than elliptical; and they lack the white tip on the dorsal fin, the cutthroatlike slash marks, and the cheek blotch. The black spots typically are irregular in shape, sometimes X- or crescent-shaped, and may be restricted to the area above the lateral line or extend to the belly. The background colors of the back vary from olive green to grey to bluish with a silvery sheen on the sides grading to white on the belly.

The fins usually are dusky; the dorsal and caudal fins are heavily spotted, and the pelvic and anal fins may be white-tipped. Lake fish may appear entirely silvery, the black spots and pink stripe being muted by deposits of guanine secreted by internal organs. All fish become darker when in spawning condition. Their spots become more prominent and the pink cheeks and lateral stripe more intense.

Males change more than do females, and large old males tend to develop a kype, or hooked lower jaw.

Scales as identifiers. Of all the different characteristics between the two groups of rainbows, the relative size of the scales, determined by lateral counts from cheek to tail and number of scale rows counted vertically, seems to be the determining factor for classifying the fish, the "bottom line," so to speak. If it is fine-scaled, the fish is considered a redband, if coarse-scaled, a coastal rainbow. Confusing combinations of other characters that cloud identification are thought to be caused by ancient introgression between the two groups or hybridization with introduced hatchery rainbows.

DISTRIBUTION

With the exception of two small populations in the headwaters of the Mackenzie River system, an Arctic drainage, rainbow trout are endemic only to the Pacific slope where they occur in all suitable watersheds from the Kuskokwim River in Alaska to the Mexican boundary. In Mexico their native distribution is limited and disjunct: one small drainage system in Baja California and the headwaters of two small rivers on the mainland, although the taxonomic status of the trout in two other drainages remains unresolved. This great spread in latitude takes in nearly all of the Temperate Zone, from near the Arctic Circle to the Tropic of Cancer.

Outside their native range, rainbows of hatchery origin have been introduced in every state of the Union. MacCrimmon stated in 1971 that they now are established in thirty-nine of these states. Rainbows also were widely introduced in Canada and Mexico beyond their native range with populations now present in all Canadian provinces and the Yukon Territory, and in fifteen of the Mexican states.

HABITAT

The extensive range of the rainbow trout in North America comprises an array of diverse climatic, topographic, and ecological regions. Yet within all this diversity, rainbows tolerate only a narrow range of conditions optimal for growth and reproduction. Clear, cool, well-oxygenated water is probably their overriding requirement.

According to Moyle, who has studied the rainbow trout of California extensively, the optimum water temperatures for growth and feeding are from 13° to 21°C (56° to 70°F), although some populations can exist at temperatures from just above freezing for six months or more in high-elevation waters or at high latitudes to 28°C (83°F) for short periods of time. Within the optimum temperature range the dissolved oxygen of the water should be at least 5 to 6 parts per million, but at the upper limits trout need amounts close to saturation, 9 to 11 parts per million.

For optimum growth slightly alkaline waters with pH values of 7 to 8 seem to be best although one subspecies, the Eagle Lake rainbow, thrives in a highly alkaline environment with pH values as high as 9.6. In acid waters, those with a pH reading of less than 6, rainbow do not reproduce.

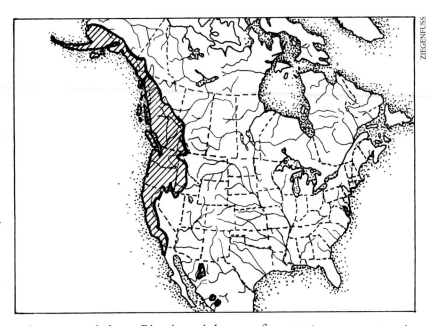

Rainbow trout are native only to the Pacific slope of North America but have been widely introduced all over the world – to every continent but Antarctica.

Streams and rivers. Riverine rainbow prefer fast-flowing streams with a high proportion of riffles to pools. They must have adequate spawning areas of clean gravel, usually in the shallow tail-out of pools or the tail of a riffle where the water velocity has slackened. There are some exceptions to this ideal habitat, however. Some populations exist in low-gradient meadow or desert streams where riffle areas are few. But for spawning they still require clean gravel areas with adequate flow.

In addition to water quality and temperature, the bottom topography and the nature of the substrate are important. Riverine rainbow prefer fast-moving streams that flow over bedrock or a freestone bottom interspersed with gravel areas. This irregular and broken substrate provides niches and crannies where invertebrates, the rainbows' primary food source, can live and feed. It also provides small eddies or slack water behind ledges or boulders where trout can hold without expending energy to breast the current. Stream rainbow are territorial and require a site where drift food is readily available with a minimum of effort and cover is nearby. Hence the more irregular and broken the substrate, the more territories available and the more trout the stream can accommodate. On the other hand, in the lower courses of many streams approaching base level, water velocity slackens with accompanying accumulations of silt so that only marginal habitat or perhaps no habitat exists for rainbow.

Rainbows usually spawn in the spring, but water temperature is the most important determining factor. If the water is warm enough, they can spawn at almost any time.

Lakes. Lacustrine rainbow live out most of their lives in still water, finding preferred temperature ranges in high-altitude lakes or in lakes or reservoirs deep enough to have cold water during the warm months. To reproduce, however, they must have a stream environment. In lakes without these streams, populations must be maintained entirely with the input of hatchery fish, although there are a few known cases of successful reproduction within a lake (typically where upwelling occurs through gravel).

In most natural lake habitats, littoral shoal areas, reefs and other shallows combine with stable water levels to provide sites where underwater vegetation can flourish, furnishing breeding places for invertebrates as well as cover for young fish. Lakes rich in nutrients are some of the most productive if the oxygen demand from decaying vegetation and algal blooms does not deplete the amount necessary to sustain trout. Thus, natural lakes are usually far more productive and provide better rainbow habitat than man-made reservoirs, which often are merely steep-sided depressions where water levels are drawn down annually during the growing season, obviating any possibility of the growth of aquatic plants.

LIFE HISTORY

Spawning. Most resident wild rainbow are spring spawners and migrate in season to gravel in spawning riffles where they themselves may have hatched out as fry. The mechanics of this process are similar to those of most other North American trout. Spawning is triggered by warming water temperatures after winter lows. Eggs are successfully incubated at temperatures ranging from 5° to 15°C (41° to 59.3°F), but below 7°C (44.7°F) embryo mortality increases inversely with the temperature. Spawning occurs usually from February to June, though in some areas it may begin earlier or be delayed until July or August. However, late-summer hatchlings may not be developed enough to survive the winter. There are even some fall spawning populations in waters warmed by thermal springs in Yellowstone Park. The great altitudinal range of the species, from near sea level to higher than 3,000 meters (10,000 feet), and the linear spread in latitude, from arctic to tropics, account for this wide range of spawning time within the species.

The number of eggs deposited by the female varies directly with her size. A fish about 13 centimeters (5 or 6 inches) long will have fewer than 200 eggs, while the large females are capable of producing 2,000 eggs per kilogram (900 per pound) of body weight. Eggs incubated at 10° to 15°C (50.2° to 59.3°F) hatch in three to four weeks (more time is required in colder water). The fry emerge from the gravel two to three weeks later upon absorption of the yolk sac. A small percentage of first-time spawners survive to spawn again, sometimes several years in succession. However, in some redband populations, as

The rainbow alevin (left) emerges from the gravel after having absorbed most of the yolk sac. Juveniles (right) may swim together for some time, but as they mature, they will become more independent.

in Pacific salmon, none survive the first spawning.

Growth. Female rainbow usually are larger than males because females typically grow faster and often reach maturity a year later than males, but the range in size at maturity is surprising. Adults can be from about 13 centimeters (5 or 6 inches) long, weighing a few ounces, to well over a meter (40 inches) in length, weighing 24 kilograms (52 pounds)! Several factors, some genetic and others environmental, account for such a span. The growth rate of rainbow generally slows or becomes negligible after maturity. Consequently trout that are genetically programmed for maturity at seven or eight years of age have a much greater opportunity to reach a larger size than do those programmed to mature at two or three years of age. The amount and quality of food is, of course, controlled by the environment, and this situation puts an effective lid on the size trout may attain in any given water. In some lacustrine habitats, however, rainbow have adapted over the millenia to feed on forage fish. Consequently they grow rapidly and they grow large. Where forage fish have been introduced for trout that were not preadapted to this source of food, the opposite result occurred: smaller adult trout. The foragers competed with the trout for food, and since any body of water can produce only so much biomass, the size of adult trout dropped.

The growth rate of rainbow in different streams varies, of course, with the available food supply and size of forage organisms. Moyle reports that in typical small California streams rainbow will reach 11 to 17 centimeters (4 to 7 inches) total length in their first year, 14 to 21 centimeters (6 to 8 inches) in their second, and 20 to 23 centimeters (8 to 9 inches) in their third, at which time most will be sexually mature. During the winter months as temperatures drop below 4° to 5°C (39° to 41°F) growth slows perceptibly or becomes negative because of lower metabolism induced by colder water. What little food is taken consists of bottom organisms, there being little drift food available, and survival until spring depends mostly on fat storage.

Behavior. As the tiny rainbow fry emerge from their natal gravel they enter a hostile world. Beset by predators large and small, by floods and droughts, they begin life fraught by hazards on every hand. Of the many that struggle up through the gravel, only a very small percentage will survive to maturity to start the process all over again.

Once free of the gravel, the fry school in the relatively slow inshore waters or quiet eddies where they can feed on small invertebrates without being swept away by the current. After several weeks of this gregarious living they begin to show their aggressive nature toward one another, the school disperses, and each fishlet must find a niche for itself. Stream rainbow are territorial in a hierarchy related to size. Thus the largest fish defends

Plunge pools created by woody debris make good nursery waters for young rainbow trout.

the best and largest territories. The situation grades down in size to young-of-the-year, which must stake out a territory in what is left, move out, or live in an exposed position, usually with fatal results. Since rainbow typically are drift feeders, at least during the warm months, a desirable territory must include a site with suitable water depth and velocity, where a fish can hold to intercept drifting invertebrates, whether in the water column or on the surface. There should also be a place to hide nearby when danger threatens—deeper water, an undercut bank, or cover of any sort.

As Moyle has reported, the trout must defend this territory against any other fish intruders, initially by an aggressive display of rigid swimming, flared cheeks, and flared fins. If this display does not sufficiently impress the trespasser, the defender will charge and give a few nips at the tail. Regardless of the tactics, if the intruder is another trout, the outcome will be decided by size and the vanquished will be forced to seek out another territory with a smaller trout in residence. If the intruder is a sucker or a cyprinid, it will not respond to the show of aggression but will be evicted by repeated rushing and tail nipping.

Hierarchies and competition. There usually is little interspecific competition for living space, as the water will be compartmentalized among the species by the selection of different microhabitats. For example, if rainbow share the water with brown trout, the rainbow will seek the riffles and faster water toward midchannel, and the browns will hold sway in the slower currents along the banks and in deep pools. Eastern brook trout and cutthroat will seek out colder water in smaller tributaries or at higher elevations in the stream than rainbow. The cyprinids and suckers will choose the warmer silty reaches lower down on the stream. Most of the competition, therefore, is among rainbow themselves, and the hierarchy is always in a state of flux because of natural predation and the removal of fish by angling.

The aggression and size hierarchy tends to break down in lacustrine populations of rainbow. Since there is no current to bring their food to them, they must cruise around as hunters either as individuals or in small schools. Growth usually is faster in lakes than in streams, and in those populations that have adapted to feeding on a forage fish base, a much greater size can be attained than in those dependent on invertebrates.

SUBSPECIES AND OTHER GEOGRAPHICAL RACES

Although no generally agreed-upon classification into subspecies currently exists for North American rainbow, for convenience they may be broken down into the following: *O. m. irideus*, *O. m. gairdneri*, and *O. m. aquilarum*. Yet within each subspecies, with the exception of *aquilarum*, which is restricted to a single lake, is a diverse array of life-history patterns, habitat preferences, and other distinctive characters that deserve recognition. In addition to the subspecies named above, there are four other groups, all interior redbands, and either they are not formally described or their classification remains in doubt. These differ from the subspecies *gairdneri* in certain morphological and genetic characters and from each other. Yet all are collectively called redbands and share many traits in common. That their differences are important in maintaining genetic diversity is now becoming increasingly apparent to fisheries managers. Several states have designated some of these diverse groups as "populations of special concern," even though their differences are not definitive. Consequently, rather than lump the subspecies together, this discussion will break out each one, again excepting *aquilarum*, into geographical units that share similar traits.

Irideus. Within the range of the subspecies *irideus*, the coastal rainbow, there are four of these geographical entities. The most southerly of these lies in the headwaters of the Rio del Presidio and adjacent Rio San Lorenzo in the Mexican state of Durango. Here on the broad top of the Sierra Madre Occidental, the topography is more plateaulike than mountainous with the headwaters wandering through gentle valleys and flats before falling into the deep gashes of the barrancas, or sheer-walled canyons, that slice through the range. At an altitude varying between 1,800 and 2,400 meters (6,000 and 8,000 feet), the country supports a pine-oak forest,

and even though it lies almost at the Tropic of Cancer, the small creeks remain cool enough to sustain trout. Very little is known about these fish and that mostly from the work of Needham and Gard published in 1959. Consequently they are only provisionally included in the coastal rainbow group, more for convenience than because of any clear-cut relationship. This study indicated that the trout in the two river systems differ from each other, and both differ from all other rainbows in some respects. In coloration and body markings they resemble redbands, those from the Rio San Lorenzo more so than those from the Rio del Presidio. In addition, the former has an extremely long adipose fin and profusion of parr marks large and small,

Riffles provide cover and help funnel drifting invertebrates to waiting trout.

SOLONSKY

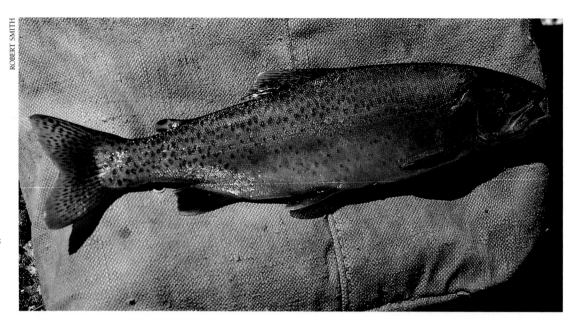

The Rio del Presidio trout is one of four geographical races of coastal rainbows (O. m. irideus). Its inclusion in this group, however, is based more on convenience than on any clear-cut relationship.

and the latter is more silvery and has a greater number of vertebrae. Behnke has written that the ancestral line leading to these trout probably had a strong redband influence, and the specimens that I saw there during a 1983 fishing expedition certainly would bear this out.

Some ichthyologists are of the opinion that these trout were hatchery introductions, but Needham and Gard reported that the native residents insisted that they had always been there and that E. W. Nelson, during one of his early faunal surveys, found them there in 1898. Furthermore, these Durango rainbows are quite different from any stocks of hatchery fish past or present.

Assuming then that these trout are actually natives, an ocean origin is indicated at some time during the Pleistocene glacial period when the Pacific was cooler and trout could roam far south of where they now occur. Since this area was never glaciated they could have invaded during any one of the four major glacial advances; an early one might account for the difference between the trout of the two drainages due to long isolation, or they may have invaded at different times from different ancestors. There also could have been some introgression between the Rio San Lorenzo trout and the Mexican golden trout of the Rio Culiacan, the next drainage to the north, as some of their headwaters almost overlap on the high plateau, making a headwater transfer a possibility.

The next geographical zone containing similar-appearing rainbows begins with the Rio Santo Domingo drainage near the village of San Quintín on the northern Baja California coast and continues north to at least the San Luis Rey River just north of Escondido, California. This area has a San Diegan type faunal zone, climate, and vegetation, and is backed by the same granitic batholith. The Rio Santo Domingo is unique on the Baja coast. Having its source on the highest range on the peninsula, the Sierra San Pedro Martir, it is the only perennial stream to reach the sea at all seasons, and the only one to contain native trout. The first specimens of this trout were collected in 1905 by Nelson, named as a full species in his honor, *Salmo nelsoni*, later relegated to subspecific status and now considered a coastal rainbow. Nelson reported it as occurring in a canyon reach from above Rancho San Antonio to the base of a barrier falls at an elevation of roughly 610 meters (2,000 feet). In later years, some of the fish were moved to the headwaters of the Santo Domingo and to a few other streams draining the west slope of the Sierra San Pedro Martir, so the range now occupied is considerably greater than the original area.

The Santo Domingo trout also strongly resemble the redband group with their brick-red band, white- or yellow-tipped fins, yellowish tinges on the lower sides, and cheek blotch. Needham and Gard even reported basibranchial teeth, a redband trait, in one specimen. They also reported a "nuchal hump," or greater-than-average body depth

Rio Santo Domingo trout
(dark phase, far left; light
phase, left) colonized this river
system by way of the sea.

behind the head. All the specimens I have seen had black spots on the iris at either side of the pupil, giving the impression of a horizontal black band across the eye, a trait shared with the Mexican golden trout, the Apache trout, and some of the redbands.

The ancestor of this trout obviously came by way of the sea. There is no other route by which it could have colonized the Rio Santo Domingo. There is some conjecture, however, as to just when this happened. According to Needham and Gard, the local residents reported that steelhead sometimes ascend the Santo Domingo during exceptionally high water conditions, probably from strays wandering down the coast from more northerly waters. Consequently, some have proposed a recent origin for the resident fish. It seems to me, however, that these trout have too many distinctive characters to be derived from a recent coastal steelhead ancestor. Among them, as Berg reported, is a unique allele found in no other trout of the genus. Furthermore, Behnke has written that he examined trout specimens from Pauma Creek, a tributary of the San Luis Rey River in California, that strongly resembled the Santo Domingo fish and suggested a strong redband influence in both populations, probably from an early introgression in the ancestral stock. Therefore, these trout probably are remnants of an original ancient population of resident fish found in all suitable waters from the Rio Santo Domingo north along the coast, possibly as far as Point Conception.

Little is known of the life history of the rainbows of the Santo Domingo. Local residents report that the fish can survive exceptionally high water temperatures, and because of the low latitude and mild climate, they are probably early spawners.

The next zone to the north is the most extensive: from Point Conception on the southern California coast to the southern edge of the Alaskan Peninsula. Within this range the coastal rainbows are both anadromous and resident fish, the steelheads being predominant except above barriers or in lakes connected to the streams. These are the classical rainbows almost everyone is familiar with: silvery, profusely spotted fish with pink cheeks and body stripes. Coloration and spotting patterns vary in fish of different drainage systems, but the group as a whole is remarkably homogeneous, especially considering more than one hundred years of indiscriminate introduction of hatchery fish. Whatever original diversity might have existed in prehatchery days is mostly gone now, at least in our three Pacific coastal states and in southern British Columbia. Some of this diversity was originally found at the north end of California's Central Valley, in the McCloud River below the barriers. These fish were highly colored, heavily spotted rainbows, and were named as a full species, *Salmo shasta*, by the early taxonomists and were thought to be the main contributor to the early stocks of hatchery fish. The original identity of this form, probably a mixture of redband and coastal rainbow, has been pretty well masked after years of hatchery introductions of various genetic strains in these waters, and it is now considered to be a coastal rainbow.

There are always exceptions, of course, as would be expected in such a huge range, one of which is the McKenzie River redside. The McKenzie, an upper Willamette River tributary heading in the high Cascades of Oregon, is home to a brightly colored rainbow with a deep-red lateral stripe: hence its local name. This would seem to indicate an ancient introgression with the redbands, which the coastal rainbows displaced in the lower Columbia system. Another oddity of the Willamette drainage: There are no resident rainbows in its western tributaries. Another slightly divergent race of coastal rainbow was described in 1896 as *Salmo beardslei* from Crescent Lake on Washington's Olympic Peninsula, but that race has since been shown to be a specialized lacustrine form of *O. m. irideus*.

In this zone there are no great deviations in life history patterns, such as age at maturity, longevity, or growth rates. The average age at maturity is three years, according to McAfee, with a typical maximum age of six or seven years. Maximum size, depending on the water and food base, varies from a few ounces in small headwater streams to more than 4.5 kilograms (10 pounds) in lakes or reservoirs with an abundant supply of forage fish.

There are still large areas of wilderness in northern British Columbia and the Alaskan Panhandle, with difficult access, where little work has been done on the fishery. Adequate study may eventually reveal some divergent strains of resident *irideus*. Captain Beardslee of the U.S. Navy gave us some tantalizing intimations of this possibility during his residence at Sitka in 1879 and 1880, but for now we can only assume that the fish in this area fall into the general pattern described above.

The last of the four geographical zones of *irideus*, the most northerly and westerly, begins on the north side of the Alaska Peninsula and continues around the Bering Sea coast to the Kuskokwim River. This area is primarily tundra, and all of the rainbows in the numerous drainages are resident fish. They also grow to be exceptionally large, old fish and are the primary attraction to the many anglers visiting the area each season. The Bristol Bay drainages receive the heaviest angler use and have therefore been most studied by the Alaska Department of Fish and Game, particularly the Lake Iliamna and Naknek River drainages. Consequently, I have relied heavily on the studies of Russell, Gwartney, and Burger for the life history of the rainbows of this area and on those of Alt for the fish of the Kuskokwim Bay drainages.

In many respects the life-history patterns of rainbows in the two areas are similar. Age at first maturity is seven years, and most spawners are eight to ten years old. Maximum longevity so far recorded is fourteen years but few survive to more than eleven. In the most northerly drainages, the Kuskokwim tributaries and those flowing to Kuskokwim Bay, the populations are entirely riverine. To the south, both riverine and lacustrine populations are present and remain distinct even though the lake fish enter the rivers to spawn and to follow the salmon runs.

These rainbows are opportunistic feeders, taking insects and other invertebrates, including clams and snails, forage fish, and even voles on occasion. However, they rely almost exclusively on salmon eggs, fry, and the flesh of dead salmon during the periods when the salmon are on their spawning runs and when their fry are available. According to Minard, growth rates and reproductive capabilities, that is, whether or not the fish will spawn in consecutive years, apparently depend upon the size of the salmon runs.

Spawning activity, as with other trout, depends upon water temperature. The timing varies from April to June from season to season. The young initially grow slowly but once they reach a size sufficient to feed on the salmon base, their growth increases rapidly. All of the fish, whether riverine or lacustrine, attain a size larger than average, but those of Lake Iliamna, known as the "Talarik strain," are the largest and often weigh more than 4.5 kilograms (10 pounds).

The riverine rainbows are colorful, profusely spotted fish and superficially resemble redbands, even to the white-tipped fins and orange slash marks on the underside of the lower jaw. The lacustrine populations acquire intense coloration only when in spawning condition. Fortunately there has been little or no introduction of hatchery rainbows in Alaska, so the native strains remain genetically undiluted.

Gairdneri. We now enter the realm of the second major group of rainbows, the redbands. This group also covers such a wide range of zoogeographic zones and habitats containing trout with diverse characteristics and life-history patterns that separate treatment of each area with its unique trout populations will be necessary.

The first of these zones to be considered is the smallest—a few tiny, often intermittent, headwaters of the McCloud River in northern California drain a heavily forested volcanic plateau just east of Mount Shasta. The trout in these streams, numbering only in the hundreds, are relict populations isolated above barriers and believed to be absolutely pure strains of the original trout to colonize the waters. Since this area was never glaciated, they could have invaded very early in the Pleistocene epoch, not just since the last push of the Wisconsin glaciation.

These unique fish were first brought to the attention of ichthyologists in 1939 when Joseph Wales, a biologist for the California Department of Fish and Game, reported "golden trout" from Tate Creek and an unnamed creek, probably Sheepheaven Creek. His identification is understandable; my first impression upon seeing these fish in 1972 was that they closely resembled the golden trout of the Kern Plateau. The trout of Sheepheaven Creek have now been the most studied taxonomically of all the redbands but are still listed as an undescribed race. They are considered by many ichthyologists to be the archetype of the redband group, the standard by which all others are judged for genetic purity. They are the most intensely colored and have distinctive morphological and genetic attributes, some of which are shared with the golden trout of the High Sierras. Sheepheaven Creek may be the most "mini" of any trout microhabitat anywhere. It originates in a tiny spring and a few sidehill seeps, flows for about a quarter of a mile and then goes underground, not to be seen again except during periods of spate. Its trout are micro as well; 15 to 18 centimeters (6 or 7 inches) is about the maximum length attained. Yet they have survived in their minus-

ROBERT SMITH

The trout of Sheepheaven Creek are considered by many experts to represent the standard for genetic purity among redbands.

cule, often harsh environment for many thousands of years—a tribute to their adaptability. But there is always the possibility that some natural catastrophe, such as a forest fire or longstanding drought, could wipe them out, so the California Department of Fish and Game has moved a few fish from the Sheepheaven Creek to two other nearby McCloud River tributaries.

Just north of the McCloud River drainage is the upper Klamath watershed in Oregon—the Klamath River above its gorge and Upper Klamath Lake with its tributary streams. This drainage system lies mostly within the same forested volcanic region, but some of the eastern tributaries reach out into the high sagebrush desert. It was from Upper Klamath Lake that the first redband was described in 1858 and named *Salmo newberrii*. But as of now these fish have been so exposed to hatchery introductions that no one is sure that the name *newberrii* is still valid. The lake fish, having a forage-fish food base, can attain a large size, and many have been taken weighing well over 9 kilograms (20 pounds). One was reported to have weighed 26 pounds. Since the Klamath system is open to the sea, coastal-rainbow steelhead once ran into the upper river before being blocked by hydroelectric dams. Hence, some fisheries workers believe that these big fish are merely landlocked steelhead. However, Behnke has written that the two races were sympatric in Upper Klamath Lake, that is, they did not hybridize, so it would seem that the present

The Deschutes redside is one of many described races of redband rainbows (O. m. gairdneri).

stock, still exhibiting strong redband characteristics, has maintained at least part of its genetic integrity despite massive introduction of hatchery fish.

The riverine populations of Klamath Basin redbands are largely restricted to the small headwater streams flowing from the southern Cascades, the isolated mountains farther to the east, and to the main Klamath River in the gorge below the lake, although the gorge is within the zone of overlap with the range of the coastal rainbow.

North of the Klamath system begins the range of the only redbands currently recognized as a valid subspecies, *O. m. gairdneri*. This range includes the mid- to upper Columbia River basin below the naturally occurring barriers to fish passage in eastern Washington, eastern Oregon, southeastern British Columbia, western Idaho, and small areas in northern Nevada and northwestern Montana; the mid- and upper Fraser River basin above Hell's Gate in British Columbia; and a few headwater tributaries of the Peace and Athabaska rivers east of the Continental Divide in both British Columbia and Alberta. This vast area includes most of the habitat types found in the Pacific Northwest: forested plateaus and mountains, parklands, and sagebrush deserts at altitudes from a few hundred to several thousand feet above sea level.

The redbands of this area were relatively late arrivals, at least in the northern part of their range, as ice of the Wisconsin stage of glaciation covered the Canadian sector until about 10,000 years ago and even intruded into the northern parts of Washington, Idaho, and Montana. McPhail and Lindsey reported in 1970 that following the retreat of the ice, the unstable drainage of the melt waters resulted in a connection between the Columbia and Fraser rivers, allowing entry of Columbia redbands into the Fraser, and that farther to the north temporary proglacial lakes in the Fraser basin allowed redbands to cross the Continental Divide into the Mackenzie system.

With such a diversity of habitats within the range of a single subspecies, one would expect a corresponding diversity in life-history patterns as the fish adapted to a variety of environmental pressures, and so it is. There are anadromous redbands as well as resident forms; riverine and lacustrine populations; and long-lived, big fish and others with short life spans and small size. There also is some variation in coloration and spotting patterns in redbands of different drainages. How much of this is due to ancestral introgression with coastal rainbows and, more recently, with hatchery introductions is unknown. Wishard and her colleagues, conducting electrophoretic studies in 1980 of eight populations of Owyhee River tributaries and adjacent streams flowing into the Snake River, found no evidence of hybridizations with hatchery rainbows. They therefore assumed that stocks of hatchery origin did not survive in the harsh environments of these waters long enough to hybridize with the native fish. But another study, by Leary and his colleagues in 1983, using a somewhat different technique, did find some evidence of hatchery influence. It seems logical to conclude that, after years of hatchery introductions, some introgression has occurred throughout the range of the subspecies, even though the harsh environment of the area studied selects against domesticated hatchery fish.

Reflecting all of this diversity, the early taxonomists described a number of races that now are considered to be synonymous with the subspecies *gairdneri*. In 1858 Suckley named a redband from the Columbia near The Dalles, Oregon, as *Salmo gibbsii*, and Jordan noted that this form was found in Columbia tributaries as far as Shoshone Falls on the Snake and was particularly common in the Deschutes River where it is still known locally as the Deschutes redside. In 1892 Jordan named a trout from Kamloops Lake in British Columbia *Salmo kamloops*. More recently, a variation of this form, a relict isolated above barriers, was described by J. R. Dymond in 1931 and named *Salmo gairdneri whitehousei*, the mountain Kamloops. The latter has many of the same traits as the redbands of Sheepheaven Creek in California and probably represents the original invaders before any introgression with coastal rainbows occurred.

The name *Kamloops trout* as a common name is well established in British Columbia where it is primarily a lake fish and known to most people as a bright silvery fish with subdued coloration except during the spawning season. The riverine populations, however, are typically colorful redbands with brick red lateral stripes. The original range has been considerably expanded in British Columbia by hatchery introductions into lakes barren of fish life but rich in food resources with some phenomenal results in the growth rates. It also has been widely stocked in the United States with indifferent results except in Lake Pend Oreille in Idaho where it grew to exceptional size.

There are some outstanding differences in the life histories of some Kamloops trout populations, of which the classic examples are the trout of Kootenay Lake in southern British Columbia. Here two separate and distinct strains of Kamloops trout live sympatrically in the same water. One strain is the "standard" Kamloops; it lives on an invertebrate food base and grows to an average size of 1 to 2 kilograms (3 or 4 pounds) and a maximum age of five or six years. The other, the Gerrard or Lardeau strain, lives on a kokanee-salmon food base, does not mature until six, seven, or even eight years of age, and attains maximum weights of more than 23 kilograms (50 pounds). It is the largest trout in North America.

Raymond, reporting on Hartman's studies, notes that this Gerrard strain selects for large size on their spawning grounds thirty miles up the Lardeau River from Kootenay Lake. Here the Lardeau flows out of Trout Lake with slightly warmer water and stable levels, allowing early maturation of the eggs and faster growth of the alevins, which gives them a competitive advantage. The current is very strong and swift so that only the very large fish are able to successfully use spawning sites. This strong flow also has scoured the substrate so that only the largest females are able to dig redds in the coarse material left. All of these factors contribute to an ongoing selective process in which the breeding stock is annually selected for greater size and greater age at maturity.

The Gerrard strain has been widely stocked in an attempt to replicate the big fish of Kootenay Lake in other waters but with only limited success, for without the kokanee food base the stocked fish can grow to only average size. The exceptions have produced some monsters, however, as at Jewel Lake in British Columbia with several fish taken weighing more than 22 kilograms (50 pounds), and at Lake Pend Oreille in Idaho that produced a fish weighing 16.8 kilograms (37 pounds) at only five years of age. The largest authenticated weight from Kootenay Lake was 23.6 kilograms (52 pounds), a female taken by an egg-collecting crew at the spawning area. But these giant trout are rare. Trout in the range of 7 to 9 kilograms (15 to 20 pounds) are far more common.

Compared with the Kamloops trout of British Columbia, the redbands in the tributaries of the Middle Snake River in eastern

Oregon, southwestern Idaho, and northern Nevada offer quite a contrast. The area is sagebrush desert with high aridity, extremes in temperatures, and low stream flows. The redbands here are small, highly colorful, stream-dwelling trout that have physiologically adapted exceedingly well to their harsh environment. Behnke reports taking specimens from an intermittent headwater of the Owyhee River in Nevada that were active and full of spirit in water of 28°C (83°F), a lethal temperature for most races of trout. Like other high desert trout, they mature early, and virtually all die after their first spawning.

Another distinctive group of redbands, still an undescribed subspecies, occupies a large tract of the high desert country of eastern Oregon and northeastern California. A part of this area lies within the drainage basin of the upper Sacramento River system. The remainder is a series of closed basins without outlets. Some of this area lies within the Columbia Plateau with the remainder in the Basin and Range province, but all areas share a similar environment with general aridity, extremes of temperature, and low, highly erratic stream flows. The trout, too, have much in common, particularly in adapting to the harsh conditions and in their life history patterns.

The closed basins of the Oregon high desert contained large lakes at the close of the Pleistocene glacial period, but now only a few remnants remain, their former size and depth still evident as fossil shorelines on surrounding hills and slopes. The trout in these lakes ate chubs and probably were very large fish, but as the lakes dessicated in the warming and drying trend following the retreat of the ice, the survivors found refuge in the few small streams that drained into the basins from the surrounding mountains and of necessity became small-stream dwellers. Many of these streams, particularly in their lower courses, were marginal trout habitat at best with low flows, high summer temperatures, and wide diurnal fluctuations, but the trout adapted to these vastly changed conditions and we know the fish today as desert redbands.

There are eight of these basins, all closed systems with no outlets to the sea except the Goose Lake basin straddling the border of Oregon and California, which has infrequently overflowed into the Pit River, a headwater tributary of the Sacramento. Two basins, the Alvord and Coyote, contain cutthroats but the other six all have redbands. Three of these basins never overflowed even at the highest lake levels so their trout populations have been isolated from each other for many thousands of years. This long isolation, together with an unknown degree of ancient introgression with coastal rainbows and more recent exposure to hatchery fish, may account for the diversity in these redband populations, for they all differ slightly from each other.

They all look like redbands, however, and share a life history pattern similar to the redbands of the Middle Snake River tributaries: None survive long after their first spawning. Hosford and Pribyl, in their 1983 studies of the Malheur Basin redbands, found that 97 percent of the fish in their sample were age three years or younger, that most spawned at age three, and that no fish had spawned twice.

It is interesting to speculate how and when these desert redbands colonized their present harsh environment, since the present closed basins had no outlets, except the Goose Lake basin, in postglacial times. There is evidence, however, of an ancient Columbia River connection prior to the Wisconsin stage of glaciation, and the trout reflect this affinity with Columbia River redbands in their high vertebral numbers. Other than this, they have a higher gill raker number and the primitive 100 allele which they share with coastal rainbows, upper Sacramento redbands, and golden trout. The Goose Lake basin fish and those in its infrequent outlet, the upper Pit River, share some of the characteristics of coastal rainbows and the Sacramento redbands as well as those of the Oregon basin fish, indicating an ancient mixing of ancestral stocks.

In the small-stream environments occupied by desert redbands, the trout are generally small, with few exceeding a length of about 26 centimeters (10 inches). When introduced into man-made reservoirs with a richer food supply, such as forage fish, however, they grow to a fairly large size though they still have a short life span.

Aquilarum. The last of the rainbow subspecies, the Eagle Lake rainbow, *O. m. aquilarum*, described by J. O. Snyder, is native only to Eagle Lake in northeastern California, a large, highly alkaline natural lake lying on the western edge of the Lahontan Basin. The rainbow's occurrence there is an enigma to zoogeographers and ichthyologists because all other native trout in the Lahontan Basin are cutthroats, and all the fish fauna in Eagle Lake except the rainbows are endemic to the Lahontan Basin. This has led some to suspect that the rainbows were introduced there by early settlers. But if this had actually happened, the introduced fish would not have survived the high alkalinity, which is lethal to all trout except the Eagle Lake rainbow. The most probable alternative is an early headwater transfer from the Pit River into Eagle Lake's only tributary, Pine Creek, after the original native cutthroat became extinct during a hyperthermal period about 5,000 years ago. This would give the Eagle Lake rainbows, many of which are preadapted to high alkalinity, a redband ancestry. Then, too, Eagle Lake, having no natural outlet, was probably less alkaline thousands of years ago when the transfer occurred and the trout adapted as the alkalinity slowly increased.

Eagle Lake rainbows have a long life span, eleven years being the oldest age recorded, and grow to large size on a tui chub food base. They are highly colorful fish at spawning time. They originally spawned in Pine Creek, but Pine Creek has become so degraded that this is no longer possible. Consequently, eggs are taken annually, propagated in hatcheries, and restocked into the lake to maintain the population. Pure populations also are maintained in three lakes in the Caribou Wilderness area in Mt. Lassen National Park, and they have been stocked in other lakes in California and elsewhere in the western states.

Snyder also described two other rainbows from nearby Lahontan waters: the royal silver trout, *Salmo regalis*, from Lake Tahoe, California, and the emerald trout, *Salmo smaragdus*, from Pyramid Lake, Nevada. Both of these probably were introduced hatchery rainbows, and both are now extinct.

Rainbows prefer fast-moving water, but they can occasionally be found in cold, clear pools.

ANDERSON

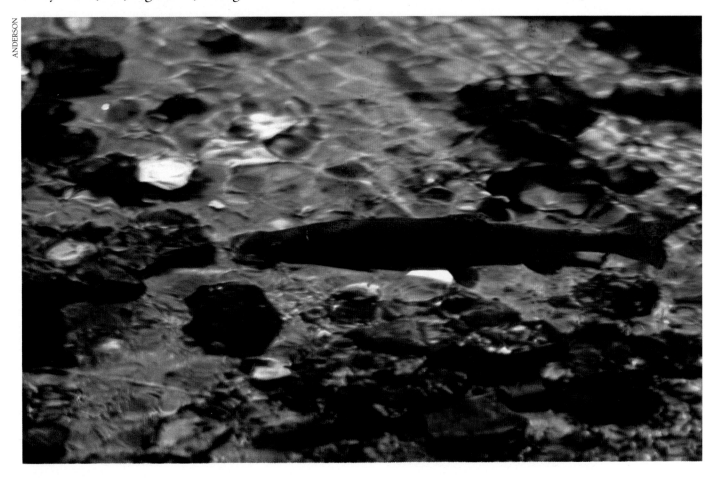

Human intervention

As a species the rainbows are doing well. Through the efforts of man the range of rainbows has been expanded across the United States to include all states except Louisiana, Mississippi, and Florida. The range also incorporates all the Canadian provinces and fifteen Mexican states. In addition rainbow populations are now established worldwide, on every continent except Antarctica. There are undoubtedly more rainbows on Earth today than at any previous time.

When we come to subspecies and discrete geographical strains of rainbows, it is a different story. Since domestic hatchery rainbows of polygenetic origins will hybridize freely with pure strains of native rainbows, our hundred-year history of indiscriminate hatchery introductions has severely compromised the genetic purity of the native races. This is particularly true in California, Oregon, Washington, Idaho, and to some extent, southern British Columbia. In these areas some races have been completely hybridized out of existence and others hang on as pure strains in a few remote headwaters. As Behnke has pointed out, what has been lost here is intraspecific diversity—the adaptive traits acquired by thousands of generations of rainbows to successfully cope with the individual demands of their habitats, such as tolerance to high water temperatures, high alkalinity, low stream flows, ability to use a specialized food base, and life history patterns governing age at maturity, maximum size, and longevity. Once lost, these genetic resources cannot be replaced.

Along with this genetic swamping by introduced hatchery rainbows, the natives have had to contend with environmental degradation of their habitats through poor land-use practices, pollution, water diversions, dams, and all the ills associated with urban development and industrialization. In the western states the greatest impact on riparian habitat has been clear-cut logging, mining, overgrazing by livestock, and water diversions for agriculture, and though we are told we are in an enlightened period of resource management, the evidence of this is not apparent.

And so today we have lots of rainbows, mostly mass-produced factory fish ill-adapted for life in the wild, and a few remnants of the real things, a tragic reminder of what we once had. The bright spots in this dismal picture are in Mexico, northern British Columbia, and Alaska where native rainbow populations exist without being affected by hatchery transplants.

—Robert Henry Smith

Steelhead

Oncorhynchus mykiss

Early fishermen named fish according to what they saw. Some say the steelhead, also called ironhead, was so named because of its hard, bony skull. Others say the beautiful steel-blue color on its head and back when it is at sea inspired the name. Early commercial fishermen called it steelhead salmon, thinking it was a salmon. In the latter part of the nineteenth century, anglers on the Pacific coast often called any trout caught in or near salt water steelhead trout. Taxonomists eventually separated the various species of trout and gave them official scientific and common names. Yet throughout all the years and throughout all the changes in trout and salmon names, the steelhead, with a hard, unbending consistency like its meaning, has persisted.

CLASSIFICATION

Steelhead, *Oncorhynchus mykiss*, is the name most commonly given to the rainbow trout that journeys to the sea as an unimpressive juvenile and returns from the sea as a large maturing adult. The steelhead, which actually spends half of its life in the ocean, is an anadromous fish. That is, it migrates from salt water to fresh water to spawn.

The scientific name of the steelhead, *Oncorhynchus mykiss*, was changed from the more familiar name, *Salmo gairdneri*, in 1988 because taxonomists determined that the native rainbow trout (including steelhead) is more closely related to Pacific salmon, *Oncorhynchus* spp., than to fish in the genus *Salmo*, which includes Atlantic salmon, *S. salar*, and brown trout, *S. trutta*.

Rainbow trout that migrate from streams into large inland freshwater lakes and later return to those streams as adult spawners are also often called steelhead. Some of these runs were started with eggs obtained from Pacific coast steelhead stocks; others apparently were from naturally reproducing runs of resident rainbow trout.

The steelhead, then, is simply a migratory strain of rainbow trout. In fact, at the juvenile stage, the steelhead is nearly impossible to distinguish from the resident rainbow. In some cases the two can be distinguished by an in-depth study of otolith characteristics, as McKern noted in 1971, or serum protein patterns, as Huzyk and Tsuyuki noted in 1974.

Steelhead also can be difficult to distinguish from their cousin, the cutthroat trout, *Oncorhynchus clarki*, of which there are likewise freshwater and anadromous strains. The two species can be difficult to distinguish for those unfamiliar with the few identifying characteristics. Steelhead lack the teeth on the back of the tongue and the red streaks beneath the jaw that characterize the cutthroat trout. In many Pacific coast streams, steelhead and cutthroat are found together. Usually the cutthroat inhabits the upper, more isolated portions of the streams, but Dougel and colleagues reported in 1973 that the two species have been known to hybridize.

DESCRIPTION

Steelhead have the typical trout body: elongated and moderately laterally compressed with a relatively small head. Spotting and color patterns vary with life stage, environment, and strain of fish. The coloration in general matches the particular strain from which the steelhead has descended. All steelhead, however, possess sharply defined black spots on the back, head, and dorsal and caudal fins. At sea, and in large clear lakes, nearly mature adult steelhead are metallic blue on the dorsal surface, or back, and bright silver on the sides grading to white on the belly. After entering streams, adult steelhead gradually take on the appearance of stream rainbow trout. The back becomes olive green and the sides and belly less silvery. These changes occur partly because pigment cells react to the different patterns of light and dark in the environment. In addition, they respond to hormonal changes occurring in the adaptation from a marine to a freshwater environment. Both steelhead and resident rainbow trout have ten to twelve fin rays in the dorsal fin, and eight to twelve rays in the anal fin. The tail, or caudal fin, is only slightly forked.

As spawning time approaches, the adults, particularly the males, darken and develop a broad pink-to-red band along the lateral line and pink coloration on the opercula, or gill covers. Mature males also develop kypes, as do mature male Pacific salmon and other salmonids.

Juvenile steelhead in streams look exactly like resident rainbow trout. Both have the black spots on the back and on the dorsal and caudal fins; the very young fish have only a few spots on the caudal fin. Juveniles of both strains have five to thirteen parr marks, which are oval or round dark blotches widely spaced along the lateral line.

DISTRIBUTION

The steelhead is native to the north Pacific Ocean and ranges at sea from northern Baja California to the Bering Sea and Japan. Historically, steelhead entered coastal streams in southern California and northern Baja California. Today, because of water diversion, which causes critically low stream flows, increased water temperatures, channelized streams, reduced living space, and increased pollution, the southern range has been reduced to the Ventura River just north of Los Angeles.

The northern range probably has not changed. Steelhead are common to coastal streams of northern California, Oregon, Washington, British Columbia, and Alaska. And many inland tributaries of the Columbia and Snake rivers in Oregon, Washington, and Idaho have steelhead populations.

Steelhead probably were introduced into the Great Lakes unintentionally. In 1876 an enterprising sportsman stocked Michigan's Au Sable River, a stream emptying into Lake Huron, with rainbow trout from the McCloud River in California. In 1883 the

THE SPECIES

Steelhead females develop a broad pink stain on their cheeks as spawning time nears, but it isn't nearly so vivid as that of the male.

The tail of a steelhead is spotted and only slightly forked, if at all.

The dramatic red of the male's gill covers and the development of a kype signal the onset of spawning.

Ontario government stocked Lake Superior streams near Sault Sainte Marie with the McCloud River rainbows. But what were thought to be resident stream rainbows soon surprised everyone. They migrated to the Great Lakes, and large steelhead returned to the stream. The upper McCloud River, it turned out, was a spawning area for steelhead as well as resident rainbow. Eggs undoubtedly were collected from both forms during hatchery spawning operations.

Steelhead runs began on the Little Manistee River, a tributary of Lake Michigan, in the 1890s. These are the first known runs in the Great Lakes area. By the early 1900s steelhead were well established in tributaries of the upper Great Lakes. Today steelhead run into tributaries of all the Great Lakes. They also have been reported recently in tributaries of the Gulf of Saint Lawrence where they are encroaching into waters of the Atlantic salmon.

Steelhead eggs were intentionally collected by the U.S. Fish Commission in 1893 for distribution to many waters of the United States. By 1900 there were steelhead present in Colorado, Connecticut, Maine, Michigan, Minnesota, Montana, New Hampshire, New Jersey, New York, Pennsylvania, Utah, Vermont, Wisconsin, and Wyoming. Many of these introductions were unsuccessful in establishing self-sustaining populations and the fish disappeared over time.

There are migratory rainbow trout populations in some tributaries of New York's Finger Lakes, but whether these fish originated from steelhead stocks is uncertain. Juvenile steelhead were stocked in Vermont tributaries of Lake Champlain as recently as 1980, and there are runs of adult fish in some Lake Champlain streams that the local anglers call steelhead. They likely are correct, because steelhead were stocked there in 1980.

LIFE HISTORY

Migrations upstream. The life history of the steelhead varies more than that of any other anadromous fish. For nearly every statement concerning a stage of life, there are exceptions. Some steelhead enter streams fully mature and spawn in a relatively short time after their upstream journey. Other steelhead are maturing as they enter the stream but do not become completely ready to spawn for eight to ten months. Generally steelhead are classified into two races: winter steelhead, which enter streams between November 1 and April 30, and summer steelhead, which enter streams between May 1 and October 30. Portions of both groups may enter spawning streams in spring or fall and are then often designated as spring- or fall-run steelhead. Some steelhead may enter large river systems such as those of the Columbia in Washington and Oregon and the Sacramento in California every month of the year.

Regardless of when they enter the streams, nearly all steelhead spawn sometime from December through June. Thus, winter-run steelhead spawn relatively soon after they migrate upstream, usually between December and February, whereas summer-run fish enter the stream immature and spawn several months later, between March and June. Although winter-run steelhead and summer-run steelhead potentially could interbreed, they probably do not because their spawning seasons do not coincide. Summer steelhead also tend to spawn in smaller streams and farther upstream than do winter-run fish.

Before dams were built on the Columbia River, some steelhead traveled as far as 744 kilometers (1,200 miles) to their spawning grounds. Steelhead spawning in tributaries of the Salmon River in Idaho have migrated 496 kilometers (800 miles) from salt water. But there also are small coastal streams where steelhead need swim only one or two miles to find suitable spawning areas.

An interesting exception to this pattern is the "half-pounder" steelhead of the Rogue River in southern Oregon and the Klamath, Mad, and Eel rivers of northern California. These unusual fish spend only a few months at sea before they migrate to fresh water. Half-pounders are immature and, unlike mature steelhead, feed extensively after entering their natal streams. These small steelhead (23 to 38 centimeters [9 to 15 inches] long) enter fresh water annually from late August to early October and are the basis of important sport fisheries. Half-pounders that survive their first upstream migration return to the ocean the following spring, then migrate

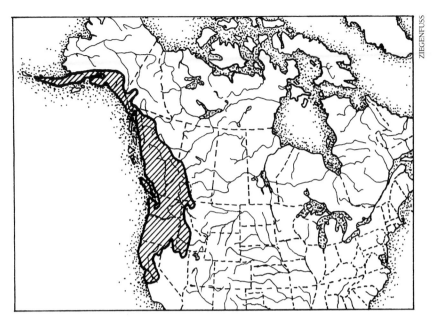

ZIEGENFUSS

back to fresh water as maturing steelhead the following summer and fall.

Steelhead, like other anadromous fish, tend to return to their parent stream to spawn. Within a few months after hatching, steelhead juveniles imprint on their home stream—that is, they "memorize" its odor—and, as returning adults, they can find their way back with remarkable consistency. The percentage of straying to other streams is quite low, especially for wild fish. Shapovalov and Taft reported in 1954 that the straying rate of steelhead during a nine-year study for two streams averaged only 3 percent and 9 percent. The homing instinct seems to depend largely on the fish's ability to sense the particular water chemistry of its natal stream; steelhead and salmon have remarkably sensitive olfactory systems.

In some cases the timing of upstream migrations of spawners appears to be correlated with freshets; each storm seems to bring in a new group of fish. This relationship is most apparent in winter steelhead runs. Steelhead ascend on both rising and falling stream levels, but cease movement during flood peaks. Some studies have shown a correlation between upstream movement and an increase in water temperatures. The occurrence of a series of high tides also seems to trigger entry into fresh water. Yet some groups of steelhead may move upstream when there are no observable changes in the environment; instead, physiological changes in the adults may be the catalyst. Upon entering fresh

Steelhead (migratory rainbow trout) are native to the north Pacific slope. Wild steelhead populations have declined during this century, especially over the last four decades, largely as a result of human activities. Dam construction, increased silt loads and water temperature changes resulting from streamside earth disturbance and logging activities, and overfishing are factors contributing to this decline.

water, hormonal changes occur that speed up the maturation of gametes in preparation for spawning. These changes apparently stimulate upstream migration toward the spawning grounds.

Individual steelhead runs on individual streams tend to occur at about the same time year after year. Over time the fish have adapted to the environmental conditions of their stream to ensure that the greatest number survive. Entry and upstream migration on some streams may be delayed by the physical conditions of the streams. Many small streams have such low flows that migration cannot occur until several storms provide enough water.

Although steelhead will move upstream during any time of the day or night, peak movement generally occurs an hour before to an hour after sunrise and again in the evening from dusk into early night.

The sex ratio of most spawning runs is about 1:1 except in streams with significant numbers of repeat spawners. Studies have shown that male steelhead dominate the early portion of some runs, and females make up the majority of the late runs. Most repeat spawners are females. Usually steelhead males each spawn with more than one female and are in the stream longer than the females; thus they expend large amounts of energy over a longer period of time, which reduces their chances of surviving the spawning season.

Because the stomachs of adult steelhead taken by anglers are usually empty, it was earlier thought that steelhead do not feed while they migrate upstream. Later studies have shown that the longer steelhead spend in fresh water, the more likely they are to have food in their stomachs. Stomachs of steelhead taken low in the drainage tend to be empty or contain only small amounts of food; stomachs of steelhead taken far upstream are sometimes full of various food items. Summer steelhead, which spend many months in a stream before spawning, enter fresh water with high body-fat content and are thus equipped to survive long periods without feeding. Nevertheless they will take food if it becomes easily available. Half-pounder steelhead do feed extensively in fresh water. Food found in the stomachs of both half-pounders and adult steelhead consists mostly of aquatic stages of caddis flies, mayflies, and stone flies; salmon eggs are not uncommon either. Somewhat surprisingly, fish are rarely found.

Spawning. Steelhead spawn in the stream where the water is cool, clear, and well-oxygenated. They are also choosy about water depth, current velocity, and size of the gravel in the streambed. The most common redd site is at the tail of a pool close to the point where the smooth surface water breaks into the riffle below.

As with other stream-dwelling salmonids, the female steelhead chooses the redd site, and builds her redd where it is rarely exposed by falling water levels. Measurements made over steelhead redds show that steelhead spawn in water of 10 to 138 centimeters (4 to 54 inches) deep where the velocity of the current is 0.6 to 1.5 meters (2 to 5 feet) per second, and the gravel is 0.64 to 13 centimeters (0.25 to 5 inches) in diameter. A large female can excavate larger gravel and swim better in stronger currents than can a smaller one, so a large female can build her redd in an area that the smaller fish cannot use. In small streams the female sometimes selects a spawning site that appears to be unfavorable, even when there are unused adequate spawning areas nearby.

The female may try several spots, digging to test each of them, only to abandon them until she locates a suitable site. She excavates a pit by repeatedly turning on her side and dislodging gravel with rapid movements of the tail fin. A large female can excavate a pit a foot deep and a foot and a half wide. Although male steelhead may be close by, they do not participate in digging the redd. Among the males will be a dominant fish, usually the largest, and one or more subordinate fish called accessory males. The dominant male divides his time between driving off accessory males and courting the female before spawning.

The actual process of spawning takes only a few seconds. The female deposits her eggs into the deepest part of the pit, and the male instantly moves alongside and deposits the milt simultaneously. The female immediately begins to cover the fertilized eggs by digging to each side and in front of the nest. The fertilization rate is high, usually exceeding 95 percent. The female excavates several redds, each one often directly upstream of the previous nest, so that digging a redd helps bury the one immediately downstream.

In high stream flow, steelhead will tend to spawn farther up in the watershed in small tributaries. They also spawn in intermittent streams. However, most of the fry emigrate to perennial streams soon after hatching. They will return to the intermittent streams to spawn. If the water is not flowing, they will spawn in larger streams nearby, usually downstream of the natal tributary.

The female steelhead generally is able to extrude nearly all of her eggs during the spawning process. The larger the female, the more eggs she will produce (that is, the greater her fecundity). On a weight basis, a 5- to 10-pound female will contain about as many eggs as she weighs in pounds multiplied by 1,000. A female in poor condition often will have a lower egg count.

Unlike salmon, steelhead do not always die just after spawning, though comparisons of condition factors, or measurements of health, of adult steelhead have shown that the longer the adults remain in the streams, the more the body condition of the fish deteriorates. After spawning, the spent steelhead that have survived the rigors of the process descend back to the sea. Anglers term those migrating to salt water *downstreamers*. Some of them return quickly to salt water; others linger in large pools for several weeks. Such fish do not appear to resume active feeding until they return to the ocean.

Some steelhead migrate to the ocean and back to their native streams to spawn once each year for several years. Along the Pacific coast, the incidence among steelhead of spawning more than once increases from north to south. The percentage of repeat spawners varies widely depending upon distance to the spawning grounds, quality of the spawning habitat, genetic factors, and angling pressure. Some runs have few repeat spawners; other runs may exceed a 30 percent ratio of repeat spawners. Fish returning to spawn a second time will make up 70 to 85 percent of repeat spawners, and third-time spawners 10 to 25 percent; fourth-time

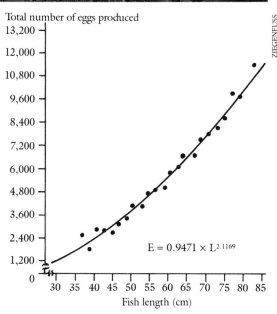

Top: *With her powerful tail, a large female steelhead can cut a redd a foot deep and 1½ feet wide.* Above: *The long migration endured by many steelhead can make them susceptible to fungal infections. Larger female steelhead tend to produce greater numbers of eggs, although numbers are not necessarily linked to fertility (older females, though large, may produce infertile eggs). A 52-centimeter (20-inch) female steelhead extrudes an average of about 3,500 eggs during spawning. An 82-centimeter (32-inch) female, about 30 percent longer, produces an average of 10,000 to 12,000 eggs— about two and a half times as many eggs as the smaller fish.*

Total number of eggs produced

$E = 0.9471 \times L^{2.1169}$

Fish length (cm)

spawners are rare. Repeat spawners do not increase greatly in size between spawning periods. They use most of their energy to restore the body loss caused by the rigors of the previous spawning and to develop new reproductive material – eggs and milt – for the next spawning.

From egg to adult. As with other salmonids, the newly fertilized steelhead egg is quite delicate and subject to "shock" by too

---

Dissolved oxygen

---

*T*he amount of dissolved oxygen in the water is critical to steelhead during the incubation period. Concentrations at or near saturation with no temporary reductions below 5 parts per million are best. Low levels of dissolved oxygen will extend the incubation period and hatching, will increase the number of abnormal embryos, and will result in smaller, weaker fry. Sustained oxygen concentrations below 2 parts per million usually result in the complete loss of eggs.

The amount of dissolved oxygen available to incubating eggs can drop if too much fine organic and inorganic material is present in the gravel. Oxygen levels may appear satisfactory, but the amount of oxygen actually reaching the embryos can be inadequate because fine sediments block the intragravel water flow and because the breakdown of organic material uses up the oxygen.

Oxygen levels in natural streams are normally near saturation, except in small tributaries that have too much decaying organic debris because of logging or other sources and in streams receiving large amounts of municipal or industrial waste. Low oxygen concentration can reduce the swimming abilities of migrating steelhead, cause them to avoid certain sections of water, and stop the migration.

– Roger A. Barnhart

---

much tumbling, as could happen in a flood that scours out the redd and exposes the eggs. However, the egg immediately begins to absorb water and is "water hardened" within twenty-four hours. After further development, the embryo eventually reaches the "eye" stage, when the eyes of the fish can easily be seen through the opaque eggshell. It is during the eyed-egg stage that hatchery steelhead eggs are moved, counted, and shipped to other areas because the eggs are most easily handled then without injury.

If the fertilized eggs are buried in gravel with a good intragravel flow of well-oxygenated water and only small amounts of silt or fine sand, most of the eggs will develop normally and hatch, and the fry will successfully emerge. The time required for the steelhead embryo to fully develop and hatch varies with water temperature. From fertilization to hatching requires only about twenty days at 15.4°C (60°F). It requires about thirty-three days at 9.9°C (50°F) and almost eighty days at 4.4°C (40°F).

Newly hatched fry spend from two to five weeks in the yolk-sac stage, depending largely upon water temperature. The yolk-sac fry at first are still buried beneath the surface of the stream bottom, surviving in spaces or interstices between the rocks. They depend solely on yolk material for nourishment and may spend two to three weeks in the gravel environment before emerging into the water column. Fry sometimes migrate several feet horizontally through the gravel medium as they work their way to the surface.

Upon emergence, the fry, also called alevins, learn to feed and for a few days live on a combination of yolk material, of which little remains, and food taken externally. By the time the yolk material is completely gone (the young steelhead are said to be buttoned up at this point), the inch-long fry are feeding and swimming actively and are well equipped to depend solely on external food for nourishment.

After emergence steelhead fry, often in small schools, will inhabit the margins of the stream until they become stronger swimmers. As the fry grow larger and more active, they begin to disperse, primarily downstream. The schools break up, and individual fish begin to establish territories (microhabitats that contain feeding lanes and resting areas), which they defend. The size of the territory for a single juvenile depends largely on the availability of food and the size of the fish.

At first steelhead fry feed primarily on microscopic organisms such as zooplankton. Under good conditions the fry grow fast and are soon large enough to eat a variety of aquatic and terrestrial insects. Growth rate is highest in the spring and early summer. In one to two months steelhead fry grow to fingerling size (fingerlings are also called parr because of the pigment blotches—parr marks—on their sides) and move into the riffle areas of the stream. Most steelhead in their first year of life live in riffles, but some larger fish inhabit pools or deep, fast runs.

Young steelhead moving about in search of suitable territories are subject to the highest predation. Instream cover such as large rocks, logs, root wads, and aquatic vegetation is important to them because it provides resting areas, visual isolation from competitive siblings, food, and protection from predators. As you might expect, densities of juvenile steelhead are highest in areas containing instream cover. However, habitat degradation has lowered the capacity of many streams to rear steelhead successfully. Excessive sedimentation, for example, reduces food production, pool depth, and cover—all important to juvenile steelhead survival.

The edge of life. Most steelhead die between the fertilized-egg stage and the downstream

If food is plentiful and weather conditions are good, steelhead fry can achieve very rapid growth.

migration. Though, under normal stream conditions, perhaps 80 percent of the fertilized eggs survive to at least the emerged-fry stage, a long-term study of steelhead in a small California coastal stream by Shapovalov and Taft showed a mean survival rate there of only 3 percent overall from egg to eventual downstream migrant.

The optimum time for emergence is just before the time of total yolk absorption. If the gravel in which the steelhead eggs are incubating becomes degraded by increased sedimentation, which reduces intragravel water flow and the level of dissolved oxygen, many eggs may not hatch. Of those that do hatch, surviving fry may be delayed in emerging from the gravel or unable to emerge at all. The condition of fry upon emergence from the gravel has an important bearing on their early survival in the wild, and although a short delay may seem inconsequential, late-emerging fry have exhausted their yolk supply and are becoming progressively weaker; they are poorer swimmers and are

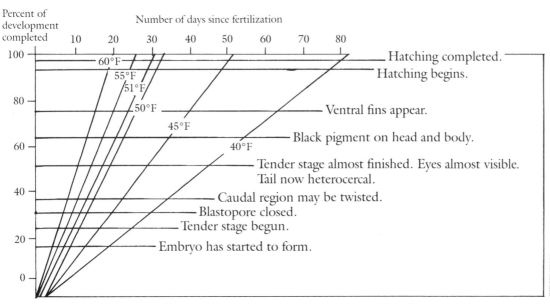

Trout eggs require certain temperature ranges to develop properly. Water temperatures of 15.4°C (60°F) will cause steelhead eggs to develop fully and hatch about 20 days (three weeks) after fertilization. In contrast, development and hatching in water at 4.4°C (40°F) takes about 80 days (2½ months), or about four times as long. Egg survival is strongly linked to water quality and temperature; habitat degradation and inappropriate temperatures can destroy the eggs.

more vulnerable to predators than fry that emerge on time.

The first few days of life in the stream, when fry begin to feed and establish themselves, are extremely critical. The newly emerged fry must soon find adequate food or they, like their late-emerging siblings who did not survive, also will weaken and become more vulnerable to predators, diseases, and starvation. The mortality rate for steelhead is highest during the first few months after fry emergence (it is not uncommon to lose 50 percent of the fry during the first month), and many investigators suggest that the relative strength or size of the year class is largely determined then.

Larger, older steelhead probably prey on fry more often than do any other species, though the fry also fall victim to other trout species, sculpins, great blue herons, belted kingfishers, mergansers, the American dipper, the common garter snake, and various mammals, such as the river otter and the raccoon.

Migrations downstream. The length of time steelhead live in streams before emigrating to the ocean varies greatly within stocks and particularly between stocks. Withler reported in 1966 that along the Pacific coast, the length of time in fresh water increases from south to north, primarily because growing seasons are longer, water temperatures higher, and stream productivity higher in southern streams. In northern streams the

Temperature

Steelhead, like other living organisms, have specific environmental requirements, which vary with each stage of life. Water temperature affects all metabolic and reproductive activities and conditions of fish, including feeding, growth, age at maturity, and time and success of spawning. A steelhead-rearing stream should have summer temperatures ranging from 4° to 10°C (40° to 50°F). Steelhead have difficulty extracting oxygen from water at temperatures exceeding 21°C (70°F), even when the water has a high oxygen content. The literature lists the preferred rearing temperatures of steelhead as 7° to 15°C (45° to 60°F), with an optimum of about 10°C (50°F) and the upper lethal limit as 23.6°C (75°F).

Low water temperatures extend the smolting period for steelhead, and high temperatures shorten the smolting process. Smolting ceases when water temperatures increase to between 13.7° and 17.6°C (57° and 64°F).

Low water temperatures during the winter affect the behavior and growth of juvenile steelhead. In northern-range streams, when water temperatures drop below 4°C (40°F), young steelhead become inactive; they hide in cover or in the substrate and stop growing. In southern-range streams, where winter temperatures are higher, juvenile steelhead are active during the day, feed when insect hatches occur, and continue to grow.

Spawning steelhead are sensitive to changes in water temperature; a sudden drop in temperature may cause spawning activity to stop. The optimum spawning temperature for steelhead is about 7°C (45°F) but they have been reported spawning at temperatures of 3.8° to 12.6°C (39° to 55°F). An increase in the water temperature of streams that have temperatures near the upper limit for incubation and rearing can increase the susceptibility of eggs, fry, and fingerlings to disease.

—Roger A. Barnhart

fish need more time to reach the physiological maturity required to adapt to saltwater existence.

The ages of downstream migrant steelhead in a central California stream ranged like this: 19 percent less than one year old; 24 percent one year old but less than two; 53 percent two years old but less than three; 4 percent three years old but less than four; and less than 1 percent were more than four years old. Conversely, the age of steelhead migrating from a small southeast Alaska stream ranged from two to five years, and 92 percent of them were three or four years old.

Most steelhead migrating out of their home stream for the first time are smolts, the term applied to an anadromous juvenile salmonid that has undergone physiological, morphological, hormonal, and behavioral changes to prepare for life in salt water. Steelhead smolts lose their parr marks and become silvery. The literature suggests that development of the smolt stage (smoltification) and seaward migration are stimulated by environmental factors, including photoperiod, water chemistry, and water temperature, according to reports by Wagner in 1974 and Kerstetter and Keeler in 1976. The most common time for steelhead smolts to migrate from streams is March through June for both summer- and winter-run races.

Downstream migrations of steelhead are not necessarily related to smolting, however. In intermittent nursery streams, steelhead fry are forced to move out as soon as streamflow, and therefore habitat, decreases. These fish move into larger streams to grow. When intermittent streams are recharged by the first storms of the wet season, juvenile steelhead will migrate back into them. These young steelhead, many of which were hatched in the same stream, make use of the newly available habitat and also avoid the heavier winter flows common to the larger streams. Some steelhead juveniles also migrate downstream in the fall with the first storms. These fish are apparently responding to the change in streamflow but have not gone through the smolting process.

In some stream systems juvenile steelhead migrate downstream into an estuary and live there from one to six months before entering the ocean. Estuaries are usually rich in food

organisms, and the young steelhead will grow faster than their siblings who remain upstream. The larger the smolt when it enters the ocean, the better its chances of survival to adulthood.

Life in the sea. When steelhead enter the ocean or large inland lakes, they begin the period of fastest growth and greatest travel. Immature steelhead can grow more than two and a half centimeters (one inch) in length each month from the time they enter the ocean until they return to fresh water. In California the average length of steelhead after two years in the ocean is 59 centimeters (23 inches), according to a 1966 report by Withler.

Biologists use a numerical system to record the number of years steelhead have spent in fresh water and in the ocean. They say, for example, that a three-year-old steelhead that has spent one year in fresh water and two years at sea is 1/2. Most half-pounders are 1/1 or 2/1. Adult wild steelhead in the southern half of the range of steelhead along the Pacific coast are generally 1/2, 2/2, 2/3 or 3/2. Most wild adult steelhead entering northern range streams are 2/2, 2/3, 3/2, or 3/3 fish.

The size of steelhead at maturity depends primarily upon how long they have lived in the ocean or in lakes. The length of time they spend at sea varies widely. Along the Pacific coast the length of residence in both fresh water and salt water increases from south to north. At the southern end of the range, young steelhead grow fast and migrate to sea

These fish are easily identified as steelhead smolts by their silvery color, a consequence of the changes they go through in preparation for life at sea.

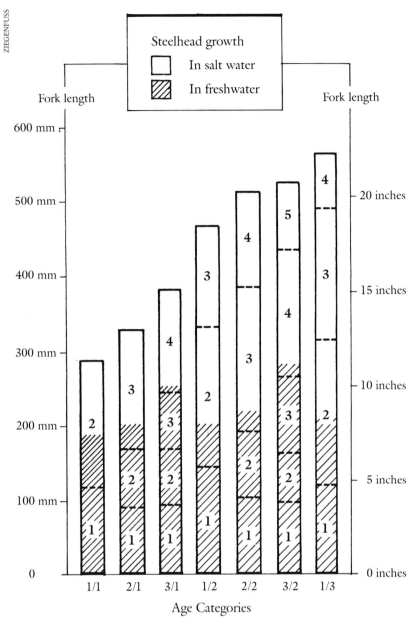

Steelhead growth
In salt water
In freshwater

Fork length

Fork length

Age Categories

Steelhead were age-classed based on the amount of time they spent in the freshwater environment of the Klamath River in northern California, as compared to time spent in the ocean. A steelhead with an age category of 3/2 spent the first three years of its life in freshwater, and then spent its fourth and fifth years of life in salt water before returning to the Klamath to spawn. The longer the ocean stay, the larger the fish—due to the increased availability of food.

at one to two years of age. They usually spend one year, occasionally two, at sea and return upstream as small adults. Conversely, at the northern end of the range, because of harsh growing conditions, juvenile steelhead spend three to four years in fresh water before they are large enough and physiologically mature enough to smolt and go to sea. These fish thus usually spend two to four years at sea and return as rather large adults. The world record for steelhead, taken in Alaska on hook and line, is about 19 kilograms (42 pounds 2 ounces), though there have been unsubstantiated claims that commercial netters fishing British Columbia waters have caught steelhead weighing up to 23 kilograms (50 pounds).

In California, adult steelhead returning to the Klamath River average three to four years in age and weigh about 2 to 3 kilograms (4 to 6 pounds). However, the California record steelhead caught by an angler is nearly 13 kilograms (28 pounds). In British Columbia and Alaska, many returning adult steelhead are five to seven years old and weigh 5 to 9 kilograms (12 to 20 pounds). The average size of steelhead taken by anglers in the Great Lakes is 1.4 to 1.8 kilograms (3 to 4 pounds), but fish up to 11.4 kilograms (25 pounds) have been caught there.

In the ocean, steelhead feed heavily on a variety of organisms, especially juvenile greenling, squids, and amphipods. They in turn are fed on by other fish and marine mammals, but the extent and effect of predation are unknown. Research has shown that ocean conditions vary from year to year, and that in years of poor upwelling, when rich nutrients are not brought to the surface because of a lack of strong, steady winds, food production is poor, and fewer salmon and steelhead survive.

Tags returned from steelhead caught at sea have helped to explain their ocean distribution and migration patterns. Distribution apparently is influenced by surface water temperatures; the fish prefer temperatures at 9° to 11.5°C (48° to 53°F). Steelhead taken incidentally by commercial fishermen apparently do not form schools as salmon do and usually swim in the upper 9 to 12 meters (30 to 40 feet) of water.

In their southern range, steelhead tend to migrate north and south along the continental shelf, a pattern that may be related to the shorter time these stocks spend in salt water. Many steelhead stocks in the northern range apparently make extensive offshore migrations. Oregon, Washington, and British Columbia steelhead commonly are taken by nets in Alaskan and Aleutian waters, and steelhead are occasionally taken off the coast of Japan. They also migrate extensively in the Great Lakes. Steelhead from Lake Michigan tributaries, for example, have been caught in northern Lake Erie.

Because adult steelhead migrate when streamflows are increasing, water depth usually does not limit their upstream migration. Steelhead are the athletes among anadro-

mous fish and are able to leap and swim over areas that most observers would consider barriers to upstream migration. However, steelhead do encounter velocity barriers in long, steep bedrock areas of streams and at precipitous culverts. An extended length of water with velocities exceeding 2.7 to 3.7 meters (9 to 12 feet) per second will stop most steelhead.

HUMAN INTERVENTION

There has been a general decline of wild steelhead populations during this century and particularly in the past forty years. The main reason is the loss of habitat through human activities. Dams have been built that block access to miles of spawning and rearing areas. Dams, too, often divert water for agriculture or urbanized areas and leave no downriver stream habitat.

Even on free-flowing, undammed rivers, steelhead habitat has been degraded by poor land-management practices, such as logging to the edges of the streams, locating logging roads in bad positions, which wash out during winter storms, and overgrazing pastures, which then erode into nearby streams. During the same period, the army of anglers has grown tremendously so that dwindling wild stocks are being overfished.

Steelhead are now fished commercially by some Washington and Oregon Indian tribes and are taken incidentally by commercial gill-net fisheries along the north Pacific coast try-

A steelhead returning to his native stream to spawn negotiates barriers that most observers would think impassable.

ing to harvest other species. Seacops, a coalition of fishermen formed to protect salmon and steelhead, estimates that 200,000 steelhead are being killed annually by the North Pacific high-seas squid driftnet fleet. Steelhead are taken by Indian gill-net fisheries in the Great Lakes. Great Lakes steelhead also have declined because of predation by sea lampreys.

With the decline of wild stocks, hatchery steelhead production has increased. Pacific coast states now stock two to eleven million smolts annually. In some rivers, steelhead fisheries would not exist without the infusion of hatchery-produced fish. However, there are concerns about the increased dependency on hatchery steelhead. There are indications that, over time, continued stocking of large numbers of hatchery steelhead does not supplement natural reproduction but gradually replaces it. Significant increases in angling pressure always accompany the successful initiation of a hatchery program, resulting in an increased harvest of the remaining wild fish. In Idaho and in many southern British Columbia streams, to protect the wild steelhead left, all hatchery-produced steelhead are marked before they are stocked and anglers must release all unmarked fish that they catch back to the stream. Reingold in 1975 and Hooten in 1987 reported that adult steelhead can be caught and released several times with little effect on the mortality rate of the population.

Experience has shown that if hatchery steelhead are stocked at a large enough size and at the right time, generally coinciding with the movement of wild steelhead smolts, they migrate rather rapidly to the ocean, thus reducing as much as possible the competition for food and space with wild juvenile steelhead rearing in the stream. If hatchery fish are released at the wrong size or time, they remain in the stream, acting like a resident fish, and therefore compete with the naturally produced fish.

A major concern today is the effect of the genetic mixing of wild and hatchery steelhead stocks. Wild steelhead have unique, desirable, genetically heritable characteristics, which should be preserved if possible. A study reported in 1977 by Reisenbichler and McIntyre compared offspring of hatchery and wild steelhead during their first year of freshwater life in a natural stream. Even though the hatchery stock originated from wild stock, the offspring of the wild adults survived better than the offspring of the hatchery adults. Hulet and Leider reported in 1989 on studies of genetic interactions of hatchery and wild steelhead in the Kalama River in Washington. They found that transplanted hatchery summer steelhead were eight to nine times less effective at producing returning adult offspring than were wild summer steelhead. They think that interbreeding of transplanted hatchery fish with wild fish is degrading the genetic makeup of the local wild stock.

Most states now stocking hatchery steelhead have a policy of not mixing stocks from one river system with those of other systems. Hatchery managers also are learning to select their spawners over the entire spawning season rather than to fill their egg quota with only the first fish of the season. This provides more variation in the hatchery population for factors such as time of sexual maturation, time of spawning return, and perhaps even growth rate—all genetically heritable characteristics.

Another method being used to minimize negative genetic effects is to collect and maintain wild broodstocks specific to individual river systems; thus, these hatchery fish should be genetically similar to their wild counterparts. Then interbreeding becomes genetically acceptable. Although this technique can lead to practical and economic difficulties associated with collecting and maintaining wild stocks, it is probably worth the effort in order to maintain pure stocks.

The steelhead, like all other seemingly inexhaustible resources, is exhaustible. Both qualitative and quantitative aspects of the fishery can be lost.

—Roger A. Barnhart

S. TURNER

The future of trout

Endangered species

Extinction of old species and their replacement by new species has always been a feature of evolution. There is a great difference, however, between natural extinction and unnatural extinction, caused by man. During the last century, the human population has been increasing at a greatly accelerated rate. At the same time, the introduction of modern technologies has created an enormous increase in the use and exploitation of Earth's natural resources—timber, minerals, soils, and water.

This situation, in turn, has created enormous increases in waste products that are polluting Earth's atmosphere and its soils and waters. The massive changes of Earth's environment, the destruction of habitat, and the conversion of large land areas from native vegetation to agriculture have caused a greatly accelerated, unnatural rate of extinction of plant and animal life on Earth—an extinction rate much more rapid than can be compensated for by the evolution of new species.

We must slow and reverse the rate of unnatural extinction for many reasons, but the one most universally applicable is that the well-being of the human species depends on the diversity of life on our planet. Lately we have devoted a lot of attention to the preservation of Earth's biodiversity.

In 1973, Congress passed the Endangered Species Act, hoping to slow and reverse the rate of extinction and thus preserve the diversity of life. Species that are listed as endangered or threatened under the Endangered Species Act receive protection from any federal agency's action that might jeopardize their continued existence. For example, a federally funded dam or irrigation project might be prohibited or modified if it would eliminate or seriously impair critical habitat necessary for the existence of an endangered or threatened species.

The diversity of life rests on the diversity within species, what we call intraspecific diversity. We can expect species that inhabit a large territory to have wide intraspecific diversity, that is, many subspecies, races, and populations, each of which has evolved under natural selection for thousands of generations to be best adapted to thrive in its specific native environment. The chinook salmon species illustrates this situation well. The species, as a whole, certainly is not endangered. Commercial fisheries harvest many millions of pounds of chinook each year. However, the winter-run chinook in California's Sacramento River is the only population or race of the species that is a spring spawner—it is a unique trait within the species and must be preserved from extinction.

Formerly, more than 100,000 winter-run chinook spawned in the upper basin of the Sacramento River. Most were lost after Shasta Dam blocked the run, and the remaining run has been drastically reduced to a few hundred fish because of highly modified winter flows in the Sacramento River resulting from

HUNTER

This stocked brown trout is in good condition and has probably lived in the stream for most of the season.

the early 1970s was that repeated stockings of hatchery trout can hurt populations of wild trout, not through "genetic pollution" as some might fear but through behavioral or competitive interaction. Wild trout do not tolerate crowding, and evidently they are not as aggressive and competitive as stocked trout.

That merely stocking trout, with no interbreeding, could harm an outstanding wild trout population was first given credibility by Richard Vincent, a fishery biologist working on the Madison River in Montana. Vincent's general observations have been widely accepted. In fact they form the foundation of a wild-trout management philosophy that says simply but emphatically: The first and most important step in managing an excellent wild-trout population is to quit stocking.

Yet, it must be recognized that not all stockings will harm all populations of wild trout, and in situations where wild trout are present but not at high levels, stocking usually is the best approach.

The need for, and the extent of, stocking varies from state to state. Not all trout stockings are good, not all are bad. Stocking has made fishing better, indeed possible, in many places, and that is good. Politically motivated and short-sighted emphasis on hatcheries and stocking have diverted monies from basic resource-oriented programs and biologically based fishery management, and that is bad. A float-stocked or specially regulated mountain stream in a state park or natural forest will have rising trout in sparkling pools, trout that would not have been there without stocking, and that is good. An opening day or a publicized stocking can be a greed-motivated mob scene, and that is bad. A hatchery trout can be a firm-fleshed, well-colored, clean-looking imitation of the wild version, and that is good. It can be a stubby-finned, colorless, fat lump of flesh, and that is bad.

The important point is to keep stocking in perspective.

—Delano R. Graff

Why not stock?

*F*or well over a century, hatcheries have provided a readily available source of fish with which to augment or replace natural reproduction when natural reproduction was considered no longer capable of producing enough fish to sustain recreational or commercial fisheries. Through the introduction of fish and the subsequent establishment of natural reproducing populations, hatcheries have helped to greatly expand the range of "desirable" species, notably brook trout, brown trout, and rainbow trout. They are now being used to preserve species from extinction. In fact, hatcheries are increasingly being used as gene banks, where we can maintain some of the genetic diversity of a threatened or endangered taxon (species or subspecies).

Before proceeding, let's define the terms that will be used in the discussion. A *native population* is one that exists within the natural range of the taxon and has always sustained itself only by *natural reproduction*, that is, reproduction in the wild. A *natural reproducing population* is one that sustains itself by natural reproduction but was established, at least partly, by the introduction of *hatchery fish*, those produced by incubating the eggs and rearing the fish in a hatchery. A natural reproducing population could be a population of fish outside its native range, a population in which interbreeding has occurred between native fish and hatchery fish not derived from them, or a population within its natural range established in rehabilitated waters or those previously barren because of barriers to dispersal. Hatchery fish could be the progeny of fish collected from the wild or the progeny of fish raised to maturity in a hatchery.

The major problems with hatcheries are potential adverse effects that the raising and introduction of hatchery fish can have on natural reproduction. These problems can be broadly classified into philosophical and biological categories, categories that are not mutually exclusive. A philosophical problem translates into a biological problem.

PHILOSOPHICAL PROBLEMS

Hatcheries can produce large numbers of fish and, through repeated introductions, provide recreational fisheries in waters no longer capable of supporting natural reproduction. Most of these "synthetic fisheries" exist close to urban areas and are economically justifiable because they now provide the only readily accessible salmonid fishery to a large number of people.

But such a practice can mislead people into thinking that we no longer need natural waters to produce fish because we can produce plenty artificially. This devaluation of natural reproduction may inadvertently divert public attention and funds away from efforts to maintain habitats capable of supporting native and natural reproducing populations. The belief that hatchery fish could always be used to provide a fishery probably has resulted in the extirpation of many native populations by preventing the use of remedial measures, such as habitat improvement, restrictive fishing, and regulations for water usage.

This concept has also existed within fish management agencies. For example, when proposed water usage was likely to have a serious adverse effect on native populations, mitigation often entailed construction of a hatchery. In some situations, other measures could have been used to minimize the effects of the proposed water usage on the fish. Such measures may not have been implemented because the hatchery was considered an acceptable replacement of the native population.

Because anglers often fish to catch and keep fish, introduction of hatchery fish can dramatically increase fishing pressure, as reported by Hoover and Johnson in 1937, Smith and Smith in 1943, Thorpe and colleagues in 1944, Cooper in 1952, and Butler and Borgeson in 1965. When introductions are made into waters containing a native or natural reproducing population, the increased fishing pressure may result in increased harvest of the naturally produced fish. This increased harvest can threaten the population's viability, as reported by Hazzard and Shetter in 1938 and 1940. In situations like this, efforts to increase natural reproduction through habitat alteration and more restrictive regulations may be more prudent and economical than reliance on a costly, long-term hatchery program.

BIOLOGICAL PROBLEMS

Williams and colleagues in 1989 reviewed the fish taxa native to North America that have received legal protection or are considered fishes of special concern. Many species and subspecies of trout, such as the Little Kern River golden trout, Paiute cutthroat trout, and greenback cutthroat trout, appear on their list. To reduce the chances of extinction, programs to establish other natural reproducing populations of some of these trout, notably the greenback cutthroat and the Colorado River cutthroat have been initiated. The establishment of a hatchery population often is an integral aspect of these restoration programs.

When a trout population is maintained in a hatchery for several generations, the fish usually acquire behavioral characteristics substantially different from those of wild fish. For example, Vincent in 1960 and Mason and colleagues in 1967 reported that the progeny of wild brook trout were much more timid and excitable in the hatchery than were progeny of fish that had remained in a hatchery environment for many generations. Shetter in 1944, Flick and Webster in 1964, and Bachman in 1984 have reported that fish from populations maintained in hatcheries for a long time had poor survival rates when introduced into the wild. Behavioral differences often are believed to be partly responsible for this phenomenon.

Unless corrected, the "domestication" of hatchery populations could reduce their value to restoration programs. Most of the introduced fish may not survive. Thus, the introduction either fails or leads to a population that is founded by only a few remaining individuals, which, as discussed by Allendorf and Ryman in 1987, results in a loss of genetic diversity. This situation will reduce the population's ability to adapt to the new environment through the process of natural selection, because genetic variation is essential for genetic adaptation. Furthermore, the loss of genetic variation can also adversely affect attributes of individuals that could further jeopardize the long-term viability of the population. Differences in survival, growth rate, and the ability of individuals to develop properly were reported to be associated with reduced genetic variation by Kincaid in 1983 and by Leary and colleagues in 1985.

In at least one case, the U.S. Fish and Wildlife Service and cooperating agencies have incorporated measures into a restoration program to alleviate these potential problems. To minimize domestication, hatchery populations of greenback cutthroat trout will periodically be crossed with wild fish. Furthermore, waters will receive multiple introductions to increase the number of individuals having a genetic contribution to the establishment of natural reproducing populations and thereby potentially increase genetic diversity.

Diseases. Unless stressed, fish tend to be rather resistant to the pathogens (bacteria, fungi, viruses, and parasites) to which they are naturally exposed. They also tend to be

If too many large trout are stocked in waters with insufficient food to sustain them, they can lose weight rapidly and die.

highly susceptible to pathogens to which they have only recently come into contact. For example, anadromous rainbow trout (steelhead) in the Columbia River drainage are quite resistant to infection by *Ceratomyxa shasta*, a parasite that exists naturally in the drainage. But steelhead from drainages where the parasite does not naturally exist are very susceptible to infection, and upon exposure, practically all the fish contract it and die, according to a 1983 report by Buchanan and colleagues.

Pathogens and parasites are a major concern of hatchery and fishery managers. The density of populations in the hatchery greatly increases the chance of an epidemic. Once this happens, the entire population may have to be destroyed. In addition, the introduction of hatchery trout into natural waters also can introduce pathogens and parasites with devastating consequences to native and natural reproducing populations. For example, the parasite that causes whirling disease is not native to North America. Apparently it was introduced in 1957 with a shipment of rainbow trout from England. According to Piper and colleagues in 1983, it is now a major disease problem for hatchery and fishery managers throughout North America.

Natural reproduction. The continued introduction of large numbers of hatchery trout can reduce natural reproduction simply by their presence. In Montana, the Madison River and its tributaries support natural reproducing populations of brown and rain-

bow trout. In 1987, Vincent reported that the introduction of catchable (21 to 31 centimeters [8 to 12 inches]) hatchery rainbow trout dramatically reduced the number of naturally produced brown and rainbow trout surviving more than two years. The presence of hatchery fish also has been reported to reduce the number of naturally produced brook trout, brown trout, and westslope cutthroat trout by Thuember in 1975, Bachman in 1982, and Petrosky and Bjornn in 1984, respectively.

We do not know how or why the presence of hatchery trout suppresses the efficiency of natural reproduction. One possibility is that larger hatchery trout may displace smaller and younger naturally produced fish from better feeding stations, as Pollard and Bjornn suggested in 1973. Hatchery trout also can disrupt the social structure in a natural population, increasing the number and length of antagonistic encounters, which in turn increases stress, according to a 1984 report by Bachman. Regardless of the mechanisms, in some situations hatchery trout represent a costly, direct replacement, not an augmentation, of natural reproduction.

Displacing native populations. The reproduction of hatchery fish or their descendants in the wild can adversely affect native populations by displacement and interbreeding. Extinction of native populations because of the introduction of trout taxa into waters outside their natural range apparently has been common. Within the past forty years, the amount of stream habitat occupied solely by native brook trout in the Great Smoky Mountains National Park has declined by 64 percent, according to a 1985 report by Larson and Moore. The expansion of nonnative, naturally reproducing rainbow trout is believed to be mainly responsible for this decline, according to a 1983 report by Moore and colleagues.

We are not sure how rainbow trout displace brook trout. One possibility is that juvenile rainbow trout can dramatically reduce the growth of juvenile brook trout. In 1986, Rose reported that this phenomenon was linked to dietary and spatial overlap between the young fishes, suggesting that the reduced growth of the brook trout was the direct result of competititon. He further suggested that the reduced size of the brook trout could lead to an increase in overwinter mortality rates, contributing to a decline in the population.

Other examples of the displacement of native trout by nonnative trout exist. Nyman in 1970 and Waters in 1973 reported the displacement of brook trout populations by brown . trout. By 1965, brown trout also had displaced populations of bull trout in Alberta, Canada, according to Nelson. And brook trout and brown trout both have displaced populations of cutthroat in western North America, according to a 1972 report by Behnke, a 1983 report by the U.S. Fish and Wildlife Service, and much anecdotal evidence. In some situations, displacement may occur more easily because of habitat alteration. The environmental changes may make the waters more suitable to the existence of the nonnative fishes, giving them a competitive or reproductive advantage over the native trout. Displacement of native populations, however, does not universally require habitat alteration, as reported by Larson and Moore in 1985.

Interbreeding. Natural reproduction of hatchery trout and their descendants results in hybridization when they interbreed with native trout. This is easiest to document when the introduced and native fish are different taxa, because substantial genetic differences often exist between them.

Hybridization between different taxa can result in either sterile or fertile offspring. In western North America, hybridization between introduced brook trout and native bull trout is common and widespread. The hybrid progeny are sterile, so this interbreeding does not directly result in a genetic alteration of bull trout populations. The production of sterile progeny, however, is a wasted reproductive effort. When hybridization is common, it represents a substantial reduction in the reproductive capacity of the parental species and creates an evolutionarily unstable situation. Reproductive isolation may evolve – that is, the two species may not interbreed and so may coexist – or reproductive isolation may not evolve and one species may become extinct.

Brook trout apparently have been able to

Deformed fins are a common problem with hatchery trout.

displace many bull trout populations. The hybridization between these two species, as well as competition and habitat alteration, may be important and interrelated causes for the extinction of the bull trout populations. This suggests that reproductive isolation does not usually evolve between these two species and that brook trout are better able tm withstand the wasted reproductive effort when hybridization occurs, possibly because they mature earlier.

Fertile hybrid progeny can reproduce among themselves and with members of the parental taxa. The latter situation introduces genes from one taxon into populations of another, a process usually referred to as introgressive hybridization, or introgression.

Pure native goldens interbreed with stocked rainbows. The result could be the extinction of the pure native population.

After a few generations of introgressive hybridization, the probability that any fish in a population contains genes only from native trout may be extremely small. Introgression that involves different taxa represents the extinction of a genetically pure population. In 1988 Allendorf and Leary reviewed the evidence showing that many native cutthroat trout populations in western North America have been extinguished because of introgression with introduced rainbow trout or other subspecies of cutthroat. Introgression with rainbow trout also is responsible for the loss of Apache trout populations, as reported by Loudenslager and colleagues in 1986.

The effects of hybridization between hatchery fish and native populations of the same taxon are likely to be highly variable. When only small genetic differences exist between the hatchery and native populations, the genetic changes induced in the native population will be slight. In this case, hybridization probably will be of little biological consequence, especially when the hatchery population was derived from the native population or a genetically similar one inhabiting the same drainage.

Appreciable genetic differences can exist between hatchery and native populations of the same taxon. This usually occurs when the hatchery population is derived from fish not native to a particular drainage system or when a native population inhabits an ecologically unusual habitat. The genetic changes induced by hybridization in these situations also may be viewed as causing extinction of native trout populations. Examples involving genetically divergent hatchery and native rainbow trout were noted by Allendorf and colleagues in 1980, and Campton and Johnson in 1985. In anadromous populations, hybridization between fishes from different drainages also has the potential to disrupt homing mechanisms, resulting in reduced natural reproduction and decreasing the populations' long-term viability.

Native populations in unusual habitats, such as small desert streams that reach daytime temperatures usually considered near-lethal for the species, represent unique and locally adapted populations. They could be extremely sensitive to hybridization because it could break down the local adaptation. In 1984, Wishard and colleagues suggested that the unusual habitat could preclude the reproduction of hatchery fish and prevent hybridization, but in 1988 Tol and Frech presented evidence that this may not always be the case.

Inherent value. In 1943, Schuck, noting the generally poor survival of hatchery fish in the wild, questioned the prevalent belief in fishery management that "natural reproduction in the wild was extremely inefficient, and that artificial reproduction, rearing, and stocking were highly efficient and therefore certain to increase the quantity of catchable fish in natural trout waters by almost any degree desired." Continued adherence to this concept, however, further devalued natural reproduction and provided justification for the introduction of vast numbers of hatchery trout, regardless of their origin, throughout the waters of North America, often with devastating consequences.

Today, increasing emphasis is now being placed on the value of natural reproduction and native trout populations, as noted by Richardson and Hamre in 1984. However, much historical damage exists. In some situations, the damage may be virtually irreparable. In others restoration is feasible. To establish viable, naturally reproducing populations, large numbers of fish will be required, and many of these fish are likely to come from hatcheries.

—Robb F. Leary

Stewardship

*T*he conservation of our trout species depends upon stewardship, taking care of the habitat. Yet human activity instead has damaged or destroyed much of the trout habitat of North America, indeed of the world. In our nation alone, since the days of our forefathers and their westward expansion, we've dammed streams, ditched and drained wetlands, paved marshes, dumped waste, developed roads excessively, logged destructively, and otherwise misused our environment in a seemingly unlimited number of ways. In recent years, public concern for the environment has brought about laws to control such abuses, and these laws have slowed the assault on the outdoors. But sadly, they have come too late for many trout streams.

Stewardship includes more than passing laws and restricting activities; it includes rolling up your sleeves as well. The best way you can help is to join a trout conservation group: Trout Unlimited, Federation of Fly Fishers, or a local angling sports club, for instance. An organized effort translates into thousands of volunteer hours, and participants have the satisfaction of multiplying their efforts and pooling their abilities. Of course, cooperating with others who are interested in solving the same problems goes further than trying to tackle those problems individually.

Those of us who love trout, whether for the enjoyment they provide us or for the mere fact of their existence, must convey that value to others. We need to show people—through the media, through contact with youth groups, schools, churches, and other organizations, and especially through example—why these fish are so important.

In addition, we must describe to our state and national political representatives the threats to water resources. We must encourage our legislators to enact tough laws to control acid rain, toxic waste, dumping, and other abuses. And we must go after the dol-

Volunteers work to stabilize the stream bank, thus improving trout habitat.

lars needed to pay for good research and professional management of our trout fisheries. These efforts cannot continue without financial support from government, industry, and you and me.

You can become active at the streamside, too, helping fisheries professionals restore or enhance trout habitat. Planting riparian cover, controlling livestock access to streams, building fish ladders, and removing silt from spawning areas all may be needed on nearby streams and rivers. Many such projects will simply continue to be needed unless you yourself help complete them.

Let's talk about planning and carrying out one of these projects. Before deciding on one and going to the trouble of gathering infor-

This rotary bypass screen keeps trout out of irrigation canals, where they can become stranded as water levels go down.

mation, contact landowners, public and private, for access to the stream and permission to work on it, and be sure you have secured the necessary government permits before you begin.

Then, learn about the stream's present condition and its potential. Many times the state fisheries department will have a history of the stream's condition, temperature information, water quality, adjacent land-use practices, fish populations, and other details. With this background and the agency's professional advice, you may be able to develop a sound program to improve the trout habitat. If the information doesn't exist, the agency may provide guidance in gathering it and will welcome your help.

Your efforts to improve the stream for trout will depend on what the stream needs. Maybe the flow of water is impeded by fallen trees. You might simply have to remove them. Suppose you find that a gully is eroding directly into the stream and causing siltation. Perhaps the gully was caused by overgrazing. In this case, the project would involve fencing the cattle from the area and stabilizing the gully.

Perhaps cover is lacking on the streambanks and the biologists tell you that willow plantings would help stabilize the banks and would help lower the water temperature by providing shade to the stream. Here you have another project.

Sometimes building instream structures is the most important way to improve the fisheries. Small log dams might be needed to allow water to spill over and provide turbulence that would create small plunge pools. Riprap might be needed on streambanks to reduce bank erosion caused by high water flows. Rock dams and deflectors can sometimes be used to create riffles or deepen channels.

With the required permissions and the information in hand, you have a good foundation for enlisting volunteers and securing donations of equipment and supplies from local businesses. Often, sawmills, brickyards, and sand and gravel companies are willing to help.

Some problems, acid mine drainage or erosion from large road construction sites, for example, could be beyond volunteer efforts. They may require petitioning a local agency to clean up the mess. If the agency does not respond, the best way to get its attention may be to show the problem to a local outdoor writer or newspaper reporter who will put the information before your neighbors so that public pressure for action develops.

We were blessed with clean, clear water and bright trout, but now many of these resources are in trouble. Your help is needed for coldwater habitats. Your help is needed for trout fisheries. In particular, your help may be needed for the individual trout stream in your own area. Get involved. Make sure we have a trout legacy to leave your children— and your children's children.

—*Robert L. Herbst*

THE FUTURE OF TROUT

References

Adron, J.W., and A.M. Mackie. "Studies on the Chemical Nature of Feeding Stimulants for Rainbow Trout, *Salmo gairdneri*, Richardson." *Journal of Fish Biology* 12 (1978): 303–310.

Aelianus, C. *De Animalium Natura*. Tiguri, apud Gesneros Fratres, 1556. A.D. 230.

Alcorn, S.R. "Temperature Tolerances and Upper Lethal Limits of *Salmo apache*." *Transactions of the American Fisheries Society* 105 (1976): 294–295.

Alderdice, D.F., J.R. Brett, D.R. Ibler, and U. Vagerlund. "Further Observations on Olfactory Perception in Migrating Adult Coho and Spring Salmon–Properties of the Repellent in Mammalian Skin." *Canadian Fisheries Research Board Progress Report, Pacific Coast Station* 89 (1954): 10–12.

Alexander, G.R., W.J. Buc, and G.T. Schnicke. *Trends in Angling and Trout Populations in the Main Au Sable and North Branch Au Sable Rivers from 1959-1976*. Michigan Department of Natural Resources, Fisheries Research Report 1865. Ann Arbor: 1979.

Alexander, G.R., and J.R. Ryckman. *Trout Production and Catch Under Normal and Special Angling Regulations in the North Branch of the Au Sable River, Michigan*. Michigan Department of Natural Resources, Fisheries Research Report 1840. Ann Arbor: 1976.

Alexander, G.R., and D.S. Shetter. "Trout Production and Angling Success from Matched Plantings of Brook Trout and Rainbow Trout in East Fish Lake, Michigan." *Journal of Wildlife Management* 33, no. 3 (1969): 682–692.

Allan, J.D. "The Effects of Reduction in Trout Density on the Invertebrate Community of a Mountain Stream." *Ecology* 63 (1982): 1444–1455.

Allen, K.R. *The Horokiwi Stream: A Study of a Trout Population*. New Zealand Marine Department of Fisheries, Bulletin 10. Wellington: 1951.

Allendorf, F.W., D.M. Espeland, D.T. Scow, and S.R. Phelps. "Co-existence of Native and Introduced Rainbow Trout in the Kootenai River Drainage." *Proceedings of the Montana Academy of Sciences* 39 (1980): 28–36.

Allendorf, F.W., and R.F. Leary. "Conservation and Distribution of Genetic Variation in a Polytypic Species, the Cutthroat Trout." *Conservation Biology* 2 (1988): 170–184.

Allendorf, F.W., N. Mitchell, N. Ryman, and G. Stahl. "Isozyme Loci in Brown Trout (*Salmo trutta* L.): Detection and Interpretation from Population Data." *Hereditas* 86 (1977): 179–190.

Allendorf, F.W., and N. Ryman. "Genetic Management of Hatchery Stocks." In *Population Genetics and Fishery Management*, edited by N. Ryman and F. Utter, 141–159. Seattle: University of Washington Press, 1987.

Allendorf, F.W., N. Ryman, A. Stennek, and G. Stahl. "Genetic Variation in Scandinavian Brown Trout (*Salmo trutta* L.): Evidence of Distinct Sympatric Populations." *Hereditas* 83 (1976): 73–82.

Alm, G. "Influence of Heredity and Environment on Various Forms of Trout." *Reports from the Swedish State Institute of Fresh-water Fishery Research, Drottningholm* 29 (1949): 29–34.

Alt, K.T. *Inventory and Cataloging of Sport Fish and Sport Fish Waters of Western Alaska*. Vol. 18. Alaska Department of Fish and Game, Study G-I-P. n.d.

Altman, J. "Observational Study of Behavior: Sampling Methods." *Behaviour* 49, nos. 3 and 4 (1974): 227–267.

Anderson, B.G., and D.L. Mitchum. *Atlas of Trout Histology*. Wyoming Game and Fish Department, 1974.

Anderson, G.J., and A.E. Bremer. *Salar: The Story of the Atlantic Salmon*. St. Andrews: International Atlantic Salmon Federation, 1976.

Andrews, C.W., and E. Lear. "The Biology of Arctic Char (*Salvelinus alpinus* L.) in Northern Labrador." *Journal of the Fisheries Research Board of Canada* 13 (1956): 843–860.

Andrusak, H., and T.G. Northcote. "Segregation between Adult Cutthroat Trout (*Salmo clarki*) and Dolly Varden (*Salvelinus malma*) in Small Coastal British Columbia Lakes." *Journal of the Fisheries Research Board of Canada* 28 (1971): 1259–1268.

Armstrong, R.H. "Age, Food and Migration of Dolly Varden Smolts in Southeastern Alaska." *Journal of the Fisheries Research Board of Canada* 27 (1970): 991–1004.

———. "Age, Food and Migration of Sea-run Cutthroat Trout, *Salmo clarki*, at Eva Lake, Southeastern Alaska." *Transactions of the American Fisheries Society* 100 (1971): 302–306.

———. "Migration of Anadromous Dolly Varden (*Salvelinus malma*) in Southeastern Alaska." *Journal of the Fisheries Research Board of Canada* 31 (1974): 435–444.

———. "Migration of Anadromous Dolly Varden Charr in Southeastern Alaska–A Manager's Nightmare." In *Biology of the Arctic Charr, Proceedings of the International Symposium on Arctic Charr*, edited by L. Johnson and B. Burns, 559–570. Symposium held in Winnipeg, May 4–8, 1981. Winnipeg: University of Manitoba Press, 1984.

Armstrong, R.H., and J.E. Morrow. "The Dolly Varden Charr, *Salvelinus malma*." In *Charrs: Salmonid Fishes of the Genus* Salvelinus, edited by E.K. Balon, 99–140. The Hague, The Netherlands: Dr. W. Junk Publishers, 1980.

Ayles, G.B., J.G.I. Lark, J. Barica, and H. Kling. "Seasonal Mortality of Rainbow Trout *(Salmo gairdneri)* Planted in Small Eutrophic Lakes of Central Canada." *Journal of the Fisheries Research Board of Canada* 33 (1976): 647–655.

Bachman, R.A. "Foraging Behavior of Free-ranging Wild Brown Trout *(Salmo trutta)* in a Stream." Ph.D. dissertation, The Pennsylvania State University, 1982.

———. "Foraging Behavior of Free-ranging Wild and Hatchery Brown Trout in a Stream." *Transactions of the American Fisheries Society* 113 (1984): 1–32.

Bacon, M., P. Brouka, M. Rode, and C. Staley. *Redband Trout* (Salmo *sp.*). Shasta-Trinity National Forest, Calif., Comprehensive Management Plan. n.d.

Baldwin, N.S. "A Study of the Speckled Trout, *Salvelinus fontinalis* (Mitchill), in a Pre-cambrian Lake." Master's thesis, University of Toronto, 1948.

Balon, E.K., ed. *Charrs: Salmonid Fishes of the Genus* Salvelinus. The Hague, The Netherlands: Dr. W. Junk Publishers, 1980.

Bannon, E., and N.H. Ringler. "Optimal Prey Size for Stream Resident Brown Trout *(Salmo trutta)*: Tests of Predictive Models." *Canadian Journal of Zoology* 64 (1986): 704–713.

Barnhart, R.A. "Symposium Review: Catch-and-Release Fishing, a Decade of Experience." *North American Journal of Fisheries Management* 9, no. 1 (1989): 74–80.

Baxter, G.T., and J.R. Simon. *Wyoming Fishes.* Wyoming Game and Fish Department, Bulletin No. 4. 1970.

Beggs, G.L., J.M. Gunn, and C.H. Olver. *The Sensitivity of Ontario Lake Trout* (Salvelinus namaycush) *and Lake Trout Lakes to Acidification.* Ontario Fisheries Technical Report Series No. 17. 1985.

Behnke, R.J. "The Systematics of Salmonid Fishes of Recently Glaciated Lakes." *Journal of the Fisheries Research Board of Canada* 29 (1972): 639–671.

———. "Monograph of the Native Trouts of the Genus *Salmo* of Western North America." U.S. Department of Agriculture, Forest Service and Bureau of Land Management. Unpublished report. Lakewood, Col.: 1979.

———. "Organizing the Diversity of the Arctic Charr Complex." In *Biology of the Arctic Charr, Proceedings of the International Symposium on Arctic Charr,* edited by L. Johnson and B. Burns, 3–21. Symposium held in Winnipeg, Manitoba, May 4–8, 1981. Winnipeg: University of Manitoba Press, 1984.

———. "About Trout: Brown Trout." *Trout* 27, no. 1 (1986): 42–47.

———. "About Trout: Atlantic Salmon." *Trout* 27, no. 3 (1986): 42–47.

———. "Brook Trout." *Trout* 28, no. 3 (1987): 42–46.

———. "How a Trout Sees." *Trout* 28, no. 3 (1987): 32–39.

———. "About Trout: Landlocked Salmon." *Trout* 28, no. 4 (1988): 42–47.

Behnke, R.J., and J. Shimizu. "Review of 'Studies on the Charrs Found in Japanese Waters.'" *Copeia,* 1962, no. 3: 674–675.

Behnke, R.J., and M. Zarn. *Biology and Management of Threatened and Endangered Western Trout.* Rocky Mountain Forest Range Experiment Station RM-28, General Technical Report. 1976.

Belghaug, R., and K.B. Døving. "Odour Threshold Determined by Studies of the Induced Waves in the Olfactory Bulb of the Char *(Salmo alpinus* L.)." *Comparative Biochemistry and Physiology* 57A (1977): 327–330.

Benoit, D.A. "Toxic Effects of Hexavalent Chromium on Brook Trout *(Salvelinus fontinalis)* and Rainbow Trout *(Salmo gairdneri)*." *Water Research* 10 (1976): 497–500.

Benoit, D.A., E.N. Leonard, G.M. Christensen, and J.T. Fiandt. "Toxic Effects of Cadmium on Three Generations of Brook Trout *(Salvelinus fontinalis)*." *Transactions of the American Fisheries Society* 105, no. 4 (1976): 550–560.

Benson, N.G. "Observations on Anchor Ice in a Michigan Trout Stream." *Ecology* 3 (1955): 529–530.

———. *Limnology of Yellowstone Lake in Relation to the Cutthroat Trout.* U.S. Department of the Interior, U.S. Fish and Wildlife Service, Bureau of Sport Fisheries and Wildlife, Research Report 56. 1961.

Berg, L.S. *Poissons de L'USSR.* Leningrad: 1932.

Berg, W.J. "Evolutionary Genetics of Rainbow Trout, *Parasalmo gairdnerii* (Richardson)." Ph.D. dissertation, University of California, Davis, 1987.

Bergeijk, W.A. van. "Introductory Comments on Lateral-Line Function." In *Lateral-Line Detectors,* edited by P.H. Cahn, 73–81. Indiana University Press, 1967.

Bergin, J.D. "Massachusetts Coastal Trout Management." In *Wild Trout III, Proceedings of the Symposium, Yellowstone National Park,* edited by F. Richardson and R.H. Hamre, 137–142. 1984.

Bergman, H.L., J.S. Mattice, and D.J.A. Brown. "Lake Acidification and Fisheries Project: Adult Brook Trout *(Salvelinus fontinalis)*." *Canadian Journal of Fisheries and Aquatic Sciences* 45 (1988): 1561–1562.

Berners, J. *A Treatyse of Fysshynge with an Angle.* First printed in the Boke of St. Albans (2d ed.). Westminster: 1496.

Bernstein, J.W., and J.F. Smith. "Alarm Substance Cells in Fathead Minnows Do Not Affect the Feeding Preference of Rainbow Trout." *Environmental Biology of Fishes* 9 (1983): 307–311.

Betteridge, G. *Movements of Rainbow Trout* (Salmo gairdneri) *and Splake* (Salvelinus fontinalis x S. namaycush) *in a Small Ontario Lake as Revealed by Ultrasonic Telemetry.* Ontario Fisheries Technical Report Series No. 18. 1985.

Bilby, R.E., and P.A. Bisson. "Relative Importance of Allochthonous vs. Autochthonous Carbon Sources as Factors Limiting Coho Salmon Production in Streams." In *Proceedings of the 1988 Northeast Pacific Chinook and Coho Salmon Workshop,* edited by B.G. Shepherd, 123–135. Penticton, British Columbia: British Columbia Ministry of Environment, 1989.

Bisson, P.A., J.L. Nielsen, R.A. Palmason, and L.E. Grove. "A System of Naming Habitat Types in Small Streams, with Examples of Habitat Utilization by Salmonids during Low Streamflow." In *Proceedings of the Symposium of Acquisition and Utilization of Aquatic Habitat Inventory Information, Portland, Oregon, October 28–30, 1981,* edited by N.B. Armantrout, 62–73. Bethesda, Md.: American Fisheries Society, 1982.

Bjornn, T.C. "Harvest, Age Structure, and Growth of Game Fish Populations from Priest and Upper Priest Lakes." *Transactions of the American Fisheries Society* 90 (1961): 27–31.

Bjornn, T.C., M.A. Brusven, M.P. Molnau, J.H. Milligan, R.A. Klamt, E. Chacho, and C. Schaye. *Transport of Granitic Sediment in Streams and Its Effects on Insects and Fish.* University of Idaho, Idaho Cooperative Fishery Research Unit, Completion Report Project B-036-IDA, Bulletin 17. Moscow, Idaho: 1977.

Bjornn, T.C., and J. Mallett. "Movements of Planted and Wild Trout in an Idaho River System." *Transactions of the American Fisheries Society* 93 (1964): 70–76.

Black, G.A., and J.B. Dempson. "A Test of the Hypothesis of Pheromone Attraction in Salmonid Migration." *Environmental Biology of Fishes* 15, no. 3 (1986): 229–235.

Booth, J.H. "The Effects of Oxygen Supply, Epinephrine, and Acetylcholine on the Distribution of Blood Flow in Trout Gills." *Journal of Experimental Biology* 83 (1979): 31–39.

Bouck, G.R., and R.C. Ball. "Influence of Capture Methods of Blood Characteristics and Mortality in the Rainbow Trout *(Salmo gairdneri)*." *Transactions of the American Fisheries Society* 95, no. 2 (1966): 170–176.

Boulva, J., and A. Simard. "Présence du *Salvelinus namaycush* (Pisces: Salmonidae) dans les eaux Marines de l'Arctique Occidental Canadien." *Journal of the Fisheries Research Board of Canada* 25 (1968): 1501–1504.

Bowler, B. "Factors Influencing Genetic Control in Lakeward Migrations of Cutthroat Trout Fry." *Transactions of the American Fisheries Society* 104 (1975): 474–482.

Boyce, F.M. "Some Aspects of Great Lakes Physics of Importance to Biological and Chemical Processes." *Journal of the Fisheries Research Board of Canada* 31 (1974): 689–730.

Bradbury, S.P., T.R. Henry, G.J. Niemi, R.W. Carlson, and V.M. Snarski. "Use of Respiratory-Cardiovascular Responses of Rainbow Trout *(Salmo gairdneri)* in Identifying Acute Toxicity Syndromes in Fish: Part 3. Polar Narcotics." *Environmental Toxicology and Chemistry* 8 (1989): 247–261.

Bradbury, S.P., J.M. McKim, and J.R. Coats. "Physiological Response of Rainbow Trout *(Salmo gairdneri)* to Acute Fenvalerate Intoxication." *Pesticide Biochemistry and Physiology* 27 (1987): 275–288.

Brannon, E.L. "Orientation Mechanisms of Homing Salmonids." In *Proceedings of the Salmon and Trout Migratory Behavior Symposium, June 3–5, 1981, First International Symposium,* edited by E.L. Brannon and E.O. Salo, 219–227. Seattle: University of Washington Press, 1982.

Brannon, E.L., and T.P. Quinn. "Odor Cues Used by Homing Coho Salmon." In *Proceedings of the Salmonid Migration and Distribution Symposium, June 23–25, 1987,* edited by E. Brannon and B. Jonsson, 30–34. 1989.

Brash, J., J. McFadden, and S. Kmiotek. *Brook Trout: Life History, Ecology, and Management.* Wisconsin Department of Natural Resources, Publication 226. 1958.

Bres, M. "The Effects of Prey Relative Abundance and Chemical Cues on Prey Selection in Rainbow Trout." *Journal of Fish Biology* 35 (1989): 439–445.

Brown, C.J.D. *Fishes of Montana.* Bozeman, Mont.: Big Sky Books, 1971.

Brown, E.H., G. Eck, N. Foster, R. Horrall, and C. Coberly. "Evidence for Discrete Stocks of Lake Trout *(Salvelinus namaycush)* in Lake Michigan." *Canadian Journal of Fisheries and Aquatic Sciences* 38 (1981): 1747–1758.

Brown, M.E. "The Growth of Brown Trout *(Salmo trutta* Linn.). I. Factors Influencing the Growth of Trout Fry." *Journal of Experimental Biology* 22 (1946): 118–155.

———, ed. *The Physiology of Fishes.* Vol. 1. New York: Academic Press, 1957.

Bryan, J.E., and P.A. Larkin. "Food Specialization by Individual

Trout." *Journal of the Fisheries Research Board of Canada* 29 (1972): 1615–1624.

Brynildson, O.M., V.A. Hacker, and T.A. Klick. *Brown Trout: Its Life History, Ecology and Management.* Wisconsin Conservation Department, Publication 324. Madison: 1963.

Buchanan, D.V., and J.R. Moring. "Management Problems with Recycling of Adult Summer Steelhead Trout at Foster Reservoir, Oregon." In *Fish Culture in Fisheries Management*, edited by R.H. Stroud, 191–200. Bethesda, Md.: American Fisheries Society, 1986.

Buchanan, D.V., J.E. Sanders, J.L. Zinn, and J.L. Fryer. "Relative Susceptibility of Four Strains of Summer Steelhead to Infection by *Ceratomyxa shasta.*" *Transactions of the American Fisheries Society* 112 (1983): 541–543.

Burdick, G.E., E.J. Harris, H.J. Dean, T.M. Walker, J. Skea, and D. Colby. "The Accumulation of DDT in Lake Trout and the Effect on Reproduction." *Transactions of the American Fisheries Society* 93, no. 2 (1964): 127–136.

Burger, C.V., and L.A. Gwartney. *A Radio Tagging Study of Naknek Drainage Rainbow Trout.* Anchorage, Alaska: U.S. National Park Service, 1986.

Burnstock, G. "The Morphology of the Gut of the Brown Trout *(Salmo trutta).*" *Quarterly Journal of Microscopical Science* 100, no. 2 (1959): 183–198.

Butler, R.L. "Some Thoughts on the Effects of Stocking Hatchery Trout on Wild Trout Populations." In *Wild Trout Management Symposium, Yellowstone National Park, 1974*, 83–87. Trout Unlimited and U.S. Department of the Interior, U.S. Fish and Wildlife Service. 1975.

Butler, R.L., and D.P. Borgeson. *California "Catchable" Trout Fisheries.* California Department of Fish and Game, Bulletin 127. 1965.

Butler, R.L., V. Hawthorne, and R. Kitchin. *The Reproductive Behavior of the Brook Trout.* 16mm, 27 min. 1971. Psychological Cinema Register.

Butler, R.L., and R.D. McCammon. "What a Fish and What the Angler See at the Air-Water Interface." *Trout* 13, no. 3 (Summer 1972): 14–15, 32.

Campton, D.E., and J.M. Johnston. "Electrophoretic Evidence for a Genetic Admixture of Native and Nonnative Rainbow Trout in the Yakima River, Washington." *Transactions of the American Fisheries Society* 114 (1985): 782–793.

Campton, D.E., and F.M. Utter. "Natural Hybridization between Steelhead Trout *(Salmo gairdneri)* and Coastal Cutthroat Trout *(Salmo clarki clarki)* in Two Puget Sound Streams." *Canadian Journal of Fisheries and Aquatic Sciences* 42 (1985): 110–119.

Carey, W.E. "Comparative Ontogeny of Photobehavioral Responses of Charrs *(Salvelinus* species)." *Environmental Biology of Fishes* 12, no. 3 (1985): 189–200.

Carey, W.E., and D.L.G. Noakes. "Development of Photobehavioral Responses in Young Rainbow Trout, *Salmo gairdneri* Richardson." *Journal of Fish Biology* 19 (1981): 285–296.

Carl, G.C. "Limnobiology of Cowichan Lake, British Columbia." *Journal of the Fisheries Research Board of Canada* 9 (1953): 417–449.

Carlander, K.D. *Handbook of Freshwater Fishery Biology.* Vol. 1. Ames: Iowa State University Press, 1969.

Carlson, R.W. "Some Characteristics of Ventilation and Coughing in the Bluegill, *Lepomis macrochirus* Rafinesque." *Environmental Pollution* (Series A) 29 (1982): 35–56.

Carpenter, S., J. Kitchell, and J. Hodgson. "Cascading Trophic Interactions and Lake Productivity–Fish Predation and Herbivory Can Regulate Lake Ecosystems." *BioScience* 35 (1985): 634–639.

Cavender, T.M. "Taxonomy and Distribution of the Bull Trout, *Salvelinus confluentus* (Suckley), from the American Northwest." *California Fish and Game* 64 (1978): 139–174.

Cederholm, C.J., and W.J. Scarlett. "Seasonal Immigrations of Juvenile Salmonids into Four Small Tributaries of the Clearwater River, Washington, 1977–1981." In *Proceedings of the Salmon and Trout Migratory Behavior Symposium, June 3–5, 1981, First International Symposium*, edited by E.L. Brannon and E.O. Salo, 98–110. Seattle: University of Washington Press, 1982.

Chapman, D.W. "Food and Space as Regulators of Salmonid Populations in Streams." *The American Naturalist* 100 (1966): 345–357.

———. "Production in Fish Populations." In *Ecology of Freshwater Fish Production*, edited by S.D. Gerking, 5–25. Oxford, England: Blackwell Scientific Publications, 1978.

Chapman, D.W., and E. Knudsen. "Channelization and Livestock Impacts on Salmonid Habitat and Biomass in Western Washington." *Transactions of the American Fisheries Society* 109 (1980): 357–363.

Chapra, S.C. "Total Phosphorus Model for the Great Lakes." *Journal of Environmental Engineering Division, American Society of Chemical Engineers* 103 (1977): 147–161.

Childerhose, R.J., and M. Trim. *Pacific Salmon.* Seattle: University of Washington Press, 1979.

Christenson, D.P. *The Revised Fishery Management Plan for the Little Kern Golden Trout.* Sacramento: California Department of Fish and Game, 1984.

Christie, G.C., and H.A. Regier. "Measures of Optimal Thermal Habi-

tat and Their Relationship to Yields for Four Commercial Fish Species." *Canadian Journal of Fisheries and Aquatic Sciences* 45 (1988): 301–314.

Clark, R.D., Jr. *Analysis of "Quality Fishing" Regulations through Mathematical Simulation of a Brown Trout Fishery.* Michigan Department of Natural Resources, Fisheries Research Report 1895. Ann Arbor: 1981.

Clark, R.D., Jr., and G.R. Alexander. "Effects of a Slotted Size Limit on the Brown Trout Fishery, Au Sable River, Michigan." In *Wild Trout III, Proceedings of the Symposium, Yellowstone National Park*, edited by F. Richardson and R.H. Hamre, 74–83. 1984.

Clark, R.D., Jr., G.R. Alexander, and H. Gowing. "Mathematical Description of Trout Stream Fisheries." *Transactions of the American Fisheries Society* 109 (1980): 587–602.

———. "A History and Evaluation of Regulations for Brook Trout and Brown Trout in Michigan Streams." *North American Journal of Fisheries Management* 1 (1981): 1–14.

Clark, R.N., D.R. Gibbons, and G.B. Pauley. "Influences of Recreation." In *Influence of Forest and Rangeland Management on Anadromous Fish Habitat in Western North America*, edited by W.R. Meehan. U.S. Department of Agriculture, Forest Service, General Technical Report PNW-178. 1985.

Cooper, E.L. "Returns from Plantings of Legal-sized Brook, Brown, and Rainbow Trout in the Pigeon River, Otsego County, Michigan." *Transactions of the American Fisheries Society* 82 (1952): 265–280.

Cooper, E.L., and R.C. Scherer. "Annual Production of Brook Trout *(Salvelinus fontinalis)* in Fertile and Infertile Streams of Pennsylvania." *Proceedings of the Pennsylvania Academy of Sciences* 41 (1967): 65–70.

Cooper, G.P., and J.L. Fuller. *A Biological Survey of Moosehead Lake and Haymock Lake, Maine.* Maine Department of Inland Fisheries and Game, Fish Survey Report No. 6. 1945.

Cooper, G.P., D.S. Shetter, and D.W. Hayne. *Results of Studies on Michigan Trout Waters with Special Angling Restrictions (Type of Lure, Size Limit, Creel Limit) 1949–59.* Michigan Department of Conservation, Fisheries Research Report 1577. Ann Arbor: 1959.

Cope, E.D., and H.C. Yarrow. "Report upon the Collection of Fishes Made in Portions of Nevada, Utah, California, Colorado, New Mexico, and Arizona, during the Years 1871, 1872, 1873, and 1874." *Report Geography Geology Exploration and Survey West of the 100th Meridian (Wheeler Survey)* 5 (1875): 635–703.

Cornett, R.J., and F.H. Rigler. "The Areal Hypolimnetic Oxygen Deficit: An Empirical Test of the Model." *Limnology and Oceanography* 25 (1980): 672–679.

Corning, R.V. "Water Fluctuations, a Detrimental Influence on Trout Streams." *Proceedings of the Annual Conference of the Southeastern Association of Game and Fish Commissioners* 23 (1969): 431–454.

Couch, J.A. "Effects of Carcinogenic Agents on Aquatic Animals: An Environmental and Experimental Overview." *Environmental Carcinogenesis Reviews* 3, no. 1 (1985): 63–105.

Craig, J.F. "A Note on Growth and Mortality of Trout, *Salmo trutta* L., in Afferent Streams of Windermere." *Journal of Fish Biology* 20 (1982): 423–429.

Crisp, D.T., R.H.K. Mann, and P.R. Cubby. "Effects of Impoundment upon Fish Populations in Afferent Streams at Cow Green Reservoir." *The Journal of Applied Ecology* 21 (1984): 739–756.

Culp, J.M. "Experimental Evidence that Stream Macroinvertebrate Community Structure is Unaffected by Different Densities of Coho Salmon Fry." *Journal of the North American Benthological Society* 5 (1986): 140–149.

Cunjak, R.A., and E.M.P. Chadwick. "Downstream Movements and Estuarine Residence by Atlantic Salmon Parr *(Salmo salar).*" *Canadian Journal of Fisheries and Aquatic Sciences* 46 (1989): 1466–1471.

Cunjak, R.A., and J.M. Green. "Habitat Utilization by Brook Char *(Salvelinus fontinalis)* and Rainbow Trout *(Salmo gairdneri)* in Newfoundland Streams." *Canadian Journal of Zoology* 61 (1983): 1214–1219.

———. "Influence of Water Temperature on Behavioural Interactions between Juvenile Brook Charr, *Salvelinus fontinalis*, and Rainbow Trout, *Salmo gairdneri.*" *Canadian Journal of Zoology* 64 (1986): 1288–1291.

Cunjak, R.A., and G. Power. "Winter Habitat Utilization by Stream Resident Brook Trout *(Salvelinus fontinalis)* and Brown Trout *(Salmo trutta).*" *Canadian Journal of Fisheries and Aquatic Sciences* 43 (1986): 1970–1981.

———. "The Feeding and Energetics of Stream-resident Trout in Winter." *Journal of Fish Biology* 31 (1987): 493–511.

Currens, K.P., C.S. Sharpe, R. Hjort, C.B. Schreck, and H.W. Li. "Effects of Different Feeding Regimes on the Morphometrics of Chinook Salmon *(Oncorhynchus tshawytscha)* and Rainbow Trout *(O. mykiss).*" *Copeia*, 1989: 689–695.

Curtis, B. "The Golden Trout of Cottonwood Lakes." *California Fish and Game* 21, no. 2 (April 1935): 101–109.

Dangel, J.R., P.T. Macy, and F.C. Withler. *Annotated Bibliography of Interspecific Hybridization of Fishes of the Subfamily Salmonidae.* U.S. Department of Commerce, NOAA Technical Memo, NMFS NWFC-1. 1973.

Davies, P.H., and W.H. Everhart. *Effects of Chemical Variations in Aquatic Environments: III. Lead Toxicity to Rainbow Trout and Testing Application Factor Concept.* U.S. Environmental Protection Agency, Water Pollution Control Research Series 18050 DYC, EPA-R3-73-011c. Washington, D.C.: 1973.

Davis, J.C. "Minimal Dissolved Oxygen Requirements of Aquatic Life with Emphasis on Canadian Species: A Review." *Journal of the Fisheries Research Board of Canada* 32 (1975): 2295-2332.

Day, F. *British and Irish Salmonidae.* London: Williams & Norgate, 1887.

de Leaniz, C.G. "Site Fidelity and Homing of Atlantic Salmon Parr in a Small Scottish Stream." In *Proceedings of the Salmonid Migration and Distribution Symposium, June 23-25, 1987,* edited by E. Brannon and B. Jonsson, 70-80. 1989.

Dempson, J.B., and A.H. Kristofferson. "Spatial and Temporal Aspects of the Ocean Migration of Anadromous Arctic Char." *American Fisheries Society Symposium* 1 (1987): 340-357.

Denton, E.J., and J.A.B. Gray. "Mechanical Factors in the Excitation of the Lateral Lines of Fishes." In *Sensory Biology of Aquatic Animals,* edited by J. Atema, R.R. Fay, A.N. Popper, and W.N. Tavolga, 595-617. New York: Springer-Verlag, 1988.

DeRoche, S.E. "Observations on the Spawning Habits and Early Life of Lake Trout." *Progressive Fish-Culturist* 31 (1969): 109-113.

Dick, T.A. "Parasites and Arctic Charr Management—An Academic Curiosity or Practical Reality?" In *Biology of the Arctic Charr, Proceedings of the International Symposium on Arctic Charr,* edited by L. Johnson and B. Burns, 371-394. Symposium held in Winnipeg, Manitoba, May 4-8, 1981. Winnipeg: University of Manitoba Press, 1984.

Dickhoff, W.W., L. Yan, E.M. Plisetskaya, C.V. Sullivan, P. Swanson, A. Hara, and M.G. Bernard. "Relationship between Metabolic and Reproductive Hormones in Salmonid Fish." *Fish Physiology and Biochemistry* 7 (1989): 147-155.

Dijkgraaf, S. "The Functioning and Significance of the Lateral Line Organs." *Biological Reviews* 38 (1962): 51-105.

Ditton, R.B., and A.J. Fedler. "Importance of Fish Consumption to Sport Fishermen: A Reply to Matlock et al." *Fisheries* 14, no. 4 (1989): 5-6.

Dolloff, C.A. "The Relationships of Wood Debris to Juvenile Salmonid Production and Microhabitat Selection in Small Southeast Alaska Streams." Ph.D. dissertation, Montana State University, Bozeman, 1983.

Donald, D.B., and D.J. Alger. "Stunted Lake Trout *(Salvelinus namaycush)* from the Rocky Mountains." *Canadian Journal of Fisheries and Aquatic Sciences* 43 (1986): 608-612.

Douglas, R.H. "Spectral Sensitivity of Rainbow Trout *(Salmo gairdneri).*" *Revue Canadienne de Biologie Experimentale* 42 (1983): 117-122.

Døving, K.B. "What the Salmon Nose Tells the Human Brain." In *Proceedings of the Salmonid Migration and Distribution Symposium, June 23-25, 1987,* edited by E. Brannon and B. Jonsson, 9-18. 1989.

Døving, K.B., P.S. Enger, and H. Nordeng. "Electrophysiological Studies on the Olfactory Sense in Char *(Salmo alpinus* L.)." *Comparative Biochemistry and Physiology* 45A (1973): 21-24.

Døving, K.B., H. Nordeng, and B. Oakley. "Single Unit Discrimination of Fish Odours Released by Char *(Salmo alpinus* L.) Populations." *Comparative Biochemistry and Physiology* 47A (1974): 1051-1063.

Dutil, J.-D. "Energetic Costs Associated with the Production of Gonads in the Anadromous Arctic Charr *(Salvelinus alpinus)* of the Nauyuk Lake Basin, Canada." In *Biology of the Arctic Charr, Proceedings of the International Symposium on Arctic Charr,* edited by L. Johnson and B. Burns, 263-276. Symposium held in Winnipeg, Manitoba, May 4-8, 1981. Winnipeg: University of Manitoba Press, 1984.

Eck, G., and E. Brown, Jr. "Lake Michigan's Capacity to Support Lake Trout *(Salvelinus namaycush)* and Other Salmonines: An Estimate Based on the Status of Prey Populations in the 1970s." *Canadian Journal of Fisheries and Aquatic Sciences* 42 (1985): 449-454.

Eck, G., and L. Wells. "Depth Distribution, Diet, and Overwinter Growth of Lake Trout *(Salvelinus namaycush)* in Southeastern Lake Michigan, Sampled in December 1981 and March 1982." *Journal of Great Lakes Research* 12 (1986): 263-269.

Edmondson, E., F.E. Everest, and D.W. Chapman. "Permanence of Station in Juvenile Chinook Salmon and Steelhead Trout." *Journal of the Fisheries Research Board of Canada* 25, no. 7 (1968): 1453-1464.

Egglishaw, H.J., and P.E. Shackley. "Growth, Survival and Production of Juvenile Salmon and Trout in a Scottish Stream, 1966-1975." *Journal of Fish Biology* 11 (1977): 647-672.

Eibl-Eibesfeldt, I., and S. Kramer. "Ethology, the Comparative Study of Animal Behavior." *The Quarterly Review of Biology* 33, no. 3 (1958): 181-211.

Elliott, J.M. "Invertebrate Drift in a Dartmoor Stream." *Archiv für Hydrobiologie* 63 (1967): 202-237.

———. "Population Dynamics of Migratory Trout, *Salmo trutta,* in a Lake District Stream, 1966-83, and Their Implications for Fisheries Management." *Journal of Fish Biology* 27, suppl. A (1985): 35-43.

———. "Spatial Distribution and Behavioural Movements of Migra-

tory Trout *Salmo trutta* in a Lake District Stream." *The Journal of Animal Ecology* 55 (1986): 907-922.

———. "The Distances Travelled by Downstream-moving Fry, *Salmo trutta,* in a Lake District Stream." *Freshwater Biology* 17 (1987): 491-499.

———, ed. "Wild Brown Trout: The Scientific Basis for Their Conservation and Management." *Freshwater Biology* 21 (1989): 1-137.

Ellis, S.L.N., and H.C. Bryant. "Distribution of the Golden Trout in California." *California Fish and Game* 6, no. 4 (October 1920): 141-152.

Emanuel, M.E., and J.J. Dodson. "Modification of the Rheotropic Behavior of Male Rainbow Trout *(Salmo gairdneri)* by Ovarian Fluid." *Journal of the Fisheries Research Board of Canada* 36 (1979): 63-68.

Embody, G.C. "Relation of Temperature to the Incubation Periods of Eggs of Four Species of Trout." *Transactions of the American Fisheries Society* 64 (1934): 281-292.

Emery, A.R. "Fish and Crayfish Mortalities Due to an Internal Seiche in Georgian Bay, Lake Huron." *Journal of the Fisheries Research Board of Canada* 30 (1970): 761-774.

Erman, D.C. "Long-term Structure of Fish Populations in Sagehen Creek, California." *Transactions of the American Fisheries Society* 115 (1986): 682-692.

Erman, D.C., and V.M. Hawthorne. "The Quantitative Importance of an Intermittent Stream in the Spawning of Rainbow Trout." *Transactions of the American Fisheries Society* 105 (1976): 675-681.

Eschmeyer, P.H. "The Reproduction of Lake Trout in Southern Lake Superior." *Transactions of the American Fisheries Society* 84 (1955): 47-74.

Eshenroder, R.L., T.P. Poe, and C.H. Olver, eds. *Strategies for Rehabilitation of the Lake Trout in the Great Lakes: Proceedings of a Conference on Lake Trout Research, August 1983.* Great Lakes Fishery Commission, Technical Report No. 40. Ann Arbor, Mich.: 1984.

Evans, D.O. *An Overview of the Ecology of the Lake Whitefish,* Coregonus clupeaformis *(Mitchill), in Lake Simcoe, Ontario.* Ontario Ministry of Natural Resources, Lake Simcoe Fisheries Assessment Unit, Report 78-1. 1978.

Evans, D.O., J. Brisbane, J.M. Casselman, K.E. Coleman, C.A. Lewis, P.G. Sly, D.L. Wales, and C.C. Willox. *Anthropogenic Stressors and Their Effects on Lake Trout Populations in Ontario Lakes.* Lake Trout Synthesis, Ontario Ministry of Natural Resources, Toronto, Canada, 1991.

Evans, D.O., J.M. Casselman, and C.C. Willox. *Effects of Exploitation, Loss of Nursery Habitat and Stocking on the Dynamics and Productivity of Lake Trout Populations in Ontario Lakes.* Lake Trout Synthesis, Ontario Ministry of Natural Resources, Toronto, Canada, 1990.

Evans, D.O., and P. Waring. "Changes in the Multispecies, Winter Angling Fishery of Lake Simcoe, Ontario, 1961-83: Invasion by Rainbow Smelt, *Osmerus mordax,* and the Roles of Intra- and Interspecific Interactions." *Canadian Journal of Fisheries and Aquatic Sciences* 44, suppl. 2 (1987): 182-197.

Evermann, B.W. "The Golden Trout of the Southern High Sierras." *Bulletin of the U.S. Bureau of Fisheries* 25, no. 1905 (1906): 1-51.

Fabricius, E. "Heterogeneous Stimulus Summation in the Release of Spawning Activities in Fish." *Reports from the Swedish State Institute of Fresh-water Fishery Research, Drottningholm* 31 (1950): 57-99.

———. "The Topography of the Spawning Bottom as a Factor Influencing the Size of the Territory of Some Species of Fish." *Reports from the Swedish State Institute of Fresh-water Fishery Research, Drottningholm* (1951): 12-48.

———. "Aquarium Observations on the Spawning Behaviour of the Char, *Salmo alpinus.*" *Reports from the Swedish State Institute of Fresh-water Fishery Research, Drottningholm* 34 (1953): 14-18.

Fahy, E., and W.P. Warren. "Long-lived Sea Trout, Sea-run 'Ferox'?" *The Salmon and Trout Magazine* 227 (1984): 72-75.

Fausch, K.D. "Profitable Stream Positions for Salmonids: Relating Specific Growth Rate to Net Energy Gain." *Canadian Journal of Zoology* 62 (1984): 441-451.

———. "Tests of Competition between Native and Introduced Salmonids in Streams: What Have We Learned?" *Canadian Journal of Fisheries and Aquatic Sciences* 45 (1988): 2238-2246.

Fausch, K.D., and R.J. White. "Competition between Brook Trout *(Salvelinus fontinalis)* and Brown Trout *(Salmo trutta)* for Positions in a Michigan Stream." *Canadian Journal of Fisheries and Aquatic Sciences* 38 (1981): 1220-1227.

———. "A Sinuous Stream Aquarium to Simulate Lotic Fish Habitat." *Progressive Fish-Culturist* 45 (1983): 113-116.

———. "Competition among Juveniles of Coho Salmon, Brook Trout, and Brown Trout in a Laboratory Stream, and Implications for Great Lakes Tributaries." *Transactions of the American Fisheries Society* 115 (1986): 363-381.

Fenderson, O.C., W.H. Everhart, and K.M. Muth. "Comparative Agonistic and Feeding Behavior of Hatchery-reared and Wild Salmon in Aquaria." *Journal of the Fisheries Research Board of Canada* 25, no. 1 (1968): 1-14.

Ferguson, A., and F.M. Mason. "Allozyme Evidence for Reproductively Isolated Sympatric Populations of Brown Trout, *Salmo trutta*

L., in Lough Melvin, Ireland." *Journal of Fish Biology* 18 (1981): 629–642.

Fisk, L. *Golden Trout of the High Sierra.* Sacramento: California Department of Fish and Game, 1983.

Fisknes, B., and K.B. Døving. "Olfactory Sensitivity to Group-specific Substances in Atlantic Salmon *(Salmo salar L.)." Journal of Chemical Ecology* 8 (1982): 1083–1092.

Flick, W.A. "Some Observations: Age, Growth, Food Habits and Vulnerability of Large Brook Trout *(Salvelinus fontinalis)* from Four Canadian Lakes." *Nature* (Canada) 104, no. 4 (1977): 353–359.

Flick, W.A., and D.A. Webster. "Comparative First Year Survival and Production in Wild and Domestic Strains of Brook Trout, *Salvelinus fontinalis." Transactions of the American Fisheries Society* 93 (1964): 58–69.

———. "Production of Wild and Domestic, and Interstrain Hybrids of Brook Trout *(Salvelinus fontinalis)* in Natural Ponds." *Journal of the Fisheries Research Board of Canada* 33, no. 7 (1976): 1525–1539.

———. *Brandon Park Fish Management Reports.* Cornell University. 1957–1987.

———. "Biomass of Fish in Adirondack Waters before and after Removal of Non-trout Species." Unpublished manuscript. 1989.

Folmar, L.C., and W.W. Dickhoff. "The Parr-Smolt Transformation (Smoltification) and Seawater Adaptation in Salmonids." *Aquaculture Magazine* 21 (1980): 1–37.

Fraley, J.J., and B.B. Shepard. "Life History, Ecology and Population Status of Migratory Bull Trout *(Salvelinus confluentus)* in the Flathead Lake and River System, Montana." *Northwest Science* 63 (1989): 133–143.

Fraser, J.M. "An Atypical Brook Charr *(Salvelinus fontinalis)* Spawning Area." *Environmental Biology of Fishes* 7 (1982): 385–388.

———. "Shoal Spawning of Brook Trout, *Salvelinus fontinalis,* in a Precambrian Shield Lake." *Le Naturaliste Canadien* 112 (1985): 163–174.

Freda, J., and D.G. McDonald. "Physiological Correlates of Interspecific Variation in Acid Tolerance in Fish." *Journal of Experimental Biology* 136 (1988): 243–258.

Frost, W.E. "The Food of Pike, *Esox lucius,* in Windermere." *The Journal of Animal Ecology* 2 (1954): 339–360.

Frost, W.E., and M.E. Brown. *The Trout.* St. James Place, London: William Collins, 1967.

Galligan, J.P. "Depth Distribution of Lake Trout and Associated Species in Cayuga Lake, New York." *New York Fish and Game Journal* 9 (1962): 44–68.

Gard, R., and G.A. Flittner. "Distribution and Abundance of Fishes in Sagehen Creek, California." *The Journal of Wildlife Management* 38 (1974): 347–358.

Garman, G.C. "Initial Effects of Deforestation on Aquatic Community Structure and Function of the East Branch Piscataquis River, Maine." Ph.D. dissertation, University of Maine, Qrono, 1984.

Giger, R.D. *Ecology and Management of Coastal Cutthroat Trout in Oregon.* Oregon State Game Commission, Fisheries Research Report 6. 1972.

Gigliotti, L.M. "No-Kill Fishing Regulations: An Assessment of the Social and Recreational Characteristics and Behaviors of Michigan Stream Trout Anglers with Special Consideration of Anglers on Selected Sections of the Au Sable River." Ph.D. dissertation, Michigan State University, 1989.

Ginetz, R.M., and P.A. Larkin. "Choice of Colors of Food Items by Rainbow Trout *(Salmo gairdneri)." Journal of the Fisheries Research Board of Canada* 30 (1973): 229–234.

Glover, G., and P. McCart. "Life History of Arctic Charr *(Salvelinus alpinus)* in the Firth River, Yukon Territory." In *Life History of Anadromous and Freshwater Fish in the Western Arctic,* edited by P.J. McCart. Canadian Arctic Gas Study, Ltd. Biological Report Series, Vol. 20. 1974.

Godin, J.-G.J. "Migrations of Salmonid Fishes during Early Life History Phases: Daily and Annual Timing." In *Proceedings of the Salmon and Trout Migratory Behavior Symposium, June 3–5, 1981, First International Symposium,* edited by E.L. Brannon and E.O. Salo, 22–50. Seattle: University of Washington Press, 1982.

Gold, J.R., and G.A.E. Gall. "The Taxonomic Structure of Six Golden Trout *(Salmo agua-bonito)* Populations from the Sierra Nevada, California (Pisces: Salmonidae)." *Proceedings of the California Academy of Sciences* 40, no. 10 (1975): 243–263.

Gold, J.R., W.J. Karel, and M.R. Strand. "Chromosome Formulae of North American Fishes." *Progressive Fish-Culturist* 42 (1980): 10–20.

Goodier, J.L. "Native Lake Trout *(Salvelinus namaycush)* Stocks in the Canadian Waters of Lake Superior prior to 1955." *Canadian Journal of Fisheries and Aquatic Sciences* 38 (1981): 1724–1737.

Goodnight, W.H., and T.C. Bjornn. "Fish Production in Two Idaho Streams." *Transactions of the American Fisheries Society* 100 (1971): 769–780.

Goodyear, C.D., T.A. Edsall, D.M. Ormsby Dempsey, G.D. Moss, and P.E. Polanski. *Atlas of the Spawning and Nursery Areas of Great Lakes Fishes.* 14 vols. U.S. Department of the Interior, U.S. Fish and Wildlife Service, FWS/OBS-82/52. Washington, D.C.: 1982.

Gordon, D.J., and H.R. MacCrimmon. "Juvenile Salmonid Production in a Lake Erie Nursery Stream." *Journal of Fish Biology* 21 (1982): 455–473.

Gowing, H. *The Effects of an Increase in the Minimum Size Limit of Trout upon Angling in the Rifle River, Rifle River Area.* Michigan Department of Conservation, Fisheries Research Report 1413. Ann Arbor: 1954.

Graham, P.J., B.B. Shepard, and J.J. Fraley. "Use of Stream Habitat Classifications to Identify Bull Trout Spawning Areas in Streams." In *Proceedings of the Symposium of Acquisition and Utilization of Aquatic Habitat Inventory Information, Portland, Oregon, October 28–30, 1981,* edited by N.B. Armantrout, 186–190. Bethesda, Md.: American Fisheries Society, 1982.

Grainger, E.H. "On the Age, Growth, Migration, Reproductive Potential and Feeding Habits of Arctic Char *(Salvelinus alpinus),* Frobisher Bay, Baffin Island." *Journal of the Fisheries Research Board of Canada* 10 (1953): 326–370.

Grant, J.W.A., A. Grant, D.L.G. Noakes, and K.M. Jones. "Spatial Distribution of Defense and Foraging in Young-of-the-Year Brook Charr, *Salvelinus fontinalis." The Journal of Animal Ecology* 58 (1989): 773–784.

Grant, J.W.A., and D.L.G. Noakes. "Escape Behavior and Use of Cover by Young-of-the-Year Brook Trout, *Salvelinus fontinalis." Canadian Journal of Fisheries and Aquatic Sciences* 44 (1987): 1390–1396.

Gresswell, R.E., ed. *Status and Management of Interior Stocks of Cutthroat Trout.* Bethesda, Md.: American Fisheries Society, 1988.

Griffith, J.S. "Comparative Behavior and Habitat Utilization of Brook Trout *(Salvelinus fontinalis)* and Cutthroat Trout *(Salmo clarki)* in Small Streams in Northern Idaho." *Journal of the Fisheries Research Board of Canada* 29, no. 3 (1972): 265–273.

———. "Utilization of Invertebrate Drift by Brook Trout *(Salvelinus fontinalis)* and Cutthroat Trout *(Salmo clarki)* in Small Streams in Idaho." *Transactions of the American Fisheries Society* 103, no. 3 (1974): 440–447.

———. "A Review of Competition between Cutthroat Trout and Other Salmonids." In *Status and Management of Interior Stocks of Cutthroat Trout,* edited by R.E. Gresswell, 134–140. Bethesda, Md.: American Fisheries Society, 1988.

Gross, M.R. "Evolution of Diadromy in Fishes." *American Fisheries Society Symposium* 1 (1987): 14–25.

Gruchy, C.G., and V.D. Vladikov. "Sexual Dimorphism in Anal Fin of Brown Trout, *Salmo trutta,* and Close Relatives." *Journal of the Fisheries Research Board of Canada* 25 (1968): 813–815.

Günther, A.C.L.G. *Catalog of the Fishes of the British Museum.* Vol. 6. London: British Museum, 1866.

Gwartney, L.A. *Naknek Drainage Rainbow Trout Study in the Katmai National Park and Preserve.* Alaska Department of Fish and Game, and U.S. Department of the Interior, National Park Service, 1985.

Hall, E.T. *The Hidden Dimension.* New York: Doubleday and Co., 1966.

Hall, J.D., and N.J. Knight. *Natural Variation in Abundance of Salmonid Populations in Streams and Its Implications for Design of Impact Studies.* Environmental Protection Agency, Report EPA-600/S3-81-021. Corvallis, Oreg.: 1981.

Hammar, J. "Ecological Characters of Different Combinations of Sympatric Populations of Arctic Charr in Sweden." In *Biology of the Arctic Charr, Proceedings of the International Symposium on Arctic Charr,* edited by L. Johnson and B. Burns, 35–63. Symposium held in Winnipeg, Manitoba, May 4–8, 1981. Winnipeg: University of Manitoba Press, 1984.

———. "Freshwater Ecosystems of Polar Regions: Vulnerable Resources." *Ambio* 18 (1989): 6–22.

Hansen, M.J., and T.M. Stauffer. "Comparative Recovery to the Creel, Movement and Growth of Rainbow Trout Stocked in the Great Lakes." *Transactions of the American Fisheries Society* 100 (1971): 336–349.

Hanson, D.L., and T.F. Waters. "Recovery of Standing Crop and Production Rate of a Brook Trout Population in a Flood-damaged Stream." *Transactions of the American Fisheries Society* 103 (1974): 431–439.

Hara, T.J. "Olfactory Responses to Amino Acids in Rainbow Trout, *Salmo gairdneri." Comparative Biochemistry and Physiology* 44A (1973): 407–416.

———. "Pheromonal Control of Fish Reproduction." In *Proceedings of the Salmonid Migration and Distribution Symposium, June 23–25, 1987,* edited by E. Brannon and B. Jonsson, 152–155. 1989.

Hara, T.J., and S.B. Brown. "Olfactory Bulbar Electrical Responses of Rainbow Trout *(Salmo gairdneri)* Exposed to Morpholine during Smoltification." *Journal of the Fisheries Research Board of Canada* 36 (1979): 1186–1190.

Hara, T.J., Y.M. Carolina Law, and B.R. Holden. "Comparison of the Olfactory Response to Amino Acids in Rainbow Trout, Brook Trout, and Whitefish." *Comparative Biochemistry and Physiology* 45A (1973): 969–977.

Hara, T.J., and S. Macdonald. "Olfactory Responses to Skin Mucus Substances in Rainbow Trout, *Salmo gairdneri." Comparative Biochemistry and Physiology* 54A (1976): 41–44.

Hara, T.J., and B. Zielinsky. "Structural and Functional Development of the Olfactory Organ in Teleosts." *Transactions of the American Fisheries Society* 118 (1989): 183–194.

Haraldstad, O., and B. Jonsson. "Age and Sex Segregation in Habitat Utilization by Brown Trout in a Norwegian Lake." *Transactions of the American Fisheries Society* 112 (1983): 27–37.

Harden Jones, F.R. *Fish Migration*. London: Edward Arnold, 1968.

Harper, K.C. "Biology of a Southwestern Salmonid, *Salmo apache* (Miller 1972)." In *Proceedings of the Wild Trout-Catchable Trout Symposium, Eugene, Oregon, February 15–17, 1978*, edited by J.R. Moring, 99–111. Portland: Oregon Department of Fish and Wildlife, 1978.

Hartman, G.F. "Nest Digging Behavior of Rainbow Trout *(Salmo gairdneri)*." *Canadian Journal of Zoology* 48, no. 6 (1970): 1458–1462.

Hartman, G.F., and T.G. Brown. "Use of Small, Temporary, Floodplain Tributaries by Juvenile Salmonids in a West Coast Rain-forest Drainage Basin, Carnation Creek, British Columbia." *Canadian Journal of Fisheries and Aquatic Sciences* 44 (1987): 262–270.

Hartman, G.F., and C.A. Gill. "Distributions of Juvenile Steelhead and Cutthroat Trout *(Salmo gairdneri* and *S. clarki clarki)* within Streams in Southwestern British Columbia." *Journal of the Fisheries Research Board of Canada* 25 (1968): 33–48.

Hartman, W.L. *Effects of Exploitation, Environmental Changes, and New Species on the Fish Habitats and Resources of Lake Erie*. Great Lakes Fishery Commission, Technical Report No. 22. 1973.

Hasler, A.D. "Fish Biology and Limnology of Crater Lake, Oregon." *The Journal of Wildlife Management* 2 (1938): 94–103.

Hasler, A.D., and A.T. Scholz. *Olfactory Imprinting and Homing in Salmon*. Berlin: Springer-Verlag, 1983.

Hausle, D.A., and D.W. Coble. "Influence of Sand in Redds on Survival and Emergence of Brook Trout *(Salvelinus fontinalis)*." *Transactions of the American Fisheries Society* 105 (1976): 57–63.

Hawkins, A.D., and A.D.F. Johnstone. "The Hearing of the Atlantic Salmon, *Salmo salar*." *Journal of Fish Biology* 13 (1978): 655–673.

Hawthorne, V., and R.L. Butler. *A Trout Stream in Winter*. 16mm, 22 min. 1979. Psychological Cinema Register. Distributed by the Audio Visual Services of The Pennsylvania State University.

Hayes, J.W. "Competition for Spawning Space between Brown *(Salmo trutta)* and Rainbow Trout *(S. gairdneri)* in a Lake Inlet Spawning Tributary, New Zealand." *Canadian Journal of Fisheries and Aquatic Sciences* 44 (1987): 40–47.

———. "Social Interactions between O+ Brown and Rainbow Trout in Experimental Stream Troughs." *New Zealand Journal of Marine and Freshwater Research* 23 (1989): 163–170.

Hazzard, A.S., and D.S. Shetter. "Results from Experimental Plantings of Legal-sized Brook Trout *(Salvelinus fontinalis)* and Rainbow Trout *(Salmo irideus)*." *Transactions of the American Fisheries Society* 68 (1938): 196–210.

Heacox, C.E. *The Compleat Brown Trout*. New York: Winchester Press, 1974.

Hearn, W.E. "Interspecific Competition and Habitat Segregation among Stream-dwelling Trout and Salmon: A Review." *Fisheries* 12, no. 5 (1987): 24–31.

Heggberget, T.G., L.P. Hansen, and T.F. Naesje. "Within-river Spawning Migration of Atlantic Salmon *(Salmo salar)*." *Canadian Journal of Fisheries and Aquatic Sciences* 45 (1988): 1691–1698.

Helm, W.T., ed. *Glossary of Stream Habitat Terms*. Logan, Utah: Utah State University, Department of Fisheries and Wildlife, 1986.

Henderson, M.A., and T.G. Northcote. "Visual Prey Detection and Foraging in Sympatric Cutthroat Trout *(Salmo clarki)* and Dolly Varden *(Salvelinus malma)*." *Canadian Journal of Fisheries and Aquatic Sciences* 42 (1985): 785–790.

Hendricks, J.D. "Chemical Carcinogenesis in Fish." In *Aquatic Toxicology*, vol. 1, edited by L.J. Weber, 149–211. New York: Raven Press, 1982.

Hestagen, T. "Movements of Brown Trout, *Salmo trutta*, and Juvenile Atlantic Salmon, *Salmo salar*, in a Coastal Stream in Northern Norway." *Journal of Fish Biology* 32 (1988): 639–653.

Heufelder, G.R., D.J. Jude, and F.J. Tesar. "Upwelling Effects on Local Abundance and Distribution of Larval Alewife *(Alosa pseudoharengus)* in Eastern Lake Michigan." *Canadian Journal of Fisheries and Aquatic Sciences* 39 (1982): 1531–1537.

Hindar, K., and B. Jonsson. "Habitat and Food Segregation of Dwarf and Normal Arctic Charr *(Salvelinus alpinus)* from Vangsvatnet Lake, Western Norway." *Canadian Journal of Fisheries and Aquatic Sciences* 39 (1982): 1030–1045.

Hitchens, J.R., and W.G.A. Samis. "Successful Reproduction by Introduced Lake Trout in 10 Northeastern Ontario Lakes." *North American Journal of Fisheries Management* 6 (1986): 372–375.

Hoar, W.S. "Smolt Transformation: Evolution, Behavior, and Physiology." *Journal of the Fisheries Research Board of Canada* 33 (1976): 1133–1252.

Hoar, W.S., and D.J. Randall, eds. *Fish Physiology*. Vol. 2. New York: Academic Press, 1969.

Hoffman, G.L., and G. Schubert. "Some Parasites of Exotic Fishes." In *Distribution, Biology, and Management of Exotic Fishes*, edited by W.R. Courtenay and J.R. Stauffer, 233–261. Baltimore: The Johns Hopkins University Press, 1984.

Holcombe, G.W., D.A. Benoit, and E.N. Leonard. "Long-term Effects of Zinc Exposure on Brook Trout *(Salvelinus fontinalis)*." *Transactions of the American Fisheries Society* 108 (1979): 76–87.

Holcombe, G.W., D.A. Benoit, E.N. Leonard, and J.M. McKim. "Long-term Effects of Lead Exposure on Three Generations of Brook Trout *(Salvelinus fontinalis)*." *Journal of the Fisheries Research Board of Canada* 33 (1976): 1731–1741.

Holcombe, G.W., G.L. Phipps, A.H. Sulaiman, and A.D. Hoffman. "Simultaneous Multiple Species Testing: Acute Toxicity of 13 Chemicals to 12 Diverse Freshwater Amphibian, Fish, and Invertebrate Families." *Archives of Environmental Contamination and Toxicology* 16 (1987): 697–710.

Honda, H. "Female Sex Pheromone of Rainbow Trout, *Salmo gairdneri*, Involved in Courtship Behavior." *Bulletin of the Japanese Society of Scientific Fisheries* 46, no. 9 (1980): 1109–1112.

Hooper, D.R. *Evaluation of the Effects of Flow on Trout Stream Ecology*. Emeryville, Calif.: Department of Engineering Research, Pacific Gas and Electric Co., 1973.

Hooten, R.S. "Catch and Release as a Management Strategy for Steelhead in British Columbia." In *Catch-and-Release Fishing: A Decade of Experience, Symposium Proceedings*, edited by R.A. Barnhart and T.D. Roelofs, 143–156. Arcata, Calif.: California Cooperative Fishery Research Unit, Humboldt State University, 1987.

Hoover, E.E., and M.S. Johnson. "Migration and Depletion of Stocked Brook Trout." *Transactions of the American Fisheries Society* 67 (1937): 224–227.

Hoover, H.E. "Experimental Modification of the Sexual Cycle in Trout by Control of Light." *Science* 86 (1937): 425–426.

Hopkins, C.L. "Production of Fish in Two Small Streams in the North Island of New Zealand." *New Zealand Journal of Marine and Freshwater Research* 5 (1971): 280–290.

Horak, D.L., and H.A. Tanner. "The Use of Vertical Gill Nets in Studying Fish Depth Distribution, Horsetooth Reservoir, Colorado." *Transactions of the American Fisheries Society* 93 (1964): 137–145.

Horner, N.J. "Survival, Density and Behavior of Salmonid Fry in Streams in Relation to Fish Predation." Master's thesis, University of Idaho, Moscow, 1978.

Horton, P.A., R.G. Bailey, and S.I. Wilsdon. "A Comparative Study of the Bionomics of the Salmonids of Three Devon Streams." *Archiv für Hydrobiologie* 2 (1968): 187–204.

Hosford, W.E., and S.P. Pribyl. *Blitzen River Redband Trout Evaluation*. Oregon Department of Fish and Wildlife, Information Reports No. 83-9. 1983.

Houghton, W. *British Freshwater Fishes*. London: G. Bell and Sons, 1884.

Hubbs, C.L. "The Specific Name of the European Trout." *Copeia*, 1930, no. 172: 86–89.

Hulbert, P.J., and R. Engstrom-Heg. "Upstream Dispersal of Fall-stocked Brown Trout in Canajoharie Creek, New York." *New York Fish and Game Journal* 29 (1982): 166–175.

Hulett, P.L., and S.A. Leider. "Genetic Interactions of Hatchery and Wild Steelhead Trout: Findings and Implications of Research at Kalama River, Washington." In *Wild Trout IV, Proceedings of the Symposium, Yellowstone National Park, September 18–19, 1989*, edited by F. Richardson and R.H. Hamre, 76–82. Washington, D.C.: U.S. Department of Agriculture, Forest Service, 1989.

Hunsaker, D., II, L.F. Marnell, and F.P. Sharpe. "Hooking Mortality of Yellowstone Cutthroat Trout." *Progressive Fish-Culturist* 32 (1970): 231–235.

Hunt, R.L. *Evaluation of Fly-fishing-Only at Lawrence Creek (A Three-Year Progress Report)*. Wisconsin Conservation Department, Miscellaneous Research Report No. 10 (Fisheries). Madison: 1964.

———. *Production and Angler Harvest of Wild Brook Trout in Lawrence Creek, Wisconsin*. Wisconsin Conservation Department, Technical Bulletin 35. Madison: 1966.

———. "Effects of Habitat Alteration on Production, Standing Crops, and Yield of Brook Trout in Lawrence Creek, Wisconsin." In *Symposium on Salmon and Trout in Streams*, edited by T.G. Northcote, 281–312. Vancouver: Institute of Fisheries, University of British Columbia, 1969.

———. *A Compendium of Research on Angling Regulations for Brook Trout Conducted at Lawrence Creek, Wisconsin*. Wisconsin Department of Natural Resources, Research Report 54. Madison: 1970.

———. "A Long-term Evaluation of Trout Habitat Development and Its Relation to Improving Management Related Research." *Transactions of the American Fisheries Society* 105, no. 3 (1976): 361–364.

Hunt, R.L., O.M. Brynildson, and J.T. McFadden. *Effects of Angling Regulations on a Wild Brook Trout Fishery*. Wisconsin Conservation Department, Technical Bulletin No. 26. Madison: 1962.

Hunter, J.G. *The Production of Arctic Char (Salvelinus alpinus Linnaeus) in a Small Arctic Lake*. Fisheries Research Board of Canada, Technical Report 231. 1970.

Hutchings, J.A. "Lakeward Migrations by Juvenile Atlantic Salmon, *Salmo salar*." *Canadian Journal of Fisheries and Aquatic Sciences* 43 (1986): 732–741.

Hutchinson, G.E. *A Treatise on Limnology*. Vol. 1, *Geography, Physics, and Chemistry.* New York: John Wiley and Sons, 1957.

Huzyk, L., and H. Tsuyuki. "Distribution of LDHB Gene in Resident and Anadromous Rainbow Trout *(Salmo gairdneri)* from Streams in British Columbia." *Journal of the Fisheries Research Board of Canada* 31 (1974): 106–108.

Ihssen, P.E., and J.S. Tait. "Genetic Differentiation in Retention of Swimbladder Gas between Two Populations of Lake Trout *(Salvelinus namaycush)*." *Journal of the Fisheries Research Board of Canada* 31 (1974): 1351–1354.

Irving, J.S., and T.C. Bjornn. *Effects of Substrate Size Composition on Survival of Kokanee Salmon and Cutthroat and Rainbow Trout.* University of Idaho, Idaho Cooperative Fisheries Research Unit, Report 84–6. 1984.

Ivlev, V.S. "The Biological Productivity of Waters." Translated by W.E. Ricker from the 1945 paper in Russian. *Journal of the Fisheries Research Board of Canada* 23 (1966): 1727–1759.

Jacobson, O.J. "Brown Trout *(Salmo trutta* L.) Growth at Reduced pH." *Aquaculture Magazine* 11 (1977): 81–84.

Jahn, L.A. "Movements and Homing of Cutthroat Trout *(Salmo clarkii)* from Open-Water Areas of Yellowstone Lake." *Journal of the Fisheries Research Board of Canada* 26 (1969): 1243–1261.

Jenkins, R.M. "The Morphoedaphic Index and Reservoir Fish Production." *Transactions of the American Fisheries Society* 111 (1982): 133–140.

Jenkins, T.M., Jr. "Night Feeding of Brown and Rainbow Trout in an Experimental Stream Channel." *Journal of the Fisheries Research Board of Canada* 26 (1969): 3275–3278.

———. "Observations on Color Changes of Brown and Rainbow Trout *(Salmo trutta* and *S. gairdneri)* in Stream Habitats, with Description of an Unusual Color Pattern in Brown Trout." *Transactions of the American Fisheries Society* 98 (1969): 517–519.

———. "Social Structure, Position Choice, and Microdistribution of Two Trout Species *(Salmo trutta* and *Salmo gairdneri)* Resident in Mountain Streams." *Animal Behaviour Monographs* 2, no. 2 (1969): 57–123.

Jenkins, T.M., Jr., C.R. Feldmeth, and G.V. Elliot. "Feeding of Rainbow Trout *(Salmo gairdneri)* in Relation to Abundance of Drifting Invertebrates in a Mountain Stream." *Journal of the Fisheries Research Board of Canada* 27 (1970): 2356–2361.

Jensen, A.J., and B.O. Johnsen. "Difficulties in Aging Atlantic Salmon *(Salmo salar)* and Brown Trout *(Salmo trutta)* from Cold Rivers Due to Lack of Scales as Yearlings." *Canadian Journal of Fisheries and Aquatic Sciences* 39 (1982): 321–325.

Jeppson, P.W., and W.S. Platts. "Ecology and Control of Columbia Squawfish in Northern Idaho Lakes." *Transactions of the American Fisheries Society* 88 (1959): 197–202.

Johnson, J.E. *Protected Fishes of the United States and Canada.* Bethesda, Md.: American Fisheries Society, 1987.

Johnson, J.E., and J.N. Rinne. "The Endangered Species Act and Southwest Fishes." *Fisheries* 7, no. 2 (1982): 1–8.

Johnson, J.H. "Production and Growth of Subyearling Coho Salmon, *Oncorhynchus kisutch,* Chinook Salmon, *Oncorhynchus tshawytscha,* and Steelhead, *Salmo gairdneri,* in Orwell Brook, Tributary of Salmon River, New York." *NOAA Fishery Bulletin* 78 (1980): 549–554.

Johnson, L. "Distribution of Fish Species in Great Bear Lake, Northwest Territories, with Reference to Zooplankton, Benthic Invertebrates, and Environmental Conditions." *Journal of the Fisheries Research Board of Canada* 32 (1975): 1989–2004.

———. "The Arctic Charr, *Salvelinus alpinus.*" In *Charrs: Salmonid Fishes of the Genus* Salvelinus, edited by E.K. Balon, 15–98. The Hague, The Netherlands: Dr. W. Junk Publishers, 1980.

Johnson, L., and B. Burns, eds. *Biology of the Arctic Charr, Proceedings of the International Symposium on Arctic Charr.* Symposium held in Winnipeg, Manitoba, May 4–8, 1981. Winnipeg: University of Manitoba Press, 1984.

Johnston, J.M. "Life Histories of Anadromous Cutthroat with Emphasis on Migratory Behavior." In *Proceedings of the Salmon and Trout Migratory Behavior Symposium, June 3–5, 1981, First International Symposium,* edited by E.L. Brannon and E.O. Salo, 123–127. Seattle: University of Washington Press, 1982.

Jones, D.E. *The Study of Cutthroat-Steelhead in Alaska.* Alaska Department of Fish and Game, Division of Sport Fish, Anadromous Fish Studies, Annual Progress Report 1973–1974, Study AFS-42-2. 1974.

Jonsson, B. "Life History Patterns of Freshwater Resident and Sea-run Migrant Brown Trout in Norway." *Transactions of the American Fisheries Society* 114 (1985): 182–194.

Jonsson, B., and J. Ruud-Hansen. "Water Temperature as the Primary Influence on Timing of Seaward Migrations of Atlantic Salmon *(Salmo salar)* Smolts." *Canadian Journal of Fisheries and Aquatic Sciences* 42 (1985): 593–595.

Jordan, D.S. "Description of the Golden Trout of Kern River." In *Twelfth Biennial Report of the State Board of Fish Commissioners of the State of California, for the Years 1891–1892,* 62–65. Sacramento: 1892.

———. "Description of the New Varieties of Trout." In *Thirteenth Biennial Report of the State Board of Fish Commissioners of the State of California, for the Years 1893–1894,* 142–143. Sacramento: 1894.

———. "Salmon and Trout of the Pacific Coast." In *Thirteenth Biennial Report of the State Board of Fish Commissioners of the State of California, for the Years 1893–1894,* 125–141. Sacramento: 1894.

———. "The Trout and Salmon of the Pacific Coast." In *Twentieth Biennial Report of the State Board of Fish Commissioners of the State of California,* 77–92. Sacramento: 1907.

———. "The Name of the Brook Trout in Europe." *Copeia,* 1926, no. 155: 140–141.

Jordan, D.S., and B.W. Evermann. *The Fishes of North and Middle America.* U.S. Museum Bulletin 47. 1896.

———. *American Food and Game Fishes.* Doubleday, Page and Co., 1923.

Jordan, D.S., B.W. Evermann, and H.W. Clark. *Report of the U.S. Commissioner of Fisheries for the Fiscal Year 1928 with Appendixes, Part II.* Washington, D.C.: U.S. Government Printing Office, 1930.

Jude, D.J., and F.J. Tesar. "Recent Changes in the Inshore Forage Fish of Lake Michigan." *Canadian Journal of Fisheries and Aquatic Sciences* 42 (1985): 1154–1157.

Jude, D.J., F.J. Tesar, S.F. DeBoe, and T.J. Miller. "Diet and Selection of Major Prey Species by Lake Michigan Salmonines, 1973–1982." *Transactions of the American Fisheries Society* 116 (1987): 677–691.

Kalleberg, H. "Observations in a Stream Tank of Territoriality and Competition in Juvenile Salmon and Trout *(Salmo salar* L. and *Salmo trutta* L.)." *Reports from the Swedish State Institute of Fresh-water Fishery Research, Drottningholm* 39 (1958): 55–98.

Kaya, C.M. "Rheotaxis of Young Arctic Grayling from Populations that Spawn in Inlet or Outlet Streams of a Lake." *Transactions of the American Fisheries Society* 118 (1989): 474–481.

Kelso, B.W., T.G. Northcote, and C.F. Wehrhan. "Genetic and Environmental Aspects of the Response to Water Current by Rainbow Trout *(Salmo gairdneri)* Originating from Inlet and Outlet Streams of Two Lakes." *Canadian Journal of Zoology* 59 (1981): 2177–2185.

Kerstetter, T.H., and M. Keeler. *Smolting in Steelhead Trout* (Salmo gairdneri): *A Comparative Study of Populations in Two Hatcheries and the Trinity River, Northern California, Using Gill Na, K, ATPase Assays.* Humboldt State University Sea Grant Project, HSU-S69. Arcata, Calif.: 1976.

Kesner, W.D., and R.A. Barnhart. "Characteristics of the Fall-run Steelhead Trout *(Salmo gairdneri gairdneri)* of the Klamath River System with Emphasis on the Half-pounder." *California Fish and Game* 58, no. 3 (1972): 204–220.

Kincaid, H.L. "Inbreeding in Fish Populations Used for Aquaculture." *Aquaculture Magazine* 33 (1983): 215–227.

Kircheis, F.W. "The Landlocked Charrs of Maine: The Sunapee and the Blueback." In *Charrs: Salmonid Fishes of the Genus* Salvelinus, edited by E.K. Balon, 749–755. The Hague, The Netherlands: Dr. W. Junk Publishers, 1980.

Krueger, C.C., A.J. Gharrett, T.R. Dehring, and F.W. Allendorf. "Genetic Aspects of Fisheries Rehabilitation Programs." *Canadian Journal of Fisheries and Aquatic Sciences* 38 (1981): 1877–1881.

Kuntz, Y.W., and E. Callaghan. "Embryonic Fissures in Teleost Eyes and Their Possible Role in Detection of Polarized Light." *Transactions of the American Fisheries Society* 118 (1989): 195–202.

Kutty, M.N., and R.L. Saunders. "Swimming Performance of Young Atlantic Salmon *(Salmo salar)* at Low Ambient Oxygen Concentrations." *Journal of the Fisheries Research Board of Canada* 30 (1973): 223–227.

Kwain, W. "Embryonic Development, Early Growth, and Meristic Variation in Rainbow Trout *(Salmo gairdneri)* Exposed to Combinations of Light Intensity and Temperature." *Journal of the Fisheries Research Board of Canada* 32 (1975): 397–402.

LaBar, G.W. "Movement and Homing of Cutthroat Trout *(Salmo clarkii)* in Clar and Bridge Creeks, Yellowstone National Park." *Transactions of the American Fisheries Society* 100 (1971): 41–49.

Lagler, K.F., and A.T. Wright. "Predation of the Dolly Varden, *Salvelinus malma,* on Young Salmon, *Oncorhynchus* spp., in an Estuary." *Transactions of the American Fisheries Society* 88 (1962): 90–93.

LaRoche, A.L., III. "The Impacts of Stocking Hatchery Reared Trout on the Native Brook Trout Populations of Two Streams in Central Virginia." Master's thesis, Virginia Polytechnic Institute and State University, Blacksburg, 1977.

Larson, G.L., and S.E. Moore. "Encroachment of Exotic Rainbow Trout into Stream Populations of Native Brook Trout in the Southern Appalachian Mountains." *Transactions of the American Fisheries Society* 114 (1985): 195–203.

Latta, W.C. "Relationship of Young-of-the-Year Trout to Mature Trout and Ground Water." *Transactions of the American Fisheries Society* 94 (1965): 32–39.

———. *The Effects of a Flies-only Fishing Regulation upon Trout in the Pigeon River, Otsego County, Michigan.* Michigan Department of Natural Resources, Fisheries Research Report 1807. Ann Arbor: 1973.

Lawson, A.C. "The Geomorphogeny of the Upper Kern Basin." *University of California Publications in Geology* 3 (1904): 291–376.

Leary, R.F., F.W. Allendorf, and K.L. Knudsen. "Consistently High Meristic Counts in Natural Hybrids between Brook Trout and Bull Trout." *Systematic Zoology* 32 (1983): 369–376.

————. *Genetic Analysis of Four Rainbow Trout Populations from Owyhee County, Idaho.* University of Montana, Department of Zoology, Population Genetics Laboratory Report 83/6. Missoula: 1983.

————. "Developmental Instability as an Indicator of Reduced Genetic Variation in Hatchery Trout." *Transactions of the American Fisheries Society* 114 (1985): 230–235.

Leary, R.F., F.W. Allendorf, S.R. Phelps, and K.L. Knudsen. "Genetic Divergence and Identification of Seven Cutthroat Trout Subspecies and Rainbow Trout." *Transactions of the American Fisheries Society* 116 (1987): 580–587.

Leclerc, J., and G. Power. "Production of Brook Charr and Ouananiche in a Large Rapid, Tributary of Caniapiscau River, Northern Quebec." *Environmental Biology of Fishes* 5 (1980): 27–32.

LeCren, E.D. "Estimates of Fish Populations and Production in Small Streams of England." In *Symposium on Salmon and Trout in Streams*, edited by T.G. Northcote, 269–280. Vancouver: Institute of Fisheries, University of British Columbia, 1969.

————. "The Population Dynamics of Young Trout (*Salmo trutta*) in Relation to Density and Territorial Behavior." *Conseil International pour L' Exploration de la Mer, Rapports et Proce's Verbaux* 164 (1973): 241–246.

Lee, A. "An Immigrant Makes Good." *Fins and Feathers* 2, no. 4 (1983): 10.

Lee, R.M., and J.N. Rinne. "Critical Thermal Maxima of Five Trout Species in the Southwestern United States." *Transactions of the American Fisheries Society* 109 (1980): 632–635.

Leider, S.A. "Precise Timing of Upstream Migrations by Repeat Steelhead Spawners." *Transactions of the American Fisheries Society* 114 (1985): 906–908.

Lennon, R.E. *The Trout Fishery in Shenandoah National Park.* U.S. Bureau of Sport Fisheries and Wildlife, Special Scientific Report–Fisheries 395. Washington, D.C.: 1961.

Leopold, A. *A Sand County Almanac.* London, Oxford, and New York: Oxford University Press, 1949.

Lewis, C., and T. Anderson. "Oscillations of Levels and Cool Phases of the Laurentian Great Lakes Caused by Inflows from Glacial Lakes Agassiz and Barlow-Ojibway." *Journal of Paleolimnology* 2 (1989): 99–146.

Libosvárský, J. "A Study of Brown Trout Population (*Salmo trutta* morpha *fario* L.) in Loućka Creek (Czechoslovakia)." *Acta Sciences Natural Brno* 2 (1968): 1–56.

Liley, N.R. "Chemical Communication in Fish." *Canadian Journal of Fisheries and Aquatic Sciences* 39 (1982): 22–35.

Linnaeus, C. *Systema Naturae.* 10th ed. 1758.

Lirette, M.G., and R.S. Hooton. *Telemetric Investigations of Winter Steelhead in the Salmon River, Vancouver Island–1986.* British Columbia Fisheries Branch, Technical Circular 82. 1988.

Loftus, K.H. "Studies on River-spawning Populations of Lake Trout in Eastern Lake Superior." *Transactions of the American Fisheries Society* 87 (1957): 259–277.

Lorenz, K. *Evolution and Modification of Behavior.* Chicago: University of Chicago Press, 1965.

Loudenslager, E.J., J.N. Rinne, G.A.E. Gall, and R.E. David. "Biochemical Genetic Studies of Native Arizona and New Mexico Trout." *The Southwestern Naturalist* 31, no. 2 (1986): 221–234.

Luton, J.R. "The First Introductions of Brown Trout, *Salmo trutta*, in the United States." *Fisheries* 10 (1985): 10–13.

McAfee, W.R. "Rainbow Trout." In *Inland Fisheries Management*, edited by A. Calhoun. California Department of Fish and Game, 1966.

McBride, J.R., D.R. Idler, R.E.E. Jonas, and N. Tomlinson. "Olfactory Perception in Juvenile Salmon. I. Observations on Response of Juvenile Sockeye to Extracts of Foods." *Journal of the Fisheries Research Board of Canada* 29 (1962): 327–334.

McCart, P., and P. Craig. "Meristic Differences between Anadromous and Freshwater Resident Arctic Char (*Salvelinus alpinus*) in the Sagavanurktok River Drainage, Alaska." *Journal of the Fisheries Research Board of Canada* 28 (1971): 115–118.

McCauley, R.W., and W.L. Pond. "Temperature Selection of Rainbow Trout (*Salmo gairdneri*) Fingerlings in Vertical and Horizontal Gradients." *Journal of the Fisheries Research Board of Canada* 28 (1971): 1801–1804.

McCleave, J.D., G.P. Arnold, J.J. Dodson, and W.H. Neill, eds. *Mechanisms of Migration in Fishes.* New York and London: Plenum Press, 1984.

McCleave, J.D., G.W. LaBar, and F.W. Kircheis. "Within-season Homing Movements of Displaced Mature Sunapee Trout (*Salvelinus alpinus*) in Flood's Pond, Maine." *Transactions of the American Fisheries Society* 106 (1977): 156–162.

McCormack, J.C. "The Food of Young Trout (*Salmo trutta*) in Two Different Becks." *The Journal of Animal Ecology* 31 (1962): 305–316.

McCormick, J.H., K.E.F. Hokansen, and B.R. Jones. "Effects of Temperature on Growth and Survival of Young Brook Trout (*Salvelinus fontinalis*)." *Journal of the Fisheries Research Board of Canada* 29 (1972): 1107–1112.

McCormick, S.D., R.J. Naiman, and E.T. Montgomery. "Physiological Smolt Characteristics of Anadromous and Non-anadromous Brook Trout (*Salvelinus fontinalis*) and Atlantic Salmon (*Salmo salar*)." *Canadian Journal of Fisheries and Aquatic Sciences* 42 (1985): 529–538.

McCormick, S.D., and R.L. Saunders. "Preparatory Physiological Adaptations for Marine Life of Salmonids: Osmoregulation, Growth, and Metabolism." *American Fisheries Society Symposium* 1 (1987): 211–229.

MacCrimmon, H.R. "World Distribution of Rainbow Trout (*Salmo gairdneri*)." *Journal of the Fisheries Research Board of Canada* 28, no. 5 (1971): 663–704.

————. "World Distribution of Rainbow Trout (*Salmo gairdneri*): Further Observations." *Journal of the Fisheries Research Board of Canada* 29 (1972): 1788–1791.

MacCrimmon, H.R., and J.S. Campbell. "World Distribution of Brook Trout, *Salvelinus fontinalis*." *Journal of the Fisheries Research Board of Canada* 26, no. 7 (1969): 1699–1725.

MacCrimmon, H.R., and B.L. Gots. *Rainbow Trout in the Great Lakes.* Ontario Ministry of Natural Resources Report. 1972.

MacCrimmon, H.R., and T.L. Marshall. "World Distribution of Brown Trout, *Salmo trutta*." *Journal of the Fisheries Research Board of Canada* 25 (1968): 2527–2548.

MacCrimmon, H.R., T.L. Marshall, and B.L. Gots. "World Distribution of Brown Trout, *Salmo trutta*: Further Observations." *Journal of the Fisheries Research Board of Canada* 27 (1970): 811–818.

McDermand, C. *Waters of the Golden Trout Country.* New York: G.P. Putnam's Sons, 1946.

McDonald, A.L., and N.W. Heimstra. "Agonistic Behavior in Several Species of Fish." *The Psychological Report* 16 (1965): 845–850.

McDonald, D.G. "The Effects of H+ upon the Gills of Freshwater Fish." *Canadian Journal of Zoology* 61 (1983): 691–703.

McDowall, R.M. "The Occurrence and Distribution of Diadromy among Fishes." *American Fisheries Society Symposium* 1 (1987): 1–13.

————. *Diadromy in Fishes.* London: Croom Helm, 1988.

Macek, K.J., K.S. Buxton, S. Sauter, S. Gnilka, and J.W. Dean. *Chronic Toxicity of Atrazine to Selected Invertebrates and Fishes.* U.S. Environmental Protection Agency, Ecological Research Series EPA-600/3-76-047. 1976.

McFadden, J.T., G.R. Alexander, and D.S. Shetter. "Numerical Changes and Population Regulation in Brook Trout, *Salvelinus fontinalis*." *Journal of the Fisheries Research Board of Canada* 24 (1967): 1425–1459.

McFadden, J.T., and E.L. Cooper. "Population Dynamics of Brown Trout in Different Environments." *Physiological Zoology* 37 (1964): 355–363.

McKern, J.L. "Steelhead Trout Otoliths for Age, Race, and Stock Analysis." Master's thesis, Oregon State University, Corvallis, 1971.

McKim, J.M., and D.A. Benoit. "Effects of Long-term Exposure to Copper on Survival, Growth, and Reproduction of Brook Trout (*Salvelinus fontinalis*)." *Journal of the Fisheries Research Board of Canada* 28 (1971): 655–662.

McKim, J.M., G.F. Olson, G.W. Holcombe, and E.P. Hunt. "Long-term Effects of Methylmecuric Chloride on Three Generations of Brook Trout (*Salvelinus fontinalis*): Toxicity, Accumulation, Distribution, and Elimination." *Journal of the Fisheries Research Board of Canada* 33 (1976): 2726–2739.

McKim, J.M., P.K. Schmieder, R.W. Carlson, E.P. Hunt, and G.J. Niemi. "Use of Respiratory-Cardiovascular Responses of Rainbow Trout (*Salmo gairdneri*) in Identifying Acute Toxicity Syndromes in Fish: Part 1. Pentachlorophenol, 2,4-Dinitrophenol, Tricaine Methanesulfonate and 1-Octanol." *Environmental Toxicology and Chemistry* 6 (1987): 295–312.

McKim, J.M., P.K. Schmieder, G.J. Niemi, R.W. Carlson, and T.R. Henry. "Use of Respiratory-Cardiovascular Responses of Rainbow Trout (*Salmo gairdneri*) in Identifying Acute Toxicity Syndromes in Fish: Part 2. Malathion, Carbaryl, Acrolein and Benzaldehyde." *Environmental Toxicology and Chemistry* 6 (1987): 313–328.

MacLean, J.A., D.O. Evans, N.V. Martin, and R.L. DesJardine. "Survival, Growth, Spawning Distribution, and Movements of Introduced and Native Lake Trout (*Salvelinus namaycush*) in Two Inland Ontario Lakes." *Canadian Journal of Fisheries and Aquatic Sciences* 38 (1981): 1685–1700.

McMurtry, M.J. *Susceptibility of Lake Trout* (Salvelinus namaycush) *Spawning Sites in Ontario to Acidic Meltwater.* Ontario Fisheries Acidification Report Series No. 86-01. 1986.

McNeil, W.J. "Survival of Pink and Chum Salmon Eggs and Alevins." In *Symposium on Salmon and Trout in Streams*, edited by T.G. Northcote, 101–117. Vancouver: Institute of Fisheries, University of British Columbia, 1969.

McNichol, R.E., E. Scherer, and E.J. Murkin. "Quantitative Field Investigations of Feeding and Territorial Behavior of Young-of-the-Year Brook Charr, *Salvelinus fontinalis*." *Environmental Biology of Fishes* 12, no. 3 (1985): 219–229.

McPhail, J.D., and C.C. Lindsey. *Freshwater Fishes of Northwestern Canada and Alaska.* Fisheries Research Board of Canada, Bulletin 173. Ottawa: 1970.

Mann, R.H.K. "The Populations, Growth, and Production of Fish in

Four Small Streams in Southern England." *The Journal of Animal Ecology* 40 (1971): 155–190.

Mann, R.H.K., J.H. Blackburn, and W.R.C. Beaumont. "The Ecology of Brown Trout, *Salmo trutta*, in English Chalk Streams." *Freshwater Biology* 21 (1989): 57–70.

Marinaro, V.C. *In the Ring of the Rise*. New York: Crown Publishers, Inc., 1976.

Marler, P. "Animal Communication Signals." *Science* 157 (August 1967): 769–774.

Marsden, J.E., C.C. Krueger, and B. May. "Identification of Parental Origins of Naturally Produced Lake Trout in Lake Ontario: Application of Mixed-Stock Analysis to a Second Generation." *North American Journal of Fisheries Management* 9 (1989): 257–268.

Martin, J.H.A., and K.A. Mitchell. "Influence of Sea Temperature upon the Numbers of Grilse and Multi-Sea-Winter Atlantic Salmon *(Salmon salar)* Caught in the Vicinity of the River Dee (Aberdeenshire)." *Canadian Journal of Fisheries and Aquatic Sciences* 42 (1985): 1513–1521.

Martin, N.V. "A Study of the Lake Trout, *Salvelinus namaycush*, in Two Algonquin Park, Ontario, Lakes." *Transactions of the American Fisheries Society* 81 (1951): 111–137.

———. "Limnological and Biological Observations in the Region of the Ungava or Chubb Crater, Province of Quebec." *Journal of the Fisheries Research Board of Canada* 12 (1955): 487–498.

Martin, N.V., and C.H. Olver. "The Lake Charr, *Salvelinus namaycush*." In *Charrs: Salmonid Fishes of the Genus* Salvelinus, edited by E.K. Balon, 205–277. The Hague, The Netherlands: Dr. W. Junk Publishers, 1980.

Mason, J.W., O.M. Brynildson, and P.E. Degurse. "Comparative Survival of Wild and Domestic Strains of Brook Trout in Streams." *Transactions of the American Fisheries Society* 96 (1967): 313–319.

Mason, J.W., and R.L. Hunt. "Mortality Rates of Deeply Hooked Rainbow Trout." *Progressive Fish-Culturist* 29, no. 1 (1967): 87–91.

Mathisen, O., and M. Berg. "Growth Rates of the Char *Salvelinus alpinus* (L.) in the Vardnes River, Troms, Northern Norway." *Reports from the Swedish State Institute of Fresh-water Fishery Research, Drottningholm* 48 (1968): 176–186.

Matlock, G.C., G.E. Saul, and C.E. Bryan. "Importance of Fish Consumption to Sport Fishermen." *Fisheries* 13, no. 1 (1988): 25–26.

May, B. "The Salmonid Genome–Evolutionary Restructuring Following a Tetraploid Event." Ph.D. dissertation, The Pennsylvania State University, 1980.

Mayer, F.L., Jr., and M.R. Ellersieck. *Manual of Acute Toxicity: Interpretation and Data Base for 410 Chemicals and 66 Species of Freshwater Animals*. U.S. Department of the Interior, U.S. Fish and Wildlife Service, Research Publication 160. Washington, D.C.: 1986.

Mayer, F.L., Jr., P.M. Mehrle, Jr., and W.P. Dwyer. *Toxaphene Effects on Reproduction, Growth, and Mortality of Brook Trout*. U.S. Environmental Protection Agency, Ecological Research Series EPA-600/3-75-013. 1975.

Maxwell, H.E. *British Fresh-water Fishes*. London: Hutchinson & Co., 1904.

Meen, V.B. "Solving the Riddle of Chubb Crater." *National Geographic Magazine* 101 (1952): 1–32.

Mehrle, P.M., and F.L. Mayer, Jr. "Toxaphene Effects on Growth and Development of Brook Trout *(Salvelinus fontinalis)*." *Journal of the Fisheries Research Board of Canada* 32 (1975): 609–613.

Merna, J.W. "Contamination of Stream Fishes with Chlorinated Hydrocarbons from Eggs of Great Lakes Salmon." *Transactions of the American Fisheries Society* 115 (1986): 69–74.

Miller, R.B. "Permanence and Size of Home Territory in Stream Dwelling Cutthroat Trout." *Journal of the Fisheries Research Board of Canada* 14, no. 5 (1957): 786–791.

Miller, R.B., and W.A. Kennedy. "Observations on the Lake Trout of Great Bear Lake." *Journal of the Fisheries Research Board of Canada* 74 (1948): 176–189.

Miller, R.R. *Notes on the Cutthroat and Rainbow Trouts with the Description of a New Species from the Gila River, New Mexico*. University of Michigan, Occasional Papers of the Museum of Zoology 529. Ann Arbor: 1950.

———. "Man and the Changing Fish Fauna of the American Southwest." *Papers of the Michigan Academy of Arts, Sciences and Letters* 46 (1961): 365–404.

———. "Classification of the Native Trouts of Arizona with the Description of a New Species, *Salmo apache*." *Copeia*, 1972, no. 3: 401–422.

Milner, N.J., A.S. Gee, and R.J. Hemsworth. "The Production of Brown Trout, *Salmo trutta*, in Tributaries of the Uppr Wye, Wales." *Journal of Fish Biology* 13 (1978): 599–612.

Minckley, W.L. *Fishes of Arizona*. Phoenix: Arizona Game Fish Department, 1973.

Moccia, R.D., J.F. Leatherland, and R.A. Sonstegard. "Increasing Frequency of Thyroid Goiters in Coho Salmon *(Oncorhynchus kisutch)* in the Great Lakes." *Science* 198 (1977): 425–426.

———. "Quantitative Interlake Comparison of Thyroid Pathology in Great Lakes Coho *(Oncorhynchus kisutch)* and Chinook *(Oncorhynchus tschawytscha)* Salmon." *Cancer Research* 41 (1981): 2200–2210.

Moore, J.W. "Distribution, Movements and Mortality of Anadromous Arctic Char, *Salvelinus alpinus* L., in the Cumberland Sound Area of Baffin Island." *Journal of Fish Biology* 7 (1975): 339–348.

Moore, K.M.S., and S.V. Gregory. "Response of Young-of-the-Year Cutthroat Trout to Manipulation of Habitat Structure in a Small Stream." *Transactions of the American Fisheries Society* 117 (1988): 162–170.

Moore, S.E., G.L. Larson, and B. Ridley. "Population Control of Exotic Rainbow Trout in Streams of a Natural Area Park." *Environmental Management* 10 (1986): 215–219.

Moore, S.E., B. Ridley, and G.L. Larson. "Standing Crops of Brook Trout Concurrent with Removal of Rainbow Trout from Selected Streams in Great Smoky Mountains National Park." *North American Journal of Fisheries Management* 3 (1983): 72–80.

Moring, J.R. *The Alsea Watershed Study: Effects of Logging on the Aquatic Resources of Three Headwater Streams of the Alsea River, Oregon. Part II–Changes in Environmental Conditions*. Oregon Department of Fish and Wildlife, Fisheries Research Report 9, part 2. 1975.

Mortensen, E. "Population, Survival, Growth and Production of Trout, *Salmo trutta*, in a Small Danish Stream." *Oikos* 28 (1977a): 9–15.

———. "The Population Dynamics of Young Trout *(Salmo trutta* L.) in a Danish Brook." *Journal of Fish Biology* 10 (1977b): 23–33.

———. "Production of Trout, *Salmo trutta*, in a Danish Stream." *Environmental Biology of Fishes* 7 (1982): 349–356.

Mortimer, C.H. "Lake Hydrodynamics." *Mitteilungen Internationale Vereinigung für Theoretische und Angewandte Limnologie* 20 (1974): 124–197.

Mount, D.R., C.G. Ingersoll, D.D. Gulley, J.D. Fernandez, T.W. LaPoint, and H.L. Bergman. "Effect of Long-term Exposure to Acid, Aluminum, and Low Calcium on Adult Brook Trout *(Salvelinus fontinalis)*. 1. Survival, Growth, Fecundity, and Progeny Survival." *Canadian Journal of Fisheries and Aquatic Sciences* 45 (1988): 1623–1632.

Moyle, P.B. "Comparative Behavior of Young Brook Trout of Domestic and Wild Origin." *Progressive Fish-Culturist* 31 (1969): 51–59.

———. *Inland Fishes of California*. Berkeley: University of California Press, 1976.

Mullen, J.W. *A Compendium of the Life History and Ecology of the Eastern Brook Trout* (Salvelinus fontinalis). Massachusetts Division of Fish and Game, Fisheries Bulletin 23. 1958.

Muller, K. "Investigations on the Organic Drift in North Swedish Streams." *Reports from the Swedish State Institute of Fresh-water Fishery Research, Drottningholm* 35 (1954): 133–148.

Naiman, R.J., S.D. McCormick, W.L. Montgomery, and R. Morin. "Anadromous Brook Charr, *Salvelinus fontinalis:* Opportunities and Constraints for Population Enhancement." *Marine Fisheries Review* 49 (1987): 1–13.

Nakano, S. "Dominance Hierarchy of Red-spotted Masu Salmon, *Oncorhynchus masou rhodurus*, in a Mountain Stream with Special Reference to Space and Food Utilization" (in Japanese). Master's thesis, Mie University, Tsu, Mie, 1986.

Nall, G.H. *Sea Trout of the River Conon*. Fisheries, Scotland, Salmon Fisheries. 4. 1937.

Narver, D.W. "Stream Management for West Coast Anadromous Salmonids." In *Stream Management of Salmonids*, 7–13. Trout Winter Supplement. Denver: 1976.

Narver, D.W., and M.L. Dahlberg. "Estuarine Food of Dolly Varden at Chignik." *Transactions of the American Fisheries Society* 94 (1965): 405–408.

Naslund, I. "Seasonal Habitat Shifts in Salmonids: Possible Mechanisms Behind Upstream Migrations." In *Proceedings of the Salmonid Migration and Distribution Symposium, June 23–25, 1987*, edited by E. Brannon and B. Jonsson, 147–151. 1989.

Needham, P.R. "Observations on the Natural Spawning of Eastern Brook Trout." *California Fish and Game* 47, no. 1 (1961): 27–40.

Needham, P.R., and R. Gard. *Rainbow Trout in Mexico and California*. Berkeley: University of California Press, 1959.

———. "Rainbow Trout in Mexico and California with Notes on the Cutthroat Series." *University of California Publications in Zoology* 67 (1959): 1–124.

———. "A New Trout from Central Mexico: *Salmo chrysogaster*, the Mexican Golden Trout." *Copeia*, 1964: 169–173.

Needham, P.R., and A.C. Jones. "Flow, Temperature, Solar Radiation and Ice in Relation to Activities of Fishes in Sagehen Creek, California." *Ecology* 40, no. 3 (1959): 465–474.

Nelson, E.W. *Lower California and Its National Resources*. Vol. 16. National Academy of Sciences, First Memoir. Philadelphia: 1920.

Nelson, J.S. "Effects of Fish Introductions and Hydroelectric Development on Fishes in the Kananaskis River System, Alberta." *Journal of the Fisheries Research Board of Canada* 22 (1965): 721–753.

Neves, R.J., and G.B. Pardue. "Abundance and Production of Fishes in a Small Appalachian Stream." *Transactions of the American Fisheries Society* 112 (1983): 21–26.

New Mexico Game Fish Department. *Handbook of Species Endangered in*

New Mexico. Santa Fe: 1985.

Nicholas, J.W. "Life History Differences between Sympatric Populations of Rainbow and Cutthroat Trouts in Relation to Fisheries Management Strategy." In *Proceedings of the Wild Trout-Catchable Trout Symposium, Eugene, Oregon, February 15-17, 1978,* edited by J.R. Moring, 181-188. Portland: Oregon Department of Fish and Wildlife, 1978.

Nickelson, T.E. "Population Dynamics of Coastal Cutthroat Trout in an Experimental Stream." Master's thesis, Oregon State University, Corvallis, 1974.

Nicola, S.J., and A.J. Cordone. "Effects of Fin Removal on Survival and Growth of Rainbow Trout *(Salmo gairdneri)* in a Natural Environment." *Transactions of the American Fisheries Society* 102 (1973): 753-758.

Nilsson, N.-A. "On the Feeding Habits of Trout in a Stream of Northern Sweden." *Reports from the Swedish State Institute of Fresh-water Fishery Research, Drottningholm* 38 (1957): 154-166.

———. "Interaction between Trout and Char in Scandinavia." *Transactions of the American Fisheries Society* 92 (1963): 276-285.

———. "Food Segregation between Salmonid Species in Sweden." *Reports from the Swedish State Institute of Fresh-water Fishery Research, Drottningholm* 46 (1965): 58-76.

Nilsson, N.-A., and T.G. Northcote. "Rainbow Trout *(Salmo gairdneri)* and Cutthroat Trout *(S. clarki)* Interactions in Coastal British Columbia Lakes." *Canadian Journal of Fisheries and Aquatic Sciences* 38 (1981): 1228-1246.

Noakes, D.L.G. "Early Behavior in Fishes." *Environmental Biology of Fishes* 3, no. 3 (1978): 321-326.

Nordeng, H. "Is the Local Orientation of Anadromous Fishes Determined by Pheromones?" *Nature* (London) 233 (1971): 411-413.

———. "A Pheromone Hypothesis for Homeward Migration in Anadromous Salmonids." *Oikos* 28 (1977): 155-159.

Northcote, T.G. "Migratory Behaviour of Juvenile Rainbow Trout, *Salmo gairdneri,* in Outlet and Inlet Streams of Loon Lake, British Columbia." *Journal of the Fisheries Research Board of Canada* 19 (1962): 201-270.

———. "Patterns and Mechanisms in the Lakeward Migratory Behaviour of Juvenile Trout." In *Symposium on Salmon and Trout in Streams,* edited by T.G. Northcote, 183-203. Vancouver: Institute of Fisheries, University of British Columbia, 1969.

———. *Some Impacts of Man on Kootenay Lake and Its Salmonoids.* Great Lakes Fishery Commission, Technical Report No. 25. 1973.

———. "Migratory Strategies and Production in Freshwater Fishes." In *Ecology of Freshwater Fish Production,* edited by S.D. Gerking, 326-359. Oxford, England: Blackwell Scientific Publications, 1978.

———. "Juvenile Current Response, Growth and Maturity of Above and Below Waterfall Stocks on Rainbow Trout, *Salmo gairdneri.*" *Journal of Fish Biology* 18 (1981): 741-751.

———. "Mechanisms of Fish Migration in Rivers." In *Mechanisms of Migration in Fishes,* edited by J.D. McCleave, G.P. Arnold, J.J. Dodson, and W.E. Neill, 317-355. New York and London: Plenum Press, 1984.

Northcote, T.G., and P.A. Larkin. "Indices of Productivity in British Columbia Lakes." *Journal of the Fisheries Research Board of Canada* 13 (1956): 515-540.

———. "Western Canada." In *Limnology in North America,* edited by D.G. Frey, 451-485. Madison: University of Wisconsin Press, 1966.

———. "The Fraser River: A Major Salmonine Production System." In *Proceedings of the International Large River Symposium,* edited by D.P. Dodge, 172-204. Canadian Special Publication of Fisheries and Aquatic Sciences 106. 1989.

Northcote, T.G., S.N. Williscroft, and H. Tsuyuki. "Meristic and Lactate Dehydrogenase Genotype Differences in Stream Populations of Rainbow Trout Below and Above a Waterfall." *Journal of the Fisheries Research Board of Canada* 27 (1970): 1987-1995.

Nunan, C.P., and D.L.G. Noakes. "Effects of Light on Movement of Rainbow Trout Embryos within, and on Their Emergence from, Artificial Redds." *American Fisheries Society Symposium* 2 (1987): 151-156.

———. "The Role of Spontaneous Activity in the Vertical Movements of Salmonid Embryos." In *Proceedings of the Salmonid Migration and Distribution Symposium, June 23-25, 1987,* edited by E. Brannon and B. Jonsson, 42-47. 1989.

Nyman, O.L. "Ecological Interaction of Brown Trout, *Salmo trutta* L., and Brook Trout, *Salvelinus fontinalis* (Mitchill) in a Stream." *The Canadian Field-Naturalist* 84 (1970): 343-350.

O'Connor, J.F., and G. Power. "Production by Brook Trout *(Salvelinus fontinalis)* in Four Streams in the Matamek Watershed, Quebec." *Journal of the Fisheries Research Board of Canada* 33 (1976): 6-18.

Olsén, H. "Chemoreceptive Behaviour in Arctic Charr *(Salvelinus alpinus* L.)." Ph.D. dissertation, University of Uppsala, 1985.

Olson, R.A., J.D. Winter, D.C. Nettles, and J.M. Haynes. "Resource Partitioning in Summer by Salmonids in South-Central Lake Ontario." *Transactions of the American Fisheries Society* 117 (1988): 552-559.

Olsson, T.I., and B.-G. Persson. "Effects of Deposited Sand on Ova Survival and Alevin Emergence in Brown Trout *(Salmo trutta* L.)." *Archiv für Hydrobiologie* 113 (1988): 621-627.

Oswalt, D. Personal communication. Montana Department of Fish, Wildlife, and Parks. 1989.

Parker, H.H., and L. Johnson. "Population Structure, Ecological Segregation and Reproduction in Non-anadromous Arctic Charr *(Salvelinus alpinus)* in Four Unexploited Lakes in the Canadian High Arctic." *Journal of Fish Biology* 38 (1991): 123-147.

Partridge, E. *Responsibilities to Future Generations.* Buffalo, N.Y.: Prometheus Books, 1980.

Pauley, G.B., B.M. Bortz, and M.F. Shepard. *Species Profiles: Life Histories and Environmental Requirements of Coastal Fishes and Invertebrates (Pacific Northwest)—Steelhead Trout.* U.S. Department of the Interior, U.S. Fish and Wildlife Service, Biological Report 82 (11.62). 1986.

Pauley, G.B., K. Oshima, K.L. Bowers, and G.L. Thomas. *Species Profiles: Life Histories and Environmental Requirements of Coastal Fishes and Invertebrates (Pacific Northwest)—Sea-run Cutthroat Trout.* U.S. Department of the Interior, U.S. Fish and Wildlife Service, Biological Report 82 (11.86). 1989.

Pennak, R.W. "Rocky Mountain States." In *Limnology in North America,* edited by D.G. Frey, 349-369. Madison: University of Wisconsin Press, 1966.

Pennant, T. *Arctic Zoology.* Vol. 1. London: Henry Hughes, 1784.

Pennsylvania Fish Commission. *Management of Trout Fisheries in Pennsylvania Waters.* Bellefonte: Division of Fisheries, 1986.

Perrin, C.J., M.L. Bothwell, and P.A. Slaney. "Experimental Enrichment of a Coastal Stream in British Columbia: Effects of Organic and Inorganic Additons on Autotrophic Periphyton Production." *Canadian Journal of Fisheries and Aquatic Sciences* 44 (1987): 1247-1256.

Peterson, D.H., H.K. Jager, G.M. Savage, G.N. Washburn, and H. Westers. "Natural Coloration of Trout Using Xanthophylls." *Transactions of the American Fisheries Society* 95 (1966): 408-414.

Petrosky, C.E., and T.C. Bjornn. "Competition from Catchables—A Second Look." In *Wild Trout III, Proceedings of the Symposium, Yellowstone National Park,* edited by F. Richardson and R.H. Hamre, 63-68. 1984.

Phillips, M.J. "The Feeding Sounds of Rainbow Trout, *Salmo gairdneri* Richardson." *Journal of Fish Biology* 35 (1989): 589-592.

Phillips, R.W., R.L. Lantz, E.W. Claire, and J.R. Moring. "Some Effects of Gravel Mixtures in Emergence of Coho Salmon and Steelhead Trout." *Transactions of the American Fisheries Society* 104 (1975): 461-466.

Pickford, G.E., and J.W. Atz. *The Physiology of the Pituitary Gland of Fishes.* New York: New York Zoological Society, 1957.

Piper, R.G., I.B. McElwain, L.E. Orme, J.P. McCraren, L.G. Fowler, and J.R. Leonard. *Fish Hatchery Management.* Bethesda, Md.: American Fisheries Society, 1983.

Pister, E.P. "Cottonwood Lakes: California's 'Gold' Mine." *Outdoor California* 25, no. 5 (1964): 7-9.

Platts, W.S., and M.L. McHenry. *Density and Biomass of Trout and Char in Western Streams.* U.S. Department of Agriculture, Forest Service, Intermountain Forest and Range Experiment Station, General Technical Report INT-241. Ogden, Utah: 1988.

Platts, W.S., and R.L. Nelson. "Fluctuations in Trout Populations and Their Implications for Land-use Evaluation." *North American Journal of Fisheries Management* 8 (1988): 333-345.

Platts, W.S., and F.E. Partridge. *Rearing of Chinook Salmon in Tributaries of the South Fork Salmon River, Idaho.* U.S. Department of Agriculture, Forest Service, Intermountain Forest and Range Experiment Station, Research Paper INT-205. Ogden, Utah: 1978.

Pollard, H.A., and T.C. Bjornn. "The Effects of Angling and Hatchery Trout on the Abundance of Juvenile Steelhead Trout." *Transactions of the American Fisheries Society* 102 (1973): 745-752.

Power, G. "The Brook Charr, *Salvelinus fontinalis.*" In *Charrs: Salmonid Fishes of the Genus Salvelinus,* edited by E.K. Balon, 141-203. The Hague, The Netherlands: Dr. W. Junk Publishers, 1980.

Pratt, K.L. "Habitat Use and Species Interactions of Juvenile Cutthroat *(Salmo clarki lewisi)* and Bull Trout *(Salvelinus confluentus)* in the Upper Flathead River Basin." Master's thesis, University of Idaho, Moscow, 1984.

Puckett, K.J., and L.M. Dill. "The Energetics of Feeding Territoriality in Juvenile Coho Salmon *(Oncorhynchus kisutch).*" *Behaviour* 92 (1985): 97-111.

Quinn, T.P. "Evidence for Celestial and Magnetic Compass Orientation in Lake Migrating Sockeye Salmon Fry." *Journal of Comparative Physiology* 137 (1980): 243-248.

———. "Intra-specific Differences in Sockeye Salmon Fry Compass Orientation Mechanisms." In *Proceedings of the Salmon and Trout Migratory Behavior Symposium, June 3-5, 1981, First International Symposium,* edited by E.L. Brannon and E.O. Salo, 79-85. Seattle: University of Washington Press, 1982a.

———. "A Model for Salmon Navigation on the High Seas." In *Proceedings of the Salmon and Trout Migratory Behavior Symposium, June 3-5, 1981, First International Symposium,* edited by E.L. Brannon and E.O. Salo, 229-237. Seattle: University of Washington Press, 1982b.

Quinn, T.P., and E.L. Brannon. "The Use of Celestial and Magnetic

Cues by Orienting Sockeye Salmon Smolts." *Journal of Comparative Physiology* 147 (1982): 547–552.

Quinn, T.P., and S. Courtenay. "Intraspecific Chemosensory Discrimination in Salmonid Fishes: Alternative Explanations." In *Proceedings of the Salmonid Migration and Distribution Symposium, June 23–25, 1987*, edited by E. Brannon and B. Jonsson, 35–41. 1989.

Raleigh, R.F. "Innate Control of Migrations of Salmon and Trout Fry from Natal Gravels to Rearing Areas." *Ecology* 52 (1971): 291–297.

Randall, R.G., M.C. Healey, and J.B. Dempson. "Variability in Length of Freshwater Residence of Salmon, Trout, and Char." *American Fisheries Society Symposium* 1 (1987): 27–41.

Randall, R.G., and U. Paim. "Growth, Biomass, and Production of Juvenile Atlantic Salmon (*Salmo salar* L.) in Two Miramichi River, New Brunswick, Tributary Streams." *Canadian Journal of Zoology* 60 (1982): 1647–1659.

Rawson, D.S. "Some Physical and Chemical Factors in the Metabolism of Lakes." *Science* 10 (1939): 9–26.

———. "Morphometry as a Dominant Factor in the Productivity of Large Lakes." *Internationale Vereinigung für Theoretische und Angewandte Limnologie* 12 (1955): 164–175.

———. "The Lake Trout of Lac la Ronge, Saskatchewan." *Journal of the Fisheries Research Board of Canada* 18 (1961): 423–462.

Raymond, S. *Kamloops, An Angler's Study of the Kamloops Trout*. Rev. ed. Portland, Oreg.: Frank Amato Publications, 1980.

Regan, C.T. *The Freshwater Fishes of the British Isles*. London: Methuen, 1911.

Regan, D. *Ecology of Gila Trout in Main Diamond Creek in New Mexico*. U.S. Department of the Interior, Bureau of Sport Fisheries and Wildlife, Technical Paper 5. 1966.

Reimers, N. "Conditions of Existence, Growth and Longevity of Brook Trout in a Small, High-Altitude Lake of the Eastern Sierra Nevada." *California Fish and Game* 44, no. 4 (October 1958): 319–333.

———. "A History of a Stunted Brook Trout Population in an Alpine Lake: A Lifespan of 24 Years." *California Fish and Game* 65, no. 4 (October 1979): 196–215.

Reimers, N., J.A. Maciolek, and E.P. Pister. *Limnological Study of the Lakes of Convict Creek Basin, Mono County, California*. U.S. Department of the Interior, U.S. Fish and Wildlife Service, Bulletin 103. Washington, D.C.: 1955.

Reingold, M. "Effects of Displacing, Hooking, and Releasing Migrating Adult Steelhead Trout." *Transactions of the American Fisheries Society* 104, no. 3 (1975): 458–460.

Reisenbichler, R.R., and J.D. McIntyre. "Genetic Differences in Growth and Survival of Juvenile Hatchery and Wild Steelhead Trout, *Salmo gairdneri*." *Journal of the Fisheries Research Board of Canada* 34 (1977): 123–128.

Reiser, D.W., and T.C. Bjornn. "Habitat Requirements of Anadromous Salmonids." In *Influence of Forest and Rangeland Management on Anadromous Fish Habitat in Western North America*, edited by W.R. Meehan. U.S. Department of Agriculture, Forest Service, General Technical Report PNW-96. 1979.

Rhein, L.D., and R.D. Cagan. "Biochemical Studies of Olfaction: Isolation, Characterization, and Odorant Binding Activity of Cilia from Rainbow and Trout Olfactory Rosettes." *Proceedings of the National Academy of Sciences of the United States of America* 77, no. 8 (1980): 4412–4416.

Richardson, F., and R.H. Hamre, eds. *Wild Trout III, Proceedings of the Symposium, Yellowstone National Park*. 1984.

Ringler, N.H. "Selective Predation by Drift-feeding Brown Trout." *Journal of the Fisheries Research Board of Canada* 36 (1979): 392–403.

———. "Variation in Foraging Tactics of Fishes." In *Predators and Prey in Fishes*, edited by D.L.G. Noakes, D.B. Lindquist, G.S. Helfman, and J.A. Ward, 159–171. The Hague, The Netherlands: Dr. W. Junk Publishers, 1983.

———. "Individual and Temporal Variation in Prey Switching by Brown Trout, *Salmo trutta*." *Copeia*, 1985: 918–926.

Ringler, N.H., and D.F. Brodowski. "Functional Responses of Brown Trout (*Salmo trutta* L.) to Invertebrate Drift." *Journal of Freshwater Ecology* 2 (1983): 45–57.

Rinne, J.N. "Development of Methods of Population Estimation and Habitat Evaluation for Management of the Arizona and Gila Trouts." In *Proceedings of the Wild Trout-Catchable Trout Symposium, Eugene, Oregon, February 15–17, 1978*, edited by J.R. Moring, 113–125. Portland: Oregon Department of Fish and Wildlife, 1978.

———. "Spawning Habitat and Behavior of Gila Trout, a Rare Salmonid of the Southwestern United States." *Transactions of the American Fisheries Society* 109 (1980): 83–91.

———. "Movement, Home Range, and Growth of a Rare Southwestern Trout in Improved and Unimproved Habitats." *North American Journal of Fisheries Management* 2 (1982): 150–157.

———. "Problems Associated with Habitat Evaluation of an Endangered Fish in Headwater Environments." In *Proceedings of the Symposium of Acquisition and Utilization of Aquatic Habitat Inventory Information, Portland, Oregon, 1981*, edited by N.B. Armantrout, 202–209. Bethesda, Md.: American Fisheries Society, 1982.

———. "Variation in Apache Trout Populations in the White Mountains, Arizona." *North American Journal of Fisheries Management* 5 (1985): 146–158.

———. "Grazing Effects on Stream Habitat and Fishes: Research Design Considerations." *North American Journal of Fisheries Management* 8 (1988): 240–247.

Rinne, J.N., and W.L. Minckley. "Patterns of Variation and Distribution in Apache Trout (*Salmo apache*) Relative to Co-occurrence with Introduced Salmonids." *Copeia*, 1985, no. 2: 285–292.

Rinne, J.N., W.L. Minckley, and J.N. Hanson. "Chemical Treatment of Ord Creek, Apache County, Arizona, to Re-establish Arizona Trout." *Journal of the Arizona-Nevada Academy of Sciences* 16 (1981): 74–78.

Rinne, J.N., B. Robertson, R. Major, and K. Harper. "Sportfishing for the Native Arizona Trout, *Salmo apache* Miller, in Christmas Tree Lake." In *Proceedings of Wild Trout II, Yellowstone National Park, Sept. 24–25, 1979*, edited by W. King. 158–164. 1979.

Rinne, J.N., R. Sorenson, and S.C. Belfit. "An Analysis of F1 Hybrids between Apache (*Salmo apache*) and Rainbow Trout (*Salmo gairdneri*)." *Journal of the Arizona-Nevada Academy of Sciences* 20 (1985): 63–69.

Roberts, R.J., ed. *Fish Pathology*. London: Bailliere Tindall, 1978.

Robinson, F.W., and J.C. Tash. "Feeding by Arizona Trout (*Salmo apache*) and Brown Trout (*Salmo trutta*) at Different Light Intensities." *Environmental Biology of Fishes* 4, no. 4 (1979): 363–368.

Rose, G.A. "Growth Decline in Subyearling Brook Trout (*Salvelinus fontinalis*) after Emergence of Rainbow Trout (*Salmo gairdneri*)." *Canadian Journal of Fisheries and Aquatic Sciences* 43 (1986): 187–193.

Rosenbauer, T. *Reading Trout Streams*. Nick Lyon Books, 1988.

Rounsefell, G.A. "Anadromy in North American Salmonidae." *Fishery Bulletin* (U.S. Fish and Wildlife Service) 58, no. 131 (1958): 171–185.

Russell, R. *Rainbow Trout Life History Studies in Lower Talarik Creek–Kvichak Drainage Job No. G-II-E*. Vol. 15. Juneau: Alaska Department of Fish and Game, n.d.

Ryder, R.A. "Chemical Characteristics of Ontario Lakes as Related to Glacial History." *Transactions of the American Fisheries Society* 93 (1964): 260–268.

———. "The Morphoedaphic Index–Use, Abuse, and Fundamental Concepts." *Transactions of the American Fisheries Society* 111 (1982): 154–164.

Ryder, R.A., and C. Edwards. *A Conceptual Approach for the Application of Biological Indicators of Ecosystem Quality in the Great Lakes Basin*. Report to the International Joint Commission's Science Advisory Board. Windsor, Ontario: 1985.

Ryman, N., and F. Utter, eds. *Population Genetics and Fishery Management*. Washington Sea Grant Program. Seattle: University of Washington Press, 1987.

Ryman, N.F., A. Allendorf, and G. Stahl. "Reproductive Isolation with Little Genetic Divergence in Sympatric Populations of Brown Trout (*Salmo trutta*)." *Genetics* 92 (1979): 247–262.

Satchell, G.H. *Circulation in Fishes*. London: Cambridge University Press, 1971.

Satou, M., and K. Ueda. "Spectral Analysis of Olfactory Responses to Rainbow Trout, *Salmo gairdneri*." *Comparative Biochemistry and Physiology* 52A (1975): 359–365.

Saunders, R.L. "Atlantic Salmon (*Salmo salar*) Stocks and Management Implications in the Canadian Atlantic Provinces and New England, USA." *Canadian Journal of Fisheries and Aquatic Sciences* 38 (1981): 1612–1625.

Savitz, J., and L. Bardygula. *Analyses of the Behavioral Bases for Changes in Salmonid Diets*. University of Illinois at Urbana-Champaign, Illinois-Indiana Sea Grant Program Report Il-In-SG-R-89-3. 1989.

Scarnecchia, D.L., and E.P. Bergersen. "Trout Production and Standing Crop in Colorado's Small Streams, as Related to Environmental Features." *North American Journal of Fisheries Management* 7 (1987): 315–330.

Scavia, D., G. Fahnenstiel, M. Evans, D. Jude, and J. Lehman. "Influence of Salmonine Predation and Weather on Long-term Water Quality Trends in Lake Michigan." *Canadian Journal of Fisheries and Aquatic Sciences* 43 (1986): 435–443.

Schill, D.J., J.S. Griffith, and R.E. Gresswell. "Hooking Mortality of Cutthroat Trout in a Catch-and-Release Segment of the Yellowstone River, Yellowstone National Park." *North American Journal of Fisheries Management* 9, no. 2 (1986): 226–232.

Schindler, D.W. "Effects of Acid Rain on Freshwater Ecosystems." *Science* 239 (1988): 149–157.

Schindler, D.W., K.H. Mills, D.F. Malley, D.L. Findlay, J.A. Shearer, I.J. Davies, M.A. Turner, G.A. Linsey, and D.R. Cruikshank. "Long-term Ecosystem Stress: The Effects of Years of Experimental Acidification on a Small Lake." *Science* 228 (1985): 1395–1401.

Scholz, A.T., C.K. Gosse, J.C. Cooper, R.M. Horrall, A.D. Hasler, R.I. Daly, and R.J. Poff. "Homing of Rainbow Trout Transplanted in Lake Michigan: A Comparison of Three Procedures Used for Imprinting and Stocking." *Transactons of the American Fisheries Society* 107 (1978): 439–443.

Schreck, C.B. "Stress and Compensation in Teleostean Fishes: Response to Social and Physical Factors." In *Stress and Fish*, edited by A.D. Pickering, 295–321. New York: Academic Press, 1981.

Schreck, C.B., and R.J. Behnke. "Trouts of the Upper Kern River Basin, California, with Reference to Systematics and Evolution of Western North American *Salmo*." *Journal of the Fisheries Research Board of Canada* 28 (1971): 987–998.

Schuck, H.A. "Survival, Population Density, Growth, and Movement of the Wild Brown Trout in Crystal Creek." *Transactions of the American Fisheries Society* 73 (1943): 209–230.

Schujif, A., and A.D. Hawkins, eds. *Sound Reception in Fish*. New York: Elsevier, 1976.

Schwartz, A.L. "The Behavior of Fishes in Their Acoustic Environment." *Environmental Biology of Fishes* 13 (1985): 3–15.

Schweibert, E. *Trout*. Vol. 1. E.P. Dutton, 1978.

Scott, W.B., and E.J. Crossman. *Freshwater Fishes of Canada*. Fisheries Research Board of Canada, Bulletin 184. Ottawa: 1973.

Scrudato, R.J., and W.H. McDowell. "Upstream Transport of Mirex by Migrating Salmonids." *Canadian Journal of Fisheries and Aquatic Sciences* 46 (1989): 1484–1488.

Sedell, J.R., and R.L. Beschta. *Bringing Back the "Bio" in Bioengineering*. Special Publication of the Bioengineering Section of the American Fisheries Society. Washington, D.C.: In press.

Sedell, J.R., and K.J. Luchessa. "Using the Historical Record as an Aid to Salmonid Habitat Enhancement." In *Proceedings of the Symposium of Acquisition and Utilization of Aquatic Habitat Inventory Information, Portland, Oregon, October 28–30, 1981*, edited by N.B. Armantrout, 210–223. Bethesda, Md.: American Fisheries Society, 1982.

Seegrist, D.W., and R. Gard. "Effects of Floods on Trout in Sagehen Creek, California." *Transactions of the American Fisheries Society* 101 (1972): 478–482.

Selset, R., and K.B. Døving. "Behaviour of Mature Anadromous Char *(Salvelinus alpinus* L.) towards Odorants Produced by Smolts of Their Own Population." *Acta Physiologica Scandinavia* 108 (1980): 113–122.

Shapovalov, L., and A.C. Taft. *The Life Histories of the Steelhead Rainbow Trout* (Salmo gairdneri gairdneri) *and Silver Salmon* (Oncorhynchus kisutch) *with Special Reference to Waddell Creek, California, and Recommendations Regarding Their Management*. California Department of Fish and Game, Fisheries Bulletin 98. 1954.

Shepherd, B.G. "Activity Localization in Coastal Cutthroat Trout *(Salmo clarki clarki)* in a Small Bog Lake." *Journal of the Fisheries Research Board of Canada* 31 (1974): 1246–1249.

Shetter, D.S. "Further Results from Spring and Fall Plantings of Legal-sized, Hatchery-reared Trout in Streams and Lakes of Michigan." *Transactions of the American Fisheries Society* 74 (1944): 35–58.

———. "The Effects of Certain Angling Regulations on Stream Trout Populations." In *Symposium on Salmon and Trout in Streams*, edited by T.G. Northcote, 333–353. Vancouver: Institute of Fisheries, University of British Columbia, 1969.

Shetter, D.S., and G.R. Alexander. "Effects of a Flies-only Restriction on Angling and on Fall Trout Populations in Hunt Creek, Montmorency County, Michigan." *Transactions of the American Fisheries Society* 91 (1962): 295–302.

———. "Angling and Trout Populations on the North Branch of the Au Sable River, Crawford and Otsego Counties, Michigan, Under Special and Normal Regulations, 1958–63." *Transactions of the American Fisheries Society* 95 (1966): 85–91.

Shetter, D.S., and L.N. Allison. *Comparison of Mortality between Fly-hooked and Worm-hooked Trout in Michigan Streams*. Michigan Department of Conservation, Research Report, Miscellaneous Publication No. 9. Ann Arbor: 1955.

———. *Mortality of Trout Caused by Hooking with Artificial Lures in Michigan Waters, 1956–57*. Michigan Department of Conservation, Research Report. Ann Arbor: 1958.

Shetter, D.S., and A.S. Hazzard. "Results of Plantings of Marked Trout of Legal Size in Streams and Lakes of Michigan." *Transactions of the American Fisheries Society* 70 (1940): 446–468.

Shuter, B.J., D.A. Schlesinger, and A.P. Zimmerman. "Empirical Predictors of Annual Surface Water Temperature Cycles in North American Lakes." *Canadian Journal of Fisheries and Aquatic Sciences* 40 (1983): 1838–1845.

Silver, S.J., C.E. Warren, and P. Doudoroff. "Dissolved Oxygen Requirements of Developing Steelhead Trout and Chinook Salmon Embryos at Different Water Velocities." *Transactions of the American Fisheries Society* 92 (1963): 327–343.

Slaney, P.A., C.J. Perrin, and B.R. Ward. "Nutrient Concentration as a Limitation to Steelhead Smolt Production in the Keogh River." *Proceedings of the Annual Conference of the Western Association of Fish and Wildlife Agencies* 66 (1986): 146–155.

Sly, P.G. "Interstitial Water Quality of Lake Trout *(Salvelinus namaycush)* Spawning Habitat." *Journal of Great Lakes Research* 14 (1988): 301–315.

Sly, P.G., and C.P. Schneider. "The Significance of Seasonal Changes on a Modern Cobble-Gravel Used by Spawning Lake Trout, Lake Ontario." *Journal of Great Lakes Research* 10 (1984): 78–84.

Sly, P.G., and C.C. Widmer. "Lake Trout *(Salvelinus namaycush)* Spawning Habitat in Seneca Lake, New York." *Journal of Great Lakes Research* 10 (1984): 168–189.

Smiley, C.W. "Loch Leven Trout Introduced in the United States." *Bulletin of the United States Fish Commission* 7 (1887): 28–48.

Smith, A.K. "Development and Application of Spawning Velocity and Depth Criteria for Oregon Salmonids." *Transactions of the American Fisheries Society* 2 (1973): 312–316.

Smith, G.R., and R.F. Stearley. "The Classification and Scientific Names of Rainbow and Cutthroat Trouts." *Fisheries* 14, no. 1 (1989): 4–10.

Smith, L.L., Jr., and B.S. Smith. "Survival of Seven- to Ten-Inch Planted Trout in Two Minnesota Streams." *Transactions of the American Fisheries Society* 73 (1943): 108–116.

Smith, L.S. *Introduction to Fish Physiology*. New Jersey: T.F.H. Publications, Inc., 1982.

Smith, M.W., and J.W. Saunders. "Movements of Brook Trout *(Salvelinus fontinalis)* between and within Fresh and Salt Water." *Journal of the Fisheries Research Board of Canada* 15, no. 6 (1958): 1403–1449.

Smith, R.C. "Biochemical-Genetic and Meristic Analyses of Populations of Little Kern River Basin Golden Trout." Ph.D. dissertation, University of California, Davis, 1981.

Smith, R.H. *Native Trout of North America*. Portland, Oreg.: Frank Amato Publications, 1984.

Smith, R.J.F. *The Control of Fish Migration*. Berlin: Springer-Verlag, 1985.

Smith, S.B. "Reproductive Isolation in Summer and Winter Races of Steelhead Trout." In *Symposium on Salmon and Trout in Streams*, edited by T.G. Northcote, 21–38. Vancouver: Institute of Fisheries, University of British Columbia, 1969.

Solomon, D.J. "A Review of Chemical Communication in Freshwater Fish." *Journal of Fish Biology* 11 (1977): 363–376.

———. "Migration and Dispersion of Juvenile Brown and Sea Trout." In *Proceedings of the Salmon and Trout Migratory Behavior Symposium, June 3–5, 1981, First International Symposium*, edited by E.L. Brannon and E.O. Salo, 136–145. Seattle: University of Washington Press, 1982.

Solomon, D.J., and R.G. Templeton. "Movements of Brown Trout, *Salmo trutta* L., in a Chalk Stream." *Journal of Fish Biology* 9 (1976): 411–423.

Sorokin, M.A., S.I. Penkin, and A.N. Lebedeva. "On the Distance of Directional Sound Discrimination by Fishes." *Journal of Ichthyology* (U.S.S.R.) 28, no. 1 (1988): 157–160.

Spigarelli, S.A., G.P. Romberg, W. Prepejchal, and M.M. Thommes. "Body-Temperature Characteristics of Fish at a Thermal Discharge on Lake Michigan." In *Thermal Ecology*, edited by J.W. Gibbons and R.R. Sharitz, 119–132. Proceedings of the Atomic Energy Commission Symposium Series, CONF-730505, Augusta, Ga., May 1973. 1974.

Spigarelli, S.A., and M.M. Thommes. "Temperature Selection and Estimated Thermal Acclimation by Rainbow Trout *(Salmo gairdneri)* in a Thermal Plume." *Journal of the Fisheries Research Board of Canada* 36 (1979): 366–376.

Sprague, J.B., and D.E. Drury. "Avoidance Reactions of Salmonid Fish to Representative Pollutants." In *Advances in Water Pollution Research, Proceedings of the 4th International Conference, Prague*, edited by S. Harvey and S.H. Jenkins, 169–179. Oxford: Pergamon Press, 1969.

Sprague, J.B., P.F. Elson, and R.L. Saunders. "Sublethal Copper-Zinc Pollution in a Salmon River–A Field and Laboratory Study." *International Journal of Air and Water Pollution* 9 (1965): 531–543.

Stabell, O.B. "Detection of Natural Odorants by Atlantic Salmon Parr Using Positive Rheotaxis Olfactometry." In *Proceedings of the Salmon and Trout Migratory Behavior Symposium, June 3–5, 1981, First International Symposium*, edited by E.L. Brannon and E.O. Salo, 71–78. Seattle: University of Washington Press, 1982.

———. "Intraspecific Pheromone Discrimination and Substrate Marking by Atlantic Salmon Parr." *Journal of Chemical Ecology* 13 (1987): 1625–1643.

Stefansson, S.O., G. Naevdal, and T. Hansen. "The Influence of Three Unchanging Photoperiods on Growth and Parr-Smolt Transformation in Atlantic Salmon, *Salmo salar* L." *Journal of Fish Biology* 35 (1989): 237–247.

Stephen, A. "Brown Trout Beginnings." *Salmon, Trout and Seatrout*. (September 1989): 38, 44.

Sternberg, D. *Freshwater Gamefish of North America*. Minnetonka, Minn.: Cy Decosse Inc., 1987.

Stewart, D.J., J.F. Kitchell, and L.B. Crowder. "Prey Fishes and Their Salmonid Predators in Lake Michigan." *Transactions of the American Fisheries Society* 110 (1981): 751–763.

Stober, Q.J. "Underwater Noise Spectra, Fish Sounds and Response to Low Frequencies of Cutthroat Trout *(Salmo clarki)* with Reference to Orientation and Homing in Yellowstone Lake." *Transactions of the American Fisheries Society* 4 (1969): 652–663.

Stringer, G.E. "Comparative Hooking Mortality Using Three Types of Terminal Gear on Rainbow Trout from Pennack Lake, British Columbia." *The Canadian Fish-Culturist* 39 (1967): 17–21.

Stuart, T.A. "Water Currents through Permeable Gravels and Their Significance to Spawning Salmonids." *Nature* 19 (1953): 407–408.

———. "Spawning Migration, Reproduction and Young Stages of Loch Trout (*Salmo trutta* L.)." *Scientific Investigations of Freshwater in Scotland* 5 (1957): 1–39.

Sutterlin, A.M. "Pollutants and the Chemical Senses of Aquatic Animals–Perspective and Review." *Chemical Senses and Flavor* 1 (1974): 167–178.

Sutterlin, A.M., and R. Gray. "Chemical Basis for Homing of Atlantic Salmon (*Salmo salar*) to a Hatchery." *Journal of the Fisheries Research Board of Canada* 30 (1973): 985–989.

Swain, W.R. "Chlorinated Organic Residues in Fish, Water, and Precipitation from the Vicinity of Isle Royale, Lake Superior." *Journal of Great Lakes Research* 4 (1978): 398–407.

———. "Human Health Consequences of Consumption of Fish Contaminated with Organochlorine Compounds." *Aquatic Toxicology* 11 (1988): 357–377.

Swales, S., F. Caron, J.R. Irvine, and C.D. Levings. "Overwintering Habitats of Coho Salmon (*Oncorhynchus kisutch*) and Other Juvenile Salmonids in the Keogh River System, British Columbia." *Canadian Journal of Zoology* 66 (1988): 254–261.

Swift, D.R. "Activity Cycles in Brown Trout, *Salmo trutta*." *Journal of the Fisheries Research Board of Canada* 21 (1974): 133–138.

Thompson, K. "Determining Stream Flows for Fish Life." In *Proceedings of the Instream Flow Requirement Workshop*, 31–50. Vancouver, Wash.: Pacific Northwest River Basins Commission, 1972.

Thorpe, L.M., H.J. Rayner, and D.A. Webster. "Population Depletion in Brook, Brown, and Rainbow Trout Stocked in the Blackledge River, Connecticut, in 1942." *Transactions of the American Fisheries Society* 74 (1944): 166–187.

Thuember, T. "Fish and the Blue Ribbon Streams." *Wisconsin Conservation Bulletin* 40 (1975): 16–17.

Tietge, J.E., R.D. Johnson, and H.L. Bergman. "Morphometric Changes in Gill Secondary Lamellae of Brook Trout (*Salvelinus fontinalis*) after Long-term Exposure to Acid and Aluminum." *Canadian Journal of Fisheries and Aquatic Sciences* 45 (1988): 1643–1648.

Tinbergen, N. "Social Releasers and the Experimental Method Required for Their Study." *Wilson Bulletin* 60, no. 1 (1948): 5–51.

Tol, D., and J. French. "Status of a Hybridized Population of Alvord Cutthroat Trout from Virgin Creek, Nevada." *American Fisheries Society Symposium* 4 (1988): 116–120.

Trewas, E. "Sea-Trout and Brown-Trout." *The Salmon and Trout Magazine* 139 (1953): 199–215.

Tripp, D., and P. McCart. *Effects of Different Coho Stocking Strategies on Coho and Cutthroat Trout Production in Isolated Headwater Streams*. Department of Fisheries and Oceans, Canadian Technical Report of Fisheries and Aquatic Sciences 1212. Vancouver, British Columbia: 1983.

Trotter, P.C. "Coastal Cutthroat Trout: A Life History Compendium." *Transactions of the American Fisheries Society* 118 (1989): 463–473.

U.S. Department of Agriculture, Forest Service. *Golden Trout Habitat and Watershed Restoration on the Kern Plateau: An Environmental Assessment*. Inyo National Forest. Bishop, Calif.: 1982.

U.S. Department of Agriculture, Forest Service. *Golden Trout Wilderness Management Plan: Alternative Approaches to Interim Management of the Golden Trout Wilderness: An Environmental Assessment*. Inyo National Forest. Bishop, Calif.: 1982.

U.S. Department of the Interior, U.S. Fish and Wildlife Service. *Arizona Trout Recovery Plan*. Albuquerque, N.Mex.: 1979a.

———. *Gila Trout Recovery Plan*. Albuquerque, N.Mex.: 1979b.

———. *Greenback Cutthroat Trout Recovery Plan*. Prepared by the greenback cutthroat trout recovery team. Denver: 1983.

Vannote, R.L., G.W. Minshall, K.W. Cummins, J.R. Sedell, and C.E. Cushing. "The River Continuum Concept." *Canadian Journal of Fisheries and Aquatic Sciences* 37 (1980): 130–137.

VanOffelen, H.K. "Performance and Behavior Characteristics of Two Strains of Brook Trout." Master's thesis, Cornell University, Ithaca, 1990.

Veith, G.D., D. DeFoe, and M. Knuth. "Structure-Activity Relationships for Screening Organic Chemicals for Potential Ecotoxicity Effects." *Drug Metabolism Reviews* 15 (1984–85): 1295–1303.

Vincent, E.R. "Effects of Stocking Catchable-size Hatchery Rainbow Trout on Two Wild Trout Species in the Madison River and O'Dell Creek, Montana." *North American Journal of Fisheries Management* 7 (1987): 91–105.

Vincent, R.E. "Some Influences of Domestication upon Three Stocks of Brook Trout (*Salvelinus fontinalis*)." *Transactions of the American Fisheries Society* 89 (1960): 35–52.

Wagner, H.H. "Photoperiod and Temperature Regulation of Smolting in Steelhead Trout (*Salmo gairdneri*)." *Canadian Journal of Zoology* 52 (1974): 219–234.

Wales, J.H. "Development of Steelhead Trout Eggs." *California Fish and Game* 27, no. 4 (1941): 250–260.

Walton, I. *The Compleat Angler*. New York: Weathervane Books, 1653.

———. *The Compleat Angler*. Edited by A. Lang. London: F.M. Dent and Co., 1896.

Ward, B.R., and P.A. Slaney. "Life History and Smolt-to-Adult Survival of Keogh River Steelhead Trout (*Salmo gairdneri*) and the Relationship to Smolt Size." *Canadian Journal of Fisheries and Aquatic Sciences* 45 (1988): 1110–1122.

Warren, C.E., J.H. Wales, G.E. Davis, and P. Doudoroff. "Trout Production in an Experimental Stream Enriched with Sucrose." *The Journal of Wildlife Management* 28 (1964): 617–660.

Waters, T.F. "Replacement of Brook Trout by Brown Trout over 15 Years in a Minnesota Stream: Production and Abundance." *Transactions of the American Fisheries Society* 112, no. 2A (1983): 137–146.

Webb, P.W. "Body Form, Locomotion and Foraging in Aquatic Vertebrates." *American Zoologist* 24 (1984): 107–120.

Webb, R.W. "Geomorphology of the Middle Kern River Basin, Southern Sierra Nevada, California." *Bulletin of the Geological Society of America* 57 (1946): 355–382.

Webster, D.A. "Artificial Spawning Facilities for Brook Trout, *Salvelinus fontinalis*." *Transactions of the American Fisheries Society* 91 (1962): 168–174.

Webster, D.A., and G. Eiriksdottir. "Upwelling Water as a Factor Influencing Choice of Spawning Sites by Brook Trout (*Salvelinus fontinalis*)." *Transactions of the American Fisheries Society* 105 (1976): 416–421.

Wedemeyer, G.A., R.L. Saunders, and W.C. Clarke. "Environmental Factors Affecting Smoltification and Early Marine Survival of Anadromous Salmonids." *Marine Fisheries Review* 42 (1980): 1–14.

Weinreb, E.L., and N.M. Bilstad. "Histology of the Digestive Tract and Adjacent Structures of the Rainbow Trout, *Salmo gairdneri irideus*." *Copeia*, 1955, no. 3: 194–204.

White, H.C. "Life History of Sea-running Brook Trout (*Salvelinus fontinalis*) of Moser River, N.S." *Journal of the Fisheries Research Board of Canada* 5, no. 2 (1940): 176–186.

White, S.E. *The Mountains*. New York: McClure, Phillips & Co., 1904.

Wiggins, W.G.B. "The Introduction and Ecology of the Brown Trout (*Salmo trutta* Linnaeus) with Special Reference to North America." Master's thesis, University of Toronto, 1950.

Willford, W., R. Bergstedt, W. Berlin, N. Foster, R. Hesselberg, M. Mac, D. Passino, R. Reinert, and D. Rottiers. *Chlorinated Hydrocarbons as a Factor in the Reproduction and Survival of Lake Trout (Salvelinus namaycush) in Lake Michigan*. U.S. Department of the Interior, U.S. Fish and Wildlife Service, Technical Paper 105. 1981.

Williams, J.E., J.E. Johnson, D.A. Hendrickson, S. Contreras-Balderas, J.D. Williams, M. Navarro-Mendoza, D.E. McAllister, and J.E. Deacon. "Fishes of North America Endangered, Threatened, or of Special Concern: 1989." *Fisheries* 14, no. 6 (1989): 2–20.

Williams, J.E., D.W. Sada, C.D. Williams, J.R. Bennett, J.E. Johnson, P.C. Marsh, D.E. McAllister, E.P. Pister, R.D. Radant, J.N. Rinne, M.D. Stone, L. Ulmer, and D.L. Withers. "American Fisheries Society Guidelines for Introductions of Threatened and Endangered Fishes." *Fisheries* 13, no. 5 (1988): 5–11.

Winter, G.W., C.B. Schreck, and J.D. McIntyre. "Meristic Comparison of Four Stocks of Steelhead Trout (*Salmo gairdneri*)." *Copeia*, 1980: 160–162.

Wishard, L.N., J.E. Seeb, F.M. Utter, and D. Stefan. *Biochemical Genetic Characteristics of Native Trout Populations of Owyhee County, Idaho*. Boise: Bureau of Land Management, 1980.

———. "A Genetic Investigation of Suspected Red Band Trout Populations." *Copeia*, 1984: 120–132.

Withler, I.L. "Variability in Life History Characteristics of Steelhead Trout (*Salmo gairdneri*) along the Pacific Coast of North America." *Journal of the Fisheries Research Board of Canada* 23, no. 3 (1966): 365–393.

Wood, C.M., R.C. Playle, B.P. Simons, G.G. Goss, and D.G. McDonald. "Blood Gases, Acid-Base Status, Ions, and Hematology in Adult Brook Trout (*Salvelinus fontinalis*) under Acid/Aluminum Exposure." *Canadian Journal of Fisheries and Aquatic Sciences* 45 (1988): 1575–1586.

Wydoski, R.S. "Relation of Hooking Mortality and Sublethal Hooking Stress to Quality Fishery Management." In *Proceedings of a National Symposium on Catch and Release Fishing*, edited by R.A. Barnhart and T.D. Roelofs, 43–87. Arcata: California Cooperative Fishery Research Unit, Humboldt State University, 1977.

Wydoski, R.S., and R.R. Whitney. *Inland Fishes of Washington*. Seattle: University of Washington Press, 1979.

Glossary-index